UNITED STATES CONSTITUTIONAL AND LEGAL HISTORY

A TWENTY VOLUME SERIES
REPRODUCING OVER 450 OF THE MOST
IMPORTANT ARTICLES ON THE TOPIC

Edited with Introductions by
KERMIT L. HALL

A GARLAND SERIES

CONTENTS OF THE SERIES

WOMEN, THE LAW, AND THE CONSTITUTION

MAJOR HISTORICAL INTERPRETATIONS

Edited with an Introduction by
KERMIT L. HALL

GARLAND PUBLISHING, INC.
NEW YORK • LONDON 1987

Library of Congress Cataloging-in-Publication Data

Women, the law, and the constitution.

(United States constitutional and legal history ; v. 10)
Bibliography: p.
1. Women—Legal status, laws, etc.—United States—History.
2. Married women—United States—History.
I. Hall, Kermit. II. Series.
KF478.A5W67 1987 346.7301'34 86-31895
ISBN 0-8240-0138-9 347.306134

The volumes in this series have been printed on acid-free, 250-year-life paper.

Printed in the United States of America.

ACKNOWLEDGMENTS

Sara Alpern and Dale Baum, "Female Ballots: The Impact of the Nineteenth Amendment." Reprinted from *Journal of Interdisciplinary History* XVI (1985), 43–67 with permission of the editors of *Journal of Interdisciplinary History* and the M.I.T. Press, Cambridge, Massachusetts..

Norma Basch, "Equity vs. Equality: Emerging Concepts of Women's Political Status in the Age of Jackson," *Journal of the Early Republic* 3 (Fall 1983): 297–318. Reprinted by permission of the *Journal of the Early Republic.*

Eleanor M. Boatwright, "The Political and Civil Status of Women in Georgia, 1783–1860," *Georgia Historical Quarterly* 25 (December 1941): 301–324. Reprinted by permission of the *Georgia Historical Quarterly.*

William B. Bosley, "Married Women's Rights in Community Property Under the Law of California." Reprinted by permission of the Yale Law Journal Company and Fred B. Rothman & Company from *The Yale Law Journal*, Vol.10, pp. 236–243.

Patricia Brito, "Protective Legislation in Ohio: The Inter-War Years," *Ohio History* 88 (Spring 1979): 173–197. Reprinted by permission of *Ohio History.*

Shirley R. Bysiewicz and Ruth E. Van de Mark , "The Legal Status of the Dakota Indian Woman," *The American Indian Law Review* 3 Winter: 255–312. Reprinted by permission of *The American Indian Law Review.*

Richard H. Chused, "Married Women's Property Law: 1800–1850," *Georgetown Law Journal* 71 (1983): 1359–1425. Reprinted by permission of the author.

Nancy F. Cott, "Divorce and the Changing Status of Women in Eighteenth-Century Massachusetts," *William and Mary Quarterly* 33 (October 1976): 586–614. Reprinted by permission of the *William and Mary Quarterly.*

Linda Grant DePauw, "Women and the Law: The Colonial Period," *Human Rights* 6 (Winter 1977): 107–114. Reprinted by permission of *Human Rights*, published by the American Bar Association Press.

Ellen DuBois, "The Radicalism of the Woman Suffrage Movement: Notes Toward the Reconstruction of Nineteenth-Century Feminism." This article is reprinted from FEMINIST STUDIES, Volume 3, nos. 1–2 (Fall 1975): 63–71, by permission of the publisher, FEMINIST STUDIES, Inc., c/o Women's Studies Program, Unviersity of Maryland, College Park, MD 20742.

William Graebner, "'Uncle Sam Just Loves the Ladies': Sex Discrimination in the Federal Government, 1917," Labor History 21 (Winter 1979–80): 75–85. Reprinted by permission of *Labor History*.

Joan R. Gundersen and Gwen Victor Gampel, "Married Women's Legal Status in Eighteenth-Century New York and Virginia," *William and Mary Quarterly* 39 (1982): 114–134. Reprinted by permission of the authors and the *William and Mary Quarterly*.

W.O. Hart, "Rights of Women in Louisiana," *Louisiana Historical Quarterly* 4 (October 1921): 437–458.

William Hodes, "Women and the Constitution: Some Legal History and a New Approach to the Nineteenth Amendment," *Rutgers Law Review* 25 (1970): 26–53. Reprinted by permission of *Rutgers Law Review*.

Joan Hoff Wilson, "The Legal Status of Women in the Late Nineteenth and Early Twentieth Centuries," *Human Rights* 6 (Winter 1977): 125–134. Reprinted by permission of *Human Rights*, published by the American Bar Association Press.

Kay Ann Holmes, "Reflections by Gaslight: Prostitution in Another Age," *Issues in Criminology* 7 (Winter 1972): 83–101. Reprinted by permission of *Crime and Social Justice*, 2701 Folsom Street, San Francisco, CA 94110.

Carol E. Jenson, "The Equity Jurisdiction and Married Women's Property in Ante-bellum America: A Revisionist View," *International Journal of Women's Studies* 2 (March–April 1979): 144–154. Reprinted by permission of the *International Journal of Women's Studies*.

Linda Kerber, "From the Declaration of Independence to the Declaration of Sentiments: The Legal Status of Women in the Early Republic, 1776–1848," *Human Rights* 6 (1977): 115–124. Reprinted by permission of *Human Rights*, published by the American Bar Association Press.

Charles O'Brien, "The Growth in Pennsylvania of the Property Rights of Married Women," *University of Pennsylvania Law Review* 49 (September 1901): 524–530. Reprinted by permission of Fred B. Rothman & Company.

Marylynn Salmon, "Women and Property in South Carolina: The Evidence from Marriage Settlements, 1730–1830," *William and Mary Quarterly* 39 (October 1982): 655–685. Reprinted by permission of the author and the *William and Mary Quarterly*.

Steven Schlossman and Stephanie Wallach, "The Crime of Precocious Sexuality: Female Juvenile Delinquency in the Progressive Era," *Harvard Educational Review*, 1978, 48:1, 65–94. Copyright (c) 1978 by the President and Fellows of Harvard College. All rights reserved.

A. Elizabeth Taylor, "The Woman Suffrage Movement in Texas," *Journal of Southern History* 17 (May 1951): 194–215. Reprinted by permission of the Southern Historical Association.

Carol Weisbrod and Pamela Sheingorn, "*Reynolds* v. *United States*: Nineteenth-Century Forms of Marriage and the Status of Women," *Connecticut Law Review* 10 (Summer 1978): 828–858. Reprinted by permission of the authors and the *Connecticut Law Review*.

CONTENTS

INTRODUCTION

"Whilst you are proclaiming peace and good will to men, [and] emancipating all nations," Abigail Adams wrote to her husband John in May 1776, "you insist upon retaining an absolute power over wives."[1] In the past two decades, the feminist movement has made American historians conscious of the need to place women fully in the context of American history. The result has been an avalanche of writing and considerable contention among those who have written it about the nature of women's experience in American history. Much of the early literature concentrated on the cult of domesticity, that body of separate, private, and domestic values which seems to have structured the world of white middle- and upper-class women, especially in the nineteenth century. More recently, however, women's history has expanded its social context, and we now have important studies of lower-class white and black women, of female juvenile delinquents, and of prostitutes. Furthermore, historians of the female sex have embarked on a quest, in the words of Norma Basch, "to understand women on their own terms and in their own words—to see history through women's eyes."[2] Interestingly, this new emphasis has brought with it a greater concern for what Basch terms "women's relationship to the state."[3]

The state and the legal system, of course, have determined only partly the social status of women. Custom, social expectations, habit, and peer-group pressure have shaped the world in which American women lived. Cultural stereotyping is particularly relevant to any historical discussion of women's rights.

Nonetheless, law in all its various forms remains an important source for understanding the history of women, and scholars have repeatedly drawn upon it. One of the earliest and most important works in women's legal history, Richard B. Morris's *Studies in the History of American Law* (1930), demonstrated the value of these materials. More than a half-century later, this book remains influential, although scholars now question Morris's positive assessment of the rights that colonial American women enjoyed.[4]

Other studies have revealed that by analyzing legal development, historians can begin to understand the formal context of rights and benefits granted by the state to women. "Since statutes and judicial precedents are a facile guide to social relationships," Marylynn Salmon has written, "historians of women study the law to learn about the status of women in times past. Through changes in the law, historians have outlined the institutional repression and gradual emancipation of the female sex."[5]

Legal historians have drawn on these sources, for example, to investigate the elaborate common law rules that governed the property rights of married women. They were considered with their husbands, Chancellor James Kent wrote in 1832, "as one person, and her legal existence and authority in a degree lost or suspended, during the continuance of the matrimonial union."[6] Single women, on the other hand, enjoyed rights similar to those of men. They could make contracts, own and dispose of property, and administer businesses. They were, of course, in the nineteenth century denied most political rights.

Yet as recent studies have shown, the traditional common law rules proved far too intricate for the American environment. As a result, there were piecemeal reforms that attempted to extend to married women the same status as that afforded to single women. Courts, for instance, expanded the concept of a separate equitable estate, a device used by English chancellors to protect widows from spendthrift husbands. Also, state legislatures, beginning with Mississippi in 1839, enacted married women's property acts. These statutes, which states continued to pass well into the twentieth century, were not designed either to give married women full legal equality or to provide them with a means by which to attack the property claims of their husbands. Instead, they rationalized the external relations of the family with creditors, by giving them a basis upon which to collect debts owed by the husband, the wife, or both. As Suzanne Lebsock found in her study of Petersburg, Virginia between 1784 and 1860, "[t]he main engine behind the passage of the initial married women's property reforms was, as with separate estates, the desire to protect women's property from seizure when indebtedness was rampant and creditors impatient."[7] The growing role of married women in the economy, combined with the pressures that destitute widows placed on the community, made such legislation necessary. But even these special protective laws inhibited the flow of capital and most states eventually came to the position of treating married women like everyone else, not because they were stirred by egalitarian sentiments, but because doing so made good economic sense.

The political rights of women protected by constitutional law also evolved gradually, and real change only began to come when women, like blacks, began to organize. The phrase "sex-discrimination law" today implies a real achievement for women and for the women's social movement. Prior to the 1960's there was no such body of law. The Constitution had never been interpreted to protect women from arbitrary, gender-based discrimination by the government, and even the adoption of the Fourteenth Amendment in 1868 did not bring significant change. The Supreme Court in the late nineteenth century regularly held that the equal protection and due process clauses did not apply to women, denying them a means of using the law to enhance their political and economic rights. "The Constitution of the United States," the Supreme Court held in the 1874 case of *Minor* v. *Happersett*, "does not confer the right of suffrage upon any one, and that the constitutions and laws of the several states which commit that important trust to men alone are not necessarily void."[8] In 1920 the Nineteenth Amendment extended the vote to women. Many of its supporters were motivated not by a commitment to equality for women, but by a belief that the "pure" nature of the female sex would make for clean politics. The idea that women as a class had a constitutional right to the equal protection of the law was first announced by the Supreme Court in the 1971 case of *Reed* v. *Reed*, but the justices have stopped short of extending to women the same level of constitutional protection that they have given to racial minorities. The Congress in 1973, following a fifty-year struggle, passed the Equal Rights Amendment, which provided a simple but comprehensive statement that women and men were equal before the law. That amendment, however, failed to gain sufficient support in the states to be ratified.

The essays in this volume treat both public and private law issues in the legal history of women. They reveal the way in which changes in underlying social values and broad economic trends have shaped women's legal status. They also reflect the continuing differences among historians about the importance of feminism. Readers will find that many of the themes raised in this volume are also treated in Volume 11, *Law, Society, and Domestic Relations*, which contains essays on private law matters, such as divorce and adoption, and Volume 12, *Civil Rights in American History*, which places the issue of gender discrimination in the context of the Supreme Court's development of the equal protection clause of the Fourteenth Amendment.

Kermit L. Hall

Notes

1. *Familiar Letters of John Adams and His Wife, Abigail Adams, During the Revolution*, ed. Charles Francis Adams (1876), pp. 3–4.
2. Norma Basch, "Equity vs. Equality: Emerging Concepts of Women's Political Status in the Age of Jackson," *Journal of the Early Republic* 3 (1983): 297.
3. Ibid.
4. Marylynn Salmon, "The Legal Status of Women in Early America: A Reappraisal," *Law and History Review* 1 (1983): 129–151.
5. Ibid., p. 131.
6. James Kent, *Commentaries on American Law*, 1st ed. (1826–1830), 2: 106.
7. Suzanne Lebsock, *The Free Women of Petersburg: Status and Culture in a Southern Town, 1784–1860* (1984), p. 84.
8. Minor v. Happersett, 21 Wallace 162 (1874).

ADDITIONAL READING

Norma Basch, *In the Eyes of the Law: Women, Marriage, and Property in Nineteenth-Century New York* (1982).

Nancy F. Cott, *The Bonds of Womanhood* (1977).

Estelle B. Freedman, *Their Sisters' Keepers: Women's Prison Reform in America, 1830–1930* (1981).

Suzanne Lebsock, *The Free Women of Petersburg: Status and Culture in a Southern Town, 1784–1860* (1984).

Richard B. Morris, *Studies in the History of American Law: With Special Reference to the Seventeenth and Eighteenth Centuries* (1930).

Mary Beth Norton, *Liberty's Daughters: The Revolutionary Experience of American Women, 1750–1800* (1980).

Journal of Interdisciplinary History, xvi:1 (Summer 1985), 43–67.

Sara Alpern and Dale Baum

Female Ballots: The Impact of the Nineteenth Amendment

The Impact of the Nineteenth Amendment Although a *Ladies' Home Journal* editorial urged women to "clean house" in the 1920 election and start "political housekeeping again with good, honestly made furniture," not all looked upon the innovation of nationwide woman suffrage with such relish. Many politicians feared the potential power of a monolithic female voting bloc even after the 1920 election did not produce one. Speaking at a League of Women Voters banquet, Nathan L. Miller, Governor of New York, criticized the concept of an organization of women voters and warned that seeking political influence in ways other than through participation in the two major political 1
parties would be a "menace" to American institutions. The League of Women Voters (created out of the disbanded membership of the National American Woman Suffrage Association) found the governor's comments to be as inappropriate as they were inaccurate. Following Carrie Chapman Catt's advice at its founding, the League was determined to remain an "educational" and "nonpartisan" organization. Neither its leadership nor its rank and file had intentions of forming a women's bloc. Yet League members, along with other women who had been active in the suffrage campaign, expected that their votes would make a difference in their society.[1]

Sara Alpern is Assistant Professor of History and Dale Baum is Associate Professor of History at Texas A&M University.

The authors would like to thank the following scholars for their helpful suggestions and criticisms: Avi Harpaz, John H. Lenihan, Allan J. Lichtman, Paula Michal-Johnson, and W. Phillips Shively. They also wish to thank Kathryn Anderson for permitting them to read an early draft of her manuscript on Anne Martin and the National Woman's Party.

0022-1953/85 $02.50

1 "The Editor's Page," *Ladies' Home Journal*, XXXVII (March 1920), 1; "The Second Thoughts of Governor Miller," *Woman Citizen*, V (19 Feb. 1921), 1009; William A. Willis, "Practical Politics," *Ladies' Home Journal*, XXXVIII (May 1921), 53. See also Stanley J. Lemons, *The Woman Citizen: Social Feminism in the 1920s* (Urbana, 1973), 98–99, 86; Eleanor Flexner, *A Century of Struggle* (Cambridge, Mass., 1959), 340. For a recent treatment of feminist politics in the 1920s, see Nancy F. Cott, "Feminist Politics in the 1920s: The National Woman's Party," *Journal of American History*, LXXI (1984), 43–68.

Recent scholarship has reiterated the high, although subsequently unrealized, expectations contained in the *Ladies' Home Journal* editorial. Lemons refers to female leaders' initial desires to "purify politics and reform political practices." Chafe, another women's history scholar, points out that by 1920 the hopes of women activists for female suffrage to promote reforms reflected their acceptance of politics as the key to a more just and egalitarian society. Their high expectations hinged on the belief that female values were distinct from those of men and that women would thus vote differently, thereby insuring a more honest and compassionate government. In her study of southern women, Scott contends that virtually all women who entered politics after woman suffrage became law believed that female ballots would facilitate reforms in their section of the country. Throughout the
2 nation, as voters and officeholders, leaders of the women's movement argued, women would be in the vanguard of those fighting to end injustice, poverty, and immorality.[2]

Did, however, the voting behavior of women differ significantly from that of men in the 1920 presidential election? Shortly after the 1920 presidential election results were known, newspaper reporters asked Mary A. Livermore, the chairperson of the Women's Republican Committee of New York, to what extent newly enfranchised women had contributed to Republican Warren G. Harding's landslide victory over Democratic candidate James M. Cox. "One half of the majority Harding vote," she replied, "was due to women's efforts." But she reminded reporters that her claim was purely speculative, since "no analysis of the division of the vote is possible." Livermore's belief in the intractability of the nationwide female vote to statistical analysis was shared by virtually all political commentators of her day. Conventional wisdom decreed that everywhere outside of Illinois (where ballots cast by women were separately tallied) male and female ballots had been fatally co-mingled. In the absence of a survey of women

2 Lemons, *Woman Citizen*, 85, 107; William H. Chafe, *The American Woman: Her Changing Social, Economic, and Political Roles, 1920–1970* (New York, 1972), 25; Anne Firor Scott, *The Southern Lady from Pedestal to Politics, 1830–1930* (Chicago, 1970), 209; Aileen S. Kraditor, *The Ideas of the Woman Suffrage Movement, 1890–1920* (New York, 1965), 38–63.

voters leaving the polls, the determination of the actual female component of each candidate's total was considered impossible.[3]

This study presents a method for measuring differences in the voting behavior of women and men in the 1920 election. The problem of uncovering the participation rates and partisan preferences of women relative to those of men in the contest between Harding and Cox is amenable to a statistical procedure only recently used by political historians: regression estimation of voter transition probabilities. By employing this device, our study presents estimates of how women voted in 1920 in three regions of the North: New England, the Mid-Atlantic states, and the Midwest (excluding Illinois). These findings and their relation to contemporary portrayals of woman suffrage, suggest the need for rethinking the traditional interpretations of the impact of the Nineteenth Amendment and its relation to the women's move- 3
ment of the 1920s.[4]

SCHOLARLY ANALYSIS OF THE 1920 ELECTION In the early 1920s a handful of academics attempted to disentangle the effects of the extension of suffrage to American women, but they encountered thorny problems inherent in the indirect measurements that they used to predict turnout and partisanship. As a consequence, for a subsequent generation little was written in an empirical vein about the female suffrage question.[5]

Many conclusions drawn in the 1920s were incorporated into standard histories of the impact of the adoption of the Nineteenth Amendment. One study has been repeatedly cited to document "American Women's Ineffective Use of the Vote." In 1924 Rice and Willey concluded that, in the twenty-one states which they analyzed outside the South, somewhere between 34.7 percent and

3 *New York Times* (Nov. 3, 1920), 4. Illinois was the only state in 1920 to print separate ballots for men and women and to require separate ballot boxes and tally sheets for each sex. The state's attorney general ordered votes to be separately recorded out of fear of a possible invalidation of the newly passed Nineteenth Amendment. See "Editorials," *Journal of Illinois State Historical Quarterly*, XIII (1920), 414.

4 On the use of ecological regressions to analyze voting patterns, see Laura Irwin Langbein and Allan J. Lichtman, *Ecological Inference* (Beverly Hills, 1978), 50–62.

5 Joel Harris Goldstein, "The Effect of the Adoption of Woman Suffrage: Sex Differences in Voting Behavior—Illinois 1914–1921," unpub. Ph.D. diss. (Univ. of Chicago, 1972), 12–13.

46.5 percent of potentially eligible women voted in the 1920 election. Their attribution of a staggering degree of apathy among America's newly enfranchised women reinforced for years the popularly held notion that women were primarily responsible for the sharp drop in voter turnout in 1920. Indeed, the assumption that women were slow to use their new vote is ingrained in several recent studies. In his classic book *The American Woman*, Chafe reinforces the assessment of a high stay-at-home tendency among women. In her study of the New Deal realignment, Anderson attributes much of the generally low turnout in the 1920 presidential race to female voter apathy.[6]

Only recently did Kleppner, a practitioner of the "new political history," empirically test the supposition that the steadily waning interest of the electorate before 1920 and the turnout
4 decline thereafter were attributable entirely to the effects of women suffrage. Amassing a wide range of relevant quantitative data, Kleppner demonstrates conclusively that neither woman suffrage alone, nor in combination with the trend in declining turnout rates before women secured the franchise, could adequately account for the low levels of voter participation in the 1920s. Kleppner's successful revisionist analysis of the relationship between female suffrage and voter turnout, however, does not attempt to uncover the male/female divisions in the partisan vote.[7]

The commonly repeated assumption that "women in general voted like their husbands if they voted at all," thus remains open to empirical investigation. Whether women would duplicate their

6 Pioneering efforts to study systematically the results of the expansion of the suffrage to women were made by William N. Ogburn and Inez Goltra, "How Women Vote," *Political Science Quarterly*, XXXIV (1919), 413–433; Stuart D. Rice and Malcolm M. Willey, "American Women's Ineffective Use of the Vote," *Current History*, XX (1924), 641–647. Rice and Willey's higher estimate of female turnout, 46.7%, was the actual, not estimated, turnout of Illinois women in the 1920 election. Their first and dismally low figure, 34.7%, was derived by estimating male turnout in 1920 by extrapolating from only two previous data points. According to their calculations, male turnout between the 1880 and 1900 elections declined by 5.7%. Thus their conclusion that women in 1920 were markedly more apathetic than their male counterparts depends on the questionable assumption that between 1900 and 1920 male turnout declined by only 5.7%. Cf. Arthur M. Schlesinger and Erik McKinley Eriksson, "The Vanishing Voter," *The New Republic*, XL (Oct. 15, 1924), 162–167, whose calculations suggest a much greater rate of decline in male turnout between 1900 and 1920. Chafe, *American Woman*, 30; Kristi Andersen, *The Creation of a Democratic Majority: 1928–1936* (Chicago, 1979), 40.

7 Paul Kleppner, "Were Women to Blame? Female Suffrage and Voter Turnout," *Journal of Interdisciplinary History*, XII (1982), 621–643.

husbands' votes was a question of some interest before the 1920 election. Although the *Ladies' Home Journal* writer who asked the question, "Does the Wife Vote Like Her Husband?" answered in the negative, the opposite assessment would prevail. Based on similar impressionistic articles which followed the election, popular belief soon held that women took their political cues from their husbands. This widely held notion, in turn, impeded the feminist movement.[8]

In 1927 Frank R. Kent, a political authority, claimed that women had promised that their votes would deliver too much. He noted that not only had women failed to become an independent force in national politics, but politically active women had joined existing political machines that felt no pressure whatsoever to grant female voters any special concessions. Moreover, according to Kent, many women did not vote at all. From these impres- 5
sions Kent concluded that women's politics merely reflected those of their husbands' or male relatives'. His argument seemed irrefutable: because women did not vote as a bloc or make independent choices at the polling places, their voting decisions were mirror images of men's political judgments.[9]

This assumption, that subsequently became accepted as fact—that women voted like men—is interesting in light of the 1924 research of Willey and Rice who found evidence of a "sex cleavage" in the 1920 election. A cursory glance at the 1920 Illinois presidential vote as reported for men and women reveals that women who voted were more emphatically in the Republican party column than men who voted. Willey and Rice demonstrated that this difference in male and female balloting in Illinois was "uniform" throughout the state to the extent that it was reflected in almost all of the state's 102 county electorates. If Illinois were typical of the nation, then the implication of their research was clear: women more than men had been responsible in 1920 for creating the most lopsided partisan victory ever achieved in the history of United States' presidential elections.[10]

8 Chafe, *American Woman*, 30; Marie Cecile Chomel, "Does the Wife Vote Like Her Husband?" *Ladies' Home Journal*, XXXVI (May 1919), 37.

9 Frank R. Kent, "Women's Faults in Politics," *Woman Citizen*, XI (March 1927), 23, 46, 47.

10 In their analysis of the Illinois returns, Willey and Rice argued that a high and positive correlation (r=+.06) across the state's 102 counties between the female Republican per-

Divergent interpretations still compete to explain women's votes in the 1920 election. In the standard historical account of the Harding-Cox contest, Bagly contradicts Willey and Rice's assessment, arguing that woman suffrage did not aid Harding substantially because the Republican ticket did not receive huge gains in states where the Nineteenth Amendment greatly increased the voting population by enfranchising women. One thing is clear from the disputes over how women voted in the 1920 presidential election: women did not vote as a bloc. However, the degree of apathy ascribed to new female voters in that election and the existence of a sex cleavage in the vote remain questions amenable to statistical analysis.[11]

6 REGRESSION ESTIMATION OF VOTER TRANSITION PROBABILITIES For the purpose of the analysis, the county electorates (adult citizens in 1920) in each region were broken down into five mutually exclusive groupings: (1) men who cast ballots for Woodrow Wilson, the Democratic candidate in 1916, (2) men who voted for the Republican candidate, Charles E. Hughes, in 1916; (3) men who voted for third party candidates in 1916; (4) men who either sat out the balloting for presidential candidates in 1916 or who were not yet eligible or old enough to vote; and (5) women who were newly enfranchised by the Nineteenth Amendment. These five groupings, along with the partisan divisions of the vote in 1920, were used as variables in a series of multiple regressions. The regression equations generated estimates of how male partisans and male nonvoters in 1916 subsequently behaved in 1920. Once the male components of the 1920 divisions of the vote were estimated, the remaining shares of the 1920 vote were attributed

---

centage of the two-party vote and the male Republican share of the combined Cox and Harding ballots demonstrated the existence of a uniform sex cleavage. See Willey and Rice, "A Sex Cleavage in the Presidential Election of 1920," *Journal of the American Statistical Association*, XIX (1924), 519–520. The first nationwide sex cleavage in a presidential race appears to have occurred in 1980. Of women voting for president, 46% cast their ballots for Ronald Reagan, 45% voted for Jimmy Carter, and the remaining 9% voted for John B. Anderson and other third party candidates. The so-called 1980 "Reagan landslide" was thus attributable almost entirely to male voters. See Kleppner, Walter Dean Burnham, Ronald P. Formisano, Samuel P. Hays, Richard Jensen, and William G. Shade, *The Evolution of American Electoral Systems* (Westport, Conn., 1981), 232.

11 Wesley M. Bagly, *The Road to Normalcy: The Presidential Campaign and Election of 1920* (Baltimore, 1962), 160.

to female ballots. The statistical procedure employed is outlined in detail in the Appendix.[12]

As an illustration, Table 1 presents estimates of individual voting behavior in the six New England states between 1916 and 1920. The estimates reveal that party lines held firm between the two elections with the exception of roughly one fifth of the 1916 Democrats who switched to the Republican party in 1920. Most of the instability in the voting patterns of males between the two elections was due to fluctuations in turnout, involving the entry of new male voters into and the departure of previous male voters from the active electorate. Since approximately 52 percent of Harding's total vote was comprised of former Hughes men and previous nonvoting males, the remaining 48 percent had to be assigned to female voters. Cox managed to attract only about half of the 1916 Democrats and received virtually no support from 7
any other grouping of men. Thus, the female component of Cox's

Table 1 Estimated Relationships between New England Voting Patterns in the 1916 and 1920 Presidential Elections (in percentages of 1920 adult citizens)

	1916:					
1920:	HUGHES	WILSON	ALL OTHERS	MEN NOT VOTING IN 1916	WOMEN NOT YET ELIGIBLE	PERCENT OF 1920 ELECTORATE
Harding	9	3	0	5	16	33
Cox	0	7	0	0	9	16
Debs and All Others	0	0	1	0	1	2
Abstaining	7	4	0	13	25	49
Percent of 1920 Electorate	16	14	1	18	51	100

NOTE: Actual N=67.
SOURCE: Political Science Archives, Univ. of Minnesota, Minneapolis.

12 The data consisted of 612 county presidential election returns for 1916 and 1920 from 16 northern states. All voting statistics were calculated on the basis of 1920 adult citizens. The data were supplied by W. Phillips Shively and are deposited in the Political Science Data Archives of the University of Minnesota, Minneapolis.

vote was derived by subtracting the Wilson men who subsequently voted for Cox from the total 1920 Democratic vote.[13]

The estimated relationships between voting patterns in the 1916 and 1920 presidential elections for the Mid-Atlantic region and the Midwest states (excluding Illinois) are presented in Tables 2 and 3. The estimated sex differences in the 1920 balloting in the New England, Mid-Atlantic, and the Midwestern states, plus the actual, not estimated, breakdown of the male and female vote in Illinois, and composite estimates for all these northern regions, are presented in Table 4 for convenient comparison.

One way to assess the effects of the extension of suffrage to women is to ask what difference female ballots made in the outcome of the 1920 election. What happened in fact compared to what would have happened if the Nineteenth Amendment had
8 not become the law of the land? If women had not voted in

Table 2 Estimated Relationships between Mid-Atlantic Voting Patterns in the 1916 and 1920 Presidential Elections[a] (in percentages of 1920 adult citizens)

	1916:					
1920:	HUGHES	WILSON	ALL OTHERS	MEN NOT VOTING IN 1916	WOMEN NOT YET ELIGIBLE	PERCENT OF 1920 ELECTORATE
Harding	16	1	0	0	17	34
Cox	0	9	0	1	6	16
Debs and All Others	0	1	1	1	0	3
Abstaining	1	3	0	16	27	47
Percent of 1920 Electorate	17	14	1	18	50	100

NOTE: Actual N=211.

SOURCE: Political Science Data Archives, Univ. of Minnesota, Minneapolis.

a New York, New Jersey, Pennsylvania, Delaware, Maryland, and West Virginia.

13 The figures in Table 1 represent the percentage of adult citizens, not the conventional percentage of votes cast. The marginals are the actual figures, not estimates. Thus, if the percentage of adult citizens voting for Harding (33%) is added to the percentage for Cox (16%) and for all other candidates (2%), the sum equals the turnout in New England for the election of 1920. Elsewhere in the tables rounding off occasionally produces totals slightly more or less than 100%.

Table 3 Estimated Relationships between Midwestern Voting Patterns in the 1916 and 1920 Presidential Elections[a] (in percentages of 1920 adult citizens)

	1916:					
1920:	HUGHES	WILSON	ALL OTHERS	MEN NOT VOTING IN 1916	WOMEN NOT YET ELIGIBLE	PERCENT OF 1920 ELECTORATE
Harding	17	5	0	0	16	38
Cox	0	8	1	0	11	20
Debs and All Others	0	0	1	0	2	3
Abstaining	0	4	0	15	20	39
Percent of 1920 Electorate	17	17	2	15	49	100

NOTE: Actual N=334. 9
SOURCE: Political Science Data Archives, Univ. of Minnesota, Minneapolis.

a Indiana, Michigan, Ohio, and Wisconsin.

Illinois and in the Mid-Atlantic states, Harding's relatively large majorities over Cox (as expressed by percentages of the ballots cast) would have decreased, slightly in Illinois and substantially in the Mid-Atlantic states (see Table 4). Thus, women helped Harding in these regions. But the opposite appears to have been the case in New England and in the Midwest (outside of Illinois). Harding's majority over Cox (again, in terms of the percentage of the popular vote) would have substantially increased had women not voted. These findings tend to support Bagly's assessment that nationwide in the 1920 election "woman suffrage did not seem to aid Harding significantly."[14]

In Illinois and in the Mid-Atlantic states, Harding fared better at the hands of female voters than at the hands of male voters (see Table 4). But in New England and the Midwest, women who voted were not more demonstrably in the Republican column than were their male counterparts at the polls. In these regions, Cox, albeit in a losing cause, fared better among women who voted than among men who voted. The results for New England and the Midwest (again, outside of Illinois) bring into serious

14 Bagly, *Road to Normalcy*, 160.

Table 4 Voting by Sex in the 1920 Presidential Election in the New England, Mid-Atlantic, and Midwestern States

	NEW ENGLAND (N=67)		MID-ATLANTIC (N=211)		MIDWEST				ALL THREE REGIONS COMBINED		
					IND., MICH., OHIO, AND WISC. (N=334)		ILLINOIS[a]		COMPOSITE ESTIMATES[b]		ACTUAL VOTING PREFERENCES OF ALL POTENTIAL VOTERS
PRESIDENTIAL CANDIDATES IN 1920:	WOMEN	MEN	WOMEN	MEN	WOMEN	MEN	WOMEN	MEN	WOMEN	MEN	
Warren G. Harding	31	35	34	34	33	43	33	49	34	37	36
James M. Cox	18	14	12	20	22	18	11	19	17	18	17
Eugene V. Debs and All Others	2	2	0	6	4	2	2	6	2	4	3
Abstaining	49	49	54	40	41	37	53	26	47	41	44

a Actual, not estimated, voting preferences of men and women.

b The composite estimates for all three regions were derived by first pooling together the northern counties outside Illinois (N=612) to gain estimates of the behavior of women versus men in all 16 states combined. When combined with the actual, not estimated, voting preferences of Illinois women and men, the estimates for the combined 16 state regions were weighted 6.97 times to equal the real voting population parameters.

question the popular belief that Harding's handsome appearance attracted many female votes. Nor do the results support the notion that Harding fared particularly well among new women voters because he was perceived to be the more "moral" candidate.[15]

The estimates in Table 4, moreover, reveal no uniform sex difference in voting in the North in the 1920 election. Although the absence of a clear-cut sex difference in northern voting patterns does not necessarily mean that women divided their vote similarly to men, the results show some significant incongruencies in male and female voting. For example, as previously noted, Cox ran slightly better among women than among men in New England and the Midwest (excluding Illinois). And according to the estimates, in the Midwest (again, excluding Illinois) third party candidates fared better among female eligibles than among 11
male eligibles (see Table 4). Although these and other regional differences in the comparative support of men and women for presidential candidates constitute interesting findings, they are difficult to explain. Contemporaries of the period seldom, if ever, commented on regional variations in the voting behavior of men versus women. Before scholars can explain the emergence of regional differences or give them historical significance, it is necessary to ascertain as accurately as possible how men and women voted. The results presented here are a step into this largely unexplored territory.

These findings should caution scholars against the assumption that women's votes were a mirror reflection of men's. Although the results in Table 4 do not permit a direct test of the widely held notion that women initially voted according to their husbands', brothers', or fathers' wishes, the estimates of relationships between voting patterns in the 1916 and 1920 Illinois presidential races permit a subtle and precise comparison of the voting behavior of the state's men and women between these two elections. According to the estimates of voting by gender in Table 5, the Illinois female electorate was only slightly less predictable (in terms of failing to repeat their same behavior, e.g., repeating a party vote or repeating not voting) between 1916 and 1920 than the state's male electorate. This greater fluctuation in the female

15 Lemons, *Woman Citizen*, 87; Willey and Rice, "Sex Cleavage," 519–520.

Table 5 Regression Estimates of Stability and Change in Party Preference Among Male and Female Voters in Illinois between 1916 and 1920 (in percentages of male and female electorates)

	REPEAT DEM	REPEAT REP	REPEAT 3RD PARTY	REPEAT NOT VOTING[a]	(TOTAL STABILITY)	REP TO DEM	DEM TO REP	NEW DEMS	NEW REPS	NEW 3RD PARTY	DEM DROPOUT	REP DROPOUT	3RD PARTY DROPOUT	DEMS TO 3RD PARTY	(TOTAL INSTABILITY[b])
Men:	19	39	3	17	(78)	—	2	—	8	1	9	—	—	2	(22)
Women:	11	23	1	39	(74)	—	—	—	10	—	10	4	1	1	(26)

NOTE: Actual N = 102.

a Repeating not voting includes those not yet eligible in 1916 who subsequently abstained in 1920.

b Total instability includes, in addition, a few other combinations of possible voter behavior between 1916 and 1920 not necessary to report here, namely segments of the respective electorates comprised of 1920 third party supporters who were either previous nonvoters or former Republicans, and former third party voters who in 1920 switched to the Republicans or Democrats.

vote was due to the larger percentage of women who voted in one election but not in the other. It was not attributable to a higher percentage of women switching parties between the two elections: only about 1 percent of the female electorate crossed party lines, whereas about 4 percent of the males switched parties.[16]

The lack of party switching among Illinois women is surprising in light of the so-called "immunization" argument which holds that those groups who begin voting will be less loyal to political parties than those groups who have been voting for years. One might expect the party loyalty of women who participated in both the 1916 and 1920 elections to be more erratic, on the whole, than that of men. However, when controlling for the level of turnout, the newly enfranchised Illinois women were not less strongly committed to a particular party than their male counter- 13
parts. One could argue, however, that the potential for the susceptibility of the Illinois female electorate to partisan realignment was greater because of the larger proportion of women not voting. Thus, as part of the "nonimmunized" population, women comprised a disproportionate share of those citizens available for future political mobilization.[17]

The most important observation to make from the estimates in Table 4 is the anomalous nature of the Illinois returns, a finding that agrees with the results of Kleppner's analysis of non-southern state turnout rates. The ratio of the rates of female to male nonvoting was much higher in Illinois than in any other region. With its ballots counted by sex, Illinois was often assumed to be typical of the nation as a whole.[18]

16 Goldstein also finds that Illinois women were less stable in their voting behavior than men, but he bases his finding on frequencies of ticket-splitting, failures to vote a complete ticket, and tendencies to vote for third party candidates—all in a relatively low-salience election for trustees of the University of Illinois. Goldstein, "Effects of the Adoption of Woman Suffrage," 135.

17 Philip E. Converse, "Of Time and Partisan Stability," *Comparative Political Studies*, II (1969), 139–171. The relationship between nonvoting and party identification is demonstrated in Angus Campbell, Converse, Warren E. Miller, and Donald E. Stokes, *The American Voter* (New York, 1960), 96–101. On the importance of "nonimmunized" women to the New Deal realignment, see Norman H. Nie, Sidney Verba, and John R. Petrocik, *The Changing American Voter* (Cambridge, Mass., 1976), 77. See also Anderson, *Creation of a Democratic Majority*, 19–72.

18 Kleppner, "Were Women to Blame?" 626–627, 633.

In Illinois only 47 percent of the women voted compared with 74 percent of the men. Yet in the Mid-Atlantic section, where a substantial number of women did not vote, there was still not as high a discrepancy between male and female abstentions (see Table 4). The estimates show that in the Mid-Atlantic region 46 percent of the women voted as compared to 60 percent of the men. In New England the estimates suggest that 51 percent of the women voted in congruence with their counterparts. (Male turnout was perhaps relatively low in New England where Republican predictions of victory before the election carried an air of certainty.) In the Midwest (excluding Illinois) 59 percent of the eligible women voted in comparison to 63 percent of the men. The conclusion seems inescapable that a substantial percentage of the turnout decline in the North in 1920 was attributable to
14 increased abstention by males.

According to the "socialization-learning" model, it is surprising that much greater percentages of the turnout decline in 1920 were not due to enfranchising women. Because potential voters allegedly become educated and politicized over time, newly enfranchised women should have had a lower probability of voting than experienced voters.[19]

Although articulate and politically competent feminist leaders were determined to reach women less educated, less politically aware, and often culturally different than they were, scholars have perceived a gap between the leaders and the masses that created a barrier to a quick integration of females into the voting population. Given that the woman suffrage amendment was not ratified until late August, 1920, with the November election rapidly approaching, and that it was handicapped by less than enthusiastic support of society, it is no wonder that women as a whole did not embrace the innovation and exercise their vote immediately. Even though the estimates point to low male-female turnout differentials in New England and the Midwest (outside of Illinois), many female leaders accepted the post-election impression that

19 For a summarization of "socialization-learning" theory, see Campbell et al., *American Voter*, 473–491. For general information on diffusion of innovation theory, see Everett M. Rogers with F. Floyd Shoemaker, *Communication of Innovations—A Cross-Cultural Approach* (New York, 1971; 2nd ed.), 6–18.

woman suffrage was a failure. Lemons calls the election of 1920 "a tremendous disappointment" to suffragists.[20]

A RE-EVALUATION OF THE IMPACT OF THE NINETEENTH AMENDMENT

Those who perceived woman suffrage as a failure did not see it in the context of a general disillusionment in post World War I America. In the early 1920s, voter participation reached all-time lows. Considerable apathy characterized the 1920 presidential contest as most Americans were tired of Wilson's idealism and his wartime cry to "Save the World for Democracy." The timing of the receipt of the vote by women was also unfortunate in that the vote was an element of representative government that lost some of its value during a war in which emergency measures abrogated civil rights on the homefront.[21]

In the 1920s tremendous attention was directed at evaluating the success or failure of woman suffrage in the presidential election and in other political contests. The *Literary Digest* took a nationwide poll of newspaper editors on the question. The *Woman Citizen*, the official publication of the League of Women Voters, reported a number of male answers to their query: "Do Women Count in Politics?" The responses soon became the sources of explanations for the assumed failure. "Why More Women Don't Vote" headed the *Literary Digest*'s report of their survey. The articles concluded that women needed "a little more education in voting." This demeaning evaluation harkened back to a *Woman Citizen* cover for September 1920. "Are You Blind Politically?" asked the front cover caption next to a drawing of a blind woman. "Are Women a Failure in Politics?" asked Emily Newell Blair, vice-chairman of the Democratic National Committee. Noting the small number of females elected to public office, Blair argued that progress was necessarily slow because it took time to capture public confidence. Furthermore, there was no women's voting bloc, and club women who had supported suffrage had become non-partisan. Women in politics, such as Blair, were by their own

20 Lemons, *Woman Citizen*, 51.

21 Declines in turnout characterized the so-called fourth party system that most political historians claim extended from 1896 to the New Deal. See Burnham, "The System of 1896: An Analysis," in Kleppner et al., *American Electoral Systems*, 145–202. See also Cicely Hamilton, "Women in Present Day Politics," *English Review*, XXXII (1921), 158–166.

admission handicapped by their brief tenure in the political in-group.[22]

Some contemporary writers judged ordinary female voters harshly. Their evaluations alleged a lack of interest in public affairs, an apathy, and an absence of concern, not so much in issues at hand, as in principles behind them. "How About the Ladies?" asked another article subtitled, "Are They Proving To The Skeptical Stronger Sex That They Can Make Good on the Dusty Battlefield of Practical Politics?" Evidently not. The author felt that American women had not advanced further in politics because the majority of women had not asked for suffrage, and, once the ballot was given to them, had not exercised their right to vote. "Women's Faults in Politics" blared out Kent's article for the *Woman Citizen*. "Mrs. Voter Does Not Yet Hold Her Own
16 With Mr. Voter in Interest, Information, Registration and Marking the Ballot." Once again women were accused of doing nothing with their vote, especially after having claimed that they would do so much with it. Kent also reinforced the assumption that women voted like their husbands and concluded that women needed more political education before they could be effective in politics.[23]

Suffrage leaders' high expectation for positive ramifications of the passage of the Nineteenth Amendment combined with exaggerated reports of nonvoting among eligible women and a paucity of females elected to public office gave a name to a 1924 article and a recurrent question to the 1920s: "Is Woman Suffrage a Failure?" In this article, which has been cited in numerous histories of the period, Charles Edward Russell declared that it would be "absurd" to consider the reform a success. Although he wrote that none of the feared disasters, like the break up of family, occurred, neither did woman suffrage bear its promised fruit, for

22 "Do Women Count in Politics?" *Woman Citizen*, VII (18 Nov. 1922), 11; "Why More Women Voters Don't Vote," *Literary Digest*, LXXXI (24 May 1924), 7; *Woman Citizen*, V (4 Sept. 1920); Emily Newell Blair, "Are Women a Failure in Politics?" *Harper's Magazine*, CLI (Oct. 1925), 513–522.

23 George Madden Martin, "American Women and Public Affairs," *Atlantic Monthly*, CXXXIII (Feb. 1924), 169–171; Anna Steese Richardson, "How About the Ladies?" *Collier's*, XXVII (Sept. 1924), 18, 39; Kent, "Women's Faults in Politics," 23, 46–48.

nothing had changed, except that "the number of docile ballot-droppers has approximately been doubled."[24]

Russell attributed part of that failure to women voting like their husbands and male relatives, but his deep-seated disappointment with the many women who "did not care enough about any public duty to vote" drove him to exaggerate the lack of participation by women in the 1920 election and to conjure up reasons for it. Russell felt that women did not vote because they did not understand the realities of pragmatic politics. Even though he judged the few women elected to public office after woman suffrage was passed to be competent, he noted that "women would not vote for women," and he predicted that this trend would continue. According to Russell, politicians had nothing to fear for there was no women's bloc vote. He concluded that, as
a consequence, men had adopted a "half-contemptuous attitude" 17
toward female voters.[25]

Historians who have recently analyzed the women's movement of the 1920s have reinforced the substance of Russell's views. Lemons concludes: "The question 'Is woman suffrage a failure?' was possible only because more had been promised during the heat of the suffrage struggle than could be delivered." But this insight has not eradicated the notion that many women did not vote and the perception that women did not vote differently than their male predecessors.[26]

Not all of the attention to the women's movement in the 1920s and subsequently focused on women's alleged failures in the political arena. Some contemporaries of the period encouraged women. "Stand Up and Be Counted," *Good Housekeeping* urged its female readers. The *Literary Digest* continued to pay attention to female political victories. The *Woman Citizen* featured a tribute to accomplishments of female voters and ran a series about "Women Who Won" and "More Women Who Won" to highlight the victories of female politicians. For the column entitled "The Women Did It," entries were requested for "best stories of the

24 Charles Edward Russell, "Is Woman Suffrage a Failure?" *Century*, CVII (March 1924), 724–730.

25 *Ibid.*, 725–729.

26 Lemons, *Woman Citizen*, 112; Chafe, *American Woman*, 30–32.

finest, most helpful and most interesting thing done by women in this season's elections." One of these stories covered the support that Pennsylvania women gave Gifford Pinchot for the Republican gubernatorial nomination against the Republican party machine candidate. Women, apparently responsible for Pinchot's nomination, thereby disproved the assumption that women merely doubled the vote. Pinchot himself acknowledged "the Influence of Women in Politics" in his nomination victory.[27]

Even though recent autopsies on the women's movement of the 1920s have dwelt on assumptions of female apathy in the political realm, they have also acknowledged at least one positive result of female voters' impact. They have credited the role of women in the 1921 passage of the Sheppard Towner bill which provided for instruction in hygiene for maternity and infant care.
18 Decidedly, women had banded together and put pressure on their elected representatives to push the legislation through Congress. In this instance their lobbying efforts succeeded. Harriet Taylor Upton, vice-chairman of the Republican National Executive Committee and head of Women's Activities, claimed that a women's bloc could exist only as a temporary phenomenon whenever women sensed a specific issue affecting them directly and cited the maternity bill as a case in point. She cautioned, however, that such action did not constitute a genuine women's bloc. Women, Upton stated, "do not want to quarrel with men; they do not want to differ from men on lines of sex distinction." She argued that women would never vote for women because of their sex; they would vote for the most qualified individuals.[28]

Many women objected to being urged into a women's bloc to vote only for women or to vote strictly on the basis of women's issues. To focus on their sex seemed to question their commonality with men as human beings. This reaction was true of some

27 "Stand Up and Be Counted," *Good Housekeeping*, LXXVII (Dec. 1923), 1; "Women Who Won," *Woman Citizen*, VII (18 Nov. 1922), 8, 9, 10, 29; "More Women Who Won," *ibid.* (2 Dec. 1922), 10, 11; "Woman's Bigger Dent in Politics," *Literary Digest* (22 Nov. 1924), 17; "More Women Laying Down the Law," *ibid.* (19 Jan. 1929), 12; "They Got Their Man: The Women Did It," *Woman Citizen*, VII (18 Nov. 1922), 12, 27; "The Women Did It," *ibid.* (3 June 1922), 7–8, 16; Gifford Pinchot, "The Influence of Women in Politics," *Ladies' Home Journal*, XXXIX (Sept. 1922), 13, 116.

28 Lemons, *Woman Citizen*, 158–180; Chafe, *American Woman*, 27–29, 43; "The Present Moment," *Woman Citizen*, V (25 Dec. 1920), 813–814; Harriet Taylor Upton, "The Machine and the Woman," *Ladies' Home Journal*, XXXIX (Oct. 1922), 13, 159.

female leaders as well. A politician who decided to drop her work in women's groups to join other politically minded women in the major parties said that the women she joined saw themselves "as human beings first, not primarily women." Moreover, she agreed with them: "Let us lump the women in one human-beings' organization where they can learn from each other, adjust, adapt, and work out their problems together; and—just maybe—shape some day a human-being's instead of a man's or woman's world."[29]

Carrie Chapman Catt, leader of the influential League of Women Voters, agreed. She persuaded her organization to take a strictly non-partisan tack and reject the idea of a women's bloc. The League would educate the general public on political issues, but would not support a candidate just because she was a woman. Neither would the League support an equal rights amendment 19
nor form a separate women's party. "No Sex Line Up" argued its journal, the *Woman Citizen*, in opposition to the Woman's Party's proposed equal rights amendment. Although Freda Kirchwey, a feminist journalist, supported an equal rights amendment, she spoke for the majority of women with a negative response to the Woman's Party's 1924 appeal to women to vote for any female candidate, regardless of party affiliation, if the candidate endorsed the equal rights amendment and a feminist program. She assessed their plan as bad politics, arguing that "women are going to vote according to the dictates of class interest and personal interest as well as sex interest." Kirchwey thought that the Woman's Party had mistakenly urged female voters "to forget they are also human beings."[30]

Indeed, many politically minded women made an effort to vote as human beings, rather than to vote in their sex's best interest. Grace Abbott, head of the Children's Bureau in the Department of Labor, evaluated the voting record of women by 1925. She found that, unlike interest groups such as manufacturers or bankers, women consciously avoided a women's bloc vote:

29 Grace Abbott, "What Have They Done?" *The Independent* (24 Oct. 1925), 475–476, 483; Elizabeth Green, "I Resign From Female Politics," *New Republic*, XLII (22 Apr. 1925), 234–235.

30 "No Sex Line Up," *Woman Citizen*, VII (3 June 1922), 13; Freda Kirchwey, unsigned editorial, *The Nation*, CXIII (5 Oct. 1921), 362–363; "A Women's Bloc?" *ibid.*, CXIX (3 Sept. 1924), 230–231.

"Women are trying hard to vote as citizens rather than as women, measuring a party or candidate in terms of their judgment on general community needs." She acknowledged that the absence of a women's bloc probably meant that female voters were not feared by politicians. According to Anne Martin, an unsuccessful candidate for a Senate seat from Nevada, the politicians were aware that individual female leaders must abide by the decisions of their party because there was no retaliation to be feared from women as a group. Martin claimed that women would "get only as much as they organize for and demand effectually as a separate political force." As early as 1921 she argued that the world could be a human world only after women received human rights equal to men, thus putting sex out of politics.[31]

Martin's minority view of the necessity for women to vote
20 as a bloc probably was the only viable path for the effective entry of women into the political scene after the passage of the Nineteenth Amendment. Yet many leaders echoed the early strategy of Blair, who wrote of women in 1925: "Confidence must be won and not demanded. She must make these men forget, if she can, that she is a woman." By 1931 Blair reversed her stance. Writing of her frustration over the lack of a women's bloc in politics, she mused, "I am discouraged because I have been ineffective in politics as a feminist."[32]

Female voters, by and large, did not vote for female politicians who campaigned for greater opportunities for women. The League of Women Voters, a logical organization to support feminist issues, provided women with education for exercising citizenship, but did not stress the need to elect feminists or to increase the number of elected females. After a decade of woman suffrage, politics remained a "male monopoly." Furthermore, many former female activists dropped the "sex line" in their campaigns. The familiar statement, " 'I am running not as a woman, but as a Democrat (or as a Republican),' " became the standard line.[33]

31 Abbott, "What Have They Done?" 476; Anne Martin, "Feminists and Future Political Action," *The Nation*, CXX (3 Feb. 1925), 185–186; "Woman's Inferiority Complex," *New Republic*, XXVII (20 July 1921), 210.

32 Blair, "Are Women a Failure?", 521; *idem*, "Why I am Discouraged About Women in Politics," *Woman's Journal*, XVI (Jan. 1931), 20.

33 *Ibid.*, 20, 22.

Wanting to be seen as competent human beings inhibited women from running for political office as conscious feminists. Yet the same female candidates who ran as political party loyalists found thousands of votes cast against them because they were women. Without a women's bloc, female political candidates thus faced a dilemma. They were voted against because of their sex; they were not recognized as viable candidates in their party because they lacked a power base. A female politician was unquestionably handicapped because of her sex. Until major party leaders saw women as a bloc to be influenced and feared, sex would necessarily remain an issue in politics.[34]

The views of feminists who advocated a women's bloc strategy were not adopted in the 1920s. Instead many female leaders assumed what they wanted to believe—that the vote had already
given them equal rights with men. They wanted to believe that 21
society saw them as human beings first, not as women first. Therefore, to call attention to their femaleness meant to acknowledge that they were not yet equal. So they stressed their human beingness in a society that still saw their femaleness as predominant. As Freedman concludes, women in the 1920s "opted for assimilation in the naive hope of becoming men's equals overnight."[35]

The prevalent belief in the 1920s that with suffrage women had achieved an as yet unrealized equality with men resulted in the failure to create a women's bloc to push for female equality. The absence of a women's bloc reinforced several societal stereotypes about women: that women did not have minds of their own and that women failed in politics. On an even deeper level this pervasive attitude undermined women's self-image and their ability to affect social change.

Analyzing actual voting returns from the election of 1920 shows that women were not as apathetic as traditionally portrayed. Many previous assessments erroneously over-generalized from the readily available Illinois data to other parts of the country. Illinois's figures are misleading in exaggerating a high differ-

34 A. Martin, "Feminists and Future Political Action," 185–186; Blair, "Are Women a Failure in Politics?" 513–522.

35 Estelle Freedman, "Separatism as Strategy: Female Institution Building and American Feminism," *Feminist Studies*, V (1979), 515

ential between female and male turnouts, distorting society's views about women and, as a consequence, negatively affecting women's self-image. Elsewhere in the North, a high percentage of turnout decline resulted from increased absenteeism of males. This study also calls into question reliance on socialization-learning theory alone to explain low voter turnout. The timing of the receipt of the vote was pertinent. Many women became voters in a legal and political milieu characterized by the declining import of the ballot.[36]

The voting behavior of women in the election of 1920 should not have thwarted the vitality of the women's movement. Women did not demonstrate a high degree of apathy (except in Illinois) when compared to male counterparts in that election. Nor did women vote as carbon copies of men. Yet stereotypical attitudes
22 that women belonged in the home and that politics should be left to men no doubt perpetuated the initial assessments of female political apathy and dependency. Rather than the actual female vote, the incorrect and long-lived exaggerations of female apathy and dependency proved detrimental to the women's movement. Such erroneous views reinforced self-effacing attitudes among women for their own sex, which in turn helps explain some of the decline of feminist activity in the 1920s.

The most telling blow to the women's movement came from the absence of a women's bloc vote during the first national political test of females as a power base. Many female leaders and female voters attempted assimilation with men in the two-party system, rather than sustaining the struggle for equality for women through a women's bloc. These women underestimated the tenacity of resistance against women's integration into the political structure. When no women's bloc materialized, party leaders could ignore females as a group to be influenced and feared. Divided over the women's bloc issue, the women's movement lost momentum. No focused strategy survived to combat remaining sexual inequalities. The belief of some female leaders that

36 See Kleppner, "Were Women to Blame?" for corraborative evidence for inordinate reliance on Illinois. For further evidence of insufficiency of socialization-learning theory, see *ibid.*; William Clagget, "The Life Cycle and Generational Models of the Development of Partisanship: A Text Based on the Delayed Enfranchisement of Women," *Social Science Quarterly*, LX (1980), 643–650.

they had become men's equals outside the polling place impeded their unfinished quest for full equality in American society.

APPENDIX

All county voting returns for 1916 and 1920 were calculated on the basis of 1920 adult citizens, a substitute measure for the actual number of potentially eligible voters in every county in the sixteen northern states included in the analyses. The regression equations were run from the 1920 election to the 1916 election or *backwards*, predicting the vote in first election from the vote in the second. This is both a valid and necessary operation for two reasons. First, causality is not posited here. The vote in 1916 does not cause the vote in 1920, any more than the latter causes the former. Second, the artifact of backward regression provides a procedure for circumventing the random error resulting from minimal county-to-county variation in the percentage of adult females. Because there is near zero variance in percent female, very little of the 23
variance in the partisan distribution of the vote can statistically be attributed to it.[37]

The regression equations used took the following form:

$$\frac{V^{M}_{ij1}}{M_{i2} + W_{i2}} = \sum_{j=0}^{J} B_j \frac{V^{M}_{ij2} + V^{W}_{ij2}}{M_{i2} + W_{i2}} + e_i$$

where: V is the vote for some candidate (or those not voting)
M is the male voting population
W is the female voting population
i is the county
j is each candidate's vote
1 denotes 1916
2 denotes 1920
and
e is the error term

The figures within the cells of the first column of Table A1 were derived by running a multiple regression with the 1916 Hughes percentage as dependent and the 1920 Harding, Cox, and "Debs and All Others" percentages as independent variables. To avoid multicollinearity, the percentage of 1920 eligibles who did not vote in the 1920 presidential election was not used. In a hypothetical voting unit where every eligible voter cast a ballot for Harding in 1920, the predicted Hughes vote in 1916 was constant plus B_1 coefficient. This sum equalled

37 Cf. Lichtman, *Prejudice and the Old Politics: The Presidential Election of 1928* (Chapel Hill, 1979), 159–165, who employs regression analysis to determine how women voted in the 1928 presidential election.

the estimated proportion of Harding voters who had voted previously for Hughes. Likewise, constant plus B_2 coefficient gave the estimated proportion of Cox voters who had voted for Hughes and constant plus B_3 coefficient gave the estimated proportion of 1920 third party voters who had voted for Hughes. The constant was the estimated proportion of those who did not vote in 1920 who had previously voted for Hughes.

The variables used in the equations were weighted by the number of adult citizens so that sparsely populated counties would not be overrepresented in the analysis. Logically, but not statistically impossible, estimates which fell outside the 0 to 100 percent range were arbitrarily set at their respective minimum or maximum limits and the values of the remaining estimates of male voting were then adjusted according to the restraints of the marginal values of the tables. In following this procedure we made no modifications in logical estimates of male voters repeating a vote for the same party in both elections. Similarly unaffected by this procedure were estimates of the percentage of previous nonvot-
24 ing males who subsequently did not vote.[38]

As a check on the estimation procedure, a similar analysis was run for Illinois. This analysis was possible because, even though Illinois women voted in 1916, the state year book reports separate vote totals by sex for each county in the 1916 presidential election. The estimation procedure overestimated female turnout for Harding by 2 percent, overestimated female turnout for Cox by 1 percent, and underestimated the percentage of women citizens who did not vote for president by 4 percent (see Table A1). The procedure underestimated the true differences in turnout between males and females: whereas the actual differential between Illinois men and women is 27 percentage points, the estimated results indicate a differential of 18 percentage points. Errors in this same direction in the New England, Mid-Atlantic, and remainder of the Midwestern states would skew the results by minimizing turnout differences between men and women. Unfortunately, it is impossible to know for certain whether the diminution of male-female differences revealed in the Illinois estimates represents a systematic bias that will be repeated elsewhere. But these methodological considerations suggest that, although the backward regression procedure is likely to uncover correctly the direction of any differences in male versus female behavior, some caution should be exercised in drawing conclusions about the magnitude of such differences.

38 For the reasons to have more confidence in these estimates than others, see Shively, "Ecological Inference: The Use of Aggregate Data to Study Individuals," *American Political Science Review*, LXIV (1969), 1191.

Table A1 A Check on the Regression Procedure: Estimated Relationships between the Voting Patterns of Illinois Men in 1916 and the Partisan Division of the Illinois Vote in 1920 (in percentages of 1920 adult citizens)

	1916:					
1920:	MALE BALLOTS FOR HUGHES	MALE BALLOTS FOR WILSON	MALE BALLOTS FOR ALL OTHERS	MEN NOT VOTING IN 1916	WOMEN THEORETICALLY NOT YET ELIGIBLE	PERCENT OF 1920 ELECTORATE
Harding	20	3	1	0	17	41
Cox	0	9	0	0	6	15
Debs and All Others	0	1	1	0	2	4
Not Voting in 1920	0	3	0	13	24	40
Percent of 1920 Electorate	20	16	2	13	49	100

NOTE: Actual N = 102. The above results produce the following estimates of voting preferences of Illinois women and men in 1920:

PERCENTAGE OF WOMEN VOTING IN 1920 FOR:

	ESTIMATED	ACTUAL
Harding	35%	33%
Cox	12%	11%
All Others	4%	2%
Not Voting	49%	53%

PERCENTAGE OF MEN VOTING IN 1920 FOR:

	ESTIMATED	ACTUAL
Harding	47%	49%
Cox	18%	19%
All Others	4%	6%
Not Voting	31%	26%

SOURCE: Political Science Data Archives, Univ. of Minnesota, Minneapolis, Minn. Illinois returns are contained in Louis L. Emmerson (ed.), *Blue Book of the State of Illinois, 1921–1922* (Springfield, Ill., 1921), 768–770; *Blue Book of the State of Illinois, 1917–1918* (Danville, Ill., 1917), 582–584.

EQUITY VS. EQUALITY: EMERGING CONCEPTS OF WOMEN'S POLITICAL STATUS IN THE AGE OF JACKSON

Norma Basch

One of the hallmarks of scholarship in women's history has been the quest to understand women on their own terms and in their own words — to see history through women's eyes. The quest has revolutionized the formulation of questions, the choice of sources, and the contours of periodization. It has yielded rich results for the period traditionally designated the Age of Jackson, the heyday of the cult of domesticity, when women were largely excluded from the extravagantly egalitarian political rhetoric of the era. Clearly Jacksonian politics, narrowly defined, were not part of woman's sphere.[1] But while emphasis on the separate, private, domestic world of white middle and upper class women has given us profound insights into their personal lives and even into their quasi-political activities, it has also diverted us from exploring emerging

---

Ms. Basch is a member of the Department of History, University College, at Rutgers University in Newark, N.J.

[1] As historians have subjected the cult of domesticity to increasingly sophisticated analyses over the past decade and a half, they have engendered controversy over its political implications and its connections to antebellum feminism. For a clear delineation of the controversy, see Ellen Carol DuBois, Mari Jo Buhle, Temma Kaplan, Gerda Lerner, and Carroll Smith-Rosenberg, "Politics and Culture in Women's History: A Symposium," *Feminist Studies*, 6 (Spring 1980), 26-64. Historical literature on the cult of domesticity is extensive. The following examples merely highlight the development of the controversy. For a critical and now classic evaluation of the cult of domesticity, see Barbara Welter, "The Cult of True Womanhood, 1820-1860," *American Quarterly*, 18 (Summer 1966), 151-174. For a more recent but still critical approach, see Ann Douglas, *The*

notions of women's relationship to the state. Perhaps the rejection of androcentric approaches and sources has led us to view the male/female, public/private dichotomy so literally as to have obscured subtle shifts in concepts about women that were emanating from the "dominant" or male legal and political cultures.[2]

This essay is an attempt to sketch some of those shifts by focusing on the connections between the legal and political cultures of the Jacksonian era. The hypothesis put forward here is that a modest transition in the legal culture (the passage of legislation granting property rights to married women) was the first stage in a significant transition in the political culture — the integration of

---

Feminization of American Culture (New York 1977). On ties between domesticity and the class structure, gender roles, and political status, see Gerda Lerner, "The Lady and the Mill Girl: Changes in the Status of Women in the Age of Jackson," *Midcontinent American Studies Journal*, 10 (Spring 1969), 5-15. On the possibilities of protofeminism in the cult of domesticity, see Carroll Smith-Rosenberg, "Beauty, the Beast and the Militant Woman: A Case Study in Sex Roles and Social Stress in Jacksonian America," *American Quarterly*, 23 (Oct. 1971), 562-584. For a pioneering exploration of the compensatory aspects of domesticity, see Kathryn Kish Sklar, *Catherine Beecher: A Study in American Domesticity* (New Haven 1973). For both the possibilities and limitations that the cult of domesticity exerted over the development of feminism, see Nancy F. Cott, *The Bonds of Womanhood: "Woman's Sphere" in New England, 1780-1835* (New Haven 1977). For the emergence of "domestic feminism," see Daniel Scott Smith, "Family Limitation, Sexual Control, and Domestic Feminism in Victorian America," in *A Heritage of Her Own: Toward a New Social History of American Women*, ed. Nancy F. Cott and Elizabeth H. Pleck (New York 1979), 222-245. In contrast, Ellen DuBois has taken historians of women to task for their failure to appreciate the political necessity for women's penetration beyond the boundaries of the domestic sphere. See "The Radicalism of the Woman Suffrage Movement: Notes toward the Reconstruction of Nineteenth-Century Feminism," *Feminist Studies*, 3 (Fall 1975), 63-71, and *Feminism and Suffrage: The Emergence of an Independent Women's Movement in America* (Ithaca 1978.) 27

[2] Scholars who have bridged the public/private gulf have done so by defining politics broadly. For an overview of this trend, see Elaine Tyler May, "Expanding the Past: Recent Scholarship on Women in Politics and Work," *Reviews in American History*, 10 (Dec. 1982), 216-217. But scholars in women's history have not pursued the activities of formal political institutions such as state legislatures with the same zeal. Some social historians, moreover, consider a focus on the relative status of women and men, and a reliance on male prescriptive sources "counterproductive." For a critique of this trend, see Hilda Smith, "Women's History and the Humanities," *OAH Newsletter*, May 1983, 14.

women into an egalitarian political ethos.[3] These transitions shed some light, moreover, on the origins of antebellum feminism.[4] The public dialogue over the property rights of married women which emerged and intensified during the second quarter of the nineteenth century unleashed two competing and overlapping clusters of ideas about the appropriate status of American women. At the core of one cluster was the concept of equity; at the core of the other was the concept of equality.

The concept of equity assumed that the property a wife brought to marriage or inherited afterward, if it were separated from the property of her husband with an appropriate legal instrument, was hers and entitled her to certain privileges, not the least of which was the insulation of her property from her husband's creditors. It also assumed that she might be considered a distinct and independent legal personality with respect to her
28 separate estate.[5] Most of the time it cohered quite comfortably with the doctrine of separate sexual spheres and, although it challenged the husband's conjugal authority, protection from creditors presented advantages to the husband. Some adherents of

---

[3] For the pathbreaking study on the married women's acts, see Elizabeth Bowles Warbasse, "The Changing Legal Rights of Married Women, 1800-1861" (Ph.D. diss., Radcliff College 1960). See also Kay Ellen Thurman, "The Married Women's Property Acts" (LL.M. diss., Univ. of Wisconsin Law School, 1966); Mary Ritter Beard, *Woman as Force in History: A Study in Tradition and Realities* (New York 1946); Peggy A. Rabkin, *Fathers to Daughters: The Legal Foundations of Female Emancipation* (Westport 1980); John D. Johnston, Jr., "Sex and Property: The Common Law Tradition, the Law School Curriculum, and Developments toward Equality," *New York University Law Review*, 47 (Dec. 1972), 1033-1092; and Lawrence M. Friedman, *A History of American Law* (New York 1973), 179-186.

[4] For problems in the various definitions of feminism, see Gerda Lerner, *The Majority Finds Its Past: Placing Women in History* (New York 1979), 4-5, 48-49. Feminism is defined here as a doctrine advocating for women the same political and legal rights granted to men — a definition that is fraught with legal and semantic ambiguities and quite narrow by contemporary standards, but that was profoundly radical in the historical context of the nineteenth century.

[5] On the wife's separate equitable estate, see William S. Holdsworth, *A History of English Law* (14 vols., London 1903), I, 395-468; V, 278-338. For early America, see Marylynn Salmon, "The Property Rights of Women in Early America: A Comparative Study" (Ph.D. diss., Bryn Mawr College 1980), and "Women and Property in South Carolina: The Evidence from Marriage Settlements, 1730 to 1830," *William and Mary Quarterly*, 3d ser., 39 (Oct. 1982), 655-685.

the equitable model demanded statutes that sheltered the wife's property as judicial precedents had done, and advocated that the wife be able to enjoy her separate estate without any specific legal device. For reasons often unrelated to the rights of women, they were willing to modify power relationships within the family to the wife's advantage. They frequently insisted, however, that the wife was represented in politics by her husband. If the equitable model was political, it was by implication only.

Proponents of equality asserted that the legal disabilities with which wives struggled were the direct result of women's political powerlessness. Only woman suffrage and (for the most radical) the concomitant right of women to serve on juries, hold political office, and be admitted to the bar, could begin to adjust the inequities of marital property. The egalitarians in the debate assumed that the ground rules for marital property and for the rights and duties of spouses — legal arrangements for the domestic 29
sphere — were inseparable from the disposition of power in the political arena. They believed that every woman, married or single, was a discrete legal and political personality and possessed an individual relationship to the state. Their position challenged the very doctrine of separate spheres and asserted that political sameness between the sexes was the first step toward legal fairness and social equality.

Neither of these spare and tidy abstractions, simplified for purposes of clarity, was new. What was new was the breadth and consistency with which they were disseminated. Furthermore, *both* concepts challenged one of the most powerful paradigms in Anglo-American law and western political theory, that of coverture. Coverture, the formal designation for the wife's status at common law, placed the wife and her property under the protection and control of her husband, thereby rendering her economically dependent and legally invisible.[6] Her political invisibility was, in

---

[6] This essay concentrates on the common law concept of coverture, but elements of coverture existed in community property systems. Although the community property systems of the civil law are considered less harsh to the wife, especially as the survivor of her husband, it is fair to say that coverture functioned as a legal and political paradigm in both systems. Community property systems in states that drew on French or Spanish origins, such as Louisiana, Texas, and California, gave control of the community during the marriage to the husband. For the increasing similarities between the two systems in nineteenth century America, see Judith T. Younger, "Marital Regimes: A Story of Compromise and

part, a corollary of her legal invisibility.[7] To consider the wife by statute as a separate, autonomous individual capable of owning and managing her own property was to undermine the paradigm of coverture, lay bare its political implications, and subject it to stresses that would be exploited in the mid-nineteenth century by the women's rights movement.

One issue that generated early debate over the legal status of married women was the conflicting nature of decisions on the wife's powers over her equitable estate. Although American courts relied extensively on the decisions of English equity, the comprehensive reporting of American cases permitted reliance on the decisions of other states, especially those of jurisdictions with separate courts of equity led by chancellors with a high degree of technical proficiency, such as James Kent of New York and Henry Desaussure of South Carolina. American cases attest to wide-
30 spread confusion over both English and American precedents. There were no clear answers for a number of critical questions. What kind of legal instrument was absolutely necessary to create a separate estate for the wife? If the deed creating her estate did not spell out her powers, might they be implied? If so, under what circumstances? What were the extent of her powers? And since a married woman was to be regarded as a single woman only with respect to her separate estate, and in all other circumstances under the disabilities and protections of coverture, when was she acting as a single woman and when as a married woman?

A Pennsylvania supreme court judge commenting on the wife's separate estate in 1829 stated, "The English decisions have unsettled everything."[8] In the same year in a case involving the wife's debts, Chancellor Desaussure complained, "This case involves a question which is too frequently occurring before the court."[9] In 1837 Chancellor Reuben Walworth of New York

---

Demoralization Together With Criticisms and Suggestions for Reform," *Cornell Law Review*, 67 (Nov. 1981), 45-102.

[7] Susan Moller Okin, *Women in Western Political Thought* (Princeton 1979), 144-146, 250-252, 272-273; Linda K. Kerber, *Women of the Republic: Intellect and Ideology in the American Revolution* (Chapel Hill 1980), 7-32.

[8] *Lancaster* v. *Dolan*, 1 Rawle 247 (Penn. 1829).

[9] *Boggs v. Reid*, cited in "Trust Estates," *Carolina Law Journal*, 1 (Jan. 1831), 330.

alluded to the fact that "conflicting decisions have taken place in England as to the power of a *feme covert* to render her separate estate liable for debts."[10] In an 1845 New Jersey case which contains an excellent overview of conflicting American and English decisions, Chancellor Daniel Haines asserted, "One of the most vexed and embarrassing questions raised in a court of chancery is that which relates to the power of disposition by a *feme covert* of her separate estate."[11]

Aside from conflicting interpretations of the wife's powers, discussions of the wife's separate estate reveal a variety of rationales for its existence. Marriage settlements, Kent asserted in a fairly traditional explanation, protect the wife from "being overwhelmed by the misfortunes, or unkindness, or vices of her husband," and proceed from "the warm and anxious affection of parents" and friends.[12] Desaussure emphasized the protection of the whole family. To objections that settlements were 31
"mischievous to creditors" and "dangerous to the peace of families," he pointed out that in "most civilized countries, the estate of the wife, is more fully protected by the general law, than they [*sic*] are in England or in America, by special contracts and marriage settlements." The woman about to marry should have a right to say, "I have property which I wish protected for the benefit of the family."[13]

Statements about the harsh effects of the common law on women and the ameliorating qualities of equity were common. Chancellor Bland of Maryland declared that the "stern and ungallant rules of the common law by which marriage so sinks the wife under the absolute sway of the husband" had been modified to a degree by equity. As a matter of policy, he argued that "more latitude of free will as to contracts and a larger extent of individuality of character in relation to the right of property" might benefit both husband and wife.[14] The common law, traditionally associated with the fundamental rights of English men, was often depicted as despotic and "feudal" with respect to American women. Judge John Bannister of Pennsylvania insisted that "in no

---

[10] *North American Coal* v. *Dyett*, 7 Paige Ch. 15 (N.Y. 1837).

[11] *Leaycraft* v. *Hedden*, 4 N.J. Equity Reports 547 (1845).

[12] Kent, *Commentaries on American Law*, ed. George F. Comstock (11th ed., 4 vols., Boston 1867), II, 157-158, 181.

[13] "Trust Estates," 332-333.

[14] *Helms* v. *Franciscus*, 2 Bland Ch. 562 (Md. 1830).

country where the blessings of the common law are felt and acknowledged, are the interests and estates of married women so entirely at the mercy of their husbands, as in Pennsylvania."[15]

Each rationale for marriage settlements engendered its own particular problems. If the purpose of the separate estate was the traditional one of protecting the interests of the wife's family of origin against the newly formed one, it made the husband the wife's enemy and cast marriage into a distinctly premodern mold.[16] If the purpose was to protect the combined assets of the marriage from the husband's creditors, it created a palpable advantage for the wealthy in an era of high risk speculation and debt, and (by inference) a disadvantage for those without the assets or foresight to separate their property.[17] If its purpose was to ease the degrading dependency and invisibility to which the common law relegated wives, it created serious doubts about the desirability of the basic
32 common law rules for marriage.

One solution was to denounce marriage settlements altogether. They smacked of a cash nexus in the marriage contract and sullied the institution that was supposed to be a buffer against the materialistic, acquisitive world. They were antidemocratic, noted a writer for the *American Law Magazine*, because they tied up property in trusts and destroyed "that just authority which nature and the laws give a man over his wife, as well as that obedience and subjection which the rules of the gospel prescribe in the deportment of woman." The wife, he warned, might contract to be free from the husband's control, thereby turning marriage into a "quasi divorce." Tampering with the old rules for marriage endangered the whole social order: "Where the female's person and happiness are entrusted, there should her property be confided

---

[15] *Watson* v. *Mercer* (1844), cited in Charles W. Dahlinger, "The Dawn of the Women's Movement: An Account of the Origin and History of the Pennsylvania Married Woman's Property Law of 1848," *Western Pennsylvania Historical Magazine*, 1 (Jan. 1918), 74.

[16] On the role of kinship in marriage settlements, see Lawrence Stone, "The Rise of the Nuclear Family in Early Modern England: The Patriarchal Stage," in *The Family in History*, ed. Charles E. Rosenberg (Philadelphia 1975), 19-20, 24-25.

[17] On shifts in debtor-creditor relations, see Peter J. Coleman, *Debtors and Creditors in America: Insolvency, Imprisonment for Debt and Bankruptcy, 1607-1900* (Madison 1974), 283-285.

also." And if perchance matrimony was somehow unsafe without these special arrangements, then, he advised, marry not at all.[18]

Marriage settlements, however, were not likely to disappear. The same law journal, which conscientiously digested English and American decisions on the married woman's estate, reached the following conclusion: "Unless all the rules of equity on this subject are overthrown, on the ground that a divided interest is inconsistent with the policy and the nature of the contract, marriage cannot be considered as an absolute election by the feme sole to merge her rights in those of the husband."[19]

The dialogue within the legal community over the status of married women helps us to understand the legal context in which married women's statutes were passed and subsequently adjudicated. With the exception of a few avid lawyer-reformers such as Thomas Herttell of New York or Timothy Walker of Ohio, both of whom attacked coverture as the source of women's political inferiority and economic dependence, most professionals did not envisage obliterating coverture, but only refining and clarifying the equitable exceptions to it with which they were familiar. That is not to suggest consensus within the profession. Codifiers clashed with common lawyers, and democrats with the defenders of an erudite, professional elite, over whether the solution to the married woman's estate was to be statutory or judicial. Nevertheless, coverture was the paradigm with which they all began. Every law student, whether he learned his law from a Blackstone and a casual apprenticeship, or whether he was among the privileged few to receive a broad and rigorous education, learned the principles of coverture first. From the legal perspective, the problem of married women was defined by coverture and the fictional unity of spouses that it mandated; the solutions lay in equity jurisprudence. The dilemma was more procedural than it was substantive.

The dialogue, however, was extended beyond procedural issues. In an 1828 *North American Review* article, Caleb Cushing remarked that "a spirit alike destitute of manliness and of gallantry, has too often presided over the formation of the laws, which fix the rights and obligations of woman in the social

---

[18] "Marriage Settlements," *American Law Magazine*, 3 (April 1844), 16-22.

[19] "The Validity of Settlements in Exclusion of the Marital Rights of a Future Husband," *ibid.*, 3 (July 1844), 297.

scheme." He criticized the husband's extensive powers, the wife's lack of legal personality, and the meager and problematic benefits of equity. It is noteworthy that Cushing added: "The maxim, that taxation and representation should go hand and hand is most salutary; but no general maxim in morals is free from exception or qualification." We do not commend "the institutions of an Amazonian republic," he protested, cautiously establishing the limits reform should take. "The constitution of nature" has "settled the question" of suffrage.[20] Political participation by women was clearly Amazonian. There was no excuse, said the *New York Mirror*, "for a female desertting [*sic*] her allotted privacy, and volunteering to encounter gladiators in the political arena."[21]

If coverture were only a legal paradigm, we would not find it discussed in conjunction with suffrage and politics. Coverture was a political paradigm as well, and therein lies the historical signif-
34 icance of the debate over married women's property rights. Denials of the connections between property holding and voting often accompanied demands for a married women's statute. In fact, the consistency of the denials is a testimony to the durability of the connections. To give married women the right to own property by statute was to create an important new class of disfranchised property owners. Americans, even as they dropped property qualifications for voting, were not so removed from Enlightenment assumptions as to have forgotten the political implications of owning property. Debate over broadening male suffrage revitalized the connections. The notion that the propertyless were dependent, without a real stake in the society, and incapable of full citizenship was inextricably intertwined with the legal disabilities of married women. It seems that in the early national period in New Jersey, a state with liberal loopholes in its earliest provisions for suffrage, the fact that some married women voted constituted a gross violation of social norms.[22]

In the "civic humanism" of the eighteenth century, the function of property was to guarantee independence, and "the end

---

[20] Cushing, "The Legal Condition of Women," *North American Review*, 26 (April 1828), 316-356; the citations are at 316, 319, 318.

[21] "Female Politicians," *New York Mirror and Repository*, 8 (Sept. 1830), 95.

[22] Sophie H. Drinker, "Votes for Women in 18th-Century New Jersey," *Proceedings of the New Jersey Historical Society*, 80 (Jan. 1962), 37.

of independence was citizenship and moral personality."[23] The reason for property qualifications, wrote Blackstone, "is to exclude such persons as are in so mean a situation as to be esteemed to have no will of their own."[24] Tenants, urban wage-earners, indentured servants, children, idiots, and married women did not possess the independence requisite for full citizenship. Single women were assumed to be similarly dependent upon the male head of the household. Consequently it was on coverture that Abigail Adams, the very model of republican motherhood, focused in 1776 when she wrote to her husband and asked him to "remember the ladies."[25] And it was on coverture that Mrs. Carter, the fictional widow living under her brother's roof, concentrated when she discussed the political status of women in Charles Brockden Brown's *Alcuin*.[26] Linda Kerber has cogently demonstrated that the persistence of coverture in the wake of revolution was inherently antirepublican; it was, then, blatantly antidemocratic, and men and 35
women of the Jacksonian era covertly or overtly perceived it as such.[27] The dilemma that confronted legislators was how to allow the married woman a separate legal estate, which was not precisely the same as an equitable one, while maintaining the validity of her virtual representation.

The law of husband and wife presented a particularly compelling example of the principle that the interests of men and women were not the same. If men truly represented women, why had they arrogated so much power to themselves in marriage? Egalitarians in the 1830s, drawing on the political culture of the American Revolution, denounced the concept of women's virtual representation. John Neal, an early advocate of woman suffrage, predicted that women were not likely to remain satisfied with virtual representation. Binding this theme to coverture, he said that "the interests of no two persons that ever lived were identical any

---

[23] J.G.A. Pocock, *Politics, Language and Time: Essays on Political Thought and History* (New York 1971), 92.

[24] Sir William Blackstone, *Commentaries on the Laws of England in Four Books*, ed. Thomas Cooley (4th ed., Chicago 1899), I, 171.

[25] Abigail Adams to John Adams, March 31, 1776, in Alice Rossi, ed., *The Feminist Papers* (New York 1974), 10-11.

[26] Brown, *Alcuin: A Dialogue*, ed. Lee R. Edwards (New York 1970), especially 29-32, which were part of the segments first published in 1798.

[27] Kerber, *Women of the Republic*, 139-155.

more than their bodies and souls."[28] In her *Letters on the Equality of the Sexes*, Sarah Grimké related the fact that woman was "a cipher in the nation" to her legal invisibility in marriage.[29] In his *Introduction to American Law*, first published in 1837, Timothy Walker moved easily from a diatribe on married women's common law disabilities to a critique of women's inferior political status. The "theory of the law," he asserted, referring to coverture, degraded American females almost "to the level of slaves . . . . We require them to contribute their share in the way of taxes, to the support of the government, but allow them no voice in its direction." Apply the same language to males, he said, and it is a form of slavery; only custom inures us to apply the language differently to females.[30] Abraham Lincoln reputedly wrote the following letter to the *Sangamon Journal* of Illinois in 1836: "I go for all sharing the privileges of the government who assist in bearing its
36 burdens. Consequently, I go for admitting all whites to the rights of suffrage who pay taxes or bear arms (by no means excluding females)."[31]

During the 1830s and the 1840s there is some evidence of impassioned appeals to the inalienable rights of women that are significantly reminiscent of the rhetoric of the American Revolution. These emotive, evocative appeals, made in the midst of broadened male suffrage, suggest a conscious effort to underscore the exclusion of women from the egalitarian implications of the revolution. When Thomas Herttell proposed a married women's bill to the New York legislature, he argued that married women "equally with males and unmarried females, possess the right of *life*, *liberty*, and PROPERTY and are equally entitled to be protected in all three." Women were deprived of their property and their full citizenship, he claimed, because they were compelled to

---

[28] Cited in August Genevieve Violette, *Economic Feminism in American Literature Prior to 1848* (Orono, Me. 1925), 51. For Neal's continued support of married women's rights and suffrage, see his *Brother Jonathan*, 5 (June 1843), 83-85, and 5 (July 1843), 304-309.

[29] Grimké, *Letters on the Equality of the Sexes, and the Condition of Woman* (Boston 1838), 74.

[30] Walker, *Introduction to American Law* (3d ed., Boston 1855), 234. See also "Walker's Introduction to American Law," *American Jurist and Law Magazine*, 18 (Jan. 1838), 375-390.

[31] Cited in Violette, *Economic Feminism*, 53.

obey laws made by men.[32] Similarly, a letter from an anonymous woman in the *United States Magazine and Democratic Review* attributed the legal disabilities of married women to the political tyranny of the male sex over the female sex.[33]

Arguments that women were victimized by the common law and that their families were subjected to economic hardship seem to have enjoyed considerable popularity. Appeals to self-evident truths, denouncements of taxation without representation, and assertions of the political tyranny of the male sex over the female sex, especially when made by females, met with ridicule or outrage. Political action by women on their own behalf was more menacing to the social order than the public activities of female abolitionists and reformers, and constituted a clearer breach of the doctrine of separate spheres. Such action, unlike the altruism of other reforms, was antithetical to the cooperative, noncompetitive, nurturing values attributed to the family. Demands that women be entitled to full political participation as individual citizens of the state without the mediation of men were often softened by assurances and probably backed by the real conviction that women would and should continue to fill their special familial roles.

John Quincy Adams' 1838 speech in Congress on behalf of the right of women to petition against the acquisition of Texas is a rare instance in which "the woman question" intruded into national politics, albeit tangentially. Although Adams' defense of political action by female abolitionists is well known, what has been overlooked are his closing remarks which reconcile such action with conventional notions of domesticity. The speech was sparked by the comments of Representative Benjamin C. Howard of Maryland, chairman of the House Foreign Affairs Committee. While attempting to introduce a gag rule against the Texas memorials, he had expressed sorrow at the women petitioners' departure from their appropriate domestic sphere, and labeled their actions "discreditable."[34]

---

[32] Thomas Herttell, *Remarks Comprising in Substance Judge Herttell's Argument in the House of Assembly of the State of New-York, in the Session of 1837, in Support of the Bill to Restore to Married Women "The Right of Property," as Guaranteed by the Constitution of this State* (New York 1839), 22-23.

[33] "The Legal Wrongs of Women," *United States Magazine and Democratic Review*, 14 (May 1844), 478.

[34] *Speech of John Quincy Adams, of Massachusetts, upon the Right of the People, Men and Women, to Petition* . . . (Washington 1838), 65.

Adams launched into a passionate defense of the right of the petitioners, the wives and daughters of his Massachusetts constituents, to engage in political action. He celebrated the women of the Old Testament, the queens of Europe, and the heroines of the revolution. For contemporary heroines, he referred to the two ladies from South Carolina, whom congressmen could readily identify as Sarah and Angelina Grimké. Caustically he urged Congress to petition Queen Victoria to abdicate because affairs of state do not belong to women. Shall women not petition because they cannot vote, he asked? "Is it so clear that they have no such right as this last! And if not, who shall say that this argument . . . is not adding one injustice to another?" In the end, however, Adams insisted that he did not countenance women stepping out of their circle except with the appropriate "motives, means and ends." A petition, he remarked, "is a prayer — a supplication — that which you address to the Almighty Being above you," and highly appropriate to the female sex.[35]

Nevertheless, Adams' models for female action provoked severe criticism, and it was not limited to southern congressmen. A writer for the *Lady's Companion* questioned Adams' choice of heroines, especially the two Catherines of Russia whom he characterized as "infamous and odious monsters of debauchery and evil." He even found that Deborah Gannett, who donned soldier's garb to fight in the revolution, imparted satisfaction only "when contemplated from a distance." The mothers of America, he said, have responded to the question of their political activity with, "Let the men take care of politics, we will fulfill our duty to our children." Summing up the woman question, he divided the spectrum of opinion into "the New Lights, clamorous for equal rights, high prerogative, and an erasure of 'to obey' from the marriage covenant; the Old lights — willing to abide by the past . . . and the Moderates."[36]

The marriage covenant actually figured prominently in all three positions. The traditionalists or Old Lights were omnipresent and their cause, buttressed by the common law and the Bible, was succinctly set forth in the *Broadway Journal*: "The true position

---

[35] *Ibid.*, 63-78, 81.

[36] Henry P. Harrington, "Female Education," *Lady's Companion*, 9 (Sept. 1838), 232, and 9 (Oct. 1838), 182.

of woman is not a disputable point; the universal sentiment of mankind has determined it; God himself has said her desire shall be unto her husband, and he shall rule over her."[37] The egalitarians or New Lights were not likely to generate much approval for married women's statutes because, like the traditionalists, they displayed an abiding awareness of the connections between women's legal and political status. Moderates, on the other hand, managed to gain ground in the 1840s by minimizing the political implications of undermining coverture, and by drawing, instead, on the time-honored rationales for the married woman's equitable estate — to protect the wife from a profligate husband and to insulate the family from pauperism. An 1843 editorial in Timothy Walker's *Western Law Journal* alleged that public opinion was shifting in favor of married women's property rights.[38] Walker was promoting a cause to which he was devoted, but there was validity to his statement. By the summer of 1848, when feminists met in Seneca Falls to launch officially the women's rights movement, nineteen states had some sort of married women's provision on their books.[39] They included northern, southern, and new western states.

To be sure, regional concerns and anomalies appear in the married women's provisions. As one might expect, slaveholding dominated the provisions of the 1839 Mississippi statute.[40] Debate preceding the New York statute of 1848 reveals concern with the ambiguities of the state's uses and trusts provisions in its *Revised Statutes*.[41] The first attempt at a state constitution in Wisconsin, which was rejected by the voters in 1847, linked the property rights of married women to homestead exemptions for debtors.[42]

---

[37] *Broadway Journal*, 1 (Mar. 1845), 182.

[38] "Law Reform," *Western Law Journal*, 1 (Mar. 1843), 281-282.

[39] Warbasse, "Changing Legal Rights," 272.

[40] *Laws of Mississippi, 1839*, chap. 46.

[41] *Revised Statutes of the State of New York, 1829* (Albany 1829), I, 727, sec. 47; Herttell, *Argument in the House of Assembly*, 12-14.

[42] "The Convention of 1846," ed. Milo M. Quaife, Wisconsin Historical Society *Collections [WHSC], 27 (1919), 631-670*; Bayrd Still, "State-Making in Wisconsin, 1846-48: An Illustration of the Statehood Process," *Wisconsin Magazine of History*, 20 (Sept. 1936), 37. For similar issues in Michigan, see *Report of the Proceedings and Debates in the Convention to Revise the Constitution of the State of Michigan* (Lansing 1850), 240, 674-682. Michigan had a married women's statute (*Michigan Acts, 1844*, no. 66) and controversy emerged, as it had in Wisconsin, over the

The one experience that cast ominous shadows over these disparate jurisdictions was the panic of 1837 and the depression beginning in 1839. Legislators were spurred to insulate some of the family's assets from the husband's creditors, and to protect the state and its taxpayers from the burdens of welfare.

Married women's acts were, among other things, debtor exemption acts. In an 1837 speech to the legislature, Governor George Paschal of Georgia found that married women's common law disabilities had inflicted a heavy financial toll on families in the state.[43] In Mississippi, which passed the first major married women's statute in the nation in 1839, T. B. J. Hadley, who had introduced the "Woman's Law" into the Mississippi legislature, introduced a bill in the same session for the relief of himself and his security, a Samuel M. Puckett.[44] On the other side of the ledger was Marshall M. Strong, a delegate to the 1846 Wisconsin con-
40 vention, who vehemently opposed a married women's clause and was said to have separated his wife's property from his own with a secure prenuptial agreement. He had, therefore, little desire to extend and democratize the redistributive aspects of the married woman's separate estate.[45] George Geddes, on the other hand, who led support for the 1848 bill in the New York Senate, had a will with a trust for his daughter with which he was dissatisfied be-

---

propriety of placing such a provision into the constitution. Texas, however, drawing on its Spanish legal origins as a former part of Mexico, placed a married women's provision into its constitution that was linked to a homestead provision in 1845 (Texas Constitution, 1845, art. 7, secs. 19 and 22). At its constitutional convention of 1849, California followed the Texas provisions verbatim. California Constitution, 1849, art. 9, secs. 14 and 15. See 'Translation and Digest of Such Portions of the Mexican Laws . . . as are Supposed to be Still in Force," in *Report of the Debates of the Convention of California on the Formation of the State Constitution . . . 1849*, ed. J. Ross Browne (Washington 1850), *xxiv-xxvii*; and Peter Thomas Conmy, *The Historic Spanish Origins of California's Community Property Law and Its Development and Adaptation to Meet the Needs of an American State* (San Francisco 1957).

[43] Eleanor M. Boatright, "The Political and Civil Status of Women in Georgia, 1783-1860," *Georgia Historical Quarterly*, 25 (Dec. 1941), 310.

[44] Elizabeth Gaspar Brown, "Husband and Wife — Memorandum on the Mississippi Woman's Law of 1839," *Michigan Law Review*, 42 (Apr. 1944), 1113-1114.

[45] Isaac P. Walker, "Address to the People of Wisconsin, March 31, 1847" in "The Struggle Over Ratification," ed. Milo M. Quaife, WHSC, 28 (1920), 602-604. Walker pointed out that the goal of the constitution was to dispense with the lawyer and the fee that marriage settlements seemed to require.

cause of uncertainties in the uses and trusts provisions of New York law.[46]

The financial circumstances of individual politicians serve to highlight the economic underpinnings of the issues. It is safe to assume that there were more Hadleys in antebellum American than there were Strongs, and it was for the relief of the former that the married women's statutes were passed. As one historian of the statutes has asserted, these reforms stood a chance because there was something in them for men, and it had nothing to do with feminism.[47]

The narrowness of the statutes supports her view. In New York the scope of the statutes was restricted by the equitable precedents on which they were based and by the economic exigencies that impelled their passage. Legal elements of coverture prevailed long after the passage of the statutes.[48] Nevertheless, there was something in the statutes for women: a legally modest but 41
symbolically significant improvement in their common law status that was more in keeping with their elevated position in the family — compensation, so to speak, for their disfranchisement that converged felicitously with economic motives.

The compensatory aspects of married women's property rights were a persistent theme in arguments for a statute. If a wife was to be her husband's helpmeet, his equal within marriage, queen of the household, arbiter of its morals, and teacher to the next generation of citizens, then she deserved something better than her childlike common law status. Governor Francis Shunk of Pennsylvania appealed to the legislature to adjust the law to a more companionate ideal of marriage. "The liberal and enlightened spirit of the age," he claimed, "has developed and secured the rights of man, and has redeemed woman and elevated her, from the degrading position she occupied, and placed her, where she always should have been, at the side of her husband, his equal in

---

[46] George Geddes to Matilda Joslyn Gage, Nov. 28, 1880, in Elizabeth Cady Stanton, Susan B. Anthony, Matilda Joslyn Gage, and Ida Husted Harper, eds., *A History of Woman Suffrage* (6 vols., Rochester and New York 1881-1922), I, 65.

[47] Suzanne D. Lebsock, "Radical Reconstruction and the Property Rights of Southern Women," *Journal of Southern History* 43 (May 1977), 197-198.

[48] For an analysis of the limitations of the married women's acts, see Norma Basch, *In the Eyes of the Law: Women, Marriage, and Property in Nineteenth-Century New York* (Ithaca 1982).

rank and dignity." Her legal status should not be defined "by the contracted and illiberal enactments of an age when her husband was her lord and he might chastise her by law as if she were a servant."[49] Shunk's rhetoric is particularly revealing because it parallels the rights of man with the elevation of woman. He associated an improvement in the legal status of married women with the rights of man while he simultaneously distinguished it from those rights. His statement exemplifies the possibilities and limitations of the equitable model.

From the available remnants of state legislative debates, and from the much fuller record of debate in the Wisconsin and New York constitutional conventions of 1846, a clear and consistent pattern of argument emerges.[50] Most proponents of a married women's provision adhered to the equitable model and argued on the grounds of debtor relief, the protection of the family, and the

elevation of women from the despotism of the common law. A few egalitarians argued on the grounds of woman's inalienable right to property and alluded to or demanded woman suffrage. So entrenched was the concept of female disfranchisement, that it was used to justify the disfranchisement of black males in the Iowa convention of 1844 and of foreigners at the Illinois convention of 1847.[51] Opponents of married women's property rights relied on the sanctity of the biblical and common law doctrine of the absolute unity of spouses, and predicted frauds against creditors, licentiousness, a rash of illegitimate children, social chaos, and woman suffrage if a married women's provision were passed.[52]

---

[49] Governor Francis Rawn Shunk, "Annual Message to the Assembly, 1848," *Pennsylvania Archives*, 4th ser., 7 (1902), 213-214.

[50] For New York, see William G. Bishop and William H. Attree, eds., *Report of the Debates and Proceedings of the Convention for the Revision of the Constitution of the State of New York* (Albany 1846), 1038-1042, 1056-1064. For Wisconsin, see WHSC, 27 (1919), 631-636, 638-640, 645-670, 702-703; and WHSC, 28 (1920), 59, 61-62, 99-100, 124-125, 174-175, 275-280, 325, 351, 360-362, 366, 384-385, 464-466, 510-513, 532, 536, 567-575, 580, 602-604, 667-669, 681, 684.

[51] Ruth A. Gallaher, *Legal and Political Status of Women in Iowa* (Iowa City 1918), 173-174; for Iowa's married women's statute, see *Laws of Iowa, 1845-1846*, chap. 5; on woman and alien suffrage in Illinois, see *The Constitutional Debates of 1847*, Illinois State Historical Library *Collections*, 14 (1919), 546.

[52] See the statements of Charles O'Conor at the New York convention in Bishop and Attree, eds., *Report of Debates*, 1056-1060.

Woman suffrage was the very embodiment of chaos, the ultimate eradication of separate sexual spheres.

All these elements of the debate appeared in Wisconsin where the married women's provision of 1846 was hotly contested at the convention and in the battle for ratification. The Racine *Advocate*, a proponent of the married women's provision and the homestead exemption clause, argued that the two measures were destined "to make men better, more stable, more equal, and to prevent uncertain and feverish speculations and grumbling."[53] David Noggle, a delegate to the 1846 convention, predicted that with the passage of the two clauses, the "little, humble cottage will no longer be the asylum of grief." The elevation of women was a persistent theme on all sides of the debate. "Elevate your wives and elevate your daughters," said Noggle, "and you elevate the race that follows."[54] William R. Smith characterized the common law status of wives as
"a remnant of the feudal system, which ought to be abolished."[55] 43
To arguments that separate property had encouraged bastardy and prostitution in France, one delegate pointed to flourishing prostitution in London and New York where the common law prevailed.[56]

A few egalitarians at the Wisconsin convention presented an amendment to the suffrage provision that would erase the word male from the suffrage requirements, but it was defeated. They also advocated a change of language in the bill of rights, which proclaimed all men free and equal, insisting that it was antithetical to the suffrage provision, which excluded women, Negroes, and mulattoes.[57] Egalitarian arguments, however, were used to attack the married women's provision and the "specious reasoning about woman's rights" on which they rested. Because suffrage was the logical component of owning property, the married women's provision must be defeated. "By parity of reasoning," went the argument, it is right that women "should vote and be eligible to the highest offices of state or nation, and thus is dissolved at once

---

[53] "The Constitution — No. 1," Racine *Advocate*, Jan. 6, 1847, in WHSC, 28 (1920), 436-437.

[54] Speech of Noggle, Dec. 7, 1846, *ibid.*, 27 (1919), 663.

[55] *Ibid.*, 631.

[56] "Remarks of Mr. Singer in the Territorial Legislature," Feb. 6, 1847, *ibid.*, 28 (1920), 278-279.

[57] *Ibid.*, 27 (1919), 214, 259, 522.

the charm, the beauty, and the glory of the female character." This provision "will tend to subvert the whole order of society." It is favored by "rogues" and "tight-fisted fathers," who view marriage not as a "sacred, indivisible union," but as "a mere matter of convenience or at best as a mutual contract of separate parties."[58]

Marshall M. Strong, who resigned from the 1846 convention during the heated debate over the married women's clause and homestead exemption clause, continued his opposition in the territorial legislature:

> The Bible says that woman shall leave father and mother and cleave unto her husband, and they twain shall be one flesh. The constitution says that they twain shall be as separate and distinct persons as any other two individuals in the community, or as any laws can make them . . . . Woman is to be transferred from her appropriate domestic sphere, taken away from her children, and
> 44 cast out rudely into the strifes and turmoil of the world, there to have her finer sensibilities blunted, the ruling motives of her mind changed, and every trait of loveliness blotted out.[59]

References made by Strong and other opponents to the legislation of other states suggest they were aware of a national trend toward married women's acts and were cognizant of state-by-state variations. The Madison *Express* reprinted a speech made by Charles O'Conor to the New York convention of 1846, a speech which closely resembled the one made by Strong to the territorial legislature in the following year.[60] The *Express* pronounced itself in favor of the 1845 Massachusetts bill, which merely recognized by statute the separate estate of a married woman if it were created by a prenuptial agreement.[61] Texas, a state which passed a married women's provision in its 1845 constitution that was similar to the Wisconsin measure, was denounced as a "noted asylum for all the desperados in the country," and a poor model for morals or laws.[62]

---

[58] "M's Views on the Rights of Married Women," Madison *Express*, Mar. 9, 1847, *ibid.*, 28 (1920), 400, 401.

[59] Speech of Marshall M. Strong in the Territorial Legislature, Feb. 5, 1847, *ibid.*, 239.

[60] "Mr. O'Connor [*sic*] on Rights of Married Women," Madison *Express*, Mar. 16, 1847, *ibid.*, 404-409.

[61] "Massachusetts Provision for the Rights of Married Women," Madison *Express*, Jan. 19, 1847, *ibid.*, 384-385.

[62] "Speech of Marshall M. Strong, On the Passage of the Article on the

Occasional debate coverage in a wide range of periodicals informed a literate middle class comprised of a variety of social aggregates. In 1845, for example, the *Massachusetts Ploughman*, an important New England agricultural journal, reprinted an article from the Cincinnati *Chronicle* that referred to bills before the Missouri, Alabama, and Georgia legislatures and supported them on the basis of debtor relief and a needed improvement in the status of women:

> The law must change because the reason of the law has changed. In all civilized society, it must be a great object to keep families together, and support them upon a homestead, because if they are not so kept together and supported, the chances are, that the public, the state itself, must contribute to their support.

The article condemned the subservience and dependence to which the common law relegated wives, and concluded that women 45
"should not be made slaves."[63]

The moderate, equitable model was attractive to those female writers and reformers who would not align themselves with an overtly political feminist position, but who sought, instead, to enlarge the influence of women within the domestic sphere. Sarah Hale backed an 1837 New York bill in her editorial column in *Godey's Lady's Book*, probably the most respectable and influential women's magazine of the period. She predicted that the bill would promote "the security and happiness of domestic life" and "preserve more indissolubly the union of hearts." The tyranny that Hale emphasized was always personal and domestic. In one of her typical attacks on the indiscretions of men, she praised the bill for its ability to prevent the husband from wasting his wife's property "on his wicked indulgences."[64]

The *Advocate of Moral Reform*, dedicated to the obliteration of prostitution, the double sexual standard, and intemperance, asserted that the husband tended to view his wife as a species of property, as "a useful article of furniture" rather than as a "helpmeet." It reprinted the married women's provision from the pro-

---

Rights of Married Women and Exemption from Forced Sale," Dec. 7, 1846, *ibid.*, 27 (1919), 647-648.

[63] "Rights of Married Women," *Massachusetts Ploughman*, Mar. 8, 1845; this journal printed the Massachusetts married women's statute on its front page of April 10, 1845.

[64] "Rights of Married Women," *Godey's Lady's Book*, 14 (May 1837), 212-214.

posed Wisconsin constitution, and characterized it as guaranteeing the wife's property "beyond the power of alienation by a drunken or otherwise profligate husband or father." Female reformers' attack on the concept that men owned property in women was important, but they did not carry their attack to its logical political conclusions. They did not reach past their personal, familial relationships to demand the right to full political participation. That task was taken up by the women's rights movement.[65]

In the 1840s women's rights advocates began uncoordinated efforts to lobby for married women's property rights in several northeastern states. This was true of Mary Upton Ferrin in Massachusetts, and of Paulina Wright, Ernestine Rose, and Elizabeth Cady Stanton in New York. Clarina Howard Nichols wrote a series of articles for the *Windham County Democrat* of Brattleboro on behalf of the 1847 Vermont statute. Jane Grey
46 Swisshelm (publisher of the Pittsburgh *Saturday Visitor*), Lucretia Mott, and Mary Grew organized support for the 1848 Pennsylvania statute.[66] Petitions grew more strident. Forty-four married women petitioned the New York legislature in March 1848 on egalitarian rather than on equitable grounds; they made their demands as women, a class of disfranchised and disaffected citizens, rather than as economically disadvantaged and victimized wives.[67] By the 1850s the drive for married women's property rights had become pivotal to the development of antebellum feminism. Feminists drew on the equitable model. But it was their reliance on and refinement of the egalitarian model that strengthened their movement, infused it with staying power, and exposed and exploited coverture for the political paradigm that it was.

---

[65] "Evils of Despotic Government," *Advocate of Moral Reform*, Feb. 15, 1838, 28; "Rights of Women — The Homestead Inalienable," *ibid.*, Feb. 15, 1847, 31. On the Female Moral Reform Society that the *Advocate* represented, see Smith-Rosenberg, "Beauty, the Beast and the Militant Woman." On the connections between men owning property in women and the double standard, see Keith Thomas, "The Double Standard," *Journal of the History of Ideas*, 20 (Apr. 1959), 195-216; and Nancy F. Cott, "Passionlessness: An Interpretation of Victorian Sexual Ideology, 1790-1850," *Signs*, 4 (Winter 1978), 219-236.

[66] *Notable American Women*, ed. Edward T. James, Janet Wilson James, and Paul S. Boyer (3 vols, Cambridge 1971, II, 625-626, III, 416; Ira V. Brown, "The Woman's Rights Movement in Pennsylvania, 1848-1873," *Pennsylvania History*, 32 (Apr. 1965), 155; Basch, *In the Eyes of the Law*, 165-168.

[67] Petition of forty-four ladies of Genesee and Wyoming, praying for the

The equity-vs.-equality dialogue suggests a few final observations. From a legal perspective, the easing of married women's common law disabilities paralleled the easing of debtors' obligations. It was part of a larger trend in family law as well. In the areas of courtship, marriage, divorce, and child custody, state judiciaries and legislatures enlarged the rights of individuals in the family at the expense of the power held by the male head of the household.[68] Yet the dialogue within the legal community, which revolved around the proper implementation of the equitable model, rarely touched on the political implications of modifying coverture. Nor does it appear to have been disseminated to or understood by the public.

As the institutional context of the dialogue shifted, the issues shifted. As discourse moved beyond the courts and the legal profession to state legislatures and constitutional conventions, it radiated in unanticipated directions. Discourse took shape in popular journals and assumed genuinely public dimensions. It became increasingly difficult to modify coverture without broaching its political implications.

From a political perspective neither the neoclassical republican culture of the revolution nor its revamped Jacksonian counterpart can be construed as congenial to the cause of women's rights. Nevertheless, as egalitarians fused fragments of the republican tradition to the drive for marital property reform, they generated severe stresses in coverture as a political paradigm. In light of the outlines of the public dialogue that they sparked, the Jacksonian era might be appropriately characterized as a transitional period with respect to the status of women in the political culture. It might be viewed as an ambiguous stage during which the political role of women was still defined by Republican Motherhood while at the same time the first steps toward integrating women into an egalitarian political ethos were being taken.[69]

---

repeal of certain laws, *Documents of the Assembly of the State of New York, 1848* (Albany 1848), V, Document 129 (March 15, 1848).

[68] For changes in family law, see Michael Grossberg, "Law and the Family in Nineteenth-Century America" (Ph.D. diss., Brandeis University 1979); Jamil S. Zainaldin, "The Emergence of a Modern American Family Law: Child Custody, Adoption, and the Courts, 1796-1851," *Northwestern University Law Review*, 73 (Feb. 1979), 1038-1089.

[69] On Republican Motherhood, see Kerber. *Women of the Republic, passim.*

The Georgia Historical Quarterly

VOLUME XXV DECEMBER, 1941 NUMBER 4

THE POLITICAL AND CIVIL STATUS OF WOMEN IN GEORGIA, 1783-1860

BY ELEANOR M. BOATWRIGHT

The philosophies, facts, practices and sentiments governing the political and civil rights of white women in Georgia between the Revolution and the Civil War were confused, fickle, contradictory, and paradoxical. The Constitution would have allowed full political
48 equality, but theory and practice granted none; whereas the statutes denied the civil existence of a married woman, yet permitted her to establish it if she chose and protected it if she did. It seems to have been a system of letting the right hand know not what the left hand did, but public opinion approved the conspiracy and guarded its secrets.

Georgia women were denied the suffrage between 1777 and 1789 otherwise they might have voted from the founding of the colony until the Civil War. The facts were that the original charter had no disqualifying clause, the Constitution of 1777 limited the franchise to males, those of 1789 and 1798 were silent on the subject, and the Constitution of 1861 barred women from the suffrage.[1] This does not mean that women voted nor that Georgia intended that they should. Neither were Negroes explicitly disqualified until 1861. The Constitution of 1789 and 1798 neither say that women may vote nor that they may not. Women are not mentioned. This failure of the framers

1. Walter McElreath, ed., *A Treatise on the Constitution of Georgia* (Atlanta, 1912), Charter of the Province, 212-237; Constitution of 1777, Art. IX, 232; Constitution of 1789, Art. IV, sec. I, 247; Constitution of 1798, Art. IV, sec. I, 264; Constitution of 1861, Art. V, sec. I, 296.

was not due to masculine liberality but to feminine insignificance. If a woman had taken advantage of the loophole and attempted to vote it is safe to wager public opinion would have left her in no condition to contest the point.

It appears that Georgia men heard, or thought they heard, the rustle of petticoats in the vogue for democracy that came with the Revolution and fortified their prerogative with the Constitution of 1777. The flutterings were so stilled by 1789 that precautions were abandoned.

Nevertheless Georgia women were not wholly negative in politics. They rarely entered into political discussions, in part because they were uninformed, or found it socially expedient to pretend so; in part, per- 49
haps, because the same code which demanded that a gentleman never contradict a lady, expected that a lady should never embarrass a gentleman with a controversial issue. When there was uniformity of public opinion, however, women who enjoyed politics had their innings. James Buckingham, an Englishman who visited the slave states and wrote of his observations, noticed that in "the struggle between the nullifiers of South Carolina and the General Government of the United States" women "took a very important part," and, according to him, long afterwards retained "more of the enthusiastic feeling of that period than the men."[2] This was not surprising. Life was drab for ante-bellum Georgia women unless they were unmarried and young.

Sometimes a woman held political power. Nancy Rumsey did. "This white female," according to her contemporary Garnett Andrews, "levied blackmail on all office-seekers in Elbert county for half a century." She began her career with a traveling restaurant which she made from an ox cart. When court was in cession

2. J. S. Buckingham, *The Slave States of America* (London, 1842), II, 182-183.

she drove her team into Elberton, hitched at the court house, and opened up for business. Nancy must have been a good cook for her profits enabled her to build a comfortable house called "Goshen" in the Chinquapin settlement near Elberton. There she established her "throne." Her talents were such that politicians sought her support. "Each got her promise of favor and she got money from each." Her practices became well known but her opposition was so feared that office seekers continued to pay their tax. During the last twenty years of her power it was said, "lawyers who were looking up business took care to say pleasant things to her as they passed, and the Judge, as he went by paid his respects."[3]

50 Feminine good will was considered important enough for women to be "flattered and appealed to by political orators, and by newspapers, whenever the occasion presented itself for so doing with effect."[4] It was common to see the ladies in the gallery of the legislature. A good murder trial was sure to find them present.[5] At one it was reported the ladies "filled the gallery and even took possession of the floor of the Senate."[6] Wives, daughters, and sweethearts were frequently taken to political celebrations, toasted at political dinners, and danced with at political balls,[7] but that was about the limit of their public activities. What political influence Georgia women had was usually individual and was exercised socially. The men of their state rarely acknowledged that any existed.

The political status of women was ignored but the civil received the most unfavorable attention. Both married and single women shared some civil disabili-

3. Garnett Andrews, *Reminiscences of an Old Georgia Lawyer* (Atlanta, 1870), 37.
4. Buckingham, *Slave States*, II, 182-183.
5. I. S. Bradwell to Adam Alexander, May 31, 1820, in mss. Letters and Papers of Adam Leopold Alexander, Washington, Georgia, in Duke University Library.
6. Milledgeville *Daily Federal Union*, Nov. 17, 1859.
7. Buckingham, *Slave States*, II, 182-183.

ties. Neither performed jury service and the testimony of both, except in criminal cases, was taken out of court.[8] There the likeness stopped. The law allowed unmarried women to contract; to sue and to be sued; to act as administrators of estates and as guardians of children; to hold bequeath, inherit, or purchase property; and to work, keep their earnings, or to spend them as they pleased. All of which they did as bountiful court evidence proves.

The ceremonial pledge of a man to his bride "with all my worldly goods I thee endow" did not have the legal significance of a valentine. For the civil law saw to it that the new-made husband lost nothing of his own at the altar and took away from it all his bride possessed—perhaps even the ring with which he made 51
his vow. For the common law of England gave a man unconditional title to his wife's personal property[9] while the Georgia Act of 1789 guaranteed him her real property on the same terms.[10]

In 1784 Georgia legally adopted all the English common law not repugnant to the State of Federal Constitution.[11] This common law gave a wife no legal civil status. It recognized the husband and wife as one person, suspended the legal existence of the woman, and put her under the protection of "her husband, her baron, or lord." Under the common law a husband could neither grant anything to his wife nor enter into an agreement with her for "the grant would suppose her separate existence, and to covenant with her would be to covenant with himself."[12]

---

8. *Acts of the General Assembly of the State of Georgia, 1829*, p. 94 (Hereafter referred to as *Acts of Georgia*); Foster Blodgett, Jr. to David L. Roath, Jan. 18, 1860, in mss. Letters of David L. Roath, Augusta, Georgia, in Office of the Ordinary of Richmond County.

9. William Blackstone, *Commentaries on the Laws of England*, with Analysis of Contents by Thomas M. Cooley, ed. by James DeWitt Andrews (Chicago, 1899), Book II, sec. 434-436.

10. Oliver H. Prince, comp., *A Digest of the Laws of the State of Georgia* (Athens, 1837), Act of 1789, p. 225; Royston *vs.* Royston, 21 Georgia 161.

11. Prince, comp., *Digest*, Act of 1784, p. 570.

12. Blackstone, *Commentaries*, Book I, sec. 442.

Georgians, following the English common law, wrote into their statutes:

"In this State the husband is the head of the family, and the wife is subject to him; her civil legal existence is merged in the husband except so far as the law recognizes her separately, either for her own protection or for her benefit, or for the preservation of public order."[13]

The estates of husband and wife were mutually responsible for debts existing at the time of marriage until the Act of 1856.[14] It left the husband responsible for his wife's debts only to the extent of the property she brought him and relieved her estate of all claims of his creditors.[15]

52 After marriage a man's financial obligations were reduced to a legal minimum. He was required to provide his wife with the "necessities suitable to her habits and conditions of life," but for "anything besides necessaries" he was not "chargeable."[16] After his death she was entitled to dower rights in his estate[17] or to her part, under the law, in its distribution if he died intestate;[18] and to a year's support for herself and their children, even though the estate was insolvent.[19] Otherwise what a wife had was her husband's, free from all rights of survivorship, to sell, dispose of, or bequeath as he wished, regardless of whether his wife's property was derived from parents, relatives, friends,[20]

---

13. R. H. Clark, T. R. R. Cobb, D. Irwin, comps., *The Code of the State of Georgia* (Atlanta, 1861), sec. 1700. (Hereafter referred to as Clark, Cobb, and Irwin, comps., *Code of 1861*.)
14. *Acts of Georgia*, 1856, p. 229.
15. Clark, Cobb, and Irwin, comps., *Code of 1861*, sec. 1705.
16. Blackstone, *Commentaries*, Book I, sec. 443.
17. Thomas R. R. Cobb, comp., *A Digest of the Statute Laws of Georgia* (Athens, 1851), Acts of: 1768, p. 163; 1807, p. 228; 1824, p. 228; 1826, p. 171; 1839, p. 230; 1850, p. 231.
18. Prince, comp., *Digest*, Acts of: 1804, p. 233; 1829, p. 253.
19. Cobb, comp., *Digest*, Act of 1838, p. 296; John Silcox and others *vs.* John Nelson and others, Richmond County Superior Court, 1842 Term, in *Decisions of the Superior Courts of the State of Georgia*, Part I (Augusta, 1843), 24-25. In De Renne Collection, University of Georgia Library. (Hereafter referred to as *Georgia Superior Court Decisions*.)
20. Penalton & Co. *vs.* Mills & *al.*, Cobb County Superior Court, 1843 Term, *ibid.*, Part II (Augusta, 1844), 116-117; Royston *vs.* Royston, 21 Georgia 161.

her former husband,[21] the child of a previous marriage,[22] or the profits of her own labor.[23] Even if a husband deserted his wife prior to 1851 he might appear periodically and collect her earnings, those of their minor children, or anything else the family which he had abandoned might have accumulated.[24]

The following wills from Wilkes County are typical of the period. John Bowen left: "to wife Rachel all that her father gave her, a slave boy Adam, the dun mare, and her bed and furniture."[25] And Samuel Jack's will reads: "Whereas at the time of our marriage my wife owned a house and lot at Chambersburg and three hundred acres . . . willed to her by her former husband Alex. Stewart, she shall hold it."[26]

A striking case that came up in the Cobb County Superior Court was that of Penalton & Co. *vs.* Mills & *al.* It is concerned with the ownership of a slave girl. She had been kept by the daughter of a widowed mother for some time. The two women had no clear understanding as to whether the negro was a gift or a loan. All went well until both of them were married. Then the mother's husband sued the daughter's husband for the return of the slave, not because she was his wife's property but because she was his own. Both mother and daughter were left out of the case. It was a question of whose husband owned the slave.[27]

The story of Fanny Kemble, the beautiful and successful English actress who married Pierce Mease Butler during her brilliant season in Philadelphia, is

21. A. Edwards and wife *vs.* B. Leigh and W. Leigh, Richmond County, Superior Court Records: Minute Book, 1805-1811, April Term, 1818, p. 246. Mss in Richmond County Superior Court Office.

22. Cobb, comp., *Digest*, Acts of: 1804, p. 291; 1845, p. 294; Uriah B. Holden and wife *vs.* David Harrell, 6 Georgia 126.

23. Gorman *et al.* *vs.* Wood, 68 Georgia 524, 73 Georgia 307; Wilson *vs.* Wilson Sewing Machine Company, 76 Georgia 104.

24. *Acts of Georgia*, 1851, p. 237.

25. Grace G. Davidson, comp., *Early Records of Georgia, Wilkes County* (Macon, 1932), I, 47. (Hereafter referred to as Davidson, comp., *Wilkes County Records.*)

26. *Ibid.*, 85.

27. Penalton & Co. *vs.* Mills & *al.*, in *Georgia Superior Court Decisions*, Part II, 116-117.

the story of a rebel against the code of her day. Theirs was a clash to two cultures which soon led to unhappiness, separation, and divorce. This niece of Mrs. Siddons with a background of Drury Lane and Covent Garden, with generation of distinguished actors behind her, who was held in adoration by two continents, and who had been married in the Unitarian Church which omitted "obey" from its ceremony, was ill designed for ante-bellum domesticity. Butler may have been bigoted but he was charming, educated, and wealthy. During their whirlwind courtship Fanny Kemble apparently never inquired the source of his wealth—slave labor on Butler's Island at the mouth of the Altamaha.[28]

54 Fanny Kemble had always disliked slavery. Her disapproval of it blazed into a burning hatred the winter she and her husband visited his plantation. The system which she so violently attacked he as jealously defended.[29] Slavery came to serve as a battle ground for all the differences that lay between them.[30]

Fanny Kemble was English, she spent only one unhappy winter in Georgia, she was an odd pattern for the mistress of a remote rice plantation, and most of her legal controversies were in Philadelphia; still she was the wife of one of Georgia's richest planters. The problem of her rights to earn, to dispose of her earnings, and to retain the custody of her children were the products of the English common law which she would have found as binding in Georgia as it was in Pennsylvania.[31]

One of their early quarrels was over Fanny Kemble's *Journal of a Residence in America.* It was an account of her first tour in this country. She had contracted for

28. Leota S. Driver, *Fanny Kemble* (Chapel Hill, 1933).
29. Frances Anne Kemble, *Journal of a Residence on a Georgian Plantation* (New York, 1863), *passim.*
30. Driver, *Fanny Kemble*, 92-114.
31. Pierce M. Butler, *Mr. Butler's Statement, Originally prepared with the aid of his Professional Council* (Philadelphia, 1850).

its publication soon after she landed here but was married before the proof was ready. When it came from the press her young husband edited and altered it in spite of her violent protest. This was his marital right and Pierce Butler knew his rights. The *Journal* appeared with the marks of his censorship still on it.[32]

It seemed to Fanny Kemble "too beneficient a provision of the law for the protection of male superiority" that "the man whose wits could not keep him half a week from starving" should be entitled to his wife's earnings.[33] But that was possible.

A case heard three times in the Georgia Supreme Court was that of a woman who had made a little money keeping boarders and from renting property belonging to her. Her husband collected her earnings, 55
invested in land, took the title to it in his own name, and subsequently lost the property. The wife protested against the seizure but the courts ruled in favor of her husband's creditors.[34]

In establishing a husband's claim to his wife's property there was one important qualification. He must "reduce it to possession" during coverture[35] for the wife had the right to her "choses in action."[36] This had its origin in common law. It meant that debts due her—such as rents, legacies, residuary personal estate, money in funds, or shares—which at the time of her marriage were in the possession of a third person, remained there unless her husband took steps to "reduce them to possession"—gain control. To do this he had to show his intentions together with some overt act to give them force—such as receiving payment on a debt

32. Butler, *Statement*, 22-24.
33. Dorothie Bobbé, *Fanny Kemble* (New York, 1931), 170, citing letter to Harriet Martineau (n. d., n. p.).
34. Gorman *et. al. vs.* Wood, 68 Georgia 524, 73 Georgia 370; Wilson *vs.* the Wilson Sewing Machine Company, 76 Georgia 104.
35. Sayre & Sayre *vs.* Flournoy, adm'r and others, 3 Georgia 541.
36. Blackstone, *Commentaries*, Book II, secs. 389, 397.

due his wife, having stock belonging to her transferred to him, or bringing action for an offence against her property in his name.

In the case of the woman with the boarding house the court held that her earnings had been reduced to possession by her husband's action. He had received and invested the money as though it were his own and had not recognized the title as being his wife's until it was attached. He had then attempted to set up her equity in the property. The decision was that a wife's earnings became her husband's if he invested them, whether he took the money with or without her consent, and "whether such earnings were made from keeping a boarding house or from washing, ironing,
56 or cooking."[37]

In another Georgia Supreme Court case, Oglesby and wife *vs.* Hall, Oglesby had permitted his wife to sell cakes and to put her earnings in the bank in Athens. She added to them with money which she borrowed from her brother and bought a negro woman and her four children. Mrs. Oglesby took the title in her own name, held the slaves as separate property, met the taxes, and paid her debt to her brother with the profits of her baking. Oglesby neither objected to her actions nor attempted to establish his claim. Nevertheless he secretly deeded the slaves away retaining for himself and his wife a life interest only. His action became known, Mrs. Oglesby contested his rights, and brought suit for the return of the slaves. At the trial Oglesby admitted he was ignorant at all times and drunk when he executed the deed, but he said he was prompted by "love and affection." The court held that since he had neither reduced his wife's earnings nor the slaves to possession that the property was hers and the deed void.[38]

37. Gorman *et. al.* *vs.* Wood, 68 Georgia 524.
38. Oglesby and wife *vs.* Hall, 30 Georgia 386.

The laws governing a married woman's property were harsh. George Paschal found during the panic of 1837 they took a grim toll in Georgia and produced "moral and social" disorders which were impossible for later generations to understand.[39] Yet a Philadelphia lawyer's remark, that the presumption of the law which gave a husband complete control over his wife's actions "in nine cases out of ten . . . resolved itself into fiction,"[40] had some foundation.

The law allowed a woman to establish a separate estate.[41] The object of this, Judge Bleckley said from the Supreme Bench of Georgia, was to guard a wife from the " 'kicks and kisses' especially the kisses of her husband."[42] The separate estate originated in the common law and did not appear on the statute books of Georgia until 1847.[43] It might be created in several ways: by conveyance to a trustee before marriage;[44] by prenuptial agreement between the parties;[45] by postnuptial settlement—under which a husband conveyed property to a third person to hold for his wife;[46] and by gift or legacy especially establishing a woman's sole ownership and disavowing her husband's claim.[47]

The common law gave a wife "without aid of statute" control over her separate estate and permitted her husband none "except as he may be trustee by implication." It bound him, even then, to follow her directions and required that he be removed if he failed to do so.[48] In Georgia an agreement creating a woman's separate estate, whether or not in writing could be enforced in the courts of equity. Both judge

39. George Paschal, *Ninety-Four Years, or Agnes Paschal* (n. p., 1871), 97.
40. Augusta *Georgia Constitutionalist*, June 8, 1846.
41. Clark, Cobb, and Irwin, comps., *Code of 1861*, secs. 1724-1729.
42. Humphrey *vs.* Copeland, 54 Georgia 543.
43. Cobb, comp., *Digest*, Act of 1847, p. 180.
44. Lydia C. Pepper and Alexander Fawnes, Chatham County Superior Court Records: Minute Book "2F," Folio 107. Mss. in Chatham County Court Office.
45. Joseph Welcher and Ann Miller, *ibid.*, Book "Z," Folio 507.
46. Clark, Cobb, and Irwin, comps., *Code of 1861*, sec. 1730.
47. Will of William Lowden, Chatham County, Inferior Court Records: Will no. 50. Mss. Chatham County Court Office.
48. Blackstone, *Commentaries*, Book I, sec. 444 (note).

and jury were inclined to be friendly to the wife's interest, and, in legal controversies, they might be expected to construe the agreement liberally.[49]

Throughout the ante-bellum period the laws to protect a married woman's property were adequate if she had safeguarded her rights in time. The weakness of the system was that it offered no shelter to those who had not. Yet, as Harriet Martineau pointed out, weak and ignorant women were the ones most likely to need legal protection and the least likely to have sought it.[50]

Little by little women in Georgia gained control of their earnings. Beginning in 1851 certain wives who applied to the legislature for "reliefs" were allowed to carry on an independent business. They were called
58 "free traders." During 1851 and 1852 there were four women so recognized, from 1853 to 1854 there were ten, and from 1855 to 1856 the number rose to fourteen.[51] After that a woman who had gained the consent of her husband was allowed to become a free trader by publishing a notice of her intentions in the paper for a month before beginning business.[52] She was then liable for her contracts and entitled to her profits.

Even when the Married Woman's Act of 1866[53] and the Constitution of 1868 insured a wife's unqualified control of her possession the courts did not relax their guardianship. In 1875 Supreme Court of Georgia decided this legislation had not modified those sections of the Code which prevented a wife from selling her estate to her husband without a court order and which prohibited his creditors buying it under any conditions.[54]

---

49. McBride *vs.* Greenwood and others, 11 Georgia 379; Kempton *et al.* *vs.* Hallowell and Co., 24 Georgia 52; Hicks *vs.* Johnson, 24 Georgia 194.

50. Harriet Martineau, *Society in America* (New York, 1837), II, 238.

51. *Acts of Georgia*, 1851-1852, pp. 515-518; 1853-1854, pp. 527-529; 1855-1856, pp. 512-514.

52. Clark, Cobb, and Irwin, comps., *Code of 1861*, sec. 1708.

53. *Acts of Georgia*, 1866, p. 146.

54. Humphrey *vs.* Copeland, 54 Georgia 543; Clark, Cobb, and Irwin, comps., *Code of 1861*, secs. 1783, 1785.

Fanny Kemble saw in the increasing liberality of the law a "possible advantage to the magnanimous sex." For according to her, it enabled dishonest men to settle extensive property on their wives and then to "baffle the claims of the creditors."[55]

In general a woman's share in her husband's estate was for life only. The laws of inheritance favored the male line and the majority of wills seem to have followed the same trend.[56] The laws regulating intestate estates made the husband the sole heir of his wife and excluded her children,[57] but only allowed a widow to choose between a child's portion and her dower. Before 1829 if a husband left no children his widow was entitled to half of his estate. The remainder went to his next of kin.[58] In that year, however, the law was altered and where there were no lineal 59
descendants the wife became sole heir of her intestate husband.[59]

The best legal protection a woman had for a share in her husband's estate was her dower. The courts defined it as the "favorite of the law" and stipulated "neither the husband nor the courts, nor any other human power can compel a wife to relinquish this right."[60] The law restricted a husband's disposal of his property during his lifetime so as to protect the wife's dower rights.[61] It established her claim to "all he died possessed of."[62] This the Supreme Court of Georgia interpreted to mean free of all mortgages that might be on the estate at the time of the husband's death—as though no encumbrances existed.[63] The law

55. Frances Anne Kemble, *Records of Later Life* (London, 1882), I, 28.
56. Davidson, comp., *Wilkes County Records*, I, II, *passim*.
57. Prince, comp., *Digest*, Act of: 1789, p. 225; 1827, p. 251.
58. *Ibid.*, Act of 1804, p. 233.
59. *Ibid.*, Act of 1829, p. 253; Clark, Cobb, and Irwin, comps., *Code of 1861*, sec. 2452.
60. Royston *vs.* Royston, 21 Georgia 161; Blackstone, *Commentaries*, Book II, sec. 129; Clark, Cobb, and Irwin, comps., *Code of 1861*, sec. 1714.
61. Cobb, comp., *Digest*, Acts of: 1760, p. 161; 1768, p. 163; 1785, p. 165; 1842, p. 179.
62. *Ibid.*, Act of 1826, p. 171.
63. Green *vs.* Causey, 10 Georgia 435; Dennis *et. al.* *vs.* Green, 20 Georgia 386.

permitted a wife to choose her dower property.[64] And it allowed her a year's support for herself and her children even though the estate was insolvent.[65]

The status of a wife under the law was, in part that of a minor whose husband was her guardian. In general public opinion accepted this theory although it was not always practiced. Like a minor her contracts were void;[66] her husband was answerable for her words and her misdemeanors;[67] if through commands, threats, coersion or persuasion he induced her to commit a crime not punishable by death or life imprisonment he must pay the penalty in her stead;[68] and, if she disobeyed he was entitled to administer punishment.[69]

60 It was explained that inasmuch as the husband was made responsible for his wife's misdemeanors the "law thought it reasonable to intrust him with the power of restraining her by domestic chastisement in the same manner that a man is allowed to correct his apprentice or children." There was a time when, for some offences, a man was permitted to "beat his wife severely with scourges and sticks," but in England the "politer reign of Charles II" brought this power of correction into "doubt,"[70] and in Georgia the law required that the stick be no larger than a man's thumb.[71]

Husbands of the upper class in Georgia did not use the lash but women were expected to obey. Something of a code of honor reinforced a husband's discipline. Probably the young ladies of LaGrange College had been reminded of their responsibilities many times before Robert Charlton told them "a woman ought not to

64. Cobb, comp., *Digest*, Acts of: 1830, p. 230; 1850, p. 231.
65. *Ibid.*, Acts of: 1838, p. 296; 1850, pp. 297-299; Hopkins *vs.* Long, 9 Georgia 261.
66. Blackstone, *Commentaries*, Book I, sec. 443-445.
67. Smith *vs.* Taylor and wife, Louise Lynch *vs.* same, 11 Georgia 20.
68. Blackstone, *Commentaries*, Book I, sec. 445.
69. Cobb, comp., *Digest*, Penal Code of 1833, Div. I, sec. VIII, 779.
70. Blackstone, *Commentaries*, Book I, sec. 445.
71. Orville A. Park, comp., *History of Georgia in the Eighteenth Century as Recorded in the Reports of the Georgia Bar Association*, reprint from the Annual Report of the Georgia Bar Association (Macon, 1921), June, 1921, 90.

speak what she pleased," because her husband must answer for her words "either by fight or by law—the first threatening his person, and the last invading his purse."[72]

Yet Georgians could say with their English ancestors "the lower ranks of people . . . still claim and exert their ancient privileges"[73] for here too husbands continued to give disobedient wives corporal punishment. Public opinion was increasingly hostile, however, and sometimes it intruded. Only a broken rail and cool headed intervention prevented a lynching when the husband of one of the mill girls in Columbus attempted to beat her.[74]

In 1857 the law made beating or mistreating a wife a penal offense. It carried a possible six months sentence and allowed the wife to testify in her own behalf.[75] But public opinion still found cause for complaint. When a husband in the factory region of Augusta was fined only "$5.00 for whipping his wife" the *Evening Dispatch* strongly protested against the "cheapness of the luxury."[76]

A wife was the property of her husband to this extent: he had the right of action against another for abducting, harboring, seducing or beating her. These were actions at common law for which the husband might collect damages.[77] Many husbands advertised their fugative wives, and warned against "dealing with, harboring, or concealing" the runaways under the penalty of the law.[78]

Women were expected to accept their lot as part of the punishment visited upon Eve, to continue the "even

72. Robert M. Charlton, *Address*, delivered at the commencement of LaGrange Female College, July, 1853 (Savannah, 1853).
73. Blackstone, *Commentaries*, Book I, sec. 445.
74. Augusta *Daily Constitutionalist*, July 14, 1847 citing *Muscogee Democrat*, 1st inst.
75. *Acts of Georgia*, 1857, p. 126.
76. Augusta *Evening Dispatch*, Feb. 1, 1859.
77. Blackstone, *Commentaries*, Book III, sec. 139-140; Clark, Cobb, and Irwin, comps., *Code of 1861*, sec. 2949.
78. Augusta *Chronicle and Gazette of the State*, Oct. 14, 1797.

as Sarah obeyed Abraham" teachings of the Jews, and to "reverence their husbands" in accordance with the theology of Paul.[79]

When Pierce Butler was preparing for his divorce he, with the aid of his lawyers, drew up his *Statement* to be used as testimony. In it he cited as "perhaps the fundamental" reason for the failure of his marriage the "peculiar views which were entertained by Mrs. Butler . . . she held that marriage should be a companionship on equal terms—partnership, in which if both partners agreed all is well—but at no time has one partner a right to control the other."[80] He claimed the things to which his wife objected were "the customary and pledged acquiescence of a wife to marital
62 control—nothing more."[81] Pierce Butler asserted that "nothing is required to show the error of this principal of equal rights in marriage. . . . No one who is not morally astray can fail to see the heedlessness of the pretension."[82]

A man was the head of his family. His wife and his minor children were his wards. The common law provided that "a mother as such is entitled to no power but only to reverence and respect," but that "the Empire of the father continues even after his death."[83] Both the statute law[84] and public opinion supported the father's authority. And this authority, Fanny Kemble discovered, "endowed" the father with the power of "supreme torture."[85] Yet she accepted her husband's right to the custody of their children.

Her ecceptance is significant of the code under which she lived. Fanny Kemble was not lacking in daring.

---

79. Mary S. Benson, *Women of the Eighteenth-Century America* (New York, 1935), 184-185, citing David Ramsey, *Memoirs of the Life of Martha Laurens Ramsey*, 41-42.
80. Butler, *Statement*, 9.
81. *Ibid.*, 9-10.
82. Bobbé, *Fanny Kemble*, 247.
83. Blackstone, *Commentaries*, Book I, sec. 454.
84. *Ibid.*, secs. 447-452, Clark, Cobb, and Irwin, comps., *Code of 1861*, sec. 1744.
85. Fanny Kemble to Harriet Martineau, Sept. 22, 1846, in Kemble, *Records of Later Life*, III, 137.

There was no doubt of her devotion to her children. Her personal conduct was unquestioned. Yet she possessed adequate proof of her husband's infidelity and made no use of it. He divorced her in 1849 and got the custody of the children.[86]

Butler himself admitted "her care and management of our children was admirable we have never disagreed once about them."[87] But both he and his wife regarded the children as a species of the father's undisputed personal property and behaved accordingly.

Fanny Kemble was planning a separation when their second child was expected. She wrote her husband that she could reach England in time for it to be born there and "if you will appoint the means for your child being brought over to you, I shall of course observe them."[88] In considering his wife's determination to leave him Butler questioned the welfare of the children without her, his own ability to care for them, and her happiness if separated from them, but not the possibility of the mother being given the guardianship of the children.[89]

The father had the right to will away the custody of his children. He might, and frequently did, name their mother as their guardian. This was the only way in which she ever gained complete control over legitimate children. If the father died without providing for their guardianship the mother was eligible for appointment by the courts, but on remarriage her authority terminated. She might be reappointed or dismissed at the discretion of the court and the father's next of kin, the new step-father, or someone else named by the court replace her.[90]

A widowed mother's estate was divided among her children but under the Act of 1804 she was entitled

86. Driver, *Fanny Kemble*, 114-156; Butler, *Statement*, *passim*.
87. Pierce Butler to Mrs. Sedgwick, May 31, 1839, *ibid.*, 38.
88. Fanny Kemble to Pierce Butler, 1838, in Butler, *Statement*, 27.
89. Pierce Butler to Mrs. Sedgwick, May 31, 1839, *ibid.*, 38.
90. Cobb, comp., *Digest*, Acts of: 1792, p. 309; 1828, p. 327; 1842, p. 335.

to nothing from an intestate legitimate child whom she might have survived. If such a child had no descendants, father, brother, and sisters shared his estate. Whole or half blood on the paternal side inherited equally. If the father was dead and the mother had remained a widow she was entitled to her husband's part of the estate, but if she had remarried the father's next kin inherited his share.[91]

The Act of 1843 was less harsh. Remarriage still barred a mother from participation in the estates of all children except her last or only one. This she might inherit unconditionally.[92]

This law took an odd turn in the settlement of the estate of William Harrell, a posthumous child who died
64 before he was three years old. His mother had married again and by that marriage had had a daughter, Mary. When the girl was two days old the boy died. Since he had inherited considerable property from his father the disposition of it became a matter for the courts. The case finally reached the Supreme Bench. It defined the "last child" as being the last surviving child of the mother and named Mary as the sole heir. Thus she inherited the estate of her mother's first husband, through a half brother, who never saw his father and who was probably never aware that his sister had been born.[93]

Illegitimate children had "no blood except that given them by the law."[94] Under it they belonged to the mother and, unless the father legally adopted them,[95] it was as though he were dead and his relatives had never existed. An illegitimate child shared equally in the estate of its mother with a legitimate one. If it died intestate, provided there were neither wife nor

---

91. Prince, comp., *Digest*, Act of 1804, p. 233.

92. Cobb, comp., *Digest*, Act of 1843, p. 297; Clark, Cobb, and Irwin, comps., *Code of 1861*, sec. 2452.

93. Uriah B. Holden and wife *vs.* David Harrell, 6 Georgia 126.

94. Clark, Cobb, and Irwin, comps., *Code of 1861*, sec. 1751.

95. *Ibid.*, sec. 1750.

lineal descendants, its estate was divided alike between mother, brothers, and sisters. If none of these existed the property went to the mother's legitimate children.[96]

The law of 1793 provided that both man and woman accused of misconduct should be indicted but the Supreme Court of Georgia left no room for doubt that the "primary object of the act . . . was to protect the county from the charge of bastard children."[97]

The mother of an illegitimate child might choose between naming the father and giving security for its support. If the father were known he was forced to provide for the expenses of the child's birth and its maintenance. Whomsoever the mother accused was held guilty unless proven innocent. The father's offence was not his paternity but his failure to pay the bills. This was held to be a misdemeanor.[98]

The fate of such children was always sad but the taxpayers were determined to protect their pocket books if possible. Most of the Bastard Bonds seem to cover the care of the child until it was fourteen years of age,[99] but among the court records are items such as: "Lucy Sheet, illegitimate child of Anna Shorter, four years old bound to Joseph Barker,"[100] which tell their own story.

With Protestanism both Church and State accepted marriage as a civil contract and divorces became permissible. They were avoided, however, if possible for there had lingered a fondness for the sacramental marriage doctrines of the Catholic Church and the causes for which divorces were allowed placed a stigma on them for either sex. And for a woman a divorce might prove socially and economically disastrous.

---

96. Clark, Cobb, and Irwin, comps., *Code of 1861*, secs. 1751-1752; Cobb, comp., *Digest*, Acts of: 1816, p. 293; 1850, p. 299.

97. Locke *vs.* the State, 3 Georgia 534.

98. Cobb, comp., *Digest*, Act of 1793, pp. 148-149; Penal Code of 1833, Div. X, sec. XXIX, 1818; Clark, Cobb, and Irwin, comps., *Code of 1861*, secs. 4640-4643.

99. Richmond County, Inferior Court Records: Bastard Bonds.

100. Davidson, comp., *Wilkes County Records*, I, 145.

The Georgia divorce code was brought from England and, in theory at least, was severe for it still bore the marks of the canon law which did not recognize divorce. The Catholic Church prohibited marriage under certain conditions. If these were not observed Rome declared the marriage void, but if both parties were qualified only death could dissolve the bond. This plan the English incorporated in their civil law—even though the recorder of the common law was "led to wonder that the same authority which enjoined the strictest celebacy to the priesthood should think itself proper judge in causes between man and wife."[101]

The English code classified divorces as complete and
66 partial. Complete divorces were given only to parties who had not made a legal contract. They were not allowed for any causes which arose after a legal marriage—not even when "it became impossible for the parties to live together; as in the case of intollerable ill temper or adultery." Partial divorces were granted for infidelity and cruel treatment. They permitted separation from "bed and board" only and prohibited remarriage.[102]

In Georgia the same distinction existed[103] but as the State Constitution of 1798 provided that divorces should be granted on "legal principles" and these were not defined by the Supreme Court for almost fifty years there was a lack of uniformity in the degree and the causes for which divorces were given. Judge Floyd, in the case of Head *vs.* Head, put a stop to the "flagrant facility" with which divorces were being granted and restricted them to the grounds recognized in the laws which the colonies had brought from England.[104]

---

101. Blackstone, *Commentaries*, Book III, sec. 93.
102. *Ibid.*, Book I, sec. 440-441.
103. Prince, comp., *Digest*, Act of 1806, p. 188.
104. Head *vs.* Head, 2 Georgia 191.

The decision necessitated a revision of the divorce code. The amendment of 1849 gave the General Assembly the right to determine the grounds for divorce.[105] The Act of 1849 recognized all divorces allowed before the decision and relieved the parties who had remarried of any possible charge of bigamy.[106] And the Act of 1850 assigned inability of the parties to contract as defined by law, incontinence, and desertion as reasons for total divorce; in cases of cruel treatment or habitual drunkenness the jury was empowered to determine whether the decree should be final or separation from bed and board only; and all other grounds permitted partial divorce only.[107]

Nevertheless the divorce code remained in confusion. The first divorce procedure in Georgia required action by both courts and legislature,[108] but in 1833 the General Assembly amended the Constitution and vested sole authority in the courts.[109] Georgians, however, did not seem to be fully aware of the change for the Legislature continued to receive frequent applications for divorce and sometimes acted upon them. Governor Brown said only one such petition had been granted since the amendment and that was to complete action begun before the alteration of the Constitution. Yet he was called upon to veto a divorce bill in 1859.[110]

The law prohibited the guilty party to a divorce suit from remarrying,[111] but the Legislature by granting a "relief" could remove the disability. It was said on the floor of the House that no petition of this character had ever been denied. In 1859 came a call for a repeal of the restriction. The discussions of the bill show that Georgians had become more charitable toward divorce.

---

105. McElreath, *Constitution of Georgia*, Constitution of 1798, amendment to Art. III, sec. IX, 278.
106. Cobb, comp., *Digest*, Act of 1849, p. 227.
107. *Acts of Georgia*, 1850, pp. 151-152.
108. McElreath, *Constitution of Georgia*, Constitution of 1798, Art. III, sec. IX, 263.
109. *Ibid.*, amendment to Art. III, sec. IX, 274.
110. Milledgeville *Daily Federal Union*, Dec. 15, 1859.
111. Prince, comp., *Digest*, Act of 1806, p. 188.

One representative dared say, "God does not put his eternal sanction on everything done by preachers and justices of the peace," and to pronounce, "continued cohabitation under the coercion of law, where there is no affection legalized adultery."[112]

As the years went by the divorce rate increased in Georgia. Oliver H. Prince counted 291 divorces granted between 1798 and the close of the legislative session of 1835. He found they averaged about four a year from 1800 to 1810. The next ten years the rate doubled —eight a year. Between 1820 and 1830 it more than doubled again—eighteen a year. And from 1830 to 1835 Georgia granted an average of twenty-eight divorces a year.[113]

68 By 1833 the weight of divorce legislation had become so great that the General Assembly stepped out from under the load and added a constitutional amendment which included their grievance in its preamble.[114] And by 1859 Representative Wallace of Taylor estimated the state had spent $200,000 on special divorce legislation.[115]

The divorce laws placed the same value on the character of the husband as they did on that of the wife, but public opinion differed. As Judge Floyd pointed out, in his Head *vs.* Head decision, society accepted the delinquency of the husband with greater grace than it was willing to allow his wife. He found this was being justified by presuming the failings of the wife to be more injurious to the home than those of the husband. Judge Floyd denied this theory and refused to believe it was "illustrative of the high esteem placed on feminine virtue." He held that the double standard was owing to the "prevelence of vice among men." And, though he deplored it, he charged that

112. Augusta *Daily Constitutionalist*, Dec. 11 1859.
113. Prince, comp., *Digest*, 187.
114. Cobb, comp., *Digest*, Preamble to the amendment of 1833, Constitution of 1798, Art. III, sec. IX, 1123.
115. Augusta *Daily Constitutionalist*, Dec. 11, 1859.

wives were required to "meekly endure" what husbands were "justified in making good cause for loathing, contempt, and repudiation."[116]

In an unhappy marriage the unsurbordinate status of women was likely to prove tragic. It is true the law granted alimony. The amount was conditioned on the wealth of the husband and the separate estate of the wife.[117] Any part of her property which he might have lost or squandered previously was forgotten by the law. There was the forlorn Elizabeth Harper, for example. She wrote of her husband to the Brothers and Sisters of Mars Hill Church, "he have taken my property and gave it to another and now is sporeting with my carecttor." But she could only be "sory" she had been driven out of her home with nothing but "a little flower and a small piece of meat" and forced to seek "sheltor" with the neighbors. There seems to have been no comfort for her destitution.[118]

Elizabeth Harper's social position was not responsible for her unhappy situation. Women of the aristocracy played with loaded dice too. There is a Charleston gentleman's own record. It appears he had killed his wife's reputed lover, probably in a duel in Georgia. Later with the full connivance of Georgia gentlemen of equal rank he attempted to secure letters which his wife had written to the dead man and which would incriminate her. He wanted them not only as testimony should he decide to sue for divorce and to exhonorate himself should he be extradited for trial, but also because there was a possibility of his "unfortunate" wife inheriting "seventy thousand pounds sterling" from her father's estate. If she did, he made no secret of

116. Head *vs.* Head, 2 Georgia 191.

117. Cobb, comp., *Digest*, Act of 1810, p. 225; Clark, Cobb, and Irwin, comps., *Code of 1861*, secs. 1676, 1688-1699.

118. Elizabeth Harper to the Brothers and Sisters of Mars Hill Church, Nov. 12, 1818, in mss. Letters and Papers of Edward Harden, Athens, Georgia in Duke University Library.

his plan to use the proof her letters contained of "her behavior and feelings" toward him to "so impress the Court of Chancery with her unworthiness as to induce them to settle the entire fortune on her children."[119]

It was common to find a husband who advertised that his wife had "left his bed and board without the least shadow of provocation,"[120] and to "forewarn all others from trading with or trusting her" as he was no longer responsible for her debts.[121] It is possible these husbands were frequently as poor risks as the wives they advertised. At least the Southern Banner seems to have been suspicious. Beginning in 1842 and continuing for years it charged for "announcing candidates for office $5.00—payable in advance," and for "hus-
70 bands advertising their wives . . . $5.00 *invariably* payable in advance." All other patrons got twelve lines of advertising for $1.00—on credit.[122]

Taken all-in-all the political status of women in Georgia from 1783 to 1860 was of microscopic importance and their civil status was capricious. That of the unmarried woman was secure but, in theory at least, a husband spoke from a burning bush and a married woman had no legal civil status. In fact, however, the law was flexible. It never intruded but if solicited it could give substantial protection to married women.

The statutes governing the relations between husband and wife were based on a mixed concept. In regard to property they were feudal—she, the vassal, surrendered all she possessed to her overlord in return for protection; in regard to a wife's conduct her relations with her husband were those of guardian and ward; and, if a wife was stolen, damaged, or abused,

119. John Rutledge to Robert MacKay, Feb. 11, 1804, in mss. Letters and Papers of Robert MacKay and W. H. H. Stiles, Savannah, Georgia, in University of North Carolina Library.

120. *Athens Gazette*, June 16, 1814.

121. Milledgeville *Georgia Patriot*, July 11, 1826.

122. Athens *Southern Banner*, June 18, 1842.

the law regarded the husband's loss as though his wife were his personal property and allowed him to collect damages.

A married woman's greatest legal liability was her lack of property rights. But here again she played hide-and-seek with the law. The law permitted her marriage vow to confiscate her possessions but did not hesitate to shut one eye, help her establish a separate estate, and maintain it during her husband's life. After her husband's death she was entitled to a year's support and to her dower. In case of divorce there was alimony. The courts were inclined to be friendly to a wife's financial interest, but expected her to keep her marriage contract and were not inclined to show mercy if she failed.

Due to the English heritage and American custom, the tendency was to keep estates in the male line. So women were in the red there. But during the antebelum period public opinion was slowly crystalizing into laws more beneficial to women. While children were the property of the father, here too a slight change in favor of the mother was in progress.

A married woman's position in Georgia before 1860 was always hazardous, frequently humiliating, and often tragic. Her true status, nevertheless, was far more commonly determined by her character, that of the man she married, their personal relations to each other, the use they made of the laws, and even by public opinion, than by the statutes alone.

MARRIED WOMEN'S RIGHTS IN COMMUNITY PROPERTY UNDER THE LAW OF CALIFORNIA.

BY WILLIAM B. BOSLEY,

OF THE SAN FRANCISCO BAR.

The first legislature of the State of California adopted, on
72 April 13, 1850, the common law of England as the rule
of decision in all the courts of the State. Four days
later "An Act defining the Rights of Husband and Wife" was
enacted whereby estates by the curtesy and estates in dower
were abolished and the institution of community property,
borrowed from the civil and Spanish law, was established. Community property of husband and wife, as defined by this statute and subsequently by our civil code, consists of all property acquired, during the existence of the marriage relation, by either husband or wife or both, except such as is acquired by gift, bequest, devise or descent. All other property, together with its rents, issues and profits, is separate property; and neither husband nor wife has any interest in the other's separate property. The Act of April 17, 1850, did, indeed, declare that the "rents and profits of the separate property of either husband or wife shall be deemed common property." But this clause of the Act was declared to be repugnant to our State Constitution in the case of *George* v. *Ransom*, 15 Cal. 322, wherein separate property of the wife is defined as "an estate held, as well in its use as in its title, for the exclusive benefit and advantage of the wife." And such has been the established law ever since.[1]

The theory underlying the legal distinction between separate and community property is that the latter is produced by the joint efforts of the husband and wife; the relation between

[1] Const. of 1849, Art. XI, Sec. 14; Const. of 1879, Art. XX, Sec. 8; Stats. of 1850, Chap. 103, Secs. 1, 2, 9 and 10; Stats. 1853, p. 165; Civil Code, Secs. 161-164, 169 and 173.

them, in respect of property, being considered as a species of partnership,[2] though, as we shall see, the wife's interest in the partnership assets is almost nominal.

The courts, in determining the character of property as community or separate, have always acted upon the presumption that all property owned by either husband or wife, or both, is community property, and have cast upon the person asserting the contrary the burden of proving, by clear and convincing evidence, its separate character. This presumption is considered not merely a rule of evidence, but a rule of property.[3] The most important exceptions to the rule that property acquired by purchase during marriage is presumed to be community property occur in cases where property is conveyed to the wife by the husband or is expressly declared to be for her sole and separate use.[4] This presumption, however, when ap- 73
plied to conveyances of land to married women, was not in harmony with the purpose of the recording laws, and not infrequently occasioned confusion in land titles. To remedy this evil the legislature in 1889, by an amendment of Sec. 164 of the civil code, provided that "whenever any property is conveyed to a married woman by an instrument in writing, the presumption is that the title is thereby vested in her as her separate property * * * and the presumption is conclusive in favor of a purchaser or incumbrancer in good faith and for a valuable consideration." The true character of property as separate or community, it will be observed from an examination of the authorities cited, does not depend much upon forms of conveyancing, but rather upon the time and mode of its acquisition.[5]

The entire management and control of the community property, and the absolute power of disposition thereof during the existence of the marriage relation are, with certain exceptions to be noted, vested in the husband.[6] Even though land or other property be granted or otherwise transferred to the

---

[2] *De Godey* v. *Godey*, 39 Cal. 157 ; *Frankel* v. *Boyd*, 106 Cal. 608.

[3] *Meyer* v. *Kinzer*, 12 Cal. 247 ; *Jordan* v. *Fay*, 98 Cal. 264 ; *Estate of Boody*, 113 Cal. 682.

[4] *Taylor* v. *Opperman*, 79 Cal. 468 ; *Carter* v. *McQuade*, 83 Cal. 274 ; *Sanchez* v. *Grace M. E. Church*, 114 Cal. 295.

[5] *Peiser* v. *Griffin*, 125 Cal. 9 ; *Jackson* v. *Torrence*, 83 Cal. 521 ; *Estate of Bauer*, 79 Cal. 305.

[6] Stats. of 1850, Chap. 103 ; Civil Code, Sec. 172.

wife, if it be in fact acquired otherwise than by gift, bequest, devise or descent, the husband can by his deed or other appropriate instrument of conveyance, and without the consent or concurrence of the wife, effectually transfer it.[7] The husband until 1891 even had the right to make a voluntary disposition of a reasonable portion of the community property, without the consent of the wife. Such a disposition was, however, voidable at the instance of the wife, if made with intent to defraud her; yet she could not, during her coverture, maintain an action to set aside such fraudulent disposition; and it is doubtful if she has any preventive remedy.[8] The legislature, by an amendment to Sec. 172 of the civil code adopted in 1891, deprived the husband of the power to make a gift of community property without the written consent of the wife. But this
74 amendment has been held inapplicable to community property theretofore acquired.[9] The husband ever since May 8, 1861, has had the right, as against his wife, to devise and bequeath one-half of the community property, but not more.[10] That the husband had the power by will to dispose of one-half of the community property before May 8, 1861, though formerly doubted, was sustained by the Supreme Court in the case of *Payne* v. *Payne*, 18 Cal. 291, 301, construing Sec. 11 of Chap. 103 of the Statutes of 1850. A different opinion was expressed as a *dictum* in the case of *Jewell* v. *Jewell*, 28 Cal. 232; though the decision in *Payne* v. *Payne*, *supra*, does not appear ever to have been overruled. Upon principles equally applicable to all kinds of property, the husband, by clearly manifesting his intention to bequeath and devise more than one-half of the community property, may put his widow to her election to take under the will or to accept the provision made for her by the law.[11] The husband may also, by his will, empower his execu-

---

[7] *Tustin* v. *Faught*, 23 Cal. 237 ; *Meyer* v. *Kinzer*, 12 Cal. 247 ; *Tolman* v. *Smith*, 85 Cal. 280 ; *Fallbrook Irrig. Dist.* v. *Abila*, 106 Cal. 355 ; *Peiser* v. *Griffin*, 125 Cal. 9.

[8] *Lord* v. *Hough*, 43 Cal. 581 ; *Greiner* v. *Greiner*, 58 Cal. 115 ; *Smith* v. *Smith*, 12 Cal. 216 ; *Corker* v. *Corker*, 95 Cal. 308 ; *Sun Ins. Co.* v. *White*, 123 Cal. 196.

[9] *Spreckels* v. *Spreckels*, 116 Cal. 339.

[10] Stats. of 1861, p. 310 ; Stats. of 1863-64, p. 363 ; Civil Code, Sec. 1402 ; *Estate of Frey*, 52 Cal. 658.

[11] *Estate of Gilmore*, 81 Cal. 240 ; *Estate of Smith*, 108 Cal. 115 ; *Estate of Stewart*, 74 Cal. 98.

tor to sell or otherwise dispose of any portion of the community property for the purpose of satisfying and discharging all of his debts and all claims and demands for which the community property may, during his lifetime, be taken in execution, but for no other purpose.[12] When the marriage is dissolved by the death of the husband, the whole of the community property becomes assets of his estate, chargeable with all of his debts, and is to be administered upon by his personal representatives.[13]

During coverture the wife has never had any power to control, manage or dispose of the community property, whether it was acquired in the name of herself or of her husband; for in either case both the legal and the equitable title is in the husband. An attempt on the part of the wife to dispose of community property, whether real or personal, is an absolute nullity.[14] 75

Under the provisions of Sec. 11, Chap. 103 of the Statutes of 1850, prior to its amendment by an act approved May 8, 1861, upon the dissolution of the marriage by the death of the wife, one-half of the community property vested absolutely in the husband, and the other half vested in the descendants of the deceased wife, or, if there were no descendants, then in the surviving husband; but in neither case did any portion of the community property become assets of the deceased wife's estate, or liable to be administered upon by her personal representative. The whole of the community property, however, remained liable to be taken for the debts previously incurred by the husband. The husband, as the survivor of the marital community, had the right to continue in possession of the community property, and to control and dispose of it for the purpose of satisfying and discharging all the liabilities which he had previously incurred. The husband, indeed, had not the power to bind the interests of his wife's descendants in the community property for any debt contracted after the wife's death. But a purchaser from the surviving husband, in good faith and for a valuable consideration, of the community property, acquired good title thereto, as against the

---

[12] *Sharp* v. *Loupe*, 120 Cal. 89.

[13] *Estate of Tompkins*, 12 Cal. 114; Stats. of 1850, Chap. 103, Sec. 11; Stats. of 1861, p. 310; Stats. of 1863-64, p. 363; Civil Code, Sec. 1402.

[14] *Peiser* v. *Griffin*, 125 Cal. 9; *Dean* v. *Parker*, 88 Cal. 283.

wife's descendants.[15] Subject to the surviving husband's right of possession and control for the purposes of satisfying existing indebtedness, the descendants of the deceased wife became tenants in common with the surviving husband, and were entitled to maintain either an action for the partition of the property in specie, or in case the property was disposed of by the surviving husband, an action for an accounting and to recover their share of the net proceeds.[16]

Ever since May 8, 1861, with the exception of the period of time from January 1, 1873, to July 1, 1874, upon the dissolution of the marriage by the death of the wife, the entire community property has vested in the husband immediately and without administration, and the wife has never had the right to devise or bequeath any of the community prop-
76 erty.[17] From January 1, 1873, until July 1, 1874, Sec.
1401 of the civil code provided that if the husband shall have abandoned his wife and lived separate and apart from her, one-half of the community property subject to the payment of the debts chargeable to it, is at the wife's testamentary disposition, and in the absence of such disposition, goes to her descendants or heirs at law, exclusive of her husband. Since July 1, 1874, any community property which may have been set apart to the wife by judicial decree for her support and maintenance, is in effect made her separate property, subject to her testamentary disposition, and in the absence of such disposition, capable of being inherited by her descendants or heirs, exclusive of her husband.

Under the statute of April 17, 1850, upon the dissolution of the marriage by the death of the husband, the wife succeeded to one-half of the community property if there were descendants of the husband, otherwise to the whole thereof, subject only to the payment of the debts of the deceased husband. This statute was amended by an act passed May 8, 1861, providing that, in the absence of descendants of the deceased husband, if he failed to exercise his right of testamentary disposition, his half of the community property, if we may so designate it, should be succeeded to in the same manner as his sepa-

---

[15] *Packard* v. *Arellanes*, 17 Cal. 525; *Cook* v. *Norman*, 50 Cal. 633; *Johnston* v. *S. F. Savings Union*, 75 Cal. 134.

[16] *Broad* v. *Broad*, 40 Cal. 493; *Ord.* v. *De La Guerra*, 18 Cal. 67.

[17] Stats. 1861, p. 310; Stats. 1863-64, p. 363; Civil Code, Secs. 1273, 1401.

rate estate; and under the general Statute of Descents and Distributions, the wife has always been, in this State, entitled to succeed, as heir, to a portion of her deceased husband's separate property; and this has been the law ever since.[18]

The courts of this State have experienced very great difficulty in attempting to define, in terms of the common law, the title by which the wife, upon the death of her husband, becomes the full and complete owner of one-half of the community property, and some confusion of thought has necessarily resulted. In the case of Burdick's Estate, *supra*, there was presented for adjudication the question whether the wife upon the death of her husband, takes title to her one-half of the property by survivorship or by succession as an heir. Dealing with this question, the Court, speaking by Mr. Justice Temple, said: "The legal title to the community property is in the husband. He has the absolute dominion and control of it, and the wife 77
has no right or title of any kind in any specific property, but a possible interest in whatever remains upon a dissolution of the community otherwise than by her own death. This cannot be classified as any species of estate known to the law." The Court held that the wife takes title by succession, that is by descent. Two of the justices, concurring specially, declared it as their opinion, that the wife upon the death of her husband, receives one-half of the community property "not as the heir of her husband, but in her own right as her half of the property which was acquired by herself and her husband during the marriage, and freed from all restrictions in its use and enjoyment, and with the same title as if the marriage had been dissolved by a decree of divorce." The doctrine of the majority of the Court *in re* Burdick's Estate, is now, however, considered as settled law.[19]

The act of April 17, 1850, provided that in case of the dissolution of the marriage by decree of any court of competent jurisdiction, the common property should be equally divided between the parties, and that the court granting the decree should make such order for the division of the common property, or the sale and equal distribution of the proceeds thereof, as the nature of the particular case should require. This stat-

---

[18] Stats. 1863-64, p. 363; Civil Code, Sec. 1402; *Jewell* v. *Jewell*, 28 Cal. 233; *Estate of Boody*, 113 Cal. 682; *Estate of Burdick*, 112 Cal. 387; *Cunha* v. *Hughes*, 122 Cal. 111.

[19] *Cunha* v. *Hughes*, *supra*.

ute was amended April 14, 1857 (Stats. 1857, p. 199), by providing that when a decree of divorce is rendered on the ground of adultery or extreme cruelty, the party found guilty thereof shall only be entitled to such portion of the common property as the court granting the decree may in its discretion deem just. The statute as amended was substantially re-enacted in sections 146 and 147 of the civil code.

Under these statutes, the effect of a decree of divorce in a case wherein no issues are presented involving the community property, and no relief in respect thereto is sought, is to make the husband and wife technically equal tenants in common of all the community property; and the parties to the divorce proceedings may thereafter have their property partitioned in the same manner as other tenants in common.[20]

When a decree of divorce is granted upon the ground of
78 adultery or extreme cruelty, the injured party is entitled at least to something more than one-half of the community property, and the court may in its discretion, award to the innocent party the whole of the community property, or a portion thereof, together with a lien upon the residue to secure any payment which the husband may be ordered to make for the support of the wife.[21]

If the court in granting a decree of divorce to the wife, assigns to her all of the community property, leaving the husband without separate property wherewith to pay his existing indebtedness, the property so assigned is taken subject to the right of creditors to enforce payment of their demands against it to the same extent as if the property had continued to belong to the husband, provided such claims arose out of transactions intended to benefit the marital community. The proper procedure for the creditor to pursue is to file a creditor's bill after the recovery of judgment against the husband.[22]

The wife may, without the concurrence of her husband, declare a homestead upon either his separate or his community property, and thereafter the property selected as a homestead is not only exempt from execution or forced sale, but also can-

---

[20] *De Godey* v. *Godey*, 39 Cal. 157; *McLeran* v. *Benton*, 31 Cal. 29; *Kirschener* v. *Dietrich*, 110 Cal. 502; *Biggi* v. *Biggi*, 98 Cal. 35; *Reid* v. *Reid*, 112 Cal. 274.

[21] *Eslinger* v. *Eslinger*, 47 Cal. 62; *Miller* v. *Miller*, 33 Cal. 353; *Brown* v. *Brown*, 60 Cal. 579; *Strozynski* v. *Strozynski*, 97 Cal. 189; *Rose* v. *Rose*, 112 Cal. 341; *Gaston* v. *Gaston*, 114 Cal. 542.

[22] *Frankel* v. *Boyd*, 106 Cal. 608.

not be conveyed or incumbered save by an instrument executed and acknowledged by both husband and wife.[23] The rights of the survivor of the marital community in the homestead differ according to whether it was selected from community or separate property; as do also the rights of the parties to a divorce suit. A discussion of the homestead law would unduly prolong this paper and must therefore be omitted. Strictly speaking, married women have no rights in community property other than those already discussed.

---

[23] Civil Code, Secs. 1238, 1240 and 1242.

PATRICIA BRITO

Protective Legislation in Ohio: The Inter-war Years

During the 1920s, protective legislation—legislation that applied only to women and was intended to preserve the health and safety of the female worker—made obvious the conflict between orthodox trade union theory and the expeditious achievement of economic goals. The American Federation of Labor and its Ohio affiliate, the Ohio State Federation of Labor, subscribed to the doctrine of "voluntarism," the idea that labor's best interests were served by voluntary organization and collective bargaining. This implied that the state should play only a minimal role in regulating economic conditions. Hence, on those issues that could be resolved through the bargaining process, the union jealously guarded its role as a spokesman for the laborer's interest.[1] The AF of L opposed legislation to set a minimum wage or maximum hours for male workers because, in its view, reliance on social welfare legislation would ultimately weaken union organization. As the AF of L Executive Council warned in 1923: "The threat of state invasion of industrial life is real. . . . The continuing clamor for extension of state regulatory powers under the guise of reform and deliverance from evil can but lead into greater confusion and hopeless entanglements."[2]

Labor's position on protective legislation for women suggests the practical limits and hidden meaning of the Federation's voluntarist ideology. As a group of largely unskilled, unorganized workers expected to remain in the work force only a short time, women posed a considerable threat to the wage level. Labor's voluntaristic philosophy suggested that improvement in wages and hours, for both sexes, should come through

Patricia Brito is a graduate student at Rice University

1. For a more complete discussion of organized labor's voluntaristic philosophy, see George Gilmary Higgins, *Voluntarism in Organized Labor in the United States, 1930-1940,* The Catholic University of America, Studies in Economics, Vol. 13 (Washington, D.C., 1944), 35-51; Max M. Kampelman, "Labor in Politics," *Interpreting the Labor Movement,* eds. George W. Brooks, Milton Derber, David A. McCabe and Philip Taft (Champaign, 1952), 171-91; Louis S. Reed, *The Labor Philosophy of Samuel Gompers* (New York, 1930); and Selig Perlman, *A Theory of the Labor Movement* (New York, 1928; reprint ed., New York, 1949).

2. American Federation of Labor, *Report of Proceedings,* Forty-third Annual Convention, 1923, 31.

collective bargaining between the employer and the employee. At the same time, union leaders believed that women were inherently difficult to organize. Thus, for male union officials there was this contradiction: women should organize and bargain for wages and working conditions, but because they were difficult to organize this approach was already doomed to failure. Complicating this, labor union officials and members shared the common assumption that a woman's role in nurturing future generations was sufficient reason that her health, safety, and morals should receive special protection. For example, the AF of L convention approved a resolution favoring restrictions on night work for women on the grounds that "there is necessity for the protection of the health of women workers; that unless this protection is given them the race cannot continue to progress as it is desired that it should."[3]

The history of the Ohio State Federation of Labor and protective legislation during the period between World Wars I and II suggests that
voluntarism, with its attendant anti-statism, was an abstraction invoked to 81
justify positions that served the interests of dominant elements within organized labor.[4] Two significant pieces of protective legislation were passed in Ohio during the inter-war period. One—the legislative prohibition of women from certain occupations—illustrates the willingness of craft unions to resort to state regulation to protect men's jobs and wages against competition from women. The second, and more important, piece of legislation was the provision of a minimum wage for women. This never received support from the Ohio State Federation of Labor. Like the AF of L, the OSF of L opposed such social welfare regulation as a violation of its voluntaristic philosophy. Those opposed to the law felt that a legislatively determined minimum wage might usurp the role of collective bargaining, especially if it were eventually extended to cover male workers. Hence, when protective legislation was written to make men's jobs secure against competition from less well-paid women, predominantly male unions accepted it. However, when such legislation threatened to interfere with what unions viewed as their self-interest, it was rejected as a violation of trade unionism and voluntaristic union philosophy.

3. AF of L., *Proceedings*, 1919, 240, 450.

4. Michael Rogin's analysis of the voluntaristic ideology of the AF of L and its practical effects reaches a similar conclusion about the national organization. See Michael Rogin, "Voluntarism: The Political Functions of an Antipolitical Doctrine," *Industrial and Labor Relations Review*, 15 (July, 1962), 521-35. In Rogin's view, Gompers' voluntaristic philosophy legitimized craft union control within the organization.

OCCUPATIONAL PROHIBITIONS

During the 1919 legislative session, the Ohio State Federation of Labor sponsored a statute in the state legislature prohibiting the employment of women in a long list of occupations. Among the occupations prohibited to women were such disparate pursuits as molding, work as baggage or freight handlers, taxi-driving, reading electric meters, and work in blast furnaces, smelters, mines, quarries, poolrooms, or establishments that catered to an exclusively male clientele and sold "substitutes for intoxicating liquors."[5]

The passage of this law can be attributed to the coincidence of several factors. During World War I, women moved into some previously male occupations. This phenomenon created alarm among male workers, who feared that women would lower prevailing wages, impede unionization, and eventually displace men. At the same time, spurred by the needs of war production, the government took an active role in coordinating and
82 overseeing industry. The government's announced policy was that workers, especially women workers, should enjoy a reasonable working day and safe and healthful workplace conditions. In the case of women, this protection sometimes took the form of restrictions on the occupations in which they were allowed to work. Such guidelines meshed neatly with the interests of the International Molders' Union, which had long attempted to bar women from foundry occupations. This union furnished the immediate impetus for the passage of the Ohio law prohibiting women from selected occupations.

During World War I, women moved out of the low-paying manufacturing industries that had traditionally employed them and into better paid positions in defense factories. In defense-related manufacturing, the absolute numbers of women workers increased dramatically over prewar levels, and as men were drafted into the armed services, women increased as a percentage of the total workforce in these industries. In the summer of 1914, they comprised 6.5 percent of the employees in defense-related manufacturing; by the late fall of 1918, they constituted 13.9 percent.[6] In almost all manufacturing defense industries, a larger proportion of firms hired at least some women during the war than had previously been the case. Hence, the increase in female employment for these industries reflects not only the addition of women in firms that had hired them before the war,

5. Ohio General Assembly, *Journal of the House of Representatives*, 83rd Gen. Assem., Reg. Sess., 1919 (Columbus, 1919); Ohio, *General Code* (Page's Compact Edition, 1920), Secs. 1008 and 1008-1; Cleveland *Citizen*, Feb. 1, 1919; Ohio State Federation of Labor, *Proceedings of the Thirty-Sixth Annual Convention*, 1919, 31-32. Hereafter referred to as OSFL, *Proceedings*.

6. U.S. Department of Labor, Women's Bureau, *The New Position of Women in American Industry*, Bull. 12 (Washington, D.C.: GPO, 1920), 34-35, 89.

but also their employment in companies where they had never before worked. However, most women in defense-related manufacturing were not new entrants into the work force. Even as defense factories added women workers, employers in traditionally female industries, such as spinning, weaving, and knitting plants, reported serious difficulty in retaining employees.[7]

As with manufacturing industries, railways and streetcar lines also employed more women. For example, in the railroad industry the number of women tripled between 1917 and October, 1918.[8] Likewise, intra-urban lines hired women in the highly visible new job of streetcar conductor, and by February 1918, 30 percent of the conductors employed by the New York Railways Company were women[9] Again, most of the women entering these new positions were not new to the labor force, but were experienced workers who transferred from traditional women's industries into better paid positions. For example, the majority of new clerks in the railroad industry had previously been clerical workers elsewhere. Women employed 83
as common laborers for the railroads had usually been recruited out of similarly unskilled work in traditional female industries such as laundries, hotels, restaurants, and domestic service.

It is difficult to determine the extent to which women in war industries were substitutes for men. Obviously, many were added to new positions, manufacturing items not previously produced, or worked in occupations already predominantly female. Statistics of the Women's Bureau show that 13 percent of all women employed in defense manufacturing in late 1918 were substituting on men's jobs. Although the Bureau felt that this figure underestimated the substitution of women for men, this still suggests that few women were directly in competition with men.[10] Likewise, in the railroad industry most women employees were in fields that had been predominantly female even before World War I. In October 1918, 72 percent of the women in the industry were in clerical positions. Traditionally female occupations such as car-cleaning, work as telephone operators, and personal service in dining rooms or kitchens accounted for most of the balance.[11] Nonetheless, the list of occupations open to women did expand, even though the numbers of women in these occupations remained small. In transportation, in addition to work as conductors on streetcar lines, new types of jobs were opened in railroads as ticket sellers,

7. *Ibid.*, 20-25, 44-47.

8. Maurine Weiner Greenwald, "Women Workers and World War I: The American Railroad Industry, A Case Study," *Journal of Social History*, 9 (Winter, 1975), 156.

9. Benjamin M. Squires, "Women Street Railway Employees," U.S. Bureau of Labor Statistics, *Monthly Review*, 6 (May, 1918), 1050.

10. Women's Bureau, *New Position*, 50, 54-55.

11. Greenwald, "Women Workers," 156-57.

telegraph operators, and electric welders. In jobs where they had already worked before the war, women often took on more responsibility than previously. For example, women had long worked as coremakers in foundries, but during the war they moved into the production of cores that were larger and more complex.[12]

Whatever the actual facts about women moving into men's occupations, the perception of male workers in Ohio was that women were rapidly displacing men. The Cleveland *Citizen*, the paper of the Cleveland Central Labor Union, wrote in September of 1918:

> What a queer world the boys in khaki will behold when they come home again! Women running streetcars, taxicabs, elevators, fire engines, locomotives, and in part also factories, mines, mills and farms! And what will the returned soldier boy say when they [sic] begin looking around for their old jobs? That's the problem, second now only to the war itself and will take first place later.[13]

84 The Toledo *Union Leader*, the publication of the Toledo Central Union, also viewed the phenomenon with alarm. In December 1918 it wrote, "But it is not mere questions of the shifting of labor that we face, puzzling as those questions are. Wholly new situations have been created. What of the women who by the thousands have taken places formerly occupied by men?"[14]

The reaction of unionized male workers to women workers in new jobs was not confined to mere editorial comment. At best, the unions tried to keep women from undercutting their wages by assuring that women in their craft got equal pay for equal work, a position that preserved men's wages as well as benefitting women. In a more direct challenge, the Motorman and Conductors Union in Cleveland struck the city's urban transport company to force the dismissal of women hired as "conductorettes." The union argued that there was no shortage of male workers for the job, and hence women should be dismissed. In this case, the male conductors made it clear that they saw the employment of women in these jobs as a threat by the streetcar companies to lower wages and replace men with a more tractable group of workers.[15]

Coinciding with this alarm among male workers that the war meant a possible incursion of women into previously male trades, defense work during World War I encouraged stricter government attention to the

12. Women's Bureau, *New Position*, 25-27, 107; Greenwald, "Women Workers," 157.
13. Cleveland *Citizen*, Sept. 14, 1918.
14. Toledo *Union Leader*, Dec. 18, 1918.
15. Cleveland *Citizen*, Aug. 31, 1918, Oct. 19, 1918; "Strike against Employment of Women as Streetcar Conductors in Cleveland," *Monthly Labor Review*, 8 (Jan., 1919), 224-30; and "Case of Woman Streetcar Conductors in Cleveland," *Monthly Labor Review*, 8 (May, 1919), 1456-58.

conditions under which women worked. Those Progressive organizations that had long advocated protective legislation provided the staff for many of the government agencies designed to oversee the entrance of women into defense-related jobs. Josephine Goldmark, research secretary of the National Consumers' League, and Dr. Alice Hamilton, a pioneer in industrial medicine, were both on the Committee on Labor of the Advisory Council to the Council of National Defense. Mary Anderson, organizer for the Women's Trade Union League and member of the Consumers' League and American Association for Labor Legislation, was assistant director of the Women in Industry Service in the Department of Labor.[16] These women had long histories as advocates of government regulation for the protection of the worker, especially the woman worker. The war provided new avenues of influence through the multiplying defense agencies and was, in a sense, the culmination of the Progressive crusade for social justice.[17]

In Ohio, the Consumers' League was the single most influential group in 85
formulating guidelines for the employment of women. The Consumers' League of Ohio was a reform-minded organization of Cleveland women that, prior to World War I, had worked with organized labor in Ohio to secure passage of maximum hours laws for women.[18] Hence, the League brought to its wartime task a strong commitment to protectionist legislation. The Committee on Women in Industry, the state's principal defense agency designated to oversee the movement of women into new industries, was for all practical purposes the Consumers' League of Ohio under another name. The Committee's chairman was Myrta L. Jones, executive committee member and later president of the League. The membership list of the Committee was composed almost exclusively of League members, and it operated from the offices of the League in Cleveland.[19] The Committee cooperated with the Industrial Commission of Ohio in developing guidelines for the employment of women workers, and the Consumers' League *Bulletin* gave great attention to publicizing these policies. The guidelines suggested by the Committee on Women in

16. "Protection of Labor Standards," *Monthly Review*, 4 (May, 1917), 650; Durward Howes ed. *American Women: The Standard Biographical Dictionary of Notable Women*, 3 (Los Angeles, 1939).

17. Allen F. Davis, "Welfare, Reform and World War I," *American Quarterly*, 19 (Fall, 967), 516-33.

18. Dennis Irven Harrison, "The Consumers' League of Ohio: Women and Reform 1909-1937" (unpublished dissertation, Case Western University, 1975).

19. Harrison, "Consumers' League," 57-58; Ohio Branch, Council of National Defense, *A History of the Activities of the Ohio Branch Council of National Defense* (Columbus, 1919), 54-56. The Ohio Committee on Women and Children in Industry was a joint committee under the Women's Committee, Ohio Branch Council of National Defense and the National Committee on Women in Industry, Advisory Commission of the Council of National Defense.

86

Myrta L. Jones. (SOCIETY COLLECTION)

Industry usually accorded with suggestions of the Women in Industry Service of the U.S. Department of Labor, the War Labor Board, and the War Labor Policies Board. Thus, the Committee acted essentially as a publicist for the views or pronouncements of federal agencies.

The policies of both the federal level war labor administration and Ohio's state Committee on Women in Industry were highly protectionist. The first tenet of both was that there should be no relaxation of legislative standards on hours and working conditions.[20] There was considerable caution about the entrance of women into new occupations: women should go into occupations only if they were safe from physical hazards, economic exploitation, and possible moral corruption. The *Bulletin* of the Consumers' League of Ohio cautioned that, "Since the war began we have heard a great deal about this being the woman's hour—'The woman's hour has struck.' Certainly we rejoice at the many opportunities for women, but

20. "Federal Standards for the Employment of Women in Industry," *Monthly Labor Review* 8 (Jan., 1919), 216-21; Consumers' League of Ohio, *Bulletin*, Nov., 1918, 2. Hereafter referred to as OCL, *Bulletin*.

we do not want to see women exploited for cheap labor, shunted wholesale into industry without preliminary provisions for training and study of suitable work and safeguards for women."[21]

Defense agencies not only emphasized the need to protect women from exploitation for women's own good, but also stressed that the introduction of large numbers of women might upset the status quo in the labor market. According to the War Labor Board, one reason for the rigid application of the equal wage principle was "to prevent more women being brought into industry than the needs of the nation demand, in order that the American home may be maintained as far as possible, as it is during the war."[22] Likewise, a War Labor Policy Board directive stipulated that "The introduction of women into positions hitherto filled by men should not be made a pretext for unnecessarily displacing men."[23] The Ohio Committee on Women in Industry and the Consumers' League echoed the sentiment. The Consumers' League remarked, " . . . we do not want women to enter
industry until there is real need, we do not want them to upset the labor 87
market, to take men's work when men are still seeking employment."[24]

The defense agencies concerned themselves not only with the protection of women's physical safety, but their morals as well. The policy of the War Labor Policies Board was that women should not replace men in occupations or places of employment where the moral atmosphere was unfit for them. Examples of such pursuits were work in barrooms or poolrooms, and employment in streetcars or elevators for females less than twenty-one years old.[25] In Ohio, the Consumers' League showed the same concern that women not be exposed to morally questionable situations. In its opinion, there were industries "which for women involve distinct moral hazards, these chiefly of course for the young worker, and when they mean night work." The seriousness which the League attached to determining which occupations posed a moral threat is shown by the considerable investigatory work which preceded the decision that work as an elevator operator was suitable for women during the daytime, when it posed "no more moral dangers . . . than other work in public places."[26]

To shield women from economic exploitation or moral corruption, the War Labor Administration and its Ohio counterpart advocated restrictions on their employment, although affected women workers did not

21. OCL, *Bulletin*, Feb. 1918, 3.

22. "Federal Policy in the Employment of Women," *Monthly Labor Review*, 7 (Nov., 1918), 1337-38.

23. "Organization of the War Labor Administration Completed," *Monthly Labor Review*, 7 (Aug., 1918), 288.

24. OCL, *Bulletin*, Feb., 1918, 3.

25. "Labor Administration Completed," *Monthly Labor Review*, 288.

26. OCL, *Bulletin*, Nov., 1918, 1.

always appreciate such protection. For example, the government's official policy was that women should not be allowed to work in jobs which were deemed too exhausting. The Ohio Consumers' League conducted an investigation of women working as section hands on railroads, and concluded that the work was much too heavy.[27] The League's conclusion was vindicated when the Women's Service Section of the Railway Administration came to the same conclusion, and the Director General of the Federal Railroad Administration ordered the railroads to discontinue completely the employment of women in such work. This protective measure was not welcomed by all women workers; a number of female section hands protested vigorously for the right to retain their jobs.[28] Similarly, the Ohio Consumers' League, like the National Consumers' League, advocated the prohibition of nightwork for women workers, even though their own investigations showed that some women workers preferred a night shift.[29]

88 The attitude that women should, in their own interest, be barred from some occupations that might be physically or morally dangerous is obvious in the guidelines for hiring women developed by the Women in Industry Committee of the Ohio Branch of the Council of National Defense and the Ohio Industrial Commission. In addition to other protective measures, these would have barred women from express driving, delivery services, freight elevators, baggage and freight handling, trucking, poolrooms, bowling alleys, and saloons, or work as bellboys, taxi drivers, or pinboys. Women under twenty-one were not to be hired as elevator operators, messengers, and street car conductors.[30] There was no effective mechanism for enforcing such guidelines. Their importance arises from the fact that they became law in 1919 when the Ohio State Federation of Labor, at the behest of Ohio locals of the International Molders' Union, adapted them to serve a much narrower purpose—the exclusion of women from work as molders.

The Ohio law was not the first instance of unionized foundry workers attempting to bar women from their crafts through legislation. The Molders' Union had long been opposed to the employment of women as coremakers or molders, since it felt that the manufacture of small, simple cores—the task most commonly assigned to women—was properly part of the training program for apprentices. Consequently, the union not only forbade membership to women, but its constitution mandated the expulsion of members who were guilty of teaching women the process of

27. OCL, *Bulletin*, Nov., 1918, 1, Feb., 1918, 2.
28. Greenwald, "Women's Work," 166-67.
29. OCL, *Bulletin*, Nov., 1918, 5-6, Oct. 1, 1920, 1-4.
30. Harrison, "Consumers' League," 57-58.

coremaking or molding.[31] Keeping women out of the union, however, was no solution to the problem of lowered wages from competition with women. The International Molders' Journal reported: "Not only has the Molders' Union been opposed to female labor on humanitarian grounds, but it has also fought it out of fear that it would result in the lowering of the standards attained by men. It is a fact well known to the student of labor problems that women can ordinarily be obtained at a less wage than men."[32]

It is not surprising, then, that local unions would eventually want legislation to prohibit women form foundry occupations. Union molders had attempted to get an absolute legislative prohibition against women coremakers in three eastern states prior to World War I. In 1910 a law to that effect was introduced into the New York legislature; similar bills were introduced in Massachusetts and New Jersey in 1911 and 1912, respectively.[33] Although union coremakers were unsuccessfull in all these states in eliminating women altogether, the State Factory Commission of New York was sufficiently impressed by the possible dangers of female employment in foundries to establish strict regulations governing the conditions under which women could work at such employment. These required the building of partitions between the core room and furnace room and limited the weight of cores and core boxes women were allowed to lift. The New York Commission that framed the legislation felt that the regulations were sufficiently stringent to prevent the extension of women's employment and would, in a few years, result in the complete elimination of women in foundries.[34]

In Ohio, a similar foundry safety code was instituted with hopes of eliminating female coremakers. In 1914 the Molders' Union received OSF of L convention approval of a bill to have the legislature establish a safety code for foundries which would, among other provisions, prohibit women

31. Frank T. Stockton, "Women in the Foundry," *International Molders' Journal*, 52 (Jan., 1916), 45; Women's Bureau, *New Position*, 107-9.

32. Stockton, "Women in the Foundry," 45.

33. *Ibid.*, 45-46; U.S. Dept. of Labor, Women's Bureau, *History of Labor Legislation for Women in Three States*, Bull. 66 (Washington, D.C.: GPO, 1921), 2, 162-64, 114-17. The support which the International gave such efforts fluctuated. For example, the Executive Board voted to give Union No. 441 of Newark, N.J. $250 reimbursement against $475.50 expenses incurred "in furthering legislation which would prohibit the employment of females in the production of cores in the state of New Jersey." Three years later when Union No. 81 of Elizabeth petitioned for financial assistance to secure passage of an act to regulate female core makers, the motion was denied. "Officers' Reports and Proceedings of the Twenty-fifth Session of the International Molders' Union of North America," published as supplement to *International Molders' Journal*, 53 (1917), 38, 99.

34. D. W. O'Connor, "Foundry Legislation in New York State," *International Molders' Journal*, 49 (April, 1913), 271-83; Women's Bureau, *History of Labor Legislation*, 162-64, 114-17; John R. O'Leary, "New York State Foundry Rules Recently Adopted," *International Molders' Journal*. 51 (July, 1915), 495-511.

coremakers and foundry workers. Eventually the request was referred to the Ohio Industrial Commission, the newly established state agency responsible for drawing up safety codes for various industries. The foundry regulations eventually developed for Ohio were almost identical to the New York code. Women were not absolutely prohibited from coremaking, but their employment was strictly regulated. For example, weightlifting limitations for female coremakers were stricter in Ohio than in New York.[35] Union coremakers evidently hoped that these regulations would not only provide safer working conditions for all foundry workers, but would eliminate women from their craft. In a resolution introduced at the OSF of L annual convention several years after the code's adoption, coremakers endorsed such regulations for "governing the employment of men and women in foundries, and if possible to eliminate the female molder and coremaker."[36]

The opposition of unionized molders to women in their craft clearly
90 predated World War I. However, the emphasis on replacing male with female workers during the war probably created fears that there would be an accelerated flow of women into foundries. At its 1917 national convention, the International Molders' Union passed a resolution vigorously condemning employers who were using the war as a pretext to employ females in foundries and other factories where men had previously worked. This was part of a resolution that instructed the incoming officers to use their "every effort to cure the abuse now obtaining where female or child labor is employed and every effort be made to prevent its extension," and that they "give their best thought and effort in opposing the employment of females and child labor in jobs recognized distinctly as men's employment."[37]

Next fall, 1918, representatives of the Molders' Union in Ohio introduced a resolution at the Ohio State Federation of Labor convention asking the state organization to endorse legislation prohibiting female molders. The molders argued that fumes, smoke, gases and the operation of cranes and pouring of metals made the molding department especially dangerous, and that the foundry was "the last place a woman should be permitted to work." The resolution instructed the OSF of L to have the Industrial Commission incorporate a law in the foundry code prohibiting the employment of women in the molding department of the foundries in

35. Foundry regulations in Ohio prevented women from making cores where the combined weight of core, corebox, and plate were more than fifteen pounds; New York set the limit at twenty-five pounds. John O'Neill, "The Ohio Foundry Code," *International Molders' Journal*, 52 (July 1916), 589-94; OSFL, *Proceedings*, 1914, 63-64, 84-85.

36. OSFL, *Proceedings*, 1920, 45.

37. "Officers' Reports and Proceedings of the Twenty-fifth Session of the International Molders' Union of North America," published as supplement to *International Molders' Journal*, 53 (1917), 183, 221, 239.

Ohio. The resolution received convention approval with no protests.[38]

The Executive Board of the OSF of L decided to meet with the state's Industrial Commission to determine the best way to carry out the intention of the Molders' resolution. This consultation resulted in an expanded measure that added molders to the list of prohibited occupations in the wartime guidelines on acceptable employment for women that had been suggested by the Industrial Commission and the Women in Industry Committee of the Ohio Branch, Council of National Defense.[39] Additional strictures against women employees in smelters, quarries, mines and blast furnaces, which simply applied laws already in force for female minors to adult women, were also included.[40] Finally, the Consumers' League of Ohio asked the cooperation of the OSF of L in securing the extension of legislation restricting hours to occupations not already covered by state laws. The Federation was already pledged by a convention resolution to support an extension of the maximum hours law which would cover women on streetcars, and at the League's request added elevator operators and ticket sellers to the list of people who should receive such protection.[41]

The final bill, therefore, showed the influence of at least three groups: the Molders' Union, which had originally wanted a prohibition against women molders, the Ohio Industrial Commission, and the Consumers' League, which had suggested an extended list of proscribed occupations and additional restrictions on hours. The bill was introduced into the Ohio legislature in the spring of 1919 and was signed by Governor James Cox on June 15 of that year. The OSF of L seemed pleased with the measure as passed. At the 1919 convention, the President mentioned in his report that, although the enforcement of protective legislation for women was still inadequate, "In line with recommendations made in the last annual report of this department [the Industrial Commission] the Legislature during the last session made some very important amendments to the child and female labor, and the compulsory education laws, which I am sure will assist very materially in the enforcement of these laws in the future."[42]

If the success of the Molders' Unions in bending protective legislation to their own ends was, in part, a product of the fact that there were no representatives of women molders to protest, similar efforts by unionized waiters provided an interesting contrast. Unlike most occupations prohibited to women by Ohio law, there were already large numbers of waitresses at work. Unlike the molders, who simply wanted to bar future

38. OSFL, *Proceedings*, 1918, 51.

39. OSFL, *Proceedings*, 1919, 31-32; Ohio General Assembly, *Journal, House of Representatives*, Reg. Sess., 1919.

40. Ohio, *General Code* (Page's Compact Edition, 1926), Secs. 1008, 1008-1.

41. OCL, *Bulletin*, June 1919, 5-6; OSFL, *Proceedings*, 1918, 65.

42. OSFL, *Proceedings*, 1919, 29.

entry of women into an occupation that was identifiably and overwhelmingly male, waiters could not hope to dislodge the large numbers of women already at work in restaurants. Furthermore, waitresses and waiters belonged to the same international—the Hotel and Restaurant Employees International Alliance and Bartenders' International League of America—but to separate local unions. Nonetheless, by "protecting" women from night work and immoral situations associated with serving alcohol, waiters could retain or increase their share of jobs. Waitresses within organized labor resisted such protection, and the prohibitive legislation eventually sanctioned by the OSF of L was much narrower than that originally requested by the waiters' unions.

Nationally, women comprised an increasing proportion of employees in the restaurant industry. In 1910 women constituted 46 percent of all waiters, but by 1930 they had increased to 59 percent. This figure was not seriously affected by the repeal of prohibition; in 1940 women were still 56
92 percent of those classified in the census as waiters or bartenders.[43] Of course, women worked for less than men, even when organized. In 1914, although union wages for Cleveland waiters were only three cents more per hour than those for waitresses, waiters received fifty cents per hour for overtime and union waitresses only twenty-five cents. In Toledo, unionized waiters were at even a greater advantage, with hourly union wage rates showing as much as an eleven cent spread between organized waiters and waitresses.[44]

The ostensible reason for controlling women's employment in the restaurant industry was that waitresses should not be exposed to the questionable moral atmosphere of establishments that served alcohol. However, the OSF of L convention discussion on a proposed regulation to limit waitresses' hours shows that, given their declining position in the industry, waiters also hoped such legislation would reserve at least certain jobs for men. In 1928 delegates from Cleveland and Cincinnati locals presented the annual OSF of L convention with a resolution to make it illegal for women to work in restaurants between the hours of ten P.M. and six A.M. In the discussion that followed, the attack on this restriction was spearheaded by Kitty Donnelly, the outspoken Vice-president of the Hotel and Restaurant Employee's International for the state. She claimed that, should such a measure become law, many women would be unable to take care of their families.[45] On the opposite side of the question, spokesmen for

43. U.S. Department of Commerce, Bureau of the Census, *Occupational Trends in the United States 1900 to 1950*, by David L. Kaplan and M. Claire Casey, Working Paper No. 5 (Washington, D.C.: GPO, 1958).

44. Ohio Industrial Commission, Department of Investigation and Statistics, *Union Scale of Wages and Hours of Labor in Ohio, May 15, 1914*, Report no. 5 (Columbus, 1915), 78.

45. OSFL, *Proceedings*, 1928, 67, 119-21.

Kitty Donnelly. (HOTEL & RESTAURANT EMPLOYEES AND BARTENDERS INTERNATIONAL UNION ARCHIVES)

the waiters' unions argued that changes in the industry hurt their union's membership and favored women. Citing declining union membership among waiters, a Cleveland delegate claimed, "We are being replaced because of conditions in our industry. They are getting away from the service restaurants to the lunch counters." Furthermore, he continued, with women replacing men, "the only chance we have to maintain our jobs is in road houses."[46] By restricting the hours of waitresses, the waiters would be able to keep those jobs in road houses where personnel were presumably required to work after ten o'clock in the evening.

The reference to road houses was an allusion to the whole question of the propriety of women working where liquor was being consumed illegally. It was in waiters' self-interest to keep women out of such establishments. Once the association between late hours and liquor could be made,

46. OSFL, *Proceedings*, 1928, 121.

however, the prohibition of nightwork became a moral issue. It could then be presented as an altruistic measure to shield women from a seamy environment rather than merely a matter of men's selfish desire to retain their jobs. Hence, a Cincinnati waiter cast the question thus:

> The people in the Union now are mostly people working in road houses, where they carry it [liquor] 'on the hip.' That isn't a place for the girls. I don't think any woman ought to work in a place where a man pulls a bottle off his hip.[47]

Because of the objections raised by women members of the Waitresses Union, the Federation's Committee on legislation took the unusual step of suggesting that the resolution to limit waitresses hours be referred back to the Hotel and Restaurant Employees International to see if a bill acceptable to the disputing interests could be constructed. There is no evidence that the waiters returned with a bill sanctioned by the International, and the matter died. However, with the repeal of prohibition
94 the question of regulating women in restaurant work returned in another form. Ohio law forbade women from working where "substitutes for intoxicating beverages" were sold. The exact nature of these substitutes remained undefined throughout the prohibition era, but with the repeal of prohibition the question of the propriety of women's serving alcoholic beverages reemerged. In December, 1933, Kitty Donnelly charged that "certain groups" were trying to mobilize public opinion against women serving drinks and warned that, "All efforts to prevent waitresses from serving alcoholic beverages in either public or private eating places will meet with vigorous opposition by Waitresses Union Local 107." Although she did not favor women as barmaids, Mrs. Donnelly argued that, "we are unable to understand why a woman who must work to support herself, and in many instances her family, should be prevented from serving beer, wine, or any other alcoholic drink."[48]

Unionized waiters were among those who were interested in keeping women from serving alcoholic drinks in restaurants and public eating places. At the 1935 annual convention of the Ohio State Federation of Labor, the Cleveland Waiters' Union introduced a resolution that, although not actually barring women from serving alcoholic beverages, would have prohibited their working where alcoholic beverages were served after ten P.M. Again, members of the Waitresses' Union campaigned against the resolution and succeeded in bringing about its defeat in the convention.[49] However, unionized waiters were undeterred in their attempts to protect women form whatever dangers were inherent in a

47. *Ibid.*
48. Cleveland *Plain Dealer*, Dec. 10, 1933.
49. OSFL, *Proceedings*, 1935, 91-92, 144.

working association with alcohol. The next year, members of the Cincinnati and Cleveland Waiters' Union introduced an even more stringent resolution at the OSF of L convention. This would have prohibited the employment of women in any place serving intoxicants. Apparently, there was once again division between the affected parties, since the convention requested that a bill "mutually agreed upon" be drafted and later presented to the Executive Board.[50]

A measure was eventually agreed upon and presented to the OSF of L Executive Board, but its provisions were much narrower than the original resolution. The bill brought to the OSF of L by the Hotel and Restaurant Workers International prohibited the employment of women only as barmaids and continued to allow their employment in establishments serving liquor. This alternative was acceptable to unionized waitresses; the previous year they had offered no objection to a similar resolution passed by the OSF of L convention at the request of bartenders. Accordingly, the Executive Board of the OSF of L voted its approval of the measure and it 95
was introduced into the Ohio Legislature in each of the next two sessions (1937-38 and 1939-40).[51] The Federation's legislative agent reported attending committee hearings in the latter session to speak in favor of the bill. In both sessions, however, efforts to pass the bill were unsuccessful.[52]

Several of the occupations from which women were legally barred in Ohio did not employ many female workers even in states in which such employment was legal. Even without a law, it is doubtful that there would have been women workers in quarries, smelters, or blast furnaces. Most of the legal prohibitions did little harm or good. Moreover, the first impetus toward such legislation seems to have been furnished by a desire to protect men's occupations. In contrast, the Ohio State Federation of Labor felt its interests threatened by the possibility of a minimum wage for women and refused to support such protective legislation.

MINIMUM WAGE

Beginning late in World War I and continuing until 1924, the Consumers' League of Ohio and the Council on Women and Children in

50. OSFL, *Proceedings*, 1936, 79, 125.

51. OSFL, *Proceedings*, 1937, 28; Ohio General Assembly, House, *A Bill to Amend Section 1008-1 of the General Code, Relative to the Employment of Females*, 92nd Gen. Assem., Reg. Sess., 1937-38, H. B. 118 and Am. H. B. 118; OSFL, *Proceedings*, 1938, 41, 137; Ohio General Assembly, *Journal of the House of Representatives*, 92nd Gen. Assem., Reg. Sess., 1937-38 (Columbus, 1938), 109-676 *passim*; Ohio General Asembly, House, *A Bill to Amend Section 1008-1 of the General Code, Relative to Prohibiting the Employment of Women in Certain Occupations or Capacities*, 93rd Gen. Assem., Reg. Sess., 1939-40, H. B. 47.

52. OSFL, *Report of the Legislative Agent*, 1939, 85.

Industry campaigned vigorously but unsuccessfully for a minimum wage for Ohio women workers.[53] Throughout, the OSF of L refused to support minimum wage legislation for women. In 1918 the question was raised with the Executive Board of the OSF of L when the legislative agent, Thomas J. Donnelley, reported that the Committee on Women and Children in Industry was advocating the creation of minimum wage boards in Ohio, and that two labor members of the committee, Nida Pangle and Kathryn Nordman, had asked whether the AF of L and OSF of L were in favor of such boards.[54] After investigation showed that the national organization had taken no official stand upon the subject, the Executive Board argued that it could not support such legislation because the membership of neither the AF of L nor the OSF of L had approved such action in a convention resolution. In taking this position, the Executive Board was either unaware of or chose to ignore a resolution approved by the 1912 OSF of L convention that instructed the Executive Board to draft and have
96 introduced into the General Assembly a bill "for the establishment of a minimum wage commission for the determination of minimum wages in the unskilled and 'sweated' industries that employ women and that element among the toilers whose wages are below the living line."[55] The Board instructed its legislative agent to take no position on minimum wage legislation, except to assure labor a position on any minimum wage commissions which might result.

In 1921 and 1923, the Consumers' League and the Council on Women and Children in Industry sponsored bills to create the necessary state agency to set and administer a minimum wage. In both instances the proposed legislation would have established a commission composed of both employers and employees to set minimum wages for female workers by industry and occupation. Both measures failed to pass the legislature. The 1921 minimum wage bill passed the House, but the Senate committee to which it was referred, the Committee on Manufactures and Commerce, reported a substitute bill which was completely unacceptable to the sponsors of the original proposal. A decision on the 1923 bill was avoided when the General Assembly voted to appoint an investigating commission to study the matter further. Only a few days after the Commission was

53. In December 1920, the wartime Committee on Women and Children in Industry became the Council on Women and Children in Industry. This was later called the Council on Women in Industry. The campaigns for a minimum wage law in Ohio are discussed briefly in Elizabeth Brandeis, "Labor Legislation," *History of Labor in the United States, 1896-1932,* Vol. III, ed. John R. Commons (New York, 1935), 519-22. For a more complete account, see Harrison, "The Consumers' League," chaps. IV, V, 90-164.

54. OSFL, *Proceedings,* 1918, 42.

55. OSFL, *Proceedings,* 1912, 103.

appointed, the Supreme Court's decision in *Adkins vs. Children's Hospital* invalidated the minimum wage law of the District of Columbia.

Despite these setbacks, the meetings of the Minimum Wage Commission continued, and the Consumers' League and the Ohio Council on Women and Children in Industry prepared an extensive brief for presentation to that Commission. The brief's few allusions to the *Adkins* decision leave the impression that the constitutionality of the state minimum wage laws was still open to question. However, as the *Bulletin* of the Council had already reported, other state minimum wage laws would undoubtedly be held invalid, and thus it seemed that the only remaining possibility was for a nonmandatory law similar to that of Massachusetts.[56] The League's efforts in behalf of such a law were to no avail; as expected, the Commission returned to the General Assembly with a report unfavorable to any minimum wage legislation. After this defeat, the issue lay dormant until depression conditions of the 1930s revived interest.

The Executive Board of the OSF of L refused to support either bill, since 97
there had been no vote to do so either in its own convention or in the AF of L. Attempts in 1921 and 1924 to pass resolutions at OSF of L conventions that would have put it on record in favor of such legislation were defeated by the substitution of resolutions for further study.[57] Therefore, the Executive Board felt that it still lacked the authorization to support such legislation, and its refusal to do so was a simple procedural matter. However, a 1921 reply to proponents of the measure suggested that its reservations may have gone deeper. In 1921 the Executive Board of the OSF of L wrote that "as the Trade Union Movement is pledged to the principle of Collective bargaining as against wages fixed by law, the Board could not co-operate at this time in advocating Minimum Wage Legislation."[58] This reduced the question to a clear conflict between voluntaristic trade union orthodoxy and state regulation.

This formulation of the controversy was echoed on the convention floor during the debate on the 1924 resolution to support the mimimum wage bill. John Frey, elected president of the OSF of L at this convention, was a strong opponent of mimimum wage laws both on the convention floor and in his position as editor of the *International Molders' Journal*. He spoke in behalf of voluntaristic orthodoxy by asserting:

56. Consumers' League of Ohio and The Council on Women in Industry, *Operation of Minimum Wage Laws: California, Wisconsin, Massachusetts.* (Brief submitted to the Ohio Legislative Committee to Investigate Minimum Wage Legislation), 1924, 47, 77, 147; Ohio Council on Women in Industry, *Bulletin*, June,1923, 1.

57. OSFL, *Proceedings*, 1921, 77, 132; OSFL, *Proceedings*, 1924, 21-22, 103-111.

58. OSFL, *Proceedings*, 1921, 21.

> . . . such a measure would not only work eventually to their [women's] disadvantage, but that in addition it will create another handicap to those of us who have placed our faith, as Trade Unionists, in collective bargaining, as the only method by which we will agree to have our terms of employment established.[59]

Although representatives of organized labor focused on the argument that a minimum wage for *women* would violate the principles of voluntarism and the role of collective bargaining, behind this was a more serious apprehension about the effects of a minimum wage for *men*. The AF of L was unalterably opposed to a legislatively determined minimum wage for men because it felt that such a measure would usurp the function of the union organization. The possibility that a minimum wage law for women would eventually include men had often been stressed by Samuel Gompers and the national AF of L. The Executive Council of the AF of L had reported to the 1915 convention that "The trade union movement has opposed the regulation of working conditions, hours of work, and wages
98 for men in private industry by law or by political agents. Where equality between men and women is established the endorsement of this principle for women becomes also a very serious menace to the liberty of the men wage-earners."[60] Gompers expressed a similar opinion that a minimum wage law could be enacted safely only if women were, in a sense, wards of the state—a status inconsistent with trade union support of women's suffrage.[61]

This same fear was evident almost a decade later in 1924, when the Ohio State Federation of Labor debated a resolution to endorse a minimum wage for women. One delegate, for example, held that

> . . . I realize that if this convention goes on record to concede that right to the Legislature to establish a minimum rate—minimum wage for women—that the Labor Movement of this country has lost its right for collective bargaining, as it will be easy to establish the same conditions for men.[62]

The issue was then changed from a question of the benefits or liabilities inherent in a minimum wage law for women to the effects of such a law for men. Hence, the endorsement of a law for women was tantamount to agreeing to the loss of collective bargaining power for men. One male spokesman justified his opposition to a minimum wage law for women because "I want to remain a free man as a wage earner, and not become a subject of the State."[63]

59. OSFL, *Proceedings*, 1924, 104-105.
60. AF of L, *Proceedings*, 1915, 63.
61. Samuel Gompers letter to John I. Nolan, reprinted in "Gompers on Minimum Wage Law," *International Molders' Journal*, 49 (April, 1913), 294-95.
62. OSFL, *Proceedings*, 1924, 107.
63. *Ibid.*, 106.

The only remedy allowed for women was organization: "They should establish these minimum wage rates in the same Trade Union manner in which the men do."[64] The argument that women were difficult to organize was not seen as sufficient reason to pass special legislation, since this might imply that unorganized male workers also should be protected by state minimum wage laws. Furthermore, a minimum wage law was held to be dangerous because it might actually retard the organization of women. John Frey first raised this point and argued that while a number of states had enacted laws creating minimum wage commissions, no trade union records showed an increase of organization among women and, in fact, in two states organization had decreased. This argument appears particularly self-serving, since Frey's own union, the International Molders, refused admission to women. Nida Pangle, a delegate from the Waitresses' Union and long an advocate of a minimum wage law, reminded the convention that trade unions had been negligent in organizing women and that delegates were thereby advocating a remedy which they were not willing to
support with funds or sustained effort.[65]

Thus, even when opponents of a minimum wage for women posed the problem as one of clear-cut theoretical objections to state intervention, most delegates felt that more concrete issues were at stake. As long as there was a chance that such a law might be extended to men, it was a threat to what many predominantly male unions perceived as their own ability to bargain. Secondarily, if legal remedies discouraged unionization among women, such remedies were counter to the interests of the OSF of L.

Although the state organization refused to endorse a minimum wage for women, it never went on record specifically in opposition. Thus labor leaders and publications were free to support the measure. Max Hayes, a long-time leader of the Socialist opposition within the AF of L and editor of the Cleveland *Citizen*, favored such legislation. As previously mentioned, Nida Pangle, a member of the Toledo Central Labor Union and of the Waitresses' Union, was an active supporter of the bill. In March 1921, she and the legislative agent of the OSF of L travelled to Cincinnati to speak before that city's Central Labor Union on the minimum wage bill and to dissuade them from the view that legislation for women only was a form of discrimination.[66]

Several labor publications also endorsed the minimum wage. For example, the Cincinnati *Labor Advocate*, the publication of the local Building Trades Council, gave support to the minimum wage in a number of ways. First, it made considerable space available to the Consumers'

64. *Ibid.*, 105
65. *Ibid.*, 106-110.
66. Harrison, "The Consumers' League," 102-114; Toledo *Union Leader*, March 18, 1921.

League of Cincinnati and the Catholic Women of Columbia, two local groups working for the minimum wage. In 1921 it published a statement and appeal by the Catholic Women of Columbia asking for help in the campaign for the minimum wage. In addition, considerable material provided by the Consumers' League in support of this legislation was published, as well as the annual report of that organization for 1922.[67]

In addition to giving interested organizations free space to present arguments in favor of minimum wage legislation, the *Labor Advocate* gave some editorial support to the measure. Although saying that the minimum wage was not a union measure because "the unions make their own minimum wage and fight to get it," the paper continued that such a measure was "only supported by union labor because it is a just cause."[68] When Mrs. Nettie B. Loughead, a Senator on the Minimum Wage Commission of the General Assembly and known to be opposed to the minimum wage, addressed the Lecture Club in Cincinnati, she was roundly criticized by the
100 *Labor Advocate.* The paper suggested that "The women of Hamilton County should elect a woman in Senator Loughead's place with a woman's desire to help her unfortunate sisters to secure wages that will protect their virtue."[69]

The Toledo *Union Leader*, the voice of that city's Central Labor Union, also gave the minimum wage measure at least favorable mention. This paper seemed unlikely to champion the measure; in 1920 it had run several short items about the failure of minimum wage commissions in other states under headlines such as "Trade Union Theory is Again Vindicated" or "Girls Must Organize to Gain Recognition." These articles featured quotations from other labor papers, the general tenor of which was to point out that "Women ought not to be obliged to rely on a political or legal mandate for their protection. Men have found that political agencies oftimes prove broken reeds when leaned upon."[70] However, in a 1921 broadside to supplement the newspaper, the *Union Leader* referred to minimum wage laws as union sponsored measures "of incalcuable worth to those to whom they relate."[71] In reporting on the 1921 minimum wage bill, it further noted that "The trade union and other progressive women of Ohio were bitterly disappointed when the Schrimper bill to establish a minimum wage commission was defeated in the state legislature last week."[72]

Nevertheless, in the 1920's the Ohio State Federation of Labor refused to

67. Cincinnati *Labor Advocate*, Feb. 26, 1921; *Ibid.*, March 5, 1921, April 14, 1923.
68. *Ibid.*, April 21, 1923.
69. *Ibid.*, April 28, 1923.
70. Toledo *Union Leader*, Oct. 22, 1920, Dec. 17, 1920.
71. *Ibid.*, Feb. 13, 1921.
72. *Ibid.*, May 20, 1921.

endorse a minimum wage bill for women workers, since male craft unions in the organization felt that such legislation was dangerous to the interests of organized labor. However, labor opinion was by no means unanimous. Several leaders within the state organization favored such legislation; moreover, some labor publications in Ohio gave space and support to its proponents. Such a division of opinion was even more apparent in the early 1930s, when the issue was raised again and Ohio did pass its minimum wage law.

After the campaign of 1923 through 1924, the Consumers' League of Ohio dropped its efforts to pass a minimum wage bill, wishing to concentrate instead on legislation for the abolition of child labor. The issue of a minimum wage commission lay dormant until the depression conditions of the 1930s revived interest. As early as 1931, the Ohio Consumers' League began publicizing the rapid drop in women's wages which had occurred since the beginning of the Great Depression.[73] In December 1932, the National Consumers' League established state 101
minimum wage laws as one of its goals. Initially, the Ohio Consumers' League deferred work on such legislation, preferring to concentrate instead on child labor restrictions and unemployment insurance.[74] However, sentiment for such a measure increased in Ohio as falling women's wages attracted public attention. A series of articles in the *Cleveland Plain Dealer* in early 1933 exposed the deplorable conditions and low wages for women workers in northeastern Ohio. Coinciding with this, the Roosevelt administration began to pressure Ohio. In March 1933, Secretary of Labor Frances Perkins called for a minimum wage bill as a necessary piece of legislation. In April, the New York Legislature passed a minimum wage for female workers in that state. Following the passage of the New York bill, President Roosevelt sent a telegram to the governors of Ohio and twelve other industrial states, commending the New York measure and recommending that they take similar action.[75]

The Ohio minimum wage bill was endorsed by William Green, president of the AF of L, even before it was introduced into the General Assembly. Green voiced his approval in an address before the Cleveland City Club in late April and afterward in a letter to the sponsor of the Ohio bill. The Cleveland *Plain Dealer* suggested that "This action of the national leader of organized labor undoubtedly will carry great weight with the Ohio and Cleveland Federations of Labor in any stand they may take on the

73. Cleveland *Plain Dealer*, June 6, 1931.

74. Harrison, "The Consumers' League," 282.

75. Cleveland *Citizen*, March 25, 1933; Robert P. Ingalls, "New York and the Minimum-Wage Movement, 1933-1937," *Labor History*, 15 (Spring, 1974), 179-198; *The Public Papers and Addresses of Franklin D. Roosevelt*, Vol. II, *The Year of Crisis 1933*, comp. Samuel I. Rosenman (New York, 1938), 133-34.

measure."[76] Some important representatives of organized labor in Ohio followed suit. On April 12, the Summit County Central Labor Union (Akron) wrote Governor George White to urge that he consider a minimum wage law for women. It was joined in its support by the Cleveland Federation of Labor, which voted unanimously to endorse the minimum wage bill and also agreed to join the Ohio Labor Standards committee, which was working for the bill's enactment. Harry McLaughlin, who was president of the OSF of L as well as the Cleveland Federation, pledged that the state federation "would be on the job at Columbus and aid in every way to push over the proposed legislation." He added, "We would like to see women and children entirely out of industry, but, since that does not seem possible at present, we do want to see them have the best working conditions that can be secured, for we are not selfish."[77]

Despite McLaughlin's pledge, the legislative agent of the OSF of L was
102 not "on the job at Columbus" when hearings were held on the bill. The Executive Board of the OSF of L decided that, in view of the failure of either the AF of L or the OSF of L to go on record in convention for minimum wage legislation, the organization's legislative agent should take no position on the bill.[78] Thus, the OSF of L officially maintained the same uncommitted stance it had assumed in the 1920s, despite the drastically changed conditions of the 1930s and the endorsement of such legislation by the presidents of both the state and national organizations.

The final passage of a minimum wage measure for women workers was the fruition of years of effort by organizations such as the Consumers' League interested in the protection of the working woman. At the critical juncture in its passage, however, the deciding influence was brought to bear by Washington rather than by any organization within Ohio. A minimum wage bill for women was introduced into the Ohio House on May 18, 1933. The bill passed the House on June 8, 1933, but the House's delay in considering the bill seemed to doom its chances of passage, for June 8 was the deadline for consideration of regular legislation.[79] However, as was so often the case in the progress of this measure, the national government intervened. A telegram from Secretary of Labor Perkins to Governor White urging the bill's passage resulted in its being placed on the Senate

76. Toledo *Union Leader*, April 28, 1933, May 5, 1933, Cleveland *Plain Dealer*, May 1, 1933.

77. Summit County Central Labor Union, letter to Gov. George White, April 14, 1933, George White Papers, Ohio Historical Society, Columbus, Ohio; Cleveland *Plain Dealer*, May 4, 1933; Cleveland *Citizen*, May 6, 1933.

78. OSFL, *Proceedings*, 1934, 42-43.

79. Ohio General Assembly, *Journal of the House of Representatives*, 90th Gen. Assem., Reg. Sess., 1933-34 (Columbus, 1934), 822-1100, *passim*; Cleveland *Plain Dealer*, June 8, 1933.

calendar. Through the strategem of stopping the clock at a quarter until midnight, the Senate officially passed the bill on June 8, the last day of the session, and it was signed by the governor on June 30.[80]

Despite some union support, Ohio's minimum wage for women was never a measure of primary importance to unions. The Cleveland press and the Consumers' League of Ohio took the initiative in again bringing the question to the public's attention in the early 1930s; the Roosevelt administration was principally responsible for its ultimate passage. The measure received almost no mention in state union publications, and the legislative agent of the OSF of L was instructed not to appear at hearings in behalf of the measure. Yet, once in effect, organized labor in Ohio was quick to assure that its interests were protected under the new minihum wage law for women. Part of its political program for the next year was a request for union representation on the minimum wage board. In 1935 the OSF of L convention at last officially endorsed a minimum wage law by passing a resolution asking that the law be made more stringent. Thus, the 103
Ohio State Federation of Labor gave its official approval to a minimum wage for women only after it was already an established fact.

Throughout the 1930s, unions continued attempts to exclude women workers when they might threaten men's jobs. As previously mentioned, waiters worked throughout the decade to curb increased employment of women in restaurants. Furthermore, in 1932 the OSF of L agreed to support the Polishers and Buffers Unions in defending against a suit that challenged the legislative exclusion of women from that occupation. As competition for jobs became more severe, married women were singled out as a particular threat to men's jobs, and the annual convention of the OSF of L approved a resolution asking the legislature to consider legal restrictions on the employment of both husband and wife.[81] Organized labor was most interested in women when they threatened men's jobs, and then its interest resulted in attempts to exclude them from occupations in which they might compete with men.

While Ohio unions finally acquiesced in a minimum wage law for women, they did not initiate the measure. This was true even though throughout the Great Depression officials of the Women's Bureau and other interested observers suggested that extremely low wages for women encouraged employers to replace male workers with females. Presumably, a minimum wage for women that narrowed the wage difference between men and women would decrease the advantage employers could hope to

80. Frances Perkins, telegram to Gov. George White, June 8, 1933, George White Papers; Cleveland *Plain Dealer*, June 9, 1933, June 10, 1933.

81. OSFL, *Proceedings*, 1932, 13, 102-104; OSFL, *Proceedings*, 1938, 80, 124.

gain by such a substitution.[82] Therefore, higher wage standards for women might protect men's jobs and wages. In the face of low-wage competition from female labor, and given the recognized necessity of raising purchasing power to combat unemployment, it is surprising that Ohio unions were not more active advocates of minimum wage bills for women. Ohio union publications did not discuss a minimum wage for women as a possible method to discourage employers from hiring female labor. This was certainly not because Ohio unions did not care about the incursion of women into occupations previously held by men. Rather, it seems probable that Ohio unions did not see a minimum wage for women as effective protection against such low-wage competition, or that the predominant craft unions did not feel particularly threatened by the largely unskilled female labor force. In those few occupations where women were seen as a threat to men's jobs, organized labor preferred specific legislative prohibitions to restrict their further entry. Whatever support Ohio labor
104 finally gave to assuring female labor a reasonable wage did not extend to assuring women an equal opportunity in the labor market.

82. For example, see statements by Mary Anderson, Director of the Women's Bureau, New York *Times*, Jan. 25, 1937, and New York *Times*, Feb. 21, 1938. Also, column by Dale Cox, Cleveland *Plain Dealer*, June 22, 1931. For an analysis that concludes that minimum wage laws did discourage women's employment, see John M. Peterson, "Employment Effects of State Minimum Wages for Women: Three Historical Cases Re-examined," *Industrial and Labor Relations Review*, 12 (April, 1959), 406-22.

THE LEGAL STATUS OF THE DAKOTA INDIAN WOMAN

*Shirley R. Bysiewicz**
and
*Ruth E. Van de Mark***

> If the pride and the virtue of the women are lost, the spring will come but the buffalo trails will turn to grass. Be strong, with the warm, strong heart of the earth. No people goes down until their women are weak and dishonored, or dead upon the ground. Be strong and sing the strength of the Great Powers within you, and all around you.
>
> *Admonition to a Dakota girl upon entering puberty.*[1]

To understand the contemporary legal status of the Dakota[2] Indian woman is to understand her position in the Dakota Nation a century ago. It is to discover how that position was misunderstood by a government imposing its own values and prejudices on an alien culture and how, as a result, treaties were signed, laws were enacted, bureaus established, and regulations promulgated which failed to recognize the Dakota woman's strength, honor, and traditional rights. Furthermore, it is to survey the effects of those treaties, statutes, and regulations as well as the effects of the jurisdictional maze and the judicial interpretation which have arisen in their wake. It is also to study the role of the Dakota Indian woman both on and off the reservation. To understand the position of the Dakota woman today is, finally, to glimpse the future of the Dakota Nation. For, as the Dakota girl was told, "the honor of the people lies in the moccasin tracks of the women."[3]

The Traditional Role of the Dakota Woman

Just as the stereotype of the Dakota Indian male as the feather-bedecked, scalp-hunting, savage warrior has represented "Indian man" in the popular imagination, so too has the stereotype of the Dakota Indian woman as the male-dominated, tight-lipped, burden-bearing squaw[4] stood for Indian woman. Both stereotypes are mis-

* B.A. 1951, Connecticut; J.D. 1954, Connecticut; M.S.L.S. 1967, Southern Connecticut State College. Head Law Librarian and Professor of Law, University of Connecticut.

** A.B. 1966, Vassar; M.T.S. 1969, Harvard; student, University of Connecticut College of Law. This author spent the summer traveling extensively throughout her native state of South Dakota collecting much of the material on which this article is based.

leading. Far from being "the personalityless squaw . . . a brown lump of a drudge, chewing buffalo hide, putting that *tipi* up and down again, carrying heavy burdens along with the dogs while the tribes moved ever onward away from the pursuing cavalry,"[5] the Dakota woman played an indispensable, highly valued, social, economic, religious, and even political role within her nomadic, but structured, buffalo-hunting *tiyospaye*.[6]

Kinship Role

Any understanding of the Dakota woman's traditional role must begin with an awareness of the structure of the *tiyospaye*. Each *tiyospaye* consisted of 10 to 20 conjugal families united by kinship ties.[7] These ties were far-reaching and extremely strong. Affinal relatives were identified as consanguineous, "so that children . . . born after a person . . . [had] . . . married into the family . . . [knew] . . . such
106 person(s) only by the latter terms."[8] A mother's sisters and her mother were also "mother" to the child. The children of the mother's sister were "brother" and "sister." The mother's brother was "uncle" (as was the sister's husband), his wife was "aunt," his children, "cousin." The mother's father was "grandfather." The relationships between the child and the father's sister, her husband, their children, the brother's wife, and the father's mother paralleled those on the mother's side. Each side was given equal weight in determining relationship.[9] For every relationship there was a prescribed code of behavior. Sisters-in-law and brothers-in-law, for example, had a "boisterously friendly and joking relationship."[10] At the other extreme, avoidance and respect characterized the relationship between a husband and his mother-in-law and that between a daughter and her father-in-law.[11]

Because it endured, one's first duty was to one's *tiyospaye*, then to one's conjugal family. Not surprisingly, then, a woman's most binding relationship was with her brothers, both siblings and cousins. In many ways, this relationship was stronger than a woman's relationship with her husband. It was of a brother's feats that a woman sang at tribal dances, his children for whom she made cradles. It was to his sister that a brother, in honor, brought the scalp stick. At the basis of the entire kinship system was a deep sense of respect and cooperation on the part of each individual toward all other members of the *tiyospaye*. Each person's prestige was measured by his or her generosity,[12] hospitality, bravery in war or skill in craft, or religious vision. Each virtue was necessary for the group's survival and all were avidly pursued. For, ultimately, "[t]o lack relatives was the great dread of the Dakota, for on kinship everything depended."[13]

In terms of this kinship structure, the Dakota woman's primary role was clearly defined. In a hunting society such as hers, the child-rearing in the early years was carried out by the child's mothers, aunts, and grandmothers. The perpetuation of the *tiyospaye* was contingent upon the education of the children by them. This education was conducted on the basis of example in an atmosphere of tenderness, affection, love, and tolerance. Corporal punishment was viewed as brutal and was never employed. Rather, very small children were humored and indulged.[14] At the same time, however, even babies were gently conditioned to learn group cooperation.[15] Baby talk was never spoken and, at a young age, children knew the correct forms of familial address for all his or her many relatives. By serving as an intermediary between persons in an avoidance/respect relation, the child soon learned the subtleties of the particular relationship. The kinship system was further reinforced when a child was given tasks consistent 107
with his or her future relationship with a sister or brother. Only older sisters, in the case of girls, and older brothers, in the case of boys, were given the liberty to scold their younger siblings. That and mild adult shaming were the only discipline ever needed or employed. Through this education, the child grew up experiencing the great security and love to be found in the *tiyospaye*, as well as learning to understand both its complex structure and its attendant behavior and duties.

In this context, a Dakota girl grew up aware that great prestige accrued to a woman who was chaste before marriage and faithful after marriage. Premarital relations were not sanctioned. Young women were usually kept under the very watchful eye of a grandmother. At night, they were sometimes tied in bed to prevent abduction.[16] The Dakota woman carried a short butcher knife with her for purposes both of work and of defense. Should anyone try to attack her, she ". . . had the duty of defending herself at all cost against attack, against any who would violate the chastity rope of soft doeskin she was always to wear when away from the lodge."[17] In fact, such violation was rare and the attacker was ostracized. Just as the Dakota male could be challenged as to his veracity about his coups in battle, so, too, could the truth of a young woman's claim to virtue be disputed. If a man could honestly claim that he had slept with a young woman, then she was barred from participation in ceremonies for which she might have been eligible as a virgin.[18] For the Dakota woman, the prestige accorded chastity was great, the humiliation of public disclosure not worth the risk.

Marriage took place either with parental approval or through elopement. The majority of marriages were arranged by a man's or a woman's parents, although parental choices were not binding and many marriages were based on the mutual consent of the parties. Because marriage to a sister or brother or cousin was prohibited, courtships flourished when several bands were encamped together.[19] These courtships were very formal. A young man would stand by the lodge door "hoping a certain girl might slip out to be enfolded in his blanket a moment for a little talk, a little joking."[20] He would probably not be alone in waiting.

If the young woman responded to his overtures and his intentions became serious, the man would perhaps tender a horse or horses to the woman's father. He might well be refused. What is referred to as a "bride price" had to do with the prestige of the young man and his family, rather than with the worth of the bride. It emphatically did not mean that a woman became chattel because of it.[21] This is made most clear in Black Elk's account of High Horse's courting. High Horse fell in love. Indeed, he was in love to the point of feeling sick.
108 Having reason to believe that she liked him "maybe a little," High Horse went to the father and offered him two good horses. The old man waved him off. He then borrowed two more horses and offered them in addition, but, again, was turned away. A talk to the girl about eloping resulted in her rejecting the idea ("You see she thought a great deal of herself, too."). With a friend, High Horse attempted stealing her. In his nervousness, however, he allowed the knife to slip while cutting the rawhide thongs and the young woman woke up screaming. Still undaunted, High Horse tried abduction again. This time the mother woke up. Thoroughly dejected, he left the village. Several days later, he came upon a Crow camp, killed the horse guard, and drove off a hundred horses.[22] High Horse fled with the herd, reached the girl's village three days later, and drove the horses in front of the father's *tipi*. "The old man did not wave him away that time. It was not the horses that he wanted. What he wanted was a son who was a real man and good for something."[23]

Frequently, the man's family added to the number of horses which were offered to the bride's family. It was ". . . not the number of horses the young man paid which was as important as the fact that he was of a respectable family whose members contributed to his gift."[24] In only one circumstance was a suitor in an approved marriage relieved of his obligation to pay the bride's price. If the prospective husband had endured the most severe torture of the Sun Dance, the highest prestige was bestowed upon him. This prestige was "equated with that of a chaste maiden whom it was fitting that he be given in marriage. He did not have to pay for her and such marriage was regarded as being very honorable."[25] If the man's suit was accepted, the couple was married. There was no formal ceremony, no vows. Rather, a *tipi* was provided by the groom's parents and decorated and equipped by the father's sister and the mother's brother's wife.[26] After possibly a brief trip with friends to visit relatives or take part in a small and not very serious hunting or war party,[27] the couple returned to their *tipi*.

Always with the Santee, and generally with the Western Dakota, the couple went to live with the bride's family.[28] This matrilocal residence meant that the husband became a son in the wife's family, a member of his wife's household, "expected to contribute certain ordinary assets: a good name, honorable and agreeable deportment and the proper honors and coups in the hunt and in war."[29] Couples who had eloped were accepted by the community upon their return, "but they knew that this was not the way for those of good family, for those who honored themselves and their people and would not set a bad face upon them."[30] 109

Despite the absence of marriage vows and formal ceremony, Dakota marriages were stable. The ideal relationship between husband and wife is probably best illustrated by the Oglala tale entitled "The Lovers."[31] A young woman died because her band moved and she was separated from her lover. A burial scaffold inside a *tipi* was erected and her body was placed upon it. Her lover, who had left his own band only to reach her in time to see her die, undid the *tipi*'s lacings and went inside to be with the body. Suddenly, the young woman was alive. His sincerity demonstrated, she had been allowed to return from the dead to be his wife. The lesson that she brought from the spiritland was related to the people:

> Neither of us must ever scold or be unkind to the other. If we show only kindness to each other all our lives, then, at the end we shall arrive full of years, together. And if we do so, then we shall have built a great lesson for the tribe, so that hereafter, when men and women take each other in marriage, they will be kind to each other.[32]

That such a relationship of kindness, trust, and respect should have existed between husband and wife is logical, given the overriding sense of cooperation that controlled all human relationships within the *tiyospaye*. The evidence is that scolds and shrews among the wives were few.[33] By the same token, mistreatment of wives was rare, not condoned, and, if the usual Dakota sanction of ridicule (in this case administered by the wive's relatives) was unsuccessful, the husband was driven from the *tiyospaye*.[34]

While most marriages were monogamous, polygamy also occurred. Far from being offended, the first wife frequently suggested the addi-

tional wife, was usually consulted in any event, and "welcomed" subsequent wives "... for additional women lightened her work load."[35] The acquisition of a new wife also meant an increase in a family's prestige. The additional wives were generally the first wife's sisters or cousins. This practice promoted "friendliness and peace in the lodge."[36] There were only two times when a man might be expected to take another wife. One occurred when his brother died. He was then expected to marry the surviving widow, if she so desired.[37] A man might also be expected to marry his wife's virginal sister should his mother-in-law die.[38] Because divorce was a relatively simple matter (see *infra*), there is no reason to doubt that a man's devotion to his first wife was any less for his taking—or having to take—an additional wife[39] Successful marriage was highly valued. The husband and wife "... enjoyed not only the private gratifications of wholesome com-
110 panionship, but the approbation of their fellow men."[40]

When a marriage was successful, the Dakota were ". . . quick to bestow high honor and acclaim: when it failed, they were compassionated enough to withhold condemnation."[41] Divorce was not difficult.[42] Since she possessed the *tipi* and usually enjoyed a matrilocal residence, a woman choosing to divorce her husband simply placed his belongings in the village circle as public notice of her intentions.[43] The husband treated this decision with fortitude and composure.[44] A man desiring to divorce his wife would beat the drum at the next dance and announce his intention. A giveaway stick might be given to a man who, even if he were not interested in marrying the woman, would see that the woman was provided with game and protection.[45] A child who was still nursing remained with the mother. Children who were five or six or older could choose with whom they wished to live. Since each child had many mothers and many fathers on both sides of his or her family, care and nurturing were assured. Girls tended to remain with their mothers, boys, with their fathers.[46]

While divorce was easy for a woman, a subsequent marriage, while tolerated, was not favored. The One Only Ones, older women who had "... been with only one man,"[47] were among the most respected members of Dakota society. "For a married woman to know one man was honorable, whether he was alive or dead, but to know more than one was shameful."[48] A woman discovered to be an adulteress could be ordered by her husband "... to take the *tipi* down and get out. . . . Women so divorced . . . [became] . . . *witkowin*, crazy women, . . . morally wild."[49] He even had the right to cut off the tip of her nose, thereby permanently marking her as an unfaithful wife.[50] If, however, the wife's seducer was the husband's brother or cousin, the husband, because of the brother relationship, did nothing to him.

Rather, he said to the offender, "Take her, my brother, since she means more to you than our relationship." Usually the guilty pair were forced by public censure to flee to another group.[51] While male fidelity did not carry with it the high prestige that a wife's faithfulness did, it was nonetheless cherished and praised.[52]

Finally, there was a place in the Dakota kinship structure for a woman who never married, but remained a life-long virgin. Such a woman was "... a boasted ornament in the family group and band."[53] A girl in her early twenties who had been courted a great deal but who had decided to remain single and chaste was frequently honored by her family by means of a Virgin Feast, which was given for the entire encampment. Sometimes the girl herself gave the feast which made the event even more prestigious.[54] Other virgins who qualified were also honored and given gifts.[55] "This was not a religious occasion, it was a happy party to celebrate the individual prestige of a girl and it 111
was made important by the giveaway of property."[56] Even if a girl honored at a Virgin Feast subsequently married honorably, she still qualified as an honored guest at other feasts. Even if widowed, should such a woman ever take another husband, however, she lost her claim to the prestige bestowed by the Virgin Feast.

Economic Role

The Dakota woman's contribution to the economy of her people was indispensable. While the man hunted the buffalo and other game, butchered the kill to bring back, protected the *tiyospaye* from foreign invasion (and himself invaded enemy camps for horses or revenge), made his weapons, assisted in digging holes for caches of food, the woman cooked, gathered or dug[57] the vegetable and fruit staples of the diet (turnips,[58] wild onions, plums, gooseberries, chokecherries[59]), preserved the buffalo meat, prepared the skins, made the clothes and coverings from the hides, secured wood and water, made, transported, erected, and oversaw all aspects of the *tipi*. While this division of labor was, for the most part, strictly adhered to, a man would gather vegetables or fruits if an abundance was discovered and there was a risk of spoilage.[60] He would also help a woman raise the *tipi* if there were no other adult woman available for the task.[61] Similarly, a woman also butchered and, if necessary, protected herself.[62] The economy of each *tiyospaye* was self-sufficient, and because giving, not accumulating, was the operating principle of the group, all goods in excess of what were actually needed by a family were given away.[63]

Within that part of the economy managed by women, there was

a further division of labor by age and degree of tedium. Along with the responsibility of being an older sister, the girl of ten was given the "less boring" parts of housework to do as well as the embroidery.[64] During her first menstrual period, she was secluded and given an intensive course in quill embroidery and moccasin making. Each subsequent period was spent using those skills. The new bride was only gradually given domestic chores after her marriage. Even so, those chores were usually only the light chores. She was relieved of much of the work by her own mother who, until she herself was past seventy, would help care for the grandchildren, do the outside work, gather berries, dig turnips, cook, and preserve. The daughter would, for example, do the porcupine quilling while the mother tanned the hides, or the mother sewed soles on the moccasins and finished them after the daughter had done the fancy work.[65] Because there was constant cooperation among the three generations, as well as among
112 all the women in the *tiyospaye*, tasks were efficiently and expertly handled.

Just as the Dakota male was exalted for his bravery in battle, the Dakota woman also was accorded high prestige for her skill in handicrafts. Paralleling the warrior societies, there were, at least among the Oglala, handicraft societies composed of ". . . skillful *tipi* cover makers and expert quill workers."[66] Membership in these societies was based solely on merit and, unlike the membership in a warrior society, could not be sold or bestowed. So highly prized were a woman's designs that, in a society where personal ownership was virtually nonexistent and where nothing else was ever inherited, they, along with a good name and a man's designs for his arrows and regalia, could be willed. The man's designs were passed to his sons, the woman's designs went to her daughters, and the good name went to both sons and daughters. "The right to use those designs belonged to the woman's line, never to be sold or bestowed. . . ."[67] Just as men kept records of their coups, Hassrick reports, ". . . so did women keep count of their accomplishments. Ambition to excel was real among females. Accomplishments were recorded by means of dots incised along handles of the polished elkhorn scraping tools."[68]

Contests were also sometimes held in conjunction with the Sun Dance or at the end of the year-long Ghost-owning rite. Women were invited to bring their quilling. Sticks were given for work done before puberty (to the left) and after puberty (to the right). The woman with the most sticks ". . . was placed before all as became her position."[69] There is no doubt that the skills required to accomplish a woman's tasks were viewed by the entire community as equally as valued as the bravery required by a man to accomplish his.[70]

Political Role

Women played no visible role in the governing system of the *tiyospaye*.[71] The reason for the male political domination is obvious. As the hunters and protectors, the men had the expertise to know the best locations for the communal buffalo hunts as well as to gauge the likelihood of invasion or attack. These were the primary decisions that rested with the councils and shirt wearers. The men also had the training to deal most effectively with the violators of the unwritten code. Even so, in reaching its decisions, the council both sought and heeded the advice of women, ". . . especially that of elderly, wise women."[72] When the necessity arose, however, women did move into active participation in the *tiyospaye* government.

> They held chieftainships when bands lost all their men of leadership stature, as in the great scourges and in the later Sioux wars, when so many good men died. Sitting Bull returned from Canada in 1881 with a couple of women among his chiefs.[73] 113

Ideally, though, ". . . women led by being women . . . and . . . held together the tribe and family by their act of being." Leadership ". . . was theirs by virtue of their existence as the core of the kinship family."[74]

Religious Role

Ultimately, the great prestige that was accorded a chaste woman, a faithful wife, a skilled worker, and anyone generous, wise, and hospitable, can only be explained in terms of the Dakota's knowledge of man, nature, and *Wakan-Tanka*, "the Great Spirit, the all-seeing god of all men."[75] "The Nation's Hoop" was based on the equal relationship of man, plant, and animal, their balance and harmony. Sometimes called "the Unitarians of the American Indian,"[76] the Dakota had no demonology, no "evil beings to be appeased or circumvented or blamed."[77] Only man's disharmony with the Great Powers brought about evil. Through visions, men and women restored harmony and gained discernment. Through visions, insight was received, the future became known, gifts were bestowed. The role of woman is at the heart of Dakota theology and is essential to its ritual. Far from being excluded from its practice, women shared its vision and promise.

Wakan-Tanka was Grandfather and Father to the Dakotan. Earth was Grandmother and Mother. "She," the Dakotan learned, "is sacred. Every step that is taken upon her should be as a prayer."[78] The central revelation of the *Wakan-Tanka* was conveyed to man by the

White Buffalo Cow Woman, a *wakan* (sacred) woman. Her coming was conceived as an event time (10 generations ago[79]). To the Dakota, she brought not only the message of the *Wakan-Tanka*, but gave to them the sacred pipe and their seven rituals as well. The message she brought was contained in her explanation of the sacred pipe:

> With this pipe you will be bound to all your relatives: your Grandfather and Father, your Grandmother and Mother. This round rock, which is made of the same red stone as the bowl of the pipe, your Father *Wakan-Tanka* has also given you. It is the Earth, your Grandmother and Mother, and it is where you will live and increase. This Earth which He has given to you is red, and the two-leggeds who live upon the Earth are red; and the Great Spirit has also given to you a red day, and a red road. All of this is sacred so
> 114 do not forget! Every dawn as it comes is a holy event, and every day is holy, for the light comes from your Father *Wakan-Tanka*; and also you must remember that the two-leggeds and all the other peoples who stand upon this earth are sacred and should be treated as such.[80]

Because of this strong sense of "inalienability from the earth and the sky and all that lies between," human virtue and natural phenomenon were interdependent. For when ". . . men are not brave the rains fail for all, and when the women lose their virtue the buffalo do not return."[81] A woman's chastity or fidelity, then, was not merely a matter of individual prestige, but, rather, a sacred duty involving the very survival of her people. The woman who walked the red road knew that "the buffalo herds wide and dark as cloud shadows moving over the prairie" followed her, as did "the spring of the yellow calves, the fall earth shaking with the coming of the fat ones, their robes thick and warm as the sun on the lodge floor."[82] Because man was no better—or worse—than all other beings, he did not take more than he needed and gave to others all that he did not need. Both generosity and hospitality were sacred duties. So, too, one did not waste that which was needed. Skill and industry were essential to the harmony between man and the rest of nature.

Of the seven rituals given to the Dakota, one involved a female central figure and another was given exclusively to women. A young girl[83] performed the *Tapa Wakan Yap* or the Throwing of the Ball rite.[84] While a girl entering puberty (usually not until fourteen, fifteen, or sixteen) had always been secluded and then purified in an *inipi* or sweat lodge for four days, the White Cow Buffalo Woman gave to the Dakota a new rite: *Ishna Ta Awi Cha Lowan*[85] or the

Preparation for Womanhood rite. Having been secluded, the young woman was taken for instruction and purification. The family then gave a feast in honor of their daughter. This feast also included a great giveaway. There was no similarly prescribed rite for males entering puberty, but many young men sought a vision by means of the *Inipi* (Rite of Purification) and *Hanblecheyapi* (Crying for a Vision).[86] In order to receive a vision, one "lamented." Unlike the Preparation for Womanhood rite, lamenting was not confined to males and puberty. "Our women also 'lament'," Black Elk reported, "after first purifying themselves in the *Inipi*; they are helped by other women, but they do not go up on a very high mountain. They go up on a hill in a valley, for they are women and need protection."[87]

Just as there were holy men gifted by their visions, so also were there holy women gifted with powers of healing and skill.[88] Women also played essential ceremonial roles in other Dakota rites. In a 115
world view that recognized the wholeness of life, both male and female were indispensable. "Out of the woman," explained Black Elk in describing the Elk Ceremony, "the people grows." But, ". . . behind the woman's power of life, is hidden the power of man." The woman, then, ". . . is the life of the flowering tree, but man must feed and care for it . . . . The power of the man encircles and protects the power of women."[89] No power was better. Each was an essential part of one life.

The Law and the Dakota Woman

By the 1850's the traditional Dakota culture was having its first significant contact with the rapidly colonizing society represented by settlers, soldiers, and Washington, D.C. A culture more antithetical to the Dakotan scarcely can be imagined. Where the Dakota Indian lived a life based upon cooperation and generosity, the nineteenth-century white American prided himself on his utter individualism and his accumulated wealth. A society which allowed its children to be children[90] and ostracized its murderers met a society which whipped its offspring and executed its transgressors. A people for whom ownership of land was an unthinkable concept encountered a nation for whom it was an all-consuming passion. Men who experienced life as an organic whole were suddenly forced to deal with men who considered themselves superior to the rest of nature and who killed buffalo for sport as if to reinforce that superiority.

Two different views of women were also meeting. The mid-nineteenth-century white woman was a woman without rights. Legally, she was her father's and her husband's. She played no role whatsoever within the political structure of white America. Her virtue was maintained by a system which both viewed sex as a necessary evil and allowed men their license. Her work was vital, but considered lowly. Her religion was patriarchal, her deity masculine, her clergy male. Far from being able to identify directly with the power of the universe and its incarnate revelation, she could associate herself directly with mankind's fall through Eve and only derivatively with its redemption through Mary. That the white man superimposed his own values and beliefs concerning woman—and, indeed, continues to do so—in dealing with Indian women can be seen, first of all, in treaties, federal legislation, and administrative rulings.

Treaties and Reservations

Between the years 1851 and 1889, a number of treaties and agreements were made between the United States and various Dakota
116 tribes. The Dakota were formidable fighters. The government was, therefore, anxious to contain and pacify the tribes. Because Indians were viewed as rank heathens, the government was also eager to civilize, *i.e.*, assimilate, Indian tribes as rapidly as possible. In dealing with what was, at best, a loose confederation of bands, the government erroneously assumed that it was dealing with a political entity composed of individual states with chiefs as hereditary monarchs. The truly democratic nature of Dakota society was never comprehended, and the role of the Dakota woman in that process was completely ignored. Treaties were negotiated with whichever male Indians the government designated as rulers. That this was an injustice to the Dakota woman can be seen by looking at three of the major treaties and agreements which were negotiated.

An early treaty,[91] dated September 17, 1851, between the United States and the Dakota tribes made the first delineation of the borders of the "Decotah" Nation. This first "Treaty of Fort Laramie" was superseded by the Laramie Treaty of April 29, 1868.[92] Negotiated primarily by Oglala Chief Red Cloud, it was a treaty well known to all the Dakota peoples. It reserved all the land west of the Missouri to the Dakota Indians for "as long as the grass should grow and the water flow."[93] In this treaty the matrilinear[94] structure of Dakota society was not acknowledged and the female dominance of agriculture was overlooked. Rather than being left to any possible tribal custom, questions of descent and alienation of property were left to future congressional action. Further, Article VI provided that "any male over eighteen years of age" was entitled—for three years of continuous occupation and two hundred dollars or more of improvements—to a patent for one hundred and sixty acres, improvements included. Indians receiving such patents became eligible for United States citizenship, "entitled to all privileges and immunities of such citizens," while, at the same time, retaining "all his rights to benefits accruing to Indians under this treaty."[95] Article XII stipulated that

> No treaty for the cession of any portion or part of the reservation herein described which may be held in common shall be of any validity or force as against the said Indians, unless executed and signed by at least three fourths of all the adult male Indians, occupying or interested in the same; and no cession by the tribe shall be understood or construed in such manner as to deprive, without his consent, any individual member of the tribe to his rights to any tract of land selected by him, as provided in Article VI of this treaty.[96]

This article proved to be significant not only because it ignored the 117
traditional role of women in the decision-making process, but because the signature of three-fourths of the adult male Indians were never secured in subsequent land cessions agreements.

On February 28, 1877, Congress ratified an agreement[97] which was dated September 26, 1876.[98] Acting under the impetus of removal to Indian territory, the Dakota, along with the Cheyenne and Northern Arapaho, agreed to cede the Black Hills. Accompanying promises of additional support and the provision that "nothing in this act shall be construed to authorize the removal of the Sioux Indians to Indian Territory,"[99] the agreement stipulated that Indians were to receive employment on the reservations. Furthermore, in order to "improve the morals and industrious habits" of the residents, non-Indians employed on the reservations were to be lawfully married and living with their families. The traditional role of the Dakota woman was not considered when the government included the stipulation that an annual census be taken ". . . and the names of each head of family and adult person be registered."[100] If it was unaware of her role before, the government learned about the position of the Dakota woman in implementing the provision. As a result of the census requirement, the Dakota were forced to adopt surnames. Because of the matrilocal residence of most families as well as the close association with the mother's family, the mother's name, not the father's, was registered. Such defiance of natural law was, of course, not tolerated, and women and children were forced to assume a husband's or father's name. "Sometimes," however, these matriarchal names ". . . stood on the roster for months, even years, before some sharp-eyed clerk caught the error."[101]

Despite the liberal land cession agreed to in 1876, the "yellow

metal that makes the *wasichus* crazy"[102] was still strong. The push for Black Hills land continued unabated. Furthermore, "thousands of hungry whites demanded that the vast reservation be alloted and the surplus land be opened to white settlement."[103] After two agreements in the early 1880's were rejected by Congress because of the clearly unconscionable means employed to secure them,[104] an agreement with the Dakota was finally ratified on March 2, 1889.[105] In it, the Dakota land was divided into the present reservations, Pine Ridge, Rosebud, Standing Rock, Cheyenne River, Lower Brule, and Crow Creek.[106] Both men and women were allowed to take their allotments in severalty. The surplus land was offered to homesteaders. This agreement reflected the policy of termination of reservations and the assimilation of Indians underlying the Dawes Act[107] which had been passed in 1887. It was viewed as "for the best interest of said Indians."[108] Because it was so much more inclusive than the Laramie
118 Treaty, the Agreement of 1889 indirectly recognized the right of women to take allotted land. Nonetheless, the largest allotments went to the presumably male heads of families. Unlike the Laramie Treaty of 1868, which required the approval of adult males,[109] the 1889 agreement's allotment provisions were ". . . not compulsory without the consent of the majority of the adult members of the tribe. . . ."[110] Where the Laramie Treaty left the devise, partition, and alienation of land to future congressional action, the 1889 agreement ruled that, in the case of the demise of an Indian who had received his allotment, determination of heirs would be made according to the state or territory where the land was located.

Interestingly enough, among all the Dakota treaties and agreements, women were mentioned only to convey reservation land ("on account of their valuable services and liberality"[111]) to men, presumably white, who otherwise probably would have been ineligible to be owners. Hence, for example, a half-section was given to the unnamed ". . . half-breed Yancton, wife of Charles Ruelo and her two sisters, the wives of Eli Bedaud and August Traverse. . . ."[112]

Federal Legislation

The first legislation which directly affected the Indian woman as woman resulted from the Supreme Court's 1883 decision in *Ex Parte Crow Dog*.[113] The political murder of Dakota Chief Spotted Tail by Crow Dog, a fellow tribe member, at the Rosebud agency, had resulted in the imposition of tribal sanctions which did not happen to include Crow Dog's execution. As a result of public outcry over the inadequacy of tribal justice, Crow Dog was arrested, convicted, and sentenced to die by the Territorial District Court. The judgment was confirmed by the Supreme Court of the Territory. The United States Supreme Court granted Crow Dog's writ of habeas corpus, ruling that lower courts lacked jurisdiction over crimes perpetrated by one Indian against another Indian in Indian territory.[114]

To prevent a recurrence of *Crow Dog,* the Congress passed the Seven Major Crimes Act on March 3, 1885.[115] The Act provided that

> . . . immediately upon and after the date of passage of this act all Indians, committing against the person or property of another Indian or other person any of the following crimes, namely, murder, manslaughter, rape, assault with intent to kill, arson, burglary, and larceny within any Territory of the United States, and either within or without an Indian reservation, shall be subject therefor to the laws of such Territory relating to said crimes, and shall be tried therefor in the same courts and in the same manner and shall 119
> be subject to the same penalties as are all other persons charged with the commission of said crimes, respectively; and the said courts are hereby given jurisdiction in all such cases; and all such Indians committing any of the above crimes against the person or property of another Indian or other person within the boundaries of any State of the United States, and within the limits of any Indian reservation, shall be subject to the same laws, tried in the same courts and in the same manner, and subject to the same penalties as are all other persons committing any of the above crimes within the exclusive jurisdiction of the United States.[116]

This meant that, after South Dakota's admission into statehood in 1889, an Indian convicted of rape on the Dakota Indian reservation was subject to federal law and the death penalty.[117]

In 1897, Congress enacted a bill "[t]o reduce the cases in which the penalty of death may be inflicted."[118] As introduced, the bill proposed to abolish capital punishment except in cases of murder, rape, and treason. In deciding such cases, the jury could choose life imprisonment in lieu of capital punishment. Rape on Indian reservations, however, was not deemed to warrant capital punishment. In Senate debate, Senator Hoar explained why rape on Indian reservations was exempted. In such cases,

> . . . the judge has no discretion where the offense of rape is committed on an Indian reservation but to sentence the prisoner to death; and there are several cases now pending where that must happen. One of the judges . . . wrote to me that there are several cases now upon trial before him of boys who did not seem to under-

> stand that they had committed any very heinous offense, and admitted the offense without any attempt to conceal it whatever, and he has to sentence those poor creatures to death.[119]

Section 5 of the bill as passed stated that ". . . any Indian male who shall commit the offense of rape within the limits of any Indian reservation shall be punished by imprisonment at the discretion of the court."[120]

As a result of the 1897 enactment, Indian males enjoyed a protected status and, unlike other males committing rape within the exclusive jurisdiction of the United States, could not be subject to capital punishment. This protected status was partially removed in 1909 when Congress decided that such exemption applied only when an Indian raped a female on the reservation.[121] In House debate on the proposed bill, the anomaly was apparent to Representative
120 Adamson, who asked:

> I should like to know why the same penalty ought not to be inflicted for the crime of rape whether it be on an Indian woman, a Negro woman, Anglo-Saxon woman, or anyone else. Why should not an Indian committing that crime against any woman suffer death?

Representative Norris offered the explanation and, in so doing, revealed a profound misunderstanding of Indian women and their culture. "I agree with the gentleman," he began,

> . . . but I think this is applied only to an Indian woman, because the committee have considered the legislation on the subject generally has been with the idea that the morals of Indian women are not always as high as those of a white woman and consequently the punishment should be lighter against her.[122]

This exemption of Indian males who rape Indian women from a stricter penalty still stands.[123] The Seven Major Crimes statute has been expanded by legislative amendment[124] and defined by judicial interpretation. Even though Section 1153 of Title 18 of the United States Code specifies that ". . . the offense of rape . . . shall be defined in accordance with the laws of the state in which the offense was committed," the majority of courts strictly interpreted an offense of rape under Section 1153 to mean common law rape and not statutory rape.[125] To remedy what it felt was a misunderstanding of congressional intent,[126] Congress passed Public Law 80-707 on November 2, 1966,[127] which amended Section 1153 to include "carnal knowledge of any female, not his wife, who has not attained the age of sixteen years," as well as "assault with intent to commit rape." Despite the revision of Section 1153, the provision that ". . . any Indian who commits rape . . . upon any female Indian within the Indian country shall be imprisoned at the discretion of the court" has never been modified or even questioned by Congress. The implication remains that Indian women are somehow "immoral" and that the rape of an Indian woman by an Indian is not as reprehensible as the rape of a non-Indian woman by an Indian man or her rape by a non-Indian man.

It was not until 1967, nearly sixty years after its inclusion in the Major Crimes Act, that the constitutionality of the provision was challenged in *Gray v. United States.*[128] The defendants, Navaho Indians, were charged with raping a non-Indian girl on the Navaho reservation in violation of Section 1153. They moved to dismiss, ". . . because the punishment prescribed was based on race and there- 121
fore denied the defendants due process of law."[129] The motion was denied and the defendants were convicted under Section 2031 of Title 18 of the United States Code.[130] On appeal, the Ninth Circuit noted, "It has long been acknowledged that Congress, in the exercise of its Constitutional power, has recognized and established for the Indian people a peculiar and protected status as awards [*sic*] of the Federal government."[131] Because Congress "has seen fit to diminish the penalty to be imposed upon an Indian who is convicted of rape upon another Indian in Indian country," the defendants, even though subject to the harsher penalty of Section 2031, were held not to have been denied due process of law. "It remains for Congress," the court concluded, "to amend or repeal the section in question, and Congress must make the decision, not the courts."[132]

The issue of the provision's constitutionality has not been directly raised since *Gray.*[133] In resorting to the special status, wardship of Indians, theory, the court clearly failed to meet the constitutional issue raised by the special provision in Section 1153. In *United States v. Boone,*[134] the District Court of New Mexico dealt with that portion of Section 1153 which includes among the major crimes assault with a dangerous weapon and specifies that such assault is to be "defined and punished in accordance with the laws of the state in which such offense was committed." A non-Indian committing a similar crime against an Indian on a reservation would be tried under Section 1152 of Title 18 of the United States Code[135] and federal law.[136] Because the federal law both requires the prosecution to prove intent and carries with it a lesser fine, the defendant argued that he was "subject to the lesser burden of proof and the greater fine" simply because of his status as an Indian and that the "racial differentiation" was "unjustifiable and therefore violative of his right to equal protection under the laws."[137] The court agreed. Citing *Bolling v. Sharpe*, the court found the racial classification to be "so unjustifiable as to be violative of due process."[138] It concluded: "This racial classification is not reasonably related to any proper governmental objective and is therefore arbitrary and invidious in violation of the Due Process Clause of the Fifth Amendment."[139]

There is no reason why the exemption from federal law which is given Indian men who rape Indian women cannot be similarly challenged by someone who, like the defendants in *Gray*, is injured by the classification.[140] There is, first of all, a racial classification. The race of the rape victim determines the punishment of the Indian rapist. Second, this classification is not related to a proper governmental objective. In fact, it serves no function and rests on the misguided and false assumptions that Indian men see nothing wrong in
122 raping Indian women and that Indian women are immoral.[141] Finally, the subject of the racial classification—the Indian woman raped by the Indian man—is injured by the classification. If stricter sanctions do have a deterring effect, then, it must be argued, the Indian woman is being denied that deterrent. Obviously, the prosecution of all rape occurring on the reservation and the punishment for those convicted must be the same for all persons, regardless of the race of the rapist or of the victim. To allow the damaging racial and sexual assumptions implicit in Section 1153 to stand does a grave injustice to both Indian men and women.

The Indian woman as woman also became the subject of a number of enactments passed after and in connection with the General Allotment Act of 1887 (otherwise known as the Dawes Act).[142] As noted in the discussion of the Dakota Agreement of 1889,[143] the enactment of the Dawes Act saw as its main objective the eventual termination of the reservations and the assimilation of all Native Americans. On August 9, 1888, Congress enacted a statute[144] designed to protect Indian women from white men who might marry them for their allotment.[145] Section 1 of the statute declared that, in the future, no white man marrying an Indian woman could thereby acquire "any right to any tribal property, privilege or interest whatever to which any member of such tribe is entitled."[146] Section 2 granted United States citizenship to Indian women who did marry United States citizens after August 9, 1888, "with all the rights, privileges, and immunities of any such citizen, being a married woman." A proviso was also added stating that this citizenship would not "impair or in any way affect the right or title of such married woman to any tribal property or any interest therein."[147] Finally, Section 3 made only circumstantial or presumptive evidence of a marriage between an Indian woman and a white man sufficient in judicial proceedings. Among the Dakota Indians, marriage to white men was disfavored.[148] While purporting to protect and help keep the individual Indian woman from unscrupulous white men, this act had the effect of encouraging such marriage and forcing the assimilation of the Indian woman. As was reiterated in the House debate,[149] a woman marrying a white man lost none of her prerogatives as an Indian, while, at the same time, United States citizenship became an automatic right.[150] Furthermore, not even a marriage license was required to reap the benefits of the statute. Should her interracial marriage in white society fail, however, and should she be forced to return to her family, the Dakota woman was forced to suffer the humiliation of group disapproval.

On February 28, 1891, Congress finally enacted legislation[151] concerning the descent and distribution of allotted land. Aware that 123
Indian customs differed from those of the dominant culture, Congress recognized, for the purpose of determining legitimate heirs, the validity of custom marriages, *i.e.*, "... whenever any male and female Indian shall have cohabited together as husband and wife according to the custom and manner of Indian life."[152] This recognition of custom marriages was necessary so that the legitimate issue of a man could be determined for purposes of descent.

While the status of the child of Indian parents followed the condition of the father, the status of children of mixed marriages was not so clear. Ten years after the passage of the Dawes Act, Congress dealt directly with the question of the rights of the children born into marriages between white men and Indian women. On June 7, 1897, a law was enacted that stated:

> All children born of a marriage solemnized prior to June 7, 1897, between a white man and an Indian woman by blood and not by adoption, where said Indian woman was on that date, or was at the time of her death, recognized by the tribe, shall have the same rights and privileges to the property of the tribe to which the mother belongs, or belonged at the time of her death, by blood, as any other member of the tribe, and no prior Act of Congress shall be construed as to debar such a child of such right.[153]

In subsequent court cases, the rights of children whose mothers maintained their tribal membership were affirmed. In *United States v. Higgins*,[154] the court noted that

> It is well-known to those who have lived here upon the frontier in America that, as a rule, half-breeds or mixed blood Indians have resided with the tribes to which their mothers belonged: that they

have, as a rule, never found a welcome home with their white relatives, but with their Indian kindred. It is but just, then, that they should be classed as Indians, and have all the rights of the Indian.[155]

The court rejected the notion that the status of the son must always necessarily follow that of the father. Rhetorically, the court asked whether it would always be true under American law that a child would be classed as the same color and race as his or her own father. No; it would not if the mother were a slave—or, it appeared, an Indian. The 1897 statute was also found to be applicable even when the member mother had left the tribe to live with her white husband. In *Vezina v. United States,*[156] the mother of the 88-year-old plaintiff-daughter had lived off the reservation after her marriage to the plaintiff's white father. Even so, the mother ". . . looked like an
124 Indian squaw; she wore no stockings, but in winter wore cloths wrapped about her legs to protect her from the inclemency of the weather." According to one report, the mother was "more like a full-blood than three-fourths." She "acted like a squaw."[157] The court concluded that the mother was a tribal member. "It should take especially strong evidence that an Indian woman has abandoned her tribe simply by living with her husband, which she ought to do by the laws of both God and man."[158] The plaintiff's claim was further strengthened by the fact that she herself had lived on the reservation after her own marriage. Unless, however, the children were recognized by the tribe or had lived with it, they lost all rights to any allotment.[159] The statute also was used to confer liabilities as well as "rights and privileges to the property of the tribe."[160] The Eighth Circuit, for example, used the provision to find that a mixed blood Indian who had received an allotment and patent and who was, in addition, a United States citizen, was an Indian for purposes of conviction under a statute which forbids the sale of intoxicants to Indians. He was held to be an Indian even though his paternal grandfather was white and because his own father had abandoned him.[161] It is entirely possible that the government was, as is suggested by the court's remarks in *United States v. Higgins, supra,* equating Indian women who married white men with slaves in allowing an exception to the rule that "the children of free parents follow the status of their father."[162] Whatever its actual rationale, the statute nonetheless reflected the traditional Dakota (and American Indian) pattern of familial identification. It had the effect of discouraging assimilation and of allowing most children of Indian mothers and white fathers legally to claim their rights as Indians.

Finally, Congress also indirectly legislated concerning Indian women in the education provisions of the June, 1897, statute. The Commissioner of Indian Affairs was given power to "... employ Indian girls as assistant matrons and Indian boys as farmers and industrial teachers in all Indian schools when it is practicable to do so."[163] This little bit of job classification on the basis of sex has never been challenged, although, presumably, it could be under Title IX of the Education Amendments of 1972, which provides that "No person in the United States shall, on the basis of sex be excluded from participation in, be denied the benefits of, or be subject to discrimination under any educational program or activity receiving Federal financial assistance."[164] According to the Director of the Office of Civil Rights, Title IX applies "only to Federally assisted education programs or activities as opposed to Federally operated programs."[165] However, because Indian schools are federally operated, a Title IX 125
challenge to the statute would seem to be barred. Nonetheless, farming and industrial arts teaching jobs are positions which should not be classified on the basis of sex. Both qualified Indian women as well as men should be able to seek and hold such positions.

Administrative Regulations

In addition to federal legislation, the Indian woman, particularly the reservation Indian woman, is also subject to the rules and regulations promulgated by the Bureau of Indian Affairs[166] and the Indian Health Service.[167] Just as the Indian woman who married a white man and the children of such a marriage were singled out for special treatment by Congress, so, too, have such women and their children been made the subject of special—and unequal—treatment by the BIA and the IHS.

According to the Bureau of Indian Affairs Manual, "General Assistance"[168] is available "... to provide necessary financial assistance to needy families and persons living on reservations under the jurisdiction of this Bureau and in jurisdictions under the Bureau of Indian Affairs in Alaska and Oklahoma."[169] General Assistance is based on the standard of need established by the state in which the reservation is located.[170] Any Indian who qualifies and whose combined income from all sources is less than that standard receives the difference in General Assistance. To qualify, a person need not be an enrolled member of a tribe, but must be

a. a descendent (son, daughter, grandchild, great-grandchild) of a person who belonged to an Indian Tribe which is recognized by the United States government and has not been "terminated," or

b. an Alaskan native.[171]

On the basis of information supplied by the Chief of Welfare, Washington, D.C., Ward and Barlow report that when ". . . an Indian (or Native) man is married to a non-Indian, the BIA gives GA to the Indian members of the family."[172] The same, however, is not true for the family of an Indian woman who is married to a non-Indian. When an Indian woman is married to a non-Indian, ". . . the family can get BIA GA only after it has asked for welfare from the State or county and been turned down. If the family meets the other eligibility conditions, the BIA may give GA to the Indian members of the family."[173] For obvious reasons, this rule is discriminatory. In the first place, the condition of poverty, as well as other eligibility criteria, have been met. There is no question of need. State and
126 county welfare programs generally pay less than the state-established standard of need.[174] The Indian woman married to a non-Indian and her family automatically, therefore, lose the higher benefits paid by BIA General Assistance if they are accepted for state or local aid. Second, only the Indian members of the family (here the mother and children) are eligible to receive the aid. BIA benefits would not be extended to non-Indians. Finally, even if the Indian woman married to a non-Indian is rejected by state and local welfare channels and does receive BIA General Assistance for herself and her children, she has had to wait[175] before receiving assistance. This delay is one not experienced by Indian women married to Indians or by Indian men. She has been denied her right to a "fast decision" because of her sex and the race of her husband.

Aside from the constitutional issues discussed *infra*, this rule must be attacked because of its ad hoc nature. Not only has it not been promulgated in the Code of Federal Regulations, but it has not even been published in the Bureau of Indian Affairs Manual. In accordance with the Administrative Procedure Act,[176] the Bureau of Indian Affairs Manual reads:

> Code of Federal Regulations: Directives which relate to the public, including Indians, are published in the Federal Register and codified in 25 Code of Federal Regulations (25 CFR). These directives inform the public of privileges and benefits available; eligibility qualifications, requirements and procedures. . . .[177]

The Bureau of Indian Affairs Manual, on the other hand, deals with "policies, procedures, and instructions which do not relate to the public but are required to govern the operations of the Bureau. . . ."[178]

There can be no doubt that a policy which demands that an Indian woman married to a non-Indian exhaust state and local welfare channels before seeking BIA General Assistance relates to "eligibility qualifications, requirements, and procedures." If, as was reported to Ward and Barlow, this is indeed an operative policy in granting aid to Indian women married to non-Indians, then it should be published in the Code of Federal Regulations. For, as noted by the Supreme Court in *Morton v. Ruiz*, an agency's power

> . . . to make rules that affect substantive individual rights and obligations carries with it the responsibility not only to remain consistent with governing legislation [citations omitted], but also to employ procedures that conform to the law . . . . No matter how rational or consistent with congressional intent a particular decision might be, the determination of eligibility cannot be made on
> an ad hoc basis by the dispenser of the funds.[179] 127

This differentiation between Indian women in general and Indian women married to non-Indians is also found in the eligibility requirements for Public Health Service care. Unlike the BIA General Assistance requirements, the Indian health requirements are published in the Code of Federal Regulations. Section 36.12 of Title 42 reads:

> (a) In general. (1) Services will be made available, as medically indicated, to persons of Indian descent belonging to the Indian community served by local facilities and program, and non-Indian wives of such persons.
>
> . . .
>
> (c) Priorities when funds, facilities, or personnel are insufficient to provide the indicated volume of service. Priorities for care and treatment, as among individuals who are within the scope of the program, will be determined on the basis of relative medical need and access to other arrangements for obtaining the necessary care.[180]

The actual effect of these rules has been not only to deny to non-Indian husbands access to Public Health Service facilities and care (while granting them to non-Indian wives), but to deny to Indian women who marry non-Indians the use of those facilities as well. As the result of numerous complaints, it was discovered that, on the basis of Section 36.12(c), Indian Health Service hospitals set their priorities so that frequently Indian women married to non-Indians lose all their eligibility. Indian men married to non-Indians do not.[181]

While neither the BIA's General Assistance rule nor the Public Health regulations fall under the prohibitions of Title IX of the 1972

Education Amendments[182] or Title VI of the Civil Rights Act of 1964,[183] both can be attacked as fifth amendment denials of the equal protection aspect of due process.[184] They involve discrimination which is based both on race and on sex. Otherwise qualified Indian women who marry non-Indians lose automatic benefits guaranteed other Indians simply because of the race of their husbands. "This is a classification drawn strictly along lines of race."[185] In 1967, the Supreme Court struck down Virginia's miscegenation law as a violation of the equal protection and due process clauses of the fourteenth amendment.[186] While that decision ". . . invalidates laws which prohibit inter-racial marriages, regulations which place special *burdens* on such marriages would," in the opinion of the Director of the Office of Civil Rights, Gilbert Roman, "seem to come within the same principle."[187] In that they are denied immediate welfare as-
128 sistance and/or health services while Indian men similarly situated are not, Indian women married to non-Indians are denied equal consideration and services because of their sex. An Idaho statute giving male survivors preference over similarly situated female survivors in determining an estate's administrator, solely for the convenience of the probate court, was held by the Supreme Court in *Reed v. Reed*[188] to be a violation of the equal protection clause of the fourteenth amendment. In *Frontiero v. Richardson*,[189] the Supreme Court dealt directly with the issue of federal legislation that discriminated on the basis of sex. Holding that it was unconstitutional discrimination, the Supreme Court struck down a law which required a military servicewoman to prove the dependency of her spouse in order to receive fringe benefits which, at the same time, made no such demands of servicemen.

In *Frontiero v. Richardson*, a plurality decision, the Supreme Court stated that a classification by sex ". . . must be reasonable, not arbitrary, and must rest upon some ground of difference having a fair and substantial relation to the object of the legislation, so that all persons similarly circumstanced shall be treated alike."[190] The Court in *Reed* and *Frontiero* held that administrative convenience is not a justification for sex differentiation. Is there, however, a legitimate governmental interest that justifies denying medical services to Indian women married to non-Indians while granting them to Indian men married to non-Indians?

> Are all Indian women who marry non-Indians less medically needy than their male counterparts? Are they automatically eligible for alternative care by virtue of their interracial marriages? Probably not. In fact this classification would seem to have no reasonable

relation to the purposes of the IHS, which is to serve medically needy Indians, male and female.[191]

Similarly, Indian women who marry non-Indians are not automatically guaranteed financial security. While it is true that reservation Indians are entitled to alternative state and county welfare,[192] such assistance is less[193] than that to which they may be entitled to receive as Indians. If the purpose of BIA General Assistance is to serve all reservation Indians, then it cannot make this aid harder for some to receive than others. Otherwise, it must demand that all reservation Indians—male and female—seek alternative aid first. Both the IHS and the BIA practices are unrelated to any reasonable purpose and are violations of the equal protection guaranteed by the fifth amendment.

In that Indian Health Service facilities frequently set their priori- 129
ties by assuming that all Indian women married to non-Indians are automatically guaranteed alternative medical care, they are also denying such women the fifth amendment right of due process. In *United States Department of Agriculture v. Murry*,[194] the Supreme Court struck down a 1971 amendment to the Food Stamp Act which denied food stamps to households in which a member of the household was over 18 years of age and had been claimed as an income tax dependent during the previous year. This provision was found to bear no relation to actual need and to have created "a conclusive presumption that the 'tax dependent's' household is not needy and had access to nutritional adequacy."[195] While it was doubtless easier to administer, a tax dependency test that "automatically—without hearing, without witnesses, without finding of fact—terminate[d] a household's claim for eligibility for food stamps"[196] lacked "critical ingredients of due process."[197] As was the case with the *Murry* plaintiffs who were poor households with tax dependent members, otherwise eligible Indian women are denied a federal benefit because of the "irrebuttable presumption often contrary to fact"[198] that, because they are married to non-Indians, they are not needy and that their health care is provided. Those Indian Health Service hospitals which establish priorities that deny services to Indian women married to non-Indians have established an automatic test indistinguishable from the tax dependency test. There are no hearings, no witnesses, no findings of fact. There is, however, a fifth amendment denial of due process.

Under the BIA General Assistance scheme, the non-Indian husbands of Indian women are in no better or worse a position than the non-Indian wives of Indian men. Neither group is eligible for as-

sistance. The same is not true under Title 42, Section 36.12, of the Code of Federal Regulations, which extends health care benefits to non-Indian wives, but not to non-Indian husbands. In *Weinberger v. Wiesenfeld*,[199] a unanimous Supreme Court found that a Social Security Act provision which awards survivor's benefits to widows but not to widowers, is a violation of the equal protection secured by the fifth amendment. The gender-based discrimination was found to be "indistinguishable from that invalidated in *Frontiero*. . . ."[200] Based on the " 'then generally accepted presumption that a man is responsible for the support of his wife and child.' "[201] the classification was not, the Court noted, "without empirical support."[202] Nonetheless, "the Constitution forbids the gender-based differentiation premised upon assumptions of dependency made in the statutes before us. . . ."[203] The purpose of survivor's benefits is, the Court found, to provide care for the deceased worker's family. This being the case,
130 "the gender-based discrimination . . . is entirely irrational. The classification discriminates among surviving children solely on the basis of the sex of the surviving parent."[204]

Like the invalidated survivor's benefits provision, the Public Health Service regulations make assumptions about dependency. They make further assumptions about capabilities as well. Not only do they assume that non-Indian wives are dependent upon their Indian husbands, but they also assume that Indian husbands are incapable of providing health care independently. At the same time, they presume that no non-Indian husbands are dependent on their Indian wives and that they always have the resources to provide for their own medical care. Such generalizations about dependency and individual capabilities are overbroad and, when considered in relation to the purposes underlying the Indian Health Service, are irrational as well. Obviously the Indian Health Service exists primarily to provide health care to Indians living on the reservation and in certain cities.[205] If this is its only function, then non-Indians should never be treated. If it also wishes, however, to provide all families with Indian members with health care, then all non-Indian spouses should be serviced. If, in fact, Indian Health Service care is predicated on the actual need and dependency of non-Indian spouses, then the dependent non-Indian spouse in need should be provided with IHS benefits regardless of his or her sex. Otherwise, such service should be available to all non-Indian spouses or to none.[206] As it now stands, the gender-based distinction found in Section 36.12(c) denies the non-Indian husbands of Indians the equal protection guaranteed by the fifth amendment.

Jurisdiction and the Dakota Woman

Federal legislation and administrative regulations do not in themselves fully explain the contemporary legal status of the Dakota woman specifically or the American Indian woman generally. Accompanying the government's frequently changing, often inconsistent Indian policy have been shifting conceptions of federal, state, and tribal jurisdictions. Not only is the law relating to similar offenses different in the three jurisdictions, but, after years of varying policies, the boundaries between the jurisdictions are unclear. Because the areas of domestic relations, inheritance, and criminal law are frequently subjects of overlapping jurisdictions and because they often directly affect the rights of Indian women, it is necessary to analyze this jurisdictional labyrinth and the rights, liabilities, and inconsistencies arising from it.[207]

131

Background

Underlying all consideration of tribal authority and jurisdiction is the basic principle that ". . . those powers which are lawfully vested in an Indian tribe are not, in general, delegated powers granted by express acts of Congress, but rather inherent powers of a limited sovereignty which has never been extinguished."[208] Treaties and statutes, therefore, have served not to bestow, but rather to limit, Indian tribal sovereignty. This congressional power of limitation was based on the "domestic dependent"[209] status of Indian nations and Congress' power "to regulate commerce with . . . the Indian tribes."[210]

As early as 1793, Congress began to limit tribal jurisdiction over offenses occurring in Indian country. In order to promote friendly relations with Indian tribes, it made crimes and trespasses committed by non-Indians in Indian territory against the person or property of Indians definable and punishable by the law of the non-Indian's home state or territory.[211] This provision was reenacted with very little modification three years later.[212] In addition, however, the 1793 act provided for the extradition of such non-Indian offenders to the territorial districts "to be proceeded against in due course of law."[213] Indian sovereignty was further restricted by an 1817 act which extended federal jurisdiction to "any Indian or other person or persons" who committed acts within Indian territory which would be crimes if committed in any place "under the sole and exclusive jurisdiction of the United States."[214] Nothing in the act, however, was to be ". . . so construed as to affect any treaty now in force between the United States and any Indian nation, or to extend to any offence committed by one Indian against another within any Indian boundary."[215]

Tribal jurisdiction was somewhat reinstated in cases involving Indian offenders in 1854 when it was legislated that punishment was not to extend "to any offence" committed by an Indian "in the Indian country who has been punished by the local law of the tribe."[216] This tribal jurisdiction over offenses perpetrated by Indians remained undisturbed until the passage of the Seven Major Crimes Act discussed earlier.[217]

Attempts to limit tribal sovereignty by the imposition of federal and state jurisdiction continued until 1934, when the government's policy changed from one of assimilation and termination to one of recognition of Indian culture and sovereignty. With the passage of the Indian Reorganization Act (otherwise known as the Wheeler-Howard Act),[218] Indian tribes were allowed to incorporate and draw
132 up formal constitutions. Because they were all based on the same model, Dakota constitutions are quite similar. Provisions for tribal courts and the appointment of judges were included in these constitutions.[219]

Following World War II, the government's Indian policy once again reversed itself and became one of relocation and termination. Consistent with this policy, Congress passed Public Law 280,[220] which gave California, Minnesota, Nebraska, Oregon, and Wisconsin full civil and criminal jurisdiction over offenses committed on most of the Indian lands within their boundaries and empowered other states desiring to assume such jurisdiction to do so by amending their state constitutions. This period was marked by jurisdictional confusion as states attempted the unilateral assumption of civil and criminal jurisdiction on reservations.[221] It also saw the termination of the Menominee Reservation, which proved disastrous both for the Menominee Indians and for the state of Wisconsin.[222] The mounting and vociferous opposition on the part of Indian leaders to the state assumption of jurisdiction over Indian lands,[223] as well as various congressional hearings on Indian constitutional rights and tribal government led to the passage of Public Law 90-284 on April 11, 1968.[224] An amendment to the 1964 Civil Rights Act, Public Law 90-284 included sections which specifically related to Indians and which both extended and limited the power of tribal self-government. Section 7 of Public law 280 was repealed and assumption of state civil and criminal jurisdiction was made contingent on "the consent of the Indian tribe occupying the particular Indian country or part thereof which could be affected by the assumption."[225]

With this option either to continue to exercise or to resume civil and limited criminal jurisdiction, came various restraints. A modified Bill of Rights was imposed by Title II[226] on tribal governments and courts. Tribal courts were further limited in the exercise of their judicial powers by a stipulation that they "in no event" could "impose for convictions of any one offense any penalty or punishment greater than imprisonment for a term of six months or a fine of $500 or both."[227] While the original Dakota Indian Reorganization Act constitutions did not have Bill of Rights provisions, amendments were added either just prior to[228] or after the passage of Public Law 90-284 which incorporated Bill of Rights provisions.[229] Since the 1968 enactment of Titles II-VII of Public Law 90-284, there has been no legislation directly affecting the judicial power or the jurisdiction of Indian tribes.

Today the majority of Dakota women living on reservations live in South Dakota. They live in a state which, with one exception, does 133
not have civil or criminal jurisdiction over Indians on reservations.[230] South Dakota reservations have their own tribal courts or operate under a court of Indian offenses.[231] By examining the code of one South Dakota reservation,[232] it is possible to see the effect of the tripartite jurisdictional structure on the legal status of the Dakota woman living on that reservation.[233]

Domestic Relations, Inheritance

Of all the powers which have been subject to congressional limitation, the tribe's power "to regulate the domestic relations of the members of the tribe"[234] has been the power least diminished by congressional enactment. This power has extended not only to the regulation of marriage and divorce, but to the offenses of bigamy, adultery, illicit cohabitation, and child custody.

As was noted earlier,[235] Congress recognized the validity of custom marriages in the late nineteenth century for purposes of determining the legitimacy of heirs. The legislatures of both the Dakota Territory and, subsequently, the state of South Dakota acknowledged that "Indians contracting marriage according to Indian custom and cohabiting as husband and wife . . . [are] . . . lawfully married."[236] Even so, the one South Dakota case touching on the validity of custom marriage found what appears to have been a traditional Dakota marriage and divorce invalid for lack of evidence. The standard set by the court was decidedly not Indian.[237]

> Granting that an agreement to live together, followed by cohabitation, constitutes the Indian custom marriage, it was necessary to prove that Sam and Alice made an express agreement of that

> character, and actually lived together pursuant thereto, and not otherwise. Such a marriage must be evidenced by words disclosing a meeting of the minds, uttered in the present tense for the purpose of establishing the relation of husband and wife, and, until they have lived together as such, the contract is not complete.[238]

Although federal statute and the Code of Federal Regulations[239] continue to recognize the legitimacy of custom marriages, such marriages no longer legally exist in terms of tribal law among the Dakota. Following the Indian Reorganization Act,[240] the drafters of the Oglala Sioux Tribal Code, for example, included in the Code the provision that "Indian custom marriage and divorce consummated after February 20, 1937, shall not be recognized."[241] Consent ". . . alone will not constitute a marriage. It must be followed by a solemnization."[242] For the most part, state statutes regulating marriage and
134 divorce have been adopted for tribal use.[243] This adoption of state laws and standards has been interpreted to mean a surrender of exclusive jurisdiction by the tribe. In two recent Montana cases, the state was found to have both subject matter and personal jurisdiction over enrolled Indians, living on reservations, in divorce actions initiated in state courts. Even though Montana does not have civil jurisdiction over its Indian reservations, the Montana Supreme Court held in *State ex rel. Iron Bear v. District Court*[244] and *Bad Horse v. Bad Horse*[245] that the 1938 and 1937 tribal adoptions of provisions requiring all marriages to be in accordance with the laws of the state of Montana relinquished tribal sovereignty over divorce action. It was further held that the failure of the state to exercise this jurisdiction would be a denial of equal protection. In light of these decisions, it is highly improbable that, where custom marriages and divorce have been replaced by marriage and divorce which conforms to state law, tribes have exclusive jurisdiction over this aspect of domestic relations any more.

Crimes such as adultery, bigamy, illicit cohabitation, which are not included among the Major Crimes, which arise out of domestic relations, and which occur among members of Indian tribes[246] within Indian country,[247] have been held by the courts to be within the exclusive jurisdiction of the tribal courts. This jurisdiction was affirmed by the United States Supreme Court in *United States v. Quiver*,[248] when it held that the federal courts did not have jurisdiction over a case of adultery committed by two Indians living on a South Dakota reservation. Congressional policy, the Court noted, dictated that "... the relations of Indians among themselves—the conduct of one toward another—is to be controlled by the customs and laws of the tribe save when Congress expressly or clearly directs otherwise."[249]

In 1955, the United States District Court for Western South Dakota found *Quiver* controlling and upheld the validity of the plaintiff's convictions and sentences for adultery which had been handed down by the Pine Ridge Oglala Tribal Court. Those convictions were not a denial of due process of law and were handed down by a "duly constituted court having jurisdiction to try, convict, and punish enrolled members of the Oglala Sioux Tribe for the crime of adultery committed on the Pine Ridge reservation."[250] Unlike cases of marriage and divorce, this exclusive jurisdiction remains intact.

As a result of this exclusive jurisdiction, the Dakota woman who is a tribal member is liable under differing codes, depending upon whether she is residing on the reservation or off it. Under state law and the tribal code, adultery and prostitution are both criminal violations. For the most part, the two offenses are similarly defined.[251] 135
Because of the maximum sentences and fine provisions of the 1968 Indian Bill of Rights,[252] however, the sanctions which are mandated are vastly different. Under state law, "[e]very person guilty of the crime of adultery shall be punished by imprisonment in the state penitentiary not exceeding five years or by a fine not exceeding five hundred dollars, or by both such fine and imprisonment."[253] The adulterer or adulteress who is convicted under the tribal code, ". . . shall be sentenced to labor for a period not to exceed six months, or to a fine not to exceed $360.00, or to both such imprisonment and fine with costs."[254] While a conviction for prostitution carries with it the same sentence and/or fine as does a conviction for adultery under the tribal code,[255] the maximum sentences and fines under state law are considerably less.[256] Furthermore, while bigamy and knowingly marrying a bigamist are crimes under the South Dakota Penal Code,[257] they are not covered and presumably are not crimes under the present Rosebud Sioux Tribal Code. On the other hand, illicit cohabitation is a crime on the Rosebud,[258] but is not illegal under state law.[259] Similarly, giving venereal disease to another and bastardy are crimes with sentences and fines attached under the Rosebud Code,[260] while, under state law, they are conditions meriting quarantine/treatment or support payments and are not criminal per se. Therefore, the rights and liabilities of Dakota women and men enrolled in a tribe are different, depending upon whether they live on the reservation or off it, whether they are subject to tribal jurisdiction or state law. These differing rights presumably reflect distinct cultural values and social concerns. That they can exist attests to the continuing sovereignty of the tribe and its jurisdiction over its members.

Tribal courts exercise probate jurisdiction over all the property the

tribe's members possess except lands which are held in trust by the United States.[261] Trust lands come under the jurisdiction of the Secretary of the Interior and wills and estates disposing of such lands are probated by the Department.[262] Wills devising trust lands must be approved by the Secretary of the Interior. The question of whether state law or tribal custom should be applied to determine the descent of nontrust property is not, on South Dakota reservations, an issue. According to the Rosebud Code, in determining heirs, ". . . shall apply the laws of the State of South Dakota unless the custom of the tribe is clearly to the contrary."[263] Since inheritance of material wealth was unknown to the Dakota peoples, it is obvious that "no custom of the tribe" could be established which is "clearly to the contrary." Absent such custom, intestate succession is the same whether the estate is probated by the tribal court or a state court.[264]
136 There are no dower or curtesy rights connected with Rosebud probate of nontrust property nor do any such rights arise under South Dakota law.[265] There is, however, a homestead exemption.[266] Since the intestate descent of trust lands involves a determination of appropriate state law and, hence, "a determination of any rights of dower, curtesy or homestead which may constitute a burden upon the interest of the heirs,"[267] the intestate descent of Dakota trust lands can be subject to the homestead exemption. Trust lands which are devised, however, are not subject to such interests. As early as 1921, Section 373 of Title 25 of the United States Code[268] was held to deny the widower of a testate Indian Oklahoma's rights of curtesy. The Supreme Court agreed with the circuit court that

> . . . it was the intention of Congress that this class of Indians should have the right to dispose of property by will under this act of Congress, free from restrictions on the part of the State as to the portions to be conveyed or as to the objects of the testator's bounty, provided such wills are in accordance with the regulations and meet the approval of the Secretary of the Interior.[269]

While frequently condemned,[270] this unfettered ability of Indians to devise restricted lands has been subsequently reaffirmed by the Supreme Court, and the Secretary's ability to disapprove such wills has been limited to wills technically deficient or irrational.[271] Under South Dakota law, the devise of a homestead is "subject to the rights of the surviving husband or wife as declared by law."[272] The devise of trust lands is not. Unless a spouse dies intestate, the surviving Dakota spouse is deprived of the financial security of a homestead interest unless trust lands were specifically willed to her or him.

Criminal Law

Without question, the greatest jurisdictional ambiguity is found between the tribal and the federal spheres of criminal law and directly involves the Indian woman. As was noted in the discussion of federal legislation earlier, the government has enumerated 13 "Major Crimes" over which it has jurisdiction when their commission occurs in Indian country and involves at least one Indian.[273] Two of the 13 Major Crimes are also offenses under the Rosebud Tribal Code.[274] Those two offenses, "Assault with Intent to Commit Rape"[275] and "Carnal Knowledge of a Female under Sixteen,"[276] carry with them the maximum sentence and/or fine of "labor for a period not to exceed six months or to a fine not to exceed $360.00 or . . . both such imprisonment and fine, with costs."

The tribal court claims jurisdiction over all offenses when committed by a member of the tribe and nonmember Indians who are members of any recognized tribe under federal jurisdiction.[277] With 137
respect to offenses "over which the Federal . . . courts may have lawful jurisdiction," the Code describes its jurisdiction as "concurrent and not exclusive."[278] Its jurisdiction is, in fact, that.[279] A Rosebud family may decide to prosecute their teenage daughter's Indian boy friend for what was probably a consensual act of intercourse. Instead of the FBI, the tribal police make the arrest and the boy is dealt with under the tribal code through the tribal courts.[280] A subsequent charge of carnal knowledge under Section 1153 of Title 18 is not brought, both because under Section 1152[281] the offender has been dealt with by the local law of the tribe, and because to bring the same charges in federal court after their disposal by the tribal court might possibly raise an issue of double jeopardy.[282]

The validity of this concurrent jurisdiction has never been directly tested. As a purely practical matter, it is unlikely that the federal courts and government prosecutors would willingly see the federal government assume exclusive jurisdiction over all petty theft, grand larceny, consensual sexual intercourse involving minor girls, as well as first-degree rape. This being the case, however, it would theoretically be possible for a tribal court to assume jurisdiction over, indict, prosecute, and convict an Indian who brutally attempted to rape an Indian woman. Even though the maximum penalty which could be imposed would be a six-month jail sentence and a $360 fine,[283] subsequent federal prosecution would be barred because the offense was committed by one Indian against the person of another Indian and because the offender had been punished by the law of the tribe.[284] If Congress were formally to acknowledge that concurrent federal-tribal jurisdiction over at least some of the Major Crimes does—and, practically, must—exist, then it could also eliminate the present ambiguities. Congress could, for example, establish guidelines stating when the jurisdiction of federal courts is preferred and when jurisdiction should be left to tribal courts. It might also provide for a binding-over procedure in cases where the tribal court penalties would be inadequate or for a formal removal process. If this were done, the problem of federal or tribal jurisdiction would be solved, not by which forum exercised its jurisdiction first, but by the seriousness and the nature of the crime.

The Dakota Indian Woman Today

Despite the government's many efforts to civilize, assimilate, and terminate it, Dakota culture did not die. As was noted before,[285] on
138 the reservation, *tiyospaye* members settled together, frequently taking adjoining allotments. Because the traditional communal functions of the *tiyospaye* have been assumed by the Bureau of Indian Affairs and/or the tribal council, the *tiyospaye* as such has become weaker and "is disappearing from Dakota life."[286] Nonetheless, the strong sense of family ties and kinship endures. Children are still, to a great extent, reared along traditional patterns, with all relatives both loving and willing to care for an individual child.[287] There is, indeed, no such thing as an unwanted Dakota child.[288] As was the case in prereservation times, the old are venerated and there is strong filial respect and devotion. Despite much effort,[289] native Dakota religion has never been totally supplanted by orthodox Christianity. At best, the Christianity at first practiced by the Dakota Indians was highly syncretistic, combining "elements" of the "native religion, such as continuous seeking for supernatural aid, divine or miraculous cures, social participation, and moral behavior."[290] It continues to be syncretistic. In addition, there is a renewed interest among many young Dakota Indians in the native religion and, especially, in the vision-seeking rites. Above all, the fundamental values of hospitality and generosity have never been extinguished. Even though Dakota reservation life has been characterized by abject poverty, no Dakota Indian would think of refusing someone in need.[291] The formal give-away is still practiced on Dakota reservations[292] and the accumulation of material possessions remains suspect.[293]

Even though the most fundamental values of Dakota culture still endure, the roles of men and women, primarily for economic reasons, have changed and shifted. When hunting, the traditional Dakota means of subsistence, was constructively prohibited, both by the es-

tablishment of reservations as well as by the wanton destruction of the buffalo herds by white settlers, the traditional role of the Dakota male was effectively destroyed. Nothing has ever satisfactorily replaced the hunting economy.[294] Agriculture had little initial appeal and, given the semi-arid conditions of the reservation lands, particularly in western South Dakota, it was and is a practical impossibility. Furthermore, the land base is simply too limited to support the population by agricultural production. Ranching, for which the land is obviously suited, was successfully practiced by reservation Indians in western South Dakota at the turn of the century and before the lands were allotted.[295] "Large tribal herds had shared the reservation lands with private herds run chiefly by mixed bloods or white men who had married into the tribe." During this period, "most of the beef issued by the government was bought from the Indians."[296] When the reservation land had been parceled and al-
lotted, the raising of individual herds on the small allotments began 139
to pose serious ecological problems.[297] Fearing the possible erosion of the land and taking advantage of the inflated World War I beef prices, the government encouraged the Indians to sell their herds. Indians "... [were] also permitted for the first time to kill their own stock for their own consumption. By 1918 most of the Indian herds had disappeared, and grazing lands were under lease to white cattlemen."[298]

Reservation lands are still, for the most part, leased to non-Indian ranchers and farmers. There is neither the capital nor the land for Dakota Indians to return to a cattle economy wholesale. With the destruction of the traditional male role came chronic unemployment, serious alcohol addiction, and more frequent divorce.[299] The role of the Dakota woman under these changed economic and social conditions was not so drastically altered as that of the man's. Her domestic and child-rearing duties continued unchanged. It was, in fact, through the exercise of the kinship structure that the cultural values were not totally destroyed. Dakota women did not actively participate in tribal government until the 1960's. Nonetheless, their traditional role as active advisers had never been abandoned and, from the beginning of reservations, women made their views known.[300] In his 1946 book, Gordon MacGregor reported:

> ... [Dakota] men have felt ... some resentment, some guilt, and much dissatisfaction, and they often become critical of and antagonistic toward women. On the other hand, the position of women in the family and in the community has risen, and their function in the family is often more important today than that of the men.[301]

While the hostility depicted by MacGregor is unquestionably overstated and inaccurate, it is nonetheless true that, over the years, many Dakota men have adopted a very traditionally white attitude toward women.[302] This attitude has been severely undermined in recent years. Two of the nine reservations in South Dakota have elected tribal chairwomen[303] and nearly all have had women judges and/or council members. Dakota women have also been the plaintiffs challenging tribal procedures under the 1968 Indian Civil Rights Act.[304] Furthermore, the leaders and organizers among the off-reservation Indian communities in South Dakota are, for the most part, women. Less publicly visible, but clearly influential, are the women leaders in the American Indian Movement. In addition to their traditional roles, Dakota women are now assuming a vocal political role in government and organizations which, unlike the traditional political structure and the male societies, both affect them as women and as
140 Dakota Indians and which can use their expertise.

The present status of the Dakota Indian woman can be assessed statistically in terms of education, occupation, income—both in relation to the Dakota Indian man and in relation to the South Dakota population generally. Within South Dakota, out of an Indian population of 32,365, there are 16,489 Dakota Indian women.[305] Of these women, 11,596 live on the reservation, 4,893 off.[306] Like their white counterparts, Indian women in South Dakota have had more formal education than their men. The median years of school completed by Indian women over 25 is 10.1 compared to 9.7 for Indian men.[307] Even so, the educational level attained by Indian women is much lower than that achieved either by the population as a whole (12.1 years) or by non-Indian South Dakota women (12.3 years). According to the 1970 census, 42.3 per cent of adult South Dakota Indians were members of the labor force[308] (compared to 56.7 per cent of the whites and 67.8 per cent of the blacks). While the unemployment rate for whites was only 3.2 per cent and was 10.7 per cent for blacks, it was 20.7 per cent for the Indians.[309] Indians, who comprise 2.7 per cent of the total work force, account for 15.3 per cent of those unemployed.[310] The census data, however, indicates that it is easier for Indian women than Indian men to get employment. In the month prior to the reporting date, only one out of eight Indian women actually seeking work was unemployed, whereas one out of every four Indian men seeking work was unemployed.[311] This is true both because there are fewer Indian women in the labor force[312] and because there are household and service jobs available to Indian women.[313]

Despite their slight educational advantage over Indian men and their lower unemployment rate, Indian women in South Dakota have personal incomes which are less than those of Indian men. The median annual income for Indian women over 16 is $1,461. For Indian men over 16, it is $1,743 while, for a white woman over 14, it is $1,616, and for such a while male, $4,780. The median personal annual income on the largest reservations (Cheyenne River, Pine Ridge, and Rosebud) reflects a similar disparity. The median personal annual income for women on those reservations averages $1,251.33 and for men it is $1,711.33.[314] Not surprisingly, then, in 1969, 64.4 per cent of Indian families with a female head lived below the poverty level, while 50.7 per cent of Indian families with a male head were below that level. Among white South Dakota families, 29.4 per cent of those with a female head and 12.3 per cent of those with a male head, subsisted on incomes below the poverty level.[315]

Any analysis of the above data underscores the difficulty all Dakota 141
Indians have in finding employment and the particular obstacles Dakota Indian women face in finding adequately paying jobs.[316] Clearly, racial and sexual discrimination accounts for a large part of the off-reservation unemployment as well as the low incomes. In addition, such discrimination is found in housing, public accommodations, education, and public services. That this discrimination does indeed exist is indicated by the complaints filed with the South Dakota Commission on Human Rights. Although they represent 2.5 per cent of the population, Dakota Indian women have lodged 14 per cent of the 145 complaints filed with the Commission between July 1, 1972, to July 1, 1974.[317] Nine of the complaints filed alleged job discrimination, seven charged housing discrimination, two alleged discrimination in public accommodations, two complained of discrimination in education, and one complaint charged discrimination in public services. All of the complaints alleged discrimination based on race and two of these complaints also included an additional allegation of discrimination because of sex. One of these two complaints was from a woman who had lost her job and the other from a woman who was denied additional public assistance.[318] In addition to the individual complaints which have been filed with the Commission on Human Rights, the Commission itself has initiated five actions on behalf of both male and female Indians. Four of those complaints involved employment and led to two cease and desist orders against the employer, one conciliation favorable to the Commission, and one dismissal for no cause. A public service complaint is pending.[319]

That complaints have been filed, actions initiated, and orders issued on behalf of Dakota Indian women does more than attest to the actual discrimination revealed by the 1970 census data. It also

attests to a new willingness on the part of both Indian women and men to challenge the society which has, for so long, misunderstood, divided, abused, and oppressed them. In a similar fashion, the demeaning statutes and presumptive regulations which have been legislated and promulgated by that society and which have their origins in nineteenth-century misconceptions about and ignorance of the Indian woman will also be challenged. For, despite the misunderstanding, division, abuse, and oppression, the Dakota woman has lost neither her strength nor her pride. It is neither surprising nor remarkable, therefore, that, with other American Indian peoples, the Dakota Nation is actively fighting existing discrimination and vigorously reasserting its sovereignty and legal rights. That which the Dakota girl was told upon entering puberty has proved to be enduringly true: "No people goes down until their women are weak and dishonoured, or dead upon the ground . . . the honor of the people lies in the
142 moccasin tracks of the women."[320]

NOTES

1. M. Sandoz, These Were the Sioux 94-95 (1961) [hereinafter cited as Sandoz].

2. "Dakota" means "an alliance of friends." An informal alliance of three subtribes, the Dakota Nation was one of 11 Siouan-speaking Indian tribes. The three major tribes within the Dakota Nation were the Teton (which spoke the Lakota dialect), the Santee (Dakota dialect), and the Yankton (Nakota dialect). The Teton and Yankton were composed of bands (the Oglala, Sans Arc, Blackfoot, Miniconjou, Twokettles, Hunkpapa, and Brulé of the Teton; the Hunkpatina and Yanktonai of the Yankton) and the Santee of clans (the Mdewakantowan, Wahpeton, Wahpekute, and Sisseton) which, in turn, were made up of extended families or *tiyospayes*. "Each *tiyospaye* was a completely independent unit which served allegiance to the band (clan) and tribe but was not governed in any way by the higher structure, except in those cases where the people formed alliances for various purposes such as hunting, summer encampments, etc. There were no band or tribal chiefs; all positions in Dakota government were found within the *tiyospaye*." *J. Satterlee & V. Malan, History and Acculturation of the Dakota Indians* 9 (Bull. 613, South Dakota State University) [hereinafter cited as Satterlee & Malan]. All three tribes are called "the Sioux," although frequently only the Teton are meant. R. Hassrick, The Sioux 6 (1964) [hereinafter cited as Hassrick]. The name "Sioux" was given by the French and was derived from the Chippewa word *Nadewisou* which meant "treacherous snake." V. Driving Hawk Sneve, The Dakota Heritage 1 (1973) [hereinafter cited as Sneve]. The traditional name, Dakota, is preferred and is used in this paper.

3. Sandoz, *supra* note 1, at 94.

4. "Squaw" is from the Algonquian word *Squaas* meaning "woman." The word was "used by white men in a derogatory sense to reflect their opinion of Indian women." Sneve, *supra* note 2, at 16.

5. Witt, *Native Women Today*, 6 Civil Rights Dig. 19 (Spring 1974).

6. Unlike the Teton and Yankton Dakota Indians, the Santee (sometimes called the "Sioux of the East") were more sedentary and were agriculturalists. They had

permanent homes "made of bark with a gabled roof, known as a *tipi-tonka*," in addition to *tipis*. Politically, the clans (*see* note 2 *supra*) were more interdependent than the autonomous bands of the Teton and Yankton. They came together, each represented by a *wakicun* or counselor, to form a band council which, in turn, appointed temporary chiefs to be in charge of battles or hunts. Because the society depended upon farming as well as hunting, trapping, and fishing, the Santee women had the additional and exclusive responsibility of "tilling the soil." Otherwise, in terms of kinship, economics, government, and religion, all three Dakota subtribes were very similar. Satterlee & Malan, *supra* note 2, at 17.

7. *Id.* at 13.

8. J. Mirsky, *The Dakota*, in Cooperation and Competition Among Primitive Peoples 292 (M. Mead ed. 1937) [hereinafter cited as Mirsky].

9. Satterlee & Malan, *supra* note 2, at 14.

10. Hassrick, *supra* note 2, at 105.

11. For the Dakota, this relationship summed up ". . . the most idealistic expression of loyalty and love." The father-in-law or mother-in-law was a constant advocate for the daughter-in-law or son-in-law and gave her or him many gifts. These gifts, of course, were never directly given. Accordingly, it was ". . . a boast among old people that they . . . [were] . . . unable to describe a certain son or daughter-in-law, as they had 143
never looked at them." Mirsky, *supra* note 8, at 402, 403. For a detailed discussion of the behavior prescribed in other familial relationships, *see id.* 394-403; Hassrick, *supra* note 2, at 104-10.

12. A person's wealth was gauged by what he or she gave away to others. Accumulation of goods implied ". . . that the owner . . . [valued] . . . material objects more than relations—that goods . . . [meant] . . . more than kin. Such a person . . . [was] . . . greedy, such a person . . . [had] . . no prestige in the tribe." Mirsky, *supra* note 8, at 387-88.

13. *Id.* at 392.

14. This was undoubtedly possible because the Dakota were a content people. As a result, conjugal families were small (three or four children at the most) and each child was nursed until he or she was three years old. As long as a mother nursed, she abstained from intercourse with her husband. "Grown persons boast of the fact that they nursed until three or four as a sign of how much their parents loved them, how their mother valued them above sex." *Id.* at 418. Practically, this also meant that no woman had more than one child too young to run in the event of an enemy attack or a buffalo stampede. See Sandoz, *supra* note 1, at 86.

15. Sandoz tells how, upon her child's first cry, the Dakota woman gently caught the baby's nose between her finger and thumb, softly singing until the crying stopped. This was repeated at the first sign of a cry. "During the newborn minutes, that newborn hour, Indian children, boy and girl, were taught the first and greatest lesson of their lives: that no one could be permitted to endanger the people by even one cry to guide a roving enemy to the village or to spoil a hunt that could mean the loss of winter meat for a whole band or even a small tribe." Sandoz, *supra* note 1, at 24.

16. As noted by Black Elk: the parents ". . . were not sure but that their daughter might really want to be stolen." J. Neihardt, Black Elk Speaks 68 (1961) [hereinafter cited as Neihardt].

17. Sandoz, *supra* note 1, at 93.

18. If the man failed to prove the accusation his property was destroyed and he was driven out of the village. *Id.* at 56.

19. Hassrick, *supra* note 2, at 115.

20. Sandoz, *supra* note 1, at 75.

21. R. Lowrie, Indians of the Plains 79 (1954) [hereinafter cited as Lowrie].

22. The highest coup for Dakota males was bestowed for stealing horses. MIRSKY, *supra* note 8, at 405.

23. NEIHARDT, *supra* note 16, at 76.

24. MIRSKY, *supra* note 8, at 386.

25. *Id.* at 411.

26. *Id.* at 386.

27. SANDOZ, *supra* note 1, at 100.

28. *Id.* at 79: "Sometimes a man already very prominent in his own band brought the new bride to his village, but even chiefs have gone to their wife's people."

29. *Id.*

30. *Id.* at 99.

31. Translated by E. DELORIA, DAKOTA TEXTS 224 ff. (1932).

32. *Id.* at 231.

33. SANDOZ, *supra* note 1, at 90.

34. *Id.* at 82.

35. SNEVE, *supra* note 2, at 16.

36. SANDOZ, *supra* note 1, at 83.

144 37. HASSRICK, *supra* note 2, at 120-21. The fact that there were widows in the community who never remarried means that a woman could refuse the second marriage.

38. MIRSKY, *supra* note 8, at 396: "Such an arrangement is not an insult to a sister already married for the girl would live with her sister in any case. By the fact of marriage an illicit relationship is circumverted. Status is provided for both before the possibility of temptation arises."

39. This devotion is illustrated by Charles Eastman when he quotes Old White Bull, who was informed that he must choose between his two wives, only one of whom would be allowed to bear his name. " 'What!' he exclaimed, 'these two women are sisters, both of whom have been my wives for over half a century. I know the way of the white man; he takes women unknown to each other and to his law. These two have been faithful to me and I have been faithful to them. Their children are my children and their grandchildren are mine. All the people know that we have been happy together, and nothing but death can separate us.' " C. EASTMAN, FROM THE DEEP WOODS TO CIVILIZATION 184-85 (1916).

40. HASSRICK, *supra* note 2, at 118.

41. *Id.* at 119.

42. Among the Santee, divorce was more difficult and virtually nonexistent. Interview with The Right Reverend Harold Jones, Suffragan Bishop of South Dakota, Sioux Falls, S.D., June 30, 1974.

43. SANDOZ, *supra* note 1, at 81.

44. *Id.* at 49.

45. *Id.* at 82; HASSRICK, *supra* note 2, at 118-19.

46. HASSRICK, *supra* note 2, at 99-100.

47. SANDOZ, *supra* note 1, at 72.

48. MIRSKY, *supra* note 8, at 410.

49. Leader Charge, quoted in HASSRICK, *supra* note 2, at 119.

50. HASSRICK, *supra* note 2, at 48.

51. MIRSKY, *supra* note 8, at 395.

52. *See* note 39 *supra*.

53. A woman was not considered chaste if she had reneged on a promise to marry a man, given a man a present, or, obviously, had an affair. MIRSKY, *supra* note 8, at 410.

54. *Id.*

55. *Id.* A girl who fraudulently attempted to join the honored guests was dragged away.

56. *Id.*

57. In the case of the Santee, the women also cultivated. *See* note 6 *supra.*

58. "The women were digging turnips" is a frequent refrain in Neihardt, *supra* note 16.

59. For an exhaustive description of the traditional Dakota diet, *see* E. Nurge, *Dakota Diet: Traditional and Contemporary*, in The Modern Sioux 36-54 (1970).

60. Hassrick, *supra* note 2, at 179.

61. Mirsky, *supra* note 8, at 395.

62. While Dakota society tolerated and had a place for the male who preferred feminine work (the *winkte* was a transvestite, skilled in woman's work), there was no comparable place for the woman who preferred a man's work. "Rare cases . . . show that such women left the group and wandered by themselves." *Id.* at 417. The active male homosexual (as distinguished from the *winkte*) was also an outcast.

63. For an analysis of the types of gift giving—solicited, voluntary, charitable—*see id.* 388-89.

64. *Id.* at 396.

65. *Id.* at 397: "If a daughter of thirty-five tans the skins while her mother does the porcupine quillwork, people will say 'She tans at her age!' 'She is still doing embroidery!' " 145

66. Lowrie, *supra* note 21, at 97.

67. Sandoz, *supra* note 1, at 105.

68. Hassrick, *supra* note 2, at 42.

69. *Id.* at 42-43.

70. Mirsky, *supra* note 8, at 410.

71. The *tiyospaye* council of the Western Dakota was composed of elderly men who had great prestige because of their proven generosity and/or bravery in the hunt or war. One of these men was chosen to be chief. Based on the advice and wisdom of the council, the "shirtwearers" or "counselors," young men elected because of their skill in hunting and bravery in war, made the day-to-day decisions. Beneath the shirtwearers, the *wakicun* served the judicial functions of both judge and jury. The *tiyospaye*'s herald publicized the shirtwearer and *wakicun* announcements; the orderlies saw to the needs of the governing bodies while they were convening; the *akitcita* were the *tiyospaye* policemen. Satterlee & Malan, *supra* note 2, at 16.

72. Sneve, *supra* note 2, at 16.

73. Sandoz, *supra* note 1, at 91.

74. S. Steiner, The New Indians 215-16 (1968).

75. Sneve, *supra* note 2, at 35.

76. Sandoz, *supra* note 1, at 106.

77. *Id.* at 107.

78. J. Brown, The Sacred Pipe: Black Elk's Account of the Seven Rites of the Oglala Sioux 6 (1972) [hereinafter cited as Brown].

79. Hassrick, *supra* note 2, at 220.

80. See Brown, *supra* note 78, at 7, for a detailed exegesis of the Dakota ritual and theology.

81. Sandoz, *supra* note 1, at 53.

82. *Id.* at 94-95.

83. In explaining the rite, Black Elk said: "First, it is a little girl, and not an older person, who stands at the center and throws the ball. This is as it should be, for just as Wakan-Tanka is eternally youthful and pure, so is this little one who has just come from Wakan-Tanka, pure and without any darkness." Brown, *supra* note 78, at 137.

84. *Id.* at 127-38.

85. "Her alone they sing over." The ritual is set forth in *id.* 116-26.

86. *See id.* at 31-36.

87. *Id.* at 46.

88. According to Mirsky, women so gifted did not marry or they received such vision after being widowed. MIRSKY, *supra* note 8, at 410.

89. NEIHARDT, *supra* note 16, at 213-15.

90. The Dakota ". . . considered the whites a brutal people who treated their children like enemies—playthings, too, coddling them like pampered pets or fragile toys, but underneath like enemies to be restrained, bribed, spied on and punished, or as objects of competition between the parents, sometimes even to open quarrellings and worse over them." SANDOZ, *supra* note 1, at 25.

91. Although never formally ratified by the Senate because tribal assent to it was never obtained, the 1851 Treaty of Fort Laramie was nevertheless implemented by means of congressional appropriations. *See* 11 Stat. 749.

92. Treaty with the Different Tribes of Sioux Indians, Apr. 29, 1868, 15 Stat. 635.

93. NEIHARDT, *supra* note 16, at 79.

94. In a society where a person's possessions were given away at his or her death, it is difficult to speak of either patrilinear or matrilinear descent. Nonetheless, the fact
146 that most Dakota Indians associated with the mother's or wife's family "owned" the *tipis* and household goods points to the matrilinear structure of the society.

95. Treaty with the Different Tribes of Sioux Indians, Apr. 29, 1868, art. VI, ¶ 4, 15 Stat. 637.

96. *Id.*, art. XII, 639.

97. Following the passage of the Indian Appropriation Act (Act of Mar. 3, 1871, ch. 120, 16 Stat. 566), Indians were no longer recognized as independent nations and, therefore, were not capable of negotiating with the government by means of treaty.

98. Act of Feb. 28, 1877, ch. 72, 19 Stat. 254.

99. *Id.* Even so, room was left for future negotiation. "Sioux Indians" were not to be removed to Indian Territory ". . . until the same shall be authorized by an act of Congress hereafter enacted. . . ." *Id.* at 254-55.

100. *Id.*, art. 10, 257.

101. SANDOZ, *supra* note 1, at 80. An old chief protested using his father's name to his agent: "We have seen that the white man makes his women like toys, like pets. Now we see they are possessions, without names of their own." *Id.*

102. NEIHARDT, *supra* note 16, at 79. *Wasichu* was a Dakota word for white men.

103. V. DELORIA, JR., OF UTMOST GOOD FAITH 52 (1971) [hereinafter cited as DELORIA].

104. *See* H. SCHELL, HISTORY OF SOUTH DAKOTA 322-23 (1968) [hereinafter cited as SCHELL].

105. Act of Mar. 2, 1889, ch. 405, 25 Stat. 888.

106. The Yankton, Flandreau, and Sisseton-Wahpeton reservations had been created earlier by other treaties and agreements.

107. Act of Feb. 8, 1887, ch. 119, 24 Stat. 388. See text accompanying note 143 *infra*.

108. Act of Mar. 2, 1889, ch. 405, § 8, 25 Stat. 890.

109. Only 10 per cent of the adult Dakota males approved the agreement of 1889.

110. Act of Mar. 2, 1889, ch. 405, § 9, 25 Stat. 891.

111. Treaty with the Yancton Tribe of Sioux, Apr. 19, 1858, art. VII, 11 Stat. 746.

112. *Id.*

113. 109 U.S. 556 (1883).

114. This was despite the fact that the Laramie Treaty of 1868 had stipulated: "If bad men among the Indians shall commit a wrong or depredation upon the person or property of anyone, white, black, or Indian, subject to the authority of the United

States, and at peace therewith, the Indians herein named solemnly agree that they will, upon proof made to their agent and notice by him, deliver up the wrong-doer to the United States, to be tried and punished according to its laws. . . ." Treaty with the Different Tribes of Sioux Indians, Apr. 29, 1868, art. I, ¶ 3, 15 Stat. 635.

115. Act of Mar. 3, 1885, ch. 341, § 9, 23 Stat. 385.

116. *Id.*

117. REV. STAT. § 5345 (1875). "Every person who, within any of the places . . . specified . . . , commits the crime of rape shall suffer death."

118. Act of Jan. 15, 1897, ch. 29, 29 Stat. 487.

119. 28 CONG. REC. 3316 (1896).

120. Act of Jan. 15, 1897, ch. 29, § 5, 29 Stat. 487.

121. Act of Mar. 4, 1909, ch. 321, § 328, 35 Stat. 1151.

122. CONG. REC. 2596 (1909). Daniel MacMeekin has suggested [21 STAN. L. REV. 1236, 1247 (1969)] that the distinction probably rested more on the notion that intercultural rape was worse than intracultural rape, rather than upon a belief that Indian women were more immoral (after all, a white man raping an Indian woman was not exempted from the death penalty). Representative Norris' expressed views would seem, however, to be ample justification for the legislation. It is, first of all, highly unlikely
that a white man would have been prosecuted for the rape of an Indian woman in 1909, 147
and even less likely that he would be convicted. Second, if a belief that intercultural rape was more heinous than intracultural rape did, in fact, underlie the 1909 amendment, then a white man's raping of a white woman within the exclusive jurisdiction of the United States should have been similarly exempted from the death penalty. Clearly, the 1909 amendment can only be explained in terms of a legislative conviction in the immorality of the Indian woman.

123. 18 U.S.C. § 1153 (1970). Offenses committed within Indian country: "As used in this section, the offense of rape and assault with intent to commit rape shall be defined in accordance with the laws of the State in which the offense was committed, and any Indian who commits the offenses of rape or assault with intent to commit rape upon any female Indian within Indian country shall be imprisoned at the discretion of the court."

124. There are now Thirteen Major Crimes. In addition to murder, manslaughter, rape, assault with intent to kill, arson, burglary, and larceny, carnal knowledge of any female not sixteen and not one's wife, incest, assault with intent to commit rape, assault with a dangerous weapon, and assault resulting in serious bodily harm are also crimes.

125. *See* United States v. Rider, 282 F.2d 476 (9th Cir. 1960); United States v. Red Wolf, 172 F. Supp. 168 (D. Mont. 1959); Petition of McCord, 17 Alas. 162, 151 F. Supp. 132 (D. Alas. 1957); United States v. Jacobs, 113 F. Supp. 203 (E.D. Wis. 1953). Virtually alone in holding that where a state law defines the carnal knowledge of a female under the age of consent and not one's wife as "rape," then its commission should be included under § 1153, was the court in United States v. Red Bear, 250 F. Supp. 633 (N.D.S.D. 1966).

126. For the legislative history of the law, *see* Senate Report No. 1770, 89th Cong., 2d Sess., U.S. CODE CONG. & ADMIN. NEWS, 3653, 3655 (1966).

127. Act of Nov. 2, 1966, Pub. L. 80-707, 80 Stat. 1100.

128. 394 F.2d 96 (9th Cir. 1967).

129. *Id.* at 97-98.

130. 18 U.S.C. 2031 (1970). Special maritime and territorial jurisdiction. "Whoever, within the special maritime and territorial jurisdiction of the United States, commits rape shall suffer death, or imprisonment for any term of years or for life."

131. 394 F.2d 96, 98 (9th Cir. 1967).

132. *Id.* at 98-99.

133. Henry v. United States, 432 F.2d 114 (9th Cir. 1970) dealt with the appeal of an Indian convicted under 18 U.S.C. § 1152 (*see* note 135 *infra*) and 18 U.S.C. § 2031 (*see* note 130 *supra*) for raping two non-Indian girls on the reservation. The court found that the indictment had been erroneously brought under § 1152 and that Henry should have been prosecuted for violation of § 1153. Nonetheless, it held that because the elements of the crime were the same under both sections, Henry had suffered no harm and was not denied due process. Although the court cited *Gray* in its decision, the issue of the constitutionality of § 1153's provision providing for different punishment depending on the race of the victim was never raised or considered.

134. 347 F. Supp. 1031 (D.N.M. 1972).

135. 18 U.S.C. § 1152 (1970). Laws governing: "Except as otherwise expressly provided by law, the general laws of the United States as to the punishment of offenses committed in any place within the sole and exclusive jurisdiction of the United States, except the District of Columbia, shall extend to the Indian country.

"This section shall not extend to offenses committed by one Indian against the person or property of another Indian, nor to any Indian committing any offense in the Indian country who has been punished by the local law of the tribe, or to any case
148 where, by treaty stipulations, the exclusive jurisdiction over such offenses is or may be secured to the Indian tribes respectively." While this exclusive jurisdiction applies to a white man committing a crime against an Indian, it does not apply to a white man committing a crime in Indian country against another white. *See* New York *ex rel.* Ray v. Martin, 326 U.S. 496 (1946); Draper v. United States, 164 U.S. 240 (1896); United States v. McBratney, 104 U.S. 621 (1881).

136. 18 U.S.C. § 113 (1970). Assaults wthin maritime and territorial jurisdiction: "Whoever, within the special maritime and territorial jurisdiction of the United States, is guilty of an assault shall be punished as follows: . . .

"(c) Assault with a dangerous weapon, with intent to do bodily harm, and without just cause or excuse, by fine of not more than $1,000 or imprisonment for not more than five years, or both."

137. 347 F. Supp. 1031, 1033 (D.N.M. 1972).

138. *Id.* at 1034, citing Bolling v. Sharpe, 347 U.S. 497, 499 (1954).

139. *Id.* at 1035. The court's statement, of course, embodies the fourteenth amendment, suspect classification (here racial) equal protection test. While the court employs an equal protection analysis, it finds a fifth amendment due process violation. This is because a federal, not a state, statute is being challenged. The court found precedent for such an analysis in Bolling v. Sharpe, 347 U.S. 497 (1954), where the Supreme Court held that racially segregated public schools in the District of Columbia deprived black pupils of due process of law under the fifth amendment. In *Bolling,* the Supreme Court concluded: "In view of our decision that the Constitution prohibits the states from maintaining racially segregated public schools, it would be unthinkable that the same Constitution would impose a lesser duty on the Federal Government." *Id.* at 500.

140. A white person prosecuted under Section 1152 for the rape of an Indian woman in Indian territory would have similar standing to question the constitutionality of Section 1153, which permits Indian men convicted of the identical crime to be "imprisoned by the discretion of the court" while he, because of his race, is subject to the death penalty under 18 U.S.C. § 2031. There is, however, no record of such a conviction having been upheld (in Williams v. United States, 327 U.S. 711 (1946), the conviction of a white man for the rape of an Indian girl "under 18" was overturned). As a result, there has never been a challenge to the punishment imposed.

141. Given the traditional Dakota views about premarital chastity and marital fidelity, no assumptions could be farther from the truth.

142. Act of Feb. 8, 1887, ch. 119, 24 Stat. 388.

143. See note 107 *supra* and accompanying text.

144. Act of Aug. 9, 1888, ch. 818, 25 Stat. 392 (codified at 25 U.S.C. §§ 181-83 (1970)).

145. 19 CONG. REC. 6885-86 (1888). The congressional debate is most illuminating:

"MR. BUCHANAN. I would like to inquire of the gentleman from Arkansas what is the overwhelming necessity for the passage of this bill, what constitutional power we have to pass it, and what great benefits to the country are to result therefrom?

"MR. ROGERS. The bill proceeds on the theory that the worst element to be found among the Indian tribes is that class of white men who are willing to sacrifice everything like civilization for the purpose of getting beyond the law and gaining headrights among the Indian tribes beyond the jurisdiction of the courts.

"Mr. Lamar stated . . . that the Department of the Interior found more trouble in preserving peace, order, and quiet among the Indian tribes because of the presence of this disturbing element than from any other cause that could be mentioned in connection with the subject.

. . .

"The object and purport of this bill, therefore, is that if these parties intermarry, if a 149
man wants to abandon civilization and going into that country and marrying a squaw to get a head-right, he shall not get it; but if he married he makes the squaw a citizen of the United States also. We are making citizens of the United States instead of making Indians of our citizens. I do not know any other reason that I could give beyond that.

"MR. BUCHANAN. If a squaw marries a white person, does she become a citizen of the United States?

"MR. ROGERS. He remains a citizen and she becomes a citizen of the United States.

"MR. BUCHANAN. Does the gentleman think that addition to our citizenship would be very desirable?

"MR. ROGERS. I think it is not highly desirable. In seven cases of ten where this class of people go into Indian Territory, instead of elevating the Indians they do them harm. They come out of there in a year with feather[s] in their hats, with revolvers buckled around them, and a pair of Texas spurs, whooping and yelling whenever they can get drink. If a white and an Indian both want to marry, let them come back into a State and we will civilize both together.

. . .

"MR. PARKER. . . . If in the State where women have the right to vote, the squaw becomes a voter. Is that so?

"MR. ROGERS. I should think so. That would be a very rare case; but I think it would be the case under this bill.

"MR. PARKER. And also that these degenerate men . . . will be citizens of the United States, while the Indian who has been so romantically described with wonderful physical capacity, would be civilized, but only have the rights of a barbarian, while the degenerate white and his degenerate progeny will become citizens of the United States.

"MR. EZRA B. TAYLOR. Is not the object of this bill to prevent the marriage of miscegenation of these degenerate whites with the Indian squaws?

. . .

MR. WEAVER. The effect of the bill is to encourage Indians to marry white men and become citizens of the United States.

"MR. PARKER. . . . . It seems to me that this is at least subject to the query whether this bill does go pretty far; and I would like the gentleman from Arkansas to state the result he expects to follow its enactment.

"MR. ROGERS. I have said about all I cared to say on this subject. I think the tendency and effect will be to keep white men out of the Indian Territory. They are deterring the Government in its efforts to civilize these people. That is my judgment as to the best result of it. I think the tendency will likewise be to prevent to a very large extent the intermarriage of these Indian women, because these men are not going to marry Indian women except for the purpose of obtaining a head-right. Many of them are fugitives from justice. Others are those who do not wish to pay their debts, and take their property there for the purpose of evading process of court. There are others who desire to marry these squaws in good faith; but let them come back to the confines of civilization, a higher civilization than there is among the tribes of Indians. These are the main benefits to be derived. It is not a bad measure. I think that it involves a great deal of genuine philosophy in the treatment of Indian tribes. I think that it will be highly beneficial to keep that class of men out of the Indian Territory. The policy of this Government has been to keep them out, as they are intruders.

"This is simply in the line of our treaties to keep these people out of that country, and, in my judgment, they ought to be kept out. There is a class of persons who go there that are highly valuable. That is the class of industrious farmers who take their families into the Territory and become tenants of these people. By them they are taught agriculture, stock-raising, and all the ways of civilized society, and they are a
150 great benefit; but the rough class, the fugitives from justice and criminals, have no business in the Indian country. Instead of having civilizing influence they have a discivilizing influence. For these reasons I think the bill is fraught with a great deal of wisdom."

[The House then discussed the constitutionality of the measure.]

"Mr. Adams. The ground on which this bill is urged is the ground last stated by the gentleman from Arkansas. Mr. Rogers, that for reasons of public policy it is desirable to discourage marriages between white men and Indian women. I do not believe that is sound public policy. In the first place, if we are to discourage such marriages for the moral welfare of the Indian woman, the answer is that the United States has nothing to do with that question; and if we are to discourage such marriages for the purpose of expediting the civilization of the Indian tribes, then I say that the white man who goes into the Indian nation and marries an Indian woman, however degraded he may be, is likely to be more an instrument of civilization than a full-blooded Indian.

. . .

"Mr. Peters. One of the motives that induce a man to marry an Indian woman is that he may obtain certain rights under the tribe into which he marries, a head-right, for instance. That, I say, is one of the baser sort to intermarry with Indians—and this is the one that actuates the baser sort to intermarry with Indians—another motive is that he may become a part of the tribe, subject to tribal law, and may thereby put himself outside of the civilized law, which he leaves when he marries into the tribe.

"In other words, the man who goes into one of these tribes and marries an Indian woman in nearly all cases becomes, as has been stated here, one of the worst and most degraded characters, even if he has not been such prior to the marriage; causes turmoil and disturbance in the tribe, and then, by reason of his superior education, or by reason of the fact that he is white man, exercises his influence over the tribe to escape the punishment that ought to be visited upon him by the tribal law, knowing at the same time that he is not amenable to the laws of the United States. Now, one of the great objects of this bill is to continue that man's responsibility for any violation of United States law that he may commit, and to hold him to the same accountability under the law that he would have been held prior to the marriage.

"Mr. Adams. Are not the children of such a marriage likely to be a little nearer to civilization—which we hope to be the ultimate outcome—than the children of a full-blood Indian marriage?

"MR. PETERS. That depends entirely upon the influences by which they are surrounded. I do not believe that the children of such a marriage, by reason of the white blood that is in them, are in any manner superior to a full-blood Indian, so far as any tendency to civilization is concerned. It depends entirely on the associations and influences that surround them whether they will be any better or nearer to civilization than full-blood Indian children.

"If they are left to grow up with the tribe and to be influenced by its customs, they are often in a certain sense greater enemies to civilization than full-blood Indians. That has been my observation in all these cases. Some of the worst characters in the Indian Territory today are the descendents of white men, who went in there and married Indian women. Some of the worst characters, the vilest outlaws, men who violate every law known to humanity as well as to Christianity, are the children of white men who went among the Indians and intermarried with them. I would rather trust my life or my property to-day in the hands of a full-blood Indian than trust it in the hands of a half-breed who has been raised in the midst of the barbarous influences that surround many of those tribes."

146. Act of Aug. 9, 1888, ch. 818, § 1, 25 Stat. 392 (25 U.S.C. § 181 (1970)).

147. *Id.* § 2 (25 U.S.C. § 182 (1970)). In 1924, all noncitizen Indians "born within 151
the territorial limits of the United States" were made citizens. The conferring of citizenship was not "in any manner" to "impair or otherwise affect the right of any Indian to tribal or other property." Act 9, June 2, 1924, ch. 233, 43 Stat. 253.

148. SANDOZ, *supra* note 1, at 76. This had not always been the case. During the early contact with white culture, Dakota culture had dominated: "Before the arrival of the English-speaking plowman on the plains, the Dakota culture appeared destined to sweep the continent and absorb the French traders and frontiersmen in the process. Many of the Hudson Bay Company men had completely assimilated the Plains Indian culture, and the early frontiersmen usually became Indians at least in thought and habit." Satterlee & Malan, *supra* note 2, at 20.

Because of this acceptance of Dakota culture, there was no resistance to intermarriage on either side. "The French fur traders attached no stigma to marriage into the tribes, and the Dakota family who had a daughter married to a trader was looked upon with envy because she had gained an honorable position." French traders are still "mentioned as a class apart from other white people with whom the Dakota have been in contact." Satterlee & Malan, *supra* note 2, at 24.

Marriages where the non-Indian partner became part of the Indian culture continued to occur. The marriages which resulted in the Indian partner leaving the group were highly disfavored. If the women of such marriages ". . . returned to their people out on the buffalo plains they usually had to live in some lone little *tipi* at the edge of the village, a hanger-on, dependent upon the meat and hides divided with the needy, for in Sioux society so long as there was meat everyone ate. But for these women the meat came without the pride of contribution—a great humiliation." SANDOZ, *supra* note 1, at 76.

149. See note 145 *supra.*

150. While the right may have been automatic, the ritual by which citizenship was conferred prior to 1924 involved a complete renunciation of Indian culture. It is also a prime example "of the utter failure of white society to comprehend the nature and meaning of culture." DELORIA, *supra* note 103, at 92. The assumptions about Indian women implicit in the citizenship ceremony for an Indian woman reveal a profound ignorance of her role in traditional society. After a few opening remarks made by a representative from the Department of Interior, the individual woman (who had been required to forswear her Indian name) was addressed. As reproduced in Deloria: "Allie Fox Duncan (white name). Take in your hand this work bag and purse." (she takes

the work bag and purse.) "This means that you have chosen the life of the white woman—and the white woman loves her home. The family and home are the foundation of our civilization. Upon the character and industry of the mother and home maker largely depends the future of our Nation. The purse will always say to you that the money you gain from your labor must be wisely kept. The wise woman saves her money, so that when the sun does not smile and the grass does not grow, she and her children will not starve.

"I give into your hands the flag of your country. This is the only flag you have ever had or will ever have. It is the flag of free men, a hundred million free men and women of whom you are now one. That flag has a request to make of you—(white name), that you will take it into your hands and repeat these words:

"For as much as the President has said that I am worthy to be a citizen of the United States, I now promise to this flag that I will give my hands, my head, and my heart to the doing of all that will make me a true American. And now beneath this flag I place upon your breast the emblem of your citizenship. Wear this badge of honor always; and may the eagle that is on it never see you do aught of which the flag will not be proud. [The audience rises and shouts: 'Allie Fox Duncan (white name) is an American citizen.']" *Id.* at 93-94.

152 151. Act of Feb. 28, 1891, ch. 383, § 5, 26 Stat. 795 (codified at 25 U.S.C. § 371 (1970)).

152. *Id.*

153. Act of June 7, 1897, ch. 3, § 1, 30 Stat. 90 (codified at 25 U.S.C. § 184 (1970)).

154. 103 F. 348 (C.C. Mont. 1900).

155. *Id.* at 352.

156. 245 F. 411 (8th Cir. 1917).

157. *Id.* at 413-14.

158. *Id.* at 420.

159. In Reynolds v. United States, 205 F. 685 (D.S.D. 1913), the mother was the daughter of an Oglala woman and a white father. Because both she and her parents had lived with the tribe until her mother's death, she was found to be entitled to an allotment. Her children, however, had not lived with the tribe and had never been recognized by it. They were not entitled to allotments.

160. Act of June 7, 1897, ch. 3, § 1, 30 Stat. 90 (codified at 25 U.S.C. § 184 (1970)).

161. Farrell v. United States, 110 F. 942 (8th Cir. 1901).

162. *Id.* at 944.

163. Act of June 7, 1897, ch. 3, § 1, 30 Stat. 83 (codified at 25 U.S.C. § 274 (1970)).

164. Act of June 23, 1972, Pub. L. 92-318, § 901 (a), 86 Stat. 373.

165. Memorandum from Gilbert D. Roman, Director, Office for Civil Rights, Dep't of Health, Education and Welfare. Subject: Sex Discrimination in the Indian Health Service, Jan. 21, 1974, at 2 [hereinafter cited as Roman Memo].

166. Transferred from the War Department to the Department of the Interior in 1849, the BIA is in charge of administering Indian affairs. In 1921, the Snyder Act (Act of Nov. 2, 1921, ch. 115, 42 Stat. 208) authorized the BIA expenditure of funds for "the benefit, care, and assistance of Indians throughout the United States." Specifically, the appropriations were for

"General support and civilization, including education.

"For relief of distress and conservation of health.

"For industrial assistance and advancement and general administration of Indian property.

"For extension, improvement, operation, and maintenance of existing Indian irrigation systems and for development of water supplies.

"For the enlargement, extension, improvement, and repair of the buildings and grounds of existing plants and projects.

"For the employment of inspectors, supervisors, superintendents, clerks, field matrons, farmers, physicians, Indian police, Indian judges, and other employees.

"For the suppression of traffic in intoxicating liquor and deleterious drugs.

"For the purchase of horse-drawn and motor-propelled passenger-carrying vehicles for official use.

"And for general and Incidental expenses in connection with the administration of Indian affairs."

This "language of the act still provides one of the best summaries of BIA activities to be found." Wittstock, *The Bureau of Indian Affairs*, 6 Civil Rights Dig. 20 (Fall 1973).

167. Formerly under the BIA, the IHS was transferred to HEW and the Public Health Service in 1955. The IHS maintains hospitals and medical personnel both on the reservation and in some cities. The IHS is also involved in a number of experimental programs involving "community development, local employment, advanced 153
communications technology." *Id.* at 24.

168. For the history and a critique of the operation of BIA cash assistance as of 1968 (such assistance itself did not begin until 1944), *see* Wolf, *Needed: A System of Income Maintenance for Indians*, 10 Ariz. L. Rev. 597, 607-16 (1968) [hereinafter cited as Wolf].

169. U.S. Dep't of Interior, Bureau of Indian Affairs Manual § 3.1.1 (1966) [cited in M. Ward & S. Barlow, Your Right to Indian Welfare 6 (CCH Publication No. 45, U.S. Comm'n on Civil Rights, 1973) (hereinafter cited as Ward & Barlow)]. The stipulation that an Indian's eligibility for General Assistance depend on his or her living on the reservation was held by the Supreme Court to be an unauthorized limitation of the Snyder Act. Accordingly, General Assistance must be given to ". . . unassimilated Indians living in an Indian community near their native reservations, and who maintain close economic and social ties with that reservation." Morton v. Ruiz, 415 U.S. 199 at 211 (1974).

170. U.S. Dep't of Interior, Bureau of Indian Affairs Manual § 3.1.7B (1966) Ward & Barlow, *supra*.

171. *Id.* at 9.

172. *Id.*

173. *Id.*

174. According to Cooper & Dodyk, "Only a minority of States pay full need." Income Maintenance 260 (2d ed. 1973).

175. "You have a right to a fast decision on your request for assistance." *Id.* at 12.

176. 5 U.S.C. § 552 (a)(1) (1970). Public information; agency rules, opinions, records, and proceedings. "(a) Each agency shall make available to the public information as follows:

"(1) Each agency shall separately state and currently publish in the Federal Register for the guidance of the public—

. . .

"(D) substantive rules of general applicability adopted as authorized by law, and statements of general policy or interpretations of general applicability formulated and adopted by the agency."

177. U.S. Dep't of Interior, Bureau of Indian Affairs Manual § 1.2 (1968) (cited in Morton v. Ruiz, 415 U.S. 199, 233 (1974)).

178. *Id.* at 234.

179. *Id.* at 199, 232.

180. 42 C.F.R. § 36.12 (a)(c) (1974).

181. Roman Memo, *supra* note 165.

182. *See* note 165 *supra* and accompanying text.

183. Act of July 2, 1964, Pub. L. 88-352, 601, 78 Stat. 252, reads: "No person in the United States shall, on the ground of race, color, or national origin, be excluded from participation in, be denied the benefits of, or be subject to discrimination under any program or activity receiving Federal financial assistance." Discrimination on the basis of sex is not, it will be noted, included and BIA General Assistance and the Indian Health Services are federally operated, not just federally assisted, programs.

184. See note 139 *supra.*

185. Roman Memo, *supra* note 165, at 4.

186. Loving v. Virginia, 388 U.S. 1 (1967).

187. Roman Memo, *supra* note 165, at 4.

188. 404 U.S. 71 (1971).

189. 411 U.S. 677 (1973).

190. 404 U.S. 71, 76 (1971), citing Guana Co. v. Virginia, 253 U.S. 412, 415 (1920).

154 191. Roman Memo, *supra* note 165, at 3.

192. The leading case establishing the right of reservation Indians to receive state and county welfare is Acosta v. San Diego, 126 Cal. App. 2d 455, 272 P.2d 92 (1954).

193. Wolf erroneously implies that, because the BIA average payment per recipient in Fiscal Year 1968 was $30.50 and the "average for the states" was $44.65, the BIA pays less. Wolf, *supra* note 69, at 612-13. Indian reservations, for the most part, are not located in the few urban states which pay the full standard of need and which also have comparatively high standards of need. Within individual states, however, BIA General Assistance pays the entire deficit between actual income and the state computed standard of need. States, on the other hand, usually pay only a percentage of the standard of the deficit. See note 174 *supra.*

194. 413 U.S. 508 (1973).

195. *Id.* at 511.

196. *Id.* at 513.

197. *Id.* at 514, citing Vlandis v. Kline, 412 U.S. 411, 452 (1972).

198. *Id.*

199. Weinberger v. Wiesenfeld, 43 U.S.L.W. 4393 (Mar. 19, 1975).

200. *Id.* at 4395.

201. *Id.* at 4396, citing Hoskins & Bixby, Women and Social Security—Law and Policy in Five Countries, Social Security Administration Research Report No. 42, 77 (1973).

202. *Id.*

203. *Id.*

204. *Id.* at 4398.

205. See note 167 *supra.*

206. This, in fact, probably will be done. "The Public Health Division of the Office of the General Counsel informs me that all of Part 36 is being revised, and that a new section 36.12 will probably reflect our office's position, either by making all non-Indian spouses eligible or by making none eligible." Letter from Margot Champagne, Office of the General Counsel, Dep't of Health, Education and Welfare, Aug. 2, 1974.

207. Because the majority of those Dakota Indians living on reservations today live in South Dakota, this analysis will be considered with references to that state and its law.

208. O. Laymon, *Survey of the Constitution and By Laws of the Oglala Sioux Tribe,*

1955 (unpublished study in the University of South Dakota Library, Vermillion, S.D.) [hereinafter cited as Laymon].

209. Cherokee Nation v. Georgia, 30 U.S. (5 Pet.) 1, 17 (1831).

210. U.S. CONST. art. I, 8.

211. Act of July 22, 1790, ch. XXXIII, § 5, 1 Stat. 138.

212. Act of Mar. 1, 1793, ch. XIX, § 4, 1 Stat. 329.

213. *Id.* § 11.

214. Act of Mar. 3, 1817, ch. 92, § 1, 3 Stat. 383.

215. *Id.* § 2.

216. Act of Mar. 27, 1854, ch. XXVI, § 3, 10 Stat. 270.

217. See text accompanying notes 115-16 *supra.*

218. Act of June 18, 1934, ch. 576, 48 Stat. 984 (codified at 25 U.S.C. § 461-79 (1970)).

219. While purporting to strengthen traditional forms of self-government, the IRA constitutions were, in fact, alien to those forms. The Oglala Pine Ridge constitution is a case in point. The traditional Dakota system of government (*see* note 70 *supra*) had endured after the establishment of the reservations. The 1936 constitution was drafted by Oglala leaders assisted by a staff anthropologist and was based on a model drawn up
by Felix Cohen. The electoral process was distrusted and viewed as a threat by the 155
traditional leaders. Furthermore, the electoral districts established by the constitution not only failed to recognize the *tiyospayes* which continued to exist, but actually divided them.

Sixty per cent of the voters cast their ballots on the question of the constitution's adoption. The vote was 1,348 for and 1,041 against.

I. Grinnell, *The Tribal Government of the Oglala Sioux of Pine Ridge*, 47-49, 1959 (unpublished M.A. thesis in the University of South Dakota Library, Vermillion, S.D.) [hereinafter cited as Grinnell].

220. Act of Aug. 15, 1953, Pub. L. 280, ch. 505, 61 Stat. 588.

221. For an account of South Dakota's involved, but eventually unsuccessful, attempt to assume jurisdiction over the Dakota reservations, *see* Abourezk, Comment, *South Dakota Indian Jurisdiction*, 11 S.D.L. REV. 101 (1966).

222. *See* Ames & Fisher, *The Menominee Termination Crisis*, 2 JOURNAL OF THE WISCONSIN INDIAN RESEARCH INSTITUTE (Dec. 1966). The Menominee Tribe was terminated June 17, 1954. Other tribes which were terminated in 1954 were the Western Oregon, Klamath, Alabama Coushatta, Utah Utes, and Utah Paiutes. The Oklahoma Wyandottes, the Peoria, and Oklahoma Ottawa were terminated in 1956, the South Carolina Catawba in 1959, and the Nebraska Ponca in 1962.

223. "Tribes have been critical of Public Law 280 because it authorizes the unilateral application of state law to all tribes without their consent and regardless of their needs or special circumstances. Moreover, it appears that tribal laws were unnecessarily preempted and, as a consequence, there was no law and order in some tribal communities." S. Rep. No. 721, 90th Cong., 2d Sess. (1968) (reprinted in U.S. CODE CONG. & ADMIN. NEWS 1865-66 (1968)). It must also be added that a well-founded fear of the imposition of state taxes on Indian lands and the possible loss of those lands through forced sales also motivated the opposition to Pub. L. 280.

224. Act of Apr. 11, 1968, Pub. L. 90-284, 82 Stat. 73.

225. *Id.* Title IV, § 401(a), 82 Stat. 78. The repeal of section 7 of Public Law 280 did not, of course, affect the exercise of state jurisdiction over Indian reservations where it existed prior to and with the passage of the 1953 statute. It did affect those states which had unilaterally assumed jurisdiction after the law's enactment and has produced jurisdictional anomalies. *See, e.g.*, Schantz v. White Lightning, 368 F. Supp. 1070 (D.N.D. 1973). North Dakota had attempted to assume jurisdiction over its

Indian reservations on the basis of tribal or individual consent. There was no tribal consent, so after the repeal of Public Law 280, the state was forced to withdraw whatever jurisdiction over individuals it had secured. In *Schantz*, no court—federal, state or tribal—was found to have jurisdiction.

226. Act of Apr. 11, 1968, Pub. L. 90-284, § 201-203, 82 Stat. 77 (codified at 25 U.S.C. §§ 1301-1303 (1970)): "Title II—Rights of Indians

"Definitions

"Sec. 210. For purposes of this title, the term—(1) Indian tribe means any tribe, band, or other group of Indians subject to the jurisdiction of the United States and recognized as possessing powers of self government;

"(2) powers of self-government means and includes all governmental powers possessed by an Indian tribe, executive, legislative, and judicial, and all offices, bodies, and tribunals by and through which they are executed, including courts of Indian offenses; and

"(3) Indian court means any Indian tribal court or court of Indian offense.

"Indian Rights

"Sec. 202. No Indian tribe in exercising powers of self-government shall—

156 "(1) make or enforce any law prohibiting the free exercise of religion, or abridging the freedom of speech, or of the press, or the right of the people peaceably to assemble and to petition for a redress of grievances;

"(2) violate the right of the people to be secure in their persons, houses, papers, and effects against unreasonable search and seizures, nor issue warrants, but upon probable cause, supported by oath or affirmation, and particularly describing the place to be searched and the person or thing to be seized;

"(3) subject any person for the same offense to be twice put in jeopardy;

"(4) compel any person in any criminal case to be a witness against himself;

"(5) take any private property for public use without just compensation;

"(6) deny to any person in a criminal proceeding the right to a speedy trial, to be informed of the nature and cause of the accusation, to be confronted with the witnesses against him, to have compulsory process for obtaining witnesses in his favor, and at his own expense to have the assistance of counsel for his defense;

"(7) require excessive bail, impose excessive fines, inflict cruel and unusual punishments, and in no event impose for conviction of any one offense any penalty or punishment greater than imprisonment for a term of six months or a fine of $500, or both;

"(8) deny to any person within its jurisdiction equal protection of its laws or deprive any person of liberty or property without due process of law;

"(9) pass any bill of attainder or ex post facto law; or

"(10) deny to any person accused of an offense punishable by imprisonment the right, upon request, to a trial by jury of not less than six persons.

"Habeas Corpus

"Sec. 203. The privilege of the writ of habeas corpus shall be available to any person, in a court of the United States, to test the legality of his detention by order of any Indian tribe."

For extended discussion of various aspects of Title II, *see The Indian Bill of Rights and the Constitutional Status of Tribal Governments*, 82 Harv. L. Rev. 1343 (1969), and Coulter, *Federal Law and Indian Tribal Law: The Right to Civil Counsel and the 1968 Indian Bill of Rights*, 3 Colum. Survey of Human Rights L. 48 (1970-71).

227. Act of Apr. 11, 1968, Pub. L. 90-284, Title II, § 202 (7), 82 Stat. 77.

228. In Colliflower v. Garland, 32 F.2d 369 (9th Cir. 1965), the Ninth Circuit found jurisdiction and granted a writ of habeas corpus to an Indian detained by a tribal court. The court reasoned that, because the tribal court was federally assisted, the federal habeas corpus statute (28 U.S.C. § 2241 (1964)) could be invoked. This

decision, along with the belief that an upgrading of legal standards would stave off state jurisdictional takeover, accounts for the pre-1968 amendments.

229. *See, e.g.*, article X of the CONSTITUTION AND BY-LAWS OF THE ROSEBUD SIOUX TRIBE OF SIOUX DAKOTA which was adopted by Amendment XI, effective, May 2, 1966.

230. The exception is the Lake Traverse Reservation. In DeCoteau v. District of Columbia, 43 U.S.L.W. 4321 (Mar. 3, 1975), the Supreme Court held that the Lake Traverse Reservation had been terminated by an 1891 cession of unallotted land and that South Dakota has both civil and criminal jurisdiction on the Reservation.

231. Tribal courts have judges which are chosen under tribal law and written codes which have been drafted by the tribe and approved by the Secretary of the Interior. Courts of Indian Offenses differ from tribal courts in that the judges are appointed by the Secretary of the Interior and operate under rules drafted by him. Fretz, *The Bill of Rights and American Indian Tribal Governments*, 6 NATURAL RESOURCES J. 583 (1966). The Court of Indian Offenses organizational structure is found in 25 C.F.R. § 11 (1974). There is, in addition, a third type of Indian court which is completely traditional. It is not found among the Dakota, but, rather, exists only in the Rió Grande pueblos. Tribal courts are, in fact, frequently very different. The Rosebud Reservation, for example, "has an attorney sitting as judge . . . and . . . the criminal
157
trials are really criminal trials with incarceration in a most unpleasant jail the result of conviction." On the Navaho Reservation, by contrast, the tribal judges "often view their role in a 'criminal' prosecution as one of mediating between the defendant and the complainant and seeking a solution under which both parties walk out of the court happy." Price, *Lawyers on the Reservation: Some Implications for the Legal Profession.* 169 LAW AND THE SOCIAL ORDER 161, 174-75 (1969).

232. The Rosebud Reservation's ROSEBUD SIOUX TRIBAL CODE (1974) is the primary source used. Reference is also made to the OGLALA REVISED CODE of the Pine Ridge Reservation which was extensively analyzed in Laymon, *supra* note 208.

233. Generalizations are dangerous. Tribal codes differ and are extremely fluid. The Rosebud Code, for instance, is in the process of being revised at this writing. Nonetheless, the Rosebud Code illustrates the problem of concurrent as well as conflicting jurisdiction. In that sense, it does have more than just local applicability.

234. All but one of the Dakota IRA constitutions contain this phrase. *See* ROSEBUD CONST. AND BY-LAWS, art. IV, § 1(p) (1935); LOWER BRULE CONST. AND BY-LAWS, art. VI, § 1(p) (1935); OGLALA CONST. AND BY-LAWS, art. IV, § 1(q) (1936); SISSETON-WAPHETON CONST. AND BY-LAWS, art. VII, § 1(c) (1946). Only the FLANDREAU SANTEE CONST. AND BY-LAWS (1936) fails to mention the regulation of domestic relations.

235. See text accompanying notes 151-152 *supra*.

236. COMP. LAWS OF THE DAKOTA TERRITORY § 2541 (1887) and the REVISED CODES OF THE STATE OF SOUTH DAKOTA 43 (1903). This section was repealed Mar. 3, 1925, ch. 196, THE LAWS PASSED AT THE NINETEENTH SESSION OF THE LEGISLATURE OF THE STATE OF SOUTH DAKOTA, 213.

237. See text accompanying notes 26-27 *supra*.

238. Henry v. Taylor, 16 S.D. 425, 432-33 (1903). This case also presents other contrasts with traditional Dakota culture. Following his mother's death, the plaintiff went to live with and was "adopted" by his maternal uncle (the strongest relation in terms of obligation in Dakota culture existed between a brother and a sister, *see* text accompanying notes 11-12 *supra*. At the death of his uncle, the plaintiff claimed an undivided one-half interest (with his uncle's widow) in the uncle's property, both as an adopted son and as a nephew. Having affirmed that adoption of an heir must be in compliance with a statute (and the plaintiff's was not, of course), the South Dakota Supreme Court made the plaintiff's illegitimacy (it was his parents' custom marriage

which was found invalid) a bar to his being an intestate heir as nephew even though there was no question that he was his mother's child.

239. 25 C.F.R. § 11.27, .28 (1974).

240. See text accompanying notes 218-19 *supra*.

241. Revised Code of the Oglala Sioux Tribe, ch. III, § 27 (1939), quoted in Laymon, *supra* note 208, at 83.

242. *Id.* § 28 (quoted in *id.*)

243. At the time of Laymon's study in 1955, the only difference between the tribal code and South Dakota law on marriage and divorce was that there were no residency requirements on the reservation. *Id.* at 86. Along with custom marriage, therefore, traditional divorce has also been abandoned. Incompatibility, the major reason for divorce in traditional society, is not grounds for divorce under South Dakota state law, *see* S.D. Comp. Laws § 25-4-2 (1967).

244. — Mont. —, 512 P.2d 1292 (1973).

245. — Mont. —, 517 P.2d 893 (1974).

246. The tribal members need not be members of the same tribe as the tribal court. Section 1 of Chapter 1 of the Rosebud Sioux Tribal Code [hereinafter cited as R.S.T.C.] reads: "Sec. 1 Jurisdiction over persons

158 "The Rosebud Sioux Tribal Court or the Rosebud Reservation shall have jurisdiction over all offenses when committed by a member of the Tribe, and non-member Indians who are members of any recognized Tribe under Federal jurisdiction."

247. 18 U.S.C. § 1151 (1970). "Indian country defined."

"Except as otherwise provided . . . the term 'Indian country', as used in this chapter, means (a) all land within the limits of any Indian reservation under the jurisdiction of the United States government, notwithstanding the issuance of any patent, and, including rights-of-way running through the reservation, (b) all dependent Indian communities within the borders of the United States whether within the original or subsequently acquired territory thereof, and whether within or without the limits of a state, and (c) all Indian allotments, the Indian titles to which have not been extinguished, including rights-of-way running through the same."

248. 241 U.S. 602 (1916).

249. *Id.* at 605-606.

250. Iron Crow v. Oglala Sioux Tribe, 129 F. Supp. 15, 16 (D.S.D. 1955). The *Iron Crow* opinion contains an excellent summary of the history of tribal courts in general and of the Oglala tribal court specifically.

251. S.D. Comp. Laws § 22-22-17 (1967) defines adultery as ". . . the unlawful voluntary sexual intercourse of a married person with one of the opposite sex other than the husband or wife of the offender, and when the crime is committed between persons, only one of whom is married both are guilty of adultery." R.S.T.C., ch. 5, § 2 reads that ". . . [Adultery has been committed when] any Indian . . . [has] . . . sexual intercourse with another person of the opposite sex either of such persons being married to a third person. . . ." *Cf.*, Prostitution, S.D. Comp. Laws § 22-23-1 (1967) with R.S.T.C. ch. 5, § 37 (1974).

252. See note 226 and accompanying text.

253. S.D. Comp. Laws § 22-22-18 (1967).

254. R.S.T.C., ch. 5, § 2.

255. *Id.* § 37.

256. *See* S.D. Comp. Laws § 22-23-1 (1967).

257. *Id.*, 22-22-15, 22-22-16.

258. R.S.T.C., ch. 5, § 28.

259. As is the case in states with similar provisions, illicit cohabitation is seldom prosecuted.

260. R.S.T.C., ch. 5, §§ 25, 5.

261. Act of Feb. 14, 1913 ch. 55, 37 Stat. 678 (codified at 25 U.S.C. § 373 (1970)). For an overview of what the authors aptly call the "Indian Heirship Tangle," *see* Gilbert & Taylor, *Indian Land Questions*, 8 ARIZ. L. REV. 102, 111-16 (1966) which discusses the problems of the descent and devise of Indian trust lands.

262. "Special Rules Applicable to Proceedings in Indian Probate, Including Hearings and Appeals" are found in Subtitle A, Subpart D, 43 C.F.R. § 4.200 (1973). Intestate succession of allotted trust lands is determined according to the law of the state in which the property is located.

263. R.S.T.C., ch. 3, § 2.

264. *See* S.D. COMP. LAWS § 29-1-5 (1967).

265. *Id.*, § 29-1-3.

266. *Id.*, § 43-31.

267. 43 C.F.R. § 4.240 (5) (1973).

268. See note 151 *supra.*

269. Blanset v. Cardin, 256 U.S. 319, 326-7 (1921).

270. The most recent condemnation is found in Akers v. Morton, 499 F.2d 44 (9th Cir. 1974). The court was required to affirm the Secretary's approval of a will and to deny the widow Montana's dower rights over the trust lands devised by her 159
Indian husband. The affirmance and denial, however, were accompanied by a strong expression of the court's "dissatisfaction with this state of the law." *Id.* at 47. *Blanset* and its progeny, the court stated, ". . . produce the anamolous result that an Indian's devise of restricted land is less restricted than an Indian's (or a non-Indian's) devise of any other realty. He or she can will that property free from any state law designed to protect a surviving spouse, and there is no federal law that fills the state law gap. Although we cannot reconcile the result with the public policy expressed by state law establishing dower and curtesy rights or with the congressional intent to provide family homes for Indian allottees and their dependents, we are unable to avoid it." *Id.* at 48.

271. Tooahnippah v. Hickel, 397 U.S. 598 (1970).

272. S.D. COMP. LAWS § 43-31-27 (1967); *see also id.* § 30-20-1.

273. 18 U.S.C. §§ 1152, 1153 (1970).

274. A third crime, "theft" (R.S.T.C., ch. 5, § 42), is, for all practical purposes the equivalent of § 1153's "larceny."

275. R.S.T.C., ch. 5, § 45.

276. *Id.*, § 46.

277. *Id.*, ch. 1, § 1.

278. *Id.*, § 1.1.

279. For a discussion of this concurrent jurisdiction, *see* P. Taylor, *The Major Crimes Act: Exclusive Federal Jurisdiction or Concurrent Federal-Tribal Jurisdiction*, 1 INDIAN LAW REPORTER 52 (Mar. 1974).

280. Interview with Terry Pechota, Director, South Dakota Legal Services, in Mission, S.D., July 17, 1974.

281. See note 135 *supra.* Taylor (*supra* note 279, at 58), argues that, "The Major Crimes Act should be read in pari materia with the General Crimes Act (*i.e.*, 18 U.S.C. § 1152) and the Major Crimes Act be construed not as a withdrawal of tribal jurisdiction over the offenses enumerated but rather as a modification of the clause in the General Crimes Acts excluding federal criminal jurisdiction."

282. The Supreme Court has held that successive federal-state and state-federal prosecutions for the same crime do not constitute a violation of the fifth amendment double jeopardy prohibition. Bartkus v. Illinois, 359 U.S. 121 (1959) and Abbate v. United States, 359 U.S. 187 (1959). Such prosecutions, particularly when identical policies and the same evidence are involved, have been sharply criticized by commen-

tators who believe that re-prosecutions for the same crime—even though by different sovereignties—are barred by the fifth amendment. *See, e.g.*, Pontikes, *Dual Sovereignty and Double Jeopardy*, 14 W. RES. L. REV. 700 (1963). In fact, it has been the policy of the Justice Department not to prosecute individuals for substantially the same act or acts if there has already been state prosecution. *See* Orlando v. United States, 387 F.2d 348 (9th Cir. 1967).

283. *See* note 227 and accompanying text.

284. 18 U.S.C. § 1152 (1970).

285. *See* note 219 *supra*.

286. Satterlee & Malan, *supra* note 2, at 34.

287. *Id.* at 35-36. According to Satterlee, attempts ". . . were made by the government agencies during the early reservation period to change Dakota ideas of child training to conform to the white pattern. Indian mothers were actually given rules to follow for the nursing of infants, along with the peculiar threat that food would be withheld if they failed to conform. In spite of this coercion, it can be assumed that the mothers followed their 'spoiling' customs when not under the watchful eye of health and other authorities."

288. Interview with Virginia Driving Hawk Sneve, author and historian, Flandreau,
160 S.D., July 5, 1974.

289. Satterlee & Malan, *supra* note 2, at 48. "In the 1860's the churches on the reservation were assigned various groups to work with, so that the Dakotas might be spared the difficulty of choosing different denominations. Agent McGillycuddy explained that this policy 'had been decreed to avoid confusing the heathen mind.' He added with a touch of humor 'that it had been ordained that the Red Cloud Indians should travel to heaven by the Episcopal route; the Catholic Church was detailed to save the souls of the Sitting Bull Indians; the Presbyterian method was prescribed to lead the Yanktons to salvation; while to the Congregationalists was assigned the responsibility of Christianizing the Lower Brule Sioux."

290. *Id.* at 49.

291. *Id.* at 41. "Whatever social cohesion still exists among the kinship group depends upon the ideal of generosity. It is not surprising that individual families find it difficult to reject this custom which prevents their accumulation of material goods. The practice may have been somewhat mitigated by the realization that most families have limited resources badly needed for their immediate requirements. But on the other hand, it is not uncommon for a family to visit relatives and depend upon their hospitality no matter what the drain on the budget might be."

292. For a description of one such contemporary giveaway—and of giveaways in general—*see* J. Cash's interview with Dorothy Lunderman in J. CASH & H. HOOVER, TO BE AN INDIAN: AN ORAL HISTORY 98-99 (1971).

293. Satterlee & Malan, *supra* note 2, at 40. "They have money" is a remark which is, in fact, "a condemnation." It implies that the family does not conform to the Dakota values and forms "a basis for social ostracism."

294. SCHELL, *supra* note 104, at 333. Early beef rations were delivered "on the hoof every fifteen days" and "afforded the Indians an opportunity to simulate a buffalo hunt. Groups of thirty mounted men would give chase to each animal, sometimes running it for two or three miles before bringing it down with rifles, the women following to dress the carcass." This practice was totally abandoned by 1890 (as, indeed, was the practice of giving full rations to everyone—only the "aged and physically disabled" and able-bodied men who worked for the agency received rations).

295. *Id.* at 334. While South Dakota reservations east of the Missouri were allotted shortly after the passage of the Dawes Act in 1887, "the Teton bands preferred to keep their tribal lands" and according to Schell, "the Indian Bureau wisely decided not to

force the issue." As a result, on the western reservations, allotment did not begin until 1904 and was not completed until 1914.

296. *Id.* at 336.

297. Satterlee & Malan, *supra* note 2, at 281.

298. SCHELL, *supra* note 104, at 336.

299. Satterlee & Malan, *supra* note 2, at 37. According to Satterlee, lack of income is "the biggest domestic problem." The wife ". . . is in no position to exert pressure on her husband to earn more while the husband never suggests that the available funds be more wisely expended. Husband and wife take little responsibility for each other's actions, and distrust between the married couple is not at all unusual. In this kind of economic and domestic situation, application of the old cultural tradition of avoiding tension as a means of adjustment results in frequent temporary and permanent separations."

300. It was frequently suggested in a number of interviews that Dakota women ran tribal governments in fact even if not in name prior to the 1960's.

301. G. MACGREGOR, WARRIORS WITHOUT WEAPONS 118 (1946). Chapter 4 of Vine Deloria Jr.'s CUSTER DIED FOR YOUR SINS (1969) is entitled "Anthropologists and Other Friends." A large portion of it is directed toward Macgregor's book. 161

302. At a meeting of the North American Indian Women's Association held in Sisseton, S.D., June 21, 1974, Dr. Bea Medicine, a Dakota Indian and anthropologist, expressed her concern about the effect of this attitude. "I'm very concerned," she said, ". . . when Indian women are made chattel by men of the dominant society and by some of their own men. [Such women] have lost the values in themselves as women that the old ways instilled in their people to give them strength and pride." Garnos, *NAIWA Meets in Sisseton*, The Watertown Public Opinion (Watertown, S.D.), June 22, 1974, at 1, col. 8.

303. Elnita Rank, Crow Creek Reservation; Agnes Ross, Flandreau Indian Reservation.

304. *See, e.g.*, the action brought by Mary Daly, Victoria Aikins, and Elnita Rank, Daly v. United States, 483 F.2d 700 (1973), and that brought by Philomene One Feather, Melvin White Eagle v. Philomene One Feather, 478 F.2d 1311 (1973).

305. M. MCELDOWNEY, WHERE WE'RE AT: STATISTICAL REPORT ON THE STATUS OF MINORITIES AND WOMEN IN SOUTH DAKOTA 7 (S.D. Comm'n on Human Rights, 1973). These statistics and those that follow are from the report *supra*. Based on the 1970 census and data supplied by the Bureau of Indian Affairs, it was compiled by Mary Ellen McEldowney, the University of South Dakota Law School. It was published by the South Dakota State Commission on Human Rights, Mary Lynn Myers, Director. The authors are indebted to both Ms. McEldowney and Ms. Myers for making the report and other data available.

306. *Id.* at 28.

307. *Id.* at 10-11.

308. The labor force, unlike the work force, includes the unemployed. *Id.* at 22.

309. The unemployment rate is higher on the reservation and is even more serious when the participation rate is considered. The following are the labor force statistics from the three reservations with Indian populations of 2,300 or more.

	Cheyenne River	Pine Ridge	Rosebud
Labor Force	835	1,951	1,179
Participation Rate, Male	64.5%	56.3%	50.2%
Participation Rate, Female	32.9%	35.9%	32.3%
Unemployment Rate, Male	19.1%	23.6%	32.2%
Unemployment Rate, Female	17.2%	5.4%	16.4%

Id. at 23. With the exception of the Yankton Reservation (where the figure is .8 per cent), the percentage of persons between the ages of 16 and 64 who do not participate in the labor force is even higher on the smaller reservations. *Id.* at 24.

310. *Id.* at 14.

311. *Id.*

312. *Id.* at 15.

313. Of the minority women in the labor force, 46.3 per cent are employed in such jobs in South Dakota as compared to 30.4 per cent of the whites. *Id.* at 37.

314. *Id.* at 46.

315. *Id.* at 44.

316. Non-Indian South Dakota women earn less than non-Indian men and, as Ms. McEldowney notes, "sex stereotyping of jobs runs high in South Dakota." *Id.* at 33.

317. Letter from Mary Lynn Myers, Director, S.D. Comm'n on Human Rights, July 25, 1974. Indian men filed a total of 11 per cent of the 161 complaints between July 1, 1972, and Aug. 15, 1974. Letter from Mary Lynn Myers, Aug. 15, 1974.

318. Letter from Mary Lynn Myers, July 25, 1974. According to Ms. Myers, "Of
the court complaints where investigation has shown merit and a settlement acceptable
to the Complainant has been reached or is being sought, three were employment cases,
162 one was a housing case. All alleged only race or national origin. Of the two complaints
which also included sex, one is under investigation, one was dismissed as to the indi-
vidual complainant, but the Commission has initiated a class action complaint on the
same subject against the same respondent."

319. Letter from Mary Lynn Myers, Aug. 15, 1974.

320. SANDOZ, *supra* note 1, at 94-95.

Married Women's Property Law: 1800-1850*

RICHARD H. CHUSED**

In the middle of the nineteenth century, numerous jurisdictions passed acts for the protection of married women's property. Many commentators hold the view that these acts were part of a concerted attack on the institution of coverture and the prevailing societal view of married women. Professor Chused takes a fresh look at this conception, tracing the development of the property rights of women in the early 1800s. In Part I, he presents archival material that reflects an increase in wives' control of family property prior to the enactment of married women's property laws. Part II presents an analysis of the legal arena in this pre-enactment period, illuminating reforms that represented a growing trend to ameliorate some of the more extreme features of coverture law. In Part III, the author uses recent literature on women in the early 1800s to show that this trend was accompanied by growth in the responsibility women had for their families. Professor Chused concludes that it is likely that the enactment of married women's property laws reflected an increase in women's family responsibilities, more than their emergence into the larger commercial and political world.

INTRODUCTION

1848 is commonly thought of as the year the women's rights movement began. That year witnessed both the Seneca Falls Convention and the adoption of the well-known New York married women's act. The dearth of literature on women's law in the 1800-1850 period[1] has made it all too easy for the legal community and the modern feminist movement to label 1848 as the pivotal year. The confluence of events in 1848 has created a mythology that the married women's acts adopted in the 1840's were a frontal attack on both the institution of coverture established by the common law and the prevailing cultural view of women as repositories of domestic virtue. Because a public women's movement and married women's legislation appeared in the same decade, it is

---

** Associate Professor of Law, Georgetown University Law Center. A number of people have worked with me intensely on this and related projects during the last two years. My colleague Wendy Williams, with whom I teach Women's Legal History, has spent so much time talking with me I have lost all ability to state the extent of her contributions to this article. My gratitude rather than a precise credit will have to suffice. Marjorie Brown, David Zolensky, Robert Stack, Elizabeth Ungar, and Robin Fradkin have provided terrific research assistance. I could not have completed this project without their help. Thanks are also due to Jim Oldham, another colleague newly immersed in legal history, for his guided tour through research into English law.

1. While the literature on women is now growing very rapidly, there is still a remarkable shortage of material on the early 19th century. The best of the general histories is E. FLEXNER, CENTURY OF STRUGGLE (rev. ed. 1975). Flexner's section on the Seneca Falls Convention describes some of the early experiences of those women who organized the meeting, particularly their exclusion from the 1840 World Anti-Slavery Convention in London which barred all women. *Id.* at 71-77. The recent release of N. BASCH, IN THE EYES OF THE LAW: WOMEN, MARRIAGE, AND PROPERTY IN NINETEENTH-CENTURY NEW YORK (1982) provides a major improvement in the state of the literature.

thought that women petitioning for change must have "caused" the state legislatures to act. As with many areas of women's history, such speculation may be flawed.

This article takes a fresh look at the development of married women's property acts by making use of three different sets of materials: Archival records, case law and legislative sources, and recent historical literature. Courthouses and archives have records of potentially enormous importance. Property ownership and trends in the disposal of property should reveal a great deal about the pressures leading to the adoption of married women's property acts. My archival work was originally structured to establish an agenda for further research rather than to be a comprehensive study, but this tentative look produced so much useful information that it is appropriate to reveal it now. Results of this work are discussed in Part I.

Part II of this article delves into the vast case law and legislative record of legal events occurring before the married women's acts were adopted. This material includes not only the married women's property acts and related cases, but also an array of legislative and judicial documents in other areas of
164 importance to women. Inheritance standards, probate codes, and divorce law, for example, tell a great deal about developments in married women's property law. In reviewing this material I placed particular emphasis on investigating the importance of English law as a model for American development, the degree to which norms existing in 1840 were actually altered by the new legislation, property law reform trends before 1840, and the relationship between the property acts and other areas of women's law in the first half of the nineteenth century.

All of this material should be viewed against the backdrop of current literature on women in the first half of the nineteenth century. Recent books present a large amount of new and useful information.[2] By and large historians have concluded that role changes for most early nineteenth-century married women involved increased family responsibilities, not greater participation in the larger commercial and political world. Such a conclusion is consistent with

---

2. Five works have provided much of the background for my own research in early reform of women's property law. Mary Beth Norton and Linda Kerber have each written a wonderful book on the changing status of women at the turn of the 19th century. M. NORTON, LIBERTY'S DAUGHTERS: THE REVOLUTIONARY EXPERIENCE OF AMERICAN WOMEN, 1750-1800 (1980); L. KERBER, WOMEN OF THE REPUBLIC: INTELLECT AND IDEOLOGY IN REVOLUTIONARY AMERICA (1980). C. DEGLER, AT ODDS: WOMEN AND THE FAMILY IN AMERICA FROM THE REVOLUTION TO THE PRESENT (1980) describes substantial developments in the history of the family during the first part of the 19th century. N. COTT, THE BONDS OF WOMANHOOD: "WOMAN'S SPHERE" IN NEW ENGLAND, 1780-1835 (1977) weaves together many of the threads of women's special sphere in the early 19th century. And Keith Melder's thesis charts the vast array of social, cultural, and political enterprises of women in the first decades of the 19th century. K. Melder, The Beginnings of the Women's Rights Movement in the United States, 1800-1840 (1965) (unpublished thesis). Other books of importance for this period include E. FLEXNER, *supra* note 1, at 1-77; B. BERG, THE REMEMBERED GATE: ORIGINS OF AMERICAN FEMINISM, THE WOMAN AND THE CITY, 1800-1860 (1978); N. BLAKE, THE ROAD TO RENO: A HISTORY OF DIVORCE IN THE UNITED STATES (1962); E. Warbasse, The Changing Legal Rights of Married Women, 1800-1861 (February 1960) (unpublished thesis); P. RABKIN, FATHERS TO DAUGHTERS: THE LEGAL FOUNDATIONS OF FEMALE EMANCIPATION (1980); M. Salmon, The Property Rights of Women in Early America (1980) (unpublished thesis); J. MOHR, ABORTION IN AMERICA: THE ORIGINS AND EVOLUTION OF NATIONAL POLICY, 1800-1900 (1978); C. DIENES, LAW, POLITICS AND BIRTH CONTROL (1972). *See also* Zainaldin, *The Emergence of a Modern American Family Law: Child Custody, Adoption and the Courts, 1796-1851*, 73 NW. U.L. REV. 1038 (1979).

the results of my own archival and legal research which suggests that the early married women's acts made only modest adjustments in coverture law, and that these adjustments generally confirmed rather than confronted prevailing domestic roles of married women. The recent literature is discussed in Part III.

As the nineteenth century began, real property owned by a married woman in a legal estate was subject to the management and control of her husband. Personal property of a wife became the property of her husband as soon as he reduced it to possession. Where equity courts existed, separate equitable estates could be created for married women's property, but the protections to be provided a wife by the equitable forum had to be specifically delineated in the document creating the estate. Although married women's property acts significantly altered the old rules by the end of the nineteenth century, the early wave of reform statutes appearing before 1850 have been given credit for accomplishing too much in the reform of married women's legal status.

In combination, the three parts of this study produce a coherent picture of the developments leading to the adoption of the early acts. The archival work suggests that use of equitable separate estates for married women increased before 1850. Analysis of legislative materials and judicial opinions shows that a number of legal norms having an economic impact on married women were modified before married women's acts appeared. Several reforms, including the liberalization of inheritance rules and divorce laws and the enlargement of benefits for widows and abandoned women, appeared in the early decades of the nineteenth century. Meanwhile, developments in the culture at large created a milieu sympathetic to changes in coverture law. Romantic notions of family formation and maintenance, introduction of industrial production, and increases in literacy and educational goals for children gave women significant family roles. When distressed economic times appeared after 1839, the moment was right for legislatures to codify a portion of the equitable separate estate tradition by insulating wives' property from their spouses' creditors. The acts, usually adopted with little lobbying from women, created a special set of assets available for family use when husbands found themselves in trouble with creditors. Only after this initial wave of debtor protection measures appeared did the women's movement get deeply and successfully involved in substantial reform of coverture law.

I. A STUDY OF WILLS AND TRUST DEEDS

A. INTRODUCTION

While it is generally (and erroneously) supposed that the first married women's property act appeared in 1839,[3] little is known about the changes in property ownership patterns and the economic status of women in the decades prior to the appearance of the new legislation. Important questions about whether the mid-century legislation "codified" existing practice, whether mar-

3. In reality the acts began to appear in 1835. *See infra* note 205 and accompanying text (Arkansas act passed in 1835). The use of 1839 or 1840 as an approximation of the beginning of a transition period, however, is appropriate. Most of the early married women's acts appeared in the 1840's. *See infra* notes 207-11 (listing acts).

ried women gained financial influence within the family before 1840 and whether married women benefitted from the separate equitable estate, are answerable only by doing a great deal of sleuthing in courthouse records.[4] For two reasons, this study was designed to search for changes in participation rates of women in the property system and in the dispositional patterns of family property, rather than for alterations in women's wealth. First, wealth studies suggest that married women's economic status did not change much relative to men's during the nineteenth century. Second, the married women's acts themselves did not legitimate any radical shifts in the economic status of women. One therefore should not expect changes in the patterns of women's wills and deeds during the early decades of the nineteenth century to display dramatic movements of money or other assets. Rather one would hypothesize that the mild changes made by the married women's acts would be preceded by some shifts in the ways families disposed of or controlled their assets. This study suggests that such shifts occurred.

What little is known about women and the economy before 1850 confirms the need to be cautious about claiming that married women's acts caused or
166 resulted from significant shifts in wealth between men and women. During the
late eighteenth century subsistence farming was giving way to commercial production and home industry, particularly spinning, needlework, and weaving.[5] Trade was becoming more pronounced and some men began to leave home to go to work. Increasing agricultural efficiency[6] and expanding markets began to separate household from work. It became possible for some women, and

---

4. Two other studies of courthouse documents are available. They are Salmon, *Women and Property in South Carolina: The Evidence From Marriage Settlements, 1730-1830*, 39 WM. & MARY Q. 655 (1982) [hereinafter Salmon, *South Carolina*], and N. BASCH, *supra* note 1, at 100-12. Salmon's study asks some of the same questions posed here and uses somewhat similar research techniques.

5. N. COTT, *supra* note 2, at 21-30. Women played a significant role in these areas, particularly in the provision of cloth for home use. An 1810 government report estimated that two-thirds of all clothing, hosiery, and linen was produced at home. *See* Summer, *History of Women in Industry in the United States*, in 9 REPORT ON CONDITION OF WOMEN AND CHILD WAGE-EARNERS IN THE UNITED STATES 37-50 (1810 & photo. reprint 1974).

6. *See* N. COTT, *supra* note 2, at 23-24. During the 19th century, yields per acre for wheat and corn stayed fairly constant. But the man-hours required to produce this yield declined substantially. Data from U.S. BUREAU OF THE CENSUS, THE STATISTICAL HISTORY OF THE UNITED STATES FROM COLONIAL TIMES TO THE PRESENT 500 (1976) [hereinafter STATISTICAL HISTORY], was used in producing this table:

	Wheat		Corn	
Year	Yield/acre	Man hrs./ 100 bushels	Yield/acre	Man hrs./ 100 bushels
1800	15*	373	25*	344
1840	15*	233	25*	276
1880	13.2	152	25.6	180
1900	13.9	108	25.9	147

* These figures are estimates.

Similar changes in the raising of cotton occurred. Some of this improvement in efficiency probably arose because of improvements in tools such as the cotton gin, scythe, and plow. *See* Rasmussen, *The Mechanization of Agriculture*, 247 SCI. AM. 76 (1982). There is much debate over the rate of increase in agricultural output in the early United States. The traditional view is that output increased moderately before 1840. Parker & Whartenby, *The Growth of Output Before 1840*, in TRENDS IN THE AMERICAN ECONOMY IN THE NINETEENTH CENTURY 191 (National Bureau of Economic Research ed. 1960). Others have argued that there was a more substantial growth in output. Gallman, *The Agricultural Sector and the Pace of Economic Growth: U.S. Experience in the Nineteenth Century*, in ESSAYS IN

necessary for others, to undertake chores in addition to those crucial for the operation of a subsistence farm. While the location of activity for most was still the home or a business attached to the home,[7] sending children off to work in others' homes, in schools, or in the towns became a possibility in some cases.[8] Although home industry diminished in importance during the first decades of the nineteenth century, teaching, domestic service, and mill work by unmarried women became commonplace by the 1830's.[9] Wages for single women rose rapidly between 1820 and 1850 when they reached fifty percent of the male level, a plateau which has remained almost unchanged to this day.[10]

But the impact of these changes on the economic standing of married women was not great. Women who did work were usually single and tended to obtain low-paying jobs. By 1840, many who had worked as young women were married and without paying jobs, carrying with them only memories of their prior work.[11] Historians have provided us vivid anecdotal descriptions of the differences between the lives of married and unmarried women to demonstrate that by 1840 many women considered marriage to be a large step from relative freedom into an important, but confining, social role.[12] Even as late as
1890 less than five percent of all married women worked,[13] and women's share 167
of the nation's wealth did not rise during the nineteenth century. Wealth studies suggest that white women constituted less than ten percent of wealth holders and that wealth holders constituted less than two percent of the total

---

NINETEENTH CENTURY ECONOMIC HISTORY: THE OLD NORTHEAST 35 (D. Klingaman & R. Vedder eds. 1975).

7. For example, shops and boarding houses both drew women's attention. N. COTT, *supra* note 2, at 42-43.

8. *Id.* at 31-36.

9. *Id.* at 36-37; S. LEBERGOTT, MANPOWER IN ECONOMIC GROWTH: THE AMERICAN RECORD SINCE 1800 520 (1964). By 1830, women and children comprised a large percentage of the industrial labor force, which they maintained despite a relative decline in the textile industry after 1830. A. GOLDIN & N. SOKOLOFF, WOMEN, CHILDREN, AND INDUSTRIALIZATION IN THE EARLY REPUBLIC: EVIDENCE FROM THE MANUFACTURING CENSUS (NBER Working Paper No. 795, 1981). Even on the frontier, working single women comprised a significant segment of the community. *See* J. JEFFREY, FRONTIER WOMEN: THE TRANS-MISSISSIPPI WEST 1840-1880 87-94 (1979). Dramatic increases in teaching employment also appeared as a result of the development of universal elementary education. *See* W. ELSBREE, THE AMERICAN TEACHER: EVOLUTION OF A PROFESSION IN A DEMOCRACY 199 (1970); 1 T. WOODY, A HISTORY OF WOMEN'S EDUCATION IN THE UNITED STATES 460-83 (1929); Bernard & Vinovskis, *The Female School Teacher in Ante-bellum Massachusetts*, 10 J. SOC. HIST. 332 (1977). Bernard and Vinovskis conclude that one out of every five antebellum Massachusetts women taught school during her lifetime, even if the total percentage of women in the entire workforce at any one time was small. Bernard & Vinovskis, *supra*, at 338.

10. A. GOLDIN & N. SOKOLOFF, THE RELATIVE PRODUCTIVITY HYPOTHESIS OF INDUSTRIALIZATION: THE AMERICAN CASE, 1820-1850 (NBER Working Paper No. 795, 1981). As of 1970, full-time white women workers earned about 59% of a male worker's wage. STATISTICAL HISTORY, *supra* note 6, at 305.

11. In fact, the proportion of working married women remained very low until recently. *See* A. GOLDIN & N. SOKOLOFF, *supra* note 10. It is unlikely that women's labor produced much wealth for most women. Wages were too low. *See id.*

12. *See* N. COTT, *supra* note 2, at 80-83.

13. STATISTICAL HISTORY, *supra* note 6, at 133. Data from STATISTICAL HISTORY at 129-34 provides additional material for this table:

population in the Revolutionary War years,[14] and that in 1860, women's and children's wealth still constituted less than ten percent of men's wealth.[15] Average men's wealth was much higher than women's.[16]

Thus, one would not expect a study of intestate and testate estates to display dramatic increases in women's wealth. Rather, discussion of the evolution of women's property law during the first half of the nineteenth century must focus on the mechanisms by which wealth was controlled. While some tentative effort is made here to look for wealth indicia in the archival data, the primary focus is on changes in the dispositional patterns for women's property.

B. METHODOLOGY

Document studies were undertaken in Dukes County, Massachusetts, and Baltimore City and County, Maryland, for the period 1800 to 1850.[17] The different sizes of the document banks available necessitated somewhat differ-

168

Year	% of labor force that is female	% of female labor force that is: single	widowed/ divorced	married
1870	14.8	—	—	—
1880	15.2	—	—	—
1890	17.2	68.2	17.9	13.9
1900	18.3	66.2	18.4	15.4
1910	19.9	60.2	15.7	24.7
1920	20.4	77.0*	—	23.0
1930	22.0	53.9	17.2	28.9

* For this entry, single also includes widowed and divorced women.

By 1979, the situation was quite different, with 60% of the female labor force married and 50% of the married women working. U.S. BUREAU OF THE CENSUS, STATISTICAL ABSTRACT OF THE UNITED STATES: 1980 402 (101st ed. 1980) [hereinafter STATISTICAL ABSTRACT].

It is possible that the five percent married women working data is misleading. Even though few unmarried women were working at any one time early in the 19th century, a large number of women worked at some time before marriage. *See supra* note 9. Perhaps by 1890, a large number of married women had worked at some point (probably before starting a family), even if only five percent of married women worked at any particular point in time.

14. A. JONES, WEALTH OF A NATION TO BE 39 (1980).

15. L. SOLTOW, MEN AND WEALTH IN THE UNITED STATES, 1850-1870 200, n.12 (1975).

16. *Compare* L. SOLTOW, THE RISE OF LITERACY AND THE COMMON SCHOOL IN THE UNITED STATES 156 (1981) *with* L. SOLTOW, *supra* note 15, at 23, 64-65, 156. This outcome is confirmed by the very tentative data available from the Dukes County wills study which show that the men's estates tended to be much larger than the women's. The average size of the nine male inventories reviewed was over $6000 (These wills were not randomly selected. Rather, they were picked because they involved petitions by women for widow's allowances). The female inventories averaged a bit less than $950. *See infra* Table 8.

17. Given the original exploratory purposes of this research, the locations were chosen for reasons of convenience. There are, however, important characteristics of these two locations which make them very useful. The Baltimore area provides both urban and rural areas for study. The lack of significant differences between the two areas is itself interesting. *See infra* note 63 (comparing Baltimore city and county results). The two areas also provide different legal milieus, with Maryland probably having a stronger equity tradition. *Compare* M. SALMON, *supra* note 2, at 162-82 (discussing Maryland's equitable enforcement of marriage settlements) *with* E. Warbasse, *supra* note 2, at 44-45 (discussing Massachusetts' refusal to create equity courts or grant equity powers to its law courts). Consistent results between the two areas give some basis for suggesting that future replicative work will reveal similar trends.

The Dukes County study was made at the Courthouse in Edgartown, Massachusetts, on Martha's Vineyard. For the years in question, the clerk took the handwritten indices and recorded document books out of her safe. There is no cataloging system. The indices are basically in chronological order. Next to each name in the index is a list of documents recorded in the case, and next to each document is

ent research techniques in the two locations. In Dukes County the Register of Probate Index provided a list of volume and page entries for matters in which documents were recorded. Prior to 1820 about one-third of the indexed matters gave only the name of the person involved in court action followed by an entry like "records not recorded." After 1820 the index was much more complete. A "no record" entry might not even involve a deceased person, because the index also included other probate matters such as guardianships and incompetencies. The total number of entries was not very large. Meaningful data therefore are useful only for periods of a decade or longer. The number of men's and women's estates (both with and without wills) and the number of "no record" entries for each decade is displayed in Table 1.

TABLE 1: DUKES COUNTY RECORDS

Years	Male Estates	Female Estates	Male No Record	Female No Record
1801-1810	44	1	21	0
1811-1820	39	3	28	2
1821-1830	88	14	5	1
1831-1840	88	17	5	1
1841-1850	92	16	0	0

All the recorded women's wills in Dukes County from 1801-1850 were read. A number of the women's estates (both testate and intestate) contained inventories; they were also read. Some men's wills involving disputes over spousal estate shares were reviewed as well.

The Baltimore study was done from a significantly larger document base. Sampling was necessary. Index data on estates with wills were taken for the years 1800, 1805, 1810, 1815, 1820, 1825, 1830, 1835, 1840, and 1846.[18] All women's wills were read for the years 1810, 1825, 1840, and 1846. A few men's wills were read for 1810, 1825, 1840, and 1846 as well.[19] Finally, a search was made in the deed index for trust documents establishing separate estates for married women. Documents discovered in the index were read for the years 1810, 1825, and 1840.

C. THE LEGAL STAGE IN 1800

As the nineteenth century opened, the status of women's property was in the

a book and page number where it may be found in the volumes of recorded documents. I simply recorded the names, documents, books, and page numbers that I was interested in and looked them up.

The same basic system operates at the Maryland Hall of Records in Annapolis, except that the volume of records was much larger, and the recorded documents were on microfilm. Indices to the Register of Wills and the land records for Baltimore were checked first. Relevant volume and page numbers were listed and the materials were read.

18. 1846, rather than 1845, was selected to provide an additional year of breathing space from the married woman's acts adopted by Maryland in 1842 and 1843.

19. The men's wills were sampled by turning the microfilm crank 10 times and reading the first male will to appear thereafter.

midst of a lengthy period of transformation. While land transfer systems had been streamlined and married women's dower rights had been modified to permit easier transfer of titles,[20] substantial reform of the testate and intestate roles of women had just begun. Reforms of the post-Revolutionary War era enhanced the ability of women and children to be beneficiaries of intestate estates. Even before primogeniture was abolished in England, many of the American colonies had rejected it. A deluge of reform statutes finished the job after the Revolutionary War.[21] New laws covering intestate succession in New England provided for descent to widows and children of both sexes.[22] These statutes were of considerable importance because the vast bulk of people never wrote wills.[23] The changes in intestacy rules, therefore, operated to provide a minimum level of economic security for some surviving widows and children.[24] Thus, well before 1800, married female children and widows could inherit property. And even though wealthier men of the early nineteenth century tended to will assets to women in life estates or other forms that insulated the property from the creditors of present or future husbands,[25] it was not uncommon for married women to own assets long before women's property acts
170 were adopted.

Most jurisdictions, however, did not pass statutes granting married women contractual or testamentary control over property held at law until well into the nineteenth century.[26] The power to dispose of property by will was granted in a few places early in the nineteenth century, but statutory reform most commonly occurred after 1850.[27] Will studies suggest that women did

---

20. *See infra* notes 157-82 and accompanying text (discussing reforms affecting ease of transfer).

21. R. MORRIS, STUDIES IN THE HISTORY OF AMERICAN LAW 72-81 (1930). England did not abolish primogeniture until 1926. *Id.* at 77. Fee tails met the same fate as primogeniture in the colonies. *Id.* at 82-103.

22. L. FRIEDMAN, A HISTORY OF AMERICAN LAW 57-60 (1973).

23. *Id.* at 220.

24. The intestate succession reforms also had some of the same effects as dower reform—land was less likely to be encumbered by future interests that would lower its marketability. Primogeniture mandated takers for a significant period of time. The new intestate succession statutes provided for estates to be divided into shares and distributed. While some assets would be distributed to tenants in common, partition was available to settle ownership disputes and, if necessary, to force sales of the disputed assets. *See* L. FRIEDMAN, *supra* note 22, at 57-58.

25. *Id.* at 220-21. This trend may have begun to disintegrate by mid-century. *See infra* Table 13.

26. Connecticut is an interesting exception, providing for wills in 1809. This is particularly puzzling because the Connecticut colony is thought to have been most restrictive of women's property rights. *See* M. SALMON, *supra* note 2, at 324-39. What, then, were women being permitted to transfer by will? A study of estate records in Connecticut should be fascinating.

27. In general, women lost their interest in personal property upon marriage and therefore had nothing to will before 1800. As to real property, instruments in the nature of wills for the disposition of equitable estates were sometimes enforced, but they were seldom written. Women could dispose of personal property with the consent of their husbands. *See* 2 J. BISHOP, COMMENTARIES ON THE LAW OF MARRIED WOMEN 421-36 (1875); M. SALMON, *supra* note 2, at 119-25. Salmon found records of decisions from the 1790's permitting women to devise their own property in Pennsylvania and Maryland. M. SALMON, *supra* note 2, at 119 n.49. In my study of Maryland wills, women began to write wills with greater frequency as the 19th century unfolded. But most of the will writers were either widows or unmarried women, and most of the property being willed was personal, not real. In general, legislation providing women with the power to write wills came slowly. While some states acted during the early decades of the 19th century, there is no clear time period in which this reform arrived. Some states had fairly well-developed equitable rules permitting married women to write wills if their deeds permitted it. *See infra* note 29. Statutes appeared in a few states at very early dates. Connecticut: Act of May, 1809, ch. VII, 1809 Conn. Pub. Acts 15 (May Sess. 1809); Florida: Act of June 29, 1823, 1825 Florida Territorial Legis. Council Acts 101 (2d Sess. 1823); Ohio: Act of Feb. 18, 1808, ch. XVIII, § 1,

not make wills in significant numbers until after 1800.[28] For the most part, a married woman's property was disposed of at death either by the operation of intestate succession laws or by the constraints contained in the equitable instrument establishing her title to the property.[29] These inheritance rules followed the more general structure of coverture law under which a married woman's real estate was subject to the management and control of her husband, and her personal property, once in the possession of her spouse, was permanently lost by the wife. While a number of exceptions to these rules arose in various areas of the United States, especially in jurisdictions with

---

1807 Ohio Acts 64 (1808). The Ohio statute was re-enacted in slightly revised versions in 1810, 1840, and 1852. While the roots of the Ohio legislation presumably were in the Northwest Ordinance, more study of this statute is needed. It is also a bit of a mystery why Connecticut moved so early. Warbasse suggests that judicial changes of heart over the old common law rules made legislative action necessary. E. Warbasse, *supra* note 2, at 15-16. Florida's statute probably resulted from its Spanish civil law heritage. A few states also adopted statutes that basically codified the common law rule that wives could write wills with their husband's consent. Maryland: Act of Mar. 10, 1843, ch. 293, § 6, 1842 Md. Laws (1843); Massachusetts: Act of Mar. 3, 1842, ch. 74, 1842 Mass. Acts 527; Pennsylvania: Act of Apr. 8, 1833, No. 128, § 2, 1833 Pa. Laws 249. Other states adopted statutes permitting women to write wills in pursuit of powers. New York: N.Y. Rev. Stat., art. 3, §§ 80, 87, 110, 1829 N.Y. Rev. Stat. 731; Pennsylvania: Act of Apr. 8, 1833, No. 128, § 2, 1833 Pa. Laws 249. A few states adopted limited wills acts in the 1840's. Alabama: Act of Feb. 4, 1846, No. 19, §§ 1-3, 1845 Ala. Acts 23, 24 (1846) (abandoned or mistreated wives only); Indiana: Act of Jan. 26, 1847, ch. LXXIX, 1846 Ind. Acts 108 (1847) (real property only); New Hampshire: Act of July 2, 1841, ch. 157, 1841 N.H. Laws 533 (deserted wives) and Act of June 27, 1845, ch. 236, 1845 N.H. Laws 235 (real property). Most states adopted general wills-enabling statutes after 1850. The exceptions include Michigan: MICH. CONST. of 1850, art. XVI, § 5; Pennsylvania: Act of Apr. 11, 1848, No. 372, §§ 5-6, 1848 Pa. Laws 536, 537; New York: Act of Apr. 11, 1849, ch. 375, 1849 N.Y. Laws 528. The later enactments include Arkansas: ARK. CONST. of 1868, art. XII, § 6; Georgia: REV. CODE § 2375 (1867); Indiana: Act of Mar. 3, 1859, ch. CXLI, 1859 Ind. Acts 245; Kansas: Act of Feb. 11, 1858, ch. 2, 1858 Kan. Territorial Sess. Laws 327; Massachusetts: Act of May 5, 1855, ch. 304, 1855 Mass. Acts 710; New Jersey: Act of Apr. 12, 1864, ch. CCCXCVI, 1864 N.J. Laws 442; New Hampshire: Act of July 8, 1854, ch. 1522, 1854 N.H. Laws 1418; Act of July 4, 1860, ch. 2342, § 3, 1860 N.H. Laws 2248; North Carolina: N.C. CONST. of 1868, art. X, § 6; Rhode Island: 1856 R.I. Pub. Laws 68 (Jan. Sess. 1856); South Carolina: Act of Dec. 12, 1866, 1866 S.C. Acts 473; Tennessee: Act of Feb. 21, 1852, ch. CLXX, § 4, 1851 Tenn. Pub. Acts 259. In some states, late enactments still prohibited married women from writing wills. *See* Kentucky: Gen. Stats., ch. 113, § 2 (1873).

28. K. LOCKRIDGE, LITERACY IN COLONIAL NEW ENGLAND 38 (1974); A. JONES, *supra* note 14, at 39. A. JONES, AMERICAN COLONIAL WEALTH: DOCUMENTS AND METHODS (1977) (3 volumes) reproduces all the inventories used in Jones' WEALTH OF A NATION TO BE. There were 82 women's estates. Forty-two wrote wills, 39 died intestate and for one woman, testacy status is not known. This 52% rate of testacy is a bit lower than that found in Dukes County. *See infra* Table 7.

29. In a number of states, early equity cases provided that married women could write wills to dispose of real property if the instrument giving title permitted it. *See* Beach v. Manchester, 56 Mass. (2 Cush.) 72 (1848); Wilkinson v. Wright, 45 Ky. (6 B. Mon.) 576 (1846); Yates Will, 32 Ky. (2 Dana) 215 (1834); Lewis v. Hudson, 6 Ala. 463 (1848); Shaw v. Dawsey, 26 S.C.L. (1 McMul.) 247 (1841); Ewing v. Smith, 3 S.C. Eq. (3 Des.) 417 (1813); Rogers v. Smith, 4 Barr 93 (Pa. 1840); Lowery v. Tiernan, 2 H. & G. 34 (Md. 1827); West v. West's Executor, 24 Va. (3 Rand.) 373 (1825); Jaques v. Methodist Episcopal Church, 17 Johns. 548 (N.Y. 1820). A will devising personal property required the husband's consent, unless an instrument under which property was held provided a right to dispose of property by will. *See, e.g.,* Lewis v. Hudson, 6 Ala. 463 (1844); Reed v. Blaisdell, 16 N.H. 194 (1844); Marston v. Norton, 5 N.H. 105 (1830); Yates Will, 32 Ky. (2 Dana) 215 (1834). *See also* 2 J. BISHOP, *supra* note 27, at 412-36.

A few states applied the equity rules very liberally, holding that general statements creating a separate estate implied the right to dispose of the property by will. Lamb v. Wregg, 8 Port. 73 (Ala. 1838); Lewis v. Hudson, 6 Ala. 463 (1844); Jaques v. Methodist Episcopal Church, 17 Johns. 548 (N.Y. 1820). Kentucky appeared to be such a jurisdiction, Yates Will, 32 Ky. 215 (1834), but a narrow rule emerged later, Wilkinson v. Wright, 45 Ky. (6 B. Mon.) 576 (1846). Maryland took the opposite trend. *Compare* Tarr v. Williams, 4 Md. 68 (1853), *with* Cooke v. Husbands, 11 Md. 486 (1857).

strong equity traditions supporting the creation of separate estates for married women, wives were treated as civilly dead persons in many situations.

Massachusetts and Maryland common law followed these general trends. In Massachusetts, case law placed severe constraints on married women's right to will property at law, prohibiting the devising of real estate and requiring the husband's consent for the devising of personal assets.[30] Both of the married women's wills found in Dukes County were written in 1810, though they were not probated until 1815 and 1821. The scarcity of married women's wills probably reflects the common law rules. A statute permitting married women to write wills with their husband's consent was adopted on March 3, 1842, but the act was construed to prohibit devises to husbands.[31] This result was overruled by statute on April 15, 1850. In 1842, Maryland adopted a statute permitting married women to write wills with their husband's consent. Married women's property acts were passed in 1842 and 1843. In both Maryland and Massachusetts the power of a wife to dispose of equitable property at death was limited to the rights granted by the instrument under which she took title.[32]

The development of inheritance rights of women and children during the
172 late eighteenth and early nineteenth centuries required some method for legitimating the holding of property by married women. Finding the methods used before 1840 is sometimes difficult. Although the Baltimore document study suggests the separate equitable estate was the logical choice in most jurisdictions, America's varied reception of equity forces legal historians to search state-by-state for the ways in which women typically held property. While English chancery had both developed rules for a wife's separate estate and declared dower inapplicable to equitable estates by the end of the eighteenth century, the colonies did not uniformly adopt chancery.[33] While the Southern colonies generally had equity courts, New England practice was spotty.[34] The Northwest Ordinance specifically called for reception of the common law, but was silent as to equity.[35] Although this omission was probably not meant to prohibit creation of equity courts,[36] not all the territories so understood it, leading to different results in the various jurisdictions.[37]

Not until well into the nineteenth century did most American states and

---

30. Osgood v. Breed, 12 Mass. 525 (1815).

31. Morse v. Thompson, 58 Mass. (4 Cush.) 562 (1849).

32. Beach v. Manchester, 56 Mass. (2 Cush.) 72 (1848); Lowery v. Tiernan, 2 H. & G. 34 (Md. 1827); Miller v. Williamson, 5 Md. 219 (1853).

33. Katz, *The Politics of Law in Colonial America: Controversies Over Chancery Courts and Equity Law in the Eighteenth Century*, in LAW IN AMERICAN HISTORY 257 (D. Fleming & B. Bailyn eds. 1971); L. FRIEDMAN, *supra* note 22, at 47-48; E. Warbasse, *supra* note 2, at 38-42; Wilson, *Courts of Chancery in the American Colonies*, in 2 SELECT ESSAYS IN ANGLO-AMERICAN LEGAL HISTORY 779 (1908); M. SALMON, *supra* note 2, at 150-233.

34. 1 J. STORY, COMMENTARIES ON EQUITY JURISPRUDENCE 62 n.1 (1836); E. Warbasse, *supra* note 2, at 39-48. M. SALMON, *supra* note 2, at 150-233, catalogues in great detail the differences in equity traditions in four states, concluding that the Southern jurisdiction she studied maintained stronger traditions than the Northern areas.

35. *See generally* Blume, *Chancery on the American Frontier*, 59 MICH. L. REV. 49 (1960).

36. *Id.* at 54.

37. Despite the terms of the Northwest Ordinance, Michigan gave its supreme territorial court equity jurisdiction as early as 1805. *Id.* at 55-56. But the early history of chancery in the territories varied, and Congress frequently had to step in later to resolve any lingering ambiguities. *See* Blume & Brown, *Territorial Courts and Law: Unifying Factors in the Development of American Legal Institutions*, 61 MICH. L. REV. 39, 54-59 (1962).

territories have chancery courts. While Story argues that equity, once adopted, was accepted with much less variation than the common law,[38] there is little modern commentary analyzing his arguments. Thus, during much of the formative period of English chancery rules on coverture,[39] America was in a state of "equitable disarray." Although some have attributed the cool reception given equity courts to antipathy to the English crown,[40] a more sophisticated explanation suggests that the desire of colonial legislatures to control chancery courts rather than leave them to the prerogatives of the crown led some areas to resist the adoption of equity. There was less opposition to the principle of equitable relief itself than to the institutions supporting it.[41] Furthermore, there is evidence that substitutes for equity, such as private bills and courts of law serving equity traditions, existed in some jurisdictions.[42]

Colonial and early American reception of equitable coverture rules reflect the variety in reception of equity law generally. Despite the contentions of Kent and Story that equity generally provided a release from the more egregious common law coverture norms,[43] there is a growing body of recent work confirming that the vagaries of local precedential and procedural settings created significant variety among the colonies and newly independent states.[44] 173
While the resistance to equity in parts of the Northeast during the late eighteenth and early nineteenth centuries[45] is one of the causes of the variety, there are also intriguing indications that private legislative bills were used in some jurisdictions to alter more traditional coverture rules,[46] and that some common

38. 1 J. STORY, *supra* note 34, at 62-65.

39. *See infra* notes 100-96 and accompanying text (discussing English developments).

40. *See* E. Warbasse, *supra* note 2, at 42-45.

41. *See* Katz, *supra* note 33, at 271-72 (resistance to equity recognized the need for such an institution but feared its abuse in the hands of the executive). Warbasse recognized that alteration of New York's equity practice arose because of complaints about the complexity of equitable procedure, not the notion of equity itself. E. Warbasse, *supra* note 2, at 217-18.

42. *See* Katz, *supra* note 33, at 283; Salmon, *Equality or Submersion?: Feme Covert Status in Early Pennsylvania*, in WOMEN OF AMERICA: A HISTORY 92 (C. Berkin & M. Norton eds. 1979).

43. J. KENT, COMMENTARIES ON AMERICAN LAW 136-49 (1826); 2 J. STORY, *supra* note 34, at 596-655. Both Kent and Story wrote without close attention to actual practice at the time in the various jurisdictions. Morris later wrote in a similar vein that equity was a general release valve from the restrictions of the coverture rules at law. R. MORRIS, *supra* note 21, at 135.

44. *Compare* M. SALMON, *supra* note 2, at 162-81; Salmon, *supra* note 42, at 92-113; *and* L. KERBER, *supra* note 2, at 139-55 *with* E. Warbasse, *supra* note 2, at 42-48; *and* J. SPRUILL, WOMEN'S LIFE AND WORK IN THE SOUTHERN COLONIES 361-64 (1938). For material on reception of equity, *see generally* Blume, *supra* note 35; L. FRIEDMAN, *supra* note 22, at 185-86; 1 R. POWELL, THE LAW OF REAL PROPERTY 447-52 (rev. ed. 1981); 1 J. STORY, *supra* note 34, at 62-64. Some of the carefully written commentary in 19th-century treatises confirms that equitable coverture rules were received in a variety of ways. *See* 1 J. BISHOP, *supra* note 27, at 16-22 (1873); J. SCHOULER, A TREATISE ON THE LAW OF DOMESTIC RELATIONS 167-69 (3d ed. 1882) [hereinafter SCHOULER, DOMESTIC RELATIONS]; 1 J. SCHOULER, TREATISE ON THE LAW OF MARRIAGE, DIVORCE, SEPARATION AND DOMESTIC RELATIONS 264-66 (rev. ed. 1921). This last work is the sixth edition, as revised by Blakemore, of a work originally written in 1870.

45. *See supra* notes 33-34 and accompanying text (discussing resistance to equity in Northeast).

46. Until the mid-19th century, private bills were sometimes passed in traditional equitable coverture areas. L. KERBER, *supra* note 2, at 150-51 (petitions for feme-sole status); J. SPRUILL, *supra* note 44, at 361-62 (petitions for feme-sole status); Zainaldin, *supra* note 2, at 1043-44 (petitions for divorce, legitimacy of birth, change of name, and adoption); E. Warbasse, *supra* note 2, at 75, 169 (petitions for feme-sole status). For an unsatisfactory history of special bills, *see* Cloe & Marcus, *Special and Local Legislation*, 24 KY. L.J. 351, 355-58 (1936). Cooley wrote at length about special bills in his famous treatise, but only those bills dealing with granting new trials, conferring power on guardians to sell

law courts acted as surrogate equity courts.[47] The use of the separate estate as a model in many of the married women's acts indicates that equity's influence grew as the nineteenth century unfolded.[48] In fact, there is some evidence that reception occurred in reverse—American treatises were being "received" in England during this period.[49]

While it is fair to suggest that the chancery picture varied in the era before the adoption of married women's acts, the lack of scholarship on private bills[50] and common law forms of equity in the coverture law makes it difficult to evaluate the situation. Furthermore, the increased use of equity precedents in the nineteenth century occurred shortly before the emergence of movements to merge law and equity,[51] to restrict legislative authority to enact private bills,[52]

---

lands, validating irregular judicial proceedings, and divorces. *See* T. COOLEY, A TREATISE ON THE CONSTITUTIONAL LIMITATIONS 103-35 (5th ed. 1883).

From my own research, the state of Alabama is an interesting example. On March 3, 1848, the state legislature enacted a law providing that abandoned married women could apply to chancery for a decree permitting them to act as feme soles. Act of Mar. 3, 1848, No. 40, 1847 Ala. Acts 100 (1848). During that same session of the legislature, private bills granted feme-sole status to 35 women. Among
174 them were acts for the relief of Mary Sitton, Act of Jan. 15, 1848, No. 368, 1847 Ala. Acts 411 (1848); Mary H. Clopton, Act of Feb. 29, 1848, No. 370, 1847 Ala. Acts 412 (1848); Margaret Craig, Act of Mar. 4, 1848, No. 372, 1847 Ala. Acts 413 (1848); Martha C. Towles, Act of Mar. 2, 1848, No. 373, 1847 Ala. Acts 414 (1848); Christian Linington Child, Act of Mar. 3, 1848, No. 374, 1847 Ala. Acts 415 (1848); Susannah C. Waldron and Kitsey Ann Stephens, Act of Feb. 22, 1848, No. 375, 1847 Ala. Acts 415 (1848); Aurelia Mary Carpenter, Act of Mar. 3, 1848, No. 377, 1847 Ala. Acts 416 (1848); Obedience Ledlow, Act of Feb. 25, 1848, No. 377, 1847 Ala. Acts 416 (1848); Mary Brame, Act of Feb. 11, 1848, No. 378, 1847 Ala. Acts 417 (1848); Susan B. Gee, Act of Feb. 28, 1848, No. 379, 1847 Ala. Acts 417 (1848); Sylvia Fowler, Act of Mar. 4, 1848, No. 380, 1847 Ala. Acts 417 (1848); Mary Peoples, Act of Mar. 6, 1848, No. 381, 1847 Ala. Acts 418 (1848); Bethaney Grimes, Act of Mar. 3, 1848, No. 383, 1847 Ala. Acts 418 (1848); Mourning Hanelson, Act of Mar. 4, 1848, No. 384, 1847 Ala. Acts 419 (1848); Elizabeth Rickard, Act of Mar. 6, 1848, No. 387, 1847 Ala. Acts 420 (1848); Olivia Lanier, Act of Feb. 21, 1848, No. 391, 1847 Ala. Acts 421 (1848); and Eliza N. Randall, Act of Feb. 4, 1848, No. 392, 1847 Ala. Acts 422 (1848). The practice of enacting private bills for abandoned wives was a longstanding habit. A review of Alabama state session laws (I did not look at territorial enactments) reveals that such private bills were enacted very frequently after 1840 and with lesser frequency as far back as 1826. The legislature did not meet in 1846. Alabama switched to biannual sessions after 1845. I found that 4 women were granted feme-sole status by such acts in the 1845 session, 35 in 1844, 10 in 1843, 10 in 1842, 5 in 1841, 2 in 1840, 2 in 1839, 2 in 1838, 6 in 1837, 3 in 1836, 3 in 1835, 4 in 1834, 4 in 1833, 2 in 1832, and 1 each in 1831, 1828, and 1826. There also was a scattering of other private acts dealing with the power of married women to sell slaves and dispose of property as guardians or administrators.

47. See the tempting generalizations by Katz, *supra* note 33, at 283, and the tidbits on Pennsylvania, Liverant & Hitchler, *A History of Equity in Pennsylvania*, 37 DICK. L. REV. 156 (1933); 1 J. BISHOP, *supra* note 27, at 9-12; and Fisher, *The Administration of Equity Through Common Law Forms in Pennsylvania*, in 2 SELECT ESSAYS IN ANGLO-AMERICAN LEGAL HISTORY 810 (1908). *See generally* M. SALMON, *supra* note 2 (discussing common law courts and equity).

48. Kent's COMMENTARIES appeared in 1827, Story's in 1836. That equity and the notion of the wife's separate equitable estate were "in the air" by the 1820's seems clear. Illustrations of its use appear in this era, even in New England. *See* Porter v. Bank of Rutland, 19 Vt. 410 (1847) (dispute over 1824 trust); Ayer v. Ayer, 33 Mass. (16 Pick.) 327 (1835) (dispute over 1824 trust involving transfer of asset from mother to daughter). *See also* Conway v. Hale, 5 Tenn. (4 Hayw.) 1 (1817).

49. *See* Simpson, *The Rise and Fall of the Legal Treatise: Legal Principles and the Forms of Legal Literature*, 48 U. CHI. L. REV. 632, 671 (1981).

50. For starters, I undertook a study of Ohio's private bills in the 19th century. Although divorce and other expected subjects were treated by private bills, there was nothing to suggest that the legislature of Ohio was a forum used to loosen the boundries of coverture. This may be because Ohio had an early and strong equity tradition, or because dower was protected. *See infra* note 173 (discussing extent of dower rights in Ohio). In any case, the dearth of bills on the subject suggests that there is vast state-by-state variation in this area.

51. M. HORWITZ, THE TRANSFORMATION OF AMERICAN LAW 265-66 (1977), suggests that the merger of law and equity in the second half of the 19th century was an effective limit on equity. To the extent this is true in coverture law it significantly complicates analysis of both equity and the role of

and to codify the law generally. The equitable separate estate, therefore, was not only a precursor to the married women's acts,[53] but was also enmeshed in the more general package of reform movements in the first half of the nineteenth century. For example, New York's enactment of substantial reforms in trust law, which made the establishment of married women's estates more difficult, is an intriguing sign of the links between married women's law reform and the early nineteenth-century movement to merge law and equity and reform pleading practices.[54] More research must now be done to link codification of coverture rules to the equitable and legislative situations extant in states other than New York.[55]

The great variety in early American chancery practice is particularly important for analysis of married women's acts. The language of separate estates became an important part of much of the legislation. The chancery model, which permitted the use of special trust instruments to provide for married women's assets, was formalized, and the complexity of early formats was abandoned in favor of simple conveyancing language. Whatever the differences between American and English chancery law may have been, there can be little doubt that the idea of a separate estate was well-known in America long before married women's acts were adopted. It also seems certain that the slow growth in the use of the married women's separate estate eventually compelled

married women's property acts. In New York, for example, the married woman's act of 1848 was adopted in the same legislative session that adopted the Field Code, two years after equity courts had been abolished and three years after the state Chancery Court had held that an active trustee was necessary in separate equitable estates. *See* L'Amoureaux v. Van Rensselaer, 1 Barb. Ch. 34, 5 N.Y. Ch. 288 (1845); E. Warbasse, *supra* note 2, at 205-29. While Horwitz's theory that equity in New York was limited may be true, it is not clear that his theory may be extended to other states. In addition, the New York equity changes were apparently not duplicated elsewhere before married women's acts were adopted. The New York setting is particularly interesting because of the clear interplay between law, equity, procedure, judicial decisions, and the reshaping of women's roles. *See generally* P. RABKIN, *supra* note 2, at 61-90 (discussing the New York setting); N. BASCH, *supra* note 1 (same).

52. C. BINNEY, RESTRICTIONS UPON LOCAL AND SPECIAL LEGISLATION IN STATE CONSTITUTIONS 6-7 (1894). It is interesting to note that far-reaching constraints were imposed on the enactment of private bills by the New York Constitution adopted in 1846, only two years before passage of New York's first married women's act. *Id.* at 7.

53. E. Warbasse, *supra* note 2, at 289, notes that states with strong equity traditions tended to lag behind other states in adopting married women's acts, thus casting doubt on any theory that equity led to enactment of the statutes. Although Warbasse's theory may be true for acts adopted after the initial wave of debt statutes, *see infra* notes 263 (listing separate estate statutes of the 1850's) and 361 (listing earnings statutes of the 1870's), she appears to be partially in error as to the early acts. The lag may simply confirm the idea that the early acts were not very far-reaching and that the later statutes found tougher sledding in the more traditional Southern legal milieu.

54. P. RABKIN, *supra* note 2, at 52-90. Rabkin's work on the relationship between the codification movement and the New York married women's act is very useful. Not only is it consistent with Horwitz's general description of the rise of codification in the first half of the 19th century, M. HORWITZ, *supra* note 51, at 17-18, but it also begins the task of linking coverture rules to other general trends in the legal arena.

55. One of the interesting questions not answered by Rabkin's work is the relationship outside of New York between changes in rules of civil procedure and the emergence of married women's acts. New York was among the first states to revamp its procedural system. To the extent that equity and law were merged, legislation might have been necessary to preserve existing equitable rights of married women. Examining equity practice prior to the adoption of married women's acts might prove a useful line of inquiry in states that adopted reforms in court practice about the same time they passed married women's legislation. At first glance, it does not appear that significant procedural reform occurred before married women's property acts were passed in other jurisdictions.

a simplification of the process by which a separate estate was created and maintained.

But just as with disposition of women's property at death, there was probably not enough married women's property held at equity in 1800 to command the attention of late eighteenth-century reformers.[56] Nor was there yet a general cultural desire to permit a married woman, rather than the person creating an equitable separate estate, to control the disposition of a separately held asset.[57] Not until separate equitable estates were routinely used by both men and women to control family wealth, rather than simply by wealthy fathers to protect their daughters from creditors of untrustworthy husbands, would the law likely respond with significant alterations in form. Therefore, one of the most important tasks for any archival study of married women's property is to investigate the changing rates at which equity was used to protect such property.[58]

D. FINDINGS

176 The proportion of recorded wills in Massachusetts and Maryland written by women rose significantly between 1800 and 1850.[59] At first glance, the data on wills in Tables 2 and 3 supports the thesis that women began to exercise more control over property as the nineteenth century developed.

TABLE 2: DUKES COUNTY[60]

Years	Number of Male Wills	Number of Female Wills	Percent of Wills Written By Females
1801-1810	40	1	2%
1811-1820	26	2	7%
1821-1830	46	10	18%
1831-1840	35	12	26%
1841-1850	45	13	22%

56. Note that women generally did not write wills before 1800, *see supra* note 28 and accompanying text, and that women held very little property before 1800. *See supra* notes 13-16 and accompanying text.

57. Even after 1800, married women's ability to dispose of their separate property was generally limited by the contents of the trust deed under which they took title. *See supra* notes 29-32 and accompanying text (discussing constraints on women's ability to dispose of their separate property).

58. A trust deed search in Dukes County is yet to be done. In addition, a large sample of male wills needs to be read. If the female wills are indicative of trends, separate estate language does begin to appear in some wills after 1830. The data is much too tentative at this point to be useful.

59. Data in both tables are from the indices for Dukes County and Baltimore. These results are fairly consistent with earlier studies suggesting that women's wills did not appear in significant numbers until after 1800. K. LOCKRIDGE, *supra* note 28, at 38, 128 (noting dearth of samples of women's handwriting); A. JONES, *supra* note 14, at 39 (showing that few women were "wealth holders" in the Thirteen Colonies in 1774).

60. This data, of course, does not include the "no record" cases. *See supra* Table 1. The reliability of the pre-1820 data is therefore more dubious, especially for men. The low number of "no record" entries for women suggests that their data are more useful.

TABLE 3: BALTIMORE CITY AND COUNTY

Year	Number of Male Wills	Number of Female Wills	Percent of Wills Written by Females
1800	68	7	9%
1805	63	13	17%
1810	75	13	15%
1815	72	27	27%
1820	68	26	28%
1825	95	19	17%
1830	96	30	24%
1835	82	28	25%
1840	71	47	40%
1846	86	53	38%

It would be improper to argue, however, that the appearance of more wo- 177
men's wills indicates that women were behaving in remarkably different ways in 1850 than they were in 1800. There were differences, but they were subtle. Though the proportion of probated wills written by women rose, it does not follow automatically that the proportion of women writing wills rose. In fact, as Table 4 indicates,[61] the proportion of women's wills in relation to the adult death rate[62] in Baltimore did not rise during this period.

TABLE 4: WOMEN'S WILL-WRITING RATE—BALTIMORE

Time Period	Avg. Number of Female Wills/Yr. for Baltimore City and County	Avg. Adult Death Rate/Yr. for Baltimore City	Female Wills as Percent of Death Rate
1815-1819	24.2	613.8	3.9%
1820-1824	25.0	948.4	2.6%
1825-1829	26.8	796.2	3.4%
1830-1834	34.4	1189.4	2.9%
1835-1839	44.2	979.2	4.5%
1840-1844	38.2	995.4	3.8%
1845-1849	50.4	1441.2	3.5%

These figures do not give true will-writing rates because the will data cover a larger geographic area[63] than the death rate data, and the death rates include

61. Death rate data for all Baltimore tables are taken from W. HOWARD, PUBLIC HEALTH ADMINISTRATION AND THE NATURAL HISTORY OF DISEASE IN BALTIMORE, MARYLAND, 1797-1920 521-23 (1924).

62. "Adult" is defined as those persons age 20 and above.

63. Will data are for both city and county. Where data was available in the wills actually read, there appeared to be no significant difference between the will-writing rates of the city and county. Since

both men and women. Nonetheless, Table 4 is very valuable as a trend indicator since the same data bases are used as measuring devices for both genders. The women's will-writing rate only kept pace with population trends. The proportion of wills written by women increased in Baltimore only because, as Table 5 suggests, men wrote fewer wills as the nineteenth century progressed.[64]

TABLE 5: MEN'S AND WOMEN'S WILL RATES FOR SELECTED YEARS—BALTIMORE

Selected Years	Number of Male Wills City & County	Number of Female Wills City & County	Baltimore City Adult Deaths	Male Wills as Percent of Deaths	Female Wills as Percent of Deaths
1815 and 1820	140	53	1267	11.8	4.2
1825 and 1830	191	49	1691	11.3	2.9
1835 and 1840	153	75	1872	8.2	4.0
1846	86	53	1234	7.0	4.3

178

The data for Dukes County are not as easily used to determine trends in will-writing rates because of the large number of male "no record" entries for the 1800-1820 period. Death rate data are also not easily available. A crude estimate may be made by tabulating a will-writing rate based on population rather than death rates. The results of such a tabulation, as can be seen in Table 6, produce much less clear data than for Baltimore. Even so, it does appear that women began writing wills at a greater rate after 1820.

---

locale was not available in the death rate data and will indices used to compile this data, I had to fudge a bit and use the wills themselves to find locale and the census to find population trends. Nonetheless, the data are quite useful as a means of discussing rate change over time, especially since there does not appear to be any significant difference in will writing rates between city and county when population is used as a rate base.

City Versus County Will-Writing Rates

Year	% of Population in City*	% Female Wills From City
1800	46%	—
1810	63%	100% (2/2)
1820	66%	—
1825	—	71% (12/17)
1830	69%	—
1840	77%	72% (26/36)
1846	—	74% (31/42)
1850	80%	—

* This figure represents the percent of the combined populations of the city and county that resided in the city. The population data is taken from the decennial census. The percent data on residence is derived from statements made in the wills about the residence of the testator.

64. The index was combed for male wills in selected years only. Nonetheless, the trends are quite clear when compared to the female data for the same selected years. As with Table 4, *infra*, Table 5 does not give true will-writing rates since the will base is city and county, the death base is city only, and will-writing rates are figured from total adult deaths, not just male or female deaths.

TABLE 6: WILL-WRITING RATES—DUKES COUNTY[65]

Years	Number of Male Wills	Number of Female Wills	Population as of Last Yr. of Decade	Male Wills as Percent of Population	Female Wills as Percent of Population
1801-1810	40	1	3118	1.3%	—
1811-1820	26	2	3290	0.8%	—
1821-1830	46	10	3517	1.3%	.3%
1831-1840	35	12	3958	0.9%	.3%
1841-1850	45	13	4540	1.0%	.3%

Just as women may have bucked the male trend to lower will-writing rates, those women with property may have died testate more frequently than their male counterparts. The Dukes County index produced some data on the proportion of probated estates that were intestate. These data certainly overstate the use of wills since many estates were not probated.[66] Table 7 gives the proportion of probated estates that were testate.

TABLE 7: TESTACY RATE—DUKES COUNTY

Years	Male Recorded Estates Testate (%)	Female Recorded Estates Testate (%)	Number of "No Record" Entries	
			Male	Female
1801-1810	91% (40/44)	— (1/1)	21	0
1811-1820	67% (26/39)	— (2/3)	28	2
1821-1830	52% (46/88)	71% (10/14)	5	1
1831-1840	40% (35/88)	71% (12/17)	5	1
1841-1850	49% (45/92)	81% (13/16)	0	0

After 1830, twenty-four percent (25/105) of the testate estates were female, but only seven percent (8/108) of the intestate estates were female.

There are at least two possible explanations for the tendency of the women's will-writing rate to stay constant while the men's declined, and for women with assets to write wills at a higher rate than men. First, it is possible that women were making a subtle statement of goals by attempting to control the disposition of their assets in the face of countervailing male trends. And second, it may be that constraints on the ability of women to hold property were being

65. Population data is taken from 2 C.E. BANKS, HISTORY OF MARTHA'S VINEYARD (1911). The population figures in Table 6 are the sums of data for each of the three non-Indian towns on the island at the relevant times. These data are in the Annals for each town contained in volume 2 of Banks' work at pages 15-16 of the Annals of Edgartown, pages 5-6 of the Annals of Tisbury, and pages 5-7 of the Annals of Chilmark.

66. Certainly the vast bulk of people never wrote wills. *See* L. FRIEDMAN, *supra* note 22, at 220 (estimating that less than five percent of the persons who died each year left wills that passed through probate). Similar data for Baltimore was not gathered for this study.

released so that the opportunities for taking dispositional control were more frequently available. Some support for both theories is present in the data.

There is something intriguing about women writing wills when the size of even their probated estates was probably smaller than that of their male counterparts. While the data is too tentative to rely upon with great confidence, there is certainly a possibility that women with small estates were taking extra care to guide the disposition of their possessions at death. The Massachusetts study revealed a number of detailed inventories, though not enough to create a large sample. The average size of the inventories of women's estates suggests some income growth among women writing wills in the nineteenth century.

TABLE 8: SIZE OF FEMALE ESTATES—DUKES COUNTY

180

Time	Number of Wills with Inventories	Average Size	Number of Intestate Estates with Inventories	Average Size
1840-1850	7	$1364	4	$540
1800-1839	3	871	4	637[67]

Nonetheless, it appears that these estates were significantly smaller than men's estates. Among the ten men's estate files examined in which widows requested an allowance out of their husband's personal estates, eight were intestate. Of these eight, six were appraised at a value over $1,000. One was appraised at almost $20,000. Both of the testate estates were very large. While this is certainly not a random sampling of men's estates, the vastness of the difference between the values of these estates and their female counterparts gives rise to the thesis that women were writing wills in situations where men would not have done so. The detailed disposition of small items such as clothing, furniture, and housewares in a large number of the women's wills in both Dukes County and Baltimore also supports the thesis that women were taking special care with the disposition of their assets.

An array of other data confirms that even if women were not consciously exercising control more frequently as the century progressed, men were becoming more willing to let them. Evidence of two sorts is available. First, data on the gender of beneficiaries demonstrate that both male and female wills tended to favor women as primary beneficiaries. Second, use of the equitable estate for married women grew over time and changed in form to permit married women greater dispositional authority.

One of the more fascinating findings of the study, as illustrated by Tables 9 and 10, is that both men and women tended to dispose of property to women rather than to men. The data gathered preclude the argument that women's preference to repose assets with women was more pronounced than men's preference to do the same thing. The primary beneficiary of each will was usually very clear. When there was doubt about a particular will, but all the possibili-

67. Two other partial inventories existed suggesting administered estates in the range of $30 and $300, respectively.

ties were of one sex, the primary beneficiary was tabulated in the "other" category for that gender. When it was not clear whether one sex or another was the primary beneficiary, the will was labeled as "mixed."[68] The years represent the year of probate, which was not always the year in which the will was written. These two tables show that both men and women favored women as primary beneficiaries in their wills and that this trend, at least in Baltimore, increased over time.

TABLE 9: PRIMARY BENEFICIARIES OF WOMEN'S WILLS

Primary Beneficiaries		Dukes County (all years)	Baltimore: 1810 and 1825	1840	1846
Females:	Daughter	7	5	11	8
	Mother	2	0	1	3
	Sister	3	3	3	6
	Other	3	4	4	8
	Total	15(50%)	12(43%)	19(49%)	25(53%)
Males:	Son	4	2	6	2
	Nephew	3	1	0	3
	Other	3	4	3	4
	Total	10(33%)	7(25%)	9(23%)	9(19%)
Mixed:	Children	2	6	4	5
	Other	3	3	7	9[69]
	Total	5(17%)	9(32%)	11(28%)	13(28%)
	Total Wills	30(100%)	28(100%)	39(100%)	47(100%)

181

68. The few cases where it was not possible to make any conclusion or the cases where the will could not be found have not been included in the tables.

69. One of these wills involved charity as the primary beneficiary.

TABLE 10: PRIMARY BENEFICIARIES OF MEN'S WILLS (BALTIMORE)[70]

Primary Beneficiaries		Total Male Wills	1810 and 1825 Wills	1840 and 1846 Wills
Female:	Wife	6	0	6
	Wife, then daughters	5	0	5
	Daughter	3	2	1
	Other female	5	4	1
	Total	19(58%)	6(46%)	13(65%)
Male:	Other male	2	2	0
	Total	2(6%)	2(15%)	0(0%)
Mixed:	Wife, then children	4	2	2
	Children	3	1	2
	Other mixed	5	2	3
	Total	12(36%)	5(38%)	7(35%)
	Total Wills	33(100%)	13(100%)	20(100%)

Of even greater importance than beneficiary trends, the wills demonstrate that testators of both genders began to grant female beneficiaries, and more importantly, married female beneficiaries, greater control over the ultimate disposition of their assets. While studies of wills have suggested that wealthy men of the early nineteenth century tended to will assets to women in life estates or other forms that would insulate the property from creditors or from present or future husbands,[71] the Baltimore data demonstrates that trend may have diminished by mid-century. None of the thirteen men's wills probated in 1810 or 1825 named a wife as the sole primary beneficiary. Of the twenty 1840 and 1846 wills, six named a wife as primary beneficiary[72] and four more provided for interests in a wife, followed by grants to daughters. Furthermore, the wills confirm that the equitable estate became an increasingly preferred device as the century progressed. This was true for both men's and women's wills, although the male sample is small. Table 11 shows the percentage of wills that either created a trust with a woman as a beneficiary, or used sole and separate estate language in a grant to a woman, or combined both devices.

70. The Baltimore male sample included 3 wills from 1810, and 10 each from 1825, 1840, and 1846. The sample was gathered by turning the microfilm crank 10 times and stopping at the next male will.

71. L. FRIEDMAN, *supra* note 22, at 220-21.

72. Five of the six were straightforward grants to wives. The other had a restriction if the widow remarried.

TABLE 11: USE OF SEPARATE ESTATE—BALTIMORE

Year of Probate	Female Wills With Separate Estate	Male Wills With Separate Estates
1810 and 1825	14% (4/29)	8% (1/13)
1840	15% (6/41)	
1846	25% (12/48)	25% (5/20)[73]

This trend is further confirmed by data on use of deeds creating separate equitable estates in Baltimore. A search of deed indices was made for January to June, 1810, 1825, and 1840. This search, as seen in Table 12, revealed that the appearance of separate estate trust deeds increased at a rate just a bit lower than women's wills.

TABLE 12: WILLS & TRUST DEEDS FOR SELECTED YEARS—BALTIMORE

Year	Number of Women's Wills	Number of Separate Estate Deeds
1810	13	8
1825	19	11
1840	46	17

Analysis of these deeds also reveals that the later instruments gave married women more dispositional authority more frequently (see Table 13).

TABLE 13: TRUST DEED DISPOSITIONAL AUTHORITY—BALTIMORE

Year of Instrument	Full Disposal Authority	Limited Disposal Authority	Life Estate With Designated Remainders
1810	4	1	3
1825	4	2	5
1840	11	4	2

The limitations on dispositional authority varied substantially from instrument to instrument. Among the limitations were a spousal consent requirement, designation of a class from whom grantees must be selected, and grant of either sale or will capacity but not both. If the 1810 and 1825 instruments are combined, fifty-eight percent (11/19) of the women obtained some disposi-

73. This entry covers both 1840 and 1846.

tional authority. Eighty-eight percent (15/17) of the 1840 instruments provided some powers of disposal to women.

Because married women rarely wrote wills in the early nineteenth century, use of will data alone to tabulate the rates at which women disposed of property at death is artificially low if nontestamentary methods of transfer were available to wives. Trust instruments granting disposal authority were just such a substitute for testation. Combining the trust deed data for 1825 and 1840 with the will data produces the intriguing, but tentative, conclusion that by 1840 the effective will-writing rate for women rose to the same level as for men. If we assume that the number of trust deeds found for the January to June periods of 1825 and 1840 represents exactly half of the rate for each year, then the following table results:

TABLE 14: WILL/TRUST DEED RATES[74]

184

Year	Male Wills Per Year	Female Wills Per Year	Trust Deeds Per Year	Baltimore City Adult Deaths	Male Wills as % of Deaths	Female Wills And Trust Deeds as % of Deaths
1825	95	19	12	772	12.3	4.0
1840	71	46	30	932	7.6	8.2

The column for Trust Deeds Per Year includes only deeds giving women some dispositional authority; the other deeds involve no substitute for testamentary capacity. Similarly, the final column adds wills to trust deeds granting some dispositional authority. Use of death rates is an artificial device for measuring trust deed rates, and the use of only a two-year sample renders the results tentative at best. At a minimum it is fair to suggest that by 1840 married women in Baltimore had obtained significantly more authority to dispose of assets at death than had previously been the case. It may be that the will-writing rate for men fell in part because women were being substituted as testamentary actors.

The Baltimore trust deed data also confirms the availability of equity as a means of limiting the impact of common law restrictions on married women. While virtually no married women's wills were found in either Dukes County or Baltimore (see Tables 15 and 16),[75] the testamentary capacity of married women did not necessarily remain unchanged between 1800 and 1850.

74. Remember that the will rates in this table are not real since the death base includes all adults in the city and the will and trust deed rates include both the city and the county. Death rates are taken from the same source as Table 4, *supra*.

75. In Tables 15 and 16 the columns labelled "probably widow or single" involve wills where the circumstances strongly suggested the woman's status, but the status was not stated explicitly. For example, a woman who willed property to her mother, and had the same last name as her mother was almost surely a single woman.

TABLE 15: MARITAL STATUS OF FEMALE TESTATORS—DUKES COUNTY

Decade of Probate	Widow or Single	Probably Widow or Single	Married	Unclear
1801-1810	1	0	0	0
1811-1820	0	0	1	1
1821-1830	7	1	1	1
1831-1840	7	2	0	3
1841-1850	9	3	0	1

TABLE 16: MARITAL STATUS OF FEMALE TESTATORS—BALTIMORE

Year of Probate	Widow or Single	Probably Widow or Single	Married	Unclear
1810	6	2	1	4
1825	8	7	0	4
1840	15	14	2	15
1846	21	18	2	7

E. CONCLUSION

The post-1820 appearance of women's wills, the growth in use of the equitable separate estate in wills by both male and female testators, and the increase in use of trust deeds with disposal powers indicates that some growth occurred in the ability or propensity of Maryland's women to dispose of property. This growth, however, occurred within very narrow bounds. The rate at which women's will-writing increased only kept pace with population growth; the proportion of wills written by women increased only because Baltimore men wrote fewer wills as the nineteenth century progressed. Married women's dispositional authority was constrained by the wishes of their grantors. The use of trust deeds with dispositional powers, if thought of as substitutes for wills, may push the women's "will-writing" rate to the level of the men's rate, but these instruments were inherently creatures of male draftsmen. All this suggests that small changes were occurring. Because women were probably not wealthier in relation to men in 1850 than they were in 1800,[76] there may have been a slow trend toward giving women dispositional authority over property at the expense of some fathers, husbands, and trustees.

---

76. General historical information suggests that women's proportion of wealth did not rise in the first half of the 19th century. *Compare* A. JONES, *supra* note 14, at 39 *with* L. SOLTOW, *supra* note 15, at 200 n.12. A complete investigation of the reasons for the different will-writing rates of Baltimore men and women is necessary, but is beyond the scope of the present study. If men of lesser wealth tended to stop writing wills over time and women of similar or growing wealth began appearing as will-writers, perhaps some rewriting of known history would be possible. If the numbers in Table 8, *supra*, hold up with larger samples, some interesting conclusions could be drawn, especially since the 1840's was a time of deflation. *See generally* A. COLE, WHOLESALE COMMODITY PRICES IN THE UNITED STATES: 1700-1861 (1938). On the other hand, whaling produced a great deal of wealth in Dukes County during this period. The increase in women's wealth, if any, may simply reflect community trends.

The results of this study confirm that research into the actual use of wills, trusts, and other forms of control over property will reveal a great deal about social patterns and customs prior to the adoption of married women's acts. But the varied reception given equity in America requires caution in drawing general conclusions from any single piece of research. Two other studies of early nineteenth-century documents, which reached somewhat different conclusions than this study, suggest an agenda for further work.

Marylynn Salmon, in her study of marriage settlements in South Carolina,[77] found that between 1730 and 1830 control of marriage settlement property by men remained fairly constant, control by women fell, and control by couples rose.[78] Authority, she found, moved from women alone toward joint management by husbands and wives. Salmon, pointing to Mary Beth Norton's conclusion that women's participation in family governance increased in the decades surrounding the turn of the nineteenth century,[79] suggested that the changes in control arose because women needed less autonomy as they "exercised more authority over the general fund of family property."[80] Salmon also found that descent of settlement property to children increased over time,
186 while control of descent by women declined.[81] She tentatively concluded that marriage settlement form became more standardized by the nineteenth century, and that the standardized children descent provisions were accepted because wives had become more secure about their financial autonomy while alive and generally desired their children to have their property at death.[82]

Both Salmon's overall finding that control of marriage settlement property in South Carolina became more egalitarian by 1830 and my conclusion that women may have gained authority over property at the expense of some men are consistent with Norton's thesis that women's role in family decisionmaking grew in importance between 1750 and 1830. But Salmon's twist that control by couples replaced control by women is different from my suggestion that control by women replaced control by men. In part this may be due to the different ways the data were gathered. Salmon looked at changes in the form of marriage settlements over time. I was interested as much in the rates at which women participated in the property transaction process as in the authority of women to dispose of trust assets. Insofar as our reviews of trust instruments alone are concerned, our results may turn out to be consistent. A larger Maryland sample of trusts may change my results. Salmon's look at a century of documents may have caught a long trend, while my look at half a century may mirror the last half of Salmon's data. Looking only at the South Carolina marriage settlements from 1800 to 1830, Salmon does appear to have found a slight increase in control by women and couples, and a slight decline in control by men.[83] In addition, my tentative conclusion that women may have replaced some men as actors in the property system arises from a look at combined

77. Salmon, *South Carolina*, *supra* note 4, at 668.

78. *Id.* at 668-72

79. M. NORTON, *supra* note 2.

80. Salmon, *South Carolina*, *supra* note 4, at 669.

81. *Id.* at 677-79.

82. *Id.* at 677.

83. *Id.* at 672.

patterns in both wills and equity instruments, rather than equity instruments alone. Further research on the rates in which women participated in all sorts of transactions, in addition to the forms of these transaction, is needed before solid conclusions may be reached about the status of women just prior to the adoption of married women's acts.

It is also possible that the studies display significant differences in the use of equity between the Deep South and the more industrialized border areas. It is logical to hypothesize that further research into Southern and border state equity documents will provide clues about why Southern states tended to adopt the first wave of married women's acts insulating wives' property from husbands' creditors, but spurned many other reforms adopted in the North after 1850, while some border jurisdictions moved quickly to revamp most major common law coverture rules.[84] If Southern equity documents show that the role of women was reduced prior to the era of married women's acts, and that married women's acts were adopted in bad economic times to solidify a fairly narrow role of married women in equitable separate estates, one would expect that further legislation to enlarge married women's autonomous role in the family would not readily be adopted. If border state documents confirm that women were seen more as autonomous persons in a marriage than as subservient financial partners, one would expect a somewhat different legislative response.

The only published study of Northeastern documents from the early nineteenth century raises as many questions as it answers. Norma Basch, in her study of New York married women's legislation,[85] undertook a small study of wills in Westchester County. Although she sampled only two years of documents, Basch found that there was little change in the content of wills between 1825 and 1850,[86] that sons were favored over daughters,[87] and that women were usually denied power over the disposition of trust assets or granted only interests for life.[88] These results conflict somewhat with my Massachusetts results, where women seemed to fare somewhat better. Basch's work, like mine, needs to be replicated with much larger samples. In addition, Basch did not focus on the possibility that women fared better in *inter vivos* trust instruments or that participation rates of women in various aspects of property decision-making may have increased, even if the contents of wills did not change.

Trust deeds were certainly used in New York, but the lack of comprehensive recording statutes led Basch not to study them except through judicial decisions.[89] Nonetheless, Basch's work confirms that the equity jurisprudence in New York[90] was underlaid with use of trusts in wills at least as early as 1825. While there is certainly the possibility, affirmed by other work,[91] that North-

---

84. *See infra* notes 204-11 and accompanying text (discussing the first wave of acts insulating wives' property); *see also infra* notes 260-73 and accompanying text (discussing reason for and extent of reforms).
85. N. BASCH, *supra* note 1, at 100-12.
86. *Id.* at 101-03.
87. *Id.* at 101, 105.
88. *Id.* at 108.
89. *Id.* at 73.
90. *See id.* at 70-100 (reviewing cases).
91. Salmon, *South Carolina*, *supra* note 4.

eastern jurisdictions with equity traditions operated more conservatively before 1850 than Southern or border states, there is now little doubt that once the reforming impulses of the abolitionist era struck with full force, many of the more rigid impulses of Northern coverture law fell.[92] If more complete explorations of the terms of Northern trusts confirm Basch's findings, it may be that the great dissonance between the reality of day-to-day property usage and the aspirations of women in a quickly industrializing region provided significant strength to the Northeastern women's movement after 1850.

II. THE ADOPTION OF MARRIED WOMEN'S PROPERTY ACTS

The Baltimore data confirm that the equitable separate estate underwent significant development from 1800 to 1850, and that the availability of equity to protect married women's property was known well before married women's acts were adopted. But equity was not the only impetus for reform of married women's property law. Like equity, many of the sources for coverture law reform had both English and American roots. The obvious relevance of Eng-
188 lish law makes it easy to underestimate the importance of American legal developments. In this section, I place English law in its proper perspective and expose the multiplicity of American legal developments during the first half of the nineteenth century that shaped the married women's acts.

A. THE ENGLISH ROOTS

While Blackstone's famous 1765 commentaries were the focus of much of the nineteenth-century public debate on women's law, there is remarkably little legal history scholarship on the influence of Blackstone, or even of English law generally, on nineteenth-century American coverture law. There is literature suggesting that English legal materials were more influential in the 1820's and 1830's than before,[93] that along with moral revivals and Jacksonian idealization of the strong male farmer came legal Anglicism, treatise writing, and codification movements.[94] Legal education, which along with education generally, developed and grew from the 1790's through 1830, was heavily influenced by the treatise writers, English law, and Blackstone.[95] Yet these very facts make it unlikely that Blackstone became the subject for public debate in the 1840's because contemporary law reflected his eighteenth-century ideas. Rather, it is likely that conservative segments of the legal and academic communities were searching British treatises for precision in an era of multiplying sources for legal rules.[96] Blackstone's writings were easily understood both by

---

92. *See infra* notes 204-11, 260-73 and accompanying text (detailing reforms).

93. Zainaldin traces the reemergence of conservative English child custody cases in the 1830's, perhaps encouraged by the heavy use of English cites in the treatises of Kent and Story. Zainaldin, *supra* note 2, at 1059-68. *See also* Nolan, *Sir William Blackstone and the New American Republic: A Study of Intellectual Impact*, 51 N.Y.U. L. REV. 731, 759-767 (1976) (discussing the growing influence of Blackstone on legal education in the period).

94. *See* P. RABKIN, *supra* note 2, at 40-60; Bloomfield, *William Sampson and the Codifiers: The Roots of American Legal Reform, 1820-1830*, 11 AM. J. LEG. HIST. 234 (1967); C. COOK, THE AMERICAN CODIFICATION MOVEMENT: STUDY OF ANTEBELLUM LEGAL REFORM (1981).

95. *See* Nolan, *supra* note 93, at 759-67 (discussing Blackstone's impact on legal education in early America).

96. *See* C. COOK, *supra* note 94, at 46-48 (noting that by 1815 sources for American law were quickly

men reading to become lawyers in a culture loosening the constraints on entry into the legal profession[97] and by women publicly criticizing the extant order.

For a number of reasons, Blackstone's vision of reality[98] is a less than satisfactory basis for measuring the influence of English coverture law. First, English law changed between the time Blackstone wrote and the opening decades of the nineteenth century. Second, by 1800 important differences between American and English law existed in conveyancing, dower, intestate succession, equity, and divorce.[99] Third, the overall impact of English law on coverture developments was diffuse. So many other influences were at work during the early nineteenth century that English law was only one of numerous factors. Well before married women's legislation appeared, American law witnessed the arrival of the codification and treatise movements, the rise and incipient decline of legislative private bills, and the appearance of efforts to merge law and equity. To ignore these and other legal developments by focusing on Blackstone's version of our English heritage is to miss the peculiarly American context of married women's property legislation.

1. Change in English Coverture Law 189

Blackstone wrote his Commentaries while the separate equitable estate of a married woman was reaching maturity in English chancery courts.[100] Decisions rendered in the late eighteenth century both subjected a wife's separate property to her debts, and narrowly construed dispositional powers in trust instruments to avoid overreaching by husbands.[101] The failure of much modern scholarship to note the changes in English law during the very era in which America began seriously to reconsider the legal status of women is quite remarkable.[102] Many have written of English law as if it were monolithic and

---

proliferating). Case reports, statutes, and books were emerging in a nation with more than twenty states. Doctrinal and theoretical diversity was becoming commonplace. Uncertainty over legal norms was becoming a real concern for many.

97. *Id.* at 158-60, 172-73. *See also* L. FRIEDMAN, *supra* note 22, at 276-78.

98. The 1803 St. George Tucker edition of BLACKSTONE'S COMMENTARIES was the most prominent of the early American editions of the 1765 English treatise. Chapter XV, part III, on the law of husband and wife, at 441-45, is the section most often chastised. There Blackstone writes that "the very being or legal existence of the woman is suspended during the marriage, or at least is incorporated and consolidated into that of the husband; under whose wing, protection and cover, she performs everything."

99. Divorce is an enormous area all by itself. I have chosen largely to pass by this area for now because so little good work has been done and the task is so enormous. Blake, *supra* note 2, does make it clear that divorce was an early and important area where the colonies differed notably from England. But the lack of work on the economics of divorce—the relative positions of men and women before, during, and after marriage—makes it very difficult to evaluate the importance of the growth of divorce between 1780 and 1840. If the major thesis of this article is correct, one should find reforms between 1800 and 1850 that provided divorced women slightly greater rights to property or money upon divorce. This would occur not because of any modern notions about protecting women, but to protect increasing numbers of children coming into the custody of women and to prevent women on the edge of poverty from becoming public charges.

100. Holdsworth writes that by 1750 property could be set aside in a separate estate or disposed of by a married woman by will or gift without a husband's consent. 12 W. HOLDSWORTH, A HISTORY OF ENGLISH LAW 275-76 (1938 & photo. reprint 1966).

101. 12 W. HOLDSWORTH, *supra* note 100, at 325-26.

102. There is a fairly large body of literature on the reception of English law. Among the more interesting items suggesting the diffuse nature of America's reception of English law are G. HASKINS, LAW & AUTHORITY IN EARLY MASSACHUSETTS 113-40 (1960); M. HORWITZ, *supra* note 51, at 3-30; D. KONIG, LAW AND SOCIETY IN PURITAN MASSCHUSETTS: ESSEX COUNTY 1629-1692 3-63 (1979); W.

unchanging.[103] Holdsworth notes that English law on married women changed substantially during the seventeenth and eighteenth centuries. The general outlines of common law coverture rules emerged in the thirteenth century.[104] Upon marriage, the husband gained power and control over his wife's freehold estate for the term of the marriage, or, upon the birth of a child, for the husband's life, and obtained ownership of his wife's personal property. A woman's ability to contract was suspended upon marriage. Equitable exceptions to these rules did not emerge until the late sixteenth century,[105] when antenuptial contracts and trusts for the separate use of the wife appeared.[106] The chancery cases also gave wives power to will their separate estates, donate them to their husbands, sell them to strangers, and perhaps deal with them by contract.[107] Though consent of the husband for the establishment of the separate equitable estate was still necessary,[108] equity courts of the late seventeenth century began to require an "equity to a settlement" to insure some financial safeguards for wives whose husbands sought to make use of assets in a separate estate.[109] This period also saw the emergence of enforceable separation agreements, support decrees for wives leaving their marital home due to the
190 fault of the husband,[110] and cases confirming the ability of married women to execute powers.[111] Not until the mid-eighteenth century did chancery courts take the crucial step of recognizing a separate estate created without the husband's consent.[112] In a related development, the courts began to examine dispositions of a separate estate more carefully to avoid coercion by husbands.[113] The separate estate became subject to the debts of married women by the end of the eighteenth century.[114]

Dower also changed dramatically from its fifteenth-century roots.[115] By the fifteenth century the one-third share was established, and it was clear that dower could be avoided if land was sold by means of a fine and the wife was

---

NELSON, AMERICANIZATION OF THE COMMON LAW: THE IMPACT OF LEGAL CHANGE ON MASSACHUSETTS SOCIETY, 1760-1830 1-64 (1975); E. Warbasse, *supra* note 2, at 3-6; Blume & Brown, *supra* note 37; DePauw, *Women and the Law: The Colonial Period*, 6 HUMAN RIGHTS 107 (1977); Nolan, *supra* note 93; Note, *The Tennessee County Courts Under the North Carolina and Territorial Governments: The Davidson County Court of Pleas and Quarter Sessions, 1783-1796, as a Case Study*, 32 VAND. L. REV. 349 (1979) [hereinafter Note, *Tennessee County Courts*]; Goebel, *Ex Parte Clio*, 54 COLUM. L. REV. 450-59 (1954) (reviewing O. CROSSKEY, POLITICS AND THE CONSTITUTION IN THE HISTORY OF THE UNITED STATES (1953)).

103. Authors often speak of the common law without reference to its modification over time. *See, e.g.*, R. MORRIS, *supra* note 21, at 128, 155, 164, 166, 173, 185, 195, 197; P. RABKIN, *supra* note 2, at 19-22; L. KERBER, *supra* note 2, at 139-41.

104. 3 W. HOLDSWORTH, A HISTORY OF ENGLISH LAW 520-33, 541-43 (1908 & photo. reprint 1966).

105. 4 W. HOLDSWORTH, A HISTORY OF ENGLISH LAW 428-29 (2d ed. 1937).

106. 5 W. HOLDSWORTH, A HISTORY OF ENGLISH LAW 310-15 (1924).

107. *Id.* at 315.

108. 6 W. HOLDSWORTH, A HISTORY OF ENGLISH LAW 645 (2d ed. 1937 & photo. reprint 1966).

109. *Id.*

110. *Id.* at 646.

111. 7 W. HOLDSWORTH, *supra* note 108, at 180-81.

112. 12 W. HOLDSWORTH, *supra* note 100, at 275-76. *See also* P. RABKIN, *supra* note 2, at 81. Rabkin notes that chancery development gradually permitted fathers to guarantee that the property they passed on to their daughters would be free from the clutches of untrustworthy husbands. It was to protect daughters, Rabkin argues, more than to free wives that the chancery acted. *Id.*

113. 12 W. HOLDSWORTH, *supra* note 100, at 276, 324-26.

114. *Id.* at 325.

115. 3 W. HOLDSWORTH, *supra* note 104, at 193.

examined separately by the court.[116] Even at this early date, other devices for avoiding dower had emerged, including the use of jointures and premarital settlements providing for life estates in the husband's lands at his death.[117] The development of jointure led to the already mentioned development of ante-nuptial contracts and trusts for the separate use of the wife. By the middle of the eighteenth century, it was clear that equitable estates were free of dower.[118] While the lack of dower at equity was reversed by statute in 1833, the same act provided for dower only in lands actually held at death by the husband.[119] Thus, the English rules governing both dower and coverture at equity underwent significant changes from the time America was first colonized in the early seventeenth century through the turn of the nineteenth century.

Coverture doctrines at law were also under stress in the same period. For some time before the turn of the eighteenth century, it was clear that married women divorced from bed and board, abandoned by their husbands, or left behind after their husband's banishment from the realm could act as single women.[120] During the eighteenth century, cases arose where women, living apart on separate maintenance provided by their husbands after a marital sep- 191
aration, pled coverture as a defense to actions by their creditors.[121] Lord Mansfield, confronted with such a dispute in *Corbett v. Poelnitz*[122] in 1785, took the opportunity gently to criticize the extant coverture rules at law, and to bind the separately maintained wife to her contract as if she were a feme-sole.[123] Though the case was overruled after Mansfield left the King's Bench,[124] it is clear from the judicial turmoil and the commentary of the day that the less central portions of the coverture rules were under attack even at law.[125] Mansfield's opinion in *Corbett* spoke of "new customs and new manners"[126] and noted the growing prevalence of deeds under which a married woman assumed the appearance of a feme-sole.[127] Mansfield's general penchant for liberalizing rules of commercial transactions meshed neatly with his attempt to reform coverture rules as they applied to married women acting independently in the business world.[128]

---

116. *Id.* at 193.
117. *Id.* at 196.
118. *Id.* at 196-97.
119. *Id.* at 197.
120. 1 J. POWELL, ESSAY UPON THE LAW OF CONTRACTS AND AGREEMENTS 75-77 (1790).
121. *See id.* at 77-93; C. FIFOOT, LORD MANSFIELD 217-18 (1936); 1 W. EVANS, A GENERAL VIEW OF THE DECISIONS OF LORD MANSFIELD 99-110 (1803); Ringstead v. Lady Lanesborough, 99 Eng. Rep. 610, 3 Douglas 197 (1783); Corbett v. Poelnitz, 99 Eng. Rep. 940, 1 Term Rep. 5 (1785); Marshall v. Rutton, 101 Eng. Rep. 1538, 8 Term Rep. 545 (1800).
122. 99 Eng. Rep. 940, 1 Term Rep. 5 (1785).
123. *Id.* at 945, 1 Term Rep. at 8.
124. Marshall v. Rutton, 101 Eng. Rep. 1538, 8 Term Rep. 545 (1800).
125. *See* J. POWELL, *supra* note 120, at 77-93. In the most widely-circulated American edition of BLACKSTONE'S COMMENTARIES, that of St. George Tucker issued in 1803, there are a number of notes critical of the Blackstone version of coverture. BLACKSTONE'S COMMENTARIES 441-45 (S.G. Tucker ed. 1803). Some of these notes are reprints of those penned by Edward Christian, who had edited an earlier English edition of the Commentaries. Tucker added a few references, including one to *Corbett v. Poelnitz*. *Id.* at 943. *See also* Nolan, *supra* note 93, at 736-37.
126. 99 Eng. Rep. at 942, 1 Term Rep. at 8.
127. *Id.* at 943, 1 Term Rep. at 9.
128. Though Mansfield apparently was not well-received in America after the Revolutionary War,

Another indication of the pressure Mansfield must have felt is revealed by cases on the custom of London, confirmed by the courts of law beginning at the end of the sixteenth century and continuing through the eighteenth century.[129] According to the custom, women could sue and be sued on debts arising out of trade in which their husbands did not intermeddle. While the cases do not reveal whether the custom was more heavily used in Mansfield's time than in prior centuries, one would certainly hypothesize that it, or some substitute, was.[130] The growth, if any, in the wealth and commercial activity of the wives of London[131] may have imposed pressures on both the coverture rules at law and on the equitable notion of the separate estate. It is quite possible that use of the custom declined rapidly in the late eighteenth century once equity had affirmed the ability of women to use separate estates free of their husbands' control.

Changes in English law were well-known in America before 1840. The most widely used edition of Blackstone, that edited by Tucker in 1803,[132] had some significant debunking notes and commentary. Even suffrage for unmarried women was implicitly approved in a note saying that women "pay taxes with-
192 out having the liberty of voting for representatives; and indeed there seems at present no substantial reason why single women should be denied this privilege."[133] "I fear," the note goes on, "there is little reason to pay compliment to our laws for their respect and favour to the female sex."[134] In addition, the early American treatises by Kent and Story[135] noted many developments, especially at equity, which had flowered in England since Blackstone's time. My archival work certainly confirms this. Furthermore, studies of court and other records in frontier areas indicate that some frontier lawyers and judges paid lavish attention to English and American precedents in the early nineteenth century, and that they had access to a wide array of case reports and treatises

---

see Goebel, *supra* note 102, at 455-56; M. HORWITZ, *supra* note 51, at 18, his work was better known and perhaps more influential by the time of Kent and the beginnings of the treatise movement in the United States. *See* 2 J. KENT, *supra* note 43, at 133-36; M. HORWITZ, *supra* note 51, at 257-58; L. FRIEDMAN, *supra* note 22, at 95.

129. Chamberlain v. Throp, 74 Eng. Rep. 121, 1 Leonard 130 (31 Eliz., 1589-1590); Bowett v. Langham, 124 Eng. Rep. 299, Hetley 9 (3 Car., 1628-1629); Langham against the wife of John Bewett, 79 Eng. Rep. 661, Croke Car. 68 (3 Car., 1628-1629); Barns v. Barns, 90 Eng. Rep. 32, Skinner 66 (34 Car. 2, 1683-1684); Fabian v. Plant, 89 Eng. Rep. 525, 1 Shower, K.B. 183 (3 W. & M., 1690-1691); Anonymous, 88 Eng. Rep. 1549, 12 Modern 603 (13 Will. 3, 1702-1703); Mrs. Pool's Case, 88 Eng. Rep. 1021, 11 Modern 253 (8 Anne, 1710-1711); Caudell v. Shaw, 100 Eng. Rep. 1065, 4 Term Rep. 361 (1791).

130. The frequency of reported cases in Viner's Abridgement goes down in the eighteenth century as compared with the seventeenth century. Perhaps this is because of the increasing utility of trusts, powers, and other devices to avoid the restrictions of the coverture rules at law. There may have been less need to dispute the legitimacy of the custom if other tools were available to women to protect their commercial interests.

131. That wives were involved in trade is fairly clear. *See* M. GEORGE, LONDON LIFE IN THE XVIIITH CENTURY 168-73, 175, 181-85, 195, 198, 202, 207-08, 427-29 (1925). It is not at all clear that the same may be said of married women in the United States, since little scholarship exists on the commercial role of married women in the early part of the century. Two works by E. Dexter, COLONIAL WOMEN OF AFFAIRS: WOMEN IN BUSINESS AND PROFESSIONS IN AMERICA BEFORE 1776 (1924) [hereinafter E. DEXTER, COLONIAL WOMEN OF AFFAIRS] and CAREER WOMEN OF AMERICA 1776-1840 (1950), pay no attention to marital status.

132. *See* Nolan, *supra* note 93, at 737 n.38.

133. 2 BLACKSTONE'S COMMENTARIES 445 (S.G. Tucker ed. 1803). The note was written by Edward Christian, an Englishman, not Tucker, shortly before Tucker did his work.

134. *Id.*

135. J. KENT, *supra* note 43; J. STORY, *supra* note 34.

within a very short time after the areas were opened for settlement.[136] Available treatises included not only the expected volumes, such as Blackstone and Kent, but also a number of now obscure American and English books.[137] There is every reason to believe that the influence in America of Blackstone's conservative commentary on coverture law was equally balanced by general knowledge of the more liberal equity concepts emerging after the Revolutionary War. As Nolan has concluded about Blackstone generally, "The Commentaries did significantly influence the evolution of American institutions, but their influence on each differed in kind and degree. In every case, however, Blackstone's influence was more oblique and more diffuse than his biographers have claimed."[138]

2. Early Differences Between English and American Coverture Law

Although our legal system was based in very substantial part on English models,[139] there were enough differences between English and American coverture law to suggest that the United States was marching to a significantly different drummer by 1800. The earliest settlers were confronted with many 193
problems not routinely dealt with by English law. There is evidence that women, sometimes even married women, received land grants in some of the Colonies.[140] While this practice may have been designed to attract women to the new Colonies,[141] it is also possible that the exigencies of colonial life sometimes forced relaxation of the strict roles of husbands and wives.[142] There is some literature suggesting that early colonial married women did not labor under legal restrictions to the extent Blackstone's commentaries would sug-

136. Brown, *Frontier Justice: Wayne County 1796-1836*, 16 AM. J. LEG. HIST. 126 (1972); Blume, *supra* note 35, at 88-95; Note, *Tennessee County Courts*, *supra* note 102, at 377-82. These studies looked at cases not generally reported by the digest system. But even in early reported opinions, the knowledge of chancery developments seems quite up-to-date. *See, e.g.,* Trustees of Methodist Episcopal Church v. Jaques, 3 Johns. Ch. 77 (N.Y. 1817); Franklin v. Creyon, 1 Harp. Eq. 243 (S.C. 1824); Trenton Banking Co. v. Woodruff, 2 N.J. Eq. (1 H.W. Green) 117 (1838); Porter v. Bank of Rutland, 19 Vt. 410 (1847).

137. Nolan's thesis that Blackstone's influence was somewhat diffuse is lent credence by Brown's work on the Michigan territorial records. *See* Brown, *supra* note 136 (suggesting that frontier lawyers possessed and used same sources of law as their metropolitan contemporaries).

138. Nolan, *supra* note 93, at 732.

139. *See* C. COOK, *supra* note 94, at 3-45. But even as to the general influence of English law, there does appear to be some agreement that legislative differences arose in great profusion. The Northwest Ordinance, for example, required the new territory's Governor and judges to adopt statutes previously enacted by one or another state "as might be necessary and best suited to the circumstances of the district." Blume & Brown, *supra* note 37, at 523. *See generally* BROWN, BRITISH STATUTES IN AMERICAN LAW: 1776-1836 (1964); Blume, *Legislation on the American Frontier*, 60 MICH. L. REV. 317 (1962). This provision governed much of the territorial development of the United States, since the Northwest Ordinance was extended from time to time to other territories. As a result, territorial statutes tended to be eclectic in origin. The tendency for legislatures to copy other statutes has appararently been a constant in American legal history. *See* L. FRIEDMAN, *supra* note 22, at 78-81. Even in 17th-century Massachusetts the practice occurred, and it was continued in the other Colonies. *See* Riesenfeld, *Law-Making and Legislative Precedent in American Legal History*, 33 MINN. L. REV. 103 (1949); Haskins, *Codification of the Law in Colonial Massachusetts: A Study in Comparative Law*, 30 IND. L.J. 1 (1954).

140. J. SPRUILL, *supra* note 44, at 9-12, 340; R. MORRIS, *supra* note 21, at 131; M. RYAN, WOMANHOOD IN AMERICA 6-7, 13 (1979). See also the numerous anecdotes of women landowners in E. DEXTER, COLONIAL WOMEN OF AFFAIRS, *supra* note 131, at 98-125. Unfortunately, Dexter did not focus on the marital status of her subjects or the impact of coverture rules.

141. J. SPRUILL, *supra* note 44, at 9-12.

142. *See* M. RYAN, *supra* note 140, at 1-40 (discussing roles of women in colonial society).

gest.[143] However significant the initial colonial land grants to women and the somewhat looser rules of the earlier colonial era, there is little disagreement that the practices were altered and that English law became more influential as the Colonies developed. The more traditional English pattern of the husband's dominance certainly governed in most places during the late seventeenth and the greater part of the eighteenth century.[144] Nonetheless, early variations in colonial practice and different traditions in colonial administration left opportunities open for novel American practices to develop.

These generalizations about married women's law coincide with the conclusions drawn in the general literature on pre-Revolutionary War use of English law in the colonies. As the colonies matured, English legal models became more important.[145] Nonetheless, substantial room was left for independent development of American legal institutions.[146] Even though American legal developments were subjected to appellate review by the Privy Council during much of the colonial era,[147] it is likely that such review was used only to protect the Crown's power to direct colonial legal institutions and to promote the economic interests of Great Britain.[148] As Goebel notes,[149] the Colonies, lack-
194 ing the centralized institutions of the English chancery system, adopted particularized procedural formats from their earliest days.[150] The diffuse system gave significantly more control to judges than in England.[151] Furthermore, the diverse needs of the Colonies, and the ability of the settlers to adopt their own legislation, naturally led to deviations from English common law practice. Much of the new law avoided Privy Council censure.[152] Finally, Goebel notes that the colonists generally acted as if they had the authority to decide which English statutes were applicable to their territory.[153]

By the end of the colonial era, therefore, the American legal system was peppered with localized procedural systems and variegated lines of cases and statutes. Judges and legislators alike considered themselves to be repositories

---

143. R. MORRIS, *supra* note 21, at 126-200; Gundersen & Gampel, *Married Women's Legal Status in Eighteenth Century New York and Virginia*, 39 WM. & MARY Q. 114 (1982).

144. J. SPRUILL, *supra* note 44, at 340-66; L. KERBER, *supra* note 2, at 119-84.

145. L. FRIEDMAN, *supra* note 22, at 42-49.

146. *See, e.g.*, Reinsch, *The English Common Law in the Early American Colonies*, in 1 SELECT ESSAYS IN ANGLO-AMERICAN LEGAL HISTORY 367 (1970); L. FRIEDMAN, *supra* note 22, at 15-16, 30-32. *See generally* G. HASKINS, *supra* note 102 (suggesting diffuse nature of America's acceptance of English law); M. KAMMEN, COLONIAL NEW YORK: A HISTORY 91-94 (1975) (same); Gundersen & Gampel, *supra* note 143 (same).

147. During the earliest years of the colonies, direct English control of American legal development was weak at best. 1 R. POWELL, *supra* note 44, at 99-102; *see* Goebel, *King's Law and Local Custom in Seventeenth Century New England*, 31 COLUM. L. REV. 416 (1931). Only after the Restoration in 1660 did the Crown begin to exercise more control over its colonial domain. This early period of relative freedom in the colonies planted the seed for much of the power exercised by the judicial and legislative authorities in the 18th century. *See* L. FRIEDMAN, *supra* note 22, at 43-45. Of course, some colonies developed legal systems from non-English roots because of the early exploration patterns of the European powers. M. KAMMEN, *supra* note 146, at 91-94.

148. Goebel, *supra* note 102, at 466.

149. Goebel's piece is a severe critique of O. CROSSKEY, POLITICS AND THE CONSTITUTION IN THE HISTORY OF THE UNITED STATES (1953).

150. *See also* G. HASKINS, *supra* note 102, at 113-40.

151. Goebel, *supra* note 102, at 464.

152. *Id.* at 464; L. FRIEDMAN, *supra* note 22, at 43. *See also* M. HORWITZ, *supra* note 51, at 1-30; W. NELSON, *supra* note 102, at 9-10.

153. Goebel, *supra* note 102, at 465; *see also* L. FRIEDMAN, *supra* note 22, at 78-81.

of substantial legal authority. Similarly, the post-war process of deciding which segments of colonial legal institutions were to be left intact gave a great deal of discretion to judges, and statutes were received if local demands warranted. The problem for revolutionary era courts was to keep legal systems operating, rather than to simply reject, or accept, English law.[154]

Modern legal historians studying coverture are now recognizing that post-war judicial and legislative decisions on the applicability of English law in the state, territorial, and federal systems were not uniform.[155] An array of recep-

---

154. Goebel, *supra* note 102, at 467-68. Although Horwitz is more sympathetic than Goebel to the idea that natural law concepts motivated much of the legal community's actions in the 18th century, the factual predicate for his theory is similar to Goebel's. *Compare* Goebel, *supra* note 102, at 456-57, *with* M. HORWITZ, *supra* note 51, at 7-9. *See also* W. NELSON, *supra* note 102, at 13-35. Horwitz, like Morris, *supra* note 21, is subject to the criticism that he makes very broad generalizations from scattered evidence. Nonetheless, his generalizations are useful categories even if only as a starting point for measurement. Horwitz argues that Revolutionary War era lawyers had great respect for the common law system, despite colonial deviations from English rules of law. *See also* L. FRIEDMAN, *supra* note 22, at 95-96. Precedent was important in the formation of norms that generally governed the human condition. M. HORWITZ, *supra* note 51, at 4-5. While common law was equated with the divination of customary practice and natural law, *id.* at 7-8, statutes were perceived as man-made instruments of the 195
Crown. While the colonists felt entitled to the common law system, if not its results, *id.* at 8, they felt free to alter English statutes. As a result, both judges pronouncing the common law and legislators enacting statutes ignored English solutions when necessary. Not until well after the Revolution did reactions set in decrying the diversity of judge-made law, *id.* at 18, and seeking the general unification and codification of legal norms, *id.* at 9-30, 253-56. The treatise tradition, which grew vigorously in the United States after 1820, also undertook to rationalize the diverse case law. The trend began with Kent's COMMENTARIES in 1827 and Story's COMMENTARIES ON EQUITY in 1836. But before the reaction, judges were emboldened to decide cases by reference to perceived public policy needs, M. HORWITZ, *supra* note 51, at 30, and legislatures felt free to adopt far-ranging alterations in English law. L. FRIEDMAN, *supra* note 22, at 97-100. By the turn of the 19th century, Horwitz argues, legal thought had moved from natural law to law as an instrument of social policy.

155. The best of the recent articles on variations during the colonial era is Salmon, *The Legal Status of Women in Early America: A Reappraisal*, 1 LAW & HIST. REV. 1 (1983). Salmon argues that modern legal historians may not with confidence rely on the general conclusions of an earlier generation of historians, including Morris, Beard, Dexter, and Bensen. Johnston opened the recent law journal debates on many of the questions taken up in this paper. Johnston, *Sex and Property: The Common Law Tradition, the Law School Curriculum and Developments Toward Equality*, 47 N.Y.U. L. REV. 1033 (1972). His cites to R. MORRIS *supra* note 21, suggest the difficulty Johnston had in deciphering the reception of English law in a culture as diverse as early America's. Even though chapter III of Morris' book has been aptly applauded as a path-breaking work, it is most certainly flawed. *See* M. SALMON, *supra* note 2, at 18-21. Morris drew a generally optimistic conclusion about the improved colonial status of women by noting a number of scattered examples of exceptions to the general English practice. Although these examples are very useful and interesting, they do not arise out of the intense cultural analysis necessary to support Morris' overall conclusion. *See* Goebel, *supra* note 147, at 416 n.3. Indeed, Morris was at times wrong in suggesting that his examples were exceptional and different from English practice. For example, Morris notes that a Mistress Margarett Brent acted as Maryland Governor Calvert's executor beginning in 1647. R. MORRIS, *supra* note 21, at 132-33. This is said to be an example of a woman acting as an attorney. But women were acting as executors of estates in England for some time before 1647. 3 W. HOLDSWORTH, *supra* note 104, at 528, 544; 7 W. HOLDSWORTH, *supra* note 108, at 180. Similarly, in an effort to make American commercial practice seem more open to women, Morris dismisses the English feme-sole trader status "merely as a local custom in some of the commercial boroughs," citing 3 W. HOLDSWORTH, *supra* note 104, at 525. But the period Holdsworth described was much earlier than the 17th century. Morris also ignores other available material on feme-sole trader status in England. *See infra* notes 183-96 and accompanying text. The custom of London can hardly be so easily dismissed. It is also not clear that Dexter's books, COLONIAL WOMEN OF AFFAIRS: WOMEN IN BUSINESS AND PROFESSIONS IN AMERICA BEFORE 1776 (1924) and CAREER WOMEN OF AMERICA 1776-1840 (1950) portray any different picture than that of London given by M. George in chapter IV of LONDON LIFE IN THE XVII CENTURY (1925). The colonies may have been more open to businesswomen than England, but Morris fails to make a case for that view. Morris also suggests that ante-nuptial contracts calling for husbands to dispose of assets by will to their wives were not clearly enforceable in England in the 17th century, while they were in the Colonies. R. MORRIS,

tion statutes was passed in the late eighteenth and early nineteenth centuries, and they differed in the era of English common law to be followed, the acceptance of equity, and the binding force of statutes.[156] Reception statutes frequently gave courts some discretion to decide which English precedents or statutes to apply. In addition, legislatures took upon themselves the task of resolving many disputes by passing private bills. In this milieu, pre-war changes in coverture-related legal norms were unlikely to be impeded by English interests. After the war, there was room for legal institutions to reexamine coverture law.

Development of Conveyance Reforms. From early in the eighteenth century, simplified documentary systems of land transfer emerged in most, but not all, of the Colonies.[157] The vast number of land transfers occurring in the eighteenth and nineteenth centuries required simple conveyancing methods. Warranty and quit claim deeds emerged in easily useable forms early in the eighteenth century.[158] The Northwest Ordinance provided for transfer of
196 property by deed, free of the technical constraints of English common law.[159]

---

supra note 21, at 135-36. Morris ignores, however, the contemporaneous development of trusts in England that served the same purposes. 5 W. HOLDSWORTH, *supra* note 106, at 312-15. Finally, Morris' examples are localized. There is no way to know the depth or breadth of the colonial practice from his discussion.

156. Although some American reception statutes referred to specific dates for determination of the English common law to be received, almost all the reception statutes allowed local judges discretion in deciding when to declare the law to be "received." Even in areas where reception statutes designated a specific date, judges were left with discretion to adopt later English case law. L. FRIEDMAN, *supra* note 22, at 97-100. It is therefore predictable that the American legal system absorbed some segments of English law and rejected others.

The most comprehensive summary of reception provisions appears to be 1 R. POWELL, *supra* note 44, at 72-363. Every state's situation is discussed. A number of states had time-specific provisions. In 1776, for example, Virginia adopted a statute providing for reception of "the common law of England, and statutes or acts of parliament made in aid of the common law prior to the fourth year of the reign of King James the First 1607, and which are of a general nature, not local to that Kingdom." 1 REVISED CODE OF THE LAWS OF VIRGINIA 135 (1819). The statutory segment of this provision was significantly narrowed in 1792 after Jefferson completed a general statutory revision project for the state. Blume & Brown, *supra* note 37, at 480. Massachusetts provided in its first constitution that "All the laws which have heretofore been adopted, used, and approved . . . and usually practised on the courts of law shall still remain and be in full force until altered or repealed by the legislature; such parts only excepted as are repugnant to the rights and liberties contained in this constitution." MASS. CONST. ch. VI, art. VI (1780). While this was later construed broadly to permit discretionary adoption of English law, Commonwealth v. Churchill, 2 Metc. 118 (Mass. 1840), it obviously lacked the certitude of Virginia's code. The Virginia Ordinance of 1776 was adopted by the territorial government of the Northwest Territories in 1795. Blume & Brown, *supra* note 37, at 39. The Northwest Ordinance itself provided simply that the territory's inhabitants should have the "benefits of . . . judicial proceedings according to the courts of the common law." *Id.*

The statutes frequently left much discretion with courts. In Vermont a fairly typical statute was passed providing for reception of common law "not repugnant to the Constitution, or to any acts of the legislature of this state." 1 Vt. 118 (1793). A contemporaneous commentary on this act by the Chief Justice of the Vermont Supreme Court noted that circumstances were different in America from England, that monarchy and aristocracy had been overthrown, and concluded that the reception statute should not be read to accept principles "which from the peculiar circumstances of that government, exist only in England." Chipman, *A Dissertation on the Act Adopting the Common and Statute Laws of England*, 1 Vt. 117, 138 (1793).

157. R. MORRIS, *supra* note 21, at 69-72; L. FRIEDMAN, *supra* note 22, at 54-57; G. HASKINS, *supra* note 102, at 171-73. New York, interestingly enough, was among the later states to alter its conveyance rules. *See* Gundersen & Gampel, *supra* note 143, at 125-27 (1982); M. SALMON, *supra* note 2, at 31-37.

158. L. FRIEDMAN, *supra* note 22, at 207-09.

159. Blume, *supra* note 139, at 326-27.

While these provisions were probably inserted in the Ordinance to benefit the Ohio Company, which was seeking rights to develop Ohio,[160] they had effects on coverture rules as well. The use of a fine and recovery to convey a married woman's interest in her husband's land gave way to joint conveyance accomplished by signature.[161] Even though many Colonies, states, and territories retained the English practice of approving a land sale only after a married woman was separately examined before a judge or magistrate,[162] the general liberalizing of conveyancing practices had substantial impact.[163] While in hindsight the ease with which a wife's dower or other interest in real property could be transferred may be viewed as a double-edged sword,[164] there is little doubt of its importance in early American women's law.[165]

Development of Dower. Among the active debates in women's legal history, that involving reception of English dower may be the most lusty. The notion that dower was imported untouched from England is universally viewed as untenable.[166] The debate concerns whether the American changes were more[167] or less[168] favorable for women than the English law. Scholars on both sides of the controversy may be correct. Nineteenth-century scholarship 197
indicates that dower was treated more favorably in some parts of the country than in others.[169] Some Colonies and states awarded dower in equitable estates; others did not.[170] Some states awarded dower in land held during coverture, others only in land held at death.[171] Although Pennsylvania law has recently been strongly criticized,[172] evidence suggests that neighboring Ohio

160. *Id.*

161. R. MORRIS, *supra* note 21, at 147-55; L. KERBER, *supra* note 2, at 145; 1 J. BISHOP, *supra* note 27, at 406-10.

162. 1 C. SCRIBNER, A TREATISE ON THE LAW OF DOWER 29-31, 37 (1867) (practice retained in Connecticut, New York, and North Carolina); 1 J. BISHOP, *supra* note 27, at 410-15; M. SALMON, *supra* note 2, at 37-83.

163. Dower, for example, was easier to defeat by conveyance than in England, at least at law. *See* 1 J. BISHOP, *supra* note 27, at 312-15; 2 C. SCRIBNER, *supra* note 162, at 268-78.

164. The use of separate examinations to protect women from overreaching husbands could act beneficially. It could also be an unnecessary hurdle, or could lapse unfairly into informality. *See* L. KERBER, *supra* note 2, at 145; Salmon, *supra* note 42, at 101-06.

165. Despite the easing of transfer restrictions, the general content of the husband-dominating coverture rules certainly continued. Married women's contracts were still not generally enforced, so promises to convey or warranties to guarantee title were frequently unenforceable. Immediate conveyances without contractual preliminaries were easier.

166. J. SPRUILL, *supra* note 44, at 359-60; L. FRIEDMAN, *supra* note 22, at 59, 375-76; L. KERBER, *supra* note 2, at 123-32, 146-48; M. HORWITZ, *supra* note 51, at 56-58; R. MORRIS, *supra* note 21, at 155-64; Salmon, *supra* note 42, at 106-08. Though not cited by the recent authors, the only significant 19th-century American treatise on dower confirms the recent work. *See* 1 C. SCRIBNER, *supra* note 162, at 23-57 (state-by-state review of dower law describing numerous state-by-state differences from English law).

167. *See generally* R. MORRIS, *supra* note 21, *and* J. SPRUILL, *supra* note 44 (arguing American changes in dower were more favorable to women).

168. *See generally* L. KERBER, *supra* note 2; M. HORWITZ, *supra* note 51; L. FRIEDMAN, *supra* note 22; and Salmon, *supra* note 42 (arguing American changes in dower were less favorable to women).

169. *See* 1 C. SCRIBNER, *supra* note 162, at 23-57; M. SALMON, *supra* note 2, at 264-98.

170. 1 C. SCRIBNER, *supra* note 162, at 382-90, 396-417.

171. *Id.* at 589-601.

172. *See* Salmon, *supra* note 42, at 108. Salmon's judgment that dower was placed in jeopardy by 18th-century Pennsylvania law may not tell the entire story. Scribner writes:

> But the courts of Pennsylvania have not left the widow to the uncertain and precarious provision contemplated by the above statute. That enactment being limited to the estate

had a lengthy tradition of protecting married women's dower interests.[173] In addition, England was limiting the impact of dower during the eighteenth century. The substantial use of equity practice in England led to very general avoidance of dower rules during the reception eras.[174] When dower reform came before Parliament in 1833, dower was extended to equitable estates, but only those actually held by the husband at death.[175] Thus, whether American law was more or less favorable to women may be impossible to assess with certainty.

The early dower statutes exhibit several interesting characteristics. They were sometimes passed in acts containing more general conveyancing reforms permitting transfer by deed,[176] or with provisions for the separate examination of married women.[177] The link between conveyance reform and dower is also illustrated by those statutes that provided widows a right to reject either dower or the provisions of their husbands' legitimate wills in favor of a statutorily prescribed share of their deceased husbands' estates.[178] Such statutes were passed in some states shortly after the Revolutionary War, and the practice existed well before the war in some areas.[179] This elective share scheme did

198

> which the husband held at his death, and in respect of which he died intestate, the courts have determined that as to lands which were aliened by him during the coverture without the concurrence of the wife, or which he attempts to dispose of by will to her prejudice, she may take her dower as by common law.[3] This doctrine is the result of judicial construction, solely, and appears to be unsupported by any express law upon the subject. It is now too well established, however, by an unbroken current of authority, to admit of serious question or doubt.
>
> While adopting the rule of the common law to the extent just stated as a part of the law of Pennsylvania, the courts have gone one step further in behalf of the widow. They have so far modified that rule as to give dower in equitable as well as legal estates. In Kelly v. Mahan, it was held that dower may be had of a mere improvement claim, and in Shoemaker v. Walker, the right of dower in equitable estates was expressly determined. "In Pennsylvania," said Tilghman, Chief Justice, after remarking upon the doctrine of common law, "the usage has been more reasonable, and more analogous to the general principles of dower."

1 C. SCRIBNER, *supra* note 162, at 410. Scribner's footnote 3 refers to a line of decisions starting with Borland v. Nichols, 12 Pa. (2 Jones) 42 (1849). The intriguing question is whether this case was a shot out of the blue or a reflection of more long-standing practice. If the latter turns out to be true, the 18th-century dower statutes in Pennsylvania may not be read to be as harsh to women as Salmon suggests. Statutes providing widows a right to elect a share of their husbands' estate were passed on Apr. 8, 1833 (1833 Pa. Laws 250, § 11) and Apr. 11, 1848 (1848 Pa. Laws 537, § 11).

173. The Northwest Ordinance provided for dower as did later territorial and Ohio state statutes. There, in contrast with Pennsylvania, dower was not subject to a husband's debts. Jointure could be waived under a Jan. 19, 1804, statute. Ch. XIV, § 2, 1804 Ohio Acts 34-35. Equitable assets held at death became subject to dower under a Feb. 12, 1805, statute. Ch. X, 1805 Ohio Acts § 1. Dower at law was not restricted to lands held at death, nor did a wife lose the benefit of the increase in value of the land from the date of its sale to the date of assignment to her. Allen v. McCoy, 8 Ohio 418, 466-67 (1838). For a more complete review of Ohio dower cases see M. Brown, *Reception of English Common Law and Chancery in Ohio* 14-22 (1981) (unpublished paper) (copy on file at *Georgetown Law Journal*).

174. 1 C. SCRIBNER, *supra* note 162, at 367-68.

175. 3 W. HOLDSWORTH, *supra* note 104, at 197.

176. 1 C. SCRIBNER, *supra* note 162, at 31, 38, 44 (New York, Georgia, and New Hampshire).

177. *Id.* at 31, 40-41 (New York, Rhode Island, and Maryland).

178. *See id.* at 27, 33, 36-42, 46, 49-50 (Massachusetts, Delaware, North Carolina, Tennessee, Georgia, Mississippi, Alabama, Maryland, Vermont, Ohio, and Illinois). *See also* 2 C. SCRIBNER, *supra* note 162, at 413-17, 464-97.

179. Many states passed such statutes in the 1820's and 1830's. *See infra* note 239. But earlier examples of the practice also exist. Kentucky passed a statute in 1797 giving widows the right to elect the share of their deceased husbands' estates they would have received under intestacy. Act of Feb. 24, 1797, § 24, 1797 Ky. Acts 162. But it is apparent that the practice described in this general enactment on wills was in existence well before that. *See* Trigg's Administrator v. Daniel, 5 Ky. (2 Bibb) 301 (1811). Similarly, Maryland's general codification of the law of wills passed in 1798 provided that a

not always give widows the right to take a share of the personal estate of their husbands prior to the payment of debts. It did, however, provide some increased access to wealth while the institution of dower was fading in significance. In cases where a woman elected to take her statutory share, she usually had to waive her dower rights. Thus these statutes also had the effect of removing dower as an encumbrance upon lands distributed to persons other than widows.[180] The same trend is displayed by the late eighteenth- and early nineteenth-century growth of statutes permitting or requiring dower to be awarded in a single cash sum upon the death of the husband.[181] Such release of dower rights freed the underlying fee simple of constraints impeding alienation. The perceived need, at least in some Colonies and states, to make land transfer as simple and as free of encumbrances as possible sometimes had the effect of reducing the scope of protection afforded married women.[182]

Feme-Sole Trading. An interesting contrast to the early developments in conveyancing and dower law is presented by the general lack of feme-sole trader acts in the Colonies. One might hypothesize that any historical trend to protect commercial dealing would carry over to permit women to act and be held accountable for business contracts. The general colonial acceptance of the law merchant[183] in the seventeenth and eighteenth centuries suggests that the colonies were not oblivious to the needs of trade. It is also clear that some women were traders in America.[184] How then can the presence of a broad feme-sole trader statute in only one colony[185] and the delay in development of trading rights for married women until late in the nineteenth century be explained?

Several hypotheses are plausible. Perhaps married businesswomen used trusts or separate estates, especially in the South.[186] Northern examples of

---

widow could reject her husband's will in favor of dower and a third of the personal estate. Act of Jan. 20, 1798, ch. 101, 1798 Md. Laws § 15. Here, too, case law suggests that the practice existed long before the statute. *See* Coomes v. Clements, 8 Md. 382, 385 (1821). *See also* North Carolina: Ch. XXXII, April 1784 Session; Virginia: Ch. LX, October 1785 Session.

180. M. HORWITZ, *supra* note 51, at 56-58, suggests that commercial pressures in early America sometimes led to significant changes in dower rules, effectively denying widows access to the increased capital values of unimproved land. *See also* L. FRIEDMAN, *supra* note 22, at 375-76.

181. *See* 2 C. SCRIBNER, *supra* note 162, at 612-55. Scribner gives a fairly detailed description of developments in Maryland and South Carolina. *See id.* at 637-46, 646-50.

182. Kerber's fascinating study of the relation between dower and the treason confiscation acts of the Revolutionary War era makes an analogous point. To the extent that the threat of losing dower upon going over to enemy territory was used as a device to influence married women's political loyalities, dower was being used for social purposes deemed more important than the economic well-being of married women. *See* L. KERBER, *supra* note 2, at 123-36.

183. L. FRIEDMAN, *supra* note 22, at 69.

184. Spruill, *supra* note 44, at 276-313; E. DEXTER, COLONIAL WOMEN OF AFFAIRS, *supra* note 131; E. DEXTER, CAREER WOMEN OF AMERICA 1776-1840 (1950); Gundersen & Gampel, *supra* note 143, at 129-33. *See also* Norton, *A Cherished Spirit of Independence: The Life of an Eighteenth Century Boston Businesswoman*, in WOMEN OF AMERICA: A HISTORY 49 (C. Berkin & M. Norton eds. 1979).

185. South Carolina was the single colony. It is described in J. SPRUILL, *supra* note 44, at 362 n.80; L. KERBER, *supra* note 2, at 148-49; 2 J. BISHOP, *supra* note 27, at 418-20. Pennsylvania also had an early (1718) feme-sole trader statute, but it was limited to wives of mariners at sea. *See* 2 J. BISHOP, *supra* note 27, at 420; J. KELLY, A TREATISE ON THE LAW OF CONTRACTS OF MARRIED WOMEN 504-05 (1881).

186. *See* J. SPRUILL, *supra* note 44, at 362-65. Equity was received more warmly in the South than in the North. *See supra* notes 33-42 and accompanying text (discussing practice of equity in the states).

feme-covert trader trusts may have existed which have not yet been uncovered.[187] Legislative private bills were used in some jurisdictions to grant women the power to trade, but extensive studies of this activity have not been done.[188] Other areas that may reveal explanations for the lack of trader statutes include the law of agency,[189] the use of arbitration,[190] and the use of specialized business tribunals for which reported decisions were not generally published.[191] The most likely explanation, however, is that many of the women operating businesses outside their homes were not married,[192] and that the few married businesswomen worked with their husbands or subjected themselves to the general rule that a wife's income belonged to her husband.[193] In contrast to the development of the custom of London in England, American law simply may not have reflected commercial reality for the few married women involved in business.[194]

Thus, by 1800 American law had freed land from some of the constraints of technical conveyance and dower rules while apparently leaving married women's business rights constrained by coverture doctrines. The reduction of home industry and the rise of a wage system for employed women may have
200 meant that there was little need to free them from commercial constraints. And certainly trading by a married woman separate from her husband and her home was likely to be subject to some public disapproval.[195] While the begin-

---

187. Some feme-sole trader trust cases do exist in the northeast. *See* North Am. Coal Co. v. Dyett, 7 Paige Ch. 9 (N.Y. Ch. 1837); Stammers v. Macomb, 10 N.Y. Common L. Rep. (2 Wend.) 454 (1829).

188. *See* J. SPRUILL, *supra* note 44, at 361-62; 2 J. BISHOP, *supra* note 27, at 475-76 (Alabama); M. BENSON, WOMEN IN EIGHTEENTH CENTURY AMERICA 241 (1935) (Virginia); L. KERBER, *supra* note 2, at 150-52 (Connecticut). It is intriguing that many states later imposed specific restrictions on passage of bills dealing with land transfers of persons under civil disabilities. *See* C. BINNEY, *supra* note 52, at 143-44.

189. Old American treatises suggest that married women may have been treated as agents of their husbands even when the relationship was established by practice and behavior rather than by express documents. *See* J. STORY, COMMENTARIES ON THE LAW OF AGENCY 8 (1844); 1 F. LIVERMORE, TREATISE ON THE LAW OF PRINCIPAL AND AGENT 28-34 (1818); J. DUNLAP, TREATISE ON THE LAW OF PRINCIPAL AND AGENT 163-64 (1847). *See also* M. BENSON, *supra* note 188, at 240.

190. J. MORSE, THE LAW OF ARBITRATION AND AWARD 26-29 (1872) has a fascinating suggestion that businessmen could voluntarily agree to arbitrate with a married woman in the early 19th century.

191. This was certainly a common practice in mercantile England, but there has been no investigation of the phenomenon here.

192. The presence of large numbers of married women in the labor force is a 20th-century phenomenon. At the end of the 19th century, less than 20% of women were in the labor force. About 40% of unmarried women, but only five percent of married women, were in the labor force. The number of married women in the labor force increased significantly during World War II, fell a bit after the war, and then began a sustained climb. STATISTICAL HISTORY, *supra* note 6, at 133 (table of women's employment). Today, over half of married women are in the labor force. STATISTICAL ABSTRACT, *supra* note 13, at 402 (table of women's employment).

193. *See* 1 J. BISHOP, *supra* note 27, at 140-42.

194. *See* L. KERBER, *supra* note 2, at 152; Gundersen & Gampel, *supra* note 143, at 131. An early Massachusetts case certainly suggests that absent use of a trust or other device, feme-sole traders operated at some risk. In Russell v. Brooks, 24 Mass. (7 Pick.) 65 (1828), Eleanor Swan operated a fur manufacturing business while her husband Joshua visited her on Sundays and lived in adultery with another woman. The case apparently arose because the husband's business had become insolvent in 1819, leaving his estate heavily indebted. The couple had separated in 1815, but had not divorced. The court held that money received and notes taken by the wife in her separately operated business prior to the 1821 death of her husband were owned by his estate. *Id.* at 67.

195. Even the most famous of 19th-century women tended to withdraw from public life upon marriage and risk censure upon reentry before divorce or widowhood. Biographers are now beginning to be quite sensitive to the problems such constraints caused. *See generally* J. FURNAS, FANNY KEMBLE: LEADING LADY OF THE NINETEENTH CENTURY STAGE (1982). Furnas devotes considerable attention

nings of reform of land transfer and inheritance rules in order to insure the economic viability of surviving widows in the face of dower's decline was perfectly compatible with the late eighteenth-century emergence of concern for family well-being,[196] feme-sole trading by married women may have been seen as quite another matter.

3. Summary

This review of reception resolves a few issues and opens up many more. While English law and equity provided substantial impetus to the development of coverture law in this country, each American jurisdiction developed variations from the general pattern. English influence, however, was not the most significant barrier to the reform of American coverture law. The more liberal aspects of English equity were also influential during the early nineteenth century. In addition, too many important differences between English and American law had appeared by 1800 to conclude that the later reform movement was simply a throwing off of colonial remnants. Rather, it appears that by 1800 American legal institutions were beginning to grapple with changing family patterns and growing commercial interests. Divorce was growing just as romantic companionate marriage emerged. New methods of providing surviving spouses and children with means of support were emerging at the same time that substantial impediments to transfer of property were being removed. The vast difference between married men and women in their job patterns and wealth made it easy to legislate separately about their property, and to create different systems of control. The very notion of a separate estate for married women, which was reaching maturity at the time historians tell us that the modern family was emerging, could be expected to grow and take on characteristics consistent with the still limited but expanding role of most early nineteenth-century married women. The unfolding of these developments is the next part of the tale.

B. THE MARRIED WOMEN'S ACTS

During the 1700's women rarely publicly expressed dissatisfaction with the legal institution of coverture.[197] Alterations in legal rules before 1800 were

---

to the marital controversies of Fanny Kemble, including property disputes, problems with her English property trust, and loss of contact with her daughters from the time of her divorce until the daughters reached the age of majority.

196. *See infra* notes 336-39 and accompanying text (discussing Degler's work on the emergence of the American family).

197. There certainly were some early examples of women pressing their male contemporaries for significant alterations in gender roles. Among the most famous of these early exchanges is that between Abigail and John Adams, Abigail writing to John that "If particular care and attention is not paid to the ladies, we are determined to foment a rebellion, and will not hold ourselves bound by any laws in which we have no voice or representation." Abigail Adams to John Adams, Mar. 31, 1777, in FAMILIAR LETTERS OF JOHN ADAMS AND HIS WIFE, ABIGAIL ADAMS, DURING THE REVOLUTION 149-50 (C. Adams ed. 1876). The correspondence is reprinted in a readily available documentary history, THE FEMINIST PAPERS 7-15 (A.S. Rossi ed. 1973). Like most women in her day, however, Abigail Adams largely kept her ideas private, in letters to her husband and to her friends. *See* L. KERBER, *supra* note 2, at 73-85. Some English materials were beginning to find their way to these shores, such as Mary Wollstonecraft's VINDICATION OF THE RIGHTS OF WOMEN (1792) and the lectures and pioneering work in education of Scotswoman Frances Wright. *See* E. FLEXNER, *supra* note 1, at 27-28. It really was not

generated more by economic needs than by any widely articulated desires to redefine the role of American women.[198] By the late 1840's the nature of the debate changed. Legal rules became subjects of public debate, statutes were adopted in a number of jurisdictions, movements arose, and controversy boiled. What happened? The roots for this change are certainly not limited to the need for simplified means of exchanging land. The married women's acts themselves reflect the complexity of developments in the first half of the nineteenth century.

According to conventional historical views,[199] Mississippi adopted the first married women's property act in 1839.[200] In fact, the acts were passed in at least three waves, beginning in 1835, and each wave arose for somewhat different reasons. The first group of statutes, passed almost entirely in the 1840's, dealt primarily with freeing married women's estates from the debts of their husbands.[201] By and large these statutes left untouched the traditional marital estate and coverture rules. The second wave of legislation, the most frequently discussed, established separate estates for married women. These statutes appeared over a long period of time beginning in the 1840's and ending after the
202 Civil War.[202] The third set of statutes took the important step of protecting women's earnings from the institution of coverture. These laws generally did not appear until after the Civil War, although Massachusetts enacted an early statute in 1855.[203]

The first wave of legislation protecting the property of married women from the debts of their husbands emerged in a deluge. Almost every state and territory then in existence adopted such legislation.[204] While there were a few general patterns to the enactments, their terminology differed and remarkably little verbatim copying occurred. The earliest statute I have found that deals

---

until the 1830's, when the Grimke Sisters surfaced, that women's issues became subjects of widespread public debate. *See infra* note 346 and accompanying text (discussing Grimke Sisters).

198. Though individual petitions were filed with legislatures, *see* L. KERBER, *supra* note 2, at 85-99, it would be a generation before more organized and overt activity would emerge.

199. The only work noting the existence of the 1835 Arkansas statute is E. Warbasse, *supra* note 2, at 159.

200. L. FRIEDMAN, *supra* note 22, at 185. *See* Brown, *Memorandum on the Mississippi Women's Law of 1839*, 42 MICH. L. REV. 1110 (1944) (discussing the origin of the Mississippi statute and the debate surrounding its passage). In fact, Florida moved well before Mississippi, and as this article later suggests, there were a number of other legislative actions which were precursors to the later women's acts. Florida's statute appears to have been the result of a desire to protect marriage arrangements made under civil law before the territory became American, since only pre-1824 married women were protected by the legislation. W. CORD, A TREATISE ON THE LEGAL AND EQUITABLE RIGHTS OF MARRIED WOMEN 719 (1861); E. Warbasse, *supra* note 2, at 77, 163.

201. *See infra* notes 204-11 and accompanying text (discussing first phase).

202. This legislative phase overlapped with the debt statutes. But the early statutes inevitably needed refinement to account for ambiguity, enlarged goals, or hostile judicial reception. For some of the separate estate statutes, see *infra* notes 207, 209, and 263.

203. Massachusetts' act was adopted on May 5, 1855. For other earnings statutes, *see infra* note 361.

204. Finding this statutory material is difficult unless one has access to the session laws and codes of all the states and territories. The session laws are now available on microfiche, but for the benefit of readers who are not fortunate enough to have access to such material, I have included in the notes that follow citations to some of the major 19th century treatises that discuss married women's acts. The treatises used are J. BISHOP, *supra* note 27; W. CORD, *supra* note 200; J. KELLY, *supra* note 185; J. ROBINSON, THE LAW OF HUSBAND AND WIFE (1890); R. TYLER, COMMENTARIES ON THE LAW OF INFANCY AND THE LAW OF COVERTURE (1873). In addition, references to these statutes by E. Warbasse, *supra* note 2, have also been included. On the New York acts, *see* P. RABKIN, *supra* note 2; N. BASCH, *supra* note 1.

directly with marital property and husband's debts was adopted by the territorial legislature in Arkansas in 1835.[205] This largely undiscussed piece of legislation protected a wife's property from debts incurred by her husband prior to marriage. Only Alabama appears to have borrowed this legal formula.[206] Following Mississippi's lead in 1839, three other states protected married women's slaves from their husband's creditors.[207] A number of jurisdictions protected only the real property of married women from debts of their husbands.[208] Most statutes, however, went further and included both real and personal property under the umbrella of protection.[209] About half of the legis-

---

205. Act of Nov. 2, 1835, 1835 Ark. Terr. Laws 34-35; E. Warbasse, *supra* note 2, at 159.

206. In 1846, after a long period of acting by private bill, Alabama adopted an act granting feme-sole status to abandoned married women. Act of Jan. 31, 1846, 1845 Ala. Acts 24 (1846). Jurisdiction to handle such cases was given to the equity courts in March 1848. The last section of the 1846 act protected the property of married women from ante-nuptial debts of the husband. This scheme lasted only two years. On March 1, 1848, Alabama adopted a separate estate married women's act. Act of Mar. 1, 1848, 1847 Ala. Acts 79 (1848).

207. Mississippi: Act of Feb. 15, 1839, ch. 46, 1839 Miss. Laws 72; 2 J. BISHOP, *supra* note 27, at 535; W. CORD, *supra* note 200, at 722-23; J. KELLY, *supra* note 185, at 427; E. Warbasse, *supra* note 2, at 138-60. Maryland: Act of Mar. 10, 1843, ch. 293, 1842 Md. Laws 33 (1843); E. Warbasse, *supra* note 2, at 203
155-59. Kentucky: Act of Feb. 23, 1846, ch. 368, 1845 Ky. Acts 42 (1846); 2 J. BISHOP, *supra* note 27, at 515-16; W. CORD, *supra* note 200, at 603-06; E. Warbasse, *supra* note 2, at 173. Arkansas: Act of Dec. 8, 1846, 1844 Ark. Acts 38 (1846); 2 J. BISHOP, *supra* note 27, at 478-79; W. CORD, *supra* note 200, at 731-32; E. Warbasse, *supra* note 2, at 159-60. The Maryland statute is very similar to Mississippi's. It added, however, sections giving married women the right to make a will and to retain up to $1,000 as separate property. Arkansas' statute is also much like Mississippi's. Kentucky took a separate path, merging its slave provisions with others protecting the real property of married women from the debts of husbands. The Mississippi, Maryland, and Arkansas statutes also have very general provisions apparently creating a separate estate in married women.

208. The earliest of these statutes was that of Maryland: Act of Mar. 1, 1842, ch. 161, 1841 Md. Laws (1842); 2 J. BISHOP, *supra* note 27, at 100. Statutes followed in Connecticut: Act of June 10, 1845, ch. XXXIX, 1845 Conn. Acts 36; 2 J. BISHOP, *supra* note 27, at 7; W. CORD, *supra* note 200, at 736; J. KELLY, *supra* note 185, at 336; E. Warbasse, *supra* note 2, at 191. Iowa: Act of Jan. 2, 1846. ch. 5, 1845 Iowa Terr. Acts 40 (1846); E. Warbasse, *supra* note 2, at 204-05. Kentucky: Act of Feb. 23, 1846, ch. 368, 1845 Ky. Acts 42 (1846); *see supra* note 207. Indiana: Act of Jan. 23, 1847, ch. VI, 1846 Ind. Acts 45 (1847); E. Warbasse, *supra* note 2, at 205. Vermont: Act of Nov. 15, 1845, No. 37, 1847 Vt. Acts 26 (1845); J. KELLY, *supra* note 185, at 526; E. Warbasse, *supra* note 2, at 192. North Carolina: Act of Jan. 29, 1849, ch. XLI, 1848 N.C. Sess. Laws 12 (1849); 2 J. BISHOP, *supra* note 27, at 555-56; J. KELLY, *supra* note 185, at 463. Tennessee: Act of Jan. 10, 1850, ch. XXXVI, 1849 Tenn. Pub. Acts 111 (1850); 2 J. BISHOP, *supra* note 27, at 569; J. KELLY, *supra* note 185, at 517-18. Maryland's statute was a very simple, one sentence enactment. In fact, Maryland adopted a more detailed statute modeled after Mississippi's about a year later. *See supra* note 207. The statutes in Connecticut, Iowa, Indiana, Vermont, North Carolina, and Tennessee are similar in content, but the language in each varies from the prior enactments.

209. Michigan: Act of Mar. 11, 1844, No. 66, 1844 Mich. Pub. Acts 77; 2 J. BISHOP, *supra* note 27, at 532-33; J. KELLY, *supra* note 185, at 416; E. Warbasse, *supra* note 2, at 202-03. Maine: Act of Mar. 22, 1844, ch. 117, 1844 Me. Acts 104; 2 J. BISHOP, *supra* note 27, at 518; R. TYLER, *supra* note 204, at 675; E. Warbasse, *supra* note 2, at 200-01. Massachusetts: Act of Mar. 25, 1845, ch. 208, 1845 Mass. Acts 531; 2 J. BISHOP, *supra* note 27, at 525; J. KELLY, *supra* note 185, at 411; E. Warbasse, *supra* note 2, at 190-91. Alabama: Act of Jan. 31, 1846, No. 20, 1845 Ala. Acts 24 (1846); W. CORD, *supra* note 200, at 725; J. KELLY, *supra* note 185, at 291; E. Warbasse, *supra* note 2, at 170 (ante-nupital debts only), and Act of Mar. 1, 1848, No. 43, 1847 Ala. Acts 79 (1848) (real and personal property generally); Florida: Act of Mar. 6, 1845, No. IX, 1845 Fla. Terr. Laws 24; Ohio: Act of Feb. 28, 1846, 1845 Ohio Laws 75 (1846); W. CORD, *supra* note 200, at 709-10; J. KELLY, *supra* note 185, at 467; E. Warbasse, *supra* note 2, at 205. New Hampshire: Act of July 10, 1846, ch. 327, 1846 N.H. Laws 307; 2 J. BISHOP, *supra* note 27, at 544; J. KELLY, *supra* note 185, at 444; R. TYLER, *supra* note 204, at 681-82; E. Warbasse, *supra* note 2, at 191. New York: Act of Apr. 7, 1848, ch. 200, 1848 N.Y. Laws 307; 2 J. BISHOP, *supra* note 27, at 545-47; W. CORD, *supra* note 200, at 649; J. KELLY, *supra* note 185, at 455; R. TYLER, *supra* note 204, at 635-36; E. Warbasse, *supra* note 2, at 205-40. Pennsylvania: Act of Apr. 11, 1848, No. 372, 1848 Pa. Laws 536; 2 J. BISHOP, *supra* note 27, at 560-61; W. CORD, *supra* note 200, at 660-63; J. KELLY, *supra* note 185, at 486-87; E. Warbasse, *supra* note 2, at 236. Missouri: Act of Mar. 5, 1849, 1848 Mo. Laws

lation also included general statements that married women could hold property separate and apart from their husbands.[210] These generalized attempts to permit married women to control their own property were frequently construed narrowly by the courts.[211] This judicial hostility made it apparent that later legislative efforts would be required to complete the married women's property reform movement.

There are a number of explanations for the appearance of the first wave of married women's acts in the 1840's. First, widespread economic problems prompted numerous changes in debtor's law and made exemptions of property from attachment by creditors a pressing concern. Second, legislation chipping away at a number of the harsher consequences of coverture law had been enacted in earlier parts of the century. Abandoned women and widows were the objects of much attention; divorce laws changed; imprisonment of women for debt disappeared; and family law developed. If further reform was to occur, the institution of coverture had to become the focus of attention. Third, the fact that public debate about the role of women in society and legislation protecting the property of married women appeared in the same decade is not
204 mere coincidence. Although it is difficult to argue that lobbying or petitioning by women or their supporters led directly to the passage of most of the debt statutes, the legal and cultural developments of the first third of the century certainly created a more sympathetic environment for their enactment.

1. The Economy of the 1840's and Debtor Legislation

The economic climate of the 1840's was established by the Panic of 1837. Some have called the depression that followed one of the worst in our history, describing devastation in virtually every phase of the economy.[212] Others argue that the economic problems were concentrated in trade and commercial

---

67 (1849); J. KELLY, *supra* note 185, at 433. Connecticut: Act of June 22, 1849, ch. XX, 1849 Conn. Acts 16; 2 J. BISHOP, *supra* note 27, at 7; W. CORD, *supra* note 200, at 737; J. KELLY, *supra* note 185, at 336; E. Warbasse, *supra* note 2, at 190. Wisconsin: Act of Feb. 1, 1850, ch. 44, 1850 Wis. Laws 29; 2 J. BISHOP, *supra* note 27, at 572; W. CORD, *supra* note 200, at 715. New Jersey: Act of Mar. 25, 1852, ch. CLXXI, 1852 N.J. Laws 407; 2 J. BISHOP, *supra* note 27, at 545. These statutes are remarkably varied in content. Those of Alabama (second act), Michigan, Maine, Massachusets, Iowa, New York, Pennsylvania, and Wisconsin each have clauses providing that a married woman's property should be hers as if she were unmarried, or in her own name. The acts of Alabama (first act), Ohio, Missouri, and Connecticut lacked such phraseology. In addition, some of the acts dealt with other subjects such as abandoned wives (Alabama's first act); intestate shares (Alabama's second act); conveyancing (Ohio); husband's trusteeship in the property of his wife (Connecticut); ante-nupital contracts, conveyancing, intestacy, wills, and trusteeships (Massachusetts and New Hamshire); conveyancing, wills, and intestacy (Pennsylvania), and wills (Wisconsin). Rhode Island, in its codification of 1844, also adopted a general debt statute. E. Warbasse, *supra* note 2, at 197.

210. *See supra* notes 204-09.

211. The hostile reception given the New York act has been told by others. *See* P. RABKIN, *supra* note 2, at 125-38; E. Warbasse, *supra* note 2, at 237-40. Warbasse also tells of similar hostility in Maine, Rhode Island, and Pennsylvania. E. Warbasse, *supra* note 2, at 201, 237, 241-44. Courts in other states may have been more favorably disposed to married women's acts. *See* M. Brown, Reception of English Common Law and Chancery in Ohio, 67-75 (1981) (unpublished paper) (copy on file with author). The state courts in Oregon also construed their acts broadly. *See* Brummet v. Weaver, 2 Or. 168 (1866). As with much of the legal history in this area, the possibility of a mixed picture is high. But there is little doubt that the narrow contents of most of the first wave of married women's acts, together with judicial hostility, necessitated the passage of more legislation in following years.

212. R. MCGRANE, THE PANIC OF 1837 1 (1965).

sectors of the economy, not in industrial and agricultural production.[213] In any case, a number of strains in the economy of the young United States appeared about this time. Extensive land speculation in the Western states and territories occurred during the 1830's. Revenues from land sales skyrocketed in the middle of the decade.[214] Government investigations of widespread land office abuses also occurred.[215] In 1836 Congress considered legislation to return to the states a budget surplus generated in significant part by land sales. In 1837, however, following a precipitous decline in land revenues, Congress found itself confronting a budget deficit.[216] Large-scale borrowing by states and territories for the construction of internal improvements occurred in the 1830's. After the panic, states heavily obligated to pay off internal improvement bonds found themselves at or near bankruptcy.[217] Textile and other manufacturing industries grew dramatically in the Northeast in the 1830's.[218] After the panic, however, industry was in general decline. Cotton sales overseas boomed in the 1830's, but by the following decade the world's cotton trade was in disarray due to falling prices.[219] Prices for slaves also fell dramatically.[220] The cause of the economic collapse is the subject of some debate, but most explanations focus on some or all of the following factors: Excessive land 205
speculation, enormous balance of trade deficits, heavy borrowing for internal improvements by states and territories, concentration of bank ownership, decline in European demand for cotton, and President Jackson's dismantling of the national bank and issuance of the *Specie Circular* in 1836.[221] Whatever the cause or causes of the panic, the resulting economic stress was the impetus for the enactment of numerous pieces of legislation on bankruptcy, banking, and debtor's rights at both the federal and state levels. A look at some of this legislative activity makes the first wave of married women's property acts a logical part of a much larger movement of economic reform.

Proposals for bankruptcy legislation at both the federal and state levels appeared frequently during the first half of the nineteenth century. Prior to 1841, Congress had enacted bankruptcy legislation only once. This early act, passed in 1800, was designed as a five-year measure, but was repealed after only three years.[222] After the onset of distressed economic times in 1839, new demands

---

213. P. TEMIN, THE JACKSONIAN ECONOMY 148-77 (1969).

214. Revenues from land sales rose from four million dollars in 1833 to almost $25 million by 1836. That extraordinarily rapid rise was followed by an even more precipitous decline to just under $7 million in 1837. Sales fell further to about $2 million a year in the mid-1840's. P. TEMIN, *supra* note 213, at 168; HAMMOND, BANKS AND POLITICS IN AMERICA 451 (1957). For a general review of land speculation see R. MCGRANE, *supra* note 212, at 43-69; HAMMOND, *supra* note 214, at 452-53; P. GATES, HISTORY OF PUBLIC LAND LAW DEVELOPMENT 177-78 (1968).

215. R. MCGRANE, *supra* note 212, at 58-61; P. GATES, *supra* note 214, at 173-75.

216. HAMMOND, *supra* note 214, at 451-52; S. REZNECK, BUSINESS DEPRESSIONS AND FINANCIAL PANICS 92-93 (1968).

217. R. MCGRANE, *supra* note 212, at 9-13, 19-24, 30-35, 112-14, 128-30.

218. *Id.* at 96-112; B. BERG, *supra* note 2, at 40-42.

219. HAMMOND, *supra* note 214, at 467-77. Cotton prices fell steadily from the late 1830's to the middle of the 1840's. G. WRIGHT, THE POLITICAL ECONOMY OF THE COTTON SOUTH 96 (1978). P. GATES, *supra* note 214, at 177-78.

220. R. MCGRANE, *supra* note 212, at 116-18.

221. *See supra* notes 212-20 (literature discussing the Panic of 1837).

222. For a short but information-laden summary of the history of federal bankruptcy legislation, see P. COLEMAN, DEBTORS AND CREDITORS IN AMERICA: INSOLVENCY, IMPRISONMENT FOR DEBT, AND BANKRUPTCY, 1607-1900 16-30 (1974). Coleman is also a rich bibliographic source.

arose for federal bankruptcy legislation. An act was adopted in 1841, and thousands of debtors found relief under its terms.[223] Though the act was quickly repealed, it did serve to relieve some of the immediate pressures on debtors. Not until the Panic of 1857, and the economic dislocations caused by the Civil War, did pressure again build for the adoption of national bankruptcy legislation.[224] Although the short-lived federal provisions of 1841 had relieved much of the need for state bankruptcy laws, a few states also adopted or modified bankruptcy laws in this period.[225] The federal government also took steps to protect merchants who were defaulting on bonds posted to cover customs charges.[226]

Although most states did not adopt bankruptcy laws during the 1840's,[227] many did enact legislation protecting debtors and eliminating abuses in banking.[228] These enactments frequently included provisions requiring that property sold at the behest of creditors be appraised and bring a minimum price,[229] extending the types and value of property exempt from execution to pay debts,[230] exempting homesteads from attachment both during life and at death,[231] abolishing imprisonment for debt,[232] and, of course, insulating mar-
206 ried women's property from the debts of their husbands.

The first wave of married women's acts meshes very nicely with this statutory reform movement. Laws exempting assets from attachment had existed in some form for decades and were simply extended in the 1840's. The married women's acts operated much like exemption laws. If the new model of family

---

223. S. REZNECK, *supra* note 216, at 96. In New York alone, 8000 debtors filed for relief under the federal act. P. COLEMAN, *supra* note 222, at 128-29.

224. P. COLEMAN, *supra* note 222, at 24.

225. Massachusetts, Connecticut, and Maryland passed such statutes. *See id.* at 50-51, 84, 171-75. Other states, such as New York and South Carolina, had long-standing insolvency relief systems. *Id.* at 105-29, 179-90.

226. S. REZNECK, *supra* note 216, at 91-92.

227. Part of the reason for the hesitancy of the states to enter the field was a fear that states could not constitutionally legislate on bankruptcy. A series of early 19th-century Supreme Court decisions had raised concern in this area. *See* P. COLEMAN, *supra* note 222, at 31-36.

228. R. MCGRANE, *supra* note 212, at 121-22; S. REZNECK, *supra* note 216, at 94-95.

229. J. MCMASTER, A HISTORY OF THE PEOPLE OF THE UNITED STATES FROM THE REVOLUTION TO THE CIVIL WAR 45-46 (1906). *See generally* P. COLEMAN, *supra* note 222 (discussing each state).

230. The vast number of bills enacted in this period makes short summaries difficult. Rather than try, it makes more sense to simply refer readers to a few sources in which this material is described. The best I have found is P. COLEMAN, *supra* note 222. The author provides a state-by-state survey of laws adopted in each jurisdiction during a period of more than 200 years. This survey describes in detail the content of bankruptcy laws, appraisal and minimum value laws, exemption statutes, and imprisonment for debt reforms. *See also* R. MCGRANE, *supra* note 212, at 91-144; S. REZNECK, *supra* note 216, at 85-96; 7 J. MCMASTER, *supra* note 229, at 45-49, 153, 183; H. FARNAM, CHAPTERS IN THE HISTORY OF SOCIAL LEGISLATION IN THE UNITED STATES TO 1860 150-52 (1938).

231. Homestead acts are thought to have appeared for the first time in this period. 2 A. CASNER, AMERICAN LAW OF PROPERTY 810-11 (1954), discusses the Texas act of 1839. Development after 1840 was quite widespread. *See* Dillon, *The Homestead Exemption*, 10 AM. L. REG. 641 (1862); Note, *State Homestead Exemption Laws*, 46 YALE L. J. 1023 (1937). P. COLEMAN, *supra* note 222, also reviews homestead laws.

232. The movement to abolish imprisonment for debt began long before the Panic of 1837. The final phase of this movement, however, occurred in the decade of the 1840's. A number of states abolished debtor imprisonment in this period. Among them were New Hampshire, Vermont, Connecticut, New York, New Jersey, Pennsylvania, Maryland, Delaware, North Carolina, and Georgia. P. COLEMAN, *supra* note 222, at 62, 68, 78, 119, 139, 149-51, 177, 210, 224, 235. The system of imprisonment no longer made sense in an era when commercial interests relied more and more on secured transactions, commercial paper, property attachments, and garnishment. *Id.* at 261-64.

finance appearing in the first half of the nineteenth century called for men to undertake financial risks for the benefit of their families, then setting aside wives' property simply provided another body of exempt assets when the risk taking went sour. The statutes themselves reflected this reality. Almost without exception, women's acts which insulated only slaves or land from attachment appeared in argicultural and Southern states, while the more urban areas adopted broader laws protecting property generally.[233] Since women generally had less property than their husbands, it was logical that legislators would see wives' property as a safe way of adding to the pool of assets insulated from attachment. While these acts may also be justified because they preserved inherited property from rapacious husbands[234] or provided married women with some independent means of support, they also provided some husbands and families with continued access to assets despite bad economic times.[235]

While the connection between the first wave of married women's acts and

---

233. The correlation between the degree of urbanization in 1850 and the content of the first wave of married women's acts is really quite remarkable. Below is a table presenting urbanization values derived from STATISTICAL HISTORY, *supra* note 6, at 24-37. Of those states adopting debt statutes protecting only slaves or real property, only Maryland was heavily urbanized. The Maryland legislation did, however, contain general statements regarding married women's separate equitable estates. Of the fourteen states passing more general legislation, only Alabama, Florida, Michigan, and Wisconsin had less than 10% of their population living in urban areas. Wisconsin was more urbanized than most of the states that passed limited statutes and Florida's act may be explained by Florida's civil law background. *See supra* note 200 (discussing Florida). *See also supra* notes 204-09 (listing state statutes).

Type of Debt Statute

State	Slave	Real Property	Property generally	% Urban in 1850
Alabama			x	4.5
Arkansas	x			0
Kentucky	x	x		7.5
Maryland	x	x		32.5
Mississippi	x			1.8
Iowa		x		5.2
Indiana		x		4.5
N. Carolina		x		2.4
Tennessee		x		5.2
Vermont		x		1.9
Connecticut			x	15.9
Florida			x	0
Maine			x	13.6
Massachusetts			x	50.7
Michigan			x	7.3
Missouri			x	11.9
New Hampshire			x	17.0
New Jersey			x	17.6
New York			x	28.2
Ohio			x	12.2
Pennsylvania			x	23.6
Rhode Island			x	55.8
Wisconsin			x	9.5

Alabama's first statute does not fit well into any particular model, since it dealt only with property held before marrige.

234. Such motivation was certainly part of the debate over some married women's acts passed later in the decade. *See* P. RABKIN, *supra* note 2, at 91-98.

235. The earliest statutes did not alter the husbands' management and control of property and a number of the later debt statutes were construed consistently with this view. *See supra* note 211 and accompanying text (describing limitations of acts).

the Panic of 1837 is impossible to dismiss,[236] other factors also must have been at work. The country had seen bad economic times before 1840, while married women's acts were a new legislative response. The fact that many of the acts had general statements adopting the notion of a separate estate for married women's property also suggests a broader purpose. The acts must therefore have been part of a larger evolution in the treatment of women by the law.[237]

2. Statutory Precursors to the Married Women's Acts

A very substantial body of legislation affecting women appeared before 1840. Probate laws were modified, abandoned wives gained greater economic protection, imprisonment of women for debt was largely abolished, and federal land grant policy displayed some desire to protect widows. By 1840 most of the obvious ways of increasing married women's access to property without altering the traditional coverture rules had been exhausted. If further reform was to occur, married women's acts would have to appear.

As previously mentioned, colonial and early territorial and state govern-
208 ments had dramatically simplified conveyancing law and had eliminated primogeniture.[238] Dower rules were swept up in this process, leading many jurisdictions to permit married women to waive dower by deed and separate examination and some jurisdictions to permit dower only in lands actually owned by the husband at death. One might hypothesize that as more women lost access to dower, inheritance rules would change to provide widows greater access to their deceased husbands' personal estates. Such a movement would still give first priority to creditors in distributing the assets of an estate, but it would also increase the likelihood that widows of solvent husbands would emerge with some assets. Probate codes adopted in many states in the first third of the nineteenth century extended the late eighteenth-century reforms in intestacy law. The new codes permitted widows to reject their husbands' wills in favor of the share of the estate mandated by law.[239] The well-known eight-

236. The connection has even been discussed in litigation. *See* Kleinert v. Lefkowitz, 271 Mich. 79, 259 N.W. 871 (1935). Some scholars have picked up the connection as well. *See* E. Warbasse, *supra* note 2, at 146-59, 202-05.

237. In fact, a good argument can be made that the 1840's was a decade of reform in a wide array of areas important to women. In addition to the emergence of married women's acts, changes appeared in divorce, child custody, and abortion laws. State statutes that significantly altered the English rule that abortions before quickening were lawful began to appear for the first time in the 1840's. *See generally* Zainaldin, *supra* note 2; J. MOHR, *supra* note 2. Both property reform and restrictions on abortion were consistent with the emerging special sphere of 19th-century women.

238. *See supra* notes 157-82 and accompanying text.

239. E. Warbasse, *supra* note 2, at 72, examines developments in New York, Pennsylvania, and Mississippi. But the changes were far more extensive than that. I have found a number of statutes that gave widows access to a share of their deceased husband's personal estate. Alabama: Act of Dec. 22, 1812, ch. 1, 1812 Ala. Acts 259; Indiana: Act of Jan. 29, 1831, ch. XXIX, 1830 Ind. Acts 209 (1831); Maine: Act of Mar. 23, 1835, ch. 180, 1835 Me. Acts 280; Maryland: Act of Jan. 20, 1798, ch. 13, 1798 Md. Laws (no page); Massachusetts: Act of Feb. 18, 1833, ch. XL, 1833 Mass. Act 547; Michigan: Act of Mar. 30, § 1, 1825 Mich. Terr. Acts 8 (statute providing for extension of debtor exemption statute to estates of husbands); Mississippi: Act of Feb. 9, 1839, ch. 24, 1839 Miss. Laws 33 (statute providing for extension of debtor exemption statute to estates of husbands); New Hampshire: Act of July 2, 1822, ch. XXXXI, 1822 N.H. Laws 30; Ohio: Act of Mar. 23, 1840, § 46, 1839 Ohio Laws 126 (1840); Pennsylvania: Act of Apr. 8, 1833, No. 143, 1832 Pa. Laws 316 (1833) (provides generally for widow's election of dower, but grants elective share of personal estate only when husband's will was drafted before marriage); Act of Apr. 11, 1848, No. 372, 1848 Pa. Laws 537 (full election); Vermont: Act of

eenth-century practice of permitting widows to reject their husbands' wills in favor of dower[240] was expanded to include access to a share of the personal estate. The entitlement was generally the same as the amount provided by intestate succession statutes. Many of these statutes also provided widows with some priority over creditors.[241] The new probate codes did not alter the traditional rules that gave a husband the right to manage his wife's real estate and the right to own outright the personal property the wife brought to the marriage. If all went well financially during the marriage, however, the probate reforms of the early nineteenth century entitled widows to receive a segment of their husbands' personal estates, perhaps regaining some of what they had lost upon marriage. Without directly attacking the coverture rules, probate reform was an avenue for altering slightly the economic impact of the common law.[242]

Early nineteenth-century legislation also eroded some of the other economic consequences of the coverture rules. Abandoned or deserted wives, left by the general content of the common law without either feme-sole status or property, were granted some relief by changes in the divorce statutes[243] or by acts specif-

Nov. 15, 1821, ch. 3, 1821 Vt. Acts 55. In addition, case law suggests that other states had long-standing practices of providing widows an elective share of the personal estate. *See* Illinois: McMurphy v. Boyles, 49 Ill. 110 (1868); Kentucky: Trigg's Adm'r v. Daniel, 5 Ky. (2 Bibb) 301 (1811); Tibbs v. Tibbs' Ex'r, 46 Ky. (7 B. Mon.) 112 (1846); Maine: Brown v. Hodgon, 31 Me. 65 (1849); Massachusetts: Crane v. Crane, 34 Mass. (17 Pick.) 422 (1835) (by a progression of statutes starting in 1783, with the final stages in 1816 and 1833); Missouri: Davis v. Davis, 5 Mo. 111 (1838) (by statute adopted in 1825). *See also* 2 C. SCRIBNER, *supra* note 162, at 257-60 (describing long-standing practice in South Carolina, and statutes in Missouri, Georgia, Pennsylvania, Massachusetts, and Vermont). Other material on this issue may be found in M. SALMON, *supra* note 2, at 264-73; 1 C. SCRIBNER, *supra* note 162, at 23-57; Cahn, *Restraints on Disinheritance*, 85 U. PA. L. REV. 139, 141 (1936); J. SCHOULER, DOMESTIC RELATIONS, *supra* note 44, at 279. Friedman erroneously writes that forced share statutes did not appear until the middle of the 19th century. Friedman, *The Law of the Living, The Law of the Dead: Property, Succession and Society*, 1966 WISC. L. REV. 340, 361.

240. *See* M. SALMON, *supra* note 2, at 257-63. Increased ability to gain access to personal property and to obtain cash in lieu of dower also appeared by 1800. *Id.* at 264-73, 298-319.

241. The statutes in Alabama provided priority only for real property, Indiana provided for a small amount of money ($100) to be free of debts, Massachusetts law provided priority to creditors, Michigan and Mississippi used the debtor exemption model as the bases for their statutes, and New Hampshire and Vermont gave the courts authority to make an allowance for a widow from an insolvent estate.

242. These statutes would obviously have limited impact where husbands disposed of their estates by gift before death, or dissipated the assets. But these problems could only be attacked by directly confronting the doctrines of coverture. In addition, there is some evidence that the statutes reflected fairly closely the habits of even the least generous husbands in writing their wills. There are few reported cases in which wives exercised their options to renounce the wills of their husbands. Studies of wills suggest that there was usually no reason to do so. Gundersen & Gampel, *supra* note 143, at 121-24. The wills of men in the Baltimore study generally confirm this, because wives were a frequent primary beneficiary. *See supra* Table 10. Nonetheless, the Dukes County wills also suggest the potential importance of the rules for widows who rejected estates. Petitions for widows' allowances that requested control over some or all of the personal estates were almost always granted. Eight out of the 10 petitions read were granted in *toto*, one in part, and the other result is not known. Though the requested amounts were usually small, they sometimes involved assets of great importance to a struggling widow. One case gave a widow furniture and both family cows; another all the furniture. Some of the decisions involved substantial amounts, such as over $1,200 in personal property in one case and a ship in another. The practice is discussed in Crane v. Crane, 34 Mass. (17 Pick.) 422 (1835).

243. There was a significant rise in the number of divorces in the first third of the 19th century. L. FRIEDMAN, *supra* note 22, at 181-84. While this did not necessarily indicate any increase in domestic dissatisfaction, *see* C. DEGLER, *supra* note 2, at 166, there is little doubt that significant changes occurred in divorce law and practice during the opening decades of the century. Desertion was among the grounds that began to find favor in this period. R. RIEGEL, AMERICAN WOMEN: A STORY OF SOCIAL CHANGE 127 (1970); N. BLAKE, *supra* note 2, at 48-63. A number of states shortened the period of desertion required to obtain a divorce. For example Alabama, which adopted a five year desertion

ically granting them some economic rights against their departed husbands.[244] This trend is demonstrated nicely by a string of Alabama private bills granting deserted wives feme-sole status.[245] The bills emerged in the mid-1820's and disappeared in the 1840's with the passage of general legislation for the benefit of deserted wives. Those husbands not fulfilling the expected obligation to provide their spouses with support began to find that the coverture rules no longer came to their aid. The reforms were not dramatic. They did little more than redefine the meaning of coverture to exclude some husbands who were not providing support for their families. But during the 1840's there was little room left for enhancing the economic status of mistreated wives unless the coverture rules themselves were altered.

The slow development of protections granted to abandoned, deserted, and divorced women in the first decades of the nineteenth century provides a context in which one would expect to find alterations in child custody and support obligations. Indeed, the case law suggests that women gained greater custodial rights during the first third of the century and that the modern "best interests of the child" test emerged more fully in the decade of the 1840's.[246] The
210 change evident in the reported case law finds even more vivid confirmation in the records of one state, Maryland, in which private bill divorces providing for custody by women began to appear after 1820.[247]

Other statutes also singled women out for special treatment.[248] During the

---

statute on March 10, 1803, shortened the period to two years by legislation passed on December 21, 1820. Blake notes that by 1850, Pennsylvania, Connecticut, New Hampshire, Vermont, Rhode Island, Tennessee, Ohio, Kentucky, and Georgia had adopted legislation providing for divorce on the ground of desertion for a time shorter than the seven year presumptive death period. Numerous private divorce bills also were passed. N. BLAKE, *supra* note 2, at 48-56.

The development of Maryland divorce law is quite revealing. A student author discovered 535 private legislative divorces between 1790 and 1850. Three divorces occurred between 1790 and 1800, 30 between 1801 and 1810, 28 between 1811 and 1820, 95 between 1821 and 1830, 295 between 1831 and 1840, and 84 between 1841 and 1849. Maryland adopted a divorce statute on March 1, 1842, displacing much of the demand for private bills. Gilpatrick, Marital Infidelity in Nineteenth Century Maryland 10 n.61 (1982) (unpublished paper) (copy on file at *Georgetown Law Journal*).

244. Other than Alabama, a number of states adopted legislation protecting abandoned married women. Iowa: Act of Jan. 17, 1840, ch. 81, 1839 Iowa Terr. Laws 152 (1840); Kentucky: Act of Feb. 7, 1843, ch. 103, 1842 Ky. Laws 19 (1843); Maine: Act of Feb. 2, 1828, ch. 380, 1828 Me. Acts 1148; Massachusetts: Act of Mar. 16, 1833, ch. 127, 1833 Mass. Laws 693; New Hampshire: Act of Dec. 24, 1840, ch. 573, 1840 N.H. Laws 488; Act of July 2, 1841, ch. 607, 1841 N.H. Laws 533; North Carolina: Ch. 44, 1828 N.C. Laws 25; Ch. 28, 1829 N.C. Laws 27; Rhode Island: Act of June 2, 1841, 1841 R.I. Laws 43; Tennessee: Act of Oct. 18, 1825, ch. 10, 1825 Tenn. Laws 8; Vermont: Act of Nov. 2, 1846, No. 128, 1846 Vt. Pub. Acts 34. *See also* 1 J. BISHOP, *supra* note 27, at 11, 140-42; R. TYLER, *supra* note 204, at 484-86. The statutes were not all designed to adapt to new family roles. Enactments indicating antipathy to early 19th-century Christian communist celibate groups also appeared. *See* Ohio: Act of Jan. 11, 1811, ch. 8, 1810 Ohio Laws 13 (1811) (act provided that a court could grant a woman a share of the estate of a man who joined "himself to any sect whose rules and doctrines require a renunciation of the marriage covenant, or forbid a man and woman to dwell and cohabit together in the conjugal relation"). These trends apparently had their American roots in disputes arising over the legal rights of women deserted during the Revolutionary War. M. SALMON, *supra* note 2, at 132-43.

245. *See supra* note 46 (listing private bills).

246. Zainaldin, *supra* note 2, at 1052-74. This is one of the most interesting and important legal history articles on women and children before 1850.

247. Private bills for divorce in Maryland began awarding custody of children to wives in the 1820's. Between 1823 and 1846, 21% of private divorce bills granted mothers custody of their children. Gilpatrick, *supra* note 243, at 18.

248. The variety of statutes is amazing. Arkansas enacted a tax exemption statute for poor widows. Act of Nov. 21, 1829, 1829 Ark. Terr. Laws 102. Connecticut provided for the support of widows pending the resolution of probate. Act of May 21, 1825, ch. 10, 1825 Conn. Laws 72. This was a fairly

1820's a number of states prohibited the imprisonment of women debtors.[249] Abolition of the practice for men generally did not occur until later.[250] A number of reforms in debt imprisonment were adopted throughout the late eighteenth and early nineteenth centuries.[251] Use of debtor oaths, extension of prison bounds to include fairly large areas beyond the jail walls, prohibition of imprisonment for petty debts, and release of debtors when creditors declined to pay the cost of imprisonment had significantly reduced the importance of debtors' prisons by the 1820's.[252] Nonetheless some women continued to be imprisoned until the practice was prohibited.[253] All these reforms may have been only symbolic, because poorhouses were growing in popularity during the same period.[254] There are some indications, however, that the abolition of debt imprisonment for women may have been related to the early nineteenth-century tendency to provide protection for widows and abandoned women. Such women were more likely to be without means of support than young unmarried women and children. During the first third of the nineteenth century, abandoned and widowed women were more likely to be isolated from extended families or friends than in the previous century. The growth of industrial cities and the opening of the Western territories provided ample occa- 211
sion for husbands to leave their families or for widows to find themselves without means of support. As the nineteenth century progressed, changes in poor laws dealt with these developments, at least in one jurisdiction, by pro-

---

common reform showing up in many state codes. Some states provided that wives of husbands under guardianship could join in suits for the partition of land. *See* Maine: Act of Feb. 1, 1831, ch. 485, 1831 Me. Acts 1269; Massachusetts: Act of Feb. 21, 1831, ch. 54, 1831 Mass. Laws 569. Many states adopted statutes permitting husbands to join suits previously being pursued by their wives when they were unmarried in order to avoid abatement of the action. *See* Michigan: Act of Mar. 27, 1835, 1834 Mich. Terr. Laws 180 (1835). A number of states also adopted acts permitting wives to insure the lives of their husbands. *See* Maryland: Act of Feb. 23, 1841, ch. 212, 1840 Md. Laws (no page) (1841). Other states provided that certain portions of a husband's estate would be exempt from creditors. *See* New York: Act of Feb. 16, 1824, ch. 44, 1824 N.Y. Laws 32.

249. Coleman provides a great mass of detail on changes in imprisonment for debt legislation. Women were freed of the possibility of debt imprisonment in Connecticut (1826), Georgia (1847), Maryland (1824), Massachusetts (1831), New Hampshire (1831), New Jersey (1818), New York (1828), North Carolina (1823), Pennsylvania (1819), and Vermont (1834). P. COLEMAN, *supra* note 222, at 77-78, 235, 177, 45, 62, 138, 119, 224, 149, 68 (respectively). Georgia was a bit late, but that state had adopted other reforms in the 1820's that virtually removed imprisonment from the list of available creditor remedies. *Id.* at 235.

250. Connecticut (1842), Delaware (1841), Georgia (1858), Maryland (1830), Massachusetts (1857), New Hampshire (1840), New Jersey (1842), New York (1831), North Carolina (1844), Pennsylvania (1842), and Vermont (1838). *See* P. COLEMAN, *supra* note 222, at 78, 210, 235, 177, 52, 62, 139, 119, 224, 151, 68 (respectively). The abolition movement was primarily a Northern enterprise, since Southern states had adopted very effective debtors' oath provisions earlier in the century. Available data suggests that by the time the reform movement got rolling, many more people were being imprisoned for debt in the North than in the South. *See* FIFTH ANNUAL REPORT OF THE BOSTON PRISON DISCIPLINE SOCIETY (1830) (2,742 debt imprisonments in the North and only 35 in the South in 1829).

251. *See* P. COLEMAN, *supra* note 222, at 9-15, 249-68.

252. Randall, *Imprisonment for Debt in America: Fact and Fiction*, 39 MISS. VALLEY HIST. REV. 89 (1952).

253. The SIXTH ANNUAL REPORT OF THE BOSTON PRISON DISCIPLINE SOCIETY 443-447 (1831) reports on a survey of jailers in Massachusetts. Although there were a number of women reported to have been jailed in Boston, a much smaller number had been jailed in other counties. The report's findings are logical as cities were likely to contain more "disconnected" women. These findings are comparable to the findings of a study of poor laws in Maryland. The Maryland study found that outpensions for widowed or deserted women were most common in Baltimore. *See infra* note 255.

254. L. FRIEDMAN, *supra* note 22, at 190-92.

viding outpensions to increasingly large numbers of such women.[255] This development is consistent with other legal developments occurring in the same period. Even in places where divorce for desertion was available, the imposition of substantial waiting periods meant long delays before women could obtain relief. Moreover, statutes like Alabama's, which provided feme-sole status to abandoned wives, would not take care of everyone. It is likely that some deserted women who were unable to work were given poor relief if their husbands left no property behind.

Finally, widows and women who headed families also appeared as something of a protected class in federal land grant policy. While some early land provisions explicitly provided benefits for white males only,[256] other legislation for the benefit of widows of deceased land claimants appeared in the early decades of the century.[257] By the 1840's land grant legislation routinely provided grants for heads of families[258] in addition to widows. Although federal land grant law never fully absorbed the married women's property move-

---

212 255. C. McKenna, Women, Welfare, and Work in Maryland: A Historical Survey of the First Two Hundred Years 25-29 (1982) (unpublished paper) (copy on file with author). McKenna found a significant increase in the number of women receiving outpensions in the first few decades of the 19th century, particularly in the cities. In addition, a number of private bills were also adopted. The pensions and private bills frequently benefitted women with children.

256. *See* Ordinance of 1785, 28 J. CONT. CONG. 375 (1785); An Act Authorizing the Grant and Conveyance of Certain Lands to the Ohio Company of Associates, 1 Stat. 257 (1792). Much early legislation was gender neutral in terminology, speaking only of "purchasers" or "settlers." It is not presently known whether women, even single women, were able to make use of such provisions. *See* An Act Providing for the Sale of the Lands of the United States, in the Territory Northwest of the River Ohio and Above the Mouth of Kentucky River, 1 Stat. 464 (1796); An Act Making Provision for the Disposal of the Public Lands in the Indiana Territory and for Other Purposes, 2 Stat. 277 (1804). This sort of legislation was sometimes amended to take care of widows and heads of families. *See* An Act to Grant Pre-emption Rights to Settlers on Public Lands, 5 Stat. 251 (1838) (amending earlier pre-emption act passed in 1830). The variety of terminology in the early land acts is staggering. It is fair to suggest that the notion of "family head" grew in prominence as the century unfolded and that early on women unaccompanied by living husbands became eligible to hold the status of "family head."

257. *See* An Act for the Relief of the Refugees From the British Provinces of Canada and Nova Scotia, 1 Stat. 547 (1798); An Act Making Provision for Certain Persons Claiming Lands Under the Several Acts for the Relief of the Refugees From the British Provinces of Canada and Nova Scotia, 2 Stat. 712 (1812) (private bill granting land to a widow and a remarried widow). By 1830 many states had statutes providing that widows would be heirs to their deceased husbands and federal land rode piggyback on these provisions. *See* An Act to Authorize the Investigation of Alleged Frauds Under the Pre-emption Laws and for Other Purposes, 5 Stat. 619 (1843); Johnson v. Collins, 12 Ala. 322 (1847). *See also* 2 J. GALES & W. SEATON, PUBLIC ACTS OF CONGRESS RESPECTING THE SALE AND DISPOSITION OF THE PUBLIC LANDS 548, 557 (1838) (discussing two Commissioner of General Land Office decisions issued in 1831 holding that Pre-emption Act of 1830, 4 Stat. 420, permits widow to act as a settler and to perfect her deceased husband's claim).

258. *See, e.g.*, An Act for Granting Lands to the Inhabitants and Settlers at Vincennes and the Illinois County, 1 Stat. 221 (1791); An Act Regulating the Grants of Land, and Providing for the Disposal of the Lands of the United States, South of the State of Tennessee, 2 Stat. 229 (1803); An Act Giving the Right of Pre-emption, in the Purchase of Lands, to Certain Settlers in the States of Alabama, Mississippi, and Territory of Florida, 4 Stat. 154 (1826); An Act to Grant Pre-emption Rights to Settlers on Public Lands, 5 Stat. 251 (1838). By the 1840's the term "head of family" was used in federal land laws. *See* An Act to Appropriate the Proceeds of the Sales of Public Lands and to Grant Pre-emption Rights, 5 Stat. 453 (1841). This Act was routinely administered to include female heads of families within its ambit. *See* 1 W. LESTER, LAND LAWS, REGULATIONS, AND DECISIONS 360-65 (1860) (Circular to Registers and Receivers of the United States Land Offices issued Sept. 15, 1841, construing Pre-emption Act of 1841 and making it clear that widows and female heads of families included within its terms). In the 1850's married women were still precluded from purchasing most federal lands unless state or territorial law permitted them to do so. *See id.* at 466.

ment,[259] it did reflect the early nineteenth-century trend to provide special treatment for female heads of families and widows.

3. Married Women's Acts, Separate Estate Trust Deeds, and a Glance at Later Developments

Legal developments between 1800 and 1840 tended to protect married women by adjusting the impacts of coverture without altering the central features of married women's status. By 1840 there was a somewhat greater likelihood that legal institutions would attempt to assist a married woman in distress because of death, abandonment, poverty, or divorce. The increase in such legal responses suggests a change in attitude toward those women who fell off the edge of the separate domestic sphere. Whether the cause of the fall was extrinsic to the marital relationship or a rupture of the marriage, recognition began to be given to the particular problems confronting some married women.

While these legislative changes were emerging, the separate equitable estate became more widely understood, and, if the Baltimore will and trust deed study reflects general trends, more widely used.[260] By 1850 the legal strands 213
began to merge. The separate estate, even before it was converted from an equitable contrivance to a statutory entitlement, was often set aside as a special class of property immune from the husband's debts and thus available to sustain the family in troubled times. Because the documents creating separate estates had long been used to insulate property from creditors,[261] thus causing courts of equity to require that husbands in debt seeking access to their wives' separate estates set aside an equity to a settlement to protect a portion of their spouses' wealth.[262] Women had long been the subject of special legislative attention, so that the earliest of the married women's acts could hardly have been perceived as radical. But they were important. Like trust instruments, they generally did not give married women control over the disposition of their separate estates, but they did set the stage for later legislation and judicial decisions that loosened the dispositional constraints.[263]

---

259. The closest federal land law came to a married women's act was the Oregon Donation Act, 9 Stat. 496 (1850), which explicitly granted land to married women. This is the only such piece of legislation I have found. It is interesting to speculate on why federal land law did not reflect the developments on the state level after 1850. It is likely that once state law developed to permit married women to contract, there was little need for federal law to change. Even if married women could not purchase land directly, they could gain title by deed after the federal patent was issued. Many, if not most, of the purchases of land by persons moving to the frontier territories were not directly from the government but from others who had already obtained title to the land. By the time state law had fully developed to permit women to control their own earnings, most of the good federal lands open for private settlement had already been sold. For background and history of federal land sales, see generally Cole, *Cyclical and Sectional Variations in the Sale of Public Lands, 1816-1860*, 9 REV. ECON. STATISTICS 41 (1927); Danhof, *Farm-Making Costs and the "Safety Valve": 1850-1860*, 49 J. POL. ECON. 317 (1941); Gates, *The Role of the Land Speculator in Western Development*, 66 PA. MAG. HIST. & BIOG. 314 (1942).

260. *See supra* notes 59-92 and accompanying text (archival study).

261. L. FRIEDMAN, *supra* note 22, at 220-22. The trust deed study confirms the same fact. *See supra* Tables 12, 13, and 14 and accompanying text.

262. Equity to a settlement had a strong tradition in England in the 17th century. 5 W. HOLDSWORTH, *supra* note 106, at 314; 6 W. HOLDSWORTH, *supra* note 108, at 645. The tradition continued here. *See* N. BASCH, *supra* note 1, at 89-96; 1 J. BISHOP, *supra* note 27, at 449-516; 2 J. STORY, *supra* note 34, at 630-50.

263. Legislation creating a separate estate for married women appeared over a wide range of years beginning in the 1840's and ending after the Civil War. Most of this legislation was enacted before the

If in 1850 there was still debate over whether women could own property without the intervention of a trustee,[264] trustees became unnecessary by 1860 in the North and 1870 in the South. If equity was a changing and sometimes uncertain means for legitimizing married women's control of property, then a legal estate created by statute could substitute nicely. If previously only wealthy men and women could afford to create the documents needed to formalize a separate estate, permit women to retain title to their personal property, insulate married women's property from creditors, and provide for its disposition at death, there was eventually room for language in a simple deed or transfer agreement to automatically serve all these and other ends. Thus, the fact that the early married women's acts fit into a network of mild reforms from 1800 on should not blind us to the significance of their arrival. They were, after all, the earliest examples of a long stream of statutes focusing specifically on the economic consequences of women's property ownership during marriage. The fact that many of the statutes adopted after the mid-1840's contained provisions that may have been intended to do more than insulate married women's property from a husband's debts gave the blossoming feminist
214 movement reason to hope that further reforms would occur.

Despite the well-known connection between legislative petitioning and lobbying by a few women in the late 1840's and the passage of a few of the married women's acts,[265] most of the early acts, modest and conservative in tone, were compatible with prior and contemporary legislation of the most ordinary sort. Even the New York act of 1848,[266] the best known of all the early statutes, was extremely narrow in scope. The first two sections of the act insulated a married woman's property from her husband's debts and also declared that the property "shall continue her sole and separate property, as if she were a single female."[267] The third section provided that property coming to married

---

war. Mississippi, Maryland, Arkansas, Alabama, Michigan, Maine, Massachusetts, Iowa, New York, and Pennsylvania each adopted debt statutes with separate estate provisions. *See supra* notes 207, 209. These acts were passed between 1839 and 1852. Another batch of separate estate statutes was adopted in the following decade in the newly burgeoning territories, and after the war in the Southern states. The states adopting such acts included Michigan: Act of Feb. 13, 1855, No. 168, 1855 Mich. Laws 420; Illinois: Act of Feb. 21, 1861, 1861 Ill. Laws 143; Ohio: Act of Apr. 3, 1861, 1861 Ohio Laws 54; Delaware: Act of Mar. 17, 1865, ch. 572, 1865 Del. Laws 663; Georgia: Act of Dec. 13, 1866, No. 204, 1866 Ga. Laws 146; Vermont: Act of Nov. 21, 1867, No. 21, 1867 Vt. Acts 29; Tennessee: Act of Mar. 2, 1870, ch. 99, 1869 Tenn. Laws 113. These statutes, especially the early ones, did not, on their face, remove the need for a trustee. Sometimes this was accomplished by later statutes, *see* Maryland: Act of May 24, 1853, ch. 245, 1853 Md. Laws 323; statutes cited *infra* note 361; and by court decision. Harris v. Harris, 42 N.C. (7 Ired. Eq.) 111 (1850); Gibson v. Walker, 20 N.Y. 476 (1859); Harding v. Cobb, 47 Miss. 599 (1873); Blood v. Humphrey, 17 Barb. 660 (N.Y. 1854); Burnett v. Hawpe's Ex'r, 25 Gratt. 481 (Va. 1874); Radford v. Carwile, 13 W. Va. 572 (1879); Maiben v. Bobe, 6 Fla. 381 (1855).

264. In New York, there was a 20-year debate over the relationship between equity and married women's estates. *See* P. RABKIN, *supra* note 2, at 61-105. Since equitable language was so often used in the statutes, it was reasonably common for courts to call upon equity precedent to construe the new statute. *See id.* at 125-38.

265. *See* E. Warbasse, *supra* note 2, at 205-36; P. RABKIN, *supra* note 2, at 106-17.

266. Act of Apr. 7, 1848, ch. 200, 1848 N.Y. Laws 307.

267. The act reads in full:

> AN ACT for the more effectual protection of the property of married women.
>
> Passed April 7, 1848.
>
> The People of the State of New York, represented in Senate and Assembly do enact as follows:
>
> § 1. The real and personal property of any female who may hereafter marry, and which she

women in the future "from any persons other than her husband" shall be held "to her sole and separate use, as if she were a single female."[268] It is this "sole and separate use" phrase which later generations have pointed to as breakthrough language.[269]

The similarity of the statute's sale and separate use phraseology to typical language in equitable instruments and its presence in sections dealing with debt made narrow construction almost inevitable. Equity courts frequently had construed trust instruments containing sole and separate use language but lacking explicit grants of dispositional authority to deny married women the right to contract about or will separate estate assets. The statute only prohibited "disposal" of a separate estate by husbands, leaving intact the range of other restrictions, providing husbands with management authority, and preventing unilateral contractual or testamentary disposal by wives. The statute's primary effect was to create a new category of exempt assets for family use. The special sphere of married women was thus largely confirmed. Assets belonging to married women were to be set aside and insulated from the harsh realities of the commercial world. Married women's property, like married women themselves, was to be specially treated and protected. Indeed, the statute 215
underscores the limited sphere of women by providing that assets received by a wife directly from her husband would not be free from her husband's debts.[270] A married woman was not easily going to become a device for insulating a husband's assets from commercial liability. These were the features of the early married women's act that finally persuaded conservative New York legislators to support the 1848 bill.[271] Neither substantial harm to creditors nor great risks of family divisiveness were likely to result from this sort of legislation.

The growing use of equitable separate estates confirms the same trends. Property management was a fairly new adventure for most married women.

---

shall own at the time of marriage, and the rents issues and profits thereof shall not be subject to the disposal of her husband, nor be liable for his debts, and shall continue her sole and separate property, as if she were a single female.

§ 2. The real and personal property, and the rents issues and profits therof of any female now married shall not be subject to the disposal of her husband; but shall be her sole and separate property as if she were a single female except so far as as the same may be liable for the debts of her husband heretofore contracted.

§ 3. It shall be lawful for any married female to receive, by gift, grant devise or bequest, from any person other than her husband and hold to her sole and separate use, as if she were a single female, real and personal property, and the rents, issues and profits thereof, and the same shall not be subject to the disposal of her husband, nor be liable for his debts.

§ 4. All contracts made between persons in contemplation of marriage shall remain in full force after such marriage takes place.

268. *Id.* § 3.

269. Other states used similar language before New York. *See supra* notes 204-09. Section 1 of Mississippi's 1839 act provided that married women become "seized and possessed of any property, real or personal, . . . in her own name, and as of her own property." Maine's 1844 statute mirrors the Mississippi language. Michigan's 1844 statute provides that after marriage, property shall be the "estate of such female after marriage to the same extent as before marriage." Despite the fact that Massachusetts was the scene of much early female agitation on both women's and slavery issues, its first married women's act was very narrow in content. It basically permitted the establishment of trusts through ante-nuptial agreements and limited the husband's control of the trust assests.

270. This provision in section 3 was judicially expanded to void conveyances made by wives directly to their husbands. White v. Wager, 25 N.Y. 328 (1862).

271. *See* E. Warbasse, *supra* note 2, at 218-29.

From receipt of inheritances in the eighteenth century, through development of income by unmarried women, to management of middle class family incomes by some married women by the middle of the century, the domestic sphere and the separate equitable estate were stretched to accommodate the presence of money and women's new role in the family. But the stretch was narrow. Independent commercial endeavors by married women were not included on the mid-century reform agenda. Married women were singled out for special treatment, their assets were subject to dispositional constraints established by others, and their property was largely controlled for the benefit of their families. The appearance of both married women's acts and separate estate instruments suggests that a married woman's property was largely viewed as a family resource or as a safeguard for a wife upon her husband's death or departure, not as mercantile or speculative wealth. Married women were still homemakers, and the gradual emergence of dispositional authority over separate property reflects women's greater activity in the home economy more than their widespread entry into the business world.

But the statutes and separate estates also reflect myriad contradictions. The
216 very device used to confirm women's special sphere—the separate estate insulated from the husband's debts—created a wedge in the coverture bastion, and confirmed for women a small degree of independence from their marriage partners. Indeed, the contradictions go deeper. Despite the prohibition on debt exemption for property coming to a wife from her husband, the New York statute, and others as well, created an incentive for husbands to use their wives' new insulation from creditors to hide assets. While a conveyance to a third party was necessary to avoid the restrictions on intramarital exchanges, extramarial property coming to a married woman was not so constrained. Those with wealth were certainly going to take the bait[272] by using straw party exchanges or causing extramarital property to be held in their wives' names. The separate equitable estate was available for similar use. The statutes and separate estates themselves contained the sorts of contradictions that would lead later reformers to urge more similar treatment of men's and women's property by refining the definitions of property owned by husbands and wives and equalizing the availability of these assets to creditors.[273]

III. THE HISTORICAL BLANKET

In her address "The Wrongs of Woman" before the 1850 Salem, Ohio, Women's Convention, J. Elizabeth Jones, like speakers at earlier gatherings, spent much of her time on law and Blackstone.[274] Jones noted that many women had conflicting feelings about their position. Some, she said, do not know they

---

272. *See* P. RABKIN, *supra* note 2, at 126-37; S. Breed, Conflicts of Interest: The Evolution of Married Women's Property Rights in Nineteenth Century New Hampshire (1982) (unpublished paper) (copy on file with author).

273. Breed's paper on women's property rights in New Hampshire, *supra* note 272, lays out this story in wonderful detail. Disputes over use of the marital property exemption eventually led to more equitable treatment and creditor access. This was the pattern followed nationally as the century unfolded. For later married women's acts, *see infra* note 361.

274. THE SALEM, OHIO 1850 WOMEN'S RIGHTS CONVENTION PROCEEDINGS 52-62 (R. Audretsch ed. 1976) [hereinafter OHIO 1850 WOMEN'S RIGHTS CONVENTION].

are "robbed of [their] rights," others feel "weak and dependent."[275] Others fear "to expose their own situation" or "dread of seeming to be out of their sphere" and therefore masculine.[276] Still others "have no sense of injury" because "all their wants have been duly supplied" or "labor for a mere pittance because they are women."[277] After making a lengthy critique of the inequities of the common law and contending that women should obtain the right of suffrage at the impending Ohio Constitutional Convention, Jones concluded:

> We but ask that our equality in point of rights be acknowledged; we ask that none shall strive to obliterate or deface the image and superscription our Creator stamped upon our souls. I am aware that the great mass of women in this country have no sympathy with the views I have expressed. I wish it were otherwise. I wish they could be led to see their true position, and be made to understand that the gallantry and devotion of man is offered them in lieu of a recognition of their rights, and that it is only in a few rare cases he approaches and converses with them as equals, as being as fully rational, intelligent and morally accountable as himself, endowed with the same rights and clothed with the same duties.
>
> But I will not further extend my remarks. I have already said enough to secure the disapprobation which is always bestowed upon a woman who thinks and speaks for herself. I have said *more* than enough for those women who are contented with their rose-covered chains and gilded prison-bars; and I could hope that I have said something to encourage to earnest action those of my sex who feel that no length of legislation can sanction and sanctify the wrongs that have been inflicted upon them; that no social usages, however time-honored, can justify the oppressions they have been compelled to endure; that no religious creed, however sanctimonious its supporters, can find the least excuse for the inequality in the church.[278]

This statement is a remarkable indication of the social pressures felt by one of the more radical of mid-nineteenth-century women.[279] Why would a public

275. *Id.* at 54.
276. *Id.*
277. *Id.*
278. *Id.* at 62 (emphasis in original).
279. Jones' speech also roundly condemned slavery and applauded by name many of the prominent feminists of her time. After 1840 she consistently turned up at important gatherings of feminists and abolitionists. Jones lobbied for the adoption of the 1861 Ohio married women's property act, lectured on health and hygiene (common interests of the feminists of her era), and for a time edited the Anti-Slavery Bugle with her husband. 2 E. JAMES, NOTABLE AMERICAN WOMEN 1607-1950, at 285-86 (J. James & P. Boyer eds. 1971).

At one point in her speech, Jones noted that she may choose not to

> exercise my right so to [vote], after it is accorded to me; indeed all who know my sentiments in relation to Constitutions and government, and you, Madam President, may not, and all whom I address may not; but that is no reason why others should judge for us, of the propriety and expediency of our so doing; *that* is a right I insist upon exercising for myself, and these 'Daniels' who have 'come to judgment' have me-thinks, assumed an air of wisdom, as foreign to their own characters as it is derogatory to us.

OHIO 1850 WOMEN'S RIGHTS CONVENTION, *supra* note 274, at 58 (emphasis in original). At first blush, this seems to be a statement that Jones would not vote because of social constraints on the role of

woman of 1850 castigate limitations on her social role while confessing to the unwillingness of most women to follow her lead?

A brief examination of the historical literature on women in the first half of the nineteenth century reveals a series of changes relevant to the mid-century emergence of married women's acts. By 1800 the importance of married women as active participants in the family was more widely recognized. Symptoms of the changes surfaced in a number of ways. Women became more involved in religious and social service activities, more literate, and more deeply involved in raising and educating their children. At the same time that married women were assuming greater importance in the family and in family-related social organizations, single women were beginning to leave home for reasons other than apprenticeship or marriage. Employment opportunities beckoned in teaching, domestic service, and the mills. As the nineteenth century unfolded, these trends accelerated, creating very substantial differences in the roles of single and married women. For many women an active unmarried life was followed by marital domesticity. Married women's acts reflected this situation. The significant features of the acts did not reject married women's
218 separate domestic sphere, but recognized the importance of women as caretakers of children and family resources.

A. THE POST-REVOLUTIONARY WAR ERA

J. Elizabeth Jones did not invent women's conflict over public and private spheres. Recent literature suggests such tension appeared at least as early as the Revolutionary War era. Both Norton and Kerber contend that the Revolutionary War was a catalyst for some redefinition of women's social position. They note that the pre-Revolutionary War domestic role of women took on a different content by the end of the eighteenth century[280] due to participation of women in the Revolutionary War political scene through economic boycotts,[281] home production,[282] and political correspondence and discussion.[283] By coping with the inevitable disruptions caused by conflict, political disagreements, and absent spouses, women sensed they were participating in important cultural developments.[284] Kerber finds that at the core of cultural values "a concensus developed around the idea that a mother, committed to the service of her family and to the state, might serve a political purpose."[285] Norton agrees, writing that the "war necessarily broke down the barrier which seemed to insulate women from the realm of politics, for they, no less than men, were caught up in the turmoil that enveloped the entire populace."[286] While Norton states that domesticity was no longer denigrated and the feminine sphere

---

women. It is probably, however, a statement typical of the radical Garrisonian wing of the Abolitionists, who perferred withdrawal from participation in a union with slavery to creation of an anti-slavery political party or to work with the existing parties. For a history of the Garrisonians, *see* W. WIECEK, SOURCES OF ANTISLAVERY CONSTITUTIONALISM IN AMERICA, 1760-1848 228-48 (1977).

280. M. NORTON, *supra* note 2, at 155-299; L. KERBER, *supra* note 2, at 157-288.

281. M. NORTON, *supra* note 2, at 157-63; L. KERBER, *supra* note 2, at 35-39.

282. M. NORTON, *supra* note 2, at 163-70; L. KERBER, *supra* note 2, at 41-45.

283. M. NORTON, *supra* note 2, at 170-77; L. KERBER, *supra* note 2, at 73-85.

284. M. NORTON, *supra* note 2, at 195-227; L. KERBER, *supra* note 2, at 455-67.

285. L. KERBER, *supra* note 2, at 283.

286. M. NORTON, *supra* note 2, at 297.

no longer subordinate,[287] Kerber prefers a less egalitarian portrayal of Republican Motherhood as a "concept that legitimized a minimum of political sophistication and interest, and only of a most generalized sort."[288] Both writers agree, however, that in contrast to the subservient role of women before 1770, the Revolutionary War era provided women with a new egalitarian vocabulary, a few well-known, if ridiculed, radical figures,[289] and a potential for limited participation in public events. The stage was set for a cultural redefinition of the married women's separate sphere.[290]

Evidence of conflict over the relationship between a married woman's public and private life appeared in a number of ways in the years just before 1800. Since public debate by women was still the extraordinary exception,[291] the evidence is largely confined to other areas. Kerber and Norton both investigated private correspondence and diaries in their efforts to sort out the effects of the Revolutionary War.[292] Just as women in the nineteenth-century tended to correspond with other women in intimate, supportive ways,[293] literate women of the eighteenth-century have left us a historical record of their friendships.[294] Female friendships and correspondence were symbolic of the larger possibilities for group female activity,[295] and consistent with the already noted tendency of women (and men) to will property to other women.[296]

Despite the basically private nature of the separate sphere, women began to participate in some worldly activities before the eighteenth-century was complete. Petitioning, particularly by widows, arose.[297] Female societies and auxiliaries to male voluntary groups appeared during the war to organize home production, nursing, and fund-drives.[298] These groups continued in a different guise after the war. Female religious, reform, and service societies proliferated in the last two decades of the century.[299] Although most female societies dealt with matters closely related to the domestic sphere[300] or religious concerns,[301] the societies inevitably led women to make public choices. The economic panics in the late eighteenth century[302] and the appearance of impoverished wo-

287. *Id.* at 298.

288. L. KERBER, *supra* note 2, at 285.

289. For a description of public reaction to Mary Wollstonecraft's VINDICATION OF THE RIGHTS OF WOMEN (1792), see L. KERBER, *supra* note 2, at 224-25, and M. NORTON, *supra* note 2, at 251-52.

290. *See* M. NORTON, *supra* note 2, at 228-55 (discussing emergence of the "reverance of self" during post-war period); L. KERBER, *supra* note 2, at 73-113 (discussing women's emerging role outside the home both during and after war). *See also* C. DEGLER, *supra* note 2, at 191-92 (attributing women's separate sphere in 18th century to society's new emphasis on freedom and individualism).

291. *But see* L. KERBER, *supra* note 2, at 99-110 (describing women's campaign to raise funds for troops during war, commonly referred to as "Philadelphia Project").

292. M. NORTON, *supra* note 2, at 309-14; L. KERBER, *supra* note 2, at 289-93.

293. C. DEGLER, *supra* note 2, at 144-50.

294. N. COTT, *supra* note 2, at 185-99.

295. M. NORTON, *supra* note 2, at 105-09.

296. *See supra* Tables 9 and 10.

297. L. KERBER, *supra* note 2, at 85-99 (petitions included requests to cross enemy lines to join husbands and claims for property left behind).

298. *Id.* at 99-105.

299. *Id.* at 111-13.

300. *Id.* at 111. Women and children in distress were of particular concern.

301. *Id.*

302. *See* P. COLEMAN, *supra* note 222, at 18-19 (economic problems even led to adoption of short-lived national bankruptcy act in 1800).

men and children, prostitution, town slums, and alcohol abuse created opportunities for many groups of middle and upper class women to become involved with social concerns.[303]

The subtle post-war changes in attitudes toward domesticity are also revealed by improvements in female literacy and education.[304] If, as both Kerber and Norton suggest, the post-war family was assigned a substantial new role in the education of children in appropriate civic virtues, then women themselves had to be literate.[305] There is no doubt that girls continued to receive lesser educations than boys long after 1800 and that expressions of support for gender equality in education met with strong disapproval.[306] Yet female academies emerged after the war and flourished with the growing public education movement after the turn of the century.[307] Literacy rates for women increased after 1780 until the first literacy census, taken in 1850, showed little difference between literacy rates for men and women.[308] Reading and writing by women exploded around the turn of the nineteenth century.[309] Ladies magazines, as well as fictional and religious reading and writing, became
220 an important part of many women's lives, though histories and the like were

303. J. FURNAS, THE AMERICANS: A SOCIAL HISTORY OF THE UNITED STATES, 1587-1914 313-17 (1969).

304. L. KERBER, *supra* note 2, at 198-99.

305. *Id.* at 199-200; M. NORTON, *supra* note 2, at 256-57. Norton adds that the exigencies of the just-completed war also suggested the need for educated women on the homefront. M. NORTON, *supra* note 2, at 256.

306. L. KERBER, *supra* note 2, at 193-221; M. NORTON, *supra* note 2, at 263-72.

307. L. KERBER, *supra* note 2, at 198-205.

308. *Id.* at 193. School enrollment among whites age 5-19 also displayed little difference by gender in 1850. About 59% of boys and 53% of girls were in school. STATISTICAL HISTORY, *supra* note 6, at 369-70. Very little work on female literacy rates in the early 19th century has been done, but what has been done suggests that vast changes occurred between 1800 and 1850. While the proportion of women signing wills in the 18th century was fairly stable at about 40%, K. LOCKRIDGE, *supra* note 28, at 38-41, men's signature rates were substantially higher. Lockridge found some evidence for literacy increases among females in the decades just before 1800. *Id.* at 38. But by 1850 differences between men and women appear to have virtually vanished. L. SOLTOW & E. STEVENS, THE RISE OF LITERACY AND THE COMMON SCHOOL IN THE UNITED STATES 157-58 (1981). *See also* GOODSELL, PIONEERS OF WOMEN'S EDUCATION IN THE UNITED STATES 1-12 (1931); 1 T. WOODY, *supra* note 9, at 159-60 (during colonial period percentage of illiteracy was greater among women than men).

309. It is perhaps not accidental that women's wills began to appear in greater numbers after women became more literate. The will studies produced some additional data on literacy. The recorded Baltimore wills noted whether wills were signed or marked. Similar notations in the Dukes County recorded wills were found to be unreliable. All the wills were probated in 1810 or later, so one would expect fairly high signature rates. The small size of the sample makes hard conclusions difficult, but over 60% of women's wills were signed. Surprisingly, no significant change appeared over time.

Women's Will Literacy (Baltimore)

Probate Year	Signed	Marked	Not Known
1810	3	5	5
1825	14	5	0
1840	23	16	4
1846	34	13	1

If the 1810 and 1825 data are merged, 63% (17/27) of the wills where information was available were signed. Similarly, 66% (57/86) of the 1840 and 1846 wills were signed. The signature rate for males among the wills read from all four of the sample years was 83% (20/24) with nine unknown. These results are compatible with the very high (90%) literacy rates of an 1860 sample of married women, L. SOLTOW & E. STEVENS, *supra* note 308, at 156, and the lower literacy rates (less than 50%) found among female will writers in the late 18th century. K. LOCKRIDGE, *supra* note 28, at 38-39.

still thought of as men's fare.[310] The movement to literacy was not without opponents fearful of introducing worldly concerns into women's lives or causing impure desires among the ladies.[311] These concerns were particularly important in an era that witnessed a substantial increase in courting freedoms and premarital pregnancy rates.[312] But female novel reading also found philosophical support in the contemporaneous rise of romanticism.[313]

With all this activity in reading, writing, and education, women began to enter teaching in new ways. The jump from household tutoring of one's own offspring to the education by unmarried women of a group of children was made by some, opposed by others, but reasonably steady in its growth.[314] By the end of the century, a middle or upper class married woman was more likely than her mother to be literate, a participant in a voluntary society or religious group, and aware of a link between her own role and the larger political culture.[315] And her female offspring were more likely to be teachers.[316]

Another link between women's domestic role and larger social activities was found in religion. The domesticity of women was linked to morality and virtue long before the Revolutionary War.[317] Women outnumbered men in churches from very early colonial days, and this trend became very noticeable by the turn of the nineteenth century.[318] Although teaching and eventually mill work provided avenues for unmarried women to leave the home, religion provided that opportunity for their mothers. Some religious groups, particularly the Quakers, provided opportunities for substantial female participation and even for religious travel.[319] Nineteenth-century revivals and camp meetings, religious fervor, religiously-based social service groups, and the Second Great Awakening had their roots in the late eighteenth century.[320] The conflicts in women's domestic role that emerged in the nineteenth-century egalitarian religious and communal movements were largely defined by the stresses

---

310. *See* L. KERBER, *supra* note 2, at 235-64 (explaining importance of reading fiction to women in the early republic); N. COTT, *supra* note 2, at 64-74 (tracing common theme of domesticity in literary works appealing to women).

311. L. KERBER, *supra* note 2, at 239.

312. C. DEGLER, *supra* note 2, at 20; L. KERBER, *supra* note 2, at 245; M. NORTON, *supra* note 2, at 51-60; Smith, *Dating the American Sexual Revolution: Evidence and Interpretation*, in THE AMERICAN FAMILY IN SOCIAL-HISTORICAL PERSPECTIVE 321 (M. Gordon ed. 1973). Smith found that premarital pregnancy rates peaked in the later 18th century and troughed in the later 19th. *Id.* at 321-22.

313. *See* N. COTT, *supra* note 2, at 76-83 (romanticism conveyed in literature influenced women to wish for ideal mate); K. MELDER, *supra* note 2, at 34-47.

314. M. NORTON, *supra* note 2, at 290-94; C. KAESTLE & M. VINOVSKIS, EDUCATION AND SOCIAL CHANGE IN NINETEENTH CENTURY MASSACHUSETTS 26-27 (1980); W. BUTTS & S. CREMINS, A HISTORY OF EDUCATION IN AMERICAN CULTURE 246-47 (1953) [hereinafter BUTTS & CREMINS].

315. M. NORTON, *supra* note 2, at 289. Norton has compiled some fascinating data on education trends over time, suggesting that among notable women, the proportion with some advanced education jumped from 18% for those born before 1770 to 65% for those born after 1770. *Id.* at 288-90.

316. *Id.*

317. *See* C. DEGLER, *supra* note 2, at 289-303 (women organized as the Social Purist to control sexuality and became involved in religion and churches).

318. N. COTT, *supra* note 2, at 126-28.

319. C. DEGLER, *supra* note 2, at 302; K. MELDER, *supra* note 2, at 77-92; M. NORTON, *supra* note 2, at 126-32.

320. *See* C. DEGLER, *supra* note 2, at 298-305 (during second awakening most converts were women and women played active role in reform organizations, religious groups, and antislavery movement); J. FURNAS, *supra* note 303, at 327-32 (discussing tactics of the leaders of the Great Awakening and camp meetings); W. MCLOUGHLIN, REVIVALS, AWAKENINGS, AND REFORM 98-140 (1978).

of the post-war era. The use of special sphere ideology to permit movement of women into religious activities related to, but outside, the home suggested both the potential for larger change and the role limitations that undoubtedly guided most married women's lives.[321]

But for most married women the combination of agricultural stability and the late eighteenth century concern over teaching young children appropriate social behavior led to concentration on child rearing rather than on activities outside the home.[322] It is, in hindsight, not surprising that the turn of the nineteenth century would see the blossoming of the domestic sphere in all of its contradictions.[323] Even though modern notions of child rearing and new techniques of manufacturing were emerging, families were still confronted with a child-rearing experience vastly different from our own. Fertility rates were extraordinarily high, with live births numbering more than twenty-five percent of the child-rearing age population.[324] The rates peaked around the turn of the century and declined thereafter.[325] The average household size was over five and one-half persons, and did not fall below five until the end of the nineteenth century.[326] Despite the large households, infant mortality rates were

222

321. *See* C. DEGLER, *supra* note 2, at 298-327 (discussing emergence of "separate sphere" for women in 19th century; protection of home and preservation of its moral character justified women's active role in outside world).

322. N. COTT, *supra* note 2, at 84-98.

323. Cott's use of the title "Bonds of Womanhood," which she explains on the first page of her book, *supra* note 2, is an appropriate signal of the potential for domesticity to be both an uplifting and binding experience.

324. Miscarriages, still births, and abortions are excluded from this high figure. It is plausible to suggest that during 1800 over one-third of the white women ages 15-44 became pregnant. Birth rates declined throughout the 19th century, with substantial declines starting after 1810. Data from STATISTICAL HISTORY, *supra* note 6, at 49, fills this table:

Year	Birth Rate for White Women 15-44 (Live births/1000 population)
1800	278
1810	274
1820	260
1830	240
1840	222
1850	194
1860	184
1870	167
1880	155
1890	137
1900	130
1930	87.1
1960	113.2
1970	84.1

325. W. GRABILL, C. KISER & P. WHELPTON, THE FERTILITY OF WOMEN IN AMERICA 1-24 (1958).

326. Household size is now well under three. Putting together material from the STATISTICAL ABSTRACT, *supra* note 13, at 45, and STATISTICAL HISTORY, *supra* note 6, at 41, yields the following table:

high, perhaps averaging fifteen percent.[327] Maternal mortality was also high.[328] The high birth rate and its attendant risks made the occurrence of pregnancy, the completion of childbirth, and the process of child rearing the focus of an enormous amount of attention. These events caused awe and fear, delight and depression with much greater frequency than today. The possibilities for tragedy were remarkably greater than we can imagine. Cott put it mildly when she wrote that "the arrival of another child posed anxieties."[329]

B. THE EARLY NINETEENTH-CENTURY

Such anxieties produced a rich variety of responses as the nineteenth century unfolded. Reproductive rates declined more noticeably after the turn of the century.[330] There seems to be little doubt that some form of birth control operated to produce the substantial decline in fertility between 1800 and 1850.[331]

Year	Average Household Size
1790	5.79
1850	5.55
1860	5.28
1870	5.09
1880	5.04
1890	4.93
1900	4.76
1930	4.11
1970	3.14
1979	2.78

327. Data from Massachusetts suggests that from 1850 until after 1900, about 15% of newborns died. Earlier rates were presumably of a similar magnitude. The somewhat lower mortality rates for the 1850's, however, suggest the possibility that rates rose contemporaneously with the decline of midwifery. There is need to explore the relationship between death rates and male entry into the birth process. Were midwives more sanitary? STATISTICAL HISTORY, *supra* note 6, at 57:

Infant Mortality For Massachusetts 1851-1970
(per 1000 live births)

Time	Rate
1851-54	131.1
1855-59	122.9
1860-64	142.5
1865-69	146.3
1870-74	170.3
1875-79	156.3
1880-84	161.3
1885-89	158.5
1890-94	163.2
1895-99	153.2
1900-04	141.4
1905-09	134.3
1910-14	116.7
1915-19	100.2
1920-24	78.7
1925-29	67.6
1970	16.8

328. Even in 1915 the rate was over 60 per 10,000 live births. The rate did not begin to fall until after 1930. Presumably 19th-century death rates were at least as high. STATISTICAL HISTORY, *supra* note 6, at 57.

329. N. COTT, *supra* note 2, at 91.

330. *See supra* notes 324 and 325 and accompanying text.

331. C. DEGLER, *supra* note 2, at 181-96, 210-16. The decline in birth rates was also attributed to improving economic status, while the primary method of birth control was probably abstinence.

Abortion appears to have been a common practice of the middle class by the 1840's when the first antiabortion laws appeared.[332] The variety in early nineteenth-century communal groups probably mirrored the tensions over childbirth present in the larger community. Some sects were celibate,[333] others openly espoused birth control, and a number adopted communal living patterns and carefully controlled programs of sexual access to handle the problems of childbirth.[334] Some groups, like the Mormons, encouraged childbirth.[335] But whether the community chose celibacy, birth control, abstinence, communal child care, or high reproduction rates, control over family formation and fertility was central to each group's self-image.

Such control is a major theme in Degler's scholarship. He argues that the period from 1780 to 1830 witnessed the emergence of the modern American family characterized by marriage based on affection and respect, greater influence and autonomy for women in the home, child rearing and home maintenance as the wife's primary role, devotion of a larger amount of parental energy and resources to young children, treatment of young children as persons different from adults and needing special treatment, love, and solicitude,
224 and smaller family size.[336] Degler and Cott suggest that the emergence of the modern family both created an opportunity for women to increase their influence within the family and established limitations on the ability of women to work in the public sphere.[337] As the separate domestic sphere grew to define middle class as well as wealthy women's roles,[338] it both legitimated domestically related activity outside the home and created a new standard for defining deviance.[339]

---

332. *See* J. MOHR, *supra* note 2, at 16-18, 86-118. Abortion probably gained in importance when mechanical means of terminating a pregnancy became preferred over taking of poisons. Abortion frequency apparently rose in the 1840's. *Id.* at 46-85. Use of instruments probably increased during the mid-19th century. *Id.* at 61, 65. In addition, infanticide probably fell off in importance around the turn of the 19th century. *See* Dellapenna, *The History of Abortion: Technology, Morality and Law*, 40 U. PITT. L. REV. 359, 392-400 (1978). It is also interesting to note that knowledge of fetal development was improving in this period. As early as the 1820's some were writing that quickening did not represent the beginning of vitality but the point where fetal growth permitted movement to be felt. W. BECK, ELEMENTS OF MEDICAL JURISPRUDENCE 199-203 (1823). Such knowledge was important to the development of the antiabortion laws. It permitted the emerging professional male doctors to argue that laws permitting abortion until quickening did not comport with either morality or medical knowledge.

333. The group best known to most 20th-century persons is the Shakers, but a number of other celibate groups existed. The most prominent during the 19th century may have been the Harmony Society. *See* K. ARNDT, GEORGE RAPP'S HARMONY SOCIETY, 1785-1847 (1971); 1 WOMEN AND RELIGION IN AMERICA 47-48, 60-66 (R. Ruether and R. Keller eds. 1981) [hereinafter RUETHER & KELLER].

334. RUETHER & KELLER, *supra* note 333, at 48-50. The Oneida Perfectionists led by John Humphrey Noyes also believed in birth control, and communal sexual access and child rearing. The Owenites, led by Robert Dale Owen and Fanny Wright were also involved in birth control and multiple partners. They were notorious in the 1830's. *Id.* at 49-50, 66-69.

335. *Id.* at 49, 69-70.

336. C. DEGLER, *supra* note 2, at 8-9.

337. *Id.* at 28; N. COTT, *supra* note 2, at 201.

338. Cott suggests that by 1830 many of the attributes of a modern family had affected middle class as well as upper class women. N. COTT, *supra* note 2, at 185. Degler goes further and argues that even lower class women were affected by the ideology of the separate sphere. C. DEGLER, *supra* note 2, at 111-43 (discussing role of Afro-American and immigrant women in 19th century).

339. *See* C. DEGLER, *supra* note 2, at 298-327 (discussing 19th century women's roles outside the home as justified by duty to act in world in order to protect morality). Degler finds that little opposition to female academies emerged while strong disapproval surfaced to women entering college. *Id.* at 309-11. Degler also describes the gradual evolution in patterns for selection of marriage partners from parental arrangements before the Revolutionary War to romantic selections with parental veto power

The rapidity of change in definitions of domesticity and deviance in the first decades of the nineteenth century is difficult to measure. But there is now little doubt that the definition of women's sphere was under greater strain in 1840 than it was at the turn of the century. The trends of the late eighteenth century in education and social services accelerated, with a large number of female academies opening after 1810.[340] Colleges open to women began to appear.[341] Social and moral reform groups emerged in great profusion, spurred by urban growth, agricultural efficiency, trade and commerce, and economic dislocations and panics.[342] Literary societies, religious charitable societies, missionary groups, associations to aid the poor, temperance societies, and societies for reform in education, prisons, and treatment of the insane emerged in greater numbers.[343] Many women found a moral foundation for their work in religion. Although some male religious leaders debated the appropriate scope of women's activities, women often found support among male religious colleagues for activities that neither challenged male leadership nor endangered appropriate feminine decorum.[344] The generally accepted notion that the virtue and morality of women was superior to that of men made religious groups a natural milieu in which to develop female leadership. 225

Many of the prominent women of the early nineteenth century found their power writing or speaking about issues of moral, religious, or ethical significance. Francis Wright came from Great Britain in 1824 with General LaFayette, met with many prominent Americans, helped establish the colony of Nashoba to aid in the emancipation of slaves, and participated with Robert Dale Owen in the New Harmony Community. In 1830 she openly advocated free thinking and infidelity, free public education for all persons, birth control, divorce, and married women's law reform.[345] She was a radical, outside the American mainstream of moral and social reform movements. When the abolitionist Grimke sisters[346] emerged from their Quaker background to speak in 1836 before women in New York and in 1837 before mixed audiences in Massachusetts, they could already point to Wright's prior speaking tours, as well as the actions of a number of other women, as the real groundbreaking. Harriet Martineau, another English woman, gave abolitionist lectures from 1834 to 1836.[347] Mixed prayer meetings occurred in the 1820's,[348] and female educators like Emma Willard, Mary Lyon, and Catherine Beecher established fe-

---

by the end of the 18th century. *Id.* at 9-25. Courtship became much less constrained, and perhaps 10% of women gave birth to children less than nine months after their marriage. *Id.* at 20. Women were acting with fewer constraints during courtship, but using marriage as the escape from social disapproval.

340. N. COTT, *supra* note 2, at 115-25. *See* BUTTS & CREMIN, *supra* note 314, at 239-51.

341. K. MELDER, *supra* note 2, at 115-18; C. DEGLER, *supra* note 2, at 310-15. After three years of separate treatment, Oberlin permitted women to enroll with men in 1837. C. DEGLER, *supra* note 2, at 310.

342. *See generally* B. BERG, *supra* note 2.

343. K. MELDER, *supra* note 2, at 77-92, 118-21.

344. *Id.* at 88-94; A. DOUGLAS, THE FEMINIZATION OF AMERICAN CULTURE 17-139 (1977).

345. K. MELDER, *supra* note 2, at 59-61.

346. Sarah Grimke migrated to Philadelphia from South Carolina in 1821 and her sister, Angelina, followed in 1829. K. MELDER, *supra* note 2, at 156, 192. *See also* G. LERNER, THE GRIMKE SISTERS FROM SOUTH CAROLINA: PIONEERS FOR WOMEN'S RIGHTS AND ABOLITION (1971).

347. K. MELDER, *supra* note 2, at 146.

348. *Id.* at 73-75.

male academies, raised funds, and lectured on women's education before 1835.[349]

The decades of work in female voluntary societies, moral reform groups, and religious activities blossomed into significant participation in the abolitionist movement in the early 1830's. Female antislavery societies emerged by the early 1830's, and women solicited signatures on antislavery petitions beginning in 1835.[350] The egalitarian rhetoric of the Revolution, the Enlightenment, and Jacksonian Democracy began to be used publicly by women. The expansion of suffrage opportunities for white men created an opportunity for radical abolitionists and feminists to focus America's attention on the appropriate role of women. Less than a decade after the Grimkes' controversial tour, discussion in mainstream newspapers on the similarity between slavery and the status of married women was possible.[351]

These developments were given added impetus by fairly constant economic developments. Economic historians generally argue that per capita wealth increased very moderately between 1800 and 1840, but none are willing to state that great increases in wealth occurred.[352] The incidence of economic contrac-
226 tions beginning in 1792, 1819, and 1839,[353] the fairly constant presence of debtor reform movements and legislative activity,[354] the lack of internal sources of capital,[355] the reliance on cotton as a major source of external trade,[356] and the enormous internal improvement debts of the 1830's suggest a growing but struggling economy, heavily reliant on the world economy for support. While certainty on these issues is not yet possible, it is logical that the collapse of European trade before the 1819 and 1839 panics, the stress of economic dislocations, and the changes in employment patterns, job descriptions, and family roles would occur side-by-side with reform movements, religious and moral revivals, radical agitation, and strong public debates.

It is tempting to conclude that the 1840's blossoming of public debates on slaves and women completely explains the arrival of married women's acts.

---

349. *Id.* at 107-15. Mary Lyon founded Mount Holyoke College in 1836. *Id.* at 111.

350. *Id.* at 176-82.

351. An anonymous article entitled *Wives and Slaves: A Bone For the Abolitionists to Pick* was published in 17 DEMOCRATIC REV. 264 (1845) and reprinted in other papers. *See* N. C. Standard, Oct. 22, 1845, at 8, col. 1.

352. For literature on the 19th-century economy see P. TEMIN, *supra* note 213; Gallman, *Gross National Product in the United States, 1834-1909*, in OUTPUT, EMPLOYMENT AND PRODUCTIVITY IN THE UNITED STATES AFTER 1800 3 (National Bureau of Economic Research ed. 1966); Lebergott, *Labor Force and Employment, 1800-1960*, in OUTPUT, EMPLOYMENT AND PRODUCTIVITY IN THE UNITED STATES AFTER 1800 117 (National Bureau of Economic Research ed. 1966); Parker & Whartenby, *supra* note 6; Goldsmith, *The Growth of Reproducible Wealth for the United States of America From 1805 to 1950*, in INCOME AND WEALTH OF THE UNITED STATES: TRENDS AND STRUCTURE 247 (S. Kuznets ed. 1952); Andreano, *Trends and Variations in Economic Welfare in the United States Before the Civil War*, in NEW VIEW ON AMERICAN ECONOMIC DEVELOPMENT 131 (Andreano ed. 1965); A. JONES, *supra* note 14.

353. P. COLEMAN, *supra* note 222, at 19; S. REZNECK, *supra* note 216, at 51-100; P. MCGRANE, *supra* note 212, at 1-42.

354. Coleman's book on debtors and creditors exhaustively catalogues the developments. *Supra* note 222.

355. Large captial inflows from overseas funded much of the 1830's boom. *See* North, *The United States Balance of Payments 1790-1860*, in TRENDS IN THE AMERICAN ECONOMY IN THE NINETEENTH CENTURY 573, 585-87 (National Bureau of Ecomonic Research ed. 1960).

356. *See* P. TEMIN, *supra* note 213, at 152.

Indeed, there is some truth in the causal link because women actively petitioned for the married women's acts adopted in New York and Pennsylvania during the later years of the decade.[357] But as we now know, the story of women's property acts is much more complex than a simple tale about progressive ideals winning out over blind forces of reaction. As Degler forcefully reminds us:

> [t]he women's movement throughout the 19th century left untouched the great mass of women, married and unmarried. At no time were more than a few thousand women actively involved in the feminist or suffrage causes. The great preponderance of women either had nothing to do with feminism, or actually scorned it as unnecessary and wrongheaded.[358]

The public exposure of contradictions in separate sphere ideology by communal groups, abolitionists, and feminists led many women to fight rather than accommodate change. The generally middle class nature of the reform movements[359] spoke peripherally to working class women, many of whom preferred the ideal image of a comfortable separate sphere at home to the potentially deviant life of a radical and frequently unmarried feminist. The tracing of reform movements therefore should not blind us to the obstacles the reformers confronted. Rather, one must hypothesize that shifts in the nation's economy, job map, family structure, agricultural productivity, banking practices, and trade structures would be mirrored by piecemeal, one step to the left, one step to the right, reforms in legal norms, and that changes would reflect generally held perceptions about women's appropriate sphere of influence.

CONCLUSION

And, of course, that is exactly what my archival and legal research suggests. Though by 1850 married women performed new legal roles within the family, property law still singled them out for special treatment and confirmed their primary role as family participants. Developments in non-property areas also confirm the patterns Degler and Cott describe. The culture's growing concentration on wifely domesticity suggests that family law reform should have been vigorous by mid-century. Indeed, by the 1840's divorce, custody, and adoption law were conforming to new notions of family and childhood development. Divorce was more prevalent and easier to obtain, women gained custody of children more frequently than in 1800, and adoption was becoming an accepted practice. Similarly, the arrival of the first antiabortion statutes in the 1840's signaled the importance attributed to married women's maternal

---

357. E. Warbasse, *supra* note 2, at 205-37. Later acts, such as those in Ohio and Massachusetts, were also supported by women. *Id.* at 265-71.

358. C. DEGLER, *supra* note 2, at 306. Degler provides an insightful chapter on why it took so long to gain women's suffrage. He discusses the reasons why suffrage was perceived as a radical step, including women's wide acceptance of the separate sphere, the perception that voting and politics threatened the family, and the substantial opposition to the amendment by women. *Id.* at 328-61. Cott also reminds us that the separate sphere was for many an acceptable level of accomplishment. N. COTT, *supra* note 2, at 197.

359. *See* C. DEGLER, *supra* note 2, at 341 (some radicals realized that giving women the vote would give middle-class women more influence but would do little to help lower class women).

role.[360] While the coexistence of married women's property acts and antiabortion laws seems strange to modern feminists, they were compatible developments in a reform era accepting domesticity as a primary ideology for rationalizing changes in legal norms.

Although organized women's groups certainly had more influence on property law after 1850, the domestic role model also gained additional authority by the Victorian era. The appearance of narrow married women's acts and abortion restrictions in the 1840's was mimicked in the 1870's by the virtually simultaneous adoption of legislation protecting married women's earnings[361] and imposing severe restrictions on the dissemination of birth control information and devices.[362] Even women's suffrage was not achievable without the aid of moral reformers, protective labor supporters, and an ideology lauding the capacity of women to make finer moral judgments than men.[363] Not until very recent times has the legal system taken seriously the notion that equality norms rather than special treatment norms should govern the outcomes of gender-based disputes. The basic thrust of Thomas Herttell's 1837 argument[364] in favor of an early version of the New York married women's act can be substi-
228 tuted for arguments made decades later in favor of protective labor legislation and women's suffrage:

> But have not women as much prudence and judgement to save and manage their property, after as before marriage? Has marriage deprived them of their senses and their wits, as well as of their rights of property which they possessed before marriage? With the additional incitement of maternal solicitude for the well-being of her children, has not a married woman even more inducement to the discreet appropriation of her property to their maintenance, than an unmarried woman, who has no such immediate motive for the prudent and due exercise of the right to possess and dispose of her property as she may please, and as by law she is authorized to do? And with such additional, natural, and maternal obligations, is not the discreet use of her property by a married woman, for the maintenance of her children,

---

360. *See supra* notes 330-35 and accompanying text (discussing abortion, birth control, and the maternal role).

361. The 1870's saw the arrival of statutes protecting earnings of married women in a number of states. Earnings statutes appeared first in the 1850's, but most of the acts were passed later. Among the states adopting earnings acts were Massachusetts: May 5, 1855; Kansas: Feb. 11, 1858 (Territorial Legislation); New York: Mar. 20, 1860; Alabama: Dec. 31, 1868 (free trader statute); Illinois: Mar. 24, 1869; Iowa: Apr. 14, 1870; Ohio: Mar. 30, 1871; Pennsylvania: Apr. 3, 1872; Delaware: Apr. 9, 1873; Kentucky: Apr. 11, 1873; Arkansas: Apr. 28, 1873; Indiana: Mar. 25, 1879. A few states also adopted limited earnings statutes, which only protected married women who were no longer living with their husbands. Pennsylvania: May 4, 1855; Minnesota: Ch. 49 (1860); Iowa: Mar. 12, 1866; Vermont: Nov. 19, 1866; Delaware: Mar. 28, 1871; New Jersey: Apr. 5, 1878. Bishop also discusses codes adopted in the 1860's and 1870's containing earnings provisions in California, Georgia, Illinois, Maine, Maryland, Massachusetts, and Mississippi. 2 J. BISHOP, *supra* note 27, at 490-91, 507, 512, 520, 524, 530, 536-37.

362. *See generally* C. DIENES, *supra* note 2.

363. Indeed, moral reformers and supporters of special workplace legislation for women, not equality minded feminists, were the major backers of women's suffrage. *See* C. DEGLER, *supra* note 2, 328-61. After the Suffrage Amendment was adopted, the Women's Party quickly became a radical fringe, a model to be picked up later in the century. *See* E. FLEXNER, *supra* note 1, 271-345 (1959).

364. Thomas Herttell, along with John Neal and Elisha Hurlbutt, was among the major male figures urging reform of women's law in New York from 1835 on.

> as much more to be relied on, than that of her husband, as maternal is more strong, constant, and unconquerable, than paternal affection? Are not the cases rare in which unmarried women waste their property? And are not the instances numerous in which men spend their fortunes in riot, intemperance, extravagance, and every species of irregularity and dissipation? And when their pecuniary resources are exhausted or impaired, is it not a common practice for men to endeavour, by marriage, to obtain the property of young, inexperienced, unsuspecting, and credulous females, with a view to the means by which to gratify their avarice, or to continue their dissolute habits of life? Does not the existing law hold out inducements to mercenary marriages, by furnishing the means by which worthless fortune-hunters are enabled to effect their iniquitous purpose? Is not the alleged law, therefore, the source of the vicious and immoral practices to which it prompts; and the cause of all the injustice and misery to which married women become the devoted victims? And is not that law justly characterized by the vice, immorality, injustice, and misery consequent on its existence and operation? 229
>
> That the affirmative are the true answers to the above questions, is as certain as that such answers prove conclusively, that married women's property would be safer in their own hands, and more certainly applied to family maintenance, than it now is, when given indiscriminately to good and bad husbands, to be disposed of as they please, or as their good or bad habits may happen to direct.[365]

The property reforms of the 1840's should not be perceived as an attack on coverture law. Though the seeds of later reforms were planted by the first wave of married women's property acts, married women's separate domestic sphere was not seriously challenged by their adoption. The legal changes of the mid-nineteenth century recognized that the women's role within the family had changed to encompass greater control over the raising of children and the disposition of family wealth. But not until this century would such increased participation in the family lead to broad participation in the political and economic fortunes of the culture at large.

---

365. Herttell, Remarks Comprising in Substance Judge Herttell's Argument in the House of Assembly of the State of New York in the Session of 1837 in Support of the Bill to Restore to Married Women the Right of Property as Guaranteed by the Constitution of this State, at 57-58 (1839) (copy on file at *Georgetown Law Journal*).

Divorce and the Changing Status of Women in Eighteenth-Century Massachusetts

Nancy F. Cott

WHEN a neighbor asked John Backus, silversmith of Great Barrington, Massachusetts, in 1784, why he kicked and struck his wife, John replied that "it was Partly owing to his Education for his father often treated his mother in the same manner."[1] John's mother may have tolerated that abuse but his wife did not: she complained of his cruelty, desertion, and adultery, and obtained a divorce.

This epitome of two generations' marital strife, one item in early Massachusetts divorce records, suggests how valuable such records may be to the interpretation of marriage and family life in the past. Divorce proceedings not only elucidate customs and ideals of marriage; they also disclose the marital behavior of the litigants. The history of divorce practice documents sex-role expectations, permits comparison between the obligations and freedoms of husbands and of wives, and provides a test of the double standard of sexual morality. Divorce records from provincial Massachusetts are especially interesting because the years they cover are those least explored in studies of marriage and family in New England. Historians have yet to explain the transition from "Puritan" to "Victorian" standards, but current research has begun to suggest that unrest and change in patterns of sexual and familial behavior were conspicuous during the eighteenth century.[2] Records of divorce in provincial Massachusetts illuminate these little-known aspects of individuals' lives.[3]

Ms. Cott is a member of the Department of History and the American Studies Program at Yale University. She wishes to acknowledge her indebtedness to David H. Flaherty and Hiller B. Zobel for helpful research suggestions, and to Douglas L. Jones for comments on an earlier draft. Shorter versions of this paper were read at the Conference on Women in the Era of the American Revolution, George Washington University, July 1975, and at Princeton University, November 1975.

[1] Deposition of William Whiting, Jr., Suffolk Court Files #129846, Suffolk County Court House, Boston, 106.

[2] Robert V. Wells, "Quaker Marriage Patterns in a Colonial Perspective," *William and Mary Quarterly*, 3d Ser., XXIX (1972), 415-442; Daniel Scott Smith, "Parental Power and Marriage Patterns: An Analysis of Historical Trends in Hingham, Massachusetts," *Journal of Marriage and the Family*, XXXV (1973), 419-439; Daniel Scott Smith and Michael Hindus, "Premarital Pregnancy in America, 1640-1966," *Journal of Interdisciplinary History*, VI (1975), 537-570.

[3] See Nancy F. Cott, "Eighteenth-Century Family and Social Life Revealed in

Massachusetts divorce proceedings between 1692 and 1786 can be fairly readily traced because they took place (with a few notable exceptions) before one body, a "court" composed of the governor and his Council.[4] One hundred twenty-two wives and 101 husbands filed 229 petitions in all (six wives petitioned twice).[5] So far as their occupational and residential characteristics are known, the petitioners included the whole range of types in the population. Slightly more than a quarter of them lived in Boston, the others in all varieties of towns, from the smallest to the largest, the most remote to the most advantageously located.[6] Almost 63 percent of the petitioners

---

Massachusetts Divorce Records," *Journal of Social History*, X (1976), where these documents are used to investigate questions about privacy and community, relations among conjugal-family and extended-family members, and romantic love and sex.

[4] In June 1692 the General Court declared that "all controversies concerning marriage and divorce shall be heard and determined by the governor and council." *Acts and Resolves, Public and Private, of the Province of Massachusetts Bay . . .* (Boston, 1869-1922), I, chap. 25, sec. 4, 61. The state constitution of 1780 confirmed 231
this practice, until "An Act for Regulating Marriage and Divorce" of Mar. 16, 1786, located jurisdiction over divorce suits in the Supreme Judicial Court held for each county. *Acts and Resolves of Massachusetts, 1784-1785* (Boston, ca. [1892]), 564-567.

[5] The most informative records are the original petitions and depositions preserved for most of the cases between 1739 and 1786 in volumes 793-796 of the Suffolk Court Files. Similar documents from some earlier cases appear in volume IX of the Massachusetts Archives, at the Archives Dept., State House, Boston. A single bound manuscript volume labeled "Divorces, 1760-1786," hereafter cited as "Divorces," located with the Suffolk Files, summarizes most of the divorce petitions and decrees between those dates. Mass. Archives, CXL, contains a fairly complete record of divorces between 1780 and 1786. Additional cases before 1780 have been recovered from the executive records of the Council, also at the Archives Dept., hereafter cited as Council Recs. Surprisingly, the Council Records do not contain the most inclusive recording of petitions and decrees; their completeness varies considerably through the years. The legislative records of the Council, a separate series in the Archives Dept. called Court Records, have been used in those cases that involved legislation.

[6] The overrepresentation of Bostonians—for the city held only 6% of the province's population in 1765—was at least partially owing to the requirement that petitioners appear before the governor and Council at their sessions in Boston. The legislation of 1786 shifted jurisdiction over divorce to the superior courts held in each county because of remote petitioners' difficulty in getting to Boston. I have estimated the geographical distribution of petitioners by using the population figures in the 1764-1765 provincial census, obviously not an exact means since the divorce cases span almost a century, but the only one available. Place of residence was disclosed in almost 90% of the suits. On the basis of 1764-1765 population figures, 24.6% of petitioners resided in towns of less than 1,000 pop.; 22.6% in towns of 1,000 to 1,999; 15.9% in towns of 2,000 to 2,999; 8.2% in towns of 3,000 to 5,000; and 28.7% in Boston. More than two-fifths of the petitioners lived in the populous counties of Suffolk and Essex; a slightly smaller proportion in the eastern counties of Middlesex, Worcester, Bristol, Plymouth, Barnstable, and Dukes; and the remainder (slightly under a fifth) in the remote and lightly populated counties of Hampshire, Berkshire,

disclosed the occupation of the man of the family. Thirty-two percent of these cases involved families of artisans or traders; 22 percent, husbandmen or yeomen; and another 22 percent, mariners or fishermen. About 17 percent originated in families in which the husbands had the more prestigious status of gentlemen, merchants, professionals, ship captains, or militia officers; and the remaining 7 percent involved families at the lower end of the occupational scale—laborers, truckmen, and servants. Although one would need to know the petitioners' wealth to ascertain their economic standing or to judge how accurately they typified the Massachusetts population, it is likely that the great majority—perhaps three-fourths—occupied the "middling ranks."[7] Whether or not they were a representative sample, the group included all varieties of the Massachusetts population, urban and rural dwellers, rich and poor.

The petitioners had an easier time gaining divorce in provincial Massachusetts than they would have had in the mother country.[8] In England
232 marital controversies were judged by the ecclesiastical courts, and these courts applied canon law, under which a valid marriage was regarded as indissoluble. True divorce (*divortium a vinculo matrimonii*), allowing the partners to remarry, was never granted unless a marriage was judged null to begin with, on grounds such as consanguinity, bigamy, or sexual incapacity. Such causes as adultery, desertion, or cruelty warranted only separation from bed and board (*divortium a mensa et thoro*), which sustained the legal obligations of marriage, excepting cohabitation, and did not allow either partner to remarry. At the end of the seventeenth century, in order to relieve the stringency of ecclesiastical rule for noblemen whose wives were adulterous, the House of Lords began to dissolve marriages by private act. Only a select group could take advantage of this avenue to divorce. The cost often

---

Cumberland, Lincoln, and York. See J. H. Benton, *Early Census Making in Massachusetts* (Boston, 1905).

[7] There are some interesting differences between the occupational levels of male petitioners and female—the latter judged by their *husbands'* occupations, however. Among the 122 wives, 73 disclosed the occupations of their husbands. Fifteen percent were esquires, gentlemen, or merchants; 4% doctors or officers; 19% husbandmen or yeomen; 16% mariners or fishermen; 37% craftsmen or traders; and 8% laborers, servants, or truckmen. Among the 101 husbands, 67 disclosed their occupations. Only 4.5% were esquires, gentlemen, or merchants; 9% professionals or officers; 25% husbandmen or yeomen; 28% mariners (reflecting the high incidence of adultery on the part of wives whose husbands were at sea for long periods); 27% craftsmen or traders; and 6% the lower occupations.

[8] They may have had an even easier time in Connecticut, which had the most liberal divorce policy of all the colonies; both judicial and legislative divorces were granted there. Between 1740 and 1789, 174 superior court divorces were recorded in Hartford County alone. Henry S. Cohn, "Connecticut's Divorce Mechanism: 1636-1969," *American Journal of Legal History*, XIV (1970), 43, n. 39.

amounted to several thousand pounds, because a petitioner was expected to have first obtained a decree of divorce *a mensa* and a civil judgment against the adulterers. The Lords passed only about ninety private acts of divorce between 1697 and 1785, all resting on adultery charges and all awarded to husbands.[9] Divorce *a vinculo* from a valid marriage was more frequent in Massachusetts during the same period. Between 1692 and 1786, 110 divorces were granted in the province on grounds other than those considered legitimate by the English ecclesiastical courts—63 to men, 47 to women—and England and Wales had a population of almost seven million in 1765, when the Massachusetts population was under 250,000.[10]

The authority of the governor and Council over divorce originated in provincial statute. No causes for divorce were codified, however, and their divorce policy combined elements of English practice, Puritan divorce theory, seventeenth-century Massachusetts precedents, and innovation. Opposing canon law, Puritan divorce theory held that marriage was a civil contract which could and should be dissolved for such breaches as adultery, long absence, or irremediable cruelty.[11] In the seventeenth century the civil courts of Massachusetts tried to effect this theoretical position, so far as is shown by the results of forty known petitions between 1639 and 1692. The county courts and the General Court, as well as the Court of Assistants (predecessor to the Council) judged petitions for divorce, even after the Code of 1660 gave jurisdiction to the assistants. They annulled marriages on grounds of consanguinity, bigamy, and sexual incapacity, and dissolved them for long absence and for adultery alone or in combination with desertion, neglect, or cruelty. No clear decrees of separate bed and board have been discovered, but

[9] This discussion of English divorce practice relies on George Elliott Howard, *A History of Matrimonial Institutions, Chiefly in the United States and England . . .* (Chicago, 1904), II, 52-57, 77-85, 92-93, 102-107; Reginald Haw, *The State of Matrimony* (London, 1952), 74-89; Oliver McGregor, *Divorce in England* (London, 1957), 1-12; Joseph W. Madden, *Handbook of the Law of Persons and Domestic Relations* (St. Paul, Minn., 1931), 256-260; and L. Kinvin Wroth and Hiller B. Zobel, eds., *The Legal Papers of John Adams*, I (Cambridge, Mass., 1965), 280-285. The several accounts of divorce in England differ slightly in their estimates of numbers of parliamentary divorces before 1800.

[10] The population figure for England and Wales is estimated from a table in J. D. Chambers, *Population, Economy, and Society in Pre-Industrial England* (London, 1972), 108.

[11] The document best illustrating Puritan divorce reform theory in England is the *Reformatio Legum Ecclesiasticarum,* authorized by Parliament and drafted by eminent divines in 1552. The *Reformatio* regarded marriage as a civil contract rather than an indissoluble sacred bond, omitted mention of separate bed and board, allowed dissolution of marriage for adultery, desertion, continued absence without news, or unmitigable enmity or cruelty by either spouse—and was never put into effect. Howard, *Matrimonial Institutions,* II, 78-79.

our knowledge of seventeenth-century divorce proceedings is probably incomplete.[12]

When the governor and Council assumed more uniform jurisdiction over divorce after 1692, they granted annulments, divorces (literally, dissolutions of marriage bonds) allowing the innocent party to remarry, and decrees of separate bed and board.[13] The years 1754 to 1757 formed a curious exception. During that period, for reasons not apparent in the historical record, the governor and Council declined to dissolve valid marriages and decreed separate bed and board for petitioners who formerly and subsequently would have been granted divorce.[14] In 1755, 1756, and 1757, six petitioners whose spouses were adulterous sought relief from the General Court and obtained legislative divorces instead of divorce decrees. These legislative divorces were the only ones enacted under the provincial charter of 1691.[15] In passing them the General Court assumed the role of Parliament in England; and in two of the six, the governor and Council filled the role of the English ecclesiastical courts by granting prior decrees of separate bed and board. Since they were legislative acts, these divorces were subject to review by the imperial Board of Trade, as was all colonial legislation. Reporting on the first three in 1758, the board called them "extraordinary" and "liable to great objections." The specific points of disapproval highlighted some of the differences between English and Massachusetts divorce policy. All three suits—two of them brought by women—rested on adultery charges. The divorces granted to the two women were called unprecedented, "the first of their kind . . . in the colonies or elsewhere." Moreover, the proofs of adultery were not clear enough; criminal conviction of the adulterers had not preceded the three divorce bills; and only one was supported by a prior decree of separate bed and board. Beyond these objections, which seemed sufficient grounds for

[12] *Ibid.*, 331-338; Edmund S. Morgan, *The Puritan Family: Religion and Domestic Relations in Seventeenth-Century New England* (New York, 1966), 35-37; John Demos, *A Little Commonwealth: Family Life in Plymouth Colony* (New York, 1970), 92-97; D. Kelly Weisberg, "Under Greet Temptations Heer: Women and Divorce in Puritan Massachusetts," *Feminist Studies*, II (1975), 183-194. Since Howard's list of divorce suits for the period 1692-1786 is incomplete (he lists only 107 suits), it is likely that his list of 40 for the period 1639-1692 is similarly fragmentary.

[13] Wroth and Zobel, eds., *Legal Papers of Adams*, I, 282, erroneously states that jurisdiction to grant divorce *a vinculo* was ambiguous after 1692 and that the governor and Council did not grant divorces between 1692 and 1760.

[14] They did so despite a law enacted by the General Court in 1755, empowering them to enforce their decrees in divorce suits by ordering imprisonment for disobedience. *Acts and Resolves, Mass. Bay*, III, chap. 15, 782.

[15] The acts are in *ibid.*, VI, 165, 169, 170, 173, 174, 177, and can be corroborated in Court Recs., XX, 337-338, 346, 351-352, 373, 379, 460, 461, 468, XXI, 97, 157, 161, 329, 497, 500, 517, 540, XXII, 40. Howard, *Matrimonial Institutions*, II, 340, errs in saying that "after 1692 the legislature does not seem to have interfered in divorce suits either on appeal or in the first instance."

disallowance, doubt existed whether any colonial legislature had the right to assume the parliamentary prerogative of granting divorces. The board referred the matter to the attorney-general and the solicitor-general for a decision whether to disallow the acts or declare them null; but no hearing took place, and these divorce bills and the subsequent three in Massachusetts were apparently allowed to stand.[16]

The interlude of legislative divorce in Massachusetts clarified the advantage the province gained through its usual practice of divorce by decree. If Massachusetts had taken the legislative route, the history of divorce there would probably have been quite different. Legislative divorces might well have been disallowed for lack of conformity to English practice, or declared null for invading the authority of Parliament. In fact, between 1769 and 1773 several colonial acts of legislative divorce, passed in Pennsylvania, New Jersey, and New Hampshire, met this fate. The crown's resentment of them resulted in a directive of 1773 to all royal governors to withhold consent from
any divorce act passed by a colonial legislature.[17] This order halted divorce in 235
the colonies other than Massachusetts until the Revolution, but in that province both petitions for and grants of divorce continued to multiply. Petitioners no longer resorted to the General Court, for in 1760, after investigating their own precedents for dissolving marriages before 1755, the governor and Council returned to the policy of decreeing divorces *a vinculo*.[18]

[16] Report of the Lords of Trade, June 6, 1758, Mass. Arch., XXII, 9-10. See also *Acts and Resolves, Mass. Bay*, VI, vi-vii, and Joseph Henry Smith, *Appeals to the Privy Council from the American Plantations* (New York, 1950), 582-585. Smith points out that in 1741 the Lords disallowed a Jamaica act of legislative divorce passed in 1739.

[17] See William Renwick Riddell, "Legislative Divorce in Colonial Pennsylvania," *Pennsylvania Magazine of History and Biography*, LVII (1933), 175-180; Thomas R. Meehan, " 'Not Made Out of Levity': Evolution of Divorce in Early Pennsylvania," *ibid.*, XCII (1968), 441-464; Leonard Woods Labaree, ed., *Royal Instructions to British Colonial Governors, 1670-1776*, I (New York, 1935), 154-155.

[18] A bill "for enabling the Governor and Council to grant Divorces from the Bands of Matrimony," passed by the House of Representatives in Aug. 1757, never became law because the Council neglected or declined to concur. Mass. Arch., IX, 419; *Journals of the House of Representatives of Massachusetts, 1757*, XXXIV (Meriden, Conn., 1961), 105. On July 30, 1759, the Council appointed four of its members to investigate the precedents of divorce actions before 1756. Why the Council had so short a collective memory—when several members had been on the Council in the early 1750s—is puzzling. The committee reported (accurately) on Nov. 10, 1759, that the Council had decreed seven divorces and one separation between 1747 and 1754. See Mass. Arch. IX, 432-434, and Council Recs., XIV, 122, 134. Another influence leading to the Council's resumption of divorce by decree may have been Gov. Thomas Pownall's message of Feb. 2, 1760, which touched on the Council's power as a divorce court. Josiah Quincy, Jr., *Reports of Cases Argued and Adjudged in the Superior Court of Judicature of the Province of Massachusetts Bay between 1761 and 1772* (Boston, 1865), 573-579.

TABLE I

NUMBER OF PETITIONS/NUMBER OF FAVORABLE DECREES, BY DECADE

Peti-tioners	1692-1704	1705-1714	1715-1724	1725-1734	1735-1744	1745-1754	1755-1764	1765-1774	1775-1786	Total
all	7/5	6/5	5/2	9/4	23/15	21/11	26/16	46/24	86/61	229/143
female	4/3	3/2	4/1	4/1	8/4	12/6	12/7	29/13	53/37	128/74
male	3/2	3/3	1/1	5/3	15/11	9/5	14/9	18/11	33/24	101/69

Note: Favorable decrees include divorce, annulment, and separate bed and board.

Divorce petitions and decrees showed a general pattern of increase during the eighteenth century in Massachusetts. As Table I indicates, more than half of the petitions and decrees between 1692 and 1786 occurred after 1764, and more than a third of them after 1774. This striking concentration took place without any change in the laws regarding divorce. What caused it? The population grew, but not nearly as rapidly as did the number of petitions. The incidence of petitions per decade increased by 77 percent from 1755-1764 to 1765-1774, and by 61 percent from 1765-1774 to 1775-1784, while the white population grew by approximately 5.7 percent from 1760 to 1770, and by approximately 14 percent from 1770 to 1780.[19]

Perhaps the governor and Council became more willing to consider and grant divorces after 1765, thus encouraging larger numbers of petitioners. In these pre-Revolutionary years the Council may have been more assertive in its divorce practice, which opposed England's, just as it became more independent of the royal prerogative in political matters, and more sympathetic to the whig leaders in the legislature.[20] Two decrees of the early 1770s in particular indicated that the Council would proceed on its own initiative in divorce actions whether or not the governor agreed. The Council alone declared Abigail Bradstreet separated from her husband in 1771, and James Richardson divorced from his wife in 1772, although Gov. Thomas Hutchinson did not judge these decrees warranted by the evidence and would not sign them.[21]

The chronological coincidence of the concentration of divorce petitions with the War for Independence suggests a causal link. We might suppose

[19] The white population of Massachusetts in 1780 was about five-and-a-half times as large as it had been in 1690, but there were twelve times as many petitions and decrees in the years 1775-1786 as in 1692-1704. Population data are from U.S. Bureau of the Census, *Historical Statistics of the United States: Colonial Times to 1957* (Washington, D.C., 1960).

[20] See Francis G. Walett, "The Massachusetts Council, 1766-1774: The Transformation of a Conservative Institution," *WMQ*, 3d Ser., VI (1949), 605-627.

[21] Abigail Bradstreet v. Joseph Bradstreet, Suffolk Files #129762, "Divorces," 68-70; James Richardson v. Hannah Richardson, Suffolk Files #129769, "Divorces," 70-72.

that wartime disruption of families led to an increase of petitions, but there is little direct evidence of this. Very few petitions originated from war-related grievances, such as a married man's adultery with a campfollower or a woman's pregnancy while her husband was absent in military service.[22] Gauged by the evidence of prenuptial pregnancy, premarital sexual relations increased dramatically during the mid- to late eighteenth century—suggesting the possibility of a similar rise in adultery—but that phenomenon antedated the war.[23]

Most likely, divorce petitions increased not because spouses more often had legitimate marital grievances but because they were more often motivated to respond to marital wrongs by seeking divorce. Perhaps, then, the rise in divorce related in a general way to the War for Independence in the sense that a certain personal outlook—one that implied self-assertion and regard for the future, one that we might label more "modern" than "traditional"—may have led a person to seek divorce and also to support American independence.[24] The evidence that aggrieved spouses desired to have their 237
marriages ended officially, rather than taking more traditional measures such as "self-divorce" through desertion, or resigning themselves to the ties of unsatisfactory marriages, suggests a modernization of attitudes.[25] Communication about the granting of divorces may also have had a cumulative effect: the more divorces were allowed, the more likely it became for a discontented spouse to consider the possibility. Especially in small towns, news of divorces being obtained must have encouraged more men and women to petition. The growth in petitions seems to indicate that more individuals were asserting control over the direction of their lives and were refusing to be ruled by unhappy fates—characteristics which are also considered "modern." In the Revolutionary period this kind of self-assertion may have gone along with an

[22] For example, Chloe Welch v. Luke Welch, Suffolk Files #129790, "Divorces," 122-125, and Andrew Gage v. Elizabeth Gage, Suffolk Files #129829, "Divorces," 192-193; see also Ann Lovell v. John Lovell, Jr., Suffolk Files #129778.

[23] See Smith and Hindus, "Premarital Pregnancy," *Jour. Interdisciplinary Hist.*, VI (1975), 537-570.

[24] See Kenneth A. Lockridge, "Social Change and the Meaning of the American Revolution," *Jour. Soc. Hist.*, VI (1973), 403-439, for several hypothetical models of "preparedness" for the War for Independence.

[25] On modernization in New England see *ibid.*, and two articles by Richard D. Brown: "Modernization and the Modern Personality in Early America, 1600-1865: A Sketch of a Synthesis," *Jour. Interdisciplinary Hist.*, II (1972), 201-228, and "The Emergence of Urban Society in Rural Massachusetts, 1760-1820," *Journal of American History*, LXI (1974), 29-51. For a typology of the "modern" personality see Alex Inkeles, "Making Men Modern: On the Causes and Consequences of Individual Change in Six Developing Countries," *American Journal of Sociology*, LXXV (1969), 208-225, and "The Modernization of Man," in Myron Weiner, ed., *Modernization: The Dynamics of Growth* (New York, 1966), 138-150.

enhanced sense of citizenship and legal rights. Not only men claimed the rights of citizens. At least one Boston woman in 1784 and another in 1785 petitioned "as a citizen of this Commonwealth" for a hearing of her case.[26]

More wives than husbands sued for divorce during the period 1692-1786, and the concentration of women's petitions during the Revolutionary years was more marked than that of men's. One can only speculate whether these figures mean that women generally had more marital grievances or that their grievances were growing faster or being more readily voiced. Several variables hindered or encouraged men and women to seek divorce. A man might hesitate because he was shy of the authorities, hated to arouse adverse publicity about his marriage, or could not afford the expense, whatever it was; or because the worth of his wife's domestic service seemed to outweigh her transgressions. Male domination of colonial public life suggests, however, that men were less shy of the authorities than were women, better able to stand adverse publicity about their marriages without risking their entire reputation, significantly more independent economically, and better equipped than women to pay legal expenses. A man could also take the initiative in acquiring a second spouse.

All the feelings that might have kept men from suing for divorce probably affected women even more intensely. Consider the doubts and anguish of Abigail Bailey as she pondered whether to seek divorce from her husband, who had committed incest with their daughter and had also had sexual liaisons with several other women. "Whether it would be consisted [*sic*] with faithfulness to suffer him to flee, and not be made a monument of civil justice, was my query. The latter looked to me inexpressibly painful. And I persuaded myself, that if he would do what was right, relative to our property, and would go to some distant place, where we should be afflicted with him no more, it might be sufficient; and I might be spared the dreadful scene of prosecuting my husband."[27]

Women apparently expected less success with their petitions than did men. While men always asked for divorce (dissolution of the bonds of marriage), women frequently equivocated; they requested divorce or, if that were not possible, whatever separation the governor and Council were willing to grant.[28] Perhaps other wives who had cause did not even petition because

[26] See Sarah Vernon v. William Vernon, Suffolk Files #129840, petition, 78, and Rebecca Simpson v. Ebenezer Simpson, *ibid.* #129854, petition, 140.

[27] *Memoirs of Mrs. Abigail Bailey . . . written by herself . . .*, ed. Ethan Smith (Boston, 1815), 58-59. Mrs. Bailey eventually did petition and obtain a divorce in 1792.

[28] For example, Mary Fairservice v. John Fairservice (1767), petition in "Divorces," 40-42; Sarah Gould v. William Gould (1773), Suffolk Files #129772, petition, 56; Sarah Kingsley v. Enoch Kingsley (1771), Suffolk Files #129773, petition, 58; Martha Air v. Adam Air (1773), Suffolk Files #129779, petition, 85.

they did not expect to win. According to the most recent study, illiteracy handicapped half or more of the female population in initiating civil actions, compared to 10 or 20 percent of the male population. The female petitioners were distinguished by their literacy: almost three-quarters of them (two-thirds of the non-Boston residents) could sign their names.[29] The high rate of literacy among female petitioners suggests that they may have been a group self-selected by stronger-than-average initiative or education, who did not fully represent the frequency of wives' dissatisfaction in marriage.

Whatever the inhibitions, powerful reasons urged unhappy wives to sue for divorce—reasons that did not so affect husbands. Self-preservation compelled wives whose husbands were physically abusive. A woman whose husband deserted or failed to provide for her gained little advantage from marriage, and the marriage contract hindered her from supporting herself because her property and earnings legally belonged to her husband. Many women pointed this out. In her petition of 1759, for example, Henrietta East Caine of Boston lamented that while her marriage contract lasted, "her 239
Friends will not supply her with Goods to carry on her business as before." Another Boston woman warned that she and her three children would become public charges if she remained subject to her husband, whereas if divorced "she apprehends she shall be able to find Friends that will place her in some business to maintain herself and children." Sarah Backus claimed in 1783 that she "would be content by the most penurious industry to gain a support for herself and Child, but every Idea of comfort is banished from her Breast when she reflects, that by Law her Person is subjected to be con-

[29] Kenneth A. Lockridge, *Literacy in Colonial New England: An Enquiry into the Social Context of Literacy in the Early Modern West* (New York, 1974), esp. tables on pp. 24 and 41, indicates that Boston women's ability to sign moved from about 40% in 1700 to a peak of 68% in 1758-1762, and then fell to 60% by 1787, while rural women's ability remained below 40% for the whole period; and that Boston men's ability to sign moved from about 75% in 1700 to 80% in 1758-1762, while rural men's ability moved from 65% to 75%. Literacy data (signature or mark) appeared for 96 female divorce petitioners and 56 male petitioners. Sixty-one percent of these female petitioners before 1765 could sign—all of the 9 Boston women, and 8 of the 19 non-Boston women. Seventy-eight percent of the female petitioners between 1765 and 1786 could sign, including 16 of the 20 Boston women and 37 (77%) of the 48 non-Boston women. Among 17 male petitioners before 1765, 94% could sign—that is, all except one black man of Boston, a servant. Of 39 male petitioners between 1765 and 1786, 95% could sign—all of the 8 Boston men and all but two of the 31 non-Boston men. If Lockridge's figures are correct for the general population, both male and female divorce petitioners, as judged by ability to sign, had literacy above the norm. For a control group independent of Lockridge's study, there are the scores of deponents who testified in the divorce cases. They suggest a different norm. The ability to sign of 495 male deponents was 98.4%; it was 100% among the 64 deponents before 1765, and 98.1% among the 431 deponents between 1765 and 1786.

TABLE II

PETITION RESULTS

	Male Petitions	Female Petitions	All
Divorce	64	51	115
Annulment	4	7	11
Separate bed and board	1	16	17
Dismissed or not granted	11	19	30
Unresolved	21	35	56
Total	101	128	229

trouled by a man possessing no one tender sentiment, but on the contrary under the entire dominion of every criminal and foul pollution."[30]

240 Sixty-eight percent of the husbands and 58 percent of the wives succeeded in gaining favorable action on their petitions, but 67 percent of the husbands gained freedom to remarry, in contrast to only 45 percent of the wives. Sixteen of the seventeen separations from bed and board granted during the period went to wives. When petitioners failed to obtain favorable action, it was more often because their suits remained unresolved than because they were dismissed. Fewer than 15 percent of the women's and 11 percent of the men's petitions were actually dismissed, but more than 27 percent of the women's and 20 percent of the men's never resulted in decrees. (See Table II.) It is unclear if the lack of resolution of these cases reflected some aim of the court or the petitioner, or whether the records are faulty or missing. No significant pattern of economic or geographic discrimination, or unusual lack of clarity in the cases, appears to account for the fate of these petitions; but the percentages reveal that women's petitions were slightly more likely than men's to suffer this end.[31]

The ability to sign of 224 female deponents was 58%; it was 68% among 50 deponents before 1765 and fell to 55.1% among the 174 deponents between 1765 and 1786. Both male and female deponents included large proportions of low-status persons, such as hired laborers and domestic servants, but the male deponents also included many of high status.

[30] Henrietta Maria East Caine v. Hugh Caine, Suffolk Files #129736, "Divorces," 2-3; Mary Hunt v. Richard Hunt (1761), "Divorces," 8-9; Sarah Backus v. John Backus, Suffolk Files #129846, 100. See also Sarah Bloget v. John Bloget, Mass. Arch., IX, 211.

[31] Ten of the unresolved petitions—seven from women and three from men—show no sign of ever having been read by the Council. If these petitions are removed from the comparison, the difference between the number of men's and the number of women's petitions left unresolved (after at least a first reading) diminishes.

Analysis of the suits by cause clarifies the comparison of men's and women's experiences and of the results of their petitions. All suits involved invalidity or breach of the marriage contract. The causes (and the numbers of petitions) can be categorized as follows:[32]

A. sexual incapacity (3 m, 4 f)
B. bigamous or fraudulent marriage (3 m, 12 f)

adultery-inclusive:

C. adultery (50 m, 6 f)
D. adultery and desertion or non-support (16 m, 12 f)
E. adultery, desertion, and cohabitation with another (10 m, 16 f)
F. desertion and remarriage (i.e., adultery) (3 m, 19 f)
G. adultery and cruelty (2 m, 19 f)
H. interracial adultery (4 m, 3 f)

I. desertion (8 m, 10 f)
J. cruelty (0 m, 23 f)
K. unknown (2 m, 4 f)[33] 241

The first two causes, sexual incapacity and invalid marriage, warranted annulment, but the governor and Council were not always consistent in wording when they granted petitions on these grounds. Two of the three men's petitions charging their wives with incapacity for coitus were granted after court-appointed "discreet Matrons" confirmed the charges, one by annulment (1739) and the other by dissolution of marriage bonds (1781). This is unremarkable, except that the one husband waited five years after marrying, and the other, eight, before petitioning for divorce.[34] Men fared better than women in this category of suits. None of the three women's

[32] In a few cases it is debatable whether the suit should be placed in one category or another: I and J in particular tend to overlap. Any of the adultery causes, C through H, might have included the charge of illegitimate offspring; as a divorce charge, this was included rather as a means of proving adultery than as a separate grievance.

[33] The records are so sparse in this category that the charges are not apparent. Rachel Draper won her divorce in 1709, and Joseph Hale's suit was dismissed in 1779; the results of the four others remain as mysterious as the charges. Rachel Draper v. John Draper, Council Recs., V, 124; Mary Parce v. John Parce, *ibid.*, XVIII, 100; Experience Simpson v. husband, *ibid.*, XXIV, 392; Elizabeth Laud v. David Laud, Mass. Arch., CXL, 194; Joseph Hale (or Hail) v. Isabella Hale, Council Recs., XXIII, 64, 76, 414; Thomas Patter v. wife, *ibid.*, XXIII, 64.

[34] Jesse Turner v. Grace Turner, Suffolk Files #129727, Council Recs., X, 331, 378; George Sherman v. Phebe Sherman, Suffolk Files #129796, Council Recs., XXIII, 92, XXIV, 206, 301, XXVI, 104, "Divorces," 137-140. Jeremiah Ingraham petitioned for divorce from Mercy Ingraham for this cause in 1733, after 15 years of marriage, but his charge was not substantiated and his petition was dismissed. Council Recs., IX, 464, 533.

petitions to the governor and Council was granted: one was dismissed and the others were left unresolved, although in one of these cases the husband acknowledged his debility. In a unique instance, however, the General Court in 1780 enacted a legislative annulment of a marriage upon proof of the wife's complaint that her husband was impotent.[35]

Twelve female and three male petitioners pursued divorce for the second cause that warranted annulment—bigamous or fraudulent marriage. Two men, in 1762 and 1770, proved their wives to be bigamists, and their marriages were declared null. Another argued that his recent marriage was invalid because he had been tricked into it, while drunk, by kinfolk of a young woman who was pregnant with his child. The governor and Council believed him and ruled the marriage null.[36] Women also had considerable success in ending bigamous marriages. Nine of the twelve wives' petitions were granted, six by annulment and three by dissolution, while three others remained unresolved.[37] Women's petitions against bigamous husbands re-
242 vealed some of the vagaries of marriage in eighteenth-century Massachusetts. In only two instances had the husband's prior marriage taken place long before and in another country.[38] In five, the husband's prior marriage occurred in another New England town between two and eight years earlier (and in one other case, fifteen years earlier).[39] Six of the bigamous husbands

[35] Sarah Maggin v. William Maggin (dismissed, 1736), Council Recs., X, 47; Elizabeth Bredeen v. Joseph Bredeen (1744), Suffolk Files #129728, Council Recs., XI, 151, 156, 174-175, 184; Judith Walker v. Simeon Walker (1773), Suffolk Files #129777; "An Act for dissolving the Marriage of Philip Turner and Mercy Turner," *Acts and Resolves, Mass. Bay*, VI, 229.

[36] William Davidson v. Hannah Davidson (1762), "Divorces," 16-17; Samuel Lefebvre v. Sarah Lefebvre (1770), Suffolk Files #129758, "Divorces," 57-59; Gill Belcher v. Mary Finney alias Belcher (1739), Suffolk Files #129726, Mass. Arch., IX, 228-229, Council Recs., X, 254-315.

[37] Annulled: Susanna T. Kennet v. Edward Kennet (1694), Council Recs., II, 290; Reliance Drew v. John Drew (1737), *ibid.*, X, 79, 122; Elizabeth Eldredge v. Ezekiel Eldredge (1751), Suffolk Files #129730, Mass. Arch., IX, 354-356, Council Recs., XII, 219; Rachel Wormley v. John Wormley (1765), Suffolk Files #129744, "Divorces," 33-34; Mary Bates v. Henry Bates (1771), Suffolk Files #129759, "Divorces," 59-62; Mehetabel Nicholson v. Joshua Nicholson (or Nickerson) (1771), Suffolk Files #129761, "Divorces," 62-64. Marriage dissolved: Rebecca Wansford v. Nicholas Wansford (1698), Council Recs., II, 562; Mary Hamilton alias Arthur v. George Arthur (1756), Mass. Arch., IX, 399-402, Council Recs., XIII, 140; Sibble Babcock v. George Babcock (1784), Suffolk Files #129835, "Divorces," 202-203. Not resolved: Abigail Hamen v. John Hamen (1748), Mass. Arch., IX, 321-323, Council Recs., XII, 46; Henrietta Maria East Caine v. Hugh Caine, Suffolk Files #129736, "Divorces," 2-3; Mary Drinkwater v. William Drinkwater (1771), Suffolk Files #129765

[38] Mary Arthur and Henrietta Maria East Caine.

[39] Abigail Hamen, Elizabeth Eldredge, Mary Bates, Mehetabel Nicholson, Mary Drinkwater, and Sibble Babcock.

TABLE III

PROPORTION OF PETITIONS RECEIVING FAVORABLE DECREES, 1692-1786

	All Causes	Adultery-Inclusive Only	Adultery-Exclusive Only
male petitioners	68%	72%	50%
female petitioners	58%	65%	47%

Note: Favcrable decrees include divorce, annulment, separate bed and board.

had also deserted, either to return to their first wives or to marry third wives.[40] These cases, especially when considered together with cases involving desertion, suggest the ease and perhaps the appeal of running away from one partner and finding another—the traditional "self-divorce." Husbands more frequently made such escapes and new starts than did wives. Twelve wives but only three husbands charged bigamy (category B); sixteen wives but only ten husbands complained of their spouses' desertion and adulterous cohabita- 243
tion with another (E); nineteen wives but only three husbands charged their partners with desertion and remarriage (F); ten wives but eight husbands petitioned on grounds of desertion alone (I). Men moved more easily from place to place, it seems; certainly, according to custom, they, and not women, took the initiative in deciding to marry or remarry.

The bulk of the petitions—84 percent of the husbands', 59 percent of the wives'—included the grievance of adultery. Men had more success than women in adultery-inclusive causes, but both sexes fared better in these causes than in others. (See Table III.) The comparison between men's and women's experiences in suing on grounds of adultery is especially interesting because it can inform us of the presence of a double standard of sexual morality. Were men's and women's infidelities considered equally cause for divorce? The cultural heritage of Massachusetts contained equivocal answers to this question. Despite the seventh commandment, English tradition enshrined the double standard, forgiving a husband's sexual transgressions but calling a wife's abhorrent. As mentioned earlier, all the parliamentary divorces for adultery in the eighteenth century were awarded to husbands, none to wives. Decorum among the aristocracy required wives to ignore their husbands' extramarital affairs.[41] In Massachusetts, however, Puritan reli-

[40] Reliance Drew, Abigail Hamen, Mary Arthur, H. M. E. Caine, Rachel Wormley, and Mary Bates. One petitioner, Mary Arthur, had already been granted separate bed and board because of her husband's cruelty. Perhaps wives would not have complained of the bigamy if their husbands had not compounded the insult with other grievances.

[41] See Keith Thomas, "The Double Standard," *Journal of the History of Ideas*, XX (1959), 195-216, and, for an example of such advice, [George Savile], *The Lady's New Year's Gift, or, Advice to a Daughter* (London, 1688).

gious values strongly infused the English tradition. Puritan ideology, partially to repudiate aristocratic manners, demanded fidelity of both partners. From the sixteenth century through the eighteenth, Puritan reformers attacked the double standard by advocating chastity before marriage, and fidelity after, for men as well as women.[42]

It is striking that in Massachusetts half of all the men's petitions named adultery as the sole major grievance (C), and that these petitions had a high rate of success: 70 percent resulted in divorce, only 4 percent were dismissed, and the remaining quarter did not result in decrees.[43] To obtain divorce a petitioner had to produce two eye-witnesses to the act of adultery or a confession from the accused spouse, or show record of criminal conviction of the adulterers, or of the failure of the accused to answer the court summons. Alternatively, a male petitioner might show that his wife had become pregnant in his absence. In England prior court conviction of the adulterers was prerequisite to a bill of divorce; but in Massachusetts civil court action
244 only seldom, and randomly, preceded or accompanied divorce suits.[44] Usually the governor and Council themselves determined the justice of the adultery charge. Since a wife's adultery was virtually sure cause for divorce, it was not unknown for a restless husband to "frame" his wife by setting up her seduction or by bribing deponents to testify that they had seen adultery committed. In several cases such plots by the husband were manifest or inferable.[45] The two husbands whose petitions were dismissed brought

[42] Thomas, "Double Standard," *Jour. Hist. Ideas,* XX (1959), 203-205.

[43] At least 17 of the 50 adulteries charged in husbands' petitions occurred while the husband was absent at sea or on a military campaign. In almost all of the cases in which bastard offspring were mentioned, the husband had been absent for a year or more. The wives' partners in adultery were neighbors, hired laborers, boarders, or, in a few cases, casual visitors or traveling companions.

[44] Only six of the male petitioners in category C gave evidence of prior court actions. Three were actions to punish the adulterers: Benjamin Bucklin v. Rebeccah Bucklin (1737), Council Recs., X, 112, 121; Thomas Gelpin v. Abigail Gelpin (1743), Mass. Arch., IX, 263-267, Council Recs., XI, 65-66, 73-74; George Raynord v. Mary Raynord (1752), Suffolk Files #129729, Council Recs., XII, 268. Three were actions for the husband to collect money damages from the wife's lover: Thomas Hammet v. Abigail Hammet (1767), Suffolk Files #129747, "Divorces," 37-40; James Dougherty v. Mary Dougherty (1768), Suffolk Files #129750, "Divorces," 45-48; Joshua Gay v. Sarah Gay (1778), Suffolk Files #129784, "Divorces," 101-103, Council Recs., XXII, 46, 48.

[45] For example, Jacob Brown v. Ruth Brown (1758), Mass. Arch., IX, 420-428, Council Recs., XIII, 350, 354; Russell Knight v. Mary Knight (1766), Suffolk Files #129745, "Divorces," 35-37, Mass. Arch., IX, 446-447; Andrew Shank v. Sarah Shank (or Schenk) (1772), Suffolk Files #129766; James Richardson v. Hannah Richardson (1772), Suffolk Files #129769, "Divorces," 70-72; William Sturgis v. Sarah Sturgis (1778), Suffolk Files #129785, "Divorces," 104-106, Council Recs., XXII, 256, 320; Samuel Hemenway v. Hannah Hemenway (1782), Suffolk Files

witnesses who incriminated the accused wives, but the court suspected bribery and believed the wives' contrary testimony.[46]

Clearly, the governor and Council would grant divorce to a man whose spouse committed adultery. Would they grant it to a woman for the same cause? There was no English precedent for such action. Only one suit from seventeenth-century Massachusetts has been found in which a wife sought and received a divorce for the sole cause of adultery—and this decree was subsequently reversed on the husband's appeal.[47] Women in eighteenth-century Massachusetts could be said to have taken a cue from these negative precedents. In contrast to the weight of men's petitions, not a single wife petitioned for the sole grievance of adultery until 1774, and only six did so between 1774 and 1786. Unless we assume that husbands displayed much more virtue than wives, the difference between the numbers of petitions from men and from women in this category (C) suggests a deeply entrenched double standard of marital fidelity. Whether individual women thought that men's adultery warranted divorce remains uncertain; but we can logically 245 conclude that before 1774 women did not expect to obtain divorce for that reason alone and so did not petition.

We can gain an approximation of the governor and Council's response to petitions grounded on husbands' adultery alone, before 1774, by looking at decrees in the other adultery-inclusive categories (D through H). Husbands' suits in these categories, dependent on their substantiation of the adultery charges, had great success. More than four-fifths of their petitions charging adultery and desertion (D), or adultery, desertion, and cohabitation (E), resulted in divorce. Few husbands petitioned on the other adultery-inclusive grounds, and only the ones who proved adultery won their suits. By contrast, the pre-Revolutionary governor and Council gave a woman very little reason to expect divorce for her spouse's infidelity. Seven out of twelve female petitioners before 1774 obtained divorces by proving their partner's desertion, adultery, and remarriage (F), but these decrees took bigamy, as well as adultery, into account.[48] Fourteen women petitioned the governor and Coun-

---

#129804. The legal process attendant on a divorce petition was meant to insure justice to the accused spouse: he or she was allowed to be present when depositions to support the petitioner were taken, and was able to bring his or her own witnesses.

[46] Andrew Shank v. Sarah Shank (1772), Suffolk Files #129766; Samuel Hemenway v. Hannah Hemenway (1782), *ibid.* #129804.

[47] Howard, *Matrimonial Institutions*, II, 334. But John Demos, *Little Commonwealth*, 97, has found in 17th-century Plymouth Colony records a divorce and favorable settlement granted to one woman who chiefly complained of her husband's "act of uncleanes" with another woman.

[48] "An Act against Adultery and Polygamy," passed June 6, 1794, made polygamy (that is, marrying again while one's first spouse was living) a felony punishable by death. *Acts and Resolves, Mass. Bay*, I, 171-172.

cil on other adultery-inclusive grounds prior to 1773. Eight of these received no decrees; one suit with apparent proof of the adultery was dismissed; and three—two of which charged adultery and cruelty—gained decrees of separate bed and board, the same decree which women's petitions charging cruelty alone could obtain.[49] Only two of the fourteen wives won divorces, and their cases were not conclusive on the question of adultery. Sarah Mitchell of Deerfield, who brought suit in 1718 on grounds of her husband's "fornication" with a black woman, obtained a divorce and the return of her marriage portion as well. The uniqueness of the decree suggests that not the adultery, but its interracial nature, was the crucial factor.[50] Hannah Rolfe of Lancaster made the other successful petition, in 1752. Her grievances included desertion, adultery, and cohabitation; her husband Ezra had been jailed for fornicating with a minor and for failing to provide for his bastard child, and he absconded to avoid answering Hannah's petition.[51]

Seventeen hundred and seventy-three was a turning point. In that year, 246 two women who petitioned on the grounds of adultery and cruelty were granted not separate bed and board, but divorce, for the specified cause of adultery. The original notation on Sarah Gould's petition recorded a unanimous decision for separate bed and board, but the formal decree of March 2, 1773, declared her marriage dissolved. Martha Air's petition a few months later resulted in an unequivocal dissolution of marriage bonds on account of Adam Air's adultery.[52] After that, women began to petition for divorce on the sole ground of adultery. The governor and Council (or the Council alone,

[49] Not decided: Ann Hall v. William Hall, category D (1753), Mass. Arch., IX, 370-373; Kezia Downing v. Nathaniel Downing, D (1765), Suffolk Files #129742; Lydia Sharp v. Boston (a black), D (1773), *ibid.* #129775; Marcy Robinson v. Leonard Robinson, E (1770), *ibid.* #129755; Sarah Wheeler v. Valentine Wheeler, E (1772), *ibid.* #129792; Hannah Medberry v. Ebenezer Medberry, G (1767), *ibid.* #129746; Eunice Mountfort v. Benjamin Mountfort, G (1771), *ibid.* #129760; Lucy Foster v. Benjamin Foster, H (1755), Mass. Arch., IX, 393-395. Dismissed: Elizabeth Shaw v. John Shaw, D (1748), *ibid.*, 324, Council Recs., XII, 57. Separate bed and board: Mary Clapham v. William Clapham, E (1754), Suffolk Files #129733, Council Recs., XII, 349; Eleanor Gray v. Samuel Gray, G (1747), Mass. Arch., IX, 296-311, Council Recs., XII, 12; Mary Fairservice v. John Fairservice, G (1767), Suffolk Files #129749, "Divorces," 40-44.

[50] Sarah Mitchell v. Michael Mitchell, Council Recs., VI, 305, 621. The older definition of adultery, incorporating the double standard, hinged on the involvement of a married *woman.* Thus a married man's sexual transgression could still be called fornication, if his partner was single.

[51] Hannah Rolfe v. Ezra Rolfe, Mass. Arch., IX, 357-358, Council Recs., XII, 218, 239.

[52] Sarah Gould v. William Gould, Suffolk Files #129772, notation on petition, 56; also "Divorces," 78-80. Martha Air v. Adam Air, Suffolk Files #129779, "Divorces," 81-82.

TABLE IV

ADULTERY-INCLUSIVE CHARGES
NUMBER OF PETITIONS/NUMBER OF FAVORABLE DECREES

		1692-1704	1705-1714	1715-1724	1725-1734	1735-1744	1745-1754	1755-1764	1765-1774	1775-1786	Total
C	men	2/1	1/1		2/1	6/6	4/2	9/5*	12/8	14/11	50/35*
	women								1/1	5/4	6/5
D	men					2/2	1/1	1/1	4/2	8/6	16/12
	women						2/0	2/2*	2/0	6/5	12/7*
E	men	1/1						2/2*	1/0	6/6	10/9*
	women					1/1	2/2*		2/0	11/8	16/11
F	men		1/1				2/0				3/1
	women	1/1		3/0	2/1	1/1	1/1	1/1	3/2	7/6	19/13
G	men							1/0		1/0	2/0
	women						1/1**		6/3**	12/7	19/11**
H	men				1/1	1/1	2/2				4/4
	women			1/1				1/0		1/1	3/2

Note: * Includes legislative divorce. ** Includes separate bed and board.

between 1776 and 1780) granted five out of the six such petitions during the next twelve years. The increasing number of wives who brought other adultery-inclusive charges also obtained divorces, and almost all of these decrees went on to the record as owing specifically to the adultery charge.[53] (See Table IV.)

These decrees were not quite as unprecedented as they may seem at first glance. In the 1750s, during the interval when the governor and Council declined to dissolve marriages, three women obtained bills of divorce from the General Court on adultery-inclusive grounds. The first was Mary Clapham, wife of a gentleman. After obtaining a decree of separate bed and board from the governor and Council because of her husband's desertion and adulterous cohabitation with a woman in Nova Scotia, she petitioned the General Court, "in whom she apprehend[ed] the Power to be vested," to

[53] Between 1774 and 1786, 5 of the 6 women who charged adultery and desertion, 8 of the 11 who brought suits on account of adultery, desertion and cohabitation, 7 of the 8 who alleged adultery, desertion and remarriage, 7 of the 13 whose grievances were adultery and cruelty, and one whose husband committed interracial adultery all obtained decrees of divorce from the governor and Council. These figures differ slightly from the 1775-1786 column of Table IV because they include the cases of 1774.

dissolve her marriage and assign her alimony. The court obliged her first request, citing as William Clapham's "Violation of his Marriage Contract" his "leaving the said Mary, cohabiting and committing adultery with Another Woman."[54] The two other women who appealed successfully to the General Court both charged their husbands with adultery and desertion. Mary Parker, also a gentleman's wife, obtained her divorce because, the bill said, "Phineas Parker has for sundry Years pass'd left the said Mary, and stands convict[ed] of committing Adultery with another woman." The act granted at the plea of Lydia Kellogg, wife of a laborer of Sunderland, declared only that "it appears to this court that the said Ephraim [Kellogg] has been guilty of the crime of adultery."[55]

The General Court seems to have been more liberal in granting divorces to women before 1773 than were the governor and Council. In enacting bills of divorce for three wives during the 1750s the court presaged actions which the Council would take during, but not before, the Revolutionary period.[56]
248 The legislative divorces, viewed together with the Council's decrees after 1773, suggest that the more whiggish and the more representative the authority, the more likely it was to treat male and female adultery equally as cause for divorce. The transformation of the Council's attitude toward male adultery would be simpler to explain if it had occurred in 1776, when the composition of the Council changed radically. Though some new members replaced old ones in 1773, specific changes in membership do not clearly account for the new pattern of decrees beginning in that year.[57]

Divorce actions in Massachusetts may have paralleled larger political

[54] Court Recs., Dec. 4, 1754, XX, 337-338; Mass. Arch., IX, 381-382; "An Act to dissolve the Marriage of Mary Clapham with William Clapham and to allow her to marry again," *Acts and Resolves,* Mass. Arch., VI, 105. The Council later awarded Mary her household furniture, worth £100. Council Recs., XII, 386.

[55] Mary Parker v. Phineas Parker, Mass. Arch., IX, 374-380, Council Recs., XII, 337, *Acts and Resolves, Mass. Bay,* VI, 169; Lydia Kellogg v. Ephraim Kellogg, Mass. Arch., IX, 403-413, *Acts and Resolves, Mass. Bay,* VI, 173. The Parker and Kellogg divorce acts, and two of the three legislative divorces obtained by male petitioners, were passed without prior decrees of separate bed and board from the governor and Council. Only in the Parker case was prior court conviction of the adulterer mentioned. The men's cases were John Farnum, Jr., v. Elizabeth Farnum, Mass. Arch., IX, 396-398, *Acts and Resolves, Mass. Bay,* VI, 170; Jonah Galusha v. Sarah Galusha, Mass. Arch, IX, 414, *Acts and Resolves, Mass. Bay,* VI, 174, Court Recs., XX, 329; and Daniel McCarthy v. Mary McCarthy, Suffolk Files, #129734, Mass. Arch., IX, 418, Council Recs., XIII, 259, 262, *Acts and Resolves, Mass. Bay,* VI, 177. The three cases reviewed by the Board of Trade in 1758 were Clapham's, Parker's, and Farnum's.

[56] Between 1760 and 1773 seven women filed adultery-inclusive petitions and none obtained divorce, although Mary Fairservice, with a plea of adultery and cruelty, obtained separate bed and board. See n. 49.

[57] "Divorces" list names of Council members present at each decision.

TABLE V

PROPORTION OF ALL PETITIONS CONTAINING ADULTERY CHARGE

	1692-1764	1765-1774	1775-1786
male petitioners	78%	94%	91%
female petitioners	40%	50%	79%

struggles, but did changes in divorce policy also move against the double standard and advance equality between the sexes? In several ways the record of petitions and decrees implies an improvement in women's status. The great increase in the number of women's petitions after 1764 suggests that women were becoming less resigned to their circumstances and were taking more initiative to end unsatisfactory marriages. Women's petitions were more concentrated in the period after 1764 than were men's.[58] The proportion of petitions including adultery charges rose for both sexes, but more emphatically for wives. (See Table V.) The higher the proportion of adultery-inclusive petitions, the greater success petitioners were likely to have. In fact, both male and female petitioners fared better between 1765 and 1786, but only on account of decrees made after independence. From 1765 through 1774 an unusually high proportion of suits remained unresolved, reducing petitioners' chances of favorable action. The proportion of unresolved petitions jumped from 23 percent for the years 1692-1764 to 41 percent for 1765-1774, and then dropped to 13 percent for 1775-1786. This noteworthy improvement in efficiency, along with the rise in the proportion of adultery-inclusive petitions, increased petitioners' likelihood of gaining favorable decrees. Because of the added factor of the new treatment of male adultery, wives' rate of success improved dramatically from 49 percent between 1692 and 1774 to 70 percent between 1775 and 1786; husbands' rate of success rose only from 66 percent to 73 percent. Wives' rate of success almost equalled that of husbands' during the decade after independence.

It is tempting to propose from this evidence that the Revolutionary era ushered in a "new deal" that recognized the injustice of the double standard, evened obligations of marital fidelity, and made redress within marriage more accessible to women. To an extent, however small, acceptance of male adultery as grounds for divorce moved in these directions. Motives for the change in the treatment of male adultery probably originated, however, more in men's political intentions than in their desire for sexual justice. Revolutionary rhetoric, in its repudiation of British "vice," "corruption," "extrava-

[58] See Table I. Half of all men's but 63% of all women's petitions occurred after 1764.

gance," and "decadence," enshrined ideals of republican virtue—of personal and national simplicity, honesty, frugality, and public spirit. In the view of Revolutionary leaders, republicanism required a moral reformation of the American people as well as a political transformation, because a republic's success depended on the virtue of its citizens. As John Adams wrote to his wife Abigail in July 1776, "the new Governments we are assuming . . . will require a Purification from our Vices, and an Augmentation of our Virtues or they will be no Blessings." Samuel Adams stated in 1777, "We shall succeed if we are virtuous. . . . I am infinitely more apprehensive of the Contagion of Vice than the Power of all other Enemies."[59] The dynamism of the words "virtue" and "vice," in Revolutionary usage, derived at least in part from their sexual connotation.[60] Rejection of British "corruption" implied a critique of the traditionally loose sexual standards for men of the British ruling class. The republican ideology of private as well as public virtue also produced an emphasis on marital fidelity, because it focused on
250 the family as the training ground of future citizens. It was wholly consistent that judges in Massachusetts, where patriotic rhetoric evoked Puritan conceptions of righteousness (and thus Puritan standards of fidelity), no longer saw male adultery as venial but called it sufficient grounds for divorce. Such a change in standards for male conduct may well have produced a divorce policy that had the appearance of improving women's marital status.

Petitioners also brought suits on account of important marital breaches other than adultery—namely, desertion (I) and cruelty (J). Desertion suits were the least successful among all the categories. Of ten wives who charged desertion—all but one abandoned for more than three years—only two achieved any favorable result. Five of the petitions were not resolved. Three more were dismissed, suggesting that the governor and Council regarded a husband's willful desertion in itself as insufficient cause to dissolve a marriage.[61] One wife who asked only for her conjugal right to restoration of

[59] John Adams to Abigail Adams, July 3, 1776, and Samuel Adams to John Langdon, Aug. 7, 1777, in Gordon S. Wood, *The Creation of the American Republic, 1776-1787* (Chapel Hill, N.C., 1972), 123-124.

[60] Ian Watt, "The New Woman: Samuel Richardson's *Pamela*," in Rose Laub Coser, ed., *The Family: Its Structure and Functions* (New York, 1964), 281-282, points out that "the eighteenth century [in England] witnessed a tremendous narrowing of the ethical scale, a redefinition of virtue in primarily sexual terms. . . . The same tendency can be seen at work on the ethical vocabulary itself: words such as virtue, propriety, decency, modesty, delicacy, purity, came to have the almost exclusively sexual connotation which they have since very largely retained."

[61] Howard, *Matrimonial Institutions*, II, 333, lists two late 17th-century cases in which women petitioned on account of their husbands' desertion and failure to provide, and the assistants declared the marriages dissolved, but no comparable 18th-

maintenance, since her husband had deserted long before, obtained her object. The court formalized the couple's agreement for yearly maintenance payments by the husband.[62] In the other successful suit Abigail Bradstreet, whose complaints included cruelty as well as desertion, won a decree of separate bed and board with maintenance payments.[63]

Among the eight men who sued because of their wives' desertion, the earlier petitioners fared better than the later. The court declared John Emery of Newbury separated from his wife in 1710 on his complaint that she slandered him and refused to live with him. Two other men obtained divorces on desertion pleas. John Ferre, a husbandman of Springfield, petitioned in 1718 and was ordered by the governor and Council to post notification that if his wife did not return within six months she would be divorced. Ferre obeyed, his wife did not return, and in 1719 the divorce was granted. Jonathan Fletcher's petition of 1734 stated that his wife had departed sixteen years earlier, after two months of marriage. In this case the
governor and Council took the unusual step of declaring both parties single 251
and free to marry, the marriage portion to be returned.[64] After 1734, however, men's desertion pleas all failed. The court gave John Williston's petition in 1737 only a first reading, apparently, and dismissed other petitions in 1739, 1740, 1743, and 1786.[65] These dismissals contradicted the implication

---

century women's suits had that result. The presumption of the law was that seven years' absence by one spouse allowed the other to remarry. The "Act against Adultery and Polygamy" of 1694 (*Acts and Resolves, Mass. Bay,* I, 171-172) exempted from its punishments any person whose spouse had been overseas for seven years or absent more than seven years, so perhaps the Council assumed that decrees of divorce were unnecessary. Two suits dismissed, however, involved absences of five and six years.

[62] That is, this was a separate bed and board arrangement by mutual consent. Ann Vansise v. Cornelius Vansise, "Divorces," 44-45.

[63] Abigail Bradstreet v. Joseph Bradstreet, Suffolk Files #129762, "Divorces," 68-70. Her lawyer, John Adams, argued her case according to canon law. See Wroth and Zobel, eds., *Legal Papers of Adams,* I, 280-285.

[64] John Emery v. Abigail Emery, Council Recs., V, 180. (Abigail also petitioned unsuccessfully for divorce from John for cruelty. Mass. Arch., IX, 162-163.) John Ferre v. Elizabeth Ferre, Council Recs., VII, 165; Jonathan Fletcher v. wife, *ibid.,* IX, 552, 565.

[65] The duration of the wife's absence is not apparent in these cases, except in the last, John Chapin v. Margaret Chapin, Suffolk Files #129856, in which it was three years. One probable reason why John's suit failed was that Margaret was willing to be divorced. Divorce was an adversary process in Massachusetts; separate bed and board, but never divorce, was decreed on the basis of a couple's mutual agreement. Any apparent collusion on the part of the couple to gain divorce invalidated the suit, so that, ironically, one way for a husband or wife to stop a divorce proceeding was to agree to it. See, for example, Sarah Rust v. Francis Rust (Jan. 1784), Suffolk Files #129833, "Divorces," 199-200; and Sarah Rust v. Francis Rust (June 1784), Suffolk Files #129836, "Divorces," 204-205. Cf. n. 80.

of the Ferre and Fletcher cases, and they force the general conclusion that desertion alone, whether by wife or husband, was not considered sufficient cause for divorce. Why not? Certainly desertion violated the marriage contract. In Puritan theory desertion warranted divorce. Under canon law, on the contrary, desertion was not even grounds for separate bed and board unless it was combined with cruelty.[66] Excepting the Ferre and Fletcher cases, the governor and Council acted as though canon law controlled their decisions on desertion.[67] Perhaps the New World offered too great opportunities for desertion for the court to wish to establish desertion as reason for divorce.

Canon law rather than Puritan precept appears to have guided the decisions in cruelty cases as well. Puritan divorce theory allowed divorce for incorrigible enmity between spouses or for dangerous abuse, but canon law prescribed only separate bed and board. Of the twenty-three Massachusetts petitions entered on grounds of cruelty, nine obtained decrees of separate bed
252 and board, three more were settled by separations based on mutual consent, six were dismissed for insufficient evidence, and five were left unresolved. Not a single one gained divorce. However, not all of these petitions asked for divorce. All of the petitioners in this category were women, and almost two-thirds of them requested only separate bed and board with maintenance. It is difficult to tell whether this reflected their pragmatism or their personal preference. Divorce was virtually impossible to obtain for this cause, but separate bed and board was possible. To gain a separation, with alimony, may have seemed a satisfactory solution to the grievance, especially for older women who did not foresee marrying again. Yet even separate bed and board was not easy to obtain, as the six dismissals attested. In all but one of these six cases the wives asked only for separation and maintenance, but the governor and council would not grant the plea.[68]

[66] Wroth and Zobel, eds., *Legal Papers of Adams,* I, 284; Howard, *Matrimonial Institutions,* II, 52-54.

[67] Possibly the change from granting of divorces for wives' desertions before 1735 to dismissing such pleas later represented an "anglicization" of divorce policy. The appearance of separate bed and board decrees during the 18th century, when none, according to Howard, was made during the previous century, supports such a theory; but the change in treatment of male adultery in 1773 opposes it. Cf. John Murrin, "Anglicizing an American Colony: The Transformation of Puritan Massachusetts" (Ph.D. diss., Yale University, 1966); Kenneth A. Lockridge, "Land, Population, and the Evolution of New England Society, 1630-1790," *Past and Present,* XXXIX (1968), 62-80; and Kenneth A. Lockridge, *A New England Town, The First Hundred Years: Dedham, Massachusetts, 1636-1736* (New York, 1970), 167-180.

[68] The records remaining for five of the six cases are not extensive enough to allow evaluation of the "sufficiency" of the cruelty alleged. One woman whose petition was dismissed sued a second time, however, bringing additional evidence, and then won separate bed and board. Mary Lobb v. George Lobb, Suffolk Files

Women who petitioned on grounds of cruelty were significantly more urban—and thus perhaps more sophisticated—than petitioners in general. Fourteen of the twenty-two[69] lived in Boston, three in towns immediately outside Boston, two in other large port towns, and only three in smaller, more remote locations. Perhaps urban women had higher standards for kind treatment in marriage than did rural women, or more readily took official steps to combat physical abuse. Urban women also predominated, though not as strongly, among wives petitioning on grounds of adultery and cruelty (G): ten of the nineteen lived in Boston and three in towns nearby.

The governor and Council usually judged requests for maintenance in cases in which they decreed separate bed and board, although a provincial statute of 1695 located jurisdiction over alimony in the Superior Court of Judicature. Alimony ordinarily took the form of regular cash payments, the amount varying with the husband's wealth.[70] Gentlemen's wives, who married with considerable portions, might ask only for the return or use of their own former property to support themselves. Mary Arthur of Boston did so in 253
1754 when she sought separation from her husband because of his nine years of abuse. After she obtained the separation, a second petition was required before the Council awarded her her household goods and the income from her Boston real estate.[71] The governor and Council assigned to another Bostonian, in lieu of the alimony she requested, the rent and profit of her

---

#129800, "Divorces," 145-148. In the sixth case, the wife gave evidence of enormous cruelty, but the governor and Council accepted her husband's promise henceforth to treat her kindly as reason to dismiss her petition. Apparently their judgment was mistaken, for the wife petitioned again less than a year later, indicating that her plight had not improved. Margaret Knodle v. Frederick Knodle (1764), Suffolk Files #129743, "Divorces," 32.

[69] There were 23 suits but only 22 petitioners, since Mary Lobb petitioned twice (n. 68).

[70] *Acts and Resolves, Mass. Bay*, I, 209. Some of the alimony awards made by the governor and Council in separate bed and board decrees were as follows: Anne Leonard v. Henry Leonard (a turner, of Boston), in 1743, 5s. per week (Mass. Arch., IX, 268-294, Council Recs., XI, 69, 113-114); Eleanor Gray v. Samuel Gray (a yeoman, of Pelham, Hampshire County), 1747, £6 per year (Mass. Arch., IX, 296-311, Council Recs., XII, 12); Mary Fairservice v. John Fairservice (a trader of Boston), 1767, £12 yearly (Suffolk Files #129749, "Divorces," 40-44); Lucy Purnam v. Scipio Purnam (a truckman, of Newburyport), 1768, 6s. per month (Suffolk Files #129751, "Divorces" 48-51). This last was the most bizarre suit on grounds of cruelty. The couple were black; Lucy accused Scipio not only of treating her cruelly but also of attempting to sell her as a slave. Scipio denied the charges and brought witnesses who impugned Lucy's character. Eventually he agreed to the official separation but objected strongly to paying alimony, claiming "she is at least as well able to support herself as he is himself and Family." See Suffolk Files #129751, 124.

[71] Mary Arthur v. George Arthur, Suffolk Files #129733b, Council Recs., XII, 371, 385.

own real property, removing it from her husband's control. Yet she was not permitted to sell the lands, which were uncultivated and produced no profit, without petitioning again for that privilege. Upon her plea, the General Court enacted a bill allowing her to sell and convey the lands as though she were single, but the Privy Council disallowed it.[72] These alimony arrangements revealed starkly how the marriage bond circumscribed the legal and economic individuality of women.[73]

In three separate bed and board decrees after 1780 the governor and Council failed to mention alimony, although the Massachusetts constitution of 1780 put the matter under their jurisdiction. They granted *divorce* with alimony to two women petitioners, however—the only two such decrees between 1692 and 1786—although no extraordinary characteristics of the cases explain why.[74] It may be that divorced women had earlier sought alimony from the superior courts. Sarah Griffin (Sarah Gould before her divorce) filed a petition for this purpose with the Superior Court of Judica-
254 ture of Suffolk County on August 31, 1773, but the court appears to have taken no action.[75]

It is doubtful how well the assignment of alimony worked to provide for separated or divorced wives. In those four cases in which the couple mutually

[72] Mary Hunt v. Richard Hunt, "Divorces," 6-11, Council Recs., XIV, 268, 270, 277; "An Act for enabling Mary Hunt to dispose and Convey her lands and interest in Holden," passed Apr. 24, 1762, disallowed by Privy Council Mar. 16, 1763, *Acts and Resolves, Mass. Bay,* VI, 187-188.

Alexander Keyssar, "Widowhood in Eighteenth-Century Massachusetts: A Problem in the History of the Family," *Perspectives in American History,* VIII (1974), esp. 100-103, 114-118, points out that widows commonly faced similar problems: as dower they received the use and profit of one-third of their husbands' real property but not the right to dispose of it. "Dozens" of widows in 18th-century Massachusetts petitioned the General Court to be enabled to dispose of real property because it was not profitable to them. Keyssar's conclusion that "the legal structure aimed at the sustenance, rather than the economic freedom, of widows" (p. 103) could apply to the position of wives separated from their husbands.

[73] Under common law all of a woman's personal property and earnings became her husband's upon marriage, and while she retained title to any real estate she owned, her husband gained the right to its use and income. A husband could not liquidate his wife's real property without her consent—this was the root of the quarrel in Bradstreet v. Bradstreet (n. 63)—but neither could she sell it of her own accord.

[74] Sarah Wheeler v. Valentine Wheeler, Suffolk Files #129792, "Divorces," 128-131, 144-145, Council Recs., XXV, 181, 400, XXVI, 118; Sarah Sawyer v. Abel Sawyer, Suffolk Files #129827, "Divorces," 188-191. Cf. Sarah Vernon v. William Vernon, Suffolk Files #129849, "Divorces," 216-217, 222-224, for an explicit refusal of alimony after a divorce decree.

[75] See Suffolk Files #91716. Her petition is in John Adams's handwriting, according to Worth and Zobel, eds., *Legal Papers of Adams,* I, 285n.

agreed to separation and maintenance no complaints followed.[76] But six of the nine decrees of separate bed and board with alimony were succeeded by further petitions from the wives, because their husbands had not made the required payments.[77] Petitioners who won separate bed and board thus had an ambiguous success, not being allowed to remarry, nor released from the economic constraints of the marriage contract, nor guaranteed current support. The husband's provision of alimony, like his support during marriage, was required by law and enforceable by compulsory process, but his performance actually depended on his own conscientiousness and goodwill.

The records of divorce in Massachusetts are most interesting for what they reveal about men's and women's respective power and advantages within marriage. The alimony petitions emphasize something the divorce suits as a whole suggest, that while marriage was a contract—a covenant, in contemporary language—it was a contract between unequals with disparate obligations. Sexual fidelity and good conduct were expected of both partners, 255
but fidelity was not regularly enforced upon husbands by the threat of divorce until the mid-1770s, and a husband's abusive conduct never warranted divorce. The husband's characteristic obligation was provision of support; the wife's, obedient service. In this, marriage resembled an indenture between master and servant; and, indeed, the marriage relation was only one of a number of dependency relations—such as parent-child and master-servant—in traditional society. The husband's obligation—enhanced by his control over his wife's property and labor—was unequivocal. In a case, for example, in which an aggrieved wife returned to her parents' household, her father sued her husband for the cost of maintaining her during that time, and his view of the husband's responsibility was upheld in court.[78] The wife performed her part in her subjection. Like a servant in relation to a master,

[76] Ann McAlpine v. William McAlpine (1763), Suffolk Files #129737—no information on amount of settlement. Ann Vansise v. Cornelius Vansise (1768), "Divorces," 44-45—alimony of £10 yearly. Ann Lovell v. John Lovell (1773), Suffolk Files #129778—wife received her own estate and earnings. Ann Gardner v. David Gardner (1783), *ibid.*, #129813, "Divorces," 168-170—settlement of £40 plus wife's retention of dower rights.

[77] See the Bradstreet, Gray, and Purnam cases cited in nn. 63 and 70, and Elizabeth Keith v. Mark Keith, Suffolk Files #129738, "Divorces," 24-27, Mass. Arch., IX, 441-442; Mary Fairservice v. John Fairservice (1770), Suffolk Files #129756, "Divorces," 56-57; Mary Hamilton alias Arthur v. George Arthur (1756), Mass. Arch., IX, 399-492, Council Recs., XIII, 140. Those that did not produce subsequent complaints were Thankfull Winehall's case of 1710, which is very sparsely documented (Council Recs., V, 238); Ann Leonard's settlement of 5s. per week; and Mary Hunt's award of her own property (see nn. 70 and 72).

[78] William Sturgis v. Sarah Sturgis, Suffolk Files #129785, "Divorces," 104-106, Council Recs., XXII, 256, 320. See also Burditch v. Sturgis, Suffolk Files #102540.

she contributed continual service and received support. Besides working in the household (many deponents in divorce cases mentioned the industry of wives), she was expected to use frugally what her husband provided. Amos Bliss of Rehoboth felt he had a valid complaint against his wife Phebe because she "behaved herself unfriendly and unsubjectedly toward him; and . . . had linked herself in friendship with her father's Family against him; who . . . had ocationed a great Deal of Trouble, as well as Loss, to his Interest: and he Represented her to be Very Disloyal towards his person: and wastefull and Careless of his provisions and goods"; but Amos was willing to invite Phebe home again if she would act the good and obedient wife and "be in subjection to him."[79] The indenture-like nature of marriage appeared in the practice of a husband's "advertising" his runaway wife, warning others not to harbor or trust her, and refusing responsibility for her debts. A husband would not be bound to provide for his wife if he could not command her services, and he could compel her services by preventing her from
256 obtaining support elsewhere.

Since marriage resembled an indenture contract, divorce should have been more readily available for varieties of nonperformance such as desertion or cruelty. That it was not suggests, first, that the sexual definition of marriage was its essence, and, second, that English divorce policy had more influence on eighteenth-century Massachusetts than might appear at first glance. Although marriage was regarded as a civil contract, and Massachusetts had no ecclesiastical courts, decisions in desertion and cruelty suits were almost entirely consistent with English application of canon law. On the whole, however, Massachusetts divorce practice diverged significantly from that of England. A much wider range of individuals—a laborer, a poor woman, a black servant—were able to obtain divorce with freedom to remarry, while in England only very rich men had that opportunity. In addition, the procedure was simpler than the parliamentary process. No prior ecclesiastical decree or criminal conviction of the adulterers was necessary in adultery cases, although the latter sufficed to warrant divorce. What was more innovative, women were able to obtain divorce with freedom to remarry and after 1773 did so on approximately the same terms as men. When in 1786 Massachusetts enacted a divorce law to codify the practice that had evolved, it allowed divorce for consanguinity, bigamy, impotency, or adultery *in either partner,* and separate bed and board for extreme cruelty.[80]

Throughout the period 1692-1786 husbands found it easier than wives to

[79] Amos Bliss v. Phebe Bliss, Suffolk Files #129799, depositions of Silvanus Martin and Eleazar Bliss, 49, 43.

[80] This law, passed Mar. 16, 1786 (*Acts and Resolves, 1784-1785,* 564-567), also stated that no divorce would be granted if the adultery or cruelty were occasioned by collusion in order to obtain divorce, or if both spouses committed adultery.

obtain divorce—not a surprising circumstance, since men also had the legal and economic independence which married women lacked, occupied all political and religious offices, were more literate than women, exercised greater control over geographic moves and choice of spouse, and by the terms of the marriage covenant could command their wives' obedience. It is more remarkable that the number of women's petitions and their rate of success accelerated during the century, so that in the decade after independence more than half again as many women as men pursued divorce, and their rate of success was almost the same. Divorce pleas by both sexes increased during the Revolutionary period, and efficiency in treating them improved, reflecting modernization of both personal values and bureaucratic procedure. The disproportionate growth in women's petitions suggests that they, even more than men, had rising expectations in marriage; and the changing treatment of their petitions implies that wives' objections were being regarded more seriously—that their status within the family had risen in the eyes of authorities.

The equalization of the consequences of adultery by either spouse, which was unmistakably the reason for the increasing success of women petitioners, may have signified a retreat from hierarchical models and an advance toward ideals of complementarity in the prevailing conception of the marriage relationship. In Hingham, Massachusetts, Daniel Scott Smith has found a consonant change in marriage patterns—a move away from parental control in the direction of individual autonomy in marriage choice—beginning markedly in the Revolutionary years. Smith sees the departure from the stable, parent-run system of selecting spouses as evidence of the "erosion and collapse of traditional family patterns in the middle to late eighteenth century."[81] Furthermore, on the basis of her analysis of New England funeral sermons Lonna Malmsheimer affirms that views of women altered significantly during these years. No longer stressing the rigid subordination of wife to husband as they had done earlier, although still insisting on the importance of the wife's domestic service, the sermons began to focus on friendship, complementarity, and emotional bonds between spouses. The seventeenth-century linkage of woman with moral evil, Eve's legacy, gave way to a new image of woman as a being ruled by conscience and religion.[82] Additionally, writers in contemporary Boston magazines seem to have been preoccupied with the reciprocal obligations and advantages of the sexes. They, too, idealized the complementary nature of men's and women's marital roles: an essayist in the Boston *Gentleman's and Lady's Town and Country*

[81] Smith, "Parental Power and Marriage Patterns," *Jour. Marriage and Family*, XXXV (1973), 426.

[82] Lonna Myers Malmsheimer, "New England Funeral Sermons and Changing Attitudes toward Women, 1672-1792" (Ph.D. diss., University of Minnesota, 1973).

Magazine, for example, of September 1784, described "matrimonial felicity" as the uniting of two congenial souls, "the man all truth, the woman all tenderness; he possessed of cheerful solidity, she of rational gaiety; acknowledging his superior judgment she complies with all his reasonable desires, whilst he, charmed with such repeated instances of superior love, endeavors to suit his requests to her inclinations."[83]

By the last quarter of the eighteenth century both parties were evidently restating the terms of the "indenture" of marriage. The divorce court's reprobation of male adultery newly defined one limit to the marital contract. This indicated an improvement in the position of wives, although it did not change their economic status, the essence of their dependency. By making men culpable for adultery, the court may also have heralded a new ideology of sexual roles—one that would encourage families in the young Republic to produce upright citizens. Stricter standards for men's marital fidelity helped enforce ideals of republican character and counteract British social models. The assumption that men could resist the temptation of adultery also implied a nontraditional view of woman[84]—not the devil-as-woman Eve, whose seductiveness absolved men of their sexual transgressions, but the angel-as-woman Pamela, who upheld and typified sexual virtue.

[83] *Gentleman's and Lady's Town and Country Magazine* (Sept. 1784), 194. See also Herman R. Lantz *et al.*, "Pre-Industrial Patterns in the Colonial Family in America: A Content Analysis of Colonial Magazines," *American Sociological Review,* XXXIII (1968), 413-426.

[84] Malmsheimer, "New England Funeral Sermons," finds this kind of shift in ideology in funeral sermons.

Articles

Symposium: Women and the Law, A Retrospective View[*]

WOMEN AND THE LAW: THE COLONIAL PERIOD

Linda Grant De Pauw†

In the beginning, ethnologists believe, women on the North American continent lived under legal and social systems that were largely matriarchal. The power of women in Native American societies began to erode during the sixteenth century, but throughout the colonial period their rights were more extensive than those enjoyed by European women. 259

Contrary to common belief, farming, not hunting provided most of the food supply for tribes in Eastern America, and women dominated the practice of agriculture. Their central economic role, as well as the legacy of matriarchal traditions, gave the Native American women great political power. Indian women as well as warriors had councils, and the women's council could veto a warriors' declaration of war. They could easily enforce this veto, should any man dare to question it, by refusing to supply the moccassins and field rations without which a war party could not move. Native American women had greater property rights than men. Although the Indians did not "own" land and therefore had a view of property different from that of Europeans, the Indian women generally built and owned Indian houses. Among the Native Americans a woman could divorce her husband by the simple ceremony of piling his belongings outside the door for him to find when he came home. The Native Americans understood how to produce abortions and commonly limited their families to two or three children at a time when European colonists often had four or five times that

* The following comments are based on a series of addresses presented at a panel discussion sponsored by the Section of Individual Rights and Responsibilities at the annual meeting of the American Bar Association in Atlanta, Georgia, August 10, 1976.

† B.A. 1961, Swarthmore College; Ph.D. 1964, Johns Hopkins University. Professor of History, George Washington University. Editor of DOCUMENTARY HISTORY OF THE FIRST FEDERAL CONGRESS, 1789-1791 (1972). Author of FOUNDING MOTHERS: WOMEN OF AMERICA IN THE REVOLUTIONARY ERA (1975).

many. Native Americans strongly disapproved of adultery, and divorce was uncommon once there were children, but unmarried women enjoyed a degree of personal freedom that horrified Europeans. "A young woman is allowed to do what she pleases," wrote a shocked observer. "Let her conduct be what it will, neither father nor mother, brother nor sister, can pretend to control her. A young woman, say they, is master of her own body, and by her natural right to liberty is free to do what she pleases."[1]

During the sixteenth, seventeenth, and eighteenth centuries, in what was one of the great movements of peoples in all recorded history, thousands of Europeans invaded the continent of North America. They brought with them legal and social traditions that assumed a much more confined role for women than that recognized by the
260 Native Americans. The legal status of women in all parts of Europe in the thousand years preceding colonization was determined by a blend of the written code of Roman law and the customs of Germanic tribes. Both of these were essentially patriarchal, but both recognized some rights for women. The Roman law was distinguished by provisions barring women from all public offices—thus denying them public rights—but also by provisions protecting women's private, family rights, particularly those to property. Germanic custom, on the other hand, allowed women to hold important positions in tribal government—thus protecting their public rights—but it denied them almost all private rights. They could not inherit property and could themselves be bought and sold. At different times and in different places these two legal traditions interacted in different ways. By chance, at the time colonization of North America began, they had blended in England in a way as favorable to women as the elements of each would permit. In sixteenth century England, the property rights of women were protected in Roman terms and their public rights were determined according to Germanic traditions that allowed public rights to property owners. In the age of Queen Elizabeth, wealthy women (whether spinsters or widows) who avoided marriage (as the queen did), could exercise the privileges of knights, hold courts, and vote for members of Parliament. So long as they held property, they also held military, legal, and political power.

---

[1] L. A. de Lom d'Arce Lahotan, 2 New Voyages to North America 453 (R. Thwaites ed. 1905).

Thus when colonization began, the legal position of English women was at a high point. Nevertheless, even at its high point the European tradition could not acknowledge full equality. The most significant limitations on women's rights were a consequence of the legal concept of coverture. Coverture is what happened to a woman when she married. Marriage made one person of two, and the person remaining after this operation was always male. The woman's legal existence disappeared. Her property rights, down to ownership of her petticoats, passed to her husband. She could not make contracts or sue in court. Indeed, she could not even commit a crime; the law assumed that whatever she did was under compulsion from her husband. This could lead, on occasion, to such peculiar legal rulings as that requiring that a husband be fined or whipped if his wife committed adultery. Since it was absurd to conceive of a single person suing itself, women could not sue for divorce; those divorce cases which were instituted had to be brought for the woman by her father or a male relative. Similarly, it was absurd to conceive of a single person making agreements or contracts with itself, so while some protection for a woman's property might be negotiated in a prenuptual agreement no postnuptual agreements were possible. The rights of the husband were absolute. Furthermore, divorce was all but impossible for a woman to obtain. Jurisdiction over matrimonial cases lay with the ecclesiastical courts, which would in extreme cases annul marriages or grant separations, but which held to the doctrine that no human law could dissolve marriages performed in accordance with God's law.

During the seventeenth century, the high tide for women's rights that had been reached during the reign of Queen Elizabeth ebbed. Unmarried, property-owning women lost most of their power, and Dutch women rather than English began to be recognized as the freest women in Europe. In the English colonies, however, frontier conditions and the mixed national background of the colonists favored retention of a wide sphere for women and even encouraged its extension.

Life in colonial America was very hard. There was no place for a leisure class, and society could not afford to restrict the activity of anyone willing and able to work. All women in colonial America were working women. In the preindustrial age, all work, for both sexes, was "in the home." Usually work meant running a farm. The

place of the farmer's wife as a full working partner in the family business, clearly entitled to her share of the profits—"butter and egg money"—a tradition that has endured in America to the present day. In the colonial period, women were full working partners not only in running farms but in any other businesses families might own. Farm girls were brought up learning to tend a dairy and poultry house. The daughters of a blacksmith learned to shoe horses. The daughters of a printer learned to set type, and the daughters of a merchant learned to keep accounts. A girl who did not learn a trade at home would be apprenticed out to learn one. When she grew up and married, she had the skills needed to make a living. Usually she married a man with whom she could work in partnership in the same business, but sometimes she would
262 have a business of her own with her husband's encouragement. Records of the colonial period show that women were active in every business activity open to men from apothecary to undertaker and that they received equal pay for their goods and services.

Under the law, of course, if the woman was married, that "equal pay" became her husband's property. Furthermore, any legal activity—contracting, suing, etc.—relating to a woman's business would have to be done in the name of her husband. In England such restriction caused no inconvenience, but in America it often did. And so the law had to bend. For instance, it was not unusual in the colonial period for a man to go off on a business trip and never be heard of again. His wife, still legally married, might find herself unable to take necessary actions with respect to her property. A woman in such a position could not get a divorce in England. But there were no ecclesiastical courts in America, and legal theory recognized that law could not be enforced where there were no courts to administer the law. So the province of Massachusetts adopted a law providing that if a person went to sea on a voyage from which he might be expected to return in three months and did not reappear within three years, his wife could be, not "divorced," but "declared single"—a state which included all the benefits of divorce including the right to remarry.

Even when legislatures did not intervene to extend the rights granted to women under the English common law, the absence both of courts and trained lawyers in America, encouraged the colonists to ignore the law when it suited them. The records are

filled with cases in which women were doing things that were clearly impermissible under English law. Women who were wives acted as though they were single. For instance wives might be counted as separate individuals and given grants of land by the colony. They sued in their own names and often acted for their husbands in contract and tort claims—an outright reversal of common law requirements. Occasionally wives joined husbands and brought joint actions. Americans came to recognize post-nuptual agreements, as, for instance, in the "truce" negotiated between the Custises in which they attempted to end their constant marital bickering. In this agreement Custis agreed that "all business property belonging to the wife shall be solely transacted by her" without his "intermeddling."[3] Colonial newspapers provide an interesting variety of illegal "legal" notices in which couples announce the terms of their own divorce 263
settlements or women announce that they will no longer be responsible for a husband's debts. Not infrequently even the form of law disappeared. When the wealthy widow Hannah Lee Corbin discovered that she would lose the estate inherited from her first husband if she remarried, she simply cohabited with her second mate, bearing several children without, it seems, causing any comment in the neighborhood.

The active economic role played by colonial women gave them political power significantly greater than that enjoyed by women in later periods. They never served as governors or sat in the legislative assemblies, however, so in contrast with Native American practices their political influence is less impressive. They did not exercise their political power by voting. But here it must be remembered that voting was a relatively insignificant political right in the colonial era. Before the Revolution, Americans believed that government was best left in the hands of an elite, the men they thought of as "natural aristocrats." Because of widespread land ownership in America, as many as 90% of the adult white male population were clearly entitled to vote. But most of these men did not go to the polls or voted as their social superiors suggested. For the record it should be noted that in the colonial period, since the right to vote depended on property ownership, women who owned property were legally entitled to the franchise. Only unmar-

[3] 4 VIRGINIA MAGAZINE OF HISTORY AND BIOGRAPHY 64-66 (1896).

ried women, at the time, could hold legal title to property, and most widows and spinsters were poor. Still, those who qualified might claim and occasionally exercise the right to vote. Hannah Lee Corbin, who certainly seems to have been quite a liberated sort, wrote to her brother Richard Henry Lee on this subject while he was a member of the Continental Congress. The estate left to her by her husband had made her a person of property and a taxpayer. She argued to her brother that as it was unfair to impose taxation without representation, widows should have the right to vote. He replied that they already had "as legal a right to vote as any other person," and if they failed to exercise it it was merely a consequence of custom not of law.[3] Before the Revolution only Pennsylvania, Delaware, and South Carolina had laws disfranchis-
264 ing women who otherwise met the property and residence requirements. Still, the custom that dictated that participation in electoral politics should be confined to society's "natural leaders" did, indeed, discourage virtually all qualified women, as well as most qualified men, from going to the polls.

In the pre-democratic era, most people relied on political organizations, rather than elections, to make their voices heard in the political process. Popular demonstrations, even violent mob actions, were considered the appropriate way for the "middling and meaner sorts" to influence political decisions. The first American women's organizations that we have record of were concerned with political issues. Not until the end of the eighteenth century did women's groups with exclusively charitable and benevolent purposes form. The colonial women's groups were counterparts of the male organizations that developed into the Sons of Liberty and later into political parties. Although women organized separately, their activities were virtually identical. Let me illustrate by describing how a group of women in Marblehead, Massachusetts influenced government policy during King Philip's War in 1677. The issue was what to do with Indian captives. The women believed that they should be killed. If they were taken alive, they felt, they would eventually escape back to their tribes and further attacks against the settlers would be encouraged. On one occasion two captives were taken alive and brought into Marblehead. One of the men responsible

[3] 2 The Letters of Richard Henry Lee 392-94 (J. C. Ballagh ed. 1914).

for the capture reported that a mob of Marblehead women "laid violent hands upon the captives, some stoning us in the meantime, because we would protect them, others seizing them by the hair, got full possession of them. . . . Then with stones, billets of wood, and what else they might, they made an end of these Indians. . . . They suffered neither constable nor mandrake, nor any other person to come near them, until they had finished their bloody purpose."[4] Similar—if less gory—examples of women's political activity can be cited for both rural and urban communities on through the time of the American Revolution.

Because the women of the colonial period were so much more
active in the economic, political, and even military affairs of their
time than the women of more recent times, there is often a tendency
to over-identify with these "founding mothers" and to set up the 265
American colonial era as a kind of feminist golden age. Let me
conclude by stating briefly why I think it would be misleading to
do so. First of all, in the European tradition, the status of women
in theory always fell short of full equity. The wide sphere of activity
colonial women enjoyed was theirs mainly because the need for
their participation was so great that laws and customs restricting
their activity could not be observed. The patriarchal traditions were
not abandoned. As one scholar, Mary P. Ryan, expresses it, colon-
ial women had "equality of function and dependency of status."[5]
Second, the circumstances that permitted women equality of
function were conditions of extreme physical hardship. Colonial
America lacked more than courts and lawyers—it lacked all the
comforts of civilized living. The restrictions on women's sphere
introduced in the late eighteenth century were accompanied by
growing wealth in America and introduction of the material com-
forts made possible by industrialization. Many women experienced
the restriction of their legal rights as an improvement in their
lives. Liberty and the opportunity to use one's talent for work to
the fullest are certainly satisfactions to be desired, but security and
physical comfort also have their attraction. In a feminist—in a
humanist—golden age it ought to be possible to have all of these.

---

[4] Axtell, *The Vengeful Women of Marblehead: Robert Roules's Deposition of 1677*, 31 Wm. & Mary Q. 647, 652 (1974).

[5] M. Ryan, Womanhood in America: From Colonial Times to the Present 22 (1975).

THE RADICALISM OF THE WOMAN SUFFRAGE MOVEMENT: NOTES TOWARD THE RECONSTRUCTION OF NINETEENTH-CENTURY FEMINISM

Ellen DuBois

The major theoretical contribution of contemporary feminism has been the identification of the family as a central institution of women's oppression.[1] On the basis of this understanding we are seeing the beginnings of a revisionist history of American feminism which challenges the significance that has traditionally been attributed to the woman suffrage movement. Aileen Kraditor and William O'Neill have suggested that the woman suffrage movement did not lead to female emancipation because it accepted women's traditional position within the home.[2] While attacking this "what-went-wrong" approach, Daniel Scott Smith has contended that suffragism should yield its claim to the central place in the history of nineteenth-century feminism to a phenomenon he calls "domestic feminism."[4] Similarly, in her study of the female moral reform movement of the 1830s, Carroll Smith-Rosenberg argues that "it can hardly be assumed that the demand for votes for women was more radical than" the moral reform movement's attack on the sexual double standard.[4]

These revisionist efforts are commendable in that they expand our sense of nineteenth-century feminism to include a much larger and more diverse group of women's activities than merely suffrage. On the other hand, I think they do an historical disservice to the woman suffrage movement. Nineteenth-century feminists and antifeminists alike perceived the demand for the vote as the most radical element in women's protest against their oppression and we are obligated to honor the perceptions of the historical actors in question. When considering nineteenth-century feminism, not as an intellectual tradition but as a social movement, as a politics that motivated people to action, twentieth-century historians are in no position to redefine what was its most radical aspect. What we can do is analyze the position of nineteenth-century women and the nature of suffragism in order to understand why the demand for the vote was the most radical program for women's emancipation possible in the nineteenth century.

I would like to suggest an interpretation of nineteenth-century suffragism that reconciles the perceived radicalism of the woman suffrage movement with the historical centrality of the family to women's condition. My hypothesis is that the significance of the woman suffrage movement rested precisely on the fact that it bypassed women's oppression within the family, or private sphere, and demanded instead her admission to citizenship, and through it admission to the public arena. By focusing on the public sphere, and particularly on citizenship, suffragists demanded for women a kind of power and a connection with the social order not based on the institution of the family and their subordination within it.

Recent scholarship has suggested that the sharp distinction between public and private activities is a relatively modern historical phenomenon. In his work on the evolution of the idea of childhood in Western Europe, Phillipe Aries demonstrates that there was considerable overlap between family life and community life in the premodern period. He traces a gradual separation of public and private life from the sixteenth century to the nineteenth century, when "family" and "society" came finally to be viewed as distinct, even hostile institutions.[5] This development seems to be have been clear and compact in American history. In seventeenth-century New England, all community functions—production, socialization, civil government, religious life—presumed the family as the basic unit of social organization.[6] The whole range of social roles drew on familial roles. The adult male's position as producer, as citizen, as member of the church, all flowed from his position as head of the family. Similarly, women's exclusion from church and civil government and their secondary but necessary role in production coincided with their subordinate position within the family.[7] A few women enjoyed unusual economic or social privileges by virtue of their family connections, but, as Gerda Lerner has pointed out, this further demonstrated women's dependence on their domestic positions for the definition of their roles in community life.[8]

By the nineteenth century, this relationship between family and society had undergone considerable change. Although the family continued to perform many important social functions, it was no longer the sole unit around which the community was organized. The concept of the "individual" had emerged to rival it. In the nineteenth century, we can distinguish two forms of social organization—one based on this new creature, the individual, the other based on the family. These overlapping but distinct structures became identified respectively as the public sphere and the private sphere. The emergence of a form of social organization not based on the family meant the emergence of social roles not defined by familial roles. This was equally true for women and men. But because women and men had different positions *within* the family, the existence of nonfamilial roles had different implications for the sexes. For women, the emergence of a public sphere held out the revolutionary possibility of a new way to relate to society not defined by their subordinate position within the family.

However, only men emerged from their familial roles to enjoy participation in the public sphere. Women on the whole did not. Women were of course among the first industrial workers, but it is important to remember that these were overwhelmingly unmarried women, for whom factory work was a brief episode before marriage. Adult women remained almost entirely within the private sphere, defined politically, economically, and socially by their familial roles. Thus, the public sphere became man's arena; the private, woman's. This gave the public/private distinction a clearly sexual character. This phenomenon, canonized as the nineteenth-century doctrine of sexual spheres, is somewhat difficult for us to grasp. We are fond of pointing out the historical durability of sexual roles into our own time and miss the enormous difference between the twentieth-century notion of sexual roles and the nineteenth-century idea of sexual spheres. The difference is a measure of the achievements of nineteenth-century feminism.

The contradiction between the alternative to familial roles that activity in the public sphere offered and the exclusion of women from such activity was particularly sharp with respect to civil government. In seventeenth-century New England, citizenship was justified on the basis of familial position; the freeholder was at once the head of the household and a citizen. By contrast, nineteenth-century citizenship was posed as a direct relationship between the individual and his government. In other words, patriarchy was no longer the *official* basis of civil government in modern industrial democracy. However, in reality only men were permitted to become citizens. The exclusion of women from participation in political life in the early nineteenth century was so absolute and unchallenged that it did not require explicit proscription. It was simply assumed that political "persons" were male. The U. S. Constitution did not specify the sex of citizens until the Fourteenth Amendment was ratified in 1869, after women had begun actively to demand the vote. Prior to that, the equation between
268 "male" and "person," the term used in the Constitution, was implicit. The same by the way was true of the founding charter of the American Anti-Slavery Society. Written in 1833, it defined the society's membership as "persons," but for six years admitted only men into that category.

The doctrine of separate sexual spheres was supreme in the nineteenth century and even sufragists were unable to challenge certain basic aspects of it. Most notably, they accepted the particular suitability of women to domestic activities and therefore their special responsibility for the private sphere, and did not project a reorganization of the division of labor within the home. Antoinette Brown Blackwell, pioneer suffragist and minister, asserted, "The paramount social duties of women are household duties, avocations arising from their relations as wives and mothers. . . . The work nearest and dearest before the eyes of average womanhood is work within family boundaries—work within a sphere which men cannot enter."[9] No suffragist of whom I am aware, including the otherwise iconoclastic Elizabeth Cady Stanton, seriously suggested that men take equal responsibilities with women for domestic activities. "Sharing housework" may be a more uniquely twentieth-century feminist demand than "smashing monogamy." To nineteenth-century feminists, domestic activities seemed as "naturally" female as childbearing, and as little subject to social manipulation.

Although suffragists accepted the peculiarly feminine character of the private sphere, their demand for the vote challenged the male monopoly on the public arena. This is what gave suffragism much of its feminist meaning. Suffragists accepted women's "special responsibility" for domestic activity, but refused to concede that it prohibited them from participation in the public sphere. Moreover, unlike the demand that women be admitted to trades, professions, and education, the demand for citizenship applied to all women and it applied to them all of the time—to the housewife as much as to the single, self-supporting woman. By demanding a permanent, public role for all women, suffragists began to demolish the absolute, sexually defined barrier marking the public world of men off from the private world of women. Even though they did not develop a critical analysis of domestic life, the dialectical relationship between public and private spheres transformed their demand for admission to the public sphere into a basic challenge to the entire sexual structure. Thus, although she never criticized women's role in the family, Stanton was still able to write: "One may as well talk of separate spheres for the two ends of the magnet as for man and woman; they may have separate duties in the same sphere, but their true place is together everywhere."[10]

Suffragists' demand for a permanent, public role for all women allowed them to project a vision of female experience and action that went beyond the family and the subordination of women which the family upheld. Citizenship represented a relationship to the larger society that was entirely and explicitly outside the boundaries of women's familial relations. As citizens and voters, women would participate directly in society as individuals, not indirectly through their subordinate positions as wives and mothers. Mary Putnam Jacobi identified this as the revolutionary core of suffragism. The American state, she explained, is based on "individual cells," not households. She went on: "Confessedly, in embracing in this conception women, we do introduce a change which, though in itself purely ideal, underlies all the practical issues now in dispute. In this essentially modern conception, women also are brought into direct relations with the State, independent of their 'mate' or 'brood'."[11] Without directly attacking women's position within the private sphere, suffragists touched the nerve of women's subordinate status by contending that women might be something other than wives and mothers. "Womanhood is the great fact in her life," Stanton was fond of saying; "wifehood and motherhood are but incidental relations."[12]

On one level, the logic behind the demand for woman suffrage in a country professing republican principles is obvious, and suffragists made liberal use of the tradition and rhetoric of the Revolution. Yet this is not sufficient to explain why suffrage became the core of a *feminist* program, why enfranchisement was perceived as the key to female liberation. I hypothesize that because enfranchisement involved a way for women to relate to society independent of their familial relations, it was the key demand of nineteenth-century feminists. It was the cornerstone of a social movement that did not simply catalogue and protest women's wrongs in the existing sexual order, but revealed the possibility of an alternate sexual order. Unlike the tradition of female protest, from the moral reformers of the 1830s to the temperance women of the 1880s, which was based in the private sphere and sought to reinterpret women's place within it, suffragism focused squarely on the public sphere.

In part, the feminist, liberating promise of enfranchisement rested on the concrete power that suffragists expected to obtain with the vote. Suffragists expected women to use the ballot to protect themselves and to impose their viewpoint on political issues. They anticipated that by strategic use of their political power women would break open new occupations, raise the level of their wage scales to that of men, win strikes, and force reforms in marriage and family law in order to protect themselves from sexual abuse, the loss of their children, and the unchecked tyranny of their husbands. The demand for suffrage drew together protest against all these abuses in a single demand for the right to shape the social order by way of the public sphere. No longer content either with maternal influence over the future voter's character or an endless series of petitions from women to law makers, suffragists proposed that women participate directly in the political decisions that affected their lives. "Like all disfranchised classes, they began by asking to have certain wrongs redressed," Stanton wrote. But suffragism went beyond what she called "special grievances" to give women's protest "a larger scope."[13]

In evaluating suffragists' expectations of the power that the vote would bring women, it is important to keep in mind the structure of political power in the nineteenth century. Political decisions were less centralized in the federal government and more significant at the local level than they are now. Herbert Gutman's analysis of the assistance which local politicians gave labor activists in nineteenth-century Patterson, New Jersey suggests that Susan B. Anthony's prediction that woman suffrage would win women's strikes had some basis in reality.[14]

Even granted the greater power of the individual voter over political decisions that would affect her or his life, suffragists did not understand the ballot as merely a weap-
270 on with which to protect their interests in the political process. They also expected enfranchisement to transform woman's consciousness, to reanchor her self-image, not in the subordination of her familial role, but in the individuality and self-determination that they saw in citizenship. This was a particularly important aspect of the political thought of Elizabeth Cady Stanton, the chief ideologue of nineteenth-century suffragism. It is developed most fully in "Solitude of Self," the speech she thought her best. She wrote there: "Nothing strengthens the judgment and quickens the conscience like individual responsibility. Nothing adds such dignity to character as the recognition of one's self-sovereignty."[15] Elsewhere, she wrote that, from the "higher stand-point" of enfranchisement, woman would become sensitive to the daily indignities which, without due appreciation for her own individuality, she ignored and accepted.[16] She developed the theme of the impact of enfranchisement on women's self-concept most fully in a speech simply titled, "Self-Government the Best Means of Self-Development."[17]

Given the impact on consciousness that suffragists expected from the vote, they generally refused to redirect their efforts toward such partial enfranchisements as municipal or school suffrage. Although these limited suffrages would give women certain political powers, they were suffrages designed especially for women and justified on the basis of women's maternal responsibilities. Their achievement would not necessarily prove women's right to full and equal participation in the public sphere. Suffragists did not simply want political power; they wanted to be citizens, to stand in the same relation to civil government as men did. As a result, it was primarily clubwomen who worked for school and municipal suffrage, while those who identified themselves as suffragists continued to concentrate on the admission of women to full citizenship.[18]

An important index to the nature and degree of suffragism's challenge to the nineteenth-century sexual order was the kind and amount of opposition that it inspired. Antisuffragists focused on the family, its position *vis-a-vis* the state, and the revolutionary impact of female citizenship on that relation. In response to suffragists' demand that modern democracy include women, antisuffragists tried to reinstate a patriarchal theory of society and the state.[19] The family, they contended, was the virtual, if not the official unit of civil government, and men represented and protected the women of their families in political affairs. Antisuffragists regularly charged that the enfranchisement of women would revolutionize the relations of the sexes and, in turn, the character and structure of the home and women's role within it. The 1867 New York Constitutional Convention expressed this fear for the future of the family when it rejected suffrage because it was an innovation "so revolutionary and sweeping, so openly at war with a distribution of duties and functions between the sexes as venerable and pervading as government itself, and involving transformations so radical in social and domestic life."[20]

Most suffragists were much more modest about the implications of enfranchisement for women's position within the family. They expected reform of family law, particularly of the marriage contract, and the abolition of such inequities as the husband's legal right to his wife's sexual services. They also anticipated that the transformation in woman's consciousness which enfranchisement would bring would improve the quality of family relations, particularly between wife and husband. Stanton argued that once women were enfranchised they would demand that democracy be the law of the family, as well as of the state.[21] Her comment suggests that, by introducing women into a form of social organization not based on patriarchal structures, she expected enfranchisement to permit women a much more critical perspective on the family itself. However, suffragists regularly denied the antisuffragists' charge that woman suffrage meant a revolution in the family. Most would have agreed with Jacobi that, if antisuffragists wanted to argue that familial bonds were mere "political contrivances," requiring the disfranchisement of women to sustain them, suffragists had considerably more faith in the family as a "natural institution," able to survive women's entry into the public sphere.[22]

Suffragists worked hard to attract large numbers of women to the demand for the vote. They went beyond the methods of agitational propaganda which they had learned as abolitionists, and beyond the skills of lobbying which they had developed during Radical Reconstruction, to become organizers. As suffragists' efforts at outreach intensified, the family-bound realities of most women's lives forced more and more domestic imagery into their rhetoric and their arguments. Yet suffrage remained a distinctly minority movement in the nineteenth century. The very thing that made suffragism the most radical aspect of nineteenth feminism—its focus on the public sphere and on a nonfamilial role for women—was the cause of its failure to establish a mass base. It was not that nineteenth-century women were content, or had no grievances, but that they understood their grievances in the context of the private sphere. The lives of most nineteenth-century women were overwhelmingly limited to the private realities of wifehood and motherhood, and they experienced their discontent in the context of those relations. The enormous success of the Women's Christian Temperance Union, particularly as contrasted with the nineteenth-century suffrage movement, indicates the capacity for protest and activism among nineteenth-century women, and the fact that this mass feminism was based in the private sphere. The WCTU commanded an army in the nineteenth century, while woman suffrage remained a guerrilla force.

Unlike the woman suffrage movement, the WCTU took as its starting point woman's position within the home; it catalogued the abuses she suffered there and it proposed reforms necessary to ameliorate her domestic situation. As the WCTU developed, its concerns went beyond the family to include the quality of community life, but its standard for nonfamilial relations remained the family and the moral values women had developed within it. The WCTU spoke to women in the language of their domestic realities, and they joined in the 1870s and 1880s in enormous numbers. Anchored in the private realm, the WCTU became the mass movement that nineteenth-century suffragism could not.

The WCTU's program reflected the same social reality that lay beyond suffragism—that the family was losing its central place in social organization to nondomestic institutions, from the saloon to the school to the legislature, and that woman's social power was accordingly weakened. Yet the WCTU, Luddite-like, defended the family and
272 women's traditional but fast-fading authority within it. Its mottos reflected this defensive goal: "For God and Home and Native Land"; "Home Protection." In 1883, the WCTU formally endorsed the demand for female enfranchisement, but justified its action as necessary to protect the home and women within it, thus retaining its family-based analysis and its defensive character. The first resolutions introduced by Frances Willard in support of suffrage asked for the vote for women in their roles as wives and mothers, to enable them to protect their homes from the influence of the saloon.[23] This was the woman suffrage movement's approach to female oppression and the problem of spheres stood on its head—women entering the public arena to protect the primacy of the private sphere, and women's position within it. Yet, the very fact that the WCTU had to come to terms with suffrage and eventually supported it indicates that the woman suffrage movement had succeeded in becoming the defining focus of nineteenth-century feminism, with respect to which all organized female protest had to orient itself. Even though the WCTU organized and commanded the forces, the woman suffrage movement had defined the territory.

Suffrage became a mass movement in the twentieth century under quite different conditions, when women's position *vis-a-vis* the public and private spheres had shifted considerably. Despite, or perhaps because of, the home-based ideology with which they operated, the WCTU, women's clubs, and other branches of nineteenth-century feminism had introduced significant numbers of women to extradomestic concerns.[24] Charlotte Perkins Gilman noted the change among women in 1903: "The socialising of this hitherto subsocial, wholly domestic class, is a marked and marvellous event, no· taking place with astonishing rapidity."[25] Similarly, Susan B. Anthony commented at the 1888 International Council of Women: "Forty years ago women had no place anywhere except in their homes, no pecuniary independence, no purpose in life save that which came through marriage. . . . [I]n later years the way has been opened to every avenue of industry—to every profession. . . . What is true in the world of worl is true in education, is true everywhere."[26] At the point that it could attract a mass base, suffragism no longer opened up such revolutionary vistas for women; they were already operating in the public world of work and politics. The scope and meaning of twentieth-century suffragism requires its own analysis, but the achievement of nineteenth century suffragists was that they identified, however haltingly, a fundamental transformation of the family and the new possibilities for women's emancipation that this revealed.

NOTES

[1]The clearest exposition of this is Juliet Mitchell, *Women's Estate* (Baltimore: Penguin Books, 1971).

[2]Aileen Kraditor, *Up From the Pedestal* (Chicago: Quadrangle Books, 1968), pp. 21-24. William L. O'Neill, "Feminism as a Radical Ideology," in *Dissent: Explorations in the History of American Radicalism*, ed., Alfred F. Young (De Kalb, Ill.: Northern Illinois University Press, 1968), p. 284.

[3]Daniel Scott Smith, "Family Limitation, Sexual Control and Domestic Feminism in Victorian America," *Feminist Studies* 1, no. 3/4 (1973): 40-57; reprinted in *Clio's Consciousness Raised*, eds., Mary Hartman and Lois W. Banner (New York: Harper Torchbooks, 1974).

[4]Carroll Smith-Rosenberg, "Beauty, the Beast, the and Militant Woman: Sex Roles and Social Stress in Jacksonian America," *American Quarterly* 23 (1971): 584.

[5]Phillipe Aries, *Centuries of Childhood: A Social History of Family Life* (New York: Vintage Books, 1962), especially pp. 365-407.

[6]Edmund Morgan, *The Puritan Family: Religion and Domestic Relations in Seventeenth-Century New England* (New York: Harper and Row, 1966), especially chapter 6. John Demos, *A Little Commonwealth: Family Life in Plymouth Colony* (New York: Oxford University Press, 1970), pp. 2-11.

[7]Morgan, *The Puritan Family*, chapter 2. Demos, *A Little Commonwealth*, pp. 82-84.

[8]Gerda Lerner, "The Lady and the Mill Girl: Changes in the Status of Women in the Age of Jackson," *Midcontinent American Studies Journal* 10 (1969): 6.

[9]Antoinette Brown Blackwell, "Relation of Woman's Work in the Household to the Work Outside," reprinted in Kraditor, *Up From the Pedestal*, p. 151.

[10]Elizabeth Cady Stanton, "Speech to the 1885 National Suffrage Convention," in *History of Woman Suffrage*, eds., Elizabeth Cady Stanton, Susan B. Anthony, and Matilda Joslyn Gage (Rochester, N.Y.: Susan B. Anthony, 1889), vol. 4, p. 58.

[11]Mary Putnam Jacobi, *"Common Sense" Applied to Woman Suffrage* (New York: Putnam, 1894), p. 138.

[12]Stanton, "Introduction," *History of Woman Suffrage*, vol. 1, p. 22.

[13]Ibid., p. 15.

[14]Herbert Gutman, "Class, Status, and Community Power in Nineteenth Century American Industrial Cities—Paterson, New Jersey: A Case Study," in *The Age of Industrialism in America*, ed., Frederic C. Jaher (New York: Free Press, 1968), pp. 263-87. For Anthony's prediction on the impact of woman suffrage on women's strikes, see "Woman Wants Bread, not the Ballot," reprinted in *The Life and Work of Susan B. Anthony*, ed., Ida Husted Harper (Indianapolis and Kansas City: Bower-Merrill Co., 1898), vol. 2, pp. 996-1003.

[15]Elizabeth Cady Stanton, "Solitude of Self," reprinted in *History of Woman Suffrage*, vol. 4, pp. 189-91.

[16]Stanton, "Introduction," *History of Woman Suffrage*, vol. 1, p. 18.

[17]Stanton, "Self-Government the Best Means of Self-Development," reprinted in *History of Woman Suffrage*, vol. 4, pp. 40-42.

[18]See Lois B. Merk, "Boston's Historical Public School Crisis," *New England Quarterly* 31(1958) 196-202.

[19]See, for instance, Orestes Brownson, "The Woman Question," in Kraditor, *Up From the Pedestal*, pp. 192-94.

[20]"Report on the Committee on Suffrage," reprinted in *History of Woman Suffrage*, vol. 2, p. 285.

[21]Elizabeth Cady Stanton, "The Family, the State, and the Church," unpublished manuscript speech, Elizabeth Cady Stanton Papers, Library of Congress, Manuscript Division.

[22]Jacobi, *"Common Sense,"* p. 108.

[23]Mary Earhart, *Frances Willard: From Prayers to Politics* (Chicago: University of Chicago Press, 1944), chapter 10.

[24]This process is described in Anne Firor Scott, *The Southern Lady: From Pedestal to Politics 1830-1930* (Chicago: University of Chicago Press, 1970), chapter 6.

[25]Charlotte Perkins Gilman, *The Home: Its Work and Influence* (New York: McClure, Phillips, & Co., 1903), p. 325.

[26]Susan B. Anthony, "Introductory Remarks," *Report of the International Council of Women* assembled by the National Woman Suffrage Association (Washington, D.C.: Rufus H. Darby, Printer, 1888), p. 31.

274 Note: I wish to thank Amy Bridges, Mari Jo Buhle, Ann D. Gordon, Linda Gordon, Carolyn Korsemeyer, and Rochell Ruthchild for their comments and suggestions on earlier versions of this article.

NOTES AND DOCUMENTS

"UNCLE SAM JUST LOVES THE LADIES": SEX DISCRIMINATION IN THE FEDERAL GOVERNMENT, 1917

By WILLIAM GRAEBNER

Early in 1917, the United States Civil Service Commission posted its regular notice of an examination for *male* stenographers for service in Federal agencies. A committee of women, assembled from offices in the capitol and each known for the ability to press a grievance, took the women's case to Senator W. L. Jones. With the energy and directness for which he was known, Jones challenged Secretary of Interior Franklin K. Lane to justify sex discrimination in his department. "What special reason is there," wrote Jones, "for filling stenographic positions entirely or almost entirely by men in the government service? Why should there be any discrimination against women solely upon the ground of their sex?" Lane handed the matter over to Chief Clerk E. J. Ayers, who turned directly to the department's thirteen chief administrative officers.[1]

The letters which follow, most written within a day after the request for information was received, do more than document the position of women in the Federal bureaucracy in 1917.[2] The confidence and authority with which their male authors both deny the existence of discrimination and define it away reveal how guiltlessly inequities may be perpetuated once the rationale is established, the needs of the system defined, and expertism

[1] *Washington Post*, Feb. 11, 1917, 14.

[2] The letters are in Record Group 48, "Records of the Department of the Interior," Office of the Secretary, Personnel Supervision and Management, 1907-1942, File 15-15-35, National Archives, Washington, D.C.

0023-656X/80/2101-0075 $01.00

harnessed to the service of the *status quo*. The *Washington Post*, in possession of several replies, brought an appropriately amazed tone to its coverage. Its headline read: "Uncle Sam Just Loves the Ladies."[3] Of the letters I have discovered, only that of William C. Taylor, Deputy Register of Wills, acknowledges the existence of sex discrimination (and then not in his own agency) and offers suggestions. His interest in retirement, while here uniquely tied to the relations between the sexes, was a staple of the efficiency-oriented Progressive era and was to come to fruition in 1920 with the Civil Service Retirement Act.

The protest responsible for these documents was vitiated in an atmosphere which assumed an enlarged role for women should the United States enter the World War. Even as women clerks
276 and stenographers sought to bring public attention to their treatment in the Federal bureaucracy, the War Department announced plans to employ women in the manufacturing of munitions in government arsenals.[4] The *Post*, the only daily which had thought the issue newsworthy in the first place, failed to keep its readers informed of further developments. One of its reporters, however, may have captured the essence of the larger story of discrimination in a mid-February interview with eighty-six year old Elizabeth Hyde, a clerk in the division of revenue of the Treasury Department. Hyde had come to the District of Columbia in December 1864 and taken a job at $800 per year. Twenty years later her salary was raised to $1200 and in 1889 to $1400. In the second week of February 1917, after fourteen years without an absence and possibly in deference to the recent accusations of sex discrimination, clerk Hyde was informed of her promotion to $1600.[5]

---

[3] *Washington Post*, Feb. 11, 1917, 14.
[4] *Washington Times*, Feb. 16, 1917, 1.
[5] *Washington Post*, Feb. 18, 1917, 10.

WASHINGTON, D.C.

February 1st, 1917.

Dear Sir:

I have the honor to acknowledge the receipt of your letter of the 30th ultimo, calling my attention to the communication from Hon. W. L. Jones, requesting information pertaining to the alleged practice of discriminating against women in the Federal Civil Service because of their sex.

It affords me pleasure to state that there is no discrimination against the employment of women in this office, the pay roll for the current month showing that sixty-two per centum of the em- 277
ployees are women.

I find that women are more amenable to discipline than men, and during my long experience in superintending employees, I can recall but two cases of women refusing to obey the rules or to improve the character or extent of their work.

What is the cause of the alleged discrimination against women?

It is with extreme reluctance and hesitation that I enter into a discussion of this subject, owing to the adverse criticism which is likely to be evoked by my views in this matter. However, you have asked for a frank statement, and in my opinion, the causes are as follows:—

1. The failure to put women on an absolute equality with men in so far as the Government Service is concerned.

2. The failure to install a proper system of work reports, showing the character and extent of the work performed by each individual, and to base promotions strictly on ability as shown by said work reports.

3. The proverbial cowardice of men when dealing with women. How many men can find courage to reprimand a woman? Science fails to give any data on this matter, and I do not find that even the renowned Hugo Münsterberg had time to settle this interesting subject.

4. How many superintendents or so-called chiefs are above the age of sixty-four? Should not the well tested rules of the Army and Navy, the warring nations of Europe, and industrial con-

cerns, to the effect that men over sixty-four should be retired from positions of direct responsibility of the management of employees, be adopted in the Civil Service?

Very respectfully,
William C. Taylor
Deputy Register of Wills.

* * * * *

DEPARTMENT OF THE INTERIOR

278 BUREAU OF MINES

January 31, 1917.

My dear Mr. Ayers:

Replying to your note of January 30th, transmitting a copy of Senator W. L. Jones' letter of January 18th addressed to Secretary Lane:

There is, as you know, no discrimination on the part of the Bureau of Mines against the employment of women because of their sex. In the Washington office of the Bureau the number of women stenographers, typewriters, and clerks is 15, and the number of male stenographers, typewriters, and clerks is 27.

At the principal field station of the Bureau of Mines, Pittsburgh, Pa., where the Bureau conducts most of its coal mining investigations, the laboratories and other work of the Bureau are located in a poor part of town in old buildings that lack proper sanitary and other accommodations. The Bureau has, therefore, never employed any women at this station. The Bureau's new half million dollar building near the Carnegie Technical School, is nearing completion, and as soon as the Bureau occupies these new quarters, due consideration will be given in filling vacancies to the selection of women for those positions in which it will be to the best interests of the service to employ them.

The personnel of the mine safety cars of the Bureau, which

travel about from one place to another training miners in the use of breathing apparatus and first aid methods, includes a stenographer and clerk, and from the nature of the surroundings and work to be done, it is obvious that these positions should be filled, as they have been, by male employees only.

With the exceptions of the positions in the Pittsburgh station of the Bureau and on the mine safety cars, women duly qualified for appointment are given the same consideration as men in the filling of vacant positions in the Bureau of Mines.

Very truly yours,
Van H. Manning
Director

279

* * * * *

DEPARTMENT OF THE INTERIOR

UNITED STATES PATENT OFFICE

January 31, 1917.

The Honorable
The Secretary of the Interior.

Sir:—

The Office is in receipt of a copy of a letter, dated the 18th instant, from Honorable W. L. Jones, United States Senate, asking to be advised as to the reasons for discrimination in sex in making appointments to positions in the civil service.

In reply thereto, upon the part of the Patent Office, I have to say that this Office is not informed as to any reasons which the Civil Service Commission may have for holding certain examinations open to men only, further than that the examinations are generally shaped to meet the requirements of the public service.

There is no sex discrimination upon the part of the Patent Office. There are, however, certain positions in the public service which can not be filled by women, and women, therefore, will not be selected for appointment to such positions.

Four classes of appointments to positions in the Patent Office, namely, assistant examiners at $1500, copyists at $720, laborers at $540 and messenger boys at $420, are made from lists of eligibles furnished by the Civil Service Commission.

The examinations for assistant examiner are open to both sexes, and no discrimination is made in the matter of appointments.

Stenographers and typewriters are selected from the male or female registers, in accordance with the needs of the service. During the year 1916, 20 males and 18 females were appointed copyists at $720, by selection from the civil service lists of eligibles. The score, therefore, has been quite evenly divided in the appointments to the 38 positions.

Women are not suitable for performing the duties pertaining to the positions of laborer, nor are they adapted to the position of messenger boy.

The following table shows the distribution of the clerical force of the Patent Office, according to sex:

Clerks,	Class 4,	$1800,	Male	9	Female	—
Clerks,	" 3,	1600,	"	5	"	4
Clerks,	" 2,	1400;	"	8	"	9
Clerks,	" 1,	1200,	"	23	"	107
Clerks,		1000,	"	27	"	63
Copyists,		900,	"	58	"	31
Copyists,		720,	"	30	"	20
			Total	160		234

Respectfully,
Thomas Ewing
Commissioner of Patents.

* * * * *

DEPARTMENT OF THE INTERIOR

UNITED STATES GEOLOGICAL SURVEY

January 31, 1917.

My dear Mr. Ayers:

In reply to your notation on the copy of the letter from Senator Jones, requesting information as to whether any discrimination against women solely upon the grounds of their sex was made by the Geological Survey: 281

As you are doubtless aware, much of the work carried on by the Survey requires field ability for which it is necessary to employ men rather than women. In the field branches, therefore, women necessarily are unable to meet the strain attendant upon constant exposure in all kinds of weather and in the strenuous physical exertions that are required of the geologists, topographers, and hydrographic engineers. There are on the rolls of the Survey 417 men, distributed as follows among the different field branches: geologists, 188; topographers, 140; water resources engineers, 74; Alaskan geologists, 15.

In the Division of Engraving and Printing, the work is necessarily of a man's type, requiring the handling of machinery, heavy lifting, dirty work and various trades to which men are especially adapted. The conditions under which much of the engraving and printing work is done is such as to preclude the employment of women. There are 126 men employed in the various non-clerical jobs in the Division of Engraving and Printing and no women.

The force of laborers, messengers, mechanics, etc., consists of 130 men and one woman. The character of the work performed is such as to practically preclude the possibility of employing women for the various duties.

From the above enumeration it will be seen that there are 646 positions in which, from the character of the work, the employment of men is necessitated.

Turning to the distinctly clerical jobs, the following table shows the distribution among the sexes of the different clerks:

Branches	Males	Females
Field	28	111
Engraving	3	0
Administrative	53	28
Total	84	139

It should be noted in the above table that the great number of males in the administrative branch is due to the inclusion of all the various administrative officers not attached to the field service, as for instance, the Chief Clerk, the Chief Disbursing Offi-
282 cer, the Chief of the Accounts Division, the Chief of the Executive Division, the Chief of the Division of Distribution, etc.

As throwing further light on this question, I have had the requests for appointment for the calendar year 1916 examined, and find that 128 appointments were requested. Of these, 35 were for females and 93 were for males. Of the requests for males, however, 14 were for geologists, chemists, topographers or hydrographic engineers; 23 were for laborers, messenger boys, mechanics, firemen, etc.; 38 were for assistant map printers, apprentices, compositors and others needed for the work of the Division of Engraving and Printing. As already stated, the work of these various positions requires the employment of men only. There were, therefore, of the clerical type of employee, 35 appointments of women and 18 appointments of men.

I think the above tables will clearly show that women are chosen for the clerical positions, in general, in preference to the men at a rate of about two to one and that so far as the Geological Survey is concerned, the spirit, as well as the letter of the law, regarding equal chance to both sexes is lived up to.

Yours very truly,
George Otis Smith
Director.

* * * * *

DEPARTMENT OF THE INTERIOR
OFFICE COMMISSIONER OF INDIAN AFFAIRS

January 31, 1917.

My dear Mr. Secretary:

I have received by your reference carbon copy of a letter from Hon. W. L. Jones, dated January 18, 1917 with which he enclosed a copy of a notice from the Civil Service Commission of an examination for male stenographers and typewriters. The Senator asks what special reason there is for filling the stenographic positions entirely or almost entirely by men, in the Government service, and why there should be any discrimination against women solely on the ground of their sex.

In this Office there are 65 stenographers and typewriters, of 283
whom 33 are male and 32 female. This is about the proportion which has been maintained in this Bureau since my incumbency, and I am advised that it is about the same ratio as existed for a number of years.

It is true, however, that male stenographers sometimes resign, but it is seldom or never that a female stenographer has resigned except in cases where they have married after coming into the service. We are, however, continually losing male stenographers through resignation, and they seem to be in demand in the outside business world. To keep up the present ratio between male and female stenographers, it would almost be necessary where resignations occur to call for male stenographers. I am not suggesting, however, that it is desirable to keep up this ratio, but we do find that the young men coming into the Office as a rule pursue courses of study in the educational institutions here in the city, which qualify them for high class clerical work. This is not the case with the female stenographers except in rare instances.

Answering specifically the inquiry as to why there should be any discrimination against women solely upon the ground of their sex, I can say positively that there has been no such discrimination in this Office.

Sincerely yours,
Cato Sells
Commissioner

DEPARTMENT OF THE INTERIOR

BUREAU OF EDUCATION

January 31, 1917.

My dear Mr. Ayers:

In reply to the letter from Senator W. L. Jones, dated January 28, 1917, which has been referred to this bureau, I beg to advise you that there are in the Bureau of Education subject to the Civil Service rules and regulations seventy-three employees. Of this

284 total number there are:

Men	Women
39	34

Of the above number fifteen are stenographers and typewriters classified as follows:

Men	Women
4	11

I believe the above statement will show that there is no discrimination against women in the Bureau of Education.

Cordially yours,
P. P. Claxton
Commissioner

* * * * *

DEPARTMENT OF THE INTERIOR

UNITED STATES RECLAMATION SERVICE

February 5, 1917.

Dear Mr. Ayers:

I have received copy of letter of January 18 by your reference of January 30, from Hon. W. L. Jones, regarding an alleged practice of discrimination against women in the Federal civil service when making appointments.

In the Reclamation Service preference has been given to male eligibles for appointment in stenographic positions on account of conditions that are found on many of the projects in the field. In the majority of appointments an understanding is had with eligibles before their employment that an assignment to any part of the field may, and frequently does, follow initial employment. The crude quarters on some projects render it inadvisable to assign women to those places as in many cases there is little privacy possible, or consideration given by the labor element to that sex, and embarrassment and discomfort would result. Whenever it is possible to foresee the permanency of locations and where either
sex would be satisfactory requests for eligibles are made accord- 285
ingly and selection without regard to sex is made.

Very truly yours,
A. P. Davis
Director and Chief Engineer

Married Women's Legal Status in Eighteenth-Century New York and Virginia

Joan R. Gundersen and Gwen Victor Gampel

A single woman in eighteenth-century British America possessed the same legal, if not political, rights as a single man, but when she married she became a feme covert, thereby undergoing a substantial change in legal status. Historians have disagreed on the meaning of coverture in the colonial period and in their assessments of the legal relationship of wives to husbands and to the system of law in general.[1]

English common law dictated the major terms of the judicial arrangements for the feme covert in the colonies. While some historians have accepted a literal interpretation of Blackstone's famous dictum that "the husband and wife are one and that one is the husband" to mean complete unity of spouses under the common law, others have rejected this notion.[2] The foremost twentieth-century English legal scholars, Sir William Holdsworth, Frederick Pollock, and Frederic William Maitland, have shown that married women often appeared as persons before the law in England.[3] Our research extends this argument to free white women in eighteenth-century New York and Virginia. We will demonstrate that matrons in

Ms. Gundersen is a member of the history faculty at Saint Olaf College, which contributed financial support for research for this paper. She did the basic research on Virginia. Ms. Gampel, who did the New York research, is a Ph.D. candidate at the University of Michigan.

[1] For positive assessments of women's status see Mary R. Beard, *Women as a Force in History: A Study in Traditions and Realities* (New York, 1946), 132; Elisabeth Anthony Dexter, *Colonial Women of Affairs: Women in Business and the Professions in America before 1776* (Boston, 1924), 190-192; Page Smith, *Daughters of the Promised Land: Women in American History* . . . (Boston, 1970), 57-76; and Richard B. Morris, *Studies in the History of American Law*, 2d ed. (New York, 1958), 200. For more negative assessments see Julia Cherry Spruill, *Women's Life and Work in the Southern Colonies* (New York, 1972 [orig. publ. Chapel Hill, N.C., 1938]), 340-366; Mary P. Ryan, *Womanhood in America: From Colonial Times to the Present* (New York, 1975), 34-36; Carol Berkin, *Within the Conjuror's Circle: Women in Colonial America* ([n.p.], 1974), 7-8; and Carol Ruth Berkin and Mary Beth Norton, eds., *Women of America: A History* (Boston, 1979), 4-15.

[2] Scholars continue to cite Blackstone as the "real" law and then note a few exceptions from Morris, Spruill, or Beard. See, for example, Linda Grant De Pauw and Conover Hunt, *Remember the Ladies: Women in America, 1750-1815* (New York, 1976), 12, 151-152.

[3] Holdsworth, *A History of English Law*, 5th ed., III (Boston, 1924), 520, 524,

these two colonies were active participants in the legal system, both because English common law was not as restrictive as has been imagined and because certain practices in the colonies deviated from those in England in ways that benefited married women.

We have chosen to compare New York and Virginia in order to broaden the scope of our study. New York was representative of the middle colonies in its rich ethnic and religious diversity as well as in the balanced nature of its commercial and agrarian economy. Virginia exemplified the more homogeneously agricultural societies of the South. New York's legal system had evolved from the grafting of English common law to an initial Dutch system. By contrast, Virginia maintained from the outset a relatively strong common law tradition. Our assumption is that if such different yet representative colonies exhibited similarities in the legal rights accorded married women and in the local implementation of the law, then historians can begin to develop a new synthesis regarding the legal status of the feme covert in colonial America.

The colonial practice of law was partly the province of amateurs and generally decentralized. Courts did not publish decisions, and legislatures were lax in printing and codifying statutes.[4] This introduces a basic paradox: while the decentralized and nonprofessional nature of the law encouraged local variations or commonsensical decisions, the only readily available written body of law was English. Thus pressures for variations and for uniformity existed side by side. The colonies did experiment, but an increased desire to comply with the British code accompanied the emergence of a trained legal profession. Women's legal status diminished by mid-century as conformity to British practices constrained the flexible colonial practices that had benefited married women. By the time of the Revolution this pressure had not managed to negate all deviations from English prescription, however, and thus to a degree, the Americanized law survived to the end of the colonial period.

A variety of sources cast light on the precepts and practices of law. Colonial statutes and English equity and common law doctrines provide a descriptive and prescriptive framework. To determine how the law actually treated the married woman, it is necessary to examine court, town, and probate records. We use several approaches to ascertain local

---

528-530. Pollock and Maitland, *The History of English Law: Before the Time of Edward I,* 2 vols., 2d ed. (Cambridge, 1968), II, 406-407.

[4] Virginia's laws were printed individually (slip laws) at the end of legislative sessions. Because it was so difficult to keep track of what statutes were in effect, the legislature started over from scratch twice in the 18th century (1705 and 1748). The first compilation of Virginia's colonial laws came in the 19th century. New York began publishing its statutes in 1691, but until 1751, when the first authorized compilation appeared, the colony faced a difficult situation. Some bills that had not passed were printed, and others that had been passed were omitted or misprinted, so that the legal information available in New York was inadequate. See William Smith and William Livingston, comps., *Laws of New York, from the Year 1691 to 1751, Inclusive . . .* (New York, 1752), ii.

practices. In Virginia we have looked intensively at the records for an area south of the James River and just west of Richmond. Originally part of Henrico County, the area later fell into Goochland, Cumberland, and Chesterfield counties. This locale seems especially appropriate because studies have suggested that the social institutions of Southside Virginia were less advanced than elsewhere in the colony. Thus if certain legal forms were followed here, it seems likely that they extended throughout Virginia. The same area provides a sample of wills that can be used to ascertain testamentary patterns. Because of the numerous ethnic enclaves in New York, we have surveyed records from all portions of the colony, including the Dutch areas of the Hudson Valley, the Puritan settlements on Long Island, and the heterogeneous society of New York City.

Our investigation explores both common and statutory law in relation to the following questions: Could a married woman dispose of her property, make contracts, or sue for debts? If widowed, was she named administratrix or executrix of her husband's estate, and did she become
288 the guardian of her children? Was the dower right enforced, and did husbands provide their wives with at least the minimum amount of real and personal property required by law? Did the colonists make any efforts to improve the legal status of wives? For example, did land conveyances change to benefit the feme covert? Last, with regard to family law, what economic options were open to the married woman? Our findings reveal that in every respect the New York and Virginia feme covert was very much involved in the legal system. Consequently, the traditional Blackstonian concept of marital unity does not apply.

Property Rights and the Married Woman

Women came in contact with the civil law in two general ways: in matters of property and contracts and of family law. In both regards, the common law definition of feme covert was the major disabling factor for women. A feme sole, the legal term for a widow or spinster, could convey property, make a valid contract, sue or be sued, execute a deed, and make a will. Technically, a feme covert could do none of these things without her husband's consent or participation.

In practice, in the early eighteenth century both New York and Virginia were willing to modify the common law restrictions when necessity or reason required. Three examples involving the rights of married women to dispose of property or to designate a guardian illustrate this flexibility. In 1709 the Henrico County Court in Virginia debated whether to admit an oral will made by Jane Durand. The court was unsure whether her husband (apparently a mariner) was dead, hence whether her will was valid. Lacking determinate information, the justices ordered the will recorded and an estate inventory taken; they also honored the woman's choice of a guardian for her child.[5] New York courts occasionally went

[5] Henrico County, Virginia, Order Book, May 2, 1709 (microfilm), Virginia State Library, Richmond, Va. Unless noted otherwise all Virginia county records are located in the Virginia State Library.

beyond English practice and recognized the wills of married women. For instance, under common law rulings a wife could not reserve the right to grant legacies from an estate placed in trust for her before marriage, even if her husband had consented. The Westchester County Court, however, honored and proved the 1759 will of Elizabeth Sands which began "By and with the advise and consent of my husband Samuel Sands, and my trustee Elisha Barton, I do make this my last Will and Testament."[6] Likewise contrary to law, Martha Smith of Long Island, though married, ran a very lucrative whaling business in the first decade of the century without resorting to equity law to declare herself a feme sole trader.[7]

Feme covert status, as interpreted by the courts of these colonies, permitted the filing of suits by married women if they acted jointly with their husbands. Court records from Goochland, Cumberland, and Henrico counties indicate that the joint suit was the normal procedure in Virginia. The Minutes of the Mayor's Court for the City of New York, 1707-1735, confirm a similar practice in that colony.[8] A joint suit covered all debts owed to a wife, whether contracted before or during the marriage. In all likelihood aspiring young New York law students learned this from a book of precedents which included the case of David and Margaret Jones. The Joneses were filing a joint suit to collect a debt of £50 incurred before Margaret married. Stephen Stockcum, the defendant, had refused to pay because he erroneously believed that, because a married woman could not make a valid contract, the debt he owed Margaret while she was single was no longer in force. The New York Supreme Court upheld the debt. Thus the would-be lawyers learned both that marriage did not invalidate contracts and that married women should file joint suits.[9]

The joint suit also served in Virginia and New York as the normal procedure to settle debts owed to an estate administered by a widow who remarried. In New York in 1736, for example, Gabriel Stelle and Margaret Stelle, widow of Isaac Carrie, filed together to collect a debt

[6] William S. Pelletreau, ed., *Early Wills of Westchester County, New York, from 1664 to 1784* . . . (New York, 1898), 163.

[7] Feme sole trader meant that with a husband's consent or a court order dispensing with the need for his assent (for example, if he had deserted her) a woman could go into business and make contracts, sue and be sued as if she were feme sole. See Linda Briggs Biemer, "The Transition from Dutch to English Law: Its Impact on Women in New York, 1643 to 1727" (Ph.D. diss., Syracuse University, 1979). Biemer believes that Martha Smith was able to circumvent English practices because of wealth and class.

[8] Minutes of the Mayor's Court . . . , microfilm, Reels MC3, MC5, Queens College Historical Documents Collection, Paul Klapper Library, Long Island, N.Y.

[9] Peter Saunders, "Forms of Sundry Precedents: Forms of Peter Saunders," microfilm, Box 5, p. 109, New-York Historical Society, New York City. This is a collection of 18th-century cases. Such books of forms were references for lawyers and training tools for students. Paul M. Hamlin, *Legal Education in Colonial New York* (New York, 1939), 66.

owed to Isaac. Likewise, a husband and wife joined suit to claim bequests made to the wife prior to marriage. "Cornelius Van Dyke who hath intermaryed with Elizabeth the Relict and Administratrix of Captain Silvester Salisbury Deceased" was co-plaintiff in a suit by Elizabeth to recover land given her under the terms of the captain's will. Rarely did a new husband sue in his own name alone for debts due his wife in her own right or as administratrix.[10]

Sometimes a remarried woman retained some independence of action as administratrix, executrix, or guardian.[11] In both New York and Virginia remarried women occasionally appear in court records as if they were still feme sole. Elizabeth Lavillain of Cumberland County, Virginia, remarried twice while administering the estate of her first husband, Anthony Lavillain. When she filed the final report, the accounting for each year appeared under her name alone. Her rapid changes of marital status had worried the men who had posted bond for her administration, and they had petitioned the court to require her last husband, Joseph Starkey, to
290 post bond for the estate. Starkey refused, and Elizabeth Lavillain Starkey presented the accounts alone. Clearly she had sole responsibility.[12]

The Dutch heritage of New York allowed another exception to English testamentary practices. Roman-Dutch law permitted husbands and wives to execute joint wills. By this system the wife automatically took immediate possession of one-half of the joint estate when her husband died. She also had the right to decide how the remainder would be divided unless the deceased husband specified otherwise. Often the joint will granted the remaining spouse the entire estate, the only restriction being a provision that half would go to the children if the widow remarried. In a sample of ninety-eight Dutch wills filed before 1700, half were joint. Unfortunately for New York married women, the custom rapidly declined in the eighteenth century, even though courts continued until the Revolution to honor any Dutch joint wills.[13] Perhaps concern over the

[10] This case is from Joseph Murray MS., Murray Collection, 61-64, Columbia Law School, New York City. Joseph Murray was a prominent 18th-century New York lawyer. The debt in the Stelle case was contracted in 1729. For the Van Dyke case see "Proceedings of the General Court of Assizes Held in the City of New York, October 6, 1680, to October 6, 1682," N.-Y. Hist. Soc., *Collections*, XLV (1912), 21-22.

[11] An administrator (administratrix) is the person appointed to handle the affairs of a person who has died without making a will. If the deceased has left a will, then the person (or persons) expressly or implicitly indicated by the terms of the will becomes the executor (executrix).

[12] The accounts showing her name changes were all registered in 1753. Cumberland County, Va., Will Book, Nov. 26, 1753.

[13] Robert W. Lee, *An Introduction to Roman-Dutch Law*, 5th ed. (Oxford, 1953), 63-69; Biemer, "Transition to English Law," 7, 250. The sample survey is from A.J.F. Van Laer, comp., *Early Records of the City and County of Albany* . . . (Albany, N.Y., 1918-1919), III, IV; Gustave Anjou, comp., *Ulster County, N.Y. Probate Records* (New York, 1906), 21-78; William S. Pelletreau, ed., *Abstracts of Wills* . . .

legality of these wills, more than anything else, led to the demise of the practice. Fear of a challenge led Margaret Van Slechtenhorst Schuyler to execute a new will in 1711. Her youngest son was "apprehensive that by the strict rules of the common law, the will made by my said husband and myself on March 4, 1683 [would] not be authentick enough to make such equal division among our eight children."[14]

In Virginia and New York, as in England, a widow normally became the administratrix of her husband's estate. By statutory law New York widows had first right (rarely refused) to administer an intestate husband's estate, and the courts upheld that right. In Virginia a wife also had first claim. Mary Anne Dutarte complained in 1709 to the Henrico County Court that Peter Chastain had been appointed administrator of her husband Lewis's estate before she arrived in Virginia. The court complied with her petition by voiding its earlier commission and issuing a new order naming her as administratrix. Nor did Virginia women give up their right of administration when they remarried. The courts did not name the new husband as administrator, although they might ask for new security.[15] 291

To mitigate the disabilities placed on married women under the common law, the courts and legislatures of the two colonies also provided protections for the feme covert consistent with English law by including her in statutes covering wards and minors. Every statute governing property conveyances, debts, or similar actions provided that femes covert, minors, and others unable to bring suit in their own names would have a period of grace, often as long as ten years, to bring suit when their coverture, wardship, or minority ended. New York statutes usually limited the period for legal action to three to seven years. For example, a 1710 act "for the better Settlement and Assureing of Lands in this Colony" gave a widow three years to bring suit or be "utterly barred" from redress.[16] Widows occasionally made use of these rights. In 1748 a

---

(N.-Y. Hist. Soc., *Colls.*, XXV-XLI [New York, 1892-1908]), I, 42-300, hereafter cited as *Abstracts of Wills*.

[14] Albany Court of Probate of Wills, Queens College Hist. Doc. Coll., Box 5; *Abstracts of Wills*, II, 73-74. See also David Narrett, "Patterns of Inheritance in Colonial New York City, 1664-1775: A Study in the History of the Family" (Ph.D. diss., Cornell University, 1981), chap. 3. According to Narrett, the shift from mutual wills to those made solely by men did affect the status of women of Dutch descent in New York City. Although the widows continued to inherit the same portion of the estate whether or not they made a joint testament in the period 1664-1725, there was a decline in granting wives sole administration of the estate. After 1751 testators of Dutch origin significantly reduced the amount of real property they bequeathed to spouses. Thus Dutch women lost the most in the transition to English inheritance practices.

[15] *The Colonial Laws of New York from the Year 1664 to the Revolution* ... (Albany, N.Y., 1894-1896), I, 9-10, 300-302, V, 616-617; Smith and Livingston, comps., *Laws of N.Y.*, 14-15.

[16] The period of grace for femes covert was above and beyond the statute of limitation governing the act. See, for example, William Waller Hening, ed., *The*

Goochland County jury awarded 5s. damages to Tabitha Evans, who had sued to recover her dower rights in land sold while she was under coverture. The courts also allowed married women to sue to protect their rights. Under equity procedures an adult "next friend" could sue to protect the rights of a minor or feme covert. Thus "Martha Clay wife of Charles Clay by Abraham Green her next friend" sued "the said Charles Clay" in Cumberland County, Virginia, in 1770.[17]

New York also followed English common law inheritance rules that protected a widow's property rights. If the husband died intestate, New York awarded the widow one-third of his personal property or one-half if there were no children. She also received her dower right to a life interest in one-third of the realty in which the husband had been seised during coverture. In other words, the widow enjoyed the use and profit of one-third of their land during her lifetime. On her death the property would then descend to the husband's heir-at-law. A statute of 1683 granted the dower within forty days, during which time a widow could remain in her
292 late husband's house. This law, however, was disallowed by the crown, and custom permitted the widow to remain as long as she desired. Necessity dictated that at times a woman enjoy the use of the entire estate during her widowhood, particularly when minor children were involved.[18]

The inheritance practices of New Netherlands helped to create a milieu that encouraged property holding and business activity among New York married women. Unlike the English law that provided a dower right as a widow's old age pension, the Dutch practice called for an equal division of marital assets. On the death of either spouse both realty and personalty were divided into equal shares. One-half belonged to the survivor, and the other could be disposed of by the decedent by will, or in the absence of a will would pass to the intestate heirs. As a result Dutch women not only automatically received half of the estate but usually a part of the intestate property. Several of New York's most notable businesswomen inherited their lands under Dutch custom. The introduction of English inheritance practices diminished the property rights of eighteenth-century wives, but the transition was not abrupt, since women who had inherited under the old Dutch system remained active in business for many years.[19]

A widow's share in Virginia was nearly identical with that under the English system in New York. For intestate estates, a Virginia widow

---

Statutes at Large; Being a Collection of All the Laws of Virginia . . . (Richmond, Va., 1809-1823), III, 522, and *Colonial Laws of N.Y.*, I, 712-713.

[17] Goochland County, Va., Order Book, July 20, 1748; Cumberland Co., Va., Order Book, Mar. 27, 1770, and Mar. 26, 1771.

[18] *Colonial Laws of N.Y.*, V, 616-617, I, 114-115.

[19] Lee, *Introduction to Roman-Dutch Law*, 82. Margaret Hardenbroeck, Maria Van Cortlandt, and Alida Schuyler Livingston all inherited large estates and businesses under Dutch customs. For a detailed account of single and married women owning and operating businesses see Jean P. Jordan, "Women Merchants in Colonial New York," *New York History*, LVIII (1977), 416-436.

received one-third of the personalty after debts were settled and a one-third life interest in the realty. If a man wrote a will, he could reduce his wife's share of the personal estate, but she could not receive less than the share given to a child. If there were only one or two children, the woman was entitled to at least one-third.

The difference between the dower one-third life interest in real estate and the unencumbered but variable share in personal property led to a unique feature of Virginia's inheritance law. In 1705 the legislature declared that slaves were real estate. The intent was to encourage landowners to consider slaves and the land they worked as a package, and provide for entail. Thus a widow would get the same share in slaves as she did in land. The numerous exceptions written into this law made clear that the assembly wanted slaves treated as chattels in every way except inheritance. The law did not work well, and the burgesses modified it in 1727 to make more explicit the wife's dower right to slaves (while vesting ownership in the husband during his life) and to prevent this movable property from leaving the colony before it passed into the hands of residual heirs. In 1748 the colony attempted to simplify inheritance by making slaves personal property. The inheritance statute enacted the same year, however, continued the widow's life interest in one-third of her husband's slaves rather than letting slaves pass to her as part of the personal estate. The crown disallowed these laws, leaving the situation as it stood in 1727. Thus Virginia widows had important rights to a one-third life interest in the family's slaves despite their lack of control of this property while their husbands lived.[20]

The law also protected widows whose husbands slighted them in wills. In both New York and Virginia, if the husband left a widow less than the share specified in law, she could renounce the bequest and sue for her dower right, the one-third life interest.[21] Women did exercise the right to claim the widow's portion when dissatisfied with their husbands' bequests. William Maxey of Virginia ordered that his plantations be rented out during his widow's lifetime and that she receive a feather bed, a horse with sidesaddle and bridle, a Negro girl named Doll, and £15 yearly for life. Mary Maxey preferred, however, to have a place to live and control of their four-hundred-acre farm. Accordingly, in 1768 she renounced the legacies and claimed her share under law.[22] She was not the only woman to take this step after mid-century, but the action remained rare. After 1750 an increase in the number of wills giving wives no interest in land indicates that women had something to gain by filing such suits, but the rarity of the suits reflects the fact that most husbands exceeded the legally required bequest.

[20] Hening, ed., *Statutes at Large*, III, 371-376, 334-335, IV, 222-228, V, 432-448, 568, VII, 118-120; Thad W. Tate, *The Negro in Eighteenth-Century Williamsburg* (Williamsburg, Va., 1965), 18-19.

[21] Hening, ed., *Statutes at Large*, III, 371-373.

[22] Cumberland Co., Va., Will Book, Aug. 22, 1768.

Under the rule of freedom of testamentary disposition, husbands could bequeath their wives whatever they pleased as long as they met the minimum dower requirements. Our sample of 131 eighteenth-century Virginia wills reveals that men usually gave their wives more than the statute governing inheritance required.[23] As the century progressed, however, the legacies changed from unencumbered ownership to life interests. There was also a trend toward granting more of the personal property and slaves to the wife while saving the land for the children. Increasingly, sons received the land and daughters got slaves or cash, reflecting a change from a more sexually neutral pattern.[24]

Only 6 percent of husbands in the Virginia sample limited their wives' inheritances to the period of widowhood, although such limitations increased later in the century. The phrase "what the Law directs," which appears in the will of Cumberland County resident Edward Bryer, also appears in a few other wills, underlining awareness of the legal requirements.[25] The shift from unencumbered interest to life interest, and the
294 more frequent use of limitation of property to widowhood, had great consequences for the freedom of widows to manage their affairs. It is

[23] The sample is not totally random. The wills, mainly from an area south of the James and upriver from Richmond, cover the years 1700-1780. They are part of a family reconstitution project that focuses on the French Huguenot parish of King William and uses a sample of English wills from the same locality as a control. By 1750 intermarriage was such that many English families were part of the King William network.

[24] Unencumbered ownership meant that there were no restrictions on transfer or sale. A life interest gave a person possession of the land for his or her lifetime, after which the land passed to another person already specified. Thus the person with a life interest did not have the sole right to sell the property. Before 1750, 26% of the wills left the wife a life interest, 14% made her sole heir, and 24% gave her an unencumbered share. The other 36% included wills of widows and widowers as well as those who received no land but were named executrixes of the estate. None were cut out entirely. After 1750, 41% received a life interest and only 3% an unencumbered share; 2% were sole heirs. The rest, 54%, included 8% executrixes only, while the rest were the wills of widows or widowers. "Dower" is the life estate to which every married woman was entitled on the death of her husband intestate, or, in case she dissented from his will, one-third in value of all lands of which the husband had beneficially seized in law or in fact, at any time during coverture. It applies to real estate exclusively. The data from Lois Green Carr and Lorena S. Walsh's study of Maryland bequests suggest a similar shift in that colony ("The Planter's Wife: The Experience of White Women in Seventeeth-Century Maryland," *William and Mary Quarterly*, 3d Ser., XXXIV [1977], 566).

[25] Henrico Co., Va., Deed Book, June 1744; Cumberland Co., Va., Will Book, Aug. 22, 1768. Daniel Blake Smith has found that after 1750 almost half of the widows with children were limited to bequests for widowhood in Albemarle County. On the other hand, before 1750 in Maryland the rate seems to have been closer to ours for Virginia. Smith, "Family Experience and Kinship in Eighteenth-Century Chesapeake Society" (Ph.D. diss., University of Virginia, 1977), 367; Carr and Walsh, "Planter's Wife," *WMQ*, 3d Ser., XXXIV (1977), 568.

possible that husbands came to put less trust in their wives' managerial abilities, indicating a changing attitude toward women. It is also possible that the men feared the effects of remarriage on the estate that would eventually pass to their children. Thus it seems that husbands increasingly worried that women would not be able to protect the estate after remarriage. There was no increase in the remarriage rate of widows to heighten this fear, nor do we find a correlation with any decrease in the availability of land.

New York men followed a more restrictive pattern than Virginians in bequeathing land to their spouses and were more likely to circumscribe their widows in other ways as well. The wills of New Yorkers were consistent over time, except for the years 1720-1740, with about two-thirds of the bequests being life interests. Between 1720 and 1740 the percentage of life interest bequests dropped to fifty-one to fifty-six, and the percentage of widows who were left no interest in land increased. Despite these limitations, in every decade at least three-quarters of the men bequeathed their wives the minimum or more required by dower and New York law.[26]

Similarly, although New Yorkers were more likely than Virginians to place such restrictions on widows as the loss of a portion of their legacies should they remarry, two-thirds of the husbands prescribed no such limits. In one common pattern the wife received the use of all real and personal property until the eldest son or all of the children came of age. At that point the widow normally retained only the use of the house or part of the house. There was a definite tendency after 1750 to bequeath a smaller portion to the widow and limit the household space she would occupy once the children came of age. New York widows relied on their roles as administratrixes of estates and as guardians of minor children to maintain their lifestyles. In these cases the estate often remained intact for many years. (As a result, when children came of age and the estate was divided, widows often found themselves in reduced circumstances in personalty and land.) The majority of wills followed the law and granted the widow her share of the personal estate. A significant minority of the women, 44 percent, received more than an equal share of the personal estate. Thus, although widows in New York were not as well provided for as those in Virginia, they still fared better than the minimum statutory requirement for both real and personal property.[27]

[26] The quantified evidence in this paragraph is based on a random sample of 120 New York wills drawn evenly by decade from the New York counties abstracted in the N.-Y. Hist. Soc. for the years 1700-1750. They are controlled for wealth and nationality. The figures for meeting dower limitations are a conservative estimate reached by combining those wills that specified life interest, a share, or the whole estate as the wife's portion. Conceivably, among those wills where the widow received "the remainder" could be some that would meet dower requirements. The percentage is also lowered because 17% of the wills could not be coded on this question.

[27] Christine H. Tompsett, "A Note on the Economic Status of Widows in

The grant of a life interest theoretically limited a widow's ability to alienate the property, but it did not eliminate the possibility of doing so in either New York or Virginia. Both colonies occasionally granted widows the right to sell land inherited under intestate laws and thus held as a life interest. The New York legislature passed several laws similar to the one of 1712 "to enable Mary Brat, widow, of Johannes Brat, late of this County Albany, to dispose of his Lands and Tenements, for Payment of his Debts, and educating his Children." The widows of both Richard Crego and John Parmyter successfully petitioned the assembly in 1715 and 1721 for permission to sell lots (one with a house) held in life tenure in New York City. The right to dispose of land was also granted to a widow who inherited by intestate succession. The motive of the legislature in passing these private acts was to aid creditors and children rather than to show respect for a widow's rights. Any holder of a life interest could sell it. For example, in 1757 Elizabeth Starkey sold for £150 her life interest in lands she held from the intestate estate of her husband Anthony Lavillain.
296 There are numerous Virginia deeds bearing the signatures of a widow and the heir to the land on her demise. These deeds conveyed both the woman's life interest and the future title in fee simple claimed by the next heir. The records do not indicate how the sellers divided the profits.[28]

Fortunately for married women, English law concerning land transfers proved cumbersome. Americans found the English attachment to an ancestral estate outmoded in a land-rich, labor-poor country. New Yorkers and Virginians speculated in land, traded estates to consolidate holdings, and sold worn-out acres in order to purchase fresh ones elsewhere. Under such circumstances a couple had to be able to dispose of any land brought to the marriage by the woman or acquired after marriage. In England conveyance of such land followed a circuitous procedure called a "fine and common recovery," in which a deed by the husband was accompanied by the wife's formal relinquishment of dower rights. Because a married woman had no independent legal existence, English law required a legal fiction to enable her to appear at court for a separate examination concerning her willingness to a sale. The process prevented a husband from selling the wife's inchoate property without her knowledge and consent, but it emphasized the subordinate status of a feme covert. About 1700 the colonies began to simplify the form of deeds, proceeding

---

Colonial New York," *N.Y. Hist.*, LV (1974), 328-329, establishes that as the century progressed widows found themselves in increasingly reduced circumstances because husbands bequeathed them less personal property and also because settlements of estates frequently required liquidation of some assets to pay debts. As a result, widows appeared on the tax rolls with less than a third of the valuation before their husbands' deaths. This probably exaggerates the plight of widows because tax assessors were inclined to undervalue estates.

[28] H. R. McIlwaine, ed., *Executive Journals of the Council of Colonial Virginia*, III (Richmond, Va., 1928), 448, 459, 414-415; Smith and Livingston, comps., *Laws of N.Y.*, 92, 116, 148; *Abstracts of Wills*, II, 77, 183-184; Cumberland Co., Va., Deeds and Wills, Mar. 28, 1757.

in a manner suggesting a conception of equality or partnership in marriage. The new form was the joint deed, an important modification of English law.[29]

The joint deed developed differently in the two colonies. While New York never enacted a joint-deed statute, Virginia made this method the statutory means of conveying land in which a married woman held an interest.[30] A joint deed named the husband and wife together as the sellers, and both signed the document. Following the English fine-and-recovery tradition, the wife was then examined to assure the court that she had not been coerced. Other colonies followed suit. In 1764 the Pennsylvania Supreme Court, for example, upheld the tradition in that colony of using the joint deed followed by a private examination. Maryland, too, made similar provisions in its laws during the eighteenth century.[31]

In Virginia the practice could vary despite the statute. Other forms of deeds are found in the records, but the joint deed was the most common. Occasionally, the wife's name does not appear in the document but is among the signatures. In other cases, the wife neither signed nor appeared 297
as a party in the deed, but invariably the court registered her private interview. County courts were repeatedly instructed to enter these interviews. Since the women did not always appear in court on the day the conveyance was registered, the records of the interviews are scattered throughout Virginia deed books, either separated from the deeds or squeezed into the margins of the entry. In a few cases the private interview did not occur in court, and a signed, witnessed affidavit was registered instead.[32]

New York land conveyances were even more diversified. A statute of 1691 and its amended form in 1771 provided only that no estate of a feme covert could be legally sold unless she previously (and privately) acknowledged the sale before a member of the council or a judge of the supreme, chancery, or common pleas courts. The examiner was to sign an endorsement to the deed certifying the separate examination. However, counties

[29] Morris, *History of Law*, 166-171; Mary Sumner Benson, *Women in Eighteenth-Century America: A Study of Opinion and Social Usage* (New York, 1935), 238-239. Joint deeds also were used occasionally in England.

[30] Hening, ed., *Statutes at Large*, III, 319. Ryan noted that some deeds had joint signatures and that some private examinations took place, but never stated that the law had changed (*Womanhood in America*, 28-29). Spruill also ignored the legal change (*Women's Life and Work*, 360).

[31] *Colonial Laws of N.Y.*, I, 247; Marylynn Salmon, "Equality or Submersion? Feme Covert Status in Early Pennsylvania," in Berkin and Norton, eds., *Women in America*, 102-103; Act of 1715 in Thomas Bacon, ed., *Laws of Maryland at Large* (Annapolis, Md., 1765), chap. 47.

[32] Deed of James Robinson to William Battersby, Goochland Co., Va., Deeds, Jan. 15, 1744/5; Susanna Robinson dower relinquished, *ibid.*, Nov. 19, 1745; Deed of William and Hester Lansdon to Thomas Turpin, *ibid.*, May 16, 1732; Power of Attorney from Susanne Michaux to William Randolph, Henrico Co., Va., Deeds and Wills, June 2, 1707.

pursued at least four methods in different periods. Some deeds before 1708 in the East Hampton town records suggest that the husband controlled all the property and conveyed it by himself. The deeds make no mention of any relinquishment of dower rights or power of thirds by the wife. Her signature does not appear, and there is no record of a private examination. After 1708 this type of conveyance lapsed in East Hampton, and probably few, if any, deeds of this kind were made elsewhere in New York.[33] Both the East Hampton town records and the Hempstead records of Queens County contain fine-and-recovery deeds. The wife is not mentioned in them, but she signed them and surrendered her dower rights. For example, "I Rachel Carpenter wife of John . . . do . . . give, grant . . . surrender up all my rights of Dowery and power of thirds. . . ." The court examined her privately, as required. The third and most popular form of conveyance in New York was the joint deed, which, as noted, used the same procedure as that in Virginia.[34] Last, in New York, the wife herself occasionally procured the conveyance because she lived apart from
298 her husband or because an antenuptial agreement had been made. Under English law a married woman could circumvent many of the common law disabilities of a feme covert through an antenuptial agreement that permitted her to retain control of property. New York women at times used such agreements. For example, by her marriage contract with John Tooker, Sr., Hannah Elton could "alienate, give and dispose of to whomever she pleases" all that estate "which at her marriage she brings to John Tooker."[35]

While the dower right potentially gave the married woman protection in real estate transactions, the common law provided less protection for personal property. On marriage, a woman's wages, livestock, clothes, jewels, furniture, and other income all became her huband's for his lifetime. Yet it must be noted that he could not bequeath her "paraphernalia" (personal possessions) to others. Even though New York and Virginia made no statutory provisions for this rule of paraphernalia, each strictly adhered to the principle. Examination of several hundred wills written in New York between 1745 and 1760 shows that no man willed such property to another person and that only one man bequeathed to his wife

[33] *Colonial Laws of N.Y.*, I, 247, V, 202-204. See, for example, *Records of the Town of East Hampton, Long Island, Suffolk Co., N.Y. . . .*, III (Sag Harbor, N.Y., 1889), 45.

[34] Benjamin D. Hicks, ed., *Records of the Towns of North and South Hempstead, Long Island, N.Y.*, III (Jamaica, N.Y., 1900), 493-496; Victor Hugo Paltsits, ed., *Minutes of the Executive Council of the Province of New York*, I (Albany, N.Y., 1910), 327.

[35] J. Wickham Case, comp., *Southold Town Records* (New York, 1882), II, 214-216; Anjou, comp., *Ulster Co., Recs.*, 29; *Abstracts of Wills*, I, 135-136, 270-271; Van Laer, comp., *Albany Recs.*, III, 271-275, 278, 285, 355-356. Virginia courts recognized separations. Spruill, *Women's Life and Work*, 361; Roger Thompson, *Women in Stuart England and America: A Comparative Study* (London, 1974), 179-180.

her own jewels and "apparell." The sample of New York wills from 1700 to 1760 reveals similar behavior.[36] In no Virginia will examined does a husband mention his wife's clothing or personal possessions, nor does the wife's apparel or jewelry appear in any estate inventory. Magdalene Trabue Chastain, for example, had several pieces of jewelry to leave her children in 1727, but these are listed in neither of her two husbands' estates.[37] The courts widely honored the rule of paraphernalia. Historian Julia Spruill found that seventeenth-century courts in the South recognized paraphernalia when selling estates, and Richard B. Morris found a similar protection in the North in debt cases.[38]

Thus in both New York and Virginia, custom and statute modified the common law concerning women's property rights. In general, the colonies took the common law concepts, such as dower, and extended them in ways that gave women more control over property than their English counterparts enjoyed. Similarly, practice indicates that women did not disappear as legal entities when they married but rather joined with their husbands to pursue legal obligations incurred before marriage. A remarried woman
retained administration rights but usually joined with her new husband in suits to recover debts. In practice, generous inheritances from husbands often left widows in control of a considerable share of property, while the honoring of a widow's rights to paraphernalia allowed her to regain control over personal effects. Life tenureship certainly limited these rights, but the widow was not stripped of her clothing and jewelry, nor could life tenureship prevent the sale of lands. Neither British common law nor colonial practice deprived the married woman of all property rights.

Rights within the Family

The legal relationship of wife and husband followed a pattern similar to that described for property rights. English practice was not totally restrictive, and colonial practice at times allowed even greater freedom. To assess the legal status of married women in the family we will focus on guardianship customs, economic rights, and powers of attorney.

While seeking to recognize the feme covert's property rights, neither New York nor Virginia tampered with traditional laws of guardianship. The common law gave the husband sole control of his children during his lifetime, and unless he specifically named someone else in his will, the courts gave preference to the mother as guardian on his death.[39] Virginia law authorized the father to bind out children to trades and to name guardians without the mother's consent. A New York father also had the

[36] *Abstracts of Wills*, V, 173-174.

[37] Henrico Co., Va., Deeds and Wills, Oct. 3, 1726, and May 1731.

[38] Morris, *History of Law*, 166-171; Spruill, *Women's Life and Work*, 360-361.

[39] Sir John Comyns, *A Digest of the Laws of England*, 4th ed., IV (Dublin, 1793), 276-280. Comyns cited a 1737 decision declaring that "children have a natural right to the care of their mother." William Blackstone, *Commentaries on the Laws of England . . .*, II (Oxford, 1765-1769), 435-436.

right to assign the custody and tuition of his children, born and unborn, to any person or persons he might select, either by deed during his lifetime or by his will.[40] However, the extant records in Virginia and New York indicate that fathers very rarely availed themselves of this right, and the provisions in wills confirm this finding. The sampled wills for both colonies almost uniformly, by their silence, left guardianship to the widow. Only one Virginia and one New York will took guardianship from the mother.[41]

Unless specific complaint arose or a child requested a different guardian, the courts left children with their mothers. Thus, in Virginia, Peter Anthony Lookado assumed that his wife Elizabeth would be their children's guardian without specifically naming her as such in 1768, when he left her a life interest in all of his land and estate "for the better support education and maintenance of my children."[42] New York husbands did likewise, and that colony's statutes clearly designated mothers as guardians of minor children in intestate administrations. The New York Chancery
300 Court showed a similar preference for the mother as guardian unless she remarried. A minority of wills made provision for the education and training of children. A few people, notably widows or widowers, eliminated the need for a guardian by declaring a teenage child of age. The one Virginia will that did specify a guardian other than the mother actually varied little from the norm. The mother, Judith Hughes, was the joint administratrix of the estate with guardian Jacob Michaux. When Michaux died a few months later, guardianship reverted to Hughes.[43] All the evidence suggests that women had control of their children in practice and that this was considered proper by courts and husbands alike.

Remarriage provides an important test of women's separate existence in law. Since coverture might limit a woman's ability to protect property eventually coming to her children, the courts had the power to intervene. Such interference was rare in New York. Before 1767 the New York Chancery Court heard only one or two guardianship suits per year. From

[40] Hening, ed., *Statutes at Large*, IV, 285, V, 449. In New York testamentary guardians were appointed by virtue of 12 Car. II c. 24, passed in 1660 and adopted in New York.

[41] The one New York will was Dutch, but this is a statistically insignificant part of the Dutch sample. Seventeenth-century studies suggest that Dutch men frequently preferred male relatives as guardians. See Berthold Fernow, ed., *The Minutes of the Orphanmasters of New Amsterdam, 1655 to 1663* (New York, 1902-1907).

[42] Cumberland Co., Va., Will Book, July 25, 1768.

[43] Kenneth Scott, ed., *Records of the Chancery Court Province and State of New York: Guardianships 1691-1815* (New York, 1971), 2-35. By law, orphan minors needed a guardian to maintain any action for an "infant legatee." Smith and Livingston, comps., *Laws of N.Y.*, 315-316. For children declared of age see the will of Magdalene Chastain, Henrico Co., Va., Miscellaneous, May 5, 1724. The guardianship transfer is recorded in the will of John Hughes, June 27, 1774, and Jacob Michaux, Aug. 22, 1774, Cumberland Co., Va., Will Book.

1767 to 1775 the court averaged twelve such cases a year. In 80 percent of these cases the court placed the children with the mother or stepfather, except in 1767-1768, when in eleven instances the court chose a guardian other than the mother or stepfather. If the mother sought guardianship, she received it. Only once did the court deny a mother's petition for guardianship, unfortunately without recording an explanation.[44]

Virginia courts took a more active interest in guardianship. The counties were empowered to hold special orphans' courts at which guardians were summoned to give an accounting of the administration of minors' estates. These orphans' court sessions gave the justices leverage to intervene. They did, but not to harass mothers.[45] Only once in our sample was a mother who had not remarried called to give an accounting. The Virginia justices, unlike those of New York, mistrusted stepfathers as guardians, and in the counties studied they seldom named a stepfather as guardian. Changes in guardianship in the southern colony were more a result of natural coming-of-age processes for orphans than of interference by the court because remarried mothers were considered unable to 301
protect their children's estates from stepfathers. Thus children changed guardians when an older brother or sister turned twenty-one and could assume guardianship, when they wished to assert independence from their mothers, or when minor women married. In all of these instances the young adult made use of common law provisions that allowed orphans fourteen years or older to choose their own guardians.[46]

Feme covert status did not prevent a married woman from participating in economic activities for her family or herself. The family, after all, was the basic economic unit of pre-industrial America, and the wife had separate economic duties within that unit. A few historians have questioned the extent of women's participation in economic affairs,[47] but evidence suggests that married women in New York and Virginia were active in at least three ways: as representatives for absent husbands, as managers of family businesses when husbands were present, and as operators of their own businesses.

The power of attorney gave wives a means to represent absent husbands or serve the couple's business and legal needs. The power of attorney was a common tool in the seventeenth century, but English pressure forced

[44] *Colonial Laws of N.Y.*, I, 145; Scott, ed., *Recs. of Chancery Court*, 2-35.

[45] The courts did not consider a father's control above question. The Cumberland County justices ordered Littleberry and Betty Epperson bound out because their father William neglected them. Cumberland Co., Va., Order Book, Mar. 23, 1756, Oct. 22, 1758, and June 27, 1757.

[46] *Colonial Laws of N.Y.*, I, 301-302. See, for example, the requests for guardians in Goochland Co., Va., Order Book, Mar. 19, 1744/5, Aug. 17, 1748, and Sept. 20, 1748. For requests of accountings see Goochland Co., Va., Order Book, Mar. 16, 1747/8, and Oct. 19, 1742. For a case where the husband became guardian see the request of Mary Farcee, *ibid.*, Mar. 16, 1747/8.

[47] For a negative assessment see Mary Beth Norton, *Liberty's Daughters: The Revolutionary Experience of American Women, 1750-1800* (Boston, 1980), 125-151.

the colonies to limit its use as the eighteenth century progressed. Official grants of power of attorney to anyone are rare in the records of Henrico, Goochland, and Cumberland counties, although married women occasionally used it to relinquish dower rights in a land sale.[48] It was fairly common in New York during the early eighteenth century for a married woman to appear as her husband's legal agent. In fact, the first case heard by the Supreme Court of Judicature on October 6, 1691, involved two wives representing their husbands.[49] Before 1750 there were numerous cases of New York women with or without power of attorney recovering debts, collecting rents, defending their husbands' good names, and suing to enforce their husbands' contracts. These examples indicate that there was more mutuality in marital relationships than scholars have usually recognized. It is significant, however, that such representation became uncommon after 1750 except among mariners' wives. Long absences of sailors made it imperative that a husband such as Arent King, "being bound to Sea with the Snow 'Dreadnought,'" appoint his "friend and wife, Jean
302 King, my true and lawful attorney."[50]

The number of women acting as agents for their husbands declined after 1750, owing chiefly to the increasing number of professional attorneys. The effect was to limit the court appearances of wives, especially upper- and middle-class women who could afford a lawyer, thus reinforcing ideas of a separate sphere for women that were developing among the "better sort."[51]

Whatever their standing in law, women were able to participate extensively in economic matters through informal agreements with their spouses. Thus wives acted as attorneys-in-fact for their husbands whether or not a power of attorney had been granted. Many women in New York and Virginia were helpmates to their husbands in business or on the farm.

[48] Spruill, *Women's Life and Work*, 347. Power of attorney of Susanne Michaux to William Randolph, Henrico Co., Va., Deeds and Wills, June 2, 1707, and Sarah Cocke to James Cocke, *ibid.*, Mar. 1, 1708/9.

[49] Paul Hamlin and Charles E. Baker, eds., "Supreme Court of Judicature of New York, 1691-1704," N.-Y. Hist. Soc., *Colls.*, I (1945), 255-258.

[50] Will dated Nov. 24, 1756, proved Feb. 24, 1763, in *Abstracts of Wills*, VI, 218; will dated Aug. 26, 1756, proved June 22, 1757, *ibid.*, V, 176. Morris stressed mutuality as a factor in the expansion of married women's rights (*History of Law*, 126).

[51] The colonies and Britain considered counsel a privilege, not a right; the accused was to rely on the judge for points of law, and innocence supposedly needed no defense in criminal suits. Civil suits were even less affected by theories of right to counsel. See Leonard W. Levy, *Origins of the Fifth Amendment: The Right Against Self-Incrimination* (New York, 1968), 375-377; Sophie H. Drinker, "Women Attorneys of Colonial Times," *Maryland Historical Magazine*, LVI (1961), 335, 351; Milton M. Klein, "The Rise of the New York Bar: The Legal Career of William Livingston," in David H. Flaherty, ed., *Essays in the History of Early American Law* (Chapel Hill, N.C., 1969), 394; and Klein, "From Community to Status: The Development of the Legal Profession in Colonial New York," *N.Y. Hist.*, LX (1979), 145-146.

Women could perform this role without knowing the complete financial arrangements of their husbands' estates. A surprisingly large number of wives were the business managers for their families. Thus Alice Christie Colden freed her husband for duties as New York's surveyor general, council member, and lieutenant governor (not to mention for pursuit of his interests as a physician and botanist) by superintending the family farm.[52] Virginia women performed the same roles. Canon law, for example, barred Anglican clergymen from doing manual labor, yet each Virginia parson had to manage a glebe farm. The parson's wife, rather than an overseer, sometimes assumed this duty, and the action excited no negative comment. Robert Carter, for instance, thought nothing of asking the Rev. Thomas Smith at church whether Mrs. Smith had 450 bushels of wheat for sale.[53]

Though common law disabilities prevented a married woman from acting on her own to make contracts, sue, recover a debt, or sell property, English equity law provided a loophole by which a feme covert could be declared a feme sole trader. What is interesting is how often both the 303
disabilities and the equity loophole were simply ignored by wives who acted on their own. Mrs. Smith, for example, had never been declared a feme sole trader, and yet Robert Carter transacted business with her and considered the wheat hers. Even the few instances where women petitioned for relief from the common law disabilities reflected the preference for granting married women informal rights rather than formal feme sole status. Susannah Cooper and Frances Greenhill both petitioned the Virginia assembly in the 1740s for private acts granting them the right to dispose of property because they had been deserted by their husbands many years before. Each woman had managed her family's affairs for over twenty years without formal feme sole status. The private act making Greenhill a feme sole in 1744 was disallowed (thus showing English disapproval of a formal change in status), but another, authorizing Cooper to dispose of her estate, passed scrutiny in England.[54] This gave Cooper the freedom she wanted without formally changing her legal status.

Wives pursued a number of economic activities outside the household in both colonies by informal agreements with their husbands. Among other trades, married women in New York were shipowners, merchants, shopkeepers, midwives, fur traders, teachers, and keepers of taverns, boardinghouses, or "disorderly houses." Even in New York City, where technically only freemen could conduct a trade or business, there was a significant number of married businesswomen. Only fifteen women were granted freeman's status from 1691 to 1728, and none after that date, yet

[52] Brooke Hindle, "A Colonial Governor's Family: The Coldens of Coldengham," *New-York Historical Society Quarterly*, XLV (1961), 237-238.

[53] Robert Carter to Mrs. Smith, Aug. 27, 1774, Robert Carter Letter Book, II (microfilm), Colonial Williamsburg Foundation, Williamsburg, Va.

[54] Henrico Co., Va., Order Book, May 2, 1709; Hening, ed., *Statutes at Large*, V, 294-295, 216-218. According to Spruill, *Women's Life and Work*, 362, the Greenhill case took place in 1752, but Hening lists it as 1742.

the newspapers make clear that many women were in business without special acts of Council or grants of freemanship.[55] Significantly, New York included women in the laws governing importation of liquor, sloop owners, and Indian traders, and used both "he" and "she" in all legislation concerning occupations. Also, although a husband jointly signed any apprenticeship indentures his wife might agree to, the indentures became void if she died before their expiration.[56]

Probably the most notable example of a married entrepreneur is Mary Alexander (died 1760), who bore ten children during two marriages while prospering in New York City as an importer of dry goods. So great was her dedication to her business that the day after giving birth to a daughter, according to her husband, she returned to her store and sold over £30 worth of merchandise. Thus neither law nor custom appears to have prevented a feme covert from making contracts or pursuing a merchant's occupation in her own name. Less well known is Elizabeth Journdaine, who in 1701 began importing a variety of merchandise while married to a
304 shipowner and operator. She remained in business after her husband died and continued to import dry goods and rum until 1729.[57]

Although it is difficult to explain the extension of women's legal rights to business management, the Dutch tradition in colonial New York undoubtedly helped create a positive milieu. The legislature recognized that single and married women (many of Dutch descent) were active in a variety of trades and occupations. Thus the statutes reflected reality by including women in all legislation governing occupations except that of surgeon.[58] Economic necessity in a labor-scarce society and the respect

[55] Minutes of the Court of Quarter Sessions of the Peace in the City and County of New York, 1691-1776, microfilm, Reels CMS1, CMS2, Queens College Hist. Docs. Coll. It is possible that the New York City charter passed in 1730 was interpreted to exclude women from freemanship. Widows of freemen were apparently granted the right to carry on a trade, though not permitted the status of freemanship. "Roll of Freemen of New York City, 1675-1866," N.-Y. Hist. Soc., *Colls.*, XVIII (1885), 54-118; "The Arts and Crafts in New York, 1728-1776," *ibid.*, LXIX (1936), 96, 271, 275, 324-325, 352.

[56] Smith and Livingston, comps., *Laws of N.Y.*, 326, 391-392; *Colonial Laws of N.Y.*, II, 207; "Indentures of Apprentices, 1718-1727," N.-Y. Hist. Soc., *Colls.*, XLII (1909), 582, 583.

[57] *Notable American Women, 1607-1950*, s.v. "Alexander, Mary Spratt Provoost"; James Alexander Papers, IV, fol. 5, 8, N.-Y. Hist. Soc.; Jean P. Jordan, "Women Merchants in Colonial New York," *N.Y. Hist.*, LVIII (1977), 416-418, 421-422, 436. According to Jordan, there were at least 106 women merchants in New York from 1660 through 1775 representing somewhat less than 2% of New York merchants. Though most New York women merchants were widows, some were married and a few were single.

[58] Lee, *Introduction to Roman-Dutch Law*, 71, 422-424; Fernow, ed., *Minutes of New Amsterdam*, I, 48, 50, 65, 170-171, 268, 315, 316, IV, 10, 139, VI, 86, 163; Alice Morse Earle, *Colonial Days in Old New York* (New York, 1896), 55; *Abstracts of Wills*, XXVII, 65-66, 389.

men displayed for businesswomen helped assure that women would not be barred from any of the governed trades and occupations.

The economic activities of married women in Virginia are less well documented, yet their activities could be essential to the prosperity of their families. Plantation mistresses sold fruits, vegetables, and poultry in local markets and did sewing, spinning, and weaving for neighbors. They received payment for these activities, but, like Thomas Smith's wife, did not request that the courts grant them feme sole trader status. The orphans' court records of Cumberland County reveal that at least two married women in that area had medical/midwifery practices. In the small towns and cities of Virginia some women ran businesses separate from those of their husbands. For example, the wife of Williamsburg printer Alexander Purdie was a milliner. Julia Spruill documented payments to Virginia wives who were in business for themselves in a number of occupations, including those of teacher, milliner, shopkeeper, and tavern-keeper. These women did not bother to have themselves declared feme sole traders.[59]

Conclusion

What did the legal codes and practices in New York and Virginia mean for the average wife? The evidence indicates that women were active participants in nearly every phase of the system. Colonial laws recognized the English principle that married women had property rights by protecting the dower and went further by encouraging the joint deed. In practice, as in England, the private examination forced men to be cognizant of their wives' interests in property and abide by their wishes, but colonial laws did not introduce the concept of legal fiction for married women despite its strong position in England. Occasionally, lawyers trained in English law used fine and recovery, but these deeds were exceptions in practice. In a number of areas, as we have noted, significant changes occurred during the eighteenth century. In general, before 1750, if the custom of these colonies differed from that of England, it was in the direction of simplicity and in favor of women.

By mid-century, however, married women in both New York and Virginia faced new obstacles. New York City women could no longer become freemen; the power of attorney was no longer a frequent tool for wives; husbands began to give their wives less control over property; widows found themselves forced to sue to gain the minimum bequests set by law; and women increasingly received smaller portions or life interests when their husbands died. These changes resulted from the efforts of lawyers to make colonial practices conform to those of England, from a growing inclination among American gentry to accept the English view of

[59] The estate administrations for orphans Mary Levillain and Margaret Bernard include payments to Mrs. Chastain for medical and midwifery services and to Mrs. Robinson as a midwife. Cumberland Co., Va., Will Book, Aug. 1755, Sept. 1756, and Aug. 1764; Spruill, *Women's Life and Work*, 258, 270, 279, 288-290.

the gentlewoman as an ornament, and from a variety of economic and demographic factors.

More restrictive interpretations of the common law by nineteenth-century jurists, feminists, and historians have obscured the actual workings of the eighteenth-century colonial legal system. The common law provided colonial wives with protections for their dower and paraphernalia as well as guardianship rights. Equity procedures could further mitigate the limitations of coverture. The records of Virginia and New York make clear that as need arose, these colonies staked out a larger sanctioned territory for wives and widows than historians have thought. The feme covert applied English precepts to good advantage and garnered further benefits from a pragmatic interpretation and application of the law by legislatures and courts.

RIGHTS OF WOMEN IN LOUISIANA

*By W. O. Hart.**

I did not know until I received the card announcing this meeting what my subject was to be, but thought it was to be "The Rights of Married Women in Louisiana"; however, as unmarried women of age and widows have never been under restraint except as to suffrage and office-holding, necessarily most of what I shall say will refer to married women.

We lawyers of Louisiana believe that next to the Constitution of the United States, the Civil Code of Louisiana is the greatest work that ever came from the mind of man, and most of those who complain of its provisions are ignorant of it and are too prejudiced against it to properly appreciate it.

Many of the inequalities under the law claimed by some opposed to the code relate to husbands as well as to wives; but when the complaint is made there is no effort to show that same are not intended as a rule as discriminations against married women. For instance, under the Civil Code as originally written and revised in 1870 (Article 1752) it was provided that a man or woman who contracts a second or subsequent marriage having children by the former, can give to his wife, or she to her husband, only the least child's portion, and that only as a usufruct, and in no case shall the portion of which the donee is to have the usufruct exceed the fifth part of the donor's estate. Now, I have heard advocates of women's rights in discussing this law, say the husband can give to his second wife not more than one-fifth of his estate and that only during his lifetime, while to a stranger he may give two-thirds, if he have but one child by the former marriage. But a second husband under this law is in the same

* A paper read before the Louisiana Historical Society March 22, 1921.

condition as the second wife, but this was never thought of in attacking the law.

I am glad to state that in the course of human events, this Article has been twice amended. First, in 1882, increasing the possible gift to one-third in full ownership, and then in 1916, so as to allow a donation to the second husband or wife to the same extent as to any other person.

Another Article of the Code (1753) also applied to husband and wife and provided that where a spouse who married again and had children by a former spouse, property coming to that spouse from the deceased spouse or from the children of the marriage should by subsequent marriage revert to the surviving children of the marriage, the surviving spouse in such a case having only the usufruct after the second marriage.

308 This law, which has since been repealed, worked endless hardships, a case now being under advisement before the Supreme Court where children are suing to recover property sold by their mother which she inherited from other children, many years ago.

Under the Inheritance Tax Law of 1906, the rate of taxation was less for ascendants and descendants than for collaterals and strangers and in the Succession of Baker, 129th La., page 74, the Supreme Court held that the wife or husband was to be considered on the same footing as a stranger regarding the rate of taxation.

The inequity of this construction was apparent and in 1912 the wife was placed on the same footing as children and ascendants and this plan is followed in the Constitution of 1921.

I simply cite these three instances, and there are others, to show that there are provisions in the law applicable alike to the husband and wife and to widows and widowers.

The Civil Code of Louisiana is based on the project of the Code Napoleon which Code is the basis of the substantive law of Continental Europe, Asia, Africa, Oceanica, the Islands of the Seas, (including the West Indies), excepting Jamaica and other British possessions, Hawaii and Newfoundland, but including Mexico, Central and South America and the province of Quebec, Canada, besides permeating the law of Scotland and many of the

States of this Union which were first governed by the laws of Spain.

It must be admitted that the original code of Louisiana was against second marriages for in addition to the two instances above quoted, Article 137 says:

> "The wife shall not be at liberty to contract another marriage, except ten months after the dissolution of the preceding marriage;

the purpose of the law being to prevent a child from having two fathers. The Supreme Court has held this law to be without effect, because it contains no prohibition. (Succession of Benton, 106th Louisiana, page 703), and a marriage contracted before the time fixed is legal and valid. It is perfectly apparent, however, that no person having the authority to celebrate marriage, 309
should do so in violation of this law.

I have heard it repeatedly stated that the wife had no testamentary power without the consent of her husband, but on this point, Article 135 of the Civil Code is worthy of quotation. It reads as follows: "The wife may make her last will without the authority of her husband," provided she be over sixteen years of age.

Wedding presents belong to the wife and not to the husband, even though they may have been given by the husband's friends and to him. (Allen vs. Segrave, No. 30,711, Division "B" Civil District Court, decided January 16, 1894.)

Later, this question was again before the Civil District Court, and was decided in the same way, when in the matter of George P. Lambert vs. Anna A. D'Hemecourt, his wife, No. 128,-298, Division "D" of the docket of the Court, on November 4, 1919, Judge Porter Parker, presiding therein, refused an injunction asked by the husband in the suit, which was for divorce, to restrain the wife from selling the wedding presents.

Usually, as we know, wedding presents, particularly when they are of money or of great value, are generally given by the parents or near relatives of the bride, and so well is the woman protected as to those that wedding presents are not subject to what in our law is known as "Collation." In Louisiana we have the law of forced heirship and equality of inheritance, so that advances made to one child, unless given as a separate portion, must be accounted for in the settlement of the estate of the donor, and may be reduced or entirely annulled if they exceed the disposable portion, but wedding presents are not subject to this law unless they exceed the disposable portion, and thus again is the woman protected. (Civil Code, 1244.)

In Louisiana "by dowry is meant the effects which the wife brings to the husband to support the expenses of marriage." (Civil Code, Article 2337), and by Article 2347 of the Code, "the dowry is given to the husband for him to enjoy the same as long as the marriage shall last." The dowry does not become the property of the husband, nor does it become community property, and "for the restitution of her dowry,—the wife has a legal mortgage on the immovables and a privilege (lien) on the movables of her husband." (Civil Code, Article 2376.)

310 By Article 2390, the wife, during marriage, may petition "for a separation of property whenever her dowry is in danger, owing to the mismanagement of her husband, or otherwise, or when the disorder of his affairs induce her to believe that his estate may not be sufficient to meet her rights and claims." For all the money that a wife brings into the marriage or gives to her husband after marriage, or the proceeds of property inherited by, or donated to her, she has a mortgage on his property, provided the claim be properly recorded, and, if the husband is in failing circumstances, while our law prohibits his preferring one creditor to another, this does not apply to the claims of his wife, for he may transfer his property to her in payment of her claims against him, even though insolvent, in preference to his other creditors, reserving of course, the rights of mortgage creditors, whose claims may have been recorded before that of the wife. (Neuman vs. Eaton, 27th Ann. 341.)

After the death of the husband, when there has been a community between the husband and wife, her linen and clothes are retained by her without any formality, and they form no part of the community estate. (Civil Code, Article 2416.)

Another statement often made is that a married woman in Louisiana cannot engage in business without the authorization of a Court,—was never the law in Louisiana; a married woman has always had the right to engage in business under her own name without the consent of anyone, and if she does so without being separate in property, then her husband would be liable with her for all the debts of the business.

Under Article 216 of the Civil Code, "a child remains under the authority of his father and mother until his majority or emancipation. In case of difference between the parents, the authority of the father prevails." How there could be any other rule I am at a loss to understand. There must be a head to all things, and unless one of the parents has the right in case of difference, the poor child would be in an anomalous condition, to say the least of it. After the death of the father, the mother cannot be deprived of the custody of her children, though she is not compelled to accept their tutorship, because the law gives her the right to let someone else be the tutor, though never depriving her of the custody of the children.

Article 253 of the Civil Code on the subject, reads as follows:

"The mother who refuses the tutorship of her children re-
tains the superintendence of them and the care of their educa- 311
tion."

The father has no such right after the death of the mother; he cannot renounce the tutorship (Succession of Watt, 111th Louisiana, 938). If a mother marries again, she cannot be retained in the tutorship save on the advice of a family meeting. (Civil Code, Article 254), which, however, is not, as is usually stated, "by the formal consent of her first husband's family."

The family meeting is composed of the nearest relatives of the children, both from the maternal and paternal sides, and the mother, who has the right to apply for the family meeting, may name other persons as friends of the minors, sufficient to out vote the relatives on the father's side who may be opposed to her retaining the tutorship after her second marriage.

Just such a case was that of the Succession of Carbajal, 111th La., page 944, where the relatives on the husband's side were in the majority, opposed to the retention of the tutorship by the mother, but the court, at her request, added her friends to the members of the family meeting sufficient to vote her the majority.

Even in cases where the mother loses the tutorship, by her remarriage, she may be reappointed after the marriage. (Succession of Faley, 34th Annual, 130), and in no event does she lose the custody of her children except for unworthiness. A trust company may be appointed as tutor of minors whose father is dead, but such appointment embraces only the control and administration of the minors' property, their custody remaining with their mother, if she be alive, and this whether she remarries or not and in such a case, one-half of the commissions allowed by law to the tutor, would go to the mother. (Act No. 45 of 1902.) Under Act 124 of 1888, when proceedings are instituted by the husband or wife for divorce or separation from bed and board, the custody of the children remains with the mother pending the trial, and even though judgment is rendered against her she may be allowed to retain the children, if the court believes it to be a greater advantage to the children or some of them. (Act 38, E. S. 1921.)

In the matter of Lasserre vs. Michael, 105th La., page 741, the Supreme Court held that during marriage "neither spouse had an absolute right to the children." (Civil Code, Art. 157.)

312 A married woman cannot become security for her husband nor can her property be used to pay his debts, and any judgment rendered against her she may annul upon showing that the debt sued for inured to her husband's benefit, or to the benefit of the community existing between them. If she wishes to mortgage her property she must be authorized by the court after an examination apart from her husband, and establish to the satisfaction of the court that the money to be secured by the mortgage is for her benefit or for the benefit of her property. If she mortgage her property without this order of court, she may show against anyone that the debt was her husband's, and even if she have the authority of the court and she has misled the court as to the use of the money, the mortgage will be null, unless the creditor who takes same and advances money on the faith thereof, shows that he had no knowledge of the nonverity of the court proceeding. (Civil Code, Articles 126, 127, and 128.)

And it is to the great credit of our present Legislature that notwithstanding pressure was brought to bear to repeal this law, it still stands and may stand forever!

Where there is a community existing between husband and wife, all the earnings of the husband and the revenues of all his separate property, including that owned by him before the marriage, fall into the community, but the revenues of the separate property of the wife do not fall into the community unless she gives the administration thereof to her husband, and she may recall at any time, that administration, after giving it. (Civil Code, Article 2387.)

When a husband, in Louisiana, dies insolvent, his widow and minor children are entitled to receive One Thousand Dollars out of the estate in preference to all his creditors, except recorded mortgage claims and if he die rich and the wife is poor, the wife is entitled to one-fourth of his estate in full ownership, if he left no children, and otherwise, to the life usufruct of one-fourth unless there were four or more children, in which event she would be entitled to the usufruct of a child's share.

Donations which a wife makes to her husband during marriage she may revoke at any time, and he cannot donate the immovables of the community without her consent. A few days ago judgment was rendered by our Civil District Court returning to a wife her share of community property donated by her husband, without her joining in the donation.

Some time ago there was an article published in one of our 313
newspapers, from a woman writer, stating that in Louisiana a husband might mortgage his wife's property without her knowledge or consent. This is absolutely incorrect. The husband cannot mortgage his wife's property because it is not his and, moreover, as before stated, to make the wife's mortgage entirely legal she must be authorized by the court, independently of her husband, to execute it.

It is true that during the existence of the marriage, community property, which embraces property acquired by the joint labor of the husband and wife, or from the revenues of the husband's property, or even from the investment of his separate property, unless in the act he especially declares that he is making a separate investment,—(See Sharp vs. Zeller, 110th Louisiana, page 61), and property donated jointly to the spouses may be sold or mortgaged by the husband without the consent or even knowledge of his wife.

From the foregoing it is perfectly apparent that the married woman in Louisiana has many rights over her property superior to those which a husband has over his.

Another forward step in protecting married women was Act No. 170 of 1912, making separate property of the wife, property which had heretofore in large measure been community property and requiring the signature of the wife where it was sought to sell or mortgage community property where the title was in her name. This act, which was prepared by Mr. R. E. Milling, reads in part, as follows:

"The earnings of the wife when living apart from her husband, although not separated by judgment of court, her earnings when carrying on a business, trade, occupation, or industry separate from her husband, actions for damages resulting from offenses and quasi-offenses, and the property purchased with all funds thus derived, are her separate property.

"Common property is that which is acquired by the husband and wife during marriage in any manner different from that above declared. But when the title to community property stands in the name of the wife, it cannot be mortgaged or sold by the husband without her written authority or consent."

Until 1902, damages recoverable for personal injuries to the wife belonged to the community and the wife was not even a competent witness in such a case, but by Act 68 of that year, all this
314 was changed so as to make such damages her separate property, and this provision was continued in the Act of 1912.

In 1916 there was passed Act No. 94, approved July 15, and which was amended in 1918 by Act 244, approved July 14, giving to married women the right of disposition over their separate property, the right to sue and be sued, and the right to contract and bind themselves, the act reading as follows:

"A married woman, whether a resident of this State or not, shall be competent to contract debts, purchase and mortgage, and to bind and obligate herself personally with reference to her separate and paraphernal property, and to appear in courts and to sue and be sued, to the same extent and in the same manner as though she were a *femme sole;* provided, that nothing herein contained shall be deemed or construed to affect in any way the statutes of this State, establishing and regulating the matrimonial community of acquets and gains, and prescribing what shall be deemed community and what shall be deemed separate property of the spouses."

The Court of Appeal for the Parish of Orleans in construing this law held that the wife could not bind herself unless she had separate property and only to the extent thereof but the Supreme Court in reversing the decree of that Court held that the married woman could contract in all respects except as security for her husband, the same as an unmarried woman. (Hicks vs. Caldwell, 148th La., 21, and Lorio vs. Gladney, 147th La., 930.)

The wife, however, was not powerless before this change in the law with reference to her separate property because she had recourse to the courts if her husband were absent, mentally incapacitated or refused his consent.

Under the Civil Code, (Art. 2406), at the death of either spouse, one-half of the community property after the payment of debts becomes vested in the survivor and no legacies made by the one first dying can affect this one-half, (Art. 915); if there were no children or parents surviving the decedent, the surviving husband or wife, as the case may be, had the life usufruct of the remaining half; if there are children of the marriage, the survivor has the usufruct of the share of these children, which usufruct terminates by a second marriage; by will, either of these usufructs may be excluded or the usufruct which would terminate
by a second marriage (Art. 916) be continued notwithstanding 315
that fact. If there are no children, but parents, the wife had no usufruct at all and the share going to the parents and the brothers and sisters, if any, went to them immediately at the death of the husband or wife.

By Act No. 57 of 1910, the surviving husband or wife, where the deceased left neither ascendants nor descendants, was given the full ownership if no disposition thereof had been made by will, of the share of the deceased in the community property and by Act No. 80 of 1916, if there were no children, but a father or mother, or both, then one-half of the share of the deceased in the community property was given to the survivor.

When before marriage the intended husband or wife make a marriage contract and therein the husband settles upon his wife certain property or money to be paid at his death, this is a debt of the succession and ranks any legacies that he may make in his will. (Succession of McCloskey, 29th Annual, 237.)

In suits for separation from bed and board, or divorce, the wife is entitled to alimony pending the suit, provided she be plaintiff, originally or plaintiff in counter-suit or "Reconventional Demand" as it is called in Louisiana, (Civil Code, Art. 148; Landreaux vs. Landreaux, 114 La., page 528), and such judgment for alimony, if rendered in a suit for separation from bed and board, extends until the wife has obtained a final divorce (Hill vs. Hill, 114th, La. 44).

By Article 160 of the Civil Code, the wife is entitled to alimony from the husband in the final judgment of divorce, which she may obtain, not to exceed one-third of his income. As originally written, the Supreme Court construed the law to mean that earnings were not to be estimated in fixing the amount of alimony (Jackson vs. Burns, 116th La., 695); but by Act No. 173 of 1916, the article was amended so as to provide that this alimony is payable "out of the property and earnings of her husband." This alimony, of course, ceases when the wife contracts a second marriage, or should it be shown that by reason of acquiring property in the meantime, she would not need the alimony.

Judgments for separation from bed and board or divorce dissolve the community as of the date of the filing of the suit, and the wife, whether plaintiff or defendant, in such a proceeding, is
316 entitled to an immediate settlement and division of the community
property by partition proceedings or otherwise.

In 1888 by Act of the Legislature of that year No. 150, approved July 12th: money or other property deposited in savings banks by married women—could be drawn out by them upon their own order or signature without other authorization.

This privilege was repeated in Act 95 of 1892, approved July 7, and by Act 63 of 1896, approved July 8, the rights of married women in this regard greatly extended in the following words:

"Any married woman shall have the right to open accounts in the different banks of this State, whether National or State banks, and in savings banks, and deposit money, checks, notes and other funds therein, and to withdraw the same by check or otherwise and without the assistance or intervention of her husband in the same manner and under the same conditions as if she was a *femme sole* or unmarried woman."

The general banking law was again amended by Act 189 of 1902, approved July 10th, and the same right was continued for married women over their deposits.

By Act 74 of 1894 approved July 7, married women were authorized to subscribe for, withdraw, or transfer, stock of building, homestead or loan association, and to deposit funds with and withdraw the same from any such association without the assistance or intervention of their husbands and in the general homestead Act No. 120 of 1902, approved July 8th, the same right was given.

Another act of great benefit to married women is Act No. 157 of 1916, approved July 5, repealing in large measure, Article 2281 of the Civil Code, which prohibited husbands and wives from testifying for and against each other; the effect of this act is to enable married women to secure many of their rights before denied to them owing to their inability to testify against their husbands.

While of little importance, women in 1908 were made competent witnesses to wills (Act No. 30) and other legal documents (Act No. 67) and in 1921 to inventories (Act No. 43, E. S.)

Probably the greatest step forward in the interest of married women is contained in Act No. 35 of the Extra Session of 1921 providing: "The designation and declaration of the family home and the manner in which the same shall be placed on record, alienated or encumbered." The effect of this Act is to preserve 317
the family home when duly designated and the designation recorded, and to prevent any sale or mortgage thereof during the marriage, by the husband without the consent of his wife.

The Constitutional Convention of 1921 was very unkind to widows of Confederate soldiers and I cannot understand how the three women members of that Body overlooked this injustice.

Under the Constitutional Amendments in force when the Convention of 1921 met, it was provided that widows of Confederate soldiers who had lived in Louisiana for five years were entitled to pensions from the State no matter from what state their husbands had enlisted nor where they had resided nor where they had died and further, that any Confederate widow marrying a Confederate Veteran for the second time would be entitled to a pension after his death.

Under the present Constitution, all widows' pensions cease upon remarriage without exception, and no widow of a Confederate veteran is entitled to a pension unless her husband was a resident of Louisiana at the time of his death.

Of all the travesties on Louisiana law, the greatest is the decision given a few months ago by then United States Attorney General Palmer, when he held in effect that community property in Louisiana was, during the existence of the community, owned one-half by the husband and the other half by the wife, and that therefore, income from community property should be divided into two parts, the husband to pay taxes on one half and the wife on the other half.

In Louisiana, community property in law belongs to the ideal being called "the Community"; in fact, it belongs to the husband, who has the control, administration, dominion, and disposition thereof with the single exception above noted, that he cannot donate the immovable property of the community without the consent of his wife.

The wife has not the slightest interest in community property during the existence of the marriage. She cannot administer it, except as the agent of her husband; she does not control it, she cannot dispose of it and she cannot touch a dollar of its revenues; payment of a community debt to a wife does not discharge the debtor, who is still liable to the husband; therefore, even if community property did belong half to the husband and half to the wife, which it does not, the decision of the learned former
318 Attorney General is entirely without foundation because income taxes are levied not on property but on income, and as before stated, the wife has not the slightest interest in the income of community property. It is absolutely certain that this decision will be recalled and where possible, back income taxes will be collected on community incomes as a whole.

It would be just as logical to say that the rights of dower, which wives have in most if not in all of the common law States, in the property of their husbands give them an ownership in such property before the dissolution of the marriage.

As the community income belongs to the husband and the tax thereon is a community debt, the wife, under the laws of Louisiana, could be responsible for no part thereof, even if she had separate property, because the separate property of the wife is in no case liable for community debts.

I think it will be found on examination that in cases where the separate returns have been made for community income, that the wife paid no part of the income taxes thereon, but that the husband paid them all and from community funds belonging to him. I know nothing about the laws in other States where the community of property exists and I speak only of Louisiana.

Several acts were passed by the Legislature in 1921, giving greater rights to women but I think some of them fall short of what was intended. Under the laws contained in the Civil Code, the only woman who can hold the office of Curatrix, as it is called in Louisiana, (meaning guardian or committee in other

States), of an insane person, or "interdict" as such person is called in Louisiana after judgment of court declaring insanity to exist, was the wife as to the husband, and Act No. 34 of the Extra Session of 1921, conferring certain rights upon women I do not believe confers the right to the position of Curatrix and Under-Curatrix, which office to a certain extent, is a check upon the other.

The law as introduced in the Legislature, reads as follows:

"Women are hereby given the same rights, authority, privileges, and immunities, and are required to perform the same obligations and duties, under the law, as men possess and are required to perform, in the holding of office."

This law, as introduced, in my judgment was entirely unneecssary because the adoption of the Nineteenth Amendment 319
had the effect of striking from the Constitutional and Statutory provisions of every State the word "male" insofar as the use of it had confined suffrage and office-holding to males, because in passing upon the Fifteenth Amendment to the Constitution, the Supreme Court of the United States held that its effect was to strike out the word "white" from all State Constitutions and laws so as to give persons of color the same rights of suffrage that white people had previous to the adoption of the amendment, and the wording of the two amendments is practically the same.

I know it has been argued by some that the right to vote does not carry with it the right to hold office, but it does in Louisiana. Under the Constitution of 1879 not only were citizens of the United States allowed to vote, but foreigners were so allowed, who had declared their intention to become citizens, but had not been naturalized. I am glad to say that this provision is not in the Constitution of 1898, 1913 and 1921, though it is in the Constitutions of several of the States of the Union with the result that during the Great World War some persons holding office under the States in which they lived were registered enemies of the United States.

In the case of Leche vs. Fowler, 41st Louisiana Annual, page 380, decided in 1889, the Supreme Court held, as follows:

"The defendant was elected to the office of coroner at the last general State election. He has all the qualifications of an elector prescribed by Art. 185 of the State Constitution.

"Previous to his election he had declared his intention to become a citizen of the United States, but he has never been naturalized. For this reason it is urged he is not a citizen of the United States, and therefore not a citizen of the State.

"A person who is a citizen of the United States is necessarily a citizen of the particular State in which he resides. But a person may be a citizen of a particular State and not a citizen of the United States. To hold otherwise would be to deny to the State the highest exercise of its sovereignty, the right to declare who are its citizens.

"The sovereignty of the citizens of a republic has its highest assertion in representative government, and is constituted in its political order in the representation of persons, and not classes or of interests. In the realization of this soverignty of the peo-
320 ple, its expression is obtained through some law regulative of political action by which the will of the people can be obtained. This is done through the instrumentality of qualified electors, who in the exercise of a free will, assert in conformity to that law the determination of the civil and political organization in which is manifested the will of the people. Electoral right is a political right and although the right to vote is primarily the right of every citizen, yet it may be denied to a certain class of individuals. Therefore a person may be a citizen of the State and may not be invested with electoral power. It is, however, difficult to conceive how a person can be an elector and not a citizen of the community in which he exercises the right to vote. The State in the exercise of its soverignty, can confer the right to vote, can make an alien an elector, and electoral power, when thus bestowed and exercised, becomes one of the most important duties and the highest and proudest privileges of citizenship.

"The elector is, therefore, one of the sovereign people, a member of the civil State and entitled to all its privileges.

"The Constitution of the State makes no distinction between citizen and elector. The words are used to signify the same thing."

And this decision was expressly affirmed a few months later in the case of Di Carlo vs. Abbott, 41st Louisiana Annual, 1096.

Therefore in this State women are eligible to every office from Governor and Chief Justice down where they have the qualifications therefor as prescribed in the Constitution and laws.

To return to the Act No. 34, I find from an inspection of the Journals that the act was amended in the Senate, so as to add thereto, these words:

"Including the civil functions of tutor, under-tutor, administrator, executor, arbitrator, notary public, and member of family meeting."

The inclusion of the words "notary public" in this act amounts to nothing because as a Notary Public is an officer under the laws of Louisiana, the right of a woman to hold that office became absolute when the Nineteenth Amendment was adopted.

While ordinarily words of enumeration in a statute are not exclusive, I do not think that rule applies when the descriptive words are offered as an amendment to an act pending before the Legislature, because in such a case the words showing the intention of the Legislature to go no further must be considered as 321
complete in themselves.

This observation applies with greater force to this law because about the time it was adopted by the Senate, another bill giving in express terms the right of women to be appointed Curatrix and Under-Curatrix, was withdrawn from the files of the Senate and these two actions of the Legislature considered together clearly show that it was not the intention of the Legislature to bestow that civil function upon women.

The Nineteenth Amendment required no enabling act, either of Congress or of any State to put its provisions into effect; the very moment the Secretary of State of the United States by proclamation announced that the requisite number of States had ratified the Amendment, it became part of the Supreme Law of the land. The State of Maryland claimed that having rejected the Nineteenth Amendment, it could have no effect in that State until the State had adopted legislation to carry it into effect but it is needless to say that the Supreme Court of the United States gave no heed to this contention.

The claim of the State of Maryland represented nuilification in its baldest form. If a Constitutional Amendment of or Act of Congress is not effective in a particular State unless that State be willing, then the United States would be driven to the condition it was in before the adoption of the Constitution of the United States, when under the articles of Confederation acts of the Continental Congress were little more than advisory to the States.

Louisiana early took notice of the adoption of the Nineteenth Amendment. In the Constitutional Convention held in this state last year, there were three women members. There are several women who are Notaries Public, Clerks of Court, on various Boards, and who hold other offices of trust and responsibility; but even before this, women held important public offices in this State. The offices of State Librarian and its two assistants have been filled by women for many years; and we have had a Factory Inspector in New Orleans, for more than a decade, who is a woman, and this last was done under an amendment to the Constitution of the State.

Some of the Truant Officers in the Juvenile Court are women and there has been a Matron in our Parish Prison (County Jail), ever since one was found willing to accept the position.

322 The proposed Twentieth Amendment to the Constitution, reads as follows:

"No political, civil, or legal disabilities or inequalities on account of sex or on account of marriage unless applying to both sexes, shall exist within the United States, or any place subject to the jurisdiction thereof."

I have already shown that no political disabilities or inequalities now exist in this country by reason of sex and marriage has no effect on such rights or absence of rights. What is meant by "civil or legal disabilities" in the Twentieth Amendment, it is hard to determine and will require construction from the courts, if the amendment should be adopted, before their meaning can be fully known. The Constitution of the United States was adopted in 1789 and we do not yet know what all of its provisions mean.

Very recently the Supreme Court of the United States held that the power of Congress to regulate commerce between the several States and with foreign countries carries with it the right to regulate commerce within the States and thus another of the rights reserved to the States has been swept away by Congressional and Judicial Action.

The objects and purposes of the Fourteenth Amendment to the Constitution of the United States, which was adopted with a view of giving some rights to former slaves, have been lost sight of in the course of time and the amendment now represents "the bulwark of the trusts."

If the proposed Twentieth Amendment is intended to mean that there are no disabilities or inequalities special to sex or married women, then many of the laws passed in the different states and some by Congress representing special legislation in favor of women, shorter hours, one day's rest in seven, prohibited employments, maternity legislation and the like, would probably be declared unconstitutional and not at the request of any women benefited thereby but at the request of corporations who do not want their labor regulated.

The two child labor laws enacted by Congress have been declared unconstitutional and by the same Judge and his opinion in the first case was affirmed by the Supreme Court of the United States, which has not yet passed on the second case; but this attack was not made by any one for the benefit of the child, but by corporations who want to exploit child labor and do not want to 323
be interfered with in so doing.

Now a few words about the so-called Blanket Bill, which the Woman's Party will urge upon every State at the next session of their respective legislatures and which reads as follows:

"Section 1. Women shall have the same privileges under the law as men with respect to:

"The exercise of suffrage.

"Holding an office or any position under the government, either state or local.

"Eligibility to examination for any position affected by civil service regulations.

"Freedom of contract.

"Choice of domicile, residence and name.

"Jury service.

"Acquiring, controlling and conveying property.

"Ownership and control of labor, and earnings.

"Care and custody of children, whether legitimate or illegitimate, and control of earnings and service of such children.

"The right to act as executors or administrators of estates of descendents.

"Grounds for divorce.

"Becoming parties litigant.

"Immunities or penalties for sex offenses.

"Quarantine examinations and treatment of diseases, and in all other respects.

"Section 2. The courts, executive and administrative officers shall make all necessary rules and provisions to carry out the intent and purposes of this statute.

"Section 3. All acts and part of acts in conflict with any of the provisions of this statute are hereby repealed."

The first three provisions therein, the right of suffrage, of holding office, and for examination under civil service regulations which is but a step to the holding of office, already exist in this State.

The fourth item, "Freedom of Contract" exists with one exception and that is that a married woman may not be security for her husband's debts and this I have previously discussed.

The fifth, "Choice of Domicile, Residence and Name", would destroy absolutely, the family life. The Legislature in 1921, must
324 have heard of this Blanket Bill when it passed Act 35 before referred to, preserving the family home, when there was inserted in said act: "In no event shall there exist, during the same period, more than one family home."

From the beginning of the world the husband has been the head of the family and if civilization is to exist, this condition must continue. If the wife has the right to establish a separate residence or domicile from the husband, what will become of the children? Where will they go? And as the husband and wife must unite under the Act of 1921 to preserve the home, with two homes the act would be ineffective and the wife, therefore, would lose the protection given by that act.

The custom of the wife adopting the husband's name is but a custom and while well nigh universal, there have been some exceptions thereto. While the law of Louisiana provides court proceedings for changing a name, these proceedings are not necessary, and anyone can take any name he or she pleases, the only question in connection therewith being one of identity; so that if Mrs. Brown chooses to call herself Mrs. Smith, no one can interfere and a law giving right to choose a name would give no rights that do not now exist.

The next item in the Bill is "Jury Service." The Constitution of 1921, in Article VII, Section 41, provides on this subject as follows:

"No woman shall be drawn for jury service unless she shall have previously filed with the Clerk of the District Court a written declaration of her desire to be subject to such service."

I have heard of no rush of women to the two District Courts in this City to register for Jury Service and I have been advised that no women have registered. Jury Service should not be forced upon any woman and when the law gives any woman a right to serve as a juror, provided she wants to, it seems to me the law goes far enough.

No doubt many of you have read of the recent "trying" not to use a stronger term, experiences of women in a mixed jury in St. Paul. In Louisiana in criminal cases the Jury cannot be separated for an instant for if they do the verdict is void and sometimes cases have taken several weeks to try in this State. Further comment on this point, it seems to me, is unnecessary.

The next two items regarding property and earnings have been
already covered and the wife's rights over her property and over
her earnings are as absolute probably as may be necessary, but 325
there can be no objections to a special statute amending the Act
of 1912 so as to provide that all earnings of the wife shall be her
separate property.

Laws in Louisiana cannot be repealed or extended by implication, and nothing in the Blanket bill will affect the Community Laws of Louisiana.

The law of Louisiana regarding children born in marriage should be a model for every State. The Articles of the Civil Code on the subject are as follows:

"215. A child, whatever be his age, owes honor and respect to his father and mother.

"216. A child remains under the authority of his father and mother until his majority or emancipation.

"In case of difference between the parents the authority of the father prevails.

"217. As long as the child remains under the authority of his father and mother, he is bound to obey them in everything which is not contrary to good morals and the laws."

To this may be added Article 223, as follows:

"Fathers and mothers shall have, during marriage, the enjoyment of the estate of their children until their majority or emancipation."

In case of separtion from bed and board or divorce, this usufruct then becomes in favor of the one who obtains the judgment. By Article 226, "This usufruct shall not extend to any estate, which the child may acquire by her own labor and industry."

Therefore, as the law of Louisiana now stands, probably the earnings of a minor child belong to the child but if further legislation on this subject is necessary then it should be done by a special law carefully drawn and after full consideration of the whole subject.

The question of illegitimate children and their rights and the rights of parents with respect thereto is too big a subject to be disposed of in one line of a general statute. This subject has been a theme of discussion in law, medicine, religion, science and social economy from the beginning of the world and should be considered separately from all other subjects when a law is to be passed determining the rights of all concerned.

As to the next item, I have never seen any objection to the
appointment of women, whether married or otherwise, as exec-
326 utors, when named in a will and as administrators of the estates
of deceased persons dying intestate, but if there was ever any doubt on the subject, it is removed under the terms of Act 34 of 1921 several times above mentioned.

As to grounds for divorce, while at one time in Louisiana grounds applicable against the wife were not always applicable against the husband, this was changed more than a half century ago.

By Article 142 of the Civil Code, it was provided that where the marriage was contracted in this State and the spouses moved to a foreign country and there the husband behaved towards his wife in such a way as to give her right under the laws of this State to a separation from bed and board, she might return to Louisiana and obtain such judgment, which "shall have force and effect in the same manner as if the parties had never left the State," and a year after this judgment of separation if the wife and her husband have not become reconciled, she might obtain a final divorce.

This right of the wife was greatly extended by Act No. 113 of 1920, which reads as follows:

"Whenever a marriage shall have been contracted in this State or elsewhere by parties either of whom are residents of this State and the matrimonal domicile shall have been established in a foreign country or in another State and if the husband shall have abandoned the wife, in the State of said marriage or elsewhere or shall behave or have behaved toward his said wife in said foreign country or in said other State, in such manner as will entitle her, under our laws, to demand a separation from bed and board, it shall be lawful for her, on returning to the domicile where said marriage was contracted, or to her domicile in this State, prior to said marriage, unless she has been absent from the State for a period of two years or more, to institute a suit against her said husband for the purposes above mentioned in the same manner as if the parties were domiciliated in such place, any law to the contrary notwithstanding."

Originally, under the law, only the successful party in a
suit for separation from bed and board could sue for a divorce
based on such judgment but by Act No. 25 of 1898, the same right
was given to the unsuccessful party except that he or she had
to wait two years to bring such suit while the successful party
was required to wait but one year. But this act preserved sub- 327
stantial rights of the wife by providing that where she had obtained a judgment of separation from her husband and he had brought suit two years thereafter for a divorce, she would have the same rights to claim alimony as though she had brought the suit for divorce, and by continuing with her the custody of the minor children, issue of the marriage.

As to the next item women married and unmarried are now allowed to become parties litigant in all cases, the same as men.

The next two items I decline to discuss for reasons that must be apparent to those who are now hearing me.

I do not believe that the so-called "Blanket Bill" if adopted, as written, would be constitutional in Louisiana. The present Constitution like most of its predecessors, provides in Article III, Section 16, "every law enacted by the Legislature shall embrace but one object, and shall have a title indicative of such object."

I do not know what is to be the title of the proposed "Blanket Bill" but it certainly embraces a multitude of objects and therefore is amenable to the prohibitions of the Constitution which have been uniformally upheld by the Supreme Court.

In a newspaper article published some time ago, in discussing inequalities of men and women under the laws of various States, it was stated that in Mississippi the husband had the legal right to "chastise the wife in moderation" and that in Florida "a husband may will away the person of an unborn child." I have consulted eminent lawyers in these two States and they tell me there are no such laws as above described. As a matter of fact, the only statute until this year in Florida was the one adopted in 1828 reading as follows: "Fathers may appoint guardians for their children during any part of infancy by deed, in writing, attested by two witnesses, or by last will and testament," but this was specifically repealed on May 17, 1921, and a law adopted in effect "that the mother jointly with the father shall be the natural guardian and may jointly appoint guardians, and that in the event of either parent's death sole guardianship should pass to the suvivor, who should have power to appoint guardians as provided in the former law."

I have not discussed the suggestion made by some that under the proposed Twentieth Amendment, if adopted, women would
328 be liable to military service, because I do not think that amendment would touch the question.

The power to declare war is, under the Constitution of the United States, vested exclusively in Congress, and this power is so broad as has been held by the Supreme Court of the United States, to include every possible contingency and practically gives Congress a free hand in dealing with all questions relating to war, and I do not think an Amendment to the Constitution, which does not specifically touch the war powers, would have any effect thereon.*

---

* It is the policy of The Quarterly not to print discussions on current problems particularly when there is a wide divergence in public opinion. The foregoing article on the Rights of Women in Louisiana is partly historical but it is also largely a polemic, as for instance the views expressed on the so called Blanket Bill. The very great interest excited by its delivery as a lecture and its real value in other respects, accounts for its appearance here. The reader will also bear in mind that The Quarterly does not hold itself responsible for the opinion of its contributors.

WOMEN AND THE CONSTITUTION: SOME LEGAL HISTORY AND A NEW APPROACH TO THE NINETEENTH AMENDMENT

W. WILLIAM HODES*

Women in the United States have been discriminated against throughout history. To this day, they remain legally, politically, and socially our second-class citizens.[1] The parallels between the status of women and the status of black men within a white-male dominated 329
society have been frequently noted.[2] Similarly, the complex and ever-changing relationship between the women's and the blacks' struggles for equal rights forms an important and informative chapter in the history of American law and society.

This note will begin with a brief restatement of the historical and sociological parallels between the two groups of second-class citizens. The discussion will then focus on the striking parallels in the legal doctrines which have been developed by white men to define the relationship between the oppressed and the oppressor. This legal history follows a path of development from slavery, to second-class citizenship, to an as yet unattained full equality. Finally, what is hoped will be a radically new approach to the question of women's rights will be developed: The 19th amendment to the Constitution, while on its face dealing only with women's suffrage, can be interpreted as an emancipation proclamation which extends the guarantees of all three Civil War Amendments to all women. The far-reaching consequences of such an approach, and the ultimate parallel to present upheavals in the law of the black man, will be the subject of a necessarily tentative, but hopefully provocative, concluding section.

---

* B.A. Harvard College, 1966; J.D. Rutgers Law School, 1969; Member of the Louisiana and New Jersey Bars; Mr. Hodes is currently an Assistant Corporation Counsel for the City of Newark.

1. *See* EPSTEIN, A WOMAN'S PLACE: OPTIONS AND LIMITS IN PROFESSIONAL CAREERS (1970); Lear, *The Second Feminist Wave*, N.Y. Times, Mar. 10, 1968, §6 (Magazine), at 24.

2. DEBEAUVOIR, THE SECOND SEX (5th ed. Parshley transl. 1964); MONTAGUE, MAN'S MOST DANGEROUS MYTH: THE FALLACY OF RACE (4th ed. 1964); MYRDAL, AN AMERICAN DILEMMA 1073 (2d ed. 1962); SPRUILL, WOMEN'S LIFE AND WORK IN THE SOUTHERN COLONIES (1938); Hacker, *Women as a Minority Group*, 30 SOCIAL FORCES 60 (1951).

I. The Woman and the Black Man

A. *Parallels in History and Sociology—"Woman as Nigger"* [3]

Power in the United States has always been firmly held in the hands of *white men.* To keep this group in power is by definition to keep those not of the group out; lowering the position of the "others" of necessity raises the position of the dominant group.[4] It is thus no accident that women have shared a history of oppression with the black man. As one commentator put it:

> Not only are race and sex entirely comparable classes, but there are no others like them. They are large, permanent, unchangeable, natural classes. No other kind of class is susceptible to implications of innate inferiority. Aliens, for instance, are essentially a temporary class, like
> 330 an age class. Only permanent and natural classes are open to those deep, traditional implications which become attached to classes regardless of the actual qualities of the members of the class.[5]

It is also possible to describe American Negro slavery and the subjugation of women as having elements of a caste system. In a caste system, one's role is defined not by ordinary criteria, such as wealth, talent, or relation to the means of production, but by mere membership in the group. The point is that a white worker might win a million dollars in a lottery, buy a factory, and thus change his *class,* but the black man or woman could not do the same and escape the effects of *caste* as well. The Negro might be called a "Tom" by some, and "uppity" by others, but his main identifying feature would remain the color of his skin. The woman would no doubt be labelled aggressive and hence "unfeminine," but her sex would still be the controlling factor in her life and social relations.

Women have recently emphasized that they constitute a separate class as well, regardless of the class position of their husband or family. Under this theory, a woman who is married to a middle class man is not herself middle class if she must slave away in the home, regardless of whether she holds another job in the outside world.[6] There are thus two distinct economies: the mainstream capitalist economy, and a

---

3. This was the significant title of a short essay distributed by a women's liberation organization in Chicago.

4. *See* deBeauvoir, *supra* note 2.

5. Crozier, *Constitutionality of Discrimination Based on Sex,* 15 B.U.L. Rev. 723, 727-28 (1935).

6. Benston, The Political Economy of Woman's Liberation (1969); Dunbar, Female Liberation as the Basis for Social Revolution (1969); Mitchell, The Longest Revolution (1966). (These booklets are distributed through the New England Free Press, Boston, Mass.).

separate homemaking economy which is technologically and socially little advanced from the frontier family unit in which the woman did the cooking and cleaning.

When women leave the home to work in the mainstream economy, they participate as workers, and join in the vicissitudes of trade unions and political life. As in the case of black workers, they suffer discrimination in hiring, firing, advancement, and wages. But in addition to this role outside the home, women are also the *only* work force for the home economy; and the male-dominated society considers this to be their primary role. In times of labor surplus, women are always expelled from the socialized economy and pushed back into the individualized and redundant [7] home economy. When Engels wrote that "within the family he (the husband) is the bourgeois and the wife represents the proletariat," [8] it may well be that he had more than a mere analogy in mind.

In order to keep the two groups of outcasts in subjection, the ruling 331
class of white men [9] developed theories, ideologies, and legal doctrines which at once justified and perpetuated the inequalities between their social positions. Since the doctrines were developd by the same people for the same purpose, it is not surprising to find antifeminism to be an echo of racism, and vice versa. Gunnar Myrdal, in his famous book, *An American Dilemma*, wrote a brief but incisive appendix dealing with the relationship between the black and the woman in America. He first made the astounding point that actually the status of women as slaves had come *first*, and was actually the model for the *later* development of Negro slavery:

> In the earlier common law, women and children were placed under the jurisdiction of the paternal power. When a legal status had to be found for the imported Negro servants in the seventeenth century, the nearest and most natural analogy was the status of women and children. The ninth commandment—linking together women, servants, mules, and other property—could be invoked, as well as a great number of other passages of Holy Scripture.[10]

Later, when the ideology and practice of slavery was challenged most sharply by the Abolitionist Movement, the status of women

---

7. Production line work in the mainstream economy may well be repetitive but work in the home economy is redundant, because each housewife must wash a load of clothes and prepare a meal, without possibility of mass production or division of labor.

8. F. Engels, The Origin of the Family, Private Property, and the State 65-6 (4th ed. 1963).

9. One does not have to be a Marxist to know that some white men exploit and oppress other white men. However, even the oppressed white man has been taught the lie of racial inequality, and even the oppressed white man, or black man for that matter, is the direct instrument of oppression of "his" woman.

10. Myrdal, *supra* note 2, at 1073.

became the rationalizing analogy as well. Myrdal quotes the following passage from a contemporary sociologist:

> "A beautiful example and illustration . . . is found in the instance of Patriarch Abraham. His wives and his children, his men servants and his maid servants, his camels and his cattle, were all equally his property . . . . Who would not desire to have been a slave of that old Patriarch, stern and despotic as he was? . . . Pride, affection, self-interest, moved Abraham to protect, love and take care of his slaves. The same motives operate on all masters, and secure comfort, competency and protection to the slave. A man's wife and children are his slaves, and do they not enjoy, in common with himself, his property?"[11]

Thus, female slavery formed the key to the social justification and the social acceptability of Negro slavery. Apparently, it did not occur
332 to many men to end *both* kinds of slavery, rather than to justify one with the other.

Once it is recognized that there is this integral connection between the caste status of women and blacks, it is not surprising to find that the everyday myths, customs, attitudes, and prejudices which have come to surround the two groups of outcasts are also all but interchangeable.[12]

---

11. *Id.* at 1073-74.

12. The following chart, which has been only slightly modified, was developed by a woman sociologist almost 20 years ago. Hacker, *supra* note 2.

BLACKS	WOMEN
Stereotype	
1. Inferior intelligence; smaller brain capacity; fewer outstanding persons in the class	1. Same
2. Emotional; primitive; child-like; great sexual prowess	2. Emotional; irrational; inconsistent; irresponsible; intuitive; sex object
3. Inferior	3. Inferior; weaker
4. Good athlete; good dancer	4. Good at cooking, typing, child-rearing, delicate manual labor
Modes of Accommodation and Survival	
1. Deferential manner	1. Flattering manner
2. Concealment of real feelings	2. Femine wiles
3. Outwit white-folks	3. Outwit menfolk, as in standard situation comedy television farce
4. Feigned ignorance	4. Helpless woman appeals to a man
Rationalization and Justification of the Status	
1. All right in his place; back of the bus; separate but equal	1. Woman's place is in the home
2. Contented Negro	2. Proud housewife; homemaking as challenging and critical occupation

The discussion has so far been largely concerned with the sociology of the caste status of women. But facts in life are always reflected in law, for law is nothing more than an institutionalized and intellectualized method of dealing with the facts of society's life. In this country, where law and lawyers play a role unequaled in any part of the world, it would be strange indeed if the law of women did not reflect the same parallels to the law of the black man. The discussion below focuses on these parallels—how the facts of discrimination against women and black Americans have been reflected in law, and how the law in turn has helped to perpetuate those very discriminations.

B. *Parallels in Early Legal Status—Woman as a Slave*

The legal history of both American women and American Negroes
is a movement from an original state of chattel slavery toward the 333
distant goal of equality with white men. A midway point has now been reached: formal citizenship in law, second-class citizenship in fact. Indeed, for women, there is still considerable discrimination in the law itself.[13] Women are just now reaching the legal position of the black man of the late 1950's and early 1960's, when the new Civil Rights Acts were being enacted.

That black men were once chattel slaves needs no demonstration—it was the most important historical facts in this country prior to the Civil War. But it is not so well known, or at least not so generally admitted, that women were then virtually chattel slaves. Dolly Madison is reputed to have said: "The Southern wife is the chief slave of the harem,"[14] presumably using the term bitterly in a lay and nontechnical sense. But it should be made clear at the outset that the term is being used here in a real legal sense. *Black's Law Dic-*

Discrimination

1. Pressure to limit education; technical schools or army training	1. Pressure to limit education; arts rather than sciences; college as marriage market
2. Confined to traditional jobs; barred from supervisory positions	2. Same; men will not take orders from better qualified women
3. Lower pay for the same job	3. Same
4. Little political influence	4. Same
5. Few precedents in own group to spur aspirations; downgrading of self-image	5. Same

13. *See* KANOWITZ, WOMEN AND THE LAW: THE UNFINISHED REVOLUTION (1968); White, *Women in the Law*, 65 MICH. L. REV. 1051 (1967); Note, *Sex Discrimination and the Constitution*, 2 STAN. L. REV. 691 (1950). The fact that 50 years after the 19th amendment gave women the vote, there is still a felt need for the Equal Rights Amendment is further proof.

14. *Quoted in* Martineau, 2 SOCIETY IN AMERICA 81 (1839).

tionary, for example, says that slavery is "[t]he condition of a slave; that civil relation in which one man has absolute power over the life, fortune and liberty of another."[15] Were women really slaves, then? Let us see.

In *Nolin v. Pearson,*[16] a case in which the Massachusetts Supreme Judicial Court was considering whether the Married Women's Property Act gave women a cause of action for alienation of affections, the court first summed up women's position before the intervention of statutes:

> The early common law recognized and upheld the doctrine that for most purposes husband and wife formed a single person, represented by the husband . . . .
>
> Personal property in her possession upon marriage passed to him, and could be levied upon for his debts, or bequeathed by him to
> 334 strangers, and he also took during coverture a sole estate in her lands which she could not alien unless he joined, or devise even with his assent, unless when exercising a power granted to her at the creating of the estate, nor derive any benefit or income therefrom by any contract which she could make separately. . . .
>
> Without her consent damages for injury to her person or reputation also might be released by him, or if collected in her lifetime they became his separate property . . . .[17]

There is little difference between this situation, and the situation of a slave, whose produce also passes directly to the master. Indeed, present day housewives still retain important features of slavery: They work far more than 40 hours a week, do not get paid a wage, get no vacations, no workmen's compensation, and receive no more reward for doing more work. Just like slaves, they are given a certain fixed amount to keep them alive and "contented," but have no incentive to work, or to work creatively.

The most definitive definition of American slavery surely must be that of the *Civil Rights Cases,*[18] for the question of what are the "badges and indicia" of slavery was to be frozen into our law from the date of that 1883 decision until a thaw was accomplished in 1968 in the case of *Jones v. Alfred H. Mayer Co.*[19] Justice Bradley wrote for the Court in 1883:

---

15. BLACK'S LAW DICTIONARY 1559 (rev. 4th ed. 1968).

16. 191 Mass. 283, 77 N.E. 890 (1906).

17. *Id.* at 284-85, 77 N.E. at 890.

18. 109 U.S. 3 (1883).

19. 392 U.S. 409 (1968). *See* Kinoy, *The Constitutional Right of Negro Freedom Revisited: Some First Thoughts on Jones v. Alfred H. Mayer Company,* 22 RUTGERS L. REV. 537 (1968).

> The long existence of African slavery in this country gave us very distinct notions of what it was, and what were its necessary incidents. Compulsory service of the slave for the benefit of the master, restraint of his movements except by the master's will, disability to hold property, to make contracts, to have a standing in court, to be a witness against a white person . . . were the inseparable incidents of the institution. . . . Congress . . . undertook to wipe out these burdens and disabilities, *the necessary incidents of slavery,* constituting its substance and visible form; and to secure to all citizens of every race and color . . . those fundamental rights which are the essence of civil freedom, namely, the same right to make and enforce contracts, to sue, be parties, give evidence, and to inherit, purchase, lease, sell and convey property, as is enjoyed by white citizens.[20]

There are few of these badges and incidents which do not apply to the common law position of women. There are other parallels; an important one being that a man is legally incapable of raping his wife, so that he can force sexual intercourse upon her at will—as 335
could the slave master upon the black slave woman.[21]

The concept of the woman as the *property* of her husband is very much with us today. It is utilized extensively in television advertizing where, for example, the wife's use of a new product assures the husband a promotion after the boss is impressed. It is universally recognized that a radiant and supporting wife is necessary for advancement in business. Her ability to be a gracious hostess or a charming guest has a real dollar value to the man on the way up, just as the slave was a main asset of the master. In a tax case,[22] two Justices of the Supreme Court suggested that when a woman accompanies her husband to a business convention *her* expenses are deductible as legitimate business expenses, since companies exert great pressure to secure the presence of the wife at such affairs, and make a great show of "involving" the woman in the man's work. In reality, of course, she is only a show piece—like a new suit of clothes, or a fine heirloom watch.

Actually, the roots of the concept of women as business assets goes far back into the common law traditions. A few years before the decision in *Nolin v. Pearson,*[23] Chief Justice Holmes of the Massa-

20. 109 U.S. at 22 (emphasis added).

21. The reason the husband escapes is that the wife is supposed to have contracted to provide this service "until death do us part," even if she later changes her mind. The slave owner escapes because the Slave South recognized precious few assaults on slaves as crimes, and did little to enforce what laws there were. *See generally* Dred Scott v. Sandford, 60 U.S. (19 How.) 393 (1857). To the victim, however, the result is the same: a rape in fact, which goes unpunished.

22. Rudolph v. United States, 370 U.S. 269, 284-87 (1962) (Douglas, J., dissenting). *See* 26 C.F.R. §1.162-2(c)(1970).

23. 191 Mass. 283, 77 N.E. 890 (1906), *discussed in,* text accompanying notes 16-17 *supra.*

chusetts Court had occasion to deal with the same problem of the woman's cause of action for alienation of affections in *Dixon v. Amerman*.[24] In *Dixon*, however, the husband's lover died by the time the case came to trial, so there was first the question of survival of the action. Under Massachusetts law, the action would survive only if it could be characterized as a "trespass against the person." Only after distinguishing the cases in which the *husband's* action *was* found to be a trespass, and thus *did* survive, did Holmes find no such trespass. Those cases, he explained, were "simply a corollary of the common law doctrine that the wife is the husband's servant, . . . and his chattel . . . , as well as part of his person."[25] The analogy is clear: Damage to the wife is an injury to the husband, just as damage to a machine is an injury to the businessman and damage to a slave is an injury to the owner, not the slave.

It should be evident that female slavery never had the utter hor-
336 ror and brutality that American Negro slavery did. For example, there was no auction block for women, although the practice of the high society families in marrying off their daughters to good business advantage is really not so far removed. And, of course, men did not have the legal power of life and death over their wives,[26] although some corporal punishment was for a long time legal, and extra-legal wife-beating continues today.

What is important is not that women were spared some of the evils of the slave system, but rather that they shared in its most direct and obvious aspects: total economic dependence upon the husband-master, and total legal inability to make decisions affecting their own lives. Woman was a chattel of man, " 'something better than her husband's dog, a little dearer than his horse.' "[27] Justice Seawell of the North Carolina Supreme Court was surely correct when he characterized the early position of women as "civil and political oppression *so akin to slavery* that we can find no adequate word to describe her present status of equality with men except emancipation . . . ."[28]

C. *A History of Struggle*

It is inconceivable that any slave, black, white or female, has ever

---

24. 181 Mass. 430, 63 N.E. 1057 (1902).

25. *Id.* at 431, 63 N.E. at 1057-58.

26. Although laws were enacted to prevent the murder or brutal treatment of slaves, there were always qualifications favoring the white slave masters. "For example, the accidental death of a slave while receiving 'moderate correction' was not homicide." And in addition, most indicted whites eventually went free. *See* STAMPP, THE PECULIAR INSTITUTION: SLAVERY IN THE ANTE-BELLUM SOUTH 218-22 (Vintage ed. 1956).

27. Doyle v. Doyle, 5 Misc. 2d 4, 6, 158 N.Y.S.2d 909, 912 (Sup. Ct. 1957).

28. State v. Emery, 224 N.C. 581, 596, 31 S.E.2d 858, 868 (1944). (Seawell, J., dissenting) (emphasis added).

acquiesced in slavery. The resistance may have its ups and downs, and there may be periods of quiet before the storm, but there is never an end to the will to be free. For this reason, American history before the Civil War is in large part the history of the freedom struggles of the black and female slaves. Slave revolts, the underground railroad, the abolitionist societies of the North, as well as feminist pamphlets and rallies, and "bloomer" skirts were happening in America. The biographies of Wendell Phillips[29] and Frederick Douglass,[30] Lucy Stone,[31] and Sojourner Truth,[32] the men and women who fought simultaneously for abolition and for feminism, epitomize an era of America's history.

It was in the abolition movement that women first learned to organize and first won the right to speak in public. It was in evolving theories of freedom and equality for the black slave that women first learned to put forward public demands for their own rights. In-
deed, it would be strange if it were otherwise, for it has been demon- 337
strated that the two groups of outcasts suffered at the hands of a common oppressor, who used two aspects of the same ideology to keep the bonds of slavery intact.

As a result of years of struggle, and because of the necessities of the new industrialism that was sweeping the country, especially in the North, some of women's bonds began to loosen. Education for women became more commonplace, and they began to enter the labor force in large numbers—exposing them even more to new ideas outside the home. Inevitably, the early women workers became early trade unionists, again increasing the pace of women's progress towards social effectiveness. By the end of the 19th century every state had passed laws allowing married women to own property separately,[33] thus freeing her from the most obvious aspect of slavery.

By the beginning of Reconstruction, then, it is accurate to say that both the woman and the black American had shed their legal status of chattel slave. The emancipation of the black man came by the sword of the Union army, and the three amendments to the Constitution; women's progress had come by gradual statutory reform, after years of agitation and organization.

---

29. Sherwin, Prophet of Liberty: The Life and Times of Wendell Phillips (1958).

30. Douglass, Life and Times of Frederick Douglass (1882); Graham, There Was Once a Slave . . . The Heroic Story of Frederick Douglass (1947).

31. *See* Flexner, Century of Struggle: The Woman's Rights Movement in the United States 68-70, 144-46 (1959); Kraditor, The Ideas of the Woman Suffrage Movement, 1890-1920, 54-55 (1965).

32. Flexner, *supra* note 31, at 90-91.

33. *See* Clark, Domestic Relations § 7.2, at 222, 224.

D. *Women After the Civil War—A Dream Deferred*

Freed from many of the shackles of their enslavement, both the black and the woman were soon to be reenslaved as second-class citizens through sociological and political developments and through judicial interpretation of the Constitution which reflected these developments in law.

The history of the "reenslavement" of the Negro—a history evoked by such historical events as the Compromise of 1877, the *Civil Rights Cases*,[34] and *Plessey v. Ferguson*[35]—is outside the scope of this note, and has been dealt with at length by both historians[36] and legal scholars.[37] The limitations on the gains of the women, however, were to come almost immediately after the end of the Civil War. In some sense they served as a model for the later reversals in the status of the freed black slaves, just as women had earlier served as the sociolog-
338 ical and legal model for black slavery itself. Once women were firmly
reentrenched in second-class citizenship, the white-male society could turn to the task of undoing the effects of what had been won by the blacks.

Women had first put forward their demand for the vote at the Seneca Falls Convention in 1848. This conference was precipitated by the fact that within the abololitionist movement itself women were being discriminated against, and at a World Anti-Slavery Convention in London, the women delegates had been barred from taking their seats and had to sit in the galleries as spectators.[38] This finds an interesting parallel today in the fact that a great number of the activists in the Women's Liberation Movement gained their early political experience in the black liberation and peace movements, but began their own caucuses and organizations after they found themselves relegated to doing typing and envelope stuffing.

At the end of the Civil War, women renewed their demand for the vote. It seemed certain that Negroes were about to receive the right to vote, and the feminists thought that they too would benefit by the new liberalism brought about by the destruction of the slave system. But they were destined to suffer great disappointment. The proposed 14th amendment provided that representation in Congress would be cut down proportionately, if any state denied to any of its *male*

---

34. 109 U.S. 3 (1883).

35. 163 U.S. 537 (1896).

36. *See generally* DONALD, THE POLITICS OF RECONSTRUCTION 1863-1867 (1965); FRANKLIN, FROM SLAVERY TO FREEDOM (1963); WOODWARD, THE STRANGE CAREER OF JIM CROW (1966); WOODWARD, REUNION AND REACTION (1951).

37. OLSON, THE THIN DISGUISE (1967); Kinoy, *The Constitutional Right of Negro Freedom*, 21 RUTGERS L. REV. 387 (1967).

38. FLEXNER, *supra* note 31, at 71-77; KRADITOR, *supra* note 21, at 2-4.

citizens the right to vote.[39] The purpose was to do away with the provision in the original Constitution that Negroes were to count as three-fifths of a person for purposes of calculating representation in Congress, but the clear implication was that *women* could be kept out of the franchise without penalty to the states. As a leading historian of suffragism wrote:

> The woman's rights leaders who had put away their cause for the duration of the Civil War believed that, when peace came, a grateful country would reward them, spurred on by the Republican party. They were still so inexperienced in politics that they failed to estimate the extent and complexity of the forces arrayed against them. While they were used to the lamentations of conservatives who foresaw the downfall of home, church, and state if women should get the vote, they were totally unprepared for the opposition of the Republican politicians. The latter had their eyes fixed on a windfall of 2,000,000
> potential male Negro voters in the South, which they had no intention 339
> of jeopardizing by stirring up an unnecessary tempest over woman suffrage. Nor did the women reckon on desertion of their cause by the abolitionists, long their staunchest allies, but now convinced that this was "the Negro's hour" and that nothing must be allowed to interfere with it.[40]

This betrayal of the woman's rights movement led to a sharp split in the movement over whether the 14th amendment should be supported, or whether the women should hold out for immediate equality with men—both black and white. Elizabeth Cady Stanton and Susan B. Anthony, the two leading suffragists of that time, finally opposed the amendment outright, and campaigned for its defeat.[41] Frederick Douglass, the great abolitionist and feminist, one of the few male signers of the Seneca Falls Declaration and the one who was the most insistent that the question of the women's suffrage be raised, supported the amendment: The ballot for the black man was a matter of survival in the South, and could not be endangered.[42] Some women believed that linking the two issues together would strengthen both, rather than weaken them, because of the historic ties between the two social movements for freedom. But the view of the later historian was probably more realistic:

> Slavery and the condition of the Negro had been a boiling national issue for thirty-five years; a war had been fought over it. No such

39. *See* Flack, The Adoption of the Fourteenth Amendment 97-127 (1908); Ten Broek, Equal Under Law (1965).

40. Flexner, *supra* note 31, at 142-43.

41. *Id.* at 144-45; Kraditor, *supra* note 31, at 3-4.

42. Flexner, *supra* note 31, at 144.

> intensity of feeling existed yet regarding the status of women, even among the women themselves, excepting in a still relatively small group. Opinion in Congress and throughout the North was concerned with assuring the vote for the Negro; it was relatively uninterested in how such a controversial measure would affect women.[43]

Most of the suffragists finally agreed that some expansion of the suffrage was better than none at all, and so supported the amendment, but an anti-Negro strain had been added to the women's suffrage movement which was never to be fully purged.[44]

Early in 1869, the 15th amendment, prohibiting governmental abridgement of the right to vote because of "race, color, or previous condition of servitude," was introduced into Congress. The women who followed Mrs. Stanton and Miss Anthony campaigned to have the word "sex" added to that list, but the result was predictably the same: The nation was simply not ready to take in two groups of
340 outcasts at once.[45]

In the earliest cases construing the new amendments to the Constitution, the Supreme Court faithfully carried out the national policy of "Negroes only." In 1870, a group of New Orleans butchers brought the famous *Slaughter-House Cases*[46] to the Court, challenging Louisiana's state-granted slaughtering monopoly under the new 14th amendment. Sharply divided, the Court, with four justices dissenting in three opinions, came to grips with the most pressing legal questions of that time: Just how much power had the Wartime Amendments transferred from the state governments to the federal? What really defined a person's citizenship? What were the "privileges or immunities of citizens of the United States,"[47] and how did they differ, if at all, from "privileges and immunities of citizens in the several States,"[48] as set out in the original Constitution? The five justices who comprised the majority read the 14th amendment narrowly, and held that it did not radically alter the structure of American federalism, so that in the main a citizen would look to his state government for the protection of his liberties, rather than the federal government. In addition, the Court, in forceful dicta, indicated that it would not be receptive to plaintiffs bringing suits under the Wartime Amendments, unless they were black.

Ironically, the *Slaughter-House Cases*[49] were later to become one of the keystones in the process of judicial interpretation which would

---

43. *Id.* at 145.
44. KRADITOR, *supra* note 31, at 179-81.
45. FLEXNER, *supra* note 31, at 147-49.
46. 83 U.S. (16 Wall.) 36, 44, 57 (1872).
47. U.S. CONST. amend. XIV, §1.
48. *Id.* art. IV, §2.
49. 83 U.S. (16 Wall.) 36 (1872).

totally undermine the effectiveness of the amendments as far as protection of even the Negro was concerned; but in 1872, the message to the women was quite clear: This was still the "Negro's hour." As one writer later explained: "If that intent was doubtful regarding application to white men, it cannot be contended that there was ever the faintest shadow of positive intent that the provision should apply to women."[50] As if to bear out this interpretation of the *Slaughter-House Cases,* the Supreme Court the next day decided *Bradwell v. State,*[51] holding that women could constitutionally be denied admission to the bar solely because of their sex. This time there was no important dissent, no wide-ranging discussions of rights of citizens and of who protects them. There was only the flat statement that the right to practice law was not a privilege or immunity of United States citizenship, and so the *Slaughter-House* opinion of the day before was dispositive of the case.

Justice Bradley's opinions in the two cases are significant commen- 341
tary on the process of judicial reenslavement. In his dissent in *Slaughter-House,* he had written:

> If my views are correct with regard to what are the privileges and immunities of citizens, it follows conclusively that any law which establishes a sheer monopoly, depriving a large class of citizens of the privilege of pursuing a lawful employment, does abridge the privileges of those citizens.
>
> . . . .
>
> In my view, *a law which prohibits a large class of citizens from adopting a lawful employment, or from following a lawful employment previously adopted, does deprive them of liberty as well as property, without due process of law.* Their right of choice is a portion of their liberty; their occupation is their property. Such a law also deprives those citizens of the equal protection of the laws, contrary to the last clause of the section.[52]

Justice Bradley apparently was unable to understand that barring an entire half of the population from the lawful employment of practicing law was also an abridgement of their privileges; a monopoly of all men was apparently quite different from a monopoly of certain men in the butchering business. For in *Bradwell,* Justice Bradley not only joined the Court's opinion upholding the monopoly of men, but wrote a concurring opinion which went far beyond the narrow issue of the case. He stated a theory of woman's place in society which is today's central enslaving theory of women:

50. Crozier, *supra* note 5, at 725.
51. 83 U.S. (16 Wall.) 130 (1872).
52. 83 U.S. (16 Wall.) at 122 (emphasis added).

> [T]he civil law, as well as nature herself, has always recognized a wide difference in the respective spheres and destinies of man and woman. Man is, or should be, woman's protector and defender. The natural and proper timidity and delicacy which belongs to the female sex evidently unfits it for many of the occupants of civil life. The constitution of the family organization, which is founded in the divine ordinance, as well as in the nature of things, indicates the domestic sphere as that which properly belongs to the domain and functions of womanhood . . . .
>
> . . . The paramount destiny and mission of woman are to fulfill the noble and benign offices of wife and mother. This is the law of the Creator. And the rules of civil society must be adapted to the general constitution of things, and cannot be based upon exceptional cases.
>
> . . . It is the prerogative of the legislator to prescribe regulations founded on nature, reason, and experience for the due admission of qualified persons to professions and callings demanding special skill and confidence . . . . [I]t is within the province of the Legislature to
> 342 ordain what offices, positions, and callings shall be filled and discharged by men, and shall receive the benefit of those energies and responsibilities, and that decision and firmness which are presumed to predominate in the sterner sex.[53]

It is fascinating that Justice Bradley dissented in the *Slaughter-House Cases,*[54] when the rights of white men were at stake, displayed strong anti-feminist views in *Bradwell v. State,*[55] *and* was the author of the *Civil Rights Cases,*[56] whose "state action" doctrine was the tour de force which enabled the Court to retreat on the promise of black freedom as well. Thus in the opinions of one Justice, an intellectual giant of his time, one can trace the development of a judicial-political strategy to reenslave first women, then blacks.

E. *Woman as Housewife—Separate but Equal*

Another important link in the chain of cases which reenslaved the black man was *Plessey v. Ferguson*[57] with its doctrine of "separate but equal." There is here another parallel to the question of women's rights, for the dominant male society has always contended that because of their physical differences women were destined from birth to be full-time wives and mothers. Just like segregationists, anti-feminists have exaggerated the physical differences and developed

---

53. 83 U.S. (16 Wall.) at 141-42 (Bradley, J., concurring).
54. 83 U.S. (16 Wall.) at 111-24 (Bradley, J., dissenting).
55. 83 U.S. (16 Wall.) at 139-42 (Bradley, J., concurring).
56. 109 U.S. 3 (1882).
57. 163 U.S. 537 (1896).

scientific justifications for relegating women to certain positions in society.

Woman's separate but equal place as homemaker is still the law of the land today, for as late as 1961, Justice Harlan was able to say without challenge in *Hoyt v. Florida:*[58] "Despite the enlightened emancipation of women from the restrictions and protection of bygone years, and their entry into many parts of community life formerly considered to be reserved to men, women are still regarded as the centers of home and family life."[59] This was the *sole* rationale by which the Court found that Florida's system of jury selection, which had the effect of sharply limiting the proportion of women on juries, was based on some reasonable classification. The exclusion of Negroes from juries has, of course, long been held to violate the due process and equal protection clauses of the 14th amendment,[60] but the Court was unable to see the analogy that to be separated into the home is to be doomed to inferiority. 343

Proponents of the theory of woman in the home do not admit that it discriminates against women. They say it states that women are merely different, not inferior. But that was exactly the theory of the Court in *Plessey*, when the doctrine of "separate but equal" was being developed. The Court said: "We consider the underlying fallacy of the plaintiff's argument to consist in the assumption that the enforced separation of the two races stamps the colored race with a badge of inferiority. If this be so, it is not by reason of anything found in the act, but solely because the colored race chooses to put that construction upon it."[61] Professor Wechsler, in his famous article, *Towards Neutral Principles of Constitutional Law,*[62] after quoting with approval the above passage from *Plessey*, sought to buttress the Court's reasoning by adding the rhetorical question: "Does enforced separation of the sexes discriminate against females merely because it may be the females who resent it and it is imposed by judgments predominantly male?"[63] Professor Wechsler, a white man, apparently thought the answer was an obvious no; the women who are organizing and agitating against oppression in the home would clearly answer with a resounding yes.[64]

---

58. 368 U.S. 57 (1961).

59. *Id.* at 61-62.

60. *See* Sims v. Georgia, 389 U.S. 404 (1967); Jones v. Georgia, 389 U.S. 24 (1967); Reece v. Georgia, 350 U.S. 85 (1955); Hernandez v. Texas, 347 U.S. 475 (1954); Patton v. Mississippi, 332 U.S. 463 (1947); Pierrce v. Louisiana, 306 U.S. 354 (1939); Norris v. Alabama, 294 U.S. 587 (1935).

61. 163 U.S. at 551.

62. Wechsler, *Toward Neutral Principles of Constitutional Law,* 73 HARV. L. REV. 1 (1959).

63. *Id.* at 33.

64. *See* FRIEDAN, THE FEMININE MYSTIQUE (1963). *See also* sources cited in note 6 *supra*.

The mistake that the Court has made consistently with respect to women is the same mistake made in *Plessey* with respect to the black man—a mistake which was, however, finally corrected in *Brown v. Board of Education.*[65] The transition from *Plessey* to *Brown* required only that the Court interpret the facts of psychology and sociology differently, and hold that segregation was *inherently* discriminatory. Speaking of this change in a later case, the Court said:

> [T]he Equal Protection Clause is not shackled to the political theory of a particular era. In determining what lines are unconstitutionally discriminatory, we have never been confined to historic notions of equality, any more than we have restricted due process to a fixed catalogue of what was at a given time deemed to be the limits of fundamental rights. . . . Notions of what constitutes equal treatment for purposes of the Equal Protection Clause *do* change. This Court in 1896 held that laws providing for separate public facilities for white
> 344 and Negro citizens did not deprive the latter of the equal protection and treatment that the Fourteenth Amendment commands. . . . When, in 1954—more than a half-century later—we repudiated the "separate-but-equal" doctrine of *Plessey* as respects public education we stated: "In approaching this problem, we cannot turn the clock back to 1868 when the Amendment was adopted, or even to 1896 when Plessey v. Ferguson was written." [66]

Why, then, cannot the Court simply change its view of the facts with respect to women? Why can't it agree with the view of two recent writers:

> To the degree women perform the function of motherhood, they differ from other special groups. But maternity legislation is not sex legislation; its benefits are geared to the performance of a special service much like the veterans' legislation. When the law distinguishes between the "two great classes of men and women," gives men a preferred position by accepted social standards, and regulates the conduct of women in a restrictive manner having no bearing on the maternal function, it disregards individuality and relegates an entire class to inferior status . . . just as separate schools for Negro and white children by their very nature cannot be "equal," classification on the basis of sex is today inherently unreasonable and discriminatory.[67]

If the Court in *Brown* was willing to accept the findings of psychologists and sociologists, why cannot it accept the findings of such writers as Betty Friedan [68] and Simone deBeauvoir,[69] that keeping

---

65. 347 U.S. 483 (1954), *reargument on relief*, 349 U.S. 294 (1955).
66. Harper v. Virginia State Bd. of Elections, 383 U.S. 663, 669-70 (1966).
67. Murray & Eastman, *Jane Crow and the Law: Sex Discrimination and Title VII*, 34 GEO. WASH. L. REV. 232, 239-40 (1965).
68. FRIEDAN, *supra* note 64.
69. DEBEAUVOIR, *supra* note 2.

the woman in the home inevitably stunts her growth and stifles her creativity and individuality?

The above suggestions show that just as in the case of discrimination against the black American, even at this late date it is possible to reinterpret the 14th amendment, and move away from the earlier narrow holdings. The difficulty lies not in the *reach* of the amendment, but in the failure of the courts to understand and accept the very real analogies that have been the subject of this discussion.

There is a difficulty in the Supreme Court's *approach* to the 14th amendment as well. The Court has always put itself in a passive role even when forging into new areas of concern. The Court sees its task as merely judging the "reasonableness" of certain state practices, but never its wisdom as a matter of policy. Thus we have *Hoyt v. Florida,*[70] wherein the Court found it not totally unreasonable for a state to consider that women are (or should be?) saddled with young
children, and thus not readily available for jury duty. The Court 345
held that the system was constitutional because there was a rational basis for it, even though it had the admitted effect of virtually eliminating women from Florida juries.

In an earlier case, *Goesaert v. Cleary,*[71] Justice Frankfurter held constitutional a Michigan law which provided that women could not be bartenders *unless* they were the wives or daughters of owners of bars. After making the questionable and unexplained assertion that "obviously" Michigan could bar *all* women from the profession of bartending, Justice Frankfurter turned to the task of determining whether there was "rhyme or reason" for the particular scheme at hand. Given such a nebulous and minimal standard, it was not difficult to conjure up a theory upon which to rationalize: The man involved could oversee and "protect" the woman.

It is submitted that as long as men are judges, and the social pressures are not yet great enough to force change, there will always be a rationalizing "rhyme or reason" available to the judicial hand. As an alternate approach, the discussion below will focus upon the 19th amendment, and a totally different way of dealing with entire areas of women's rights in constitutional law.

II. A New Approach to the 19th Amendment

A. *The Starting Point: Minor and Dred Scott*

After the Civil War, the Supreme Court was engaged in limiting the scope of the new constitutional amendments.[72] In *Minor v. Happer-*

70. 368 U.S. 57 (1961); *see* text accompanying notes 58-59 *supra*.
71. 335 U.S. 464 (1948).
72. *See* sources cited in notes 34-37 *supra* and accompanying text.

sett [73] the Court held that a state could deny women the right to vote in either state or federal elections—a decision which was not reversed until the adoption of the 19th amendment nearly a half century later. Leaving aside for the moment the substantive result reached by the court in the *Minor* case, the most striking feature of the opinion is its obvious similarity to Chief Justice Taney's opinion in *Dred Scott v. Sandford.*[74] From the style, the method of approach to the legal issues, the organization, and the oblique references and paraphrases, it appears that Chief Justice Waite had *Dred Scott* in front of him when he wrote *Minor.* Here is the ultimate statement of woman as slave. To assess better the significance of the case, and the corresponding significance of the 19th amendment which overruled it, this parallel must be considered in some greater detail.

The first item of similarity is the almost inexorable drive in both opinions to reach all of the issues, and to announce the broadest pos-
346 sible rule to settle an entire area of the law for all time. In the first 30 pages of his *Dred Scott* opinion, the Chief Justice concluded that the lower court had not had jurisdiction over Dred Scott's suit for freedom; but rather than being the end of the case, this was only the beginning, for Taney went on to treat all of the substantive issues in the case. After doing so, and announcing a broad national law of slavery, the Chief Justice finally came back to where he could have left off in the first place, and remanded with orders to dismiss the case. Taney was certainly aware of the extraordinary step he was taking in reaching the merits after deciding that the court had no jurisdiction, for he went to great lengths to spin out a new theory of appellate jurisdiction to fit the needs of the case—the *entire* record is presented to the higher court and *any* error may be corrected. The *Minor* court did not take such a roundabout path in justifying its decision to reach the merits when the constitutional issue could have been avoided; the first paragraph of the opinion stated bluntly that it would do so.

> We might, perhaps, decide the case upon other grounds [than the constitutional issue], but this question is fairly made. From the opinion we find that it was the only one decided in the court below, and it is the only one which has been argued here. The case was undoubtedly brought to this court for the sole purpose of having that question decided by us, and in view of the evident propriety there is of having it settled . . . we have concluded to waive all other considerations and proceed at once to its determination.[75]

This is hardly the role that the Court usually casts itself in; normally the Court does not sit to hear contrived cases, or to decide issues which

---

73. 88 U.S. (21 Wall.) 162 (1874).
74. 60 U.S. (19 How.) 393 (1857).
75. 88 U.S. (21 Wall.) at 165.

the parties force upon it. Clearly, the Court in *Minor*, just as it did in *Dred Scott*, had a desperate need to reach the merits of the case.

The first point that the plaintiff in *Minor* had to make was that she was a citizen of the United States, and so entitled to certain privileges and immunities under the 14th amendment. Since the case arose after the passage of the amendment, it was self-evident that the plaintiff, being a person born or naturalized in the United States, was indeed a citizen. The Court so acknowledged. But since *Dred Scott* was to be the model, the discussion could not and did not end with that simple statement, for in *Dred Scott* the major portion of the opinion dealt with the question of who were citizens of the United States. Obligingly, Chief Justice Waite in *Minor v. Happersett* added a totally gratuitous section dealing with the same topic although, as we have seen, the issue was irrelevant to the outcome of the case, not as in *Dred Scott* where it was crucial. It is submitted that the only reason for this discussion in *Minor* is that it appeared in *Dred* 347
Scott! In *Dred Scott*, Chief Justice Taney argued that all who were the "people of the United States," as those words are used in the preamble of the Constitution, became citizens at the instant the new nation was formed. His conclusion was that Negroes were not "persons" at all, but "beings of an inferior order, and altogether unfit to associate with the white race." [76] In *Minor*, Chief Justice Waite, not surprisingly, reached the same conclusion with regard to the question of how citizenship was to be determined—the "people of the United States" are its citizens.[77] Then, seemingly to insure that no one would miss the parallels to the *Dred Scott* opinion, Waite added: "Disputes have arisen as to whether or not certain persons or certain classes of persons were part of the people at the time, but never as to their citizenship if they were." [78] The dispute was, of course, *Dred Scott*, and there again appears to be no reason for the allusion, other than that the Chief Justice had the case on his mind as he wrote.

In Waite's attempt to prove that women have always at least been considered citizens of the United States, he made another obvious reference to the *Dred Scott* opinion. He wrote:

> [B]y the Constitution, the judicial power of the United States is made to extend to controversies between citizens of different states. Under this *it has been uniformly held* that the citizenship necessary to give the courts of the United States jurisdiction of a cause must be affirmatively shown on the record. Its existence as a fact may be put in issue and tried. If found not to exist the case must be dismissed.[79]

---

76. 60 U.S. (19 How.) at 407.
77. 88 U.S. (21 Wall.) at 166.
78. *Id.* at 167.
79. *Id.* at 169 (emphasis added).

His proof then consisted of showing that women had often sued in federal courts without challenge, and so clearly must have been citizens all along.[80] But the doctrine that citizenship must be affirmatively shown was not a "uniform" holding at all; it, in fact, originated with *Dred Scott*! Taney had gone to great lengths to establish the doctrine in the face of what seemed to be contrary precedent, so that he could reopen the question of the slaves' ability to sue in the federal courts, and thus the question of citizenship.

The main issue in the *Minor* case was whether women citizens had the right to vote as a privilege and immunity of citizenship. After the *Slaughter-House Cases* and *Bradwell v. Illinois* the year before, the Court could easily have answered this question in the negative without further ado, since the very limited nature of privileges and immunities had already been established by a 5 to 4 majority.[81] But instead, the Court followed the organization and style of *Dred Scott*,
348 and launched into an historical discussion of the status of the right to vote at the time of the adoption of the Constitution. The parallel is once again clear: In *Dred Scott* the question was whether the black man was a citizen; in *Minor* the question was whether citizens were necessarily voters; in both cases, the historical answer was no. Taney cited the plight of the black man in the nonslave states; Waite cited the universal practice of limiting the suffrage to a small group of propertied, lettered, and *male* citizens.

Perhaps the most interesting parallel of all is the narrow view which both Courts took of their role in American politics. Both Courts correctly interpreted history, and both refused to move forward from there. The Taney Court in *Dred Scott* said: "It is not the province of the court to decide upon the justice or injustice, the policy or impolicy, of these laws. The decision of that question belonged to the political or law-making power; to those who formed the sovereignty and framed the Constitution." [82] And the Waite Court echoed in *Minor*:

> Our province is to decide what the law is, not to declare what it should be . . . . If the law is wrong, it ought to be changed; but the power for that is not with us . . . . No argument as to woman's need of suffrage can be considered. We can only act upon her rights as they exist. It is not for us to look at the hardship of withholding. Our duty is at an end if we find it within the power of a State to withhold.[83]

The studied parallelism between *Dred Scott* and *Minor* inevitably raises a crucial question for an evaluation of the latter case. Why

---

80. *Id.*
81. *See* text accompanying notes 46-56 *supra*.
82. 60 U.S. (19 How.) at 405.
83. 88 U.S. (21 Wall.) at 178.

would the Chief Justice of the United States choose the most discredited case in American law for his model, only a few years after the Civil War and the Wartime Amendments had erased it? Was Waite taunting the women with *Dred Scott,* telling them that their situation was as hopeless of legal solution as was that of the prewar slave? Was he telling them they must take the route of civil war or constitutional amendment before they too could be free? Perhaps it was a sardonic protest against the position of women—his way of shaming society by showing it what position had in fact been forced upon the women. Perhaps it was merely an effective way of showing women that this was still the "Negro's hour," and that they could not hope to share in the Negro's emancipation from the law of *Dred Scott.*

But whatever the actual reason, the significance of the parallels should give one pause. *Minor v. Happersett* established that women were second-class citizens—citizens with less legal rights than other
citizens. As in the case of *Dred Scott,* the historical position of the 349
oppressed class was ratified by the Supreme Court, given the sanction of the Constitution, and thus immeasurably strengthened. In both cases, it would take many years of struggle and, in the end, constitutional amendments to undo the effects of the Supreme Court's holding. This suggests that the 19th amendment can be viewed as more than a suffrage measure, for not only did it give women the same right to vote as men; but it also reversed *Minor,* women's *Dred Scott.* Therefore, a further parallel may be suggested. The 19th amendment did not merely add the word "sex" to the 15th amendment, but it actually performed for women the same function that the Wartime Amendments had for the blacks—to obliterate the former inferior status. In this view, the 19th amendment has, as has the 13th, "a reflex character also, establishing and decreeing universal civil and political freedom throughout the United States."[84] That is the central argument of this article—all "badges and indicia" of the pre-1920 status of women must now be destroyed. Under this analysis, we have not the "rhyme or reason" test of the 14th amendment, but the sharp thrust of the 13th amendment.[85]

B. *The Women's Emancipation Proclamation*

An examination of the history of the 19th amendment also suggests that viewing it as a broad emancipation proclamation is not so farfetched. The amendment was ratified and became part of the Con-

---

84. Civil Rights Cases, 109 U.S. 3, 20 (1883).

85. *See* Plessey v. Ferguson, 163 U.S. 537, 552-64 (1896) (Harlan, J., dissenting); Civil Rights Cases, 109 U.S. 3, 26-62 (1883) (Harlan, J., dissenting); Kinoy, *supra* note 19.

stitution in 1920, 72 years after Seneca Falls, and 46 years after the decision in *Minor v. Happersett.*[86] During those years, women attained most of the formal goals for which they struggled: Women were more or less able to obtain an education and to enter the professions; they could own property and sign contracts. But at the same time, male America steadfastly refused to concede ground on the question of suffrage for women. From 1867, when the first state referendum on women's suffrage failed in Kansas, to 1920, when the amendment was finally adopted, there were 55 referenda, 480 campaigns to induce state legislatures to submit such referenda to the public, 277 campaigns to persuade state party conventions to include women suffrage planks in their platforms, and 19 campaigns for a federal amendment.[87]

What, then, was different about the vote? The answer probably lies in the fact that the vote came to symbolize the final dividing line between women as part of the family organization and women as
350 independent and equal citizens in American life. In a democratic society, where the majority rules, a large group without the vote is ultimately dependent upon the voting group for favors, and can only ask for, rather than demand, further change. A recent study of the rationale of antisuffragism shows the special importance of the vote, as seen by those who would limit it to men only:

> [the] "separate but equal" doctrine of the respective spheres of man and woman was a central part of the sociological argument against woman suffrage, which declared that social peace and the welfare of the human race depended upon woman's staying home, having children, and keeping out of politics. *Voting implied much more than simply dropping a ballot in a box once a year.* It meant on the part of the woman an entire intellectual reorientation. Having the right to vote imposed the duty of exercising that right competently, which required *doing whatever was necessary to become politically intelligent.* At the very least it meant that women must become informed on political issues, and the inevitable discussions on such subjects between spouses would cause disagreements which in turn would raise the divorce rate. Woman suffrage would lead to neglect of children by politically active mothers and, thereby, to increased juvenile delinquency, because the franchise would inexorably draw women into political organization and even into office.[88]

The traditional idea of the American family in which the man was its representative in public and the woman its leader at home was being challenged by the drive for woman's suffrage; if suffrage were

---

86. 88 U.S. (21 Wall.) 162 (1874).
87. FLEXNER, *supra* note 31, at 157-239, 248-93; KRADITOR, *supra* note 31, at 219-48.
88. KRADITOR, *supra* note 31, at 22-23 (emphasis added).

granted, it would be individuals, rather than families, who would receive political representation.

> For this reason, the vote would not be merely a quantitative addition to all the other rights women had acquired in the preceding two generations. *The franchise was not just another new right* to add to higher education, equal guardianship of children, and ownership of one's own earnings in the march of women toward full equality with men. *Suffrage meant a qualitative change* in the social and familial role of women, antis believed, and the demand for it consequently met with more determined resistance than did women's struggles for other rights.[89]

In all of this, there is once more an interesting parallel to the condition of the black man, for the history of the post-Reconstruction South is primarily a history of disenfranchisement of the Negro. The "grandfather clause,"[90] the white primary,[91] the literacy test,[92] and 351
still later the racial gerrymander[93] were each a primary tool of subjugation, for without the vote, black America would forever remain powerless. In this regard, a speech that Senator James O. Eastland, a plantation owner and a long-time symbol of segregation, made to the joint session of the Mississippi House and Senate early in 1948 is particularly revealing.[94] After reviewing the historical developments which led to the end of Reconstruction, the Senator said:

> During that time we built up a racial system in the south that is the envy of any section in the world where the two races in great numbers live side by side. Of course, it is built upon a segregation . . . . Every decent southerner wants the Negro to enjoy the fruits of his labor. Every decent southerner wants the Negro to prosper and do well and make a good citizen. *The only rule that we of the south lay down is that he must stay out of politics,* because he would use the power of the

89. *Id.* at 25 (emphasis added).

90. *See, e.g.,* Lane v. Wilson, 307 U.S. 268 (1939); Myers v. Anderson, 238 U.S. 368 (1915); Guinn v. United States, 238 U.S. 347 (1915); Giles v. Harris, 189 U.S. 475 (1903).

91. *See, e.g.,* Terry v. Adams, 345 U.S. 461, *rehearing denied,* 345 U.S. 1003 (1953); Smith v. Allwright, 321 U.S. 649, *rehearing denied,* 322 U.S. 769 (1944); Nixon v. Herndon, 273 U.S. 536 (1927); Love v. Griffith, 266 U.S. 32 (1924).

92. *See, e.g.,* Lassiter v. Northhampton County Bd. of Elections, 360 U.S. 45 (1959); Davis v. Schnell, 81 F. Supp. 872 (S.D. Ala.), *aff'd per curiam,* 336 U.S. 933 (1949).

93. *See, e.g.,* Gomillion v. Lightfoot, 364 U.S. 339 (1960); Sims v. Baggett, 247 F. Supp. 96 (M.D. Ala. 1965). *See also* TAPER, GOMILLION v. LIGHTFOOT: THE TUSKEEGEE GERRYMANDER CASES (1962); Lucas, *Dragon in the Thicket: A Perusal of Gomillion v. Lightfoot,* 1961 S. CT. REV. 194.

94. JOURNAL OF THE HOUSE OF REPRESENTATIVES OF THE STATE OF MISSISSIPPI AT A REGULAR SESSION THEREOF 168-77, Jan. 6-April 14, 1948. The speech was given on January 29, 1948.

> ballot to destroy the laws on which our social structure is built. We have got to give him better schools—we have got to give him better hospitals—we have got to give him better health programs, but the only question is that he stay out of political office.[95]

At the turn of the 20th century, male America apparently felt the same way about women: "reforms, yes; votes, no."

By the time the 19th amendment approached passage, the question of woman's suffrage was truly "a boiling national issue," as the question of Negro emancipation had been before the Wartime Amendments were passed. The suffragists were engaged in speaking tours, petitioning and lobbying; the antisuffragists were hard at work writing pamphlets and organizing countercampaigns. President Wilson finally spoke out in favor of suffrage and even took the unprecedented step of addressing Congress when it had the amendment under considera-
352 tion. Despite the best efforts of the opposition, the amendment finally passed, was ratified and became part of the law of the land; *Minor v. Happersett* was overturned.[96]

Seemingly, the 19th amendment gave to the women a single new right—the right not to be denied the vote solely on the basis of their sex. Looking only at the literal wording of the amendment, it seems as if all that happened was that the 15th amendment itself was amended by adding the word "sex". But from the foregoing discussion, it is clear that much more than the right to vote was at stake—a whole new way of life was being established for women. According to the hopes of its sponsors, and the fears of its opponents, the granting of the vote was to have a revolutionary impact on American society.

Was this not then "the woman's hour?" Was not the 19th amendment a statement by the nation that at long last women were to be equal—just as the nation had promised equality to the freed black slave at the end of the Civil War? If the Chief Justice of the United States thought that *Dred Scott* was the proper model for writing the leading decision on the status of women, did not the overturning of *Minor v. Happersett* mean that the new will of the nation was that henceforth women should no longer be comparable to the pre-Civil War slave? Did not the 19th amendment in fact declare that the second-class citizenship of women was at an end, that women should no longer be "separate but equal" in their status as wife and mother? Did not the 19th amendment thus establish a new national right not to be discriminated against on the basis of sex *in any area*? Did not the national government now have the power to eradicate all "badges and indicia" of second-class citizenship?

---

95. *Id.* ,at 173.
96. *See* FLEXNER, *supra* note 31, at 308-24.

This approach to the 19th amendment is the ultimate parallel in the law of the woman to the law of the black man. The question of the nature of the Wartime Amendments, and how much power they gave to the national government in enforcing the rights there secured has long been a question of great controversy. Some have taken the expansive view suggested above, saying that the Wartime Amendments gave to the national government the power, if not the duty, to affirmatively make the black man equal to white men in all respects, no matter who challenges his right to equality or in what manner.[97] Traditionally, the Supreme Court has taken a more passive view, holding that the new rights of equality granted by the Wartime Amendments are still to be protected by the state governments in the first instance.[98] However, recent opinions of the Supreme Court seem to indicate the Court is rethinking its views on this subject,[99] and it may well be that there will soon be a reinterpretation of those amendments in a more forceful fashion. In *Jones v. Alfred H. Mayer Co.*,[100] 353
the Court took a major step towards redefining the "badges and indicia of slavery," and reactivating the 13th amendment. This decision was, no doubt, influenced by increased pressures from the black community for greater liberties. In the same manner, if the voice of women is loud enough, the Court will find a way to break through years of inaction and rationalization. It is not too unrealistic to think that the 19th amendment will provide a vehicle for the Court to provide for additional rights for females. Just as *Dred Scott* was followed in *Minor v. Happersett* a woman's rights case will one day follow *Jones*.

III. Some Consequences of a Radical Approach to the 19th Amendment

The analysis above has suggested that the 19th amendment really had very little to do with the vote, but instead established the total equality of women with men. Under such an interpretation, there is a national right in all women to suffer no discriminations of any kind *because of their sex*. Under such an interpretation, one need only demonstrate that a certain practice discriminates against women as a class, or that it is a "badge and indicia" of the pre-1920 status of

---

97. *See* Jones v. Alfred H. Mayer Co., 392 U.S. 409 (1968); Plessey v. Ferguson, 163 U.S. 537, 552-64 (1896) (Harlan, J., dissenting); Civil Rights Cases, 109 U.S. 3, 26-62 (1883) (Harlan, J., dissenting); Singleton v. Jackson Munic. Separate School Dist., 348 F.2d 729 (5th Cir. 1965); Kinoy, *supra* note 19.

98. *See* Bell v. Maryland, 378 U.S. 226 (1964); Civil Rights Cases, 109 U.S. 3 (1883).

99. *See* United States v. Price, 383 U.S. 787 (1966); United States v. Guest, 383 U.S. 745 (1966).

100. 392 U.S. 409 (1968). *See* Kinoy, *supra* note 19.

second-class citizen, in order to find primary corrective power in the national government.

Ideally, it should be the women, rather than the predominantly male courts, who decide what discriminates against women, and what is a reasonable regulation which has a legitimate relation to the admitted physical difference between men and women. There is now in the United States a real "second wave" of feminism which is attempting to define its goals, and to organize women and sympathetic men. Many of the women are veterans of the civil rights struggles of the early 1960's, so that they are frequently both militant and politically sophisticated. They have begun to set forth some of the things which they find discriminatory in our society, and to suggest methods of solution. Since the binding of women to the home is the real basis of the inferior position of women in our society, and since it is where the traits of slavery are still most visible, it is not surprising to find
354 that many of their demands center on ways to deal with the problems which women face as a result of their unavoidable childbearing function.

A prime example is the question of abortion. The new feminists argue that women must have an absolute right to an abortion, even as an after-the-fact method of birth control, for otherwise a woman would be forced to undergo nine months of unwanted inconvenience and discomfort, while her husband would not suffer any of the physical inconvenience or discomfort. The position is even stronger, of course, when an illegitimate pregnancy is involved, for in that case the women alone would have to bear the entire burden, including the social stigma, when she and her lover had both violated society's mores. In addition, laws which forbid abortions force the woman with an unwanted pregnancy to abort herself or to find an unethical and unsanitary back-alley abortionist—the result being a staggering number of abortion deaths each year; the men involved, of course, do not suffer that ultimate penalty. Under the approach suggested in this note, an argument could be made that all abortion laws violate the 19th amendment, because they discriminate against the woman.[101]

Another example is the question of maternity leave without loss of seniority. Since it is evident that in the present state of scientific advancement women alone will perform the childbearing function, it

---

101. It is interesting to note in this regard that some abortion suits which have been brought by male doctors have focussed on the vagueness of the criminal statutes, whereas suits brought by women directly challenge the law on the grounds that it abrogates the woman's right to control her own existence. *Compare* People v. Belous, 71 Cal. 2d 954, 458 P.2d 194, 80 Cal. Rptr. 354 (Sup. Ct. 1969), *cert. denied*, 397 U.S. 915 (1970), California v. Robb, Case Nos. 149005 and 159061, Orange County, Cal., Municipial Court, Jan. 9, 1970 *and* District of Columbia v. Vuitch, Crim. Nos. 1043-68 and 1044-68, D.O.C. Nov. 10, 1969 *with* the plaintiffs' brief in Abramowicz v. Lefkowitz, 69 Civ. 4469 (5 D.N.Y.) *and* complaint in Abramowicz v. Kugler (N.J.).

would seem that men should not be allowed to profit economically by it. This means that an employer should not be able to discriminate against women because they will occasionally have to retire from society for a time in order to give birth. Just as society imposes the responsibility upon employers to contribute to the old age pensions of their workers under the social security plans, and requires that they participate in a workmen's compensation plan, so too they could be required to compensate women for the valuable service which they perform for society when they must leave their employment to have children. Such legislation could be upheld under the 19th amendment, for it is legislation which seeks to equalize the position of women and men.

Since the main basis of woman's inferior position in society is her continued enslavement in the home, particularly in caring for the children, the 19th amendment may require that the government act affirmatively to establish universally available, free childcare centers, 355
open to all who wish to make use of them. That is conceptually no different from establishing free public schools, and surely it is required if the woman is to be fully emancipated under the command of the 19th amendment.

Since the 19th amendment declares that women shall be equal, it would seem to be of no constitutional importance from whence the discriminations came. Like the amendment which outlawed slavery for the blacks, the 19th amendment would seem to be immune from the limiting concept of "state action," which has been the subject of so much controversy when the 14th amendment is involved. In particular, it would seem that legislatures and courts would have the power under the 19th amendment to regulate much that takes place in the home. Since the concept that woman's work is in the home is the basis of the enslavement of the woman, it is not too far-fetched to suggest that a man who forbids his wife to work outside the home is attempting to foist second-class citizenship upon her, and is reachable under the amendment. If it is a badge or indicia of Negro slavery to refuse to let a black man rent an apartment, why is it not a badge or indicia of female slavery for a man to refuse to do the dishes? If husband and wife both work during the day, does not the man exploit the woman if she must come home and do the cooking for both of them? If the 19th amendment really does have the power suggested, why could not the refusal of the husband to share in the often burdensome task of childrearing be grounds for divorce, the basis of a tort, or, in the last resort, a crime?

At this point in history, such suggestions seem radical, outlandish, and impossible.[102] But who would have thought at the time *Dred*

102. This expanded theory of the 19th amendment is beginning to gain acceptance by members of the judiciary. *See* State v. Hall, 187 So. 2d 861, 871 (Miss. 1966) (Ethridge, C.J., dissenting).

Scott was written, when it was illegal in many states to teach a black child to read, that integration in education would be the law of the land? Who would have thought when *Plessey v. Ferguson* was written that one day the federal government would pass laws which forbid segregation in the smallest of restaurants, and forbid discrimination in the sale of a one-family house? Ideas have a way of living a life of their own, and once a concept takes hold there is no telling where it will lead, or what the results will be.

To think of government regulating family affairs seems radical because it challenges the very basis of our society. But let people once see that that basis is really the enslavement of our women, then few measures aimed at eradicating the effects of that slavery will seem unwarranted or unwanted. When that time comes, the 19th amendment will be viewed as the great emancipation proclamation, a tool in the hands of those who really believe with the first suffragists
356 at Seneca Falls that all men and women are created equal.

THE LEGAL STATUS OF WOMEN IN THE LATE NINETEENTH AND EARLY TWENTIETH CENTURIES

JOAN HOFF WILSON*

The period 1865 to 1920 marks the first time that women systematically tried to obtain equality of treatment in the courts. While they did not succeed, in retrospect their attempts are interesting for a number of reasons. First, the few cases of major significance involving women clearly indicate the overwhelming legal obstacles that the several generations of women of these years faced, almost regardless of the issues being discussed. Second, judicial patterns or preferences that emerged by 1920 from these 357
cases lingered for many years—some down to the present. Third, there was also a subtle interaction between the political and legal activities of women reformers during this period. Their relationship has been largely ignored by both legal historians and historians of women's history.

It is now possible to trace how these two types of activity varied in intensity depending upon how women perceived their legal status at any given time. In fact, I would argue that to the degree the courts discouraged female legal reform, women often responded by taking political action as a form of compensation. Such compensatory political actions were often more conservative in nature than their initial court cases were. A similar but possibly less obvious relationship continues to exist today because women have still not found adequate legal means for obtaining equality of treatment.

Equality of treatment in the late nineteenth and early twentieth centuries, as well as now, inevitably means that at various levels the courts were being asked to question standard sex stereotyped assumptions. According to Professor Laurence Tribe of Harvard Law School, the Supreme Court is almost always reluctant when asked to "identify areas of moral flux and normative transition"

---

* B.A. 1957, University of Montana; M.A. 1959, Cornell University; Ph.D. 1966, University of California at Berkeley. Professor of History, Arizona State University. Co-author of SEXISM AND THE LAW: MALE BELIEFS AND LEGAL BIAS IN BRITAIN AND THE UNITED STATES (1977).

and "to facilitate . . . the evolution of moral and thus legal consciousness."[1] Tribe has pointed out in a recent article that there is still no satisfactory way for the courts to do this for citizens in general, let alone for women. He suggests moving beyond the suspect classification and strict judicial scrutiny of the equal protection clause and beyond procedural and substantive due process to what he calls "structural due process".[2] This concept, as Tribe defines it, would take into consideration the fact that "the structures through which policies are both formed and applied [are] formed in the very process of being applied."[3] He recommends, therefore, that the Supreme Court should consciously begin to consider the relationship between policy and process and begin to structure the "process of change in constitutional principles
358 without dictating the end products."[4] Admittedly Tribe's concept of "structural due process" is a very tenuous one, but in the event that ERA *is not* ratified it may prove a seminal suggestion. I simply want to point out how few legal options for change were available to women immediately following the Civil War, compared to today, despite the passage of the fourteenth amendment. This resulted primarily from an excessive use of pure judicial preference.

In fact, the most overtly sexist decisions on the part of the Supreme Court occurred *after* the Civil War, as women attempted to improve their legal status under the fourteenth amendment. This is not to say that the Married Women's Property Acts, which were passed in nine states *before* the Civil War, were liberally interpreted by the lower courts. Professor Linda Kerber has referred to the conservative nature of these pre-war acts[5] and the post-war ones were generally not more liberating in terms of either motivation or an expansion of married women's rights. The significance of these very legally limited and narrowly interpreted Married Women's Property Acts lies in the fact that they represented one of

---

[1] Tribe, *Structural Due Process*, 10 HARV. C.R.-C.L. L. REV. 269, 319, 321 (1975).

[2] *Id.* at 269.

[3] *Id.* at 291.

[4] *Id.* at 296.

[5] *See* Kerber, *From the Declaration of Independence to the Declaration of Sentiments: The Legal Status of Women in the Early Republic 1776-1848*, 6 HUMAN RIGHTS 115, 118-20 (1977).

the major traditional instruments whereby legal reform could be achieved for women, namely, through the passage of legislation at the state level.[6] By 1900 they constituted the most significant advance in the status of married women with respect to property. They also represented the most viable legal alternative for women before the appearance of substantive due procss, which did not occur until the early twentieth century when the Supreme Court adopted the use of "judicial notice" and accepted facts deemed "common knowledge."

In other words, all of the other legal means women pursued to obtain equality of treatment between 1865 and 1900 had failed. Let us review the major Supreme Court cases that arose after the passage of the Reconstruction Amendments. As I have said they are few in number and in some instances are well known for reasons 359
other than their impact on women. They are: *Bradwell v. Illinois,*[7] which held that the right to practice law was not a privilege and immunity of citizenship for a woman; the *Slaughter House Cases,*[8] which also very narrowly interpreted the Privileges and Immunity clause of the fourteenth amendment and remains well known for its definition of national citizenship and the denial that the Equal Protection clause could be applied in other than race cases; *Minor v. Happersett,*[9] which declared that historically women constituted a very special category of citizens whose inability to vote did not infringe upon their rights as citizens; and *Ex parte Yarbrough,*[10] which technically overruled the *Minor* decision by setting the stage for the proposition that voting for a federal official was, indeed, a privilege and immunity of national citizenship.

Remember, that it was also during these years from 1865 to 1900, that in those states where the first women's rights movement was the most actively organized, Married Women's Property Acts

---

[6] The other basic ways in which such reform or change had occurred since the colonial period was through equity jurisprudence and legal fictions. For the latest in-depth discussion of these and of the significance of Married Women's Property Acts in general, *see* Rabkin, The Silent Feminist Revolution: Women and the Law in New York State from Blackstone to the Beginnings of the American Women's Rights Movement (1975) (unpublished Ph.D. dissertation, presented at State University of New York, Buffalo).

[7] 83 U.S. (16 Wall.) 130 (1873).

[8] 83 U.S. (16 Wall.) 36 (1873).

[9] 88 U.S. 162 (1875).

[10] 110 U.S. 651 (1884).

were more comprehensive than before the Civil War. These statutes, however, were still subjected to severely restrictive judicial interpretations by the end of the century. These are the same years that women united around the long struggle for passage of women's suffrage at the state level. This effort finally led to the passage of the nineteenth amendment at the end of World War I. It was also the period in which the country celebrated its Centennial in 1876. Professor Kerber has alluded to the famous document that Susan B. Anthony and others insisted on presenting in Philadelphia that July 4—[11] called a Women's Declaration of Rights. Beginning with the words: "The history of our country the past hundred years has been a series of assumptions and usurpations of power over woman, in direct opposition to the principles of just government . . . ,"[12] it
360 called for the impeachment of American leaders. Thus, we can see that women reformers resorted to political activities when they failed to improve their legal status through the courts following the passage of the fourteenth and fifteenth amendments. These same women had unsuccessfully employed every effort to get Republican leaders to eliminate the word "male" from the first section of the former and to add the word "sex" to the latter. Taken together these two amendments to the Constitution of the United States implied that women were not citizens. Female activists lost no time testing both in the courts in some of the cases cited above. In a very real sense, therefore, passage of the fourteenth and fifteenth amendments, and their subsequent negative interpretation by courts, as far as women were concerned, forced all post-war female reformers —whether they considered themselves radical or moderates—to concentrate on what had never been their primary pre-war goal: suffrage.

So the legal and political implications of the Reconstruction Amendments for the first women's movement were enormous. The Civil War itself had disrupted the momentum of the women's rights movement since 1848. When the post-war political efforts of the more militant reformers, like Anthony and Stanton, failed to expressly include women in the fourteenth and fifteenth amendments,

---

[11] *See* Kerber, *supra* note 5, at 123-24.

[12] A copy of the "Women's Declaration of Rights" for 1876 can be found in ONE HALF THE PEOPLE: THE FIGHT FOR WOMAN SUFFRAGE 91-95 (A.F. Scott & A.M. Scott eds. 1975).

they immediately began the first of a series of systematic attempts by several generations of women to use the courts to improve their legal and political status—first through the Privileges and Immunities clause, then through the Due Process clause, and finally, continuing down to the present, through the Equal Protection clause. To date none of these efforts has been completely successful and the initial attempts, as reflected in the cases mentioned above, were particularly discouraging.

For example, one of the worst aspects of the Myra Colby Bradwell case was not simply that she was denied the right to practice as a lawyer in Illinois. Its worst feature was the language that Justice Bradley used in his concurring opinion. In the Blackstone tradition, Bradley insisted that women had no legal existence separate from that of their husbands, despite the passage of a number of 361
Married Women's Property Acts. His opinion stated:

> The civil law, as well as nature itself, has always recognized a wide difference in the respective spheres and destinies of man and woman. Man is, or should be, woman's protector and defender. . . . The domestic sphere . . . properly belongs to the domain and functions of womanhood. The harmony . . . of interests and ties which belong, or should belong, to the family institution is repugnant to the idea of a woman adopting a distinct and independent career from that of her husband. . . . The paramount destiny and mission of woman are to fulfill the noble and benign offices of wife and mother. This is the law of the creator. And the rules of civil society must be adapted to the general constitution of things, and cannot be based upon exceptional cases.[13]

Another interesting feature of *Bradwell* is its relationship to the *Slaughter House Cases*. Since both were considered by the Supreme Court during the same fourteen month period, it is entirely possible that the narrow interpretation of privileges and immunities with respect to a choice of occupation for the butchers in *Slaughter House* was probably "influenced by the Court's realization that a broad interpretation would necessarily change the status of women."[14] Justice Bradley's position on these two cases is also noteworthy. He argued against Myra Bradwell's right of choice of occupation. But in his dissenting opinion in the *Slaughter House*

---

[13] Bradwell v. Illinois, *supra* note 7, at 141-42 (Bradley, J., dissenting).

[14] B. Babcock, A. Freedman, E. Norton, & S. Ross, Sex Discrimination and the Law: Causes and Remedies 8 (1975).

Cases, he argued for the butchers having that same right, saying that a "law which prohibits a large class of citizens from adopting lawful employment . . . does deprive them of liberty as well as property without due process of law."[15] Obviously by the word "citizens," Justice Bradley did not mean women. Mathew Carpenter, one of the best known advocates of the day, took similarly irreconcilable positions in these two cases. He was, unlike Bradley, arguing against the butchers and for Bradwell. His opinions were as inconsistent as Bradley's, albeit for different legal reasons. Nonetheless, both men used standard sexist arguments.

One might wonder why such inconsistencies were never seriously questioned by the Court or any historian until recently. Was Bradwell's case simply considered less important because of pre-
362 vailing "natural male dominance" theories of the time? Did the general political climate of the Reconstruction Era play a more important role than gender discrimination in the *Bradwell* and *Slaughter House* decisions? Regardless of the exact reasons, one thing is clear. The decisions and precedents set in these two cases created insurmountable obstacles for a broadening of women's rights through the courts in the early post-Civil War decades.

About the same time that Bradwell was bringing suit to practice law, other women were taking more direct and disruptive action by actually trying to vote. In 1871 and 1872 over 100 women voted in nine different states. The most famous of all these attempts resulted in the trial of Susan B. Anthony,[16] who with thirteen other women tried to vote on November 5, 1872, in Rochester, New York. All of the women were arrested under a provision of the Federal Civil Rights Act of 1870 which was designed to prevent white voters from cancelling out black votes by voting more than once. The misuse of this law against Anthony and other women in the 1870s brings to mind the parallel of the similarly novel use of federal statutes in the 1960s against demonstrators. It was also a clear indication of the political nature of her trial. The Anthony case never reached the Supreme Court because of two legal technicalities. Therefore, interest in the case today remains largely historical because of the increased interest in Anthony

[15] Slaughter House Cases, *supra* note 8, at 122 (Bradley, J., dissenting).

[16] United States v. Anthony, 24 F. Cas. 829 (C.C.N.D.N.Y. 1873) (No. 14459).

as a militant feminist. Moreover, the legal issues it raised were more clearly developed in *Minor v. Happersett* in 1875.[17]

Using parallel reasoning to *Dred Scott v. Sandford*,[18] the *Minor* court declared women a special category similar to that of children and specifically denied that the right to vote for national officials was a privilege and immunity of national citizenship as implied in the *Slaughter House Cases*. The *Minor* decision, like the *Dred Scott* decision of twenty years before, could only be bypassed by a constitutional amendment, even though the *Minor* case was unofficially overruled in the *Yarbrough* case of 1884.[19] What is curious here is that *Dred Scott* has for some time been considered a blot on constitutional law, but *Minor* and *Bradwell* have yet to receive the same deserved castigation by the legal profession. Again, the question must be asked—why? Is it because of Reconstruction politics 363
or judicial sexism, or both? Little wonder that Anthony and other radical women protested at the 1876 Centennial celebration in Philadelphia. These women knew what was happening to their rights in courts. Many, like Bradwell, were involved in writing and agitating for Married Women's Property Acts. So they took up the cause of suffrage with a vengeance and conservatism that had not generally characterized their court actions.[20]

By the first decade of the twentieth century, however, some women reformers were ready to try the courts again. This time they were eager to test the legality of protective legislation. By 1908 there were nineteen laws setting maximum hours for women and/or prohibiting night work for women. Their constitutionality was in question because of a previous decision denying a limit on working hours for male bakers in *Lochner v. New York*.[21] The

---

[17] *Supra* note 9.

[18] 60 U.S. (19 How.) 393 (1857). Chief Justice Taney's exact words in Dred Scott were: "Undoubtedly, a person may be a citizen, that is, a member of the community who form the sovereignty, although he exercises no share of the political power, and is incapacitated from holding particular offices. Women and minors who form a part of the political family, cannot vote. . . ." *Id.* at 422.

[19] *Supra* note 10.

[20] Historians currently disagree on whether or not suffrage falls into the category of conservative political activity. I personally think it was, except for the original generation of women who advocated it immediately preceding and following the Civil War. Ellen DuBois has made the strongest case for the radical nature of the suffrage movement. *See* DuBois, *The Radicalism of the Woman Suffrage Movement: Notes Toward the Reconstruction of Nineteenth-Century Feminism*, 3 FEMINIST STUDIES 63-71 (1975).

[21] 198 U.S. 45 (1905).

Court's *Lochner* decision clearly stood in the way of protective legislation for women as well as men. Therefore, in the next protective legislation case to reach the Supreme Court, which involved a woman, a new defense had to be devised. That case turned out to be *Muller v. Oregon*.[22] Louis D. Brandeis could have argued his case against Muller (who had been convicted of requiring a female employee to work more than ten hours in violation of a state law) in one of two ways. First, he could have tried to displace the "common knowledge" or "common understanding" argument in *Lochner*, about the lack of health dangers in bakeries or any industrial job, by using sociological evidence to show that any such job performed steadily for more than ten hours a day was dangerous to a worker's health. Second, he could have argued that, because women were in-
364 volved, there was reason to make an exception to *Lochner's* doctrine of liberty of contract on the grounds that women need "special protection."

Theoretically, the very famous 113-page "Brandeis Brief" combined both approaches by presenting statistical and sociological data from nonjudicial sources. In actuality, however, the brief (and later the decision) focused primarily on the physical differences between men and women. Thus, the majority opinion did not really consider the individual working woman involved in the case in terms of either her working conditions or her performance on the job. Instead, the Court concentrated on her procreative functions and those of all American working women. In ruling in favor of the state, the Supreme Court used sexist language and attitudes reminiscent of the *Anthony*, *Bradwell* and *Minor* cases. In addition, it incorporated the *Dred Scott* argument that "women as citizens" constituted a special category. In retrospect, as a judicial precedent, the *Muller* decision represented the worst of all possible legal arguments in terms of equality of treatment of women, although this is seldom noted in legal texts. Beyond any doubt *Muller* opened the door to the discriminatory application of protective legislation to women workers. At the time, however, the decision was welcomed by Progressive reformers in general because it did improve some of the harsh conditions women faced in an unregulated factory system. But like the Married Women's Prop-

[22] 208 U.S. 412 (1908).

erty Acts of the previous century, this improvement came without changing any traditional ideas about male supremacy, which have prevailed in court decisions down to the present.

Moreover, further protective legislation that followed in the wake of *Muller* convinced a number of women reformers that their needs were being met by the courts. This belief actually lulled the vast majority of female activists into ccmplacency. Only a handful of the most militant feminists saw the future danger of a decision like *Muller* which could be used to keep women from advancing on the job and out of so-called men's jobs. These were the same perspicacious women who drafted the first ERA amendment in the 1920s to overcome traditional gender discrimination by the courts. For the most part, their warnings and activities were ignored until
a new generation of women began to take them up again in the 365
last decade.

By 1920, therefore, American women had more political, legal, educational and economic opportunities than they had had in 1865. But they still had not achieved equality before the law with men. They had tried in recent years to obtain equality of treatment through the Equal Protection clause of the fourteenth amendment. Despite *Frontiero v. Richardson,*[23] in which the Court condemned "romantic paternalism," it has been most reluctant to face the Equal Protection issue in subsequent cases and to declare unequivocally that sex is, indeed, a suspect classification requiring close judicial scrutiny. In the event that the ERA is not ratified and the Equal Protection clause continues to prove a dead end for expanding women's rights, it may well be that Professor Tribe's concept of "structural due process," as reflected in *Witherspoon v. Illinois,*[24] and *Roe v. Wade,*[25] will prove less threatening than the Equal Protection clause, as a way for the Supreme Court to advance the principle of equality for women. In fact, as recently as July 1, 1976, in *Planned Parenthood v. Danforth,*[26] the Court upheld its previous position on viability of the fetus (*Roe v. Wade*) in terms of what Tribe is calling "structural due process."

Whatever happens in the next few years, it is to be hoped that

---

[23] 411 U.S. 677 (1973).
[24] 391 U.S. 510 (1968).
[25] 410 U.S. 113 (1973).
[26] 96 S.Ct. 2831 (1976).

women will not end up as they did in 1920 with too little too late. By this I mean that it is entirely possible that women obtained the right to vote, not in the nineteenth century when it would have been truly significant in terms of grassroots Jacksonian politics, but in the twentieth at the very time when electoral politics was breaking down into meaningless choices. With technological advancements making traditional labor increasingly obsolete, it looks as though women are at long last going to receive equal pay for equal work and equal opportunity to compete for jobs in the 1970's. Only time and hopefully the passage of the ERA will determine whether this latest women's struggle will end with too little too late, as it has so many times in the past.

ISSUES IN CRIMINOLOGY, VOLUME 7, NUMBER 1 (WINTER, 1972)

Reflections by Gaslight: Prostitution in Another Age

Kay Ann Holmes

The movie industry, with a pat on the head and a pat on the butt, has urged the cameo portrait of the prostitute out onto the stage before 367
millions. In films like *Never on Sunday, Irma La Douce, Sweet Charity,* and *The First Time,* the whore with the heart of gold, earthy wisdom, honesty, and other sterling qualities similar to those of the Virgin Mary, Saint Joan, and Florence Nightingale, mercilessly steals her audiences' hearts for the short period of two hours. For even though the audience may laugh at the antics and weep at the misfortunes of the "painted lady" on the screen—somehow in the middle-American mind the association between the girl on the screen and the girl on the street is never made. The two characters are not one and the same. To that hard core "we shall not be moved, and besides it is in the Bible so it must be true" moralistic segment of our population prostitution is bad, evil, nasty, unAmerican, and must be searched out and eliminated with untiring vigilance.

This process takes the form of laws aimed directly at the prostitute making her occupation punishable by incarceration and fine. Such laws exist in all 50 states.

Despite each new police chief's effort to impress the public with his new "Clean up the streets and return to law and order" program, these laws and their enforcement are not new. Their first enforcement goes back 70 years to a period when the popular image of a prostitute (despite the efforts of a group of reformers during this same period of time to change it), was that of a totally immoral, foreign feebleminded, syphilitic, nymphomaniac, running rampant through the

*Kay Ann Holmes received her A.B. from the School of Criminology at the University of California, Berkeley in 1971. She also received the Departmental citation for that year and is a Phi Beta Kappa.

slums mating with others of her kind and misguided, weak, upper-class boys who were improperly socialized. Little better than an animal, she was a threat to the very structure of the country, as constantly having intercourse and being perpetually fertile, she brought into the world offspring who genetically inherited all the vices and mental facilities of the mother.

Our laws still stem from this image even though the vast majority of successful prostitutes are not infected with venereal disease, do not get pregnant, and are no more feebleminded than any other occupational group. The only remaining stigma is moral and this too is in a period of change.

It is the purpose of this article to show that during the periods of law enforcement discussed what appears to be a complete humanitarian movement at the turn of the century, an international crusade of the compassionate toward the women who receive neither pity nor con-
368 sideration and have so long been judged without a hearing (Adams, 1912:218), was in fact made up of two different groups, holding different and contradictory thoughts on the prostitute and methods of controlling her trade. The purpose of the one was the rescue of misguided girls; the purpose of the other was the preservation and protection of the "moral upper classes" from a potentially expandable and "dangerous class." Our present laws are based on the latter.

Prostitution itself was not regarded as an offense in either English or American Common Law, and came into conflict with the law only when it was associated with street soliciting or the operation of a bawdy house as to be annoying to the passerby. In other words, the test of the offense was the fact of annoyance. This is clearly indicated by one of the conditions of disorderly conduct enumerated in an early New York State Statute, which defined as a disorderly person, "every common prostitute or night walker loitering or being in any thoroughfare or public place for the purpose of prostitution or solicitation to the annoyance of inhabitants or passerby" (Waterman, 1932:12).

It follows that the only person who can be guilty of offenses concerned with prostitution are those who are active participants, and are guilty only when their activities have resulted in "annoyance of inhabitants or passerby." It is to this distinction that the prevelance of "red light" districts in the United States can be traced. The toleration of these districts is based upon the opinion that if the disorders of behavior frequently associated with prostitution are segregated within a given area of town, the reputable and sedate members of the community can avoid the district. The disorderly elements of society are thus herded together, and other citizens, by avoiding contact with the district, do not have their sensibilities outraged by being forced to be spectators of obscenity and disorder (Waterman, 1932:13).

And so were formed the "sections" which existed in almost every large city in the United States. New Orlean's Basin Street, San Francisco's Barbary Coast, Denver's Market Street Line, New York's Bowery and Five Points, all offered women and "good time" in all types of settings from the most wretched to the most lavish.

Women were arrested during this period but they were, by the vast majority, the streetwalkers. Old, alcoholic, deformed, part-time, or new in the business, unable or unwilling to work within the security of a house, they were arrested when they came into conflict with the "solicitation and public nuisance" clause. Hanging around a street corner, yelling obscenities, fighting over a customer, bothering respectable women, public eyesore, forcing attentions on a gentleman were all grounds for arrest.

Brothel girls were rarely bothered. Sometimes the whole house 369
was arrested and taken down to the station and fined during a yearly or semi-annual ceremony, but more often money was simply passed to the proper member of the police force and the outward trappings of penance became unnecessary. The law was always potentially enforceable, but simply given lip service to the agreement of all involved.

Little was instituted to alter this mutual co-operation system until one Sunday morning in 1892, The Reverend Charles E. Pankhurst took the pulpit of a local New York church and proclaimed with the wrath of God behind him that the police department was in league with prostitutes and racketeers (Murtaugh and Harris, 1957:211). Each Sunday he continued his accusations and backed up his information with statistics gathered through "personal research." The majority of officials in any type of public position knew the arrangement between the police and the Houses, but there were certain people, not in public positions, who were unaware of the situation and they were becoming upset. It has always been difficult to espouse a position that the Church damns and this was no exception. The police department came under fire and the old police chief was replaced (Murtaugh and Harris, 1957:213).

Prostitution was slowly, reluctantly being pushed into the light of public scrutiny.

It is highly doubtful that if this one blast from "the man of God" had been the only bad publicity that prostitution had received, that this in itself would have caused enough indignation to close the brothels. Too many men used the brothels from time to time and enjoyed the service they rendered. Likewise, respectable ladies didn't talk of sex much less immoral sex of the type that was going on in the sections. The local power structure, its officials and police, certainly knew the existence of the situation, but for a time at least, it served their interest in that they personally profited from it. Without their becoming "officially" upset there simply was no place for the cause against prostitution to take hold. The catalyst was publicity. When a few people become noticeably upset over an existing situation, it becomes necessary for politicians' and "upright citizens'" images to become upset also. A disposable scapegoat is demanded, every evil is blamed on him, he is "lynched" and the relative status of the politicians and "upright citizens" remains unaltered regardless of their previous tacit or actual involvement with the "evil" situation. In this case New York scapegoated her police chief and, had it not been for publicity factors which helped to enrage public opinion, the segregated, police protected districts probably would not have been changed at all.

370 At this time, most men knew of venereal disease, what it was and where you got it—most women did not. It is difficult to discern whether syphilis made a notable rise during this period (1890-1915) bringing it to national attention as it rose to epidemic proportions, or whether people simply began to deal with it as a public health problem rather than a lightening bolt from heaven—adequate statistics are not available. But, whatever the reason, the result was that syphilis and like diseases were beginning to be dealt with on some sort of a national level.

Statistics concerning the results of the disease were becoming common knowledge. Statistics such as: 70% of all female patients in New York hospitals are respectable married women infected innocently by their husbands, 90% of all syphilitic infection in men is derived from prostitutes, 100% of locomotor ataxia comes from syphilitic infection, 2 out of every 13 deaths in the United States is related to syphilis (Funk, 1921:47), 3,500,000 out of a population of 70,000,000 in 1893 were estimated to be infected (Sanger, 1897:687). All cases of blindness at birth of infants, and all miscarriages were also attributed to the disease.

If these "facts" were not enough to instill fear—"professionals" pressed their opinions that these numbers were only a small portion of the total infected. S. Philip Goodhart, PhD. M.D. Chief of Nervous Disease Clinic Mount Sinai Hospital, New York:

> Computation of the number of cases can only have a relative value, and the estimate of 5-20% which is given by various writers as the proportion of population infected is probably an underestimate, since from the very nature of things, secrecy is invariably a factor (1913:414).

The appeal was an emotional one. Men were told that once infected they were not safe from fresh outbreaks for a period varying in medical opinion from 2-5 years (Creighton, 1914:25).

So opinion was formed—syphilis and prostitution were synonymous, and the cry was; "Sir, for a moment of evil pleasure—think of your chaste, blushing bride and unborn child."

Organizations began to form with the sole purpose of education of the public to the results of the "Social Diseases" and to put pressure on legislatures to "do something" about this "Social Evil," prostitution which was the cause of venereal disease. Some of the organizations formed were:

> The Society of Sanitary & Moral Prophylaxis (this was one of the largest anti-prostitution organizations with branches in Pennsylvania, Chicago, Maryland, St. Louis, Spokane, Colorado, California, Detroit, Indiana, West Virginia, Connecticut, Texas, New Jersey, and Seattle.)
> Bureau of Social Hygiene
> American Social Hygiene Association
> Illinois Vigilance Association
> New York Society for the Prevention of Crime

All printed pamphlets which were sent to schools and businesses. They formed lecture teams and went out into the community to give talks before clubs and church groups. Women began to get involved in the crusade. Jane Adams states the view of these early women as to their goals of dislodging their reticent sisters:

> The very fact that the conditions and results of the social evil lie so far away from the knowledge of good women is largely responsible for the secrecy and hypocrisy upon which it thrives. Most good women will probably never consent to break through their ignorance save under a sense of duty which has ever been the incentive to action to which even timid women have responded. At least a promising beginning would be made toward more effective social control, if the mass of conscientious women were once thoroughly convinced that a knowledge of local vice conditions was a matter of civic obligation (1912:196).

The hypothesis was that the general public was just ignorant—if given the needed information they would rise up and join forces to control the dread disease.

That syphilis was bad and prostitution was its cause seemed to be the one point of total agreement within the ranks of the warriors against the social evil. After this point a split begins to form and two dstinct groups begin to take shape. I have labeled them the "control group" and the "humanitarians" for ease in handling.

Although individuals from the East, Midwest, and Southwest (the author found only one writer from the South) belonged to both groups, the centralization of both was in the East and in large metropolitan areas.

In respect to occupation and social class, the members of both groups were in the middle and upper classes. Occupations tended to be of a professional nature, including a large number of doctors in both groups. Also represented in both groups were lawyers, social workers, probation workers and wives of professional men. The only distinguishable feature between the two was the large number of women, especially in positions of power in the Humanitarian group and the large number of administrators of training schools, mental hospitals, and clinics in the other.

THE CONTROL GROUP

372 The most salient fact to come out of this group was the view of the prostitute as an animal, as something less than human. They saw the occupation as a seething, mangled stew of all the vilest, miserable dregs of society.

But even this view, added to the fact of the prostitute as a health menace, was not in itself enough to foster the plan for control brought forth by this group. There were other problems involved.

Besides being syphilitic, these women were pictured as an ethnic, economic, and intellectual group of the lowest level, a group that conventional society could well do without. That group was also in a period of rapid expansion, for while a lady of breeding and refinement might have intercourse with her husband once a month, the prostitute was having intercourse perhaps 10 times a day or more—7 days a week. Her chances of conceiving a child were greatly increased. Add this to the fact that the characteristics she was said to possess—syphilitic infection, feeblemindedness, low intelligence, poverty, foreign origin, immorality, disregard for Christian ethics, were transferred to the offspring, and that the prostitute was capable of conceiving a "defective" infant every nine months—you have a cause for concern.

One of the most important hypotheses put forth by this group was that women became prostitutes because they wanted to be prostitutes. No coercion was involved. "Women are attracted rather than forced into prostitution—the earnings the rich attire, and more luxurious mode of life is a strong attraction." This was stated by the Committee of 15, a commission formed in Chicago in 1910 to study the prostitution "problem" (1902:7). What they were actually saying was that the women who became prostitutes were of weak character and will. They held the same goals the rest of society did, the goals of the obvious outward appearance of wealth, but they refused to work, scrimp, sweat and slave for the extra crumb as the Bible taught. They saw an easier way and took it. They defied the Protestant Ethic. They owned a commodity in demand and sold it, thus taking part in a "voluntary act known by everyone to be immoral" (1902:65). They liked their work and would change it for no other. In Sanger's survey of prostitutes in New York City in 1898, of the 2,000 girls interviewed more than half said they became prostitutes because of inclination. "Inclination to this work, said Sanger, is in itself such an answer as would imply an innate depravity, a want of womanly feeling which is truly incredible" (1897:488).

These women were all from the lower classes. They were looked upon by the Control group as a "class of women who may be said to have been trained for prostitution from earliest childhood. Foundlings, orphans, offsprings of the miserably poor, they grow up in wretched tennements, contaminated by constant familiarity with vice at its lowest forms, without training mental or moral they remain ignorant and disagreeable, slovenly, and uncouth, good for nothing in the social or economic organism" (Committee of Fifteen, 1902:10). The previous jobs listed by these women were never of a professional nature, they were menial labor types of jobs: servants, factory workers, sales clerks, seamstresses, umbrella makers, and waitresses. These jobs paid as little as $2.00 for an 80 hour week. The Control group concluded:

> First among these is the fact that one pauper family has a tendency to marry to other pauper families. Secondly, the evidence is clear that successive generations of the same family contain a due proportion of paupers. This points to the conclusion that pauperism is due to inherent defects which are hereditarily transmitted. Thirdly, the experiences of the Committee is quite clear that paupers whom they have examined individually, are characterized by some obvious vice or defect such as drunkeness, theft, persistent laziness, mental deficiency, deliberate moral obliquity or general weakness of character (Council of the Eugenics Education Society, 1910:187).

The majority of these women were foreign born. In Sanger's study 5/8 of those interviewed were not American citizens (1897:460). Estimates of the number of foreign prostitutes goes as high as 80% of the total.

Another reason for becoming a prostitute was feeblemindedness. Between 30% - 56% of all prostitutes were said to be of the imbecile and moron level (Funk, 1921:47). Great concern was placed on the heredity of this trait, and articles were written by staff of Kings Park State Hospital, New York (Rosanoff, 1911:22); Manhatton State Hospital, New York (Kirby, 1913:156); Presbyterian Hospital, New

York (Fisher, 1913:163); and the Russell Sage Foundation (Hart, 1914:1).

Concern was also shown to the breeding habits of the feeble-minded. "Their increasing numbers is apparent in our statistics and the expense of maintenance grows annually. Each feebleminded person who lives will certainly produce his kind and bring blight and disease into the blood of normal character" (Hurty, 1912:4). "These people are unfit to be parents and if they have children, the latter will curse the day they were born. And so, it is not humanity, it is not christianity, it is not good government to permit the children to become parents" (Hurty, 1912:8).

From this assumption, plus the image of the prostitute - animal - non-person, the method of control by sterilization was a logical step.

As Francis Galton said (Blacker, 1952:111) in 1908: "The first
374 object of Eugenics is to check the birth rate of the unfit, instead of
allowing to come into being, though doomed in large numbers to perish prematurely." This is just what the Control group hoped to do.

The idea of sterilization of the "unfit" is not of American origin. The first recorded operation of this type was done in Switzerland at the Cantonal Asylum at Wil in 1909. The operation was performed on four individuals, two women and two men, who though mentally "slightly" abnormal or defective were not strictly insane, and the medical authorities wished to discharge them. Both women had each given birth to two children, two of which were "epileptic idiots." The men were said to have strong sex inclinations (Nacke, 1909:6).

By 1911 sterilization laws were passed in California, Connecticut, Indiana, Iowa, New Jersey, and Washington (Smith and Wilkinson, 1914:34). But the process was still in the experimental stage; few cases were actually being unsexed. Americans were reticent about plunging in.

On December 14, 1911, The American Society of Sanitary and Moral Prophylaxis, one of the largest anti-syphilis, anti-prostitution organizations of the time met in New York for its annual meeting. At the proceedings, Dr. John N. Nurty, Secretary of the Indiana State Board of Health and State Health Commissioner rose to the occasion and chastised Americans for not doing more about sterilization of the "unfit":

> How passing strange are many of our acts. We organize society, we institute governments, we establish schools and churches, we build prisons, almshouses, jails, insane hospitals, and idiot asylums all for the purpose of training, directing, protecting, and controlling ourselves. We

> declare against the evils of alcohol and drugs, we pass pure food laws, we establish a system whereby we may know if we are receiving fair weight and measure, we organize societies to care for the unfortunate, we enact laws prohibiting the violation of physical sancity, but when it comes to the core of the question, the prevention of the causes of these evils and misfortunes, we restrain from wise and practical action by prudery.
>
> We are permitting thousands, ten thousands, hundreds of thousands to marry and reproduce their own kind, when at the time of their marriage they are deviates or they are afflicted with syphilis or with gonorrhoea or possibly with both, which diseases will not cause death, but will visit themselves into the third and fourth generation in the forms of blindness, bone disease, insanity, imbecility, nervous wrecks, moral degenerates, and perverts. We are doing this because we will not stop it, not because we cannot. We are filling our almshouses, hospitals, jails, penitentiaries and homes for the morally and physically unfortunate by our refusal to meet the social question, the sex question, the prevention of the procreation of degenerates in an honest, sensible, pure-minded manner. Would it not be worth something to this nation in dollars and cents 375
> to raise men and women who are physically sound? Does not the future and the perpetuity of our nation, politically and commercially depend upon a generation that is clean limbed and clear-headed, possessed of brain, brawn, nerve, and are free from taint and weakness?
>
> The burden of degeneracy, defectiveness, syphilis and gonorrhea may in great degree be lifted by a united effort to keep hell out of men rather than trying to keep men out of hell. We must away with prudery. We must sterilize all lily livered loons who would prate of an individual right to perpetuate defectiveness and spread horrible diseases which bring pain, sorrow, agony, torture, and anguish to the tender and innocent and which may destroy the race!! (Hurty, 1912:16-18)

Following the lecture, the former superintendent of the New York State Reformatory, Elmira, New York; the superintendent and psychologist of the Training School for Feebleminded Children, Vineland, New Jersey; the Superintendent of the New Jersey State Village for Epileptics; the superintendent of the New Jersey State Reformatory; the Secretary of the New York Board of Charities; and two private physicians lauded Dr. Hurty's speech. Only one individual present offered a dissent, the President of the Board of Trustees for the Society of Medical Jurisprudence (Hurty, 1912:19).

Similar talks and pamphlets were put out by the First National Conference on Race Betterment, Battle Creek, Michigan; the American Prison Association (Hart, 1913:1); the American Social Hygiene Association; and the Russell Sage Foundation.

The stand of the Control Group was then, that the prostitute was a depraved criminal. She must be sought out and punished severely.

Girls now in the business must be directed into other work and would-be novices must be discouraged. The women who still refused to leave the profession must be imprisoned and sterilized whenever possible to prevent the passing on of unwanted traits, which were harmful to society, and the next generation.

THE HUMANITARIANS

The Humanitarians, while lacking little in zeal and belief in purpose, did not have the national organizations of the Control Group. While the Humanitarians did work through such organizations as the Y.M.C.A., Y.W.C.A., the Salvation Army, and the National Purity Council, their strength lay in the strong personalities of such people as Jane Adams, Maude Miner, Louise Creighton, and in the local metro-
376 politan "rescue missions" that sprung up in most of the large cities.
These were staffed by local church groups.

The first public appearance of their work was in September, 1909 issue of *Womans' World,* (then the largest woman's magazine in circulation) and gave the views and aims of the Humanitarians.

The nucleus of their argument was that no woman was a prostitute because she wanted to be. That the social problems of the society as a whole, the treachery of evil souls wanting to make money off the weakness of men, and the ignorance of young girls, forced women into the occupation of prostitute. There was no special predisposed "type" to this profession—all were basically good women, and almost any woman in the same position would succumb.

They first chastised society as a whole for the existence of the "double standard." The standard which condoned and even admired sex on the part of the young man asserting his blossoming masculinity and at the same time condemned the young woman who was his partner. This formed the market for prostitution:

> Society has accepted prostitution as a necessity. To this day many will tell you that it has always existed, that it is useless to expect that it will ever cease to exist. The majority probably have never stopped to think what its existence involves. The young man who sins lightly because others do it, because someone suggests it, because he has drunk a little too much, because no one has ever taught him the duty of self-control, never stops to think that the thoughtless act which he and so many others like him commit means the degradation of women, means the existence of a shameful trade out of which men and women grow rich through the ruin of young girls in order to supply him with a passing gratification (Creighton, 1914:28-29).

> The respectable women safe in their own sheltered existence have not only for the most part in the past refused to concern themselves in any way for their fallen sisters and have been content to assume the ignorance of evil was in itself purity; they have openly disbelieved in the possibility of chastity for men (Creighton, 1914:58).

The Humanitarians called for the spiritual uplift of the entire population. Desires of the flesh should be talked of as little as possible for this was the only way to keep lusts in check. Wholesome recreation for young and old was a way of diverting the thoughts of the sensual and keep idleness at a minimum. Sex should be taken out of movies, plays, and literature for it forced the mind to dwell on unwholesome subjects.

In this same line, the Humanitarians espoused sex education in the home for all children as; "children should not be kept in ignorance about the functions of the body or the laws of reproduction, for ignorance arouses curiosity and curiosity leads to more unwholesome thought in these matters than simple information" (Creighton, 1914:74). They did talk of segregated (by sex) classes on sex education on the college level for young people who failed to receive the needed information from home. But universal sex education on the secondary level or primary level was not a part of their program. They felt this responsibility lay with the parents and the school should enter only when the parents completely failed to do the job (they never answer the argument that most children who "get into trouble" sexually do so well before college age, say 13-17 years, and furthermore, that only a small part of the total population during this period of time ever reached college where they could get this information—this does not seem to be their concern).

In short, there was a need for prostitution set forth by a society which failed to properly socialize its young men—and where the majority of young women were chaste. Where was the supply to come from?

The White Slave Trade was the Humanitarians' answer. Their literature on the illicit trade in young girls got more publicity than any other aspect of prostitution. It not only appealed to the tender-hearted, but it was also the "dirty book" of the time. There was more implied sex and tales of sin in these social protest novels than in many of the cheap, escape thrillers of the day. Thousands of people read these stories; some read them because they were shocked and knew nothing of the "situation," and others read them for sexual "kicks." But whatever the reasons for reading the material, no one could remain in ignorance about the source of prostitution as seen by the Humanitarians.

Brothel prostitutes were White Slaves—all of them—this was the Humanitarians simple statement. The girls were kidnapped; seduced

into marriage to a slaver; thought they were becoming actresses with a traveling show; seduced by offers of higher wages and easier work and not told the nature of the work; immigrant girls traveling alone were stolen right off the boat; lonely girls in the city who were seduced by young men who offered companionship—the list goes on. Once in the brothels their street clothes were taken from them and they were given gaudy finery unsuitable for the street. They were beaten, kept in so called debt to the House Madame for keep and clothing, and kept in constant fear of her "husband," procurer, or house bouncer. The girl could not go out, was forced to write letters to relatives saying that she was well and had a good job, and was never allowed to keep any of her wages. After several months she was allowed to go out of the house, because by that time she was so degraded, humiliated, and resigned to her life of fear that she would not run away—she would even admit staying "in the life" by choice if asked. She would live from 4-6 years
378 finally dying a horrible death from syphilitic infection.

Thousands of pages were written in this vein. Books like: *Fighting the Traffic in Young Girls* by Ernest Bell, *The Girl That Goes Wrong* by Reginald W. Kauffman, *House of Bondage* by the same author, *White Slave Traffic in America* by Edward Janney, *Panderers and the White Slaves* by Clifford Roe, *The White Slave Trade Versus the American Home* by Madeline Southard are just a few.

An example of the type of writing (Roe, 1910:11):

> A thin, frail young girl aided by a physician walked slowly into the court room and took her place on the witness stand. She said that she had lived with her parents on the North Side of Chicago; that she was twenty years old and was a high school graduate.
>
> "Do you remember meeting a certain young man about a month ago?" I asked her.
>
> "Yes," she answered. "I was then employed in an office downtown and one of the girls working in the same building with me suggested that we attend a dance on Saturday night. This dance was held at a dance hall, I believe near the corner of Thirty-first Street and Indiana Avenue. It was there I met the young man whose name was John."
>
> John invited her to have a drink of lemonade.
>
> "When I began to drink the lemonade I noticed a peculiar taste about it. After drinking it I felt dizzy. It seemed as though my head was whirling round and round. I was sick, and in a few minutes I entirely forgot where I was."
>
> When she regained consciousness she found herself in a bed in an entirely strange room.
>
> "My head was sore and I put up my arm to feel for something and my hand clutched bedclothing. In a moment a door opened and a bright

light shone into the room and a person passed through the door toward me. She came over and put her hand upon my head and soothingly said, "Dearie, how are you?" I tried to answer, but my voice failed me. I lay still for a while, and finally gasped out, "Where am I?"

"You are all right," said the negress, "and you will like it here."

"I asked for my clothes that I might go home and she told me that the madam had them locked up."

"Please let me see the madam," I cried out, for I was becoming terribly frightened. The negress disappeared and came back with a stout blond woman wearing a kimono and a great many diamonds and many other jewels."

The woman came up to me and took me by the hand and said, "Why you know where you are; you can't go home now. You owe me a debt and until the debt is paid you cannot leave this house."

"I owe you a debt," I cried, "and for what?"

"Why don't you think you owe me anything for taking care of you here and for the clothes I have brought you and for the money I have paid the young man who brought you here for his trouble and expense? Of course, you do."

"They knocked me about and even whipped me. They watched me as a cat does a mouse for fear that I would say something or tell something which I had been forbidden to tell."

"At first they sent a man to me, whom I thought from his manner I could trust, and I told him of my trouble, and he sympathized with me in my terrible plight and said he would help me to escape and tell my family where I was. It was for this that I was whipped, for I found out that he was what they call a "ringer" and had been sent to me purposely to see whether or not I would tell that I was being kept in this place against my will."

"The girls are cowed into submission this way and are afraid and suspicious of every man they meet, and they have been whipped and have seen others whipped until their spirits are broken. They are forced into a life which they cannot escape."

The Humanitarians (Sanger, 1897:526) admitted that some women did become prostitutes by choice, forced into the life by poverty, low wages, and scarcity of jobs for women:

> If women are compelled to undergo merely the slavery of life no moral advancement can ever be expected of them. If every approach to renumerative employment is sytematically closed to them, nothing but degradation can ensue, and the moralist who shuddered with horror at the bare possibility of a woman being allowed to earn a competent living in a respectable manner will ejaculate, "What awful depravity exists in the female sex!" He and others of his class drive women to starvation by refusing to give her employment, and then condemn her maintaining a wretched existence at the price of virtue.

Other social conditions were cited as contributions to prostitution: overcrowded home conditions (Cocks, 1912:19), long working hours (Adams, 1912:167), broken homes, lack of sympathy and understanding from parents, seasonal work, working with men, and liquor (Sanger, 1897:53-79).

So the impetus behind the Humanitarian Movement was that the prostitute herself was not the cause of prostitution, society in fact promoted it. Control, therefore, had to come from society. Moral standards required uplifting while brothel keepers and procurers were to be incarcerated rather than fined. The lighter sentence of a fine was thought to breed disrespect for the law. The prostitute, herself, required wholesome work and recreation in a strong family-type situation rather than either fines or incarceration. Rehabilitation was the goal. The police forces also had to be investigated and staffed with incorruptible men while society in general was to be educated on the evils of
380 prostitution and venereal disease.

Through the combined efforts of both groups, public opinion was swayed. In every large city in the U.S. investigations and boards were formed to look into each city's particular "red light" district. One after another the segregated sections in large cities were closed (Mayer, 1918:199):

CITY	INVESTIGATION	CLOSING
Chicago	1910	1912
Atlanta	1912	1912
Denver	1913	1913
Philadelphia	1912	1913
St. Louis	1914	1914
New York	1912	1916
Portland	1912	1913
Honolulu	1913	1917
Baltimore	1913	1915
Cleveland	1911	1915
Lexington	1915	1915

With the closing of the brothels, several other measures were instituted to help control prostitution. One such measure was the formation of specialized courts to deal with offenders.

The Morals Court was a branch of the Chicago Municipal Court. It was created by an act of the Illinois Legislature in 1905 at the request of the Chicago Vice Commission, The Committee of Fifteen. It put pressure on city authorities and the State's Attorney to compel them to enforce the laws and wipe out the segregated vice districts in Chicago. By bringing all such cases into one court, it was possible for the general public without much difficulty to observe in what manner the authorities enforced the laws. It heard cases on keeping a disorderly house, procuring a female for a house of prostitution, fornication, adultery, and vagrancy (Worthington and Topping, 1925:4).

Other similar courts instituted in this period were: the Misdemeanant's Division of the Philadelphia Municipal Court (1913) and the Women's Day Court of New York (1918) (Worthington and Topping, 1925:83).

In respect to actual laws passed, many more laws were instituted against the procurer and brothel keeper than against the prostitute herself.

The Injunction and Abatement Act often called the Red Light Abatement Act was first passed in the state of Iowa in 1909. It stated that any private citizen could maintain an equitable action to abate a house of prostitution without having to show particular damage or injury. When a citizen affirmatively established the existence of the nuisance, the court would issue an abatement order by virtue of which the furniture, fixtures, and other contents of the building were to be sold and the premises sealed under judicial supervision for a one year period. If the owner paid the cost of proceedings and posted bond, usually in an amount equal to the value of the property and conditioned on the immediate abatement of the nuisance, the court could release the premises from the abatement order (Slovenko, 1965:650).

New York passed a similar act in March, 1914. This act not only made the definition of the nuisance sweepingly inclusive, but it also enumerated those who could be enjoined as guilty of maintaining such a nuisance. It included whoever might erect, establish, maintain, use, own, or lease a place for the purpose forbidden in the act. This compelled property owners to assume some of the responsibility for the use to which their buildings were being put (Waterman, 1932:24).

In New York the earlier Tenement Act of 1901 provided that: "A tenement house shall be subject to a penalty of one thousand dollars if it or any part of it shall be used for the purpose of a house of prostitution or assignation of any description with the permission of the owner, or his agent, and said penalty shall be a lien upon the house and the lot upon which the house is situated" (Waterman, 1932:27).

In Portland, Oregon in 1913 the Tin Plate Ordinance made use of the element of publicity by requiring the owners of any building which was used for hotel purposes, as a saloon or dance hall, to attach a plate on the outside of the building near the main entrance giving the name and adress of the owner (Waterman, 1932:27).

All states passed and still have laws against pimping; that is living off the wages of a prostitute. For example New York's White Slave Act states:

> Section 1090 of the Penal Law, relating to the prostitution of a wife, provides that any man who by force, intimidation, or threats places or leaves or procures any other person or persons or places or leaves his wife in a house of prostitution shall be guilty of a felony and upon conviction shall be imprisoned for not more than 10 years.
>
> Section 2460 of the Penal Law relating to placing women in custody of another for immoral purposes, provides that any person who shall place any female in charge of another for immoral purposes or in a house of prostitution or shall compel any woman to reside with him or any other person for immoral purposes or shall compel any woman to reside in any such house of prostitution or live the life of a prostitute is punish-
> 382 able by such fine of not more than $5,000 or by imprisonment for not less than one year nor more than three years, or both (Waterman, 1932:16).

In 1910 The Mann Act was adopted making it illegal to import aliens for immoral purposes and permitting deportations of aliens engaged in prostitution.

In addition to laws prohibiting the acts of those associated with the prostitute; her pimp, landlord, client etc.; more laws which generally employed a scientific medical model used to control her behavioral and attendant health problems were also passed. The former types of laws can be seen as the results of the Humanitarians' efforts, the latter as by and large the results of the Control groups' work against the prostitute herself.

By 1913, twelve states had laws on the books allowing sterilization of criminals, idiots, the feebleminded, imbeciles, syphilitics, moral and sexual perverts, epileptics and rapists (Waterman, 1932:34).

New York's Venereal Disease of 1918 states:

> Every citizen arrested for vagrancy as defined under subdivision 3 or 4 section 887 of the code of criminal procedure (prostitution clause) of the tenement house law or under any statute or ordinance for any offense of the nature specified in subdivision 4 of section 887 of the code of criminal procedure, or arrested and charged with a violation of section 1146 of the penal law or 1148 of the penal law or any person arrested for living in a disorderly house or houses of prostitution, shall be reported within 24 hours by the court or magistrate before whom such person is arraigned to the board of health or health officer and shall be examined in accordance with the provisions of the proceeding

section. For the purpose of examination such person may be detained until the results of such an examination are known. No such person if convicted shall be released from the jurisdiction of such court or magistrate until the person so convicted has been examined as provided for in the proceeding section (Waterman, 1931:36).

New York's Wayward Minors Act:

Any person between the ages of 16 and 21 who either (1) habitually addicted to the use of drugs or the intemperate use of intoxication liquors, or (2) habitually associates with dissolute persons, or (3) is found of his or her own free will and knowledge in a house of prostitution or assignation of ill fame, or (4) habitually with thieves, prostitutes, pimps, or procurers or disorderly persons, or (5) is willfully disobedient to the reasonable lawful commands of parents or other custodians and is morally depraved or is in danger of becoming morally depraved may be deemed a wayward minor (Waterman, 1932:39).

Seventy years have passed and little has changed in respect to America's attitude towards prostitution. The attempt by the little group to make the prostitute appear as a human being with feelings and dignity of soul has failed. Like bubble gum on the bottom of its shoe, Moral America is still trying to remove the glob by rubbing it as hard as it can against an immovable object: the police force.

All the laws passed at the turn of the century against prostitution, those directed towards the panderers and procurers originated by the Humanitarians and those aimed directly at the prostitute promulgated by the Control Group are still, in fact, law. But the majority of the laws aimed against the panderers and procurers have fallen away, so to speak, because of the lack of enforcement. The only laws that are still in full swing are the "Control" laws against the prostitute herself. Despite the "Reform" movement of the turn of the century, despite the movie media, despite all attempts to relax the harassment towards the world's first legislated against "minority group," we continue to view the prostitute as the animal, non-person, the woman with a piece missing out of her personality. It appears that the Control Group has won.

REFERENCES

Adams, Jane
1912 A New Conscience and an Ancient Evil. New York: McMillan Co.

Blacker, C. P.
1962 Eugenics–Galton and After. London: Gerald Duckworth and Co.

Cocks, Orrin
1912 The Social Evil and Methods of Treatment. New York: Associated Press.

Committee of Fifteen
1902 The Social Evil. New York: G. P. Putnam's Sons.

Council of the Eugenics Education Society
1910 Eugenics Review 2:2 (July):186-204.

Creighton, Louise
1914 The Social Disease. London: Longmans, Green and Co.

Fisher, Irving C.
1913 "The Necessity for Social and Statutory Recognition of Syphilis." Social Diseases 4:114.

Funk, John C.
1921 Vice and Health. Philadelphia: J. B. Lippincott and Co.

Goddard, Henry H.
1910 "Heredity of Feeblemindedness." American Breeders Magazine 1:3:165-178.

384

Goodhart, S. Philip
1913 Social Diseases 4:113.

Hart, Hastings H.
1913 Meeting the Problem of Mental Defectiveness. New York: Russell Sage Foundation.
1913 Sterilization as a Practical Measure. New York: Russel Sage Foundation.

Hurty, John H.
1912 "The Sterilization of Criminals and Defectives." Social Diseases 3:1(January) :1-18.

Kirby, George H.
1913 "Syphilis and Insanity." Social Diseases 4:4(October) :156-162.

Meyer, Joseph
1918 "Passing of the Red Light Districts." Social Hygiene 4:199.

Miner, Maude E.
1916 The Slavery of Prostitution. New York: McMillan Co.

Murtagh, John M. and Sara Harris
1957 Cast the First Stone. New York: McGraw Hill.

Nacke, P.
1909 "Die Ersten Kastration aus Sozialen Gruden auf Europaiachem Boden." Neurologisches Centralblatt (March).

Roe, Clifford
1911 The Prodigal Daughter. Chicago: L. W. Walter Co.

Rosanhoff, A. J.
1912 "A Study of Heredity of Insanity in the Light of Mendelian Theory." American Journal of Insanity 68:2:221-261.

Sanger, W. W.
1897 The History of Prostitution. New York: The Medical Publishing Co.

Slovenko, Ralph
1965 Sexual Behavior and the Law. Springfield, Ill.: Thomas.

Smith, Stevenson and Madge Wilkinson
1914 A Summary of Laws of the Several States Concerning Sterilization. Seattle: University of Washington Press.

Waterman, Willoughby
1931 Prostitution and Its Repression in New York City. New York: Columbia University Press.

Worthington, George
1925 Specialized Court Dealing with Sex Delinquents. New York: Hitchcock.

THE EQUITY JURISDICTION AND MARRIED WOMEN'S PROPERTY IN ANTE - BELLUM AMERICA: A REVISIONIST VIEW

CAROL ELIZABETH JENSON

ABSTRACT

General textbook discussions of the legal status of women in the United States during the early nineteenth century often contain a sentence or a paragraph maintaining that the equity jurisdiction aided married women in the protection of their property. These same references often base their analysis upon Mary Beard's 1946 publication, Women As Force in History, *in which she accused early women's movement leaders of an ignorance of the law and of the rights available to them under the equity system. Close examination of the equity systems present in the pre-Civil War state judiciaries reveals that Beard's analysis was superficial and misleading. Equity proves to have been a complicated system* 386 *not applicable to all forms of property and available at best to wealthy and upper middle class women who were not allowed to administer the procedures in their own behalf. Equity, like the common law, assumed that married women were unable to manage property interests responsibly and that they required the protective assistance of male benefactors.*

MARY BEARD'S ANALYSIS

During World War II Mary Ritter Beard's interest in the role which women played in American defense led her to examine *Woman as Force in History*. (1) Published in 1946 the work devoted considerable space to a discussion of the legal status of women in mid-nineteenth century America and dismissed as mere myth the contention that women have been subjugated by men. Despite the fact that the total absence of footnotes makes a critique of her work difficult, she provides one of the few analyses ever attempted on the subject of married women's property rights; and she leads the reader to raise a number of questions regarding the property protection which the equity jurisdiction offered to married women. (2)

Beard's analysis focused on the influence of the British jurist Sir William Blackstone, whom she saw as the chief perpetrator of what she regarded as a great misconception. In his famed *Commentaries* which first appeared in 1765, Blackstone declared that "By marriage, the husband and wife are one person in law," (3) thus suspending all legal rights of the married woman. However, said Beard, Blackstone's observation did not adequately represent the property status of married women because he willfully ignored another system of jurisprudence - the equity jurisdiction. (4) According to her view this system granted to women the right to hold and maintain property as well as the ability to contract, to sue, and to pursue other remedies closely related to the administration of property.

Furthermore, Beard alleged that the early feminists in their search for a bill of grievances were misled into accepting Blackstone's dictum and into using it as the basis for protests such as the Declaration of Sentiments issued from Seneca Falls in 1848. Because of their ignorance of the law:

> . . . leaders in the woman movement took Blackstone's metaphorical words about the civil death of the married woman as inescapable law, took it to heart as if it were the supreme truth for marital relations and advertised it throughout the Western world . . . (5)

Out of what she assumed was an absence of legal knowledge and an acceptance of Blackstone's analysis, women ". . . adopted a myth and made a frontal assault on that;" (6) and in their ignorance they overlooked the relief offered by the equity system. She completed her criticism of the early woman's movement with her contention that the married women's property acts which began to appear in the late 1830s ". . . merely transformed generally accepted equity principles into statutory provisions." (7)

In her insistence that the idea of women's subjugation was a myth, Beard attempted to demonstrate the thesis that the presence of the equity jurisdiction provided considerable remedies to mitigate the harshness of the common law. Her analysis leads to four basic questions regarding the exact nature of the judicial remedies which could be utilized by married women in relation to their property. How available was the equity jurisdiction to the average woman? What property did the equity jurisdiction cover, and how much protection did this provide for women? What procedures had to be utilized to secure equity protection? What was the relationship between equity and other developments in American jurisprudence during the early and middle decades of the nineteenth century? In answering these points, there is considerable evidence to support the contention that equity did not provide a parity of legal status between men and women and that as a result legal reforms were badly needed to correct the imbalance.

THE EQUITY SYSTEM

The equity system which Beard praised so highly dated from mid-thirteenth century England and the separation of the Chancery from the *curia regis.* (8) By the time of the Tudors, equity, which derived from continental civil law rather than from English common law, had developed its own system of courts later abolished by the Long Parliament. The Restoration of 1660 brought the return of equity in the Court of Chancery (9) which remained a separate jurisdiction until the Judicature Act of 1873 fused the courts of law and equity without fusing their systems of rules. (10)

Over the years the equity jurisdiction came to be regarded as a far more flexible institution than the common law and adapted itself in particular to new developments in commerce and business. (11) In England equity evolved the procedures surrounding the trust, the injunction, new types of contracts, transferable stocks, improved procedures for relief against frauds, guardianships for infants, lunatics, and idiots, as well as the married woman's separate estate. (12) In America, 7 colonies - the two Carolinas, Maryland, Virginia, New York, New Jersey, and Delaware - had separate chancery courts; but during the colonial period as well as later equity principles were also applied where separate courts did not exist. (13) The equity procedures were often criticized by eighteenth century colonists who saw equity's ties to Roman law, the absence of a jury system, and the close association with the executive authority of royally-appointed governors as a denial of basic English rights. Nevertheless, the equity system survived the Revolution; (14) and as Joseph Story observed in his well-known *Commentaries on Equity Jurisprudence* first published in 1836, "The jurisdiction of a Court of Equity is, therefore, sometimes concurrent with the jurisdiction of a Court of law; it is sometimes exclusive of it; and it is sometimes auxiliary to it." (15)

Obviously, then, there is little doubt regarding the presence of the equity system in ante-bellum America. Article III of the Constitution extended the judicial power of the one system of federal courts ". . . to all Cases in Law and Equity." In the federal courts equity actually made gains against the common law. During the same term in 1812 the United States Supreme Court denied the federal government criminal jurisdiction in common law cases (16) but acknowledged the validity of equity proceedings involving trusts. (17) In later cases the High Court accepted the application of equity ". . . according to such rules and principles as governed the action of the Court of Chancery in England . . ." and as established by an act of Congress in 1792. (18)

At the state level where most property cases were adjudicated, equity was also very much present during the first five decades of the nineteenth century. The constitutions of 25 of the 33 states admitted to the Union before 1860 at some time allowed for the exercise of equity jurisdiction or equity procedures. Eighteen of these states at some time had constitutions which called for the establishment of chancery courts. Of the original 13 states, Massachusetts, New Hampshire, Connecticut, and Georgia were the holdouts against including equity in their constitutions; (19) and before 1848 when the Field Code movement began gaining gound only Georgia and Texas had abolished the distinction between law and equity. (20) Among the 20 states which joined the original 13, only the constitutions of Illinois, Maine, Michigan, Oregon, and Louisiana at no time allowed specifically for the establishment of some form of equity. Furthermore, the broad discretionary power which constitutions extended to state legislatures regarding the establishment of state judiciaries during the early years of the republic made possible an allowance for the use of equity (21) even if it were not specified in the constitution. The only firm exception to the use of equity developed in Louisiana which based its law upon French code and practice and which adopted a version of the Napoleonic Code in 1825. (22)

Equity and Married Women

However, the presence of either a chancery court or the possibility of the use of equity procedures in most states does not answer fully the question regarding the availability of equity to the average woman. The complexities and the vague nature of equity practices made it confusing to anyone - woman or man. Furthermore, equity could not be exercised without the aid of a skilled attorney, placing it out of the financial reach of many persons, particularly women since they had little economic power and usually possessed little knowledge about litigatory procedures since they were not allowed to learn the law. Although many of the equity proceedings of the early nineteenth century have gone unreported, one can turn to one of equity's greatest students, Joseph Story, for an opinion on the availability of the system. Story was quick to acknowledge equity's complexities, ". . . a very refined species of logic, which it requires great talents to master in all its various distinctions and subtle contrivances." (23) His analysis would seem to put to rest any contention that any country lawyer could manipulate the rules of equity for the benefit of any farmer's wife and would substantiate the conclusion of Lawrence Friedman and other legal historians that the equity system usually helped only wealthy landowners. "Plantation owners of the South were . . . able to adapt to the law of settlement and trusts. But these devices were far too intricate for the average person to handle, even the average landowner, and even when aided by the average lawyer." (24) In short, it is reasonable to conclude that equity relief was not readily available to the average woman.

For those women to whom equity relief was available, devices for the protection of married women's property can be placed into several categories - trusts and marriage settlements which together created the separate equitable estate, contracts and business agreements, and wills. Under common law, a *femme sole* held the same property rights as a man. However, when a woman married, her husband came into possession and management of all of her land and chattels, he could sue and recover her choses in action which included debts owed to her as well as stocks and bonds, (25) he took into his possession all of her personal property including any money she might have had. In turn, the husband was responsible for all of her debts including those acquired before coverture. (26) However, it was possible in equity for a *femme sole* contemplating marriage to draw up a settlement which would place her lands and chattels in trust during her coverture. (27) Her prospective husband had to consent to this *ante-nuptial* agreement, and any secrecy on her part would void the settlement in a court of equity. (28) The very fact that a woman attempting to protect her property had to seek out an attorney to aid her in negotiating, with her prospective husband's permission, special agreements not required of a man questions at the outset Beard's conclusion that the equity system did much to equalize the legal situation between men and women.

Trusts and Marriage Agreements

Ante-nuptial agreements usually involved the appointment of trustees whose approval was necessary in most cases before a *feme covert* could act. However, trustees were not always appointed, and if so the husband could serve in that capacity provided he attempted to no "special privilege" regarding his wife's property. (29) The one control a wife could retain over her separate estate in equity was the power to assign it with full title granted to her assignee. (30) In other words she could sell or will property; but she could not manage it without the aid of trustees, a circumstance which hardly assumed female competence or responsibility. Both Story's and Kent's *Commentaries* referred to *post-nuptial* agreements, but these did not have equal status with the *ante-nuptial* and usually amounted to gifts between husband and wife. (31) If a wife acquired real property during coverture, most likely through inheritance, the will had to stipulate expressly that she was to have the power of disposal through a separate estate before a court of equity could recognize her ownership over that of her husband. (32) Since a wife's equity rights could not extend to property in the hands of third parties, they could not be applied to choses in action, thereby excluding any protection for securities she might have held as a *feme sole*; for this income could be placed ". . . directly in the husband's hands without the intervention of a suit." (33)

The intricacies of the separate equitable estate, which are analyzed here only in part, confused even the best of legal minds. According to Story, trusts had to be certain and definite before they could be administered in courts of equity. At times such courts refused to enforce marriage settlements because of inconsistency, uncertainty, or because they were unintelligible. (34) The lengths to which a married woman had to go to protect her property involved a tremendous effort, assumed her incapacity to handle business matters, and provided little certainty. These circumstances seem to deny what equity's defender, Chancellor James Kent termed ". . . a pure and perfect justice, which courts of law are unable to reach." (35)

390

Contracts and Business Agreements

Establishment of a separate equitable estate was also related to a married woman's ability, or perhaps it is more accurate to say inability, to contract. A *feme covert's* contractual rights did not exist at all in common law, for the husband ". . . performs her contracts." (36) In equity, as well, she was not generally able to bind her person or property. However, equity did provide a married woman some protection in dealing with outside parties provided she had established a separate estate. Through a complicated procedure she could charge debts and incumbrances to her separate estate. This was not considered as a contract but as a power of appointment ". . . incident to the power of enjoyment of her separate property." (37) In equity a wife could make an agreement with her husband to go into business via the establishment of a separate estate in which she in a sense acted as his agent. If the agreement were ***ante-nuptial*** the husband and his creditors were bound to discharge the debts of the business. If they established the separate estate after marriage the agreement bound the husband and was void against creditors. Both situations denied the responsibility of the woman and assumed the protective nature of husband over wife. The treatment of creditors pretty much precluded any vigorous business activity. Some states, most notably North Carolina, completely excluded the establishment of trading under a separate estate. (38)

Wills and Inheritance

The subject of wills established one of the greatest ironies in common law treatment of women. At law the only person from whom a married women could inherit was her husband because upon his death her legal status reverted to that of a *feme sole*. In most states a woman's dower rights entitled her to at least one-third of her husband's estate, a subject which caused much controversy since she was not bound to pay her dead husband's creditors who held claims against that portion of his estate. (39) As stated earlier a woman could inherit property during coverture provided the will specifically expressed the formation of a trust for her benefit. Otherwise, her husband received the inheritance. (40) The administration of any trust created by a will rested completely within the jurisdiction of the courts of equity. (41) Marriage nullified any will made by a woman as a *feme sole* (42) but had no similar effect upon a will made by a single man. In equity a woman could will property protected by an *ante-nuptial* agreement separate estate without the aid of trustees. (43) In the absence of an *ante-nuptial* agreement a husband could grant his wife the right to make a will. (44) However, since the absence of an *ante-nuptially*-created separate estate meant the absence of property, this became a moot point.

Wages and Salaries

One crucial area in which the equity system did not apply to married women's property was in relation to wages. Legal sources of the pre-Civil War period offer virtually no comment on the sŭbject of wages earned by married women, thus reflecting the upper and middle class background of the legal commentators and their lack of communication with the problems of the ever-increasing numbers of women employed in factories. Since under the common law money was personal property, all money earned by the wife automatically belonged to the husband. (45) Statistics on the numbers of married women employed in the early days of American industry are difficult to find since most reports on the subject are concerned mainly with working conditions of women and children.
Also, they do not discuss their legal status. Edith Abbott's *Women in Industry* cited census figures and other data to indicate that in 1831, 68% of the employees in the cotton mills were women; in 1850, 64% , and 1860 62%. (46) Unfortunately, the census did not report how many of those women were married. In a sense this is a moot issue in the discussion since few working class women had access to the resources of the equity system. Furthermore, the near-necessity for *ante-nuptial* protection of women's property precluded any protection for wages earned by a woman during coverture; and her inability to contract prevented her from negotiating any wage or salary agreement.

WOMEN AND EQUITY PROCEDURES

Many of the complexities and intricacies involved with the third question, that of equity procedures, have been mentiond already; and Story's assessment indicated that the process ". . . requires various talents, long experience, vast learning, and a clearness and acuteness of perception, which belong only to a few gifted minds." (47) A married woman could initiate a suit in her own name both in law and equity and receive treatment as a *feme sole* under certain conditions - banishment or exile of her husband, imprisonment of the husband for a felony, enemy alien status of the husband, and in some states, desertion. (48) Otherwise, in law she could not sue anyone including her husband, and he could not sue her because she was considered under his protection; ". . . and a suit representing her rights or interests must be with the assent and cooperation of her husband." (49) In equity the situation was very similar. Under certain conditions in equity a woman could sue her husband and vice versa provided she had property protected by a separate estate. (50) In one sense, then, the equity system presented a disadvantage to women because their husbands could bring suit in that jurisdiction whereas in common law a husband could not sue his wife. A wife could also bring suit against other parties. However, whenever a married woman initiated a suit in equity she could not act individually in her own behalf as a man could, a point Beard overlooked. If her husband were not her adversary in the suit he ". . . ordinarily . . . must be joined . . ." with her. (51) If the wife were suing her husband or if he were abroad, banished, exiled, or imprisoned ". . . she was allowed to seek the protection of some other person, who acted as her next friend" (52) and hired her attorney to proceed with the action. In no instance in either law or equity could a husband or wife testify against one another. (53) Furthermore, in equity the marriage of a female plaintiff caused abatement of a suit in progress. The marriage of a female defendant did not require abatement, but her husband was to joined with her in the subsequent proceedings. (54) Finally, if a married woman - or an infant, idiot, or lunatic - bringing suit did not name a next friend, the defendant could demur; and the suit would most likely be dropped on grounds of improper procedure.

In the case of a husband's desertion or ill-treatment of a wife, equity courts did not have general jurisdiction to decree separate maintenance although this situation was corrected gradually by statute in a number of states. However, equity courts could intervene through the establishment of trustees to protect a wife's separate estate or to secure maintenance from that property. Again, this procedure demonstrated a necessity for
392 long-range planning in the establishment of a separate estate, a luxury usually reserved only for the astute and the wealthy. Equity's reluctance to enter into litigation of this type was based upon opposition to separation and divorce and a commitment to the reconciliation of married partners. (56)

A final point in the area of procedures concerns the situation of a wife who maintained a separate estate becoming involved in a case concerning a tort or a fraud. In such an instance she was not held responsible. If the punishment were a fine, the husband was jointly liable, but if the punishment were a prison term the ". . . husband is alone liable . . ." unless the prison term were imposed by a criminal rather than a civil action. Then the wife alone was to be punished. (56) This analysis of the basic rules governing procedures by married women in equity courts contributes further to demonstrating the equity system's assumption that women could not act competently and responsibly in the administration of property, hardly a representation of parity between legal rights of men and of women. Joseph Story's assessment of the role of equity courts summarized the pre-Civil War attitude very well:

> And here, on the subject of married women as well as in the exercise of the jurisdiction in regard to infants and lunatics, we cannot fail to observe the parental solicitude, with which Courts of Equity administer to the wants and guard the interests, and succor the weakness of those who are left without any other protectors, in a manner which the common law was too rigid to consider or too indifferent to provide for. (57)

On the question regarding equity's relationship to legal developments, Mary Beard's assessment of early nineteenth century American legal history as a battleground between an ever-expanding equity system and Blackstone's version of the common law is open to criticism on the grounds that it offered an overly-simplified view. Although few would deny the influence of Blackstone upon the law in the early years of the republic, his was not a singular effect. The internal evolutionary nature of law countered the influence of Blackstone especially after expansion of manufacturing and transportation enterprises created a need for new procedures governing commerce, trade, and contracts. (58) During the period between 1820 and 1860 a movement developed to Americanize the law, to make it less dependent upon Blackstone. Kent's and Story's famed *Commentaries* were a part of this movement to make the law, and also equity, more accessible (59) as was Timothy Walker's well-known textbook *Introduction to American Law* which appeared in 1837. (60) American society became increasingly concerned about an ever-broadening range of legal topics - individual rights in business, safeguards for independent persons, new bankruptcy procedures, creditor's rights, recognition of the legal status of labor unions, prison reform, and a desire to curb the powers of judges. (61) New business developments demanded change, and legal reformers responded to this challenge by initiating a movement for codification and hence Americanization and simplification of the law, an issue which was to divide the American bar for several decades (62) and strangely enough a point Beard ignored even though she mentioned codification reforms suggested by Jeremy Bentham in England. In 1837 Joseph Story himself headed a Massachusetts commission which recommended in favor of the codification of the state's criminal law. (63) Ironically enough, it was the work of men like Story and Kent in making the common law and equity more adaptable and understandable which provided a counter-force to the codification movement which is usually associated with the work of David Dudley Field.

Field's code of procedure was first adopted by the state of New York in 1848 after a constitutional convention two years previous had abolished the Court of Chancery and called for a systematic merger of law and equity. (64) The Field codification movement begun in 1837 reflected a desire on the part of legal reformers to end the confusion and uncertainty of maintaining two systems of law and equity and also demonstrated the Jacksonian reform impulse to utilize the legislature as the institution designed to be the most responsive to the needs of the people. (65) Adoption of the code abolished ". . . distinction between actions at law and suits in equity, and provided one form of civil action for the enforcement or protection of private rights and the redress of private wrongs." (66) Prior to the Civil War 13 additional states and territories adopted its provisions, (67) thus merging law and equity into one system of procedures and at the same time recognizing an Americanization of jurisprudence and a movement away from the influence of Blackstone. In those states which adopted the Field Code equity ceased to supplement and to compete with the common law and merged with it, a development which is in contrast to the dichotomous struggle described by Beard.

CONCLUSION

Perhaps the chief value of Mary Beard's provocative analysis of married women and their property has been to prompt students of the history of American jurisprudence to examine more carefully the position of married women's legal status in ante-bellum America. For the most part that closer look shows her analysis to be inaccurate and overly-simplified. The equity system which she praised as an equalizing force between the property rights of men and women assumed a married woman's inability to manage her interests and her need for protectors - husband, trustees, or a next friend. For those few wealthy and landholding women to whom equity was available its use required careful and long-range planning by a skilled attorney and did not extend to all types of property and procedures. In her great effort to discredit early woman's movement leaders as both victims and perpetrators of Blackstone's myth, Beard overlooked many of the influences of a changing society and the impact of codification, one of the greatest legal reform movements of the pre-Civil War period. After careful consideration of Beard's analysis one can conclude that the supporters of the changes proposed by the married women's property acts saw the immediate situation far more realistically than did Beard a century later. Although the advocates of women's property law reform did not always act out of concern for women's rights, they agreed with law professor and codification advocate Timothy Walker that even with the presence of the equity jurisdiction the legal relationship possible between husband and wife in the United States was ". . . a disgrace to any civilized nation." (68)

Carol E. Jenson, Associate Professor, Department of History
The University of Wisconsin - La Crosse, WI 5 :601

NOTES

(1) Mary R. Beard, *Woman as Force in History* (New York: Macmillan, 1946).

(2) A thorough discussion of Mary Beard's entire work can be found in Bernice A. Carroll, "Mary Beard's *Woman as Force in History*: A Critique," *Massachusetts Review*, 13 (Winter-Spring, 1972), 125-143. This analysis concludes that the chief contribution of the book rests with its provocative and questioning presentation. In contrast to the Carroll work my analysis attempts to deal solely with Beard's contentions regarding the effects of legal developments upon women.

(3) William Blackstone, *Commentaries on the Laws of England*, I (Oxford: Clarendon Press, 1765), p. 430.

(4) Beard, p. 84.

(5) Ibid., p. 114.

(6) Ibid., p. 115.

(7) Ibid., p. 132.

(8) William Holdsworth, *A History of English Law*, I (London: Methuen, 1966), p. 395.

(9) Ibid., pp. 409-16.

(10) William Holdsworth, "Blackstone's Treatment of Equity," *Harvard Law Review*, 43 (1929-1930), 27.

(11) Joseph Story, *Commentaries on Equity Jurisprudence as Administered in England and America*, I (Boston: Charles C. Little and James Brown, 1839), p. 27.

(12) Holdsworth, *History*, I, pp. 466-67.

(13) Story, I, p. 62 provided this list in a footnote. Lawrence M. Friedman, *A History of American Law* (New York: Simon and Schuster, 1973), p. 47, does not include Virginia on his list.

(14) Friedman, pp. 47-48. The quotation is from p. 48.

(15) Story, I, pp. 32-33.

(16) *United States* v. *Hudson and Goodwin*, 7 *Cranch* 32 (1812).

(17) *Russell* v. *Clarke's Executors*, 7 *Cranch* 69 (1812).

(18) *United States* v. *Howland*, 4 *Wheaton* 115 (1812); and *Boyle* v. *Zacharie*, 6 *Peters* 657-658 (1832).

(19) These figures are based upon a survey of all of the constitutions of the states admitted to the Union before 1860. This material is available in Benjamin Perley Poore, *The Federal and State Constitutions, Colonial Charters, and Other Organic Laws of the United States*, 2 vols. (New York: Burt Franklin, 1924).

(20) Friedman, p. 130.

(21) Poore, state-by-state analysis.

(22) Ibid., I, pp. 704-05; Friedman, p, 153.

23) Joseph Story, *Commentaries on Equity Pleadings* (Boston: Charles C. Little and James Brown, 1838), p. 11, hereafter cited as Story, *Pleadings*. Since reports of this period are by no means complete and usually involve only appellate courts, it would be an endless task to trace the effects of equity on a case-by-case basis. Therefore, this analysis relies heavily on the work of legal commentators and teachers like Story, Kent, and Timothy Walker, men whose collections served as the basis for many rulings and decisions by equity courts.

(24) Friedman, p. 185.

(25) James Kent, *Commentaries on American Law*, II (New York, 1840), pp. 133-34.

(26) Kent, II, p. 143.

(27) Ibid., II, p. 163.

(28) James Schouler, *A Treatise on the Laws of Domestic Relations* (Boston: Little, Brown and Company, 1870), pp. 268-269.

(29) Story, II, p. 606; and Schouler, p. 266.

(30) Story, II, p. 238.

(31) Kent, II, p. 178; Story, II, p. 601; and Schouler, p. 276.

(32) Story, II, p. 617.

(33) Schouler, p. 128.

(34) Story, II, p. 243; and Schouler, p. 267.

(35) Kent, II, p. 165.

(36) Ibid., p. 133.

(37) Story, II, pp. 625-27.

(38) Schouler, pp. 243-47.

(39) Friedman, p. 376.

(40) Story, II, p. 617.

(41) Ibid., II, 319.

(42) Schouler, p. 251; and Kent, II, p. 171.

(43) Kent, II, pp. 170-72.

(44) Schouler, p. 252.

(45) Ibid., p. 111.

(46) Edith Abbott, *Women in Industry* (New York: D. Appleton and Co., 1926), p. 10.

(47) Story, *Pleadings*, p. 11.

(48) Schouler, p. 209. Although this is not a subject to be covered in this paper, this circumstance is one example which indicates a difference between equity practice and subsequent statutes, thereby contradicting Beard's contention that statutes merely enacted equity procedures. In 1821 the Maine Legislature authorized women deserted by their husbands to act as *feme soles*. By 1850 New Hampshire, Vermont, Tennessee, Kentucky, and Michigan had enacted similar laws.

(49) Story, *Pleadings*, pp. 61, 11. The quotation is from p. 11.

(50) Ibid., pp. 61-63.

(51) Ibid., p. 72.

(52) Kent, II, p. 163.

(53) Ibid., p. 178.

(54) Story, *Pleadings*, pp. 289, 384.

(55) Story, II, pp. 649-54.

(56) Kent, II, pp. 148-49.

(57) Story, II, pp. 654-55.

(58) Friedman, pp. 233, 244. William E. Nelson, *Americanization of the Common Law: The Impact of Legal Change in Massachusetts Society, 1760-1830* (Cambridge: Harvard University Press, 1975), offers a valuable one-state analysis of developments mentioned above.

(59) Francis R. Aumann, *The Changing American Legal System* (New York: Da Capo Press, 1969), pp. 120-25.

(60) Timothy Walker, *Introduction to American Law* (Boston: Charles C. Little and James Brown, 1873).

(61) Charles Warren, *A History of the American Bar* (Boston: Little, Brown and Company, 1911), p. 466; and Friedman, pp. 186, 255.

(62) Maxwell Bloomfield, "William Sampson and the Codifiers," *American Journal of Legal History*, 11 (1967), 248.

(63) Aumann, p. 125.

(64) Mildred V. Coe and Lewis W. Morse, "Chronology of the Developments of the David Dudley Field Code," *Cornell Law Quarterly*, 27 (February 1942), 238; and Alison Reppy, "The Field Codification Concept," in *David Dudley Field Centenary Essays* (Dobbs Ferry, New York: Oceana, 1949), pp. 31-32.

(65) Titus M. Coan, Editor, *Speeches, Arguments, and Miscellaneous Papers of David Dudley Field*, 3 vols. (New York: D. Appleton and Co., 1870), pp. 239-240; and A.P. Sprague, *Speeches, Arguments, and Miscellaneous Papers of David Dudley Field*, I (New York: D. Appleton and Co., 1884), pp. 201-06.

(66) Reppy, p. 49.

(67) Reppy, p. 45; and Friedman, p. 343. The list of states includes Missouri, California, Iowa, Minnesota, Indiana, Kentucky, Ohio, Wisconsin, Oregon, and Kansas. The territories include Washington, Nebraska, and Nevada. In addition, Georgia and Texas earlier had abolished the distinction between law and equity; and the revised Michigan Consitution of 1850 prohibited a court of chancery in that state, Poore, I, pp. 704-05.

(68) Walker, p. 260.

International Journal of Women's Studies, Vol. 2, No. 2, 144-154.

FROM THE DECLARATION OF INDEPENDENCE TO THE DECLARATION OF SENTIMENTS: THE LEGAL STATUS OF WOMEN IN THE EARLY REPUBLIC 1776-1848

LINDA K. KERBER*

> When, in the course of human events, it becomes necessary for one portion of the family of man to assume among the people of the earth a position different from that which they have hitherto occupied, but one to which the laws of nature and of nature's God entitle them, a decent respect to the opinions of mankind requires that they should declare the causes that impel them to 397
> such a course.[1]

The rhetoric of the opening text of the Seneca Falls Declaration of Sentiments suggests a failure of literary imagination. One would expect Elizabeth Cady Stanton to have formulated her own statement of the women's case, rather than proffer a tepid echo of Thomas Jefferson. Stanton apparently confirmed the subordinate place of women at the moment she condemned it.

There was, however, an obvious rhetorical purpose to Stanton's use of borrowed rhetoric; an alternative reading of the Declaration of Sentiments seems more plausible. By tying the complaints of women to the most distinguished political statement the nation had made she implied that the women's demands were no more or less radical than the American Revolution had been; that they were in fact an implicit fulfillment of the commitments already made. The familiar phrases represented an effort to deflect hostility and to make the claims of the Seneca Falls women as self-evident as the other truths which Americans had once proclaimed to a candid world.

---

* A.B. 1960, Barnard College; Ph.D. 1968, Columbia University. Professor of History, University of Iowa. Author of FEDERALISTS IN DISSENT: IMAGERY AND IDEOLOGY IN JEFFERSONIAN AMERICA (1970). The author is currently writing a book about women in the early republic, which is partially supported by a grant from the American Bar Association.

[1] 1 HISTORY OF WOMEN SUFFRAGE 70 (E. Stanton, S. Anthony, & M. Gage eds. 1881).

Jefferson's litany of complaints against King George was echoed by Stanton's litany of complaints against mankind; many of which related directly to women's legal status.

> He has never permitted her to exercise her inalienable right to the elective franchise.
> He has compelled her to submit to laws, in the formation of which she had no voice . . .
> He has made her, if married, in the eye of the law, civilly dead.
> He has taken from her all right in property, even to the wages she earns.
> He has so framed the laws of divorce, as to what shall be the proper causes, and in the case of separation, to whom the guardianship of the children shall be given, as to be wholly regardless of the happiness of women—the law, in all cases, going upon a
> 398 false supposition of the supremacy of man . . .
> After depriving her of all rights as a married woman, if single, and the owner of property, he has taxed her to support a government which recognizes her only when her property can be made profitable to it.[2]

The Declaration goes on to protest the conditions of women's education, women's inferior position in church governance, the use of a double moral standard, the exclusion of women from the professions. But the first, and most firmly voiced complaints related directly to women's inferior *legal* status: the denial of the suffrage, the economic and physical subordination of married women to their husbands, the vulnerability of women in divorce cases. These were the most substantial and serious of the women's resentments, and they would take more than a century to rectify.

Subordinate legal status seemed the more outrageous because it was publicly unacknowledged. The political rhetoric of the Revolution spoke generically of mankind. Women had taken political identities as Whigs or Tories; they had served the revolutionary army in substantial numbers as nurses and cooks, and in small numbers as combatants and spies; they had raised money for the war effort. Neither the Declaration of Independence nor the Constitution made invidious distinctions between men and women or required that women's status under the law be different from that of men.

---

[2] *Id.* at 70-71. The Seneca Falls Declaration was a product of the first women's rights convention in the United States. Organized by Elizabeth Cady Stanton and Lucretia Mott, it was held on July 19, 1848 in Seneca Falls, N.Y.

It was popularly supposed, as the Connecticut judge Zephaniah Swift put it in 1795, that "in no country, is a greater share of domestic felicity enjoyed, than in this."[3] But with the single exception of New Jersey, whose state constitution briefly permitted all free adult inhabitants to vote, the Revolution had no direct impact on the theoretical legal status of women.

Occasional voices identified the legal realities, but they were ignored. Abigail Adams' famous demand that the ladies be "remembered" in the new code of laws because they were determined not to give allegiance to a government that excluded them, was voiced only in a private letter to her husband, and her husband found the plea amusing.[4] He did not act on it. A pamphlet demanding equal legal status signed by "A Matron of Connecticut" at the turn of the century has long since been forgotten except by rare 399
book collectors.[5] The most ringing public attack on the inadequacies of the post-revolutionary political situation came, not from a political activist, but from a novel. Charles Brockden Brown in 1798 put in the mouth of his fictional Mrs. Carter as sharp a statement as any that would be made at Seneca Falls a half century later. Mrs. Carter announces to Alcuin:

> What have I, as a woman, to do with politics? Even the government of our country, which is said to be the freest in the world, passes over women as if they were not. We are excluded from all political rights without the least ceremony. Lawmakers thought as little of comprehending us in their code of liberty, as if we were pigs, or sheep . . . this constitution is unjust and absurd . . .
> I am conscious of being an intelligent and moral being . . . I see myself denied . . . the exercise of my own discretion; incapable of separate property; subject in all periods of my life, to the will of another, on whose bounty I am made to depend for food, raiment, and shelter . . . I see myself, in my relation to society, regarded merely as a beast, or an insect; passed over, in the distribution of public duties . . . they generously admit me into the class of existence, but affirm that I exist for no purpose but the convenience of the more dignified sex; that I am not to be intrusted with

---

[3] 1 Z. Swift, A System of the Laws of the State of Connecticut 192 (1795).

[4] Letter from Abigail Adams to John Adams (March 31, 1776), *reprinted in* 1 Adams Family Correspondence 369-70 (L. Butterfield ed. 1965); Letter from John Adams to Abigail Adams (April 14, 1776), *reprinted in id.* at 381-83.

[5] The Female Advocate (1801).

> the government of myself; that to foresee, to deliberate and decide, belongs to others, while all my duties resolve themselves into this precept, "listen and obey;" it is not for me to smile at their tyranny, or receive, as my gospel, a code built upon such atrocious maxims.[6]

If we search for the sources of these resentments, and ask in what ways men and women were unequal under the law in the years after the Revolution, there is a simple answer: in all three ways listed in the Seneca Falls Declaration—and many more that were not listed.

I. They were unequal because women did not vote. Apart from some scattered anecdotal evidence of women voting in some local elections, and with the conspicuous exception of New Jersey be-
400 tween 1790 and 1807, women were by definition political dependents.

II. Their continued political dependency was said to be justified by women's economic dependence on their fathers and their husbands; a subordination which was implied by English common law and continued by American practice. Because Americans based their claims to political rights on the Lockean notion that only those who owned a stake in the community properly had a voice in its affairs, the married women whose control over her property had passed by marriage to her husband had also conceded her political voice. The most readily available guide to the legal implications of marriage was Blackstone's *Commentaries*, published in England between 1765 and 1769, and quickly reprinted in America.[7] Blackstone was not without his own contemporary critics; his summary of the common law was a conservative one. But for colonies with a dearth of law books it was an enormously convenient codification of what British courts had been doing, and it was widely accepted and used. Even after independence, it served as a guide to those portions of the common law which had not been specifically revised by American statute.

The common law, as Blackstone described it, derived from feudal traditions in which the desire to guarantee manorial property led to giving the husband lifetime control of the wife's lands,

---

[6] C. BROWN, ALCUIN 29-30 (1970).

[7] The first American edition of Blackstone was published in Philadelphia in 1771. *See* Nolan, *Sir William Blackstone and the New American Republic: A Study of Intellectual Impact*, 51 N.Y.U. L. REV. 731 (1976).

and absolute ownership of her personal property, wages and income. By common law tradition, there were few limits on the husband's control; he might spend her property, punish her physically, and provide her with only minimal food, clothing and shelter. She had no recourse. "By marriage, the husband and wife are one person in law," Blackstone wrote, "the very being or legal existence of the woman is suspended during the marriage, or at least incorporated and consolidated into that of the husband."[8]

Blackstone must not be read too literally. The rigor of the common law was in fact substantially mitigated both in England and the colonies by courts of equity, which proceeded with looser rules, gave more initiative to the judges, and handled the bulk of cases in which wives disputed the way husbands handled their property. The common law rights of the husband might, for example, be 401
circumvented by prenuptial contracts or marriage settlements, in which the property which women brought to their marriages was confined to their own separate use. Women might even sue their own husbands (and husbands their wives,) through the legal fiction of the *prochein amy*.[9]

Stanton and other supporters of the women's rights movement have therefore often been accused of overstating their complaints. It is certainly true that both tradition and the courts of equity gave women more legal options than a superficial reading of Blackstone suggests. But these options were most realistic for women who could have the benefit of sophisticated legal advice and had substantial property to protect. They were not readily available to those who needed them most. The demand for legislation which would confirm the right of married women to the property they had brought into their marriages and to wages and income earned during the marriage was not a self-indulgent demand; it reflected a real need. Ironically, the first Married Women's Property Acts, in Mississippi in 1839 and in New York in 1848, were supported by male legislators out of a desire to confirm the power of married daughters against spend-thrift sons-in-law; four out of the five sections of the Mississippi act broadened the rights of married women

[8] *Quoted in* L. KANOWITZ, WOMEN AND THE LAW: THE UNFINISHED REVOLUTION 35 (1969). *See also* R. MORRIS, STUDIES IN THE HISTORY OF AMERICAN LAW ch. 4 (1964).

[9] *See* Jelineau v. Jelineau, 2 S.C. Eq. (2 Des.) 45 (1801); Taylor v. Taylor, 4 S.C. Eq. (4 Des.) 167 (1811).

over their own slaves.[10] The major source of support for these acts came out of a desire to recognize the broad rights of a *creditor* to collect debts out of property owned by wives. And even after these acts were passed, antebellum courts still regularly upheld the claims of husbands to control the earnings of their wives. Despite the Pennsylvania Married Woman's Property Act of 1848 for example, a state court ruled in 1853 that the savings of one Mrs. Raybold, who ran a boardinghouse, "enured to the benefit of her husband," although her industry and frugality had been "meritorious."[11]

III. The third major complaint of the Seneca Falls Declaration was against the limited availability of divorce and the likelihood that post-separation settlements and child custody arrangements would favor the man. Freedom to separate from tyrannical hus-
402 bands seemed as appropriate a claim as freedom to separate from tyrannical kings; but on the eve of the Revolution bills to ease divorce procedures in Pennsylvania, New Jersey and New Hampshire were disallowed by the Privy Council. South Carolina permitted no divorce at all.[12] Well into the nineteenth century legislative divorces—the most cumbersome and crude method, requiring the greatest degree of political sophistication to manage successfully—were still among the most commonly available.

In some states, statutes did provide for divorce, handled through the courts on clear and fixed grounds. In Connecticut the grounds were adultery, desertion, and missing and presumed dead.[13] That these relatively obvious grounds were not widely available elsewhere suggests the number of unhappy marriages that must have persisted. Cruelty, for example, was not grounds for divorce. Even in states with relatively easy divorce procedure, post-divorce property settlements were not systematized, and the dearth of records suggests that it required considerable political sophistication to get a property settlement. In Massachusetts the divorced woman retained her dower right in her husband's estate but had to claim it in a separate legal action.[14]

---

[10] 1839 Miss. Laws ch. 46, at 72-73; 1848 N.Y. Laws ch. 200, at 307-08.

[11] Raybold v. Raybold, 20 Pa. 308, 311 (1853), *cited in* M. BLOOMFIELD, AMERICAN LAWYERS IN A CHANGING SOCIETY 114 (1976).

[12] N. BLAKE, THE ROAD TO RENO: A HISTORY OF DIVORCE IN THE UNITED STATES chs. IV, V (1962).

[13] 1808 Conn. Pub. Acts 236.

[14] Smith v. Smith, 13 Mass. 230 (1816).

It is true that divorce is a procedure that affects both men and women. But where divorce was available, one of the most common grounds was desertion, and most desertion petitions were by women. How much collusion there was in these desertions is impossible to estimate. A situation in which the only statutory grounds are adultery, fraudulent contract or desertion suggests that the easiest way to be free of an unhappy marriage was to walk away from it. A court that had earned the reputation of routinely granting divorces if the claims fit the statute requirement, would surely be presented with cases that fit the statute requirement.

But if desertion may often have meant collusion, it must also have implied desperation. Through the stilted legal formulae of the women's petitions rings the note of suffering: the woman left with no one to support her though she is "Bigg with Child"; the 403
woman with the large family left "destitute of the Necessary Supports of Life."[15] Divorce was not a mark of liberation; it was the gambit of the desperate.

The Seneca Falls Declaration was accurate in identifying three major ways in which women were not equal before the law in the early republic. There were other modes of legal inequality which bore on women quite as heavily, and which relate to the differential *impact* of the law on men and on women. We are only beginning to identify them.

I. The professionalization of the bar and the exclusion of women from formal legal training meant the absence of women as attorneys. They were also absent from juries, which meant, of course, that accused women did not have a trial before their peers. The implications of this exclusion on the judgments of juries are difficult to identify. But surely there was some effect. A common murder charge against women, for example, was infanticide—usually desperate unmarried women suffocating newly born babies.[16] Often they were treated with sympathy by male juries; whether women on juries would have supported stiffer penalties or more leniency is hard to say, but it seems likely that their presence would have had some impact on the outcome of the trials.

---

[15] *See*, e.g., Divorce Petitions of Huldah Archer (1782), Aehsah Evans (1788), Susannah Whiting (1792) (Record Group 3, Connecticut State Library).

[16] 2 Z. SWIFT, *supra* note 3, at 303; *see also* New Haven Criminal Court Files, 1797-1822 (located at Connecticut State Library).

II. There were apparently differences in the type and frequency of crimes committed by women and by men, and in the extent to which women and men were convicted and punished. Witchcraft was a woman's crime; infanticide appears to have been a woman's crime. In New York, in the years before the Revolution, women were most frequently accused of theft and of running disorderly houses—crimes which, as Douglas Greenberg has commented, "the social boundaries of society made available to them." Marriage was so surely the mark of respectability that single women were, conversely, an object of suspicion and antagonism; fully 87% of the New York women who appeared as defendants were unmarried.[17] Michael Hindus' study of crimes and punishments of black slaves in antebellum South Carolina shows that prosecutions for 404 harboring fugitives and runaways were more frequent against black women than against black men; and except in crimes against the person (where women received more lashes), women and free blacks received lighter sentences than male slaves.[18] It is probable that other studies of crimes and punishments would reveal continuing differences between the sexes in the extent to which laws were applied to them.

III. Finally, it is clear that there were in effect multiple codes of law in antebellum America. The poor and the enslaved were subject to heavier burdens than others. Within these categories women were not always treated as men were.

1) Apprenticeship contracts for boys, which provided schooling along with the teaching of a trade, were not replicated for girls. Girls were rarely taught complicated skills; they were usually taken as unskilled servants. Apprenticeship contracts for girls that provided for formal schooling were exceptional and rare; it was not rare to find a contract that promised that the girl would be taught to read and write signed with her master's mark, revealing his own illiteracy.

2) Towns, in New England and elsewhere, had early accepted responsibility for providing charity for legal residents who were incapable of supporting themselves. But this was accompanied by a

---

[17] D. Greenberg, Crime and Law Enforcement in the Colony of New York 1691-1776 (1976).

[18] Hindus, *Black Justice under White Law: Criminal Prosecutions of Blacks in Antebellum South Carolina*, 63 J. Am. Hist. 575-99 (1976).

desire to keep the locality free from as many claims for charitable assistance as possible, an extraordinary caution about entertaining poor strangers, a skepticism of vagrants, and an insistence that each person establish clearly his or her right to "legal settlement." The care with which the laws of settlement were enforced had direct implication for married women, whose right to settlement in a town, and whose implicit claim to town charity, was far more vulnerable than that of men. A married woman could have no settlement separate from her husband, nor could she transfer her right of settlement to her husband. If she married a man who had a settlement in any other state, she had to follow him, "though she had never been there"; if a married woman became destitute elsewhere she could not return to the town of her birth and throw herself on the town's charity. In such a case, one jurist wrote, "the law 405
will not admit the separation of husband and wife. They must both be considered as vagrants wherever they are."[19] Therefore, the fact that a poor woman *might* throw herself on public charity, severely compromised her freedom to travel.

It remains to be admitted that millions of women, rich and poor, lived out their lives thinking that these constraints were not particularly burdensome. If one was on good terms with her husband, perhaps it did not matter much who "owned" the boardinghouse that she operated. But as interest in abolition naturally turned reformist women's minds to questions of legal status, and as more and more women entered the public work force, the legal constraints on women's political and economic behavior became more and more abrasive. These constraints were real and they would persist. When the Centennial celebrations were held in Philadelphia a hundred years ago, it was not by accident that the women of Seneca Falls turned up there, to hold a counter-Centennial and to read a longer, far more detailed and intense version of the Declaration of 1848. Susan B. Anthony was the orator, and she concluded, familiarly enough, with the demand for the impeachment of all officers of the government, on the ground that they had been false to the promises of the Revolution. Her closing words are ones that —in a year that still has not seen the passage of the Equal Rights Amendment—are worth reading again: "[N]ow, at the close of a

[19] 1 Z. Swift, *supra* note 3, at 169-71; *see also* New Haven Criminal Court Files, 1797-1822 (located at Connecticut State Library).

hundred years . . . , we declare our faith in the principles of self-government . . . . We ask no special favors . . . . We ask justice, we ask equality, we ask that all the civil and political rights that belong to the citizens of the United States be guaranteed to us and our daughters forever."[20]

[20] HISTORY OF WOMEN SUFFRAGE, *supra* note 1, at 34.

THE GROWTH IN PENNSYLVANIA OF THE PROPERTY RIGHTS OF MARRIED WOMEN.*

In the extremely brief space permitted this paper on such a broad subject, it will only be possible to point out the marked contrast between existing legal conditions and what formerly constituted the law.

At the old common law of England, from which we in this State have drawn the substance of the principles of our law, when a woman entered the state of matrimony, the theory arose that her person in the eyes of the law became merged in that of her husband's. As a consequence her property was transferred by virtue of this legal fiction to him as follows: he became the absolute owner of whatever personal property was in possession of the wife, and such other personal property as bonds, notes and other choses in action; he could acquire complete property in them by reducing them to possession or, in other words, by taking such legal steps as were necessary to substitute himself in his wife's position as the holder of the legal or equitable title he acquired, under certain conditions, what is termed his curtesy in her real estate, the amount of this interest being a freehold estate not of inheritance in the wife's real property; and he became absolute master of the profits of her land during coverture.

At common law it was generally said marriage destroyed all powers of the woman to enter into a contract, and this was an effect also of the same theory of the destruction and obliteration of the legal existence of a married woman.

It would seem, however, that this theory, considered from the mere standpoint of a legal theory causing legal results to flow from its operation, is not entirely flawless, because it was possible for a married woman to have received a gift or a purchase provided she had her husband's assent to the transaction, and her choses in action remained in her legal

* This article was delivered as an address at the Commencement of the Temple College Law School in June, 1901, and as it was intended for a non-professional audience it was the author's effort to make it popular in form.

possession until such time as the husband reduced them to his possession; again, it was possible for a married woman to enter into a contract, and this was not absolutely void, though generally said to be so, but only became void at her election, or the election of her husband when he chose to interfere.

In connection with the last proposition, it would seem the theory suggested, *obiter dictum,* by Mr. Justice Woodward, and also by other jurists and legal authorities, that a married woman is in law supposed to be *sub potestate viri* and therefore incapable of making a contract, is perhaps a more logical theory so far as her making and enforcing of contracts is concerned, though it is not generally approved.

Whether these criticisms are sound or not, the practical
408 results were as stated, and in substance her property and contractual rights as a single woman were almost entirely destroyed, her legal existence for most purposes suspended. and other legal disabilities not to be properly considered here added to her estate when she became a married woman.

Such legal servitude was incompatible with the spirit of the founders of the Commonwealth and their descendants, and as was said in an opinion by Mr. Justice Agnew in 1864: "Even before the passage of the Act of 1848, custom and the common sense of justice had materially mitigated the rigor of that fiction, and equity had consistently refused to recognize the logical effect of a legal unity wherever by its rank injury it became legal folly."

Time cannot be taken in a paper of this general character to consider the smaller ameliorations effected by liberal judges, but only some of the larger and more important emancipations accomplished by legislative action can be briefly examined, without even indulging in the interesting study of the manner in which the various Acts were expounded and received their present construction by the Supreme Court.

The first legislative step for this purpose was the Act of 1718, and it had in view the case of a wife left to shift for herself where her husband had gone to sea. It provided that such wife should have the right to trade as a *feme sole,* contract as such and sue or be sued without joining her husband.

This Act had its provisions extended by the Act of 1855 to cases of *desertion* by or *neglect* of the *husband* to *support* his wife. But, under both Acts it was held that the wife, to become entitled to the benefit of the provisions, should be engaged in some trade, business or employment pursued as a means of livelihood; and if this were not so, she could not contract, sue or be sued under their provisions. The scope and purpose of these Acts are evidently to ameliorate the unfortunate condition of a woman under any of the above recited conditions, who otherwise might not be able to earn her living by any trade or business occupation. In this connection we might examine the Act of 1872 which provides that the earnings of *any* married woman "*shall accrue to and inure to the separate benefit of said married woman*" and not be subject to any legal claim of her husband. It was 409
contended that this Act enabled *any* married woman to engage in trade or business, and by virtue of that circumstance she became a *feme sole* trader, but Mr. Justice Paxson in 1882 held that the Act of 1872 only secured to her her separate earnings and that there is no *feme sole* trading with us except those licensed under the Acts of 1718 and 1855. And further, that the Act of 1872 by *implication* gave her the right to engage in business, and that to the extent of her rights and liabilities in *relation to the business itself* she is to be considered a *feme sole.* Before this Act of 1872 and notwithstanding the Act of 1848, to which immediate reference will be made, the earnings of a married woman on their receipt by her became the property of her husband.

In 1848 the legislature took a long step towards freeing married woman from their disabilities to *hold* their *own* property; in substance it was enacted that "*every species of property which may be owned by a single woman shall continue to be her property as fully after marriage as before . . and all property which shall accrue during coverture shall be owned, used and enjoyed by such married woman as her own separate estate . . . and shall not be subject to levy and execution for her husband's debts . nor encumbered or conveyed by her husband without her written consent.*" One might, reading these provisions, be inclined to think that the very obvious purpose of the

Act, after preserving her separate estate to her own use, was to enable a married woman to do almost anything she pleased with it. But this Act, as well as those which so far have been adverted to, is in derogation of the common law and therefore to be construed strictly. And when the words are carefully analyzed and considered, no general powers are found contained in them, but only certain *special* powers given, and such has been the effect given to the Act by the courts when appealed to. In a case where it was strongly urged that the Act gave general powers of contract to a married woman we find such language as this denying such proposition. First, alluding to the disabilities prior to the Act, the court said: "And the Act of 1848 did not and was not intended to change the law in this respect except to bind her separate estate in special cases and in the manner therein
410 specified." The Act was therefore limited to its terms, and it was held that all the Act *expressly* did was to enable a married woman to *own, use* and *enjoy* her property as a married woman as if the property had been settled to her *sole* and *separate* use during coverture: and that such ownership involved no contractual powers of any kind except such as were indispensible to preserve such estate from ruin, and these rights rested upon the theory that the privelege to own, use and enjoy gave by *implication* the power to take care of it, and if this were not so the privilege would be an empty one; as was said in a *per curiam* opinion in 1875: "If the roof of her house be blown off by storm or sink in utter decay so that the building becomes untenantable, what is to become of it if she cannot repair it." This narrow construction, however, was only reached after considerable doubt by the profession and it was thought by many that a more liberal one should have been given.

Prior to the Act of 1848 the property of a married woman could be taken in execution for the debts of her husband by his creditors. This Act put an end to that injustice, though it did not in any way interfere with the husband's right of curtesy in her estate. Against this interest in his wife's land his creditors still issued execution, but of course could not get possession until the wife's death. To remedy this evil the legislature in 1850 enacted that the husband's interest in his wife's land shall not be subject to *execution and* sale during the wife's life. This Act, however, made no mention of the lien of judgments against the husband attaching to his interest in the wife's property. To remedy this the legislature enacted in 1863 that the lien of no such judgment should attach to the real estate of the wife, nor upon the husband's interest as tenant by curtesy in her property during the lifetime of the wife.

The spirit of freedom which pervades our society had up to this point been aiming at the *mere protection* of married women, and had found expression in the legislative acts which have been cursorily examined. But the same spirit called for greater strides in the direction of freeing married women from the legal trammels that marriage imposed upon them. *Mere protection* had been accomplished, but had become insufficient to satisfy the growth of public sentiment which in innumerable ways was recognizing the legal, economic and personal equality of men and women in the married state. Accordingly,in 1887, an Act was passed which was intended not merely to protect the wife's property from the rapaciousness of her husband and his creditors, but aimed at giving to a married woman as large property and contractual rights as would be consistent with a proper protection, necessary for the inexperience in business affairs and easily influenced character of her sex.

The terms of this Act were by far the most sweeping of any of a similar kind that had been passed up to the time of its enactment, and indicated the clear purpose of the legislature that it should be construed in the same spirit as all prior ones of a similar kind had been, but that it was to be an enabling and an enlarging Act, and therefore it should receive such liberal and fair constructon as, in the words of Judge Endlich, in his book on the interpretation of statutes, "would advance the remedy aimed at by it so long as it does not go beyond its real object and scope." In 1891 Paxson, C. J., speaking of the Act of 1887 and of the powers given by it to a married woman, said: "So general is her power to contract now, that her inability is the exception rather than the rule." These words of the Chief

Justice were adopted by Justice Green in 1893, and fairly represent what was the attitude of our highest tribunal towards the Act. A few years of working experience under the Act showed that it was not as satisfactory as could be desired, and the profession saw that many points had been raised and could be still further raised, that were not fully covered by its terms. According, in 1893 an Act was passed intended to cover the discrepancies of the Act of 1887, accomplish in a better way the same objects as the Act of 1887, and which by its very terms repealed all laws inconsistent with it. The Act of 1893 gave the same powers to a married woman to *acquire, enjoy* and *dispose* of any property as if she were an unmarried person, except she cannot convey or mortgage her real
412 property without the joinder of her husband. She may make any contract, except she may not become accommodation indorser, maker, guarantor or surety for another. She may sue and be sued as an unmarried woman, but she may not sue her husband except under certain conditions and for certain objects. Thus at one blow almost all the remaining disabilities existing at common law in the case of a married woman were swept away. The *purpose* of this act is well stated by Mr. Justice Green in a case decided in 1895. He said: "The Act of 1893 was intended to place the rights of a married woman upon a broader, more comprehensive and better defined basis than was accomplished by the Act of 1887." And the *effect* of the Act is well stated by Justice Dean in 1895. He said: "Formerly her *capacity* to *contract* was *exceptional* and her *disability* general; now her disability is exceptional and her capacity general."

These very words were incorporated in an opinion by President Judge Rice, of the Superior Court, in a case decided in 1897. Together they are a good reflection of the mind of our courts of highest jurisdiction on the *meaning* of the Act of 1893 and the *effect* to be given to it.

The Acts of 1848, 1887 and 1893 gave with certain restrictions to married women the power to dispose of their property by will and testament.

Of necessity it has only been possible in this paper to notice the most important of the forty odd Acts of legislature passed with a view to emancipate married women from their legal disabilities.

The brief paper, which is the condensed result of considerable labor, is a good exemplification of the fact that the law is a progressive science, and shows that as economic and social conditions change, the law, as an integral part of the government, also changes, to keep step with the new and constantly arising necessities of the people and the State.

Charles O'Brien.

Women and Property in South Carolina: The Evidence from Marriage Settlements, 1730 to 1830

Marylynn Salmon

DURING the eighteenth and early nineteenth centuries two distinct sets of legal principles—those of the common law and equity law—governed the status of women in the British-American colonies and the American states. Complications arose when the rules contradicted each other, as they did, for example, with regard to property ownership. Under the common law, a married woman (feme covert) could not own property, either real or personal. All personalty a woman brought to marriage became her husband's. He could spend her money, sell her stocks or slaves, and appropriate her clothing and jewelry. He gained managerial rights to her lands, houses, and tenements and decided if land was to be farmed by the family or leased.[1] He also controlled the rents and profits from all real estate. With regard to conveyances, however, women held a single note of power. No husband could sell real property without the consent of his wife. The common law sanctioned conveyances only when wives freely agreed to them, although "free" consent was sometimes quite difficult to determine in court.[2]

Ms. Salmon is a member of the Department of History at the University of Maryland Baltimore County. She wishes to thank Mary Maples Dunn, Mary Beth Norton, and the members of the 1979-1980 seminar of the Philadelphia Center for Early American Studies for their critical comments on this and an earlier version of the article. The invaluable technical assistance of Joseph O'Rourke is also gratefully acknowledged.

[1] William Blackstone, *Commentaries on the Laws of England* . . . , 4 vols. (Oxford, 1765-1769), II, 132, 136, 255, 293, 355; Thomas Smith, *De Republica Anglorum: A Discourse on the Commonwealth of England,* ed. Leonard Alston (Cambridge, 1906), 127; William Holdsworth, *A History of English Law,* 16 vols. (London, 1903-1966), III (5th ed.), 193, 195-196, 249; *An Essay on the Nature and Operation of Fines and Recoveries* (London, 1728), 68-69; *The Laws Respecting Women* . . . (Dobbs Ferry, N.Y., 1974 [orig. publ. London, 1777]), 181; James Kent, *Commentaries on American Law,* 4 vols. (New York, 1826-1830), II, 151-154; Samuel Church, "Lectures on Law by Tapping Reeve, Esq." (1806) (unpubl. notebook, Cornell University Law Library, Ithaca, N.Y.).

[2] Tapping Reeve, *The Law of Baron and Femme, of Parent and Child, of Guardian and Ward, of Master and Servant, and of the Powers of Courts of Chancery* . . . (New Haven, Conn., 1816), 98; *Laws Respecting Women,* 70-72; Marylynn Salmon, "The Property Rights of Women in Early America: A Comparative Study" (Ph.D. diss., Bryn Mawr College, 1980), 27-84.

Since women could not own property under the common law, they could not exercise legal controls over it. A feme covert could not make a legally binding contract. She could not sell or mortgage property that she brought to the marriage or that she and her husband acquired. She possessed no power to execute a deed of gift or write a will unless her husband consented, and even then her power was restricted to personal property. During widowhood, the law allowed women only a life interest in one-third of the family's real property, no matter what proportion of that property had been hers before marriage. With regard to personal property, widows could claim absolute ownership of one-third, but only if the estate were free of debts. If a husband died heavily indebted or insolvent, his wife lost all her personal property (and in some jurisdictions her real property as well), even though she had exercised no control over the accumulation of her husband's debts. Regarding property, then, women were virtually powerless under the common law.[3]

Equity law as administered by the British and American courts of chancery was not similarly harsh. Through formal contracts called marriage settlements, femes covert owned and controlled property.[4] In their various forms, marriage settlements allowed women full or partial managerial rights over property. Separate clauses gave women the right to sell or mortgage property, give it away, or write wills. Some marriage settlements stated explicitly the traditional rights that men relinquished by signing them. Many settlements barred husbands from "intermeddling" with their wives' estates in any way and, perhaps most important, stated that settlement property could not be taken by creditors to pay a husband's debts. Separate estates for women also frequently included clauses guaranteeing the inheritances of children. Once women or their

[3] No comprehensive study of the legal status of early American women has yet been written. The best general discussion is still Reeve, *Baron and Femme. Laws Respecting Women* is a good survey of English law and is available in a reprint edition. Holdsworth's impressive overview of the history of English law is also helpful. The most commonly cited discussion of the legal rights of early American women is Richard B. Morris, *Studies in the History of American Law, with Special Reference to the Seventeenth and Eighteenth Centuries* (New York, 1930), chap. 3. This should be used with care, however, since it is only a cursory study and unreliable.

[4] Holdsworth cited *Avenant* v. *Kitchen* (1581) as the first case in which an equity court supported the right of a woman to hold property separately from her husband by the force of a prenuptial contract. Within a short period of time, the Chancery Court permitted women to exert active control over settlements. Decisions recognized the right of women to enter into binding contracts (1582), write wills (1594), make presents to their husbands (1614), and convey to strangers (1619). Holdsworth, *History of English Law,* I (7th rev. ed.), 494, V, 303, 310-315; Richard Francis, *Maxims of Equity . . .* (London, 1728), 5; Reeve, *Baron and Femme,* 222-223, 238; *Laws Respecting Women,* 179; Zephaniah Swift, *A System of the Laws of the State of Connecticut: In Six Books,* 2 vols. (New Haven, Conn., 1795-1796), I, 200-201.

relations protected property from the possible business misfortunes of a husband, it could safely be passed through the maternal line.

Marriage settlements were designed, then, to serve several functions. They gave women a measure of financial security during marriage and widowhood. They protected a portion of family property from creditors. They provided grandparents with the assurance that family fortunes would not be spent before grandchildren came of age. Historians of aristocratic society in seventeenth- and eighteenth-century England have tended to emphasize this last function of marriage settlements. They have found that beginning in the late sixteenth century, fathers created trust estates for their daughters in an effort to prevent sons-in-law from controlling, and perhaps squandering, family fortunes. For a man who wanted to guarantee the inheritances of his grandchildren, a trust presented an alternative to turning property over to an outsider—his daughter's husband. According to this interpretation, the primary purpose of English marriage settlements was to create and preserve large family estates.[5]

416 Historians of early America have tended to discount the importance of the British perspective on trust estates. Instead, scholars such as Richard B. Morris and Mary R. Beard stressed the utilitarian function of settlements for the feme covert. Pointing to the existence of equity law and trust estates, Beard and Morris claimed that in America (and Beard also applied the argument to England), women functioned virtually on a legal par with men. If a woman could own property, make contracts, and write wills under equity law, then common law restrictions on her activities lost meaning.[6] Thus the most generally accepted interpretation of equity law in America has emphasized its ability to elevate the legal status of women from subservience to relative independence.

Historians of women in early America have relied on this interpretation of equity law to help define the status of the feme covert. The hypothesis of equality has contributed to the assumption that colonial women enjoyed a legal and social status superior to that of both their English contemporaries and their nineteenth-century descendants.[7] For if, as

[5] Christopher Clay, "Marriage, Inheritance, and the Rise of Large Estates in England, 1660-1815," *Economic History Review*, 2d Ser., XXI (1968), 503-518; H. J. Habakkuk, "Marriage Settlements in the Eighteenth Century," Royal Historical Society, *Transactions*, 4th Ser., XXXII (1950), 15-31; Lawrence Stone. *The Crisis of the Aristocracy, 1558-1641* (Oxford, 1965).

[6] Morris, *History of American Law*, 126-155; Beard, *Woman as Force in History: A Study in Traditions and Realities* (New York, 1962 [orig. publ. 1946]).

[7] In fact, historians usually depict the colonial period as a golden age for women. In addition to Morris's legal study, books by Elisabeth Anthony Dexter (*Colonial Women of Affairs: Women in Business and the Professions in America before 1776* [Boston, 1924] and *Career Women of America, 1776-1840* [Francestown, N.H., 1950]) and Mary Sumner Benson (*Women in Eighteenth-Century America: A Study of Opinion and Social Usage* [New York, 1935]) helped to build the theory of a liberal legal and social climate for colonial women. More recently the theory has been supported by the work of John Demos in *A Little Commonwealth: Family Life in Plymouth Colony* (New York, 1970); Roger Thompson in *Women in Stuart*

Morris claimed, marriage settlements were "widely employed" in America, and if, as Beard believed, they were interpreted liberally, then women of all classes in the colonies enjoyed the rights of wealthy Englishwomen. In the view of these historians, the common use of settlements in the eighteenth century reflected a beneficial legal climate for American women. Similarly, the decline of equity law in the nineteenth century demonstrated the advantages enjoyed by eighteenth-century matrons.[8]

Neither Morris nor Beard studied marriage settlements in detail. They knew that equity law contained rules allowing women to own property and that some marriage settlements existed, but they did not know how frequently settlements were employed or what specific powers women exercised through them. Historical understanding of equity law and the use of marriage settlements has been based on scant research and impressionistic evidence. The current lively debate over the nature of women's legal and social status in the colonial and early national periods makes it important, however, to understand equity law more precisely.[9]
We must learn who used marriage settlements, how often they were used,
and for what purposes. Such information should reveal the degree to

---

England and America: A Comparative Study (London, 1974); Mary P. Ryan in *Womanhood in America: From Colonial Times to the Present* (New York, 1975); Ann D. Gordon and Mari Jo Buhle in "Sex and Class in Colonial and Nineteenth-Century America," in Berenice A. Carroll, ed., *Liberating Women's History: Theoretical and Critical Essays* (Urbana, Ill., 1976), 278-300; and Joan R. Gundersen and Gwen Victor Gampel, "Married Women's Legal Status in Eighteenth-Century New York and Virginia," *William and Mary Quarterly*, 3d Ser., XXXIX (1982), 114-134. In her pathbreaking study of American women between 1750 and 1800, Mary Beth Norton revises significantly the old interpretations, for she concludes that women possessed both a low status and a low self-image during the colonial period. The status of women changed as a result of the American Revolution, improving on some points such as self-esteem, but remaining ambiguous in the areas of politics and law (*Liberty's Daughters: The Revolutionary Experience of American Women, 1750-1800* [Boston, 1980]). Linda K. Kerber has also demonstrated that women's lives changed after the American Revolution, but she emphasizes points on which women lost rights, especially in the law (*Women of the Republic: Intellect and Ideology in Revolutionary America* [Chapel Hill, N.C., 1980]). Kerber's contention that the legal status of women deteriorated in the 19th century is not proved. For a revisionist study of the legal rights of women, see Salmon, "Property Rights."

[8] Morris, *History of American Law*, 138; Beard, *Woman as Force*, 151.

[9] There appears to be a growing split among women's historians concerning the changing status of women after 1800. Scholars such as Norton, and Kerber to a lesser degree, see a widening of the female sphere during the early national period away from the subservience and dependency of colonial women. Other historians still maintain that colonial women occupied a privileged position compared to 19th-century women, who lost status and economic power with the rise of industrialism. Most recently, Gerda Lerner has made the latter argument in a review of the Norton and Kerber books, "What the Revolution Meant for Women," *Washington Post Book World*, XV (Jan. 4, 1981), 9.

which settlements provided women with financial security and whether they were written to benefit women, or children and grandchildren, or all three groups.

Before the role of equity law in America can be understood, many separate studies of settlements must be conducted, because each colony and state handled principles of equity law differently.[10] Large numbers of settlement deeds must also be scrutinized, even though the informality of American recording practices frequently makes such analysis difficult. This article reports findings for South Carolina, for which a wealth of information is available. The extent of the documentation makes South Carolina a good place to begin an investigation into the nature of equity law. The legal record reveals remarkably liberal attitudes toward women's property rights—quite possibly the most liberal of all the colonies and states, although that supposition must be tested by comparative study.[11]

In 1720 the colony established a court of chancery that handled cases concerning marriage settlements in a sophisticated manner, imitating the
418 English Chancery Court in style and decisions.[12] The court kept good records and remained active throughout the colonial and early national periods. The legislature did not require registration of marriage settlements until 1785, but before that date prudent persons frequently recorded their settlements with the secretary of state in Charleston. After 1785, all settlements had to be recorded within three months of their creation to be considered valid.[13] Altogether some 2000 settlements have survived from the colonial and early national periods.[14] For this study, an attempt was made to discover and analyze all recorded marriage settlements for the colonial and Revolutionary periods. For the period 1785-1830, when the law required settlements to be recorded and the number increased accordingly, a sample consisting of all deeds registered in Charleston in every fifth year has been analyzed, for a total of 638 (see

[10] Some colonies, such as Massachusetts, Connecticut, and Pennsylvania, did not have separate courts of equity in the English fashion. On the problem of equity law in early America, see Stanley N. Katz, "The Politics of Law in Colonial America: Controversies over Chancery Courts and Equity Law in the Eighteenth Century," *Perspectives in American History*, V (1971), 257, and Swift, *A System*, II, 419-460. For a full discussion of regional comparisons on the administration of marriage settlements, see Salmon, "Property Rights," 150-234.

[11] Salmon, "Property Rights," 150-256.

[12] Anne King Gregorie, ed., *Records of the Court of Chancery of South Carolina, 1671-1779* (Washington, D.C., 1950), 5-7.

[13] "An Act to oblige persons interested in Marriage Deeds and Contracts, to record the same in the Secretary's office of this state," in Thomas Cooper and David J. McCord, eds., *The Statutes at Large of South Carolina* (Columbia, S.C., 1836-1841), IV, 656-657.

[14] Marriage Settlements, Vols. 1-10 (1785-1830); Records of the Register of the Secretary of the Province, Vols. A-I (1721-1733); Miscellaneous Records of the Secretary of State, Charleston Series, Vols. AB, BB-XX (1735-1789). All manuscripts cited are located in the South Carolina State Archives, Columbia, unless noted otherwise.

TABLE I
MARRIAGE SETTLEMENT SAMPLE SIZE

Years	*N*	*% of Total*
1730-1740	23	4
1741-1750	35	5
1751-1760	55	9
1761-1770	107	17
1771-1780	107	17
1781-1790	88	14
1791-1800	51	8
1801-1810	54	8
1811-1820	49	8
1821-1830	69	11
1730-1780	327	51
1781-1830	311	49
1730-1830	638	100

Table I). Each settlement gives the names of the parties, the dates of creation and recording, the type of property settled, and the terms of the settlement. Also frequently noted are the occupations of the parties, their residence, their marital status, the name of the owner(s) of the property, and the location and amount of the property.

Proper marriage settlements were complicated documents, usually made in the form of trusts. Before the English case of *Rippon* v. *Dawding* (1769), all valid settlements were required to include trustees who nominally owned the property in the name of the feme covert (the *cestui qui trust*).[15] After 1769, in England and in some American jurisdictions, simple marriage settlements—contracts made directly between a man and a woman without the intervention of trustees—also sufficed to create separate estates.[16] In their handling of simple marriage settlements, equity courts initially referred to the husband as trustee for his wife. This language soon disappeared from most cases, however, perhaps as courts realized the irony of naming husbands trustees for their wives' separate estates. In South Carolina, judges disliked simple agreements, and trusts remained the most common form for separate estates. Trust estates composed 91 percent (582) of the deeds studied. Only 9 percent (56)

[15] *Rippon* v. *Dawding*, Ambler, 565 (1769).

[16] Reeve reported in 1816 that settlements without trustees had become "no uncommon thing" (*Baron and Femme*, 163). One of the earliest American cases dealing with a simple marriage settlement appeared on the docket of the Pennsylvania Supreme Court in 1793. See *Barnes Lessee* v. *Hart*, 1 Yeates 221 (1793). The case is analyzed in Marylynn Salmon, "Equality or Submersion? *Feme Covert* Status in Early Pennsylvania," in Carol Ruth Berkin and Mary Beth Norton, eds., *Women of America: A History* (Boston, 1979), 91-113.

were simple marriage settlements, indicating the reluctance of South Carolinians to abandon the formality of trusts.[17]

To create a trust estate in the normal fashion, the man, woman, and trustee(s) all joined in the execution of an "indenture tripartite," a contract stipulating the terms of the settlement. This form guaranteed the knowledge and consent of the parties, as required by law. In cases involving separate estates, equity standards demanded that men be fully apprised of the terms of their wives' settlements. Judges refused to support a woman who deceived her fiancé or husband into expecting property at marriage, only to secure it to herself through a trustee.[18] They viewed such action as a fraud against the husband's marital rights and held that "he [or she] that hath committed Iniquity, shall not have Equity."[19]

Settlements granting women separate estates could be written either before or after marriage, but most couples executed them prior to marriage. For the period under study, 87 percent (552) of the settlements were prenuptial. There was no significant change in this pattern over time,
420 indicating the constancy of women's desire to secure separate property at the point when they exercised the greatest bargaining power over men.[20] Postnuptial settlements usually resulted when a wife inherited property unexpectedly, or when her husband encountered financial difficulties that made it necessary to secure some family property against creditors.

For understandable reasons, creditors disliked trust estates, particularly those made after marriage. They resented the ability of a feme covert to deny them access to her separate estate and argued that husbands as well as wives could find protection under the terms of marriage settlements. A man who lost his own estate through business misfortunes or extravagant living, they claimed, could fall back on the income from his wife's trust property. Indebted or insolvent husbands might even attempt to preserve a portion of their own fortunes by fraudulently settling property on their wives.[21]

[17] South Carolina courts preferred women to use formal trusts rather than direct agreements with their husbands. In *Barret* v. *Barret*, 4 S.C. Eq. (4 Des.) 491 (1814), and *Dupree* v. *McDonald*, 4 S.C. Eq. (4 Des.) 209 (1812), the judges noted their disapproval of settlements made without trustees. See also the arguments of counsel in *Executors of Smelie* v. *Executors of Smelie*, 2 S.C. Eq. (2 Des.) 72 (1802).

[18] Holdsworth, *History of English Law*, V, 313; George W. Keeton and L. A. Sheridan, *Equity* (London, 1969), 442-443; Reeve, *Baron and Femme*, 236. In the South Carolina case of *Cape* v. *Adams*, 1 S.C. Eq. (1 Des.) 567 (1797), a man tried to create a settlement of his wife's property for his own benefit without her knowledge or consent. The court disallowed his deed.

[19] Francis, *Maxims of Equity*, 5.

[20] Reeve noted the significant role of parents and guardians in bargaining with the suitors of young women (see *Baron and Femme*, 174).

[21] Some men did attempt to settle property on their families after contracting debts. Examples of cases involving fraudulent trusts include *Drayton* v. *Pritchard* (1816), Charleston District Equity Decrees, 3, 161; *Peigne* v. *Snowden*, 1 S.C. Eq. (1 Des.) 591 (1800); *Peace* v. *Spierin*, 2 S.C. Eq. (2 Des.) 500 (1807); and *Croft* v. *Townsend's Administrators*, 3 S.C. Eq. (3 Des.) 223 (1811).

Evidence from South Carolina undermines the argument that settlements commonly benefited husbands rather than wives. Women who wrote marriage settlements usually wanted to control the property they brought to their marriages, not their husbands' property. Eighty-two percent (523) of the settlements studied included only the wife's estate; 11 percent (68), only the estate of the husband; and 5 percent (35), property from both the husband and wife. (In 12 cases, 2 percent, it is unknown who owned the property.) No man put his entire estate into a trust for his wife. These figures demonstrate no general attempt by men to protect their property through marriage settlements. They benefited, of course, when women held property that could not be confiscated for family debts, but they did not usually safeguard their own estates. The need for credit in money-scarce economies gave men reasons to avoid trusts. In addition, by the end of the eighteenth century strict recording requirements made deceit difficult, for creditors could easily discover the status of a family's estate and refuse to extend credit on settled property.

Cases of fraudulent trusts demonstrate judicial solicitude for the rights 421
of creditors. The recording statute of 1785 served primarily as a means of informing creditors about separate estates. In addition, chancellors refused to enforce trusts made to deny creditors their just claims.[22] But the South Carolina Court of Chancery also demonstrated sensitivity to the needs of debtors who wanted to create trust estates. A debtor could execute a valid settlement for the benefit of another person if he possessed assets to repay his debts above the value of the trust property.[23]

In the case of *Tunno* v. *Trezevant* (1804), to take a well-documented example, we find that a man consented to the marriage of his niece only after her fiancé agreed to create a settlement including all her property and some of his own.[24] The young man was a merchant whose credit appeared to be good at the time of his marriage (the uncle made inquiries), but within a year he became an insolvent debtor hounded by creditors who demanded payment out of both his business and his private property. From testimony the court found that he had not created his marriage settlement with any fraudulent purpose in mind. Both he and his bride-to-be had honestly believed that their financial position was secure when they executed the deed. In situations such as theirs, when a settlement was

[22] The preamble to the recording statute of South Carolina noted the problem. It read, "The practice prevailing in this State of keeping marriage contracts and deeds in the hands of those interested therein, hath been oftentimes injurious to creditors and others, who have been induced to credit and trust persons under a presumption of their being possessed of an estate subject and liable to the payment of their just debts" (Cooper and McCord, eds., *South Carolina Statutes*, IV, 656).

[23] Reeve, *Baron and Femme*, 176. In *Croft* v. *Townsend's Administrators*, Chancellor Desaussure ruled against a settlement that included too much of an indebted man's property. See especially his comments on p. 2. In *Taylor* v. *Heriot*, 4 S.C. Eq. (4 Des.) 227 (1812), a legal opinion noted that indebted men were fully justified in creating settlements of their future wives' estates before marriage.

[24] *Tunno* v. *Trezevant*, 2 S.C. Eq. (2 Des.) 264 (1804).

created for the "valuable consideration" of marriage, the court of chancery enforced it against the claims of creditors. In this instance the judges regarded the settlement as "a *bona fide* discharge of a moral duty" and refused to "weigh it too nicely." They did not attach the settlement property to discharge the husband's debts, acting on the fundamental principle that "marriage is not only a *bona fide* and valuable consideration, but the very highest consideration in law; this Court will therefore always support marriage settlements, if there is no particular evidence of fraud made out, showing an intention to deceive or defraud creditors."[25]

Tunno v. *Trezevant* clearly demonstrates the advantages of separate estates for women and their children. Through marriage settlements, families possessed a source of income that was free from obligations of the male head, either business or, if the estate were so designed, personal. Since separate estates could prove so beneficial, it is important to know how many women actually employed them. In this regard the documentation for colonial South Carolina is sadly limited. Before 1785, the absence
422 of a recording statute makes it impossible to discover the total number of settlements. For the period 1785-1810, however, when virtually all marriage settlements were recorded in Charleston and when accurate census records are available for the state, it is possible to arrive at a rough estimate of the number of couples with settlements. During those years, approximately 1-2 percent of marrying couples created separate estates.[26] Settlements apparently were far from the common occurrence that some historians have believed, at least in South Carolina. Few women had either means or reason to utilize them.

Who, then, did create marriage settlements? Perhaps the small number of deeds indicates use of settlements only among the wealthy, landed families of South Carolina in the manner of the English aristocracy. Fortunately, the detailed information available in the deeds allows us to discover something about the status of couples who employed trust estates and marriage settlements. This can be done by analyzing the value of settled property and by noting the occupations of husbands. (We cannot consider the occupations of wives, because few identified themselves by

[25] *Ibid.*, 269-271.

[26] There are no accurate marriage rates for South Carolina in the period under study. Population figures are available, however, and by applying the earliest available marriage rate, that of 1860 (1/115), we can arrive at a rough percentage of marrying couples with settlements. Thus in 1790 when the white population was 140,000, the estimated number of marriages was 1610. Twenty-two settlements were written in that year and therefore the percentage of marrying couples with settlements was 1.4. The next federal census (1800) revealed a population figure of 196,000, making the estimated number of marriages 2254. Since 28 settlements were written in 1800, the percentage of marrying couples with settlements was 1.2. *The Statistical History of the United States: From Colonial Times to the Present* (New York, 1976), 1168; *Population of the United States in 1860* (Washington, D.C., 1869), xxxvi.

occupation.) The following discussion investigates property values first, and then turns to male occupations.

Analysis of property values presents some difficulty. Many settlements do not specify the amount or type of property, but refer to it as "everything" or "all her property both real and personal." When these deeds are excluded, 456 (71 percent) remain for analysis, but even these, while listing specific types of property such as slaves, cattle, or land, rarely give property values. Consequently, only broad, comparative categories will be considered here, and not specific property valuations.[27]

The upper ranks of South Carolina society relied on settlements more often than people of middling status. It appears that 69 percent (316/456) of the estates that specified types of property included property worth more than £500 sterling, or more than five slaves, or more than one town lot with appurtenances, or a plantation of more than three hundred acres.[28] Settlements of more than ten slaves and hundreds of pounds sterling were common. One settlement included one hundred slaves,
another £50,000 sterling, and still another forty-four slaves and over four 423
thousand acres of land. A number of settlements included more than ten slaves, land, and at least one town lot with appurtenances—the traditional estate of a wealthy South Carolina planter family.

Although the elite employed marriage settlements most often, persons with small amounts of property also used them. Settlements sometimes included only one or two slaves, a few articles of household furniture, or the woman's clothing and household goods. Approximately 9 percent (41/456) of the settlements included property estimated to be worth less than £150 sterling, or included only one slave, or a part of a house. Another 22 percent (99) included property estimated at £151-500 sterling, or contained two to five slaves, or one house, or 100 to 299 acres of land. The

[27] For determining the approximate values of property included in marriage settlements, the work of Alice Hanson Jones was indispensable. See *American Colonial Wealth: Documents and Methods*, 2d ed., 3 vols. (New York, 1977). Equally useful for determining exchange rates for South Carolina in the 18th century was John J. McCusker, *Money and Exchange in Europe and America, 1600-1775: A Handbook* (Chapel Hill, N.C., 1978), 223-224. Throughout the 18th century, approximately £7 South Carolina currency equaled £1 sterling.

[28] For the purpose of making comparative statements concerning settlement property, I assigned estimated values to certain types of property, based on information provided in Jones, *American Colonial Wealth*, III. A slave was valued at £85, one acre of improved land at £1, one head of cattle at £10, one riding horse at £75, one town lot with appurtenances at less than £500, and more than one town lot with appurtenances at more than £500. Settlements with a single slave were all classified as containing property of a value less than £150, as were settlements containing only part of a house. Settlements including only slaves, numbering two to five, were all classified in the £150-500 range. All pounds are pounds sterling. Although estimated valuations such as these are extremely unreliable for determining absolute wealth, they enable us to distinguish between individuals of great and middling wealth.

settlement of John Darrell and Elizabeth Legeaux is typical of contracts made by persons from the middling ranks of society:

> This is to certify to all whom it may concern that I John Smith Darrell of the city of Charleston and State aforesaid Mariner being now about to be joined in the holy Bond of Wedlock to Miss Elizabeth Browne Legeaux conceiving it just and right that she should continue after marriage to hold what property she might have at that time I do therefore by this Instrument Secure to her and the heirs of her body for ever all right and title to Two Negroes left to her by her Father (Vizt.) the Woman Named Constant and her son Caesar together with any other Issue that the said Constant may have. I do also secure to her her Bed Bedding and the household furniture that she now possesses reserving to myself the Services of the said Negroes during my Natural life.[29]

424 While Elizabeth Legeaux's estate of two slaves might have been enviable by eighteenth-century standards, it was hardly that of an heiress. The motivation for creating a trust estate of small value undoubtedly stemmed from more than a desire to protect the inheritances of future generations. A woman who went to the trouble and expense of creating a separate estate for her household furniture was concerned about herself and her own position in life at least as much as with the well-being of her children. Although the desire to protect family property for future generations may have motivated some of the wealthy couples with settlements, the preservation of family status was not the dominant consideration for all. Given the wide range of individuals with separate estates—from a woman with one slave, to an heiress with one hundred—we cannot rely on the traditional English interpretation of settlements.

Most women who made settlements owned personal rather than real property. Very few of the settlements included real estate to the exclusion of personalty (10/456), and only one-third (147) included some real estate. The other two-thirds (301) involved only personal property. In South Carolina, women's marriage settlements most often included slaves, money, cattle, and household goods, but not land. Such a pattern may indicate that fathers gave their land to sons, while daughters received slaves or money. In the absence of comparative probate materials, it is impossible to be sure. What is clear, however, is that settlements consisting entirely of personal property appeared twice as often in the sample as settlements including any real property. Given the fact that under the common law men acquired absolute ownership of their wives' personal estates at marriage, while they exercised only managerial rights over real property, this is not surprising. Settlements were more useful to women who owned personal property.

[29] Marriage Settlement between Elizabeth Legeaux and John Smith Darrell (1809), Marriage Settlements, 5, 522-523.

This consideration may explain why a substantial number of settlements involved slaves. Eighty-two percent (372) of the deeds that specify the nature of the property included at least some slaves, and 28 percent (129) included only slaves. No other type of property appears so frequently in the settlements. Moreover, settlements including only a few slaves appeared in the sample as often as those with many slaves. When settlements including only slaves are singled out, we learn that fully 32 percent (41/129) contained five slaves or fewer, and that an additional 19 percent contained six to ten slaves. Women with slaves appreciated the importance of protecting their property.

More may be learned about the function of settlements by studying the occupational status of the men who made them. Of the whole number of deeds analyzed, 68 percent (434) noted the husband's occupation (see Table II). Over half of these (228) involved planters (30 percent, N = 131) or gentlemen (22 percent, N = 97). From the settlements, we can learn no more about the status of these men than the words they used to describe themselves. We do not know, for example, how many of the planters were large landowners and therefore considered members of the social elite. The word planter stood for all farmers and landowners in South Carolina, large and small. The fact that 22 percent of the sample referred to themselves as "gentlemen," however, reveals the high social standing of a significant proportion of settlement holders.

Merchants composed the next largest group of men with settlements, 13 percent (58/434). Perhaps the volatile fortunes of merchant families gave them special incentives to protect their property from creditors. Indentures tripartite involving merchants frequently alluded to the financial risks of trade. The settlement of William Edwards and Elizabeth Moore in 1774, for example, gave the couple joint control over her property—seven slaves and a £6000 current money bond—"unless it shall happen that the said William Edwards shall become Bankrupt or meet with losses or misfortunes in Trade or Business so as to be unable to support himself and family."[30] In that case, Elizabeth Edwards would have full managerial rights, free from "interference" by her husband. In 1787 James Stephenson and Elizabeth Scott were equally careful. Their settlement stated that if James became insolvent "by losses in trade or otherwise by accumulation of debts by accident or misfortune," the trustees would give Elizabeth £350 current money for her separate use, "to the intent that the said Elizabeth may have a resource left."[31] The overseas expeditions of merchants could place wives and children in precarious financial situations. Before Josiah Smith left on a "sea voyage," he took out the 1789

[30] Marriage Settlement between Elizabeth Moore and William Edwards (1744), Miscellaneous Records, RR, 212-213.

[31] Marriage Settlement between Elizabeth Scott and James Stephenson (1787), Marriage Settlements, 1, 338.

Table II
Male Occupations

Title	*N*	%
Planter	131	30
Gentlemen and Professionals		
Gentleman, Esquire	97	22
Merchant	58	13
Physician	30	7
Lawyer, Judge	13	3
Minister	6	1
Schoolmaster	2	—
Shipmaster	1	—
Officials		
Military Officer	6	1
Government Official	3	1
Shopkeepers and Innholders		
Shopkeeper	5	1
Factor	5	1
Clerk	5	1
Innholder, Tavernkeeper	3	1
Trader	1	—
Indian Trader	1	—
Grocer	1	—
Artisans		
Carpenter	10	2
Cordwainer	9	2
Tailor	8	2
Blacksmith	4	1
Cabinetmaker	4	1
Baker	3	1
Bricklayer	3	1
Butcher	1	—
Cooper	1	—
Breechesmaker	1	—
Watchmaker	1	—
Frame Mole Knitter	1	—
Carver	1	—
Spinner	1	—
Saddler	1	—
Coachmaker	1	—
Wheelwright	1	—
Periwigmaker	1	—
Shipwright	1	—
Painter	1	—
Distiller	1	—
Mariner	10	2
Free Black	1	—
Total	434	100

equivalent of flight insurance. He settled six slaves on his wife for her sole and separate use, free from his debts, if he never returned.[32] The case of *Tunno* v. *Trezevant*, discussed above, suggests that it was wise for a woman to be wary when entering marriage with a South Carolina merchant.

Almost as many artisans, innkeepers, and mariners made marriage settlements as gentlemen—20 percent (86/434). Although we cannot learn the economic standing of these men from the settlements (and some of them may have owned considerable amounts of property), the fact that they identified themselves by trade rather than by status indicates that they were not a part of the South Carolina elite. Even persons at the lowest social level could make use of equity law, as demonstrated by the appearance of a free black man in the sample. On the basis of male occupations, then, it is possible to state that marriage settlements were not made exclusively by the South Carolina aristocracy. Couples from the middling and even the lower ranks of society also sometimes took the precaution of establishing separate estates for wives.

It is easy to understand why the wife of a merchant or a mariner might 427
want a separate estate, yet not all merchants' wives utilized equity provisions, and not all mariners followed in the footsteps of John Darrell, whose settlement appears above. Moreover, it is not as obvious why a planter's wife, or a physician's or a cordwainer's, might desire this special protection. Why did a particular gentleman and his fiancée step into the office of the secretary of state to register a settlement, given the fact that most genteel families did not? The motivations of individuals cannot be conclusively established; but by investigating the provisions for control and descent of settlement property and by analyzing the court cases concerning specific disputes over settlement terms, we may learn more about the use of separate estates.

Each marriage settlement contained various clauses for delineating control over settlement property. Couples could place property under the management of trustees, or they could give trustees no managerial powers at all, reducing them to figureheads. Some husbands retained control over their wives' estates, and in many cases, as will be shown below, femes covert managed their own property. The powers retained by women became significant for determining their level of independence. Some trusts gave women extensive authority over their own property, while others gave them none at all but instead directed trustees to pay them the rents and profits of their estates. Some settlements gave women one privilege of control while denying others. For example, if a deed granted a feme covert the right to devise, she could not also sell or mortgage her estate; those powers had to be granted in a separate clause. In the same vein, a woman whose settlement gave her rights to the rents and profits of

[32] Marriage Settlement between Mary Smith and Josiah Smith (1789), *ibid.*, I, 446-447.

her property could not regulate the principal, which remained in the hands of trustees who made all investment decisions.[33]

Although most South Carolina settlements were trust estates, trustees rarely managed property. Only 3 percent (16) of the deeds gave trustees sole powers of control. In 93 percent (591) trustees were vested with minimal powers, such as the right to approve a property sale initiated by the feme covert, or were not employed at all. In 5 percent of the settlements (31), control was shared by the trustee and the couple, or the arrangement is unknown. Settlement terms demonstrate that many creators of separate estates, whether parents, relatives, or the women themselves, wanted women rather than trustees—or husbands—to manage their own property. Over the entire period studied, 40 percent (254) of the women administered their estates alone. In 28 percent (180) of the deeds, husbands and wives managed settlement property together, and in 25 percent (157), men possessed exclusive managerial rights (see Table III).

428 Some change in this division of authority occurred over time (see Figure 1). There was a small but steady decline in the number of women who managed their own estates, offset by an increase in the number of husbands and wives who shared control. With the exception of a slight rise between 1780 and 1800, the number of men who managed settlement property alone remained fairly constant, at about 22 percent. What we see then, is a shifting pattern, away from exclusive privileges for women and toward joint privileges for couples.

A plausible explanation for this pattern may be found in Mary Beth Norton's study of marital relationships in the eighteenth and early nineteenth centuries. Norton discovered that before the Revolution wives rarely played an active role in family business beyond their sphere of domestic concerns. They deferred to their husbands on most questions and relied on men to manage family finances. By the end of the century, however, this deferential relationship was changing. Marriages became more egalitarian, as wives abandoned passivity to participate in broader decisions concerning family affairs. The need for female autonomy in regulating separate estates would decrease as relationships between spouses became more equal over time. Femes covert might no longer desire total independence in managing their own estates precisely because they exercised more authority over the general fund of family property.

For the 180 settlements involving coadministration, we cannot know who actually managed the property. Perhaps men dominated in all cases, and the figure should be combined with that for sole male control. Total freedom for all husbands in this category is unlikely, however, for many of the joint control settlements restricted husbands in various ways. Some

[33] Reeve, *Baron and Femme*, 162-163, 170-173; *Price* v. *Michel* (1821), Charleston District Equity Decrees, 3, 377; Kent, *Commentaries on American Law*, II, 164-165.

Table III
Control of Settlement Property

	Woman		Man		Couple		Trustee		Mixed/Unknown		
Years	N	%	N	%	N	%	N	%	N	%	*No. Deeds*
1730-1740	12	52	7	30	4	17	0	0	0	0	23
1741-1750	20	57	6	17	6	17	0	0	3	9	35
1751-1760	29	53	12	22	9	16	3	5	2	4	55
1761-1770	44	41	25	23	32	30	2	2	4	4	107
1771-1780	44	41	25	23	31	29	4	4	3	3	107
1781-1790	34	39	28	32	22	25	1	1	3	3	88
1791-1800	14	27	18	35	16	31	2	4	2	4	51
1801-1810	19	35	13	24	18	33	2	4	2	4	54
1811-1820	17	35	8	16	16	33	1	2	7	14	49
1821-1830	21	30	15	22	26	38	1	1	6	9	69
Total	254	40	157	25	180	28	16	3	31	5	638

FIGURE I

CONTROL OF SETTLEMENT PROPERTY

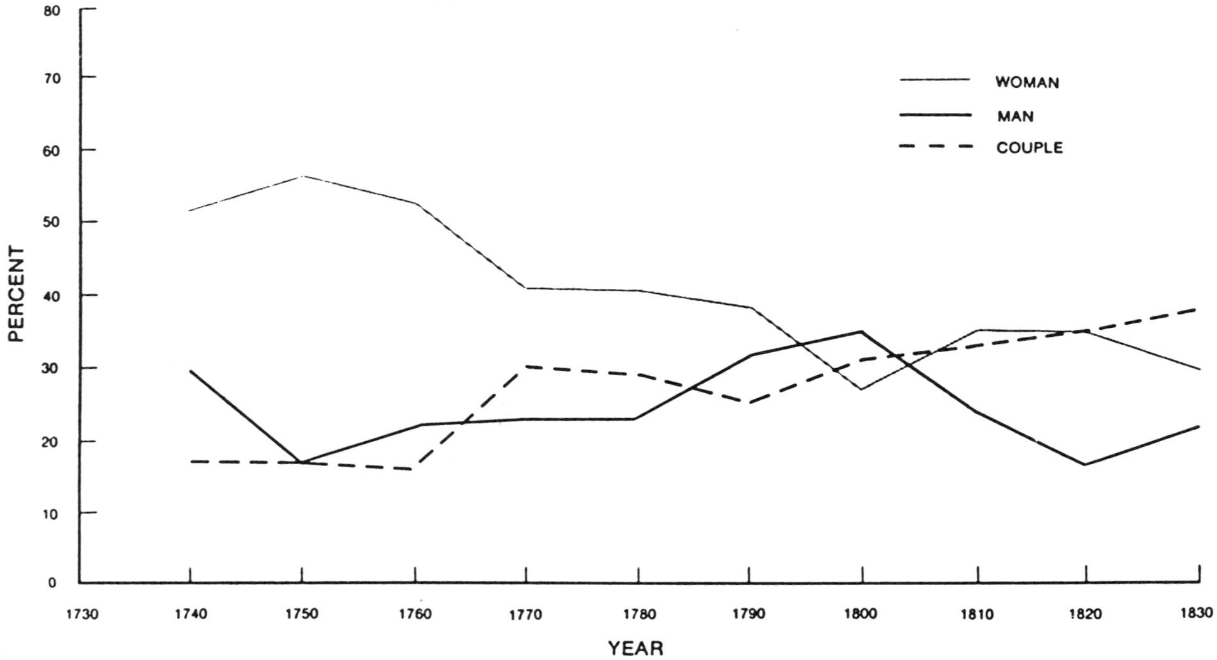

required that the wife consent to all conveyances made by her husband (16 percent, N = 29). In others, either the trustee or both the trustee and the wife had to consent to all transactions (5 percent, N = 9). More important, the fact that a feme covert wielded authority with her spouse says a great deal about the way she wanted the property handled, that is, under her management as well as her husband's. Since many women did possess managerial rights, we can assume they wanted to take part in decisions concerning their property. At the very least they exercised a veto power over sales and investments stronger than that provided by the common law, which offered only weak protection in the form of private examinations.

Most important for limiting the degree of power exercised by men in joint-control settlements were clauses restricting creditors' interests. Although the principal sums of settlements could never be taken to pay husbands' debts, rents and profits could be so applied if the settlement terms gave men access to them. To avoid this danger, yet still allow husbands the use of separate estates, many couples relied on clauses that explicitly denied creditors' rights. Martha Baker and Allen Bolton wrote such a settlement in 1765. They agreed that Allen, a planter, could "have Receive and take the use enjoyment profits and interest" of Martha's £5000 estate as long as he continued "in good Circumstances." If his affairs suffered, however, Martha would be permitted to take over management of her own estate. The settlement specified her right to act "without the Controul or Intermeddling of the said Allen Bolton or any Creditors of his in the same manner as if she were sole and unmarried and no part [of her estate] thereof or the interest thereof shall be thereafter liable to any Debts Contracts or engagements of the said Allen Bolton."[34]

Another woman and her fiancé took similar precautions. Although Thomas Bee considered himself a "gentleman," he and Susanna Holmes thought it wise to place £1000 of her money in a trust as protection against future insolvency. The settlement terms allowed the couple full use of the money, unless "by misfortunes or losses (which God avert) the present occupation calling or business of him the said Thomas Bee as a Planter or otherwise, shall fail or decline very considerably, and there shall be manifest danger, or probability, that he will be reduced and obliged to surrender quit or deliver up his Estate and Effects for the Satisfaction of his Creditors."[35] In that case, the money went into the hands of the couple's trustees, who were directed to pay them the annual interest, safe from creditors' demands. Similar stipulations commonly appeared in settlements throughout the period. Over half (51 percent, N = 326) of the women demanded this explicit protection. Without clauses denying creditors' claims on settlement property, husbands' debts, poor business

[34] Marriage Settlement between Martha Baker and Allen Bolton (1765), Marriage Settlements, I, 110.

[35] Marriage Settlement between Susanna Holmes and Thomas Bee (1761), *ibid.*, I, 170.

decisions, fraud, or, simply, financial misfortunes could destroy the utility of a separate estate.

Carefully constructed settlements specified each restriction or power of control separately and included sections allowing or disallowing certain basic changes in the settled property. For example, when creating trusts for the benefit of daughters or other female relatives, some individuals perceived a need to forbid future changes in the settlements. They feared the power of their beneficiaries to annul the protective function of their trusts by conveying them to their husbands or making use of the principal.[36] To protect women from male coercion or prevent them from making damaging business decisions, creators of settlements sometimes employed clauses forbidding changes or certain kinds of potentially harmful dispositions. A deed of settlement might state that it could not be altered in any way, or it might include provisions allowing a feme covert control over the rents and profits but not the principal of her estate.

432 When settlements did not include provisions restricting the right of a woman to control her own property, she could change or even dissolve her marriage settlement at any time.[37] Although some women wanted to alter settlement terms for the benefit of their husbands, more often wives acted to transfer controls from husbands to themselves. At the time of marriage it might seem appropriate for a woman to give her husband powers of active control over her property, without any reference to contingency arrangements in the event he encountered difficulties. Many women, unlike Martha Baker and Susanna Holmes, did not express

[36] In any case in which it appeared conclusively that a man forced his wife to transact a certain agreement against her will, she was not held liable for the agreement. Reeve, *Baron and Femme*, 165; *Bethune* v. *Beresford*, 1 S.C. Eq. (1 Des.) 174 (1790). The evidence had to be positive, however, for once a woman possessed separate property jurists defined her as a feme sole rather than a feme covert and did not regard her as susceptible to coercion. In the mid-19th century a debate arose in Maryland and South Carolina over the need for women with trust estates to undergo private examinations when conveying their property. Maryland decided that women did not need private examinations because they were legally femes sole. South Carolina decided just the opposite. See *Tiernan* v. *Poor*, 1 G. & J. 216 (1829); *Brundige* v. *Poor*, 2 G. & J. 1 (1829); *Ewing* v. *Smith*, 3 S.C. Eq. (3 Des.) 467 (1811). The South Carolina stance indicates concern with protecting women from male coercion. See Marylynn Salmon, " 'Life, Liberty, and Dower': The Legal Status of Women after the American Revolution," in Carol R. Berkin and Clara M. Lovett, eds., *Women, War, and Revolution* (New York, 1980), 85-106.

[37] Reeve, *Baron and Femme*, 162-163; *Curtis* v. *Duncan* (1821), Charleston District Equity Decrees, 3, 468; *Price* v. *Michel* (1821), *ibid.*, 3, 377; *Garner* v. *Garner's Executors*, 1 S.C. Eq. (1 Des.) 477 (1795); *Dupree* v. *McDonald*, 4 S.C. Eq. (4 Des.) 209 (1812). In *Garner*, the court corrected nonsensical words in a deed of settlement that had the effect of denying a woman all rights to her property until after her own death. The court opinion noted that it was the duty of a chancellor to correct such errors. In *Dupree*, the court interpreted a poorly worded settlement to benefit the feme covert and her son against the claims of the woman's second husband, who attempted to seize all of her property after her death.

publicly their fears for the future. But if a husband later suffered financial setbacks threatening his wife's estate, she might want to rescind his powers. By inserting a clause in her settlement allowing unspecified changes in her trust, a woman who initially wanted to leave property in her husband's hands could do so, confident that at a future date she could use her power to restrict his managerial capacity.

Such was the case for Charlotte Poaug, whose prenuptial settlement gave her husband control over the rents and profits of her real property.[38] John Poaug was a merchant who became indebted several years after his marriage. In 1771, to prevent John's creditors from seizing their estate, the Poaugs changed the terms of their settlement. In the new document, Charlotte retained all powers of control for herself. Clearly, a safety valve of this nature was invaluable for families with uncertain fortunes.

Unfortunately, some individuals did not understand the importance of precision. They wrote loose documents, failing to delineate specific powers of control. Occasionally, friends or relatives failed to clarify the fact that they were creating a separate estate for a feme covert through a deed of gift or a devise. They gave a woman property, meant for her separate use, but failed to say so explicitly. In South Carolina, when settlements were vague and disputes brought couples into court, judges in equity did everything in their power to protect women. The intent of settlements, gifts, or wills, however haphazardly designed, governed judicial decisions.

Court records indicate that by the early nineteenth century, South Carolina jurists interpreted unclear words in a deed of gift or marriage settlement consistently for the benefit of women. For example, following the English Chancery case of *Tyrrel* v. *Hope* (1743), the South Carolina court ceased requiring the specific words "to her sole and separate use" for the creation of a separate estate.[39] Instead, chancellors began to assume that any conveyance to a married woman was meant for her own use, whether the donor said so explicitly or not. If it appeared from other evidence, either parol evidence concerning the donor's intent or the wording of the document in question, that the property was intended for the sole use of a woman, the standard phrase could be omitted.

The South Carolina case of *Johnson* v. *Thompson* (1814) exemplifies judicial practice in this regard.[40] Here a father made a bequest of personal property to his married daughter. Her husband claimed the property and disposed of it. After the woman's death, her children contested his disposition. They stated that their grandfather intended the property to descend to his daughter as a separate estate, free from the control of her husband. In deciding favorably for the children, the court of appeals noted

[38] Marriage Settlement between Charlotte Poaug and John Poaug (1771), Marriage Settlements, 1, 78.

[39] *Tyrrel* v. *Hope*, 2 Atkyns 561 (1743); Reeve, *Baron and Femme*, 164; *Lowndes' Trustee* v. *Champneys' Executors* (1821), Charleston District Equity Decrees, 3, 354.

[40] *Johnson* v. *Thompson*, 4 S.C. Eq. (4 Des.) 498 (1814).

that since the devise was made to a feme covert, its wording had to be examined closely to determine intent. Here the words "fairly inferred" that the estate was designed to be a separate one, and therefore the woman's husband possessed no right to dispose of it. The implementation of this liberal policy in South Carolina indicates strong support for marriage settlements as a legal form.

South Carolina chancellors also interpreted unclear words in settlements for the benefit of married women. When coercion was not an issue, judges assumed that the absence of restrictive clauses meant freedom to exercise control.[41] In *Lowndes' Trustee* v. *Champneys' Executors* (1821), the chancellor declared that it was "immaterial in what form or phrase a trust of this nature creating a seperate [*sic*] estate for the Wife is described—technical language is not necessary—All that is requisite is that the intention of the gift should appear manifestly to be for the wife's seperate enjoyment."[42] An inference, or the circumstances of a gift or devise, could induce the court to rule in favor of separate estates.

434 The favorable perspective on marriage settlements in South Carolina equity courts is also demonstrated by acceptance of the doctrine called "equity to a settlement." Settlements became so respectable, and chancellors supported them so wholeheartedly, that by the mid-eighteenth century in England and by 1762 in South Carolina, equity courts regarded them as a positive right for all married women.[43] Under certain circumstances, chancellors ordered men to give their wives separate estates. Most often chancellors made such orders when the executor of an estate refused to give a woman her proper inheritance under a will, thereby forcing her and her husband to sue in Chancery for possession. Before awarding them the property, the chancellor would order the husband to settle all or part of it on his wife. The amount of the settlement depended on the man's financial situation. In this way, chancellors knew that they were not giving property to men who could take it for themselves, providing their wives—the rightful owners—no benefits from it.

South Carolina equity courts closely followed English law on the wife's equity to a settlement. Chancellors maintained that any man who sued in an equity court for the property of his wife assumed a moral obligation to settle at least a part of it on her as a separate estate. Thus in *Mathewes and others* v. *The Executors of Mathewes et al.* (1762), the court ordered the

[41] During the period under study, only one case indicated a judicial reluctance to support female powers of control, and there the controversial subject of divorce clouded the issue. See *Barret* v. *Barret*, 4 S.C. Eq. (4 Des.) 491 (1814).

[42] *Lowndes' Trustee* v. *Champneys' Executors* (1821), Charleston District Equity Decrees, 3, 354.

[43] Reeve, *Baron and Femme*, 9, 178-179. Favorable decisions include *McPike* v. *Hughes and Rumph* (1816), Charleston District Equity Court Decrees, 3, 175; *Tatnell* v. *Fenwick's Executors*, 1 S.C. Eq. (1 Des.) 147 (1786); *Greenland* v. *Brown*, 1 S.C. Eq. (1 Des.) 196 (1791); and *Postell and Smith* v. *Skirving's Executors*, 1 S.C. Eq. (1 Des.) 158 (1789).

creation of a trust for Mary Lloyd.[44] Her husband, Thomas, had refused to appear in court for hearings concerning the execution of his father-in-law's estate. What other transgressions Thomas may have committed are unclear, but the court refused to give him Mary's inheritance. The chancellor ordered division of the deceased's estate and distribution among the heirs, "except the Share and proportion claimed by the Defendant Thomas Lloyd in right of his said Wife Mary." His share was ordered invested, and the proceeds paid to Mary "for her own and separate use, and after her Death the said Money to go to and become the property of the said Thomas Lloyd the Son, if he be then living, if not, then the Interest of said Money shall be paid to the said Thomas Lloyd the Defendant during his Natural life."[45]

Chancellors ordered the creation of a separate estate when the financial situation of a husband caused them concern for his wife's well being. Men of good standing in the community were not usually handled as harshly as Thomas Lloyd. When William Henry Drayton, a prosperous planter, member of the Governor's Council, and subsequently chief justice of 435
South Carolina, won a chancery suit against his father-in-law's executors, he did not have to place the property into a trust.[46] Undoubtedly the court believed that his respectable position, added to the fact that his wife already possessed a settlement, made the order unnecessary.

In another similar case, the court ordered no settlement for Mrs. Postell, a plaintiff with her husband in the suit of *Postell and wife, and Smith and wife* v. *The Executors of James Skirving* (1789).[47] The chancellor explained his omission carefully for the record. "The court having in private examined Mrs. Postell, who has attained twenty-one years of age, and the said Mrs. Postell being very desirous that no settlement should be made on her; and it appearing to the court that Mr. and Mrs. Postell have constantly lived together in the greatest harmony; and he being a gentleman of fortune in his own right, it is not requisite that he should make any settlement on his said wife."[48] With regard to the other plaintiff, Mrs. Smith, the court was not so trusting of the husband. She received a settlement, and the words of the chancellor demonstrate his opinion about the importance of female separate estates. "With regard to Mr. O. B. Smith," he wrote, "his wife is not of age to make such request as Mrs. Postell has done, (although the court entertains a similar opinion of him as of Mr. Postell), they find themselves bound to order that the said O. B. Smith do make the usual settlement on his wife, of the fortune she is entitled to from her father."[49] The "usual" settlement gave the Smiths

[44] Gregorie, ed., *Chancery Records*, 507-511.

[45] *Ibid.*, 510.

[46] *Ibid.*, 551-552; Marriage Settlement between Dorothy Golightly and William Henry Drayton (1764), Marriage Settlements, 2, 185-192.

[47] *Postell and Smith* v. *Skirving's Executors*, 1 S.C. Eq. (1 Des.) 158.

[48] *Ibid.*, 158.

[49] *Ibid.*, 158-159.

joint control over her property, with descent to the survivor and then to their children. Presumably in a case of this nature, Mrs. Smith could void her own trust upon reaching her majority. As previously noted, such action could be taken under the law and occasionally was.

On one point South Carolina chancellors were not willing to make liberal interpretations. Unless a settlement explicitly gave a feme covert power to write a will, she could not do so.[50] Women and their benefactors were careful, therefore, to include this right as a clause in settlements. It appeared frequently, particularly during the first two decades under study, when 62 percent (36/58) of the women specified the power to make a will. The figure rises to 71 percent if we include those women who possessed the right to bequeath in the event they outlived their husbands. Over the course of the eighteenth century, this figure fell, but until 1800 more than half of the women with settlements possessed testamentary powers. After the turn of the century the figure declined until fewer than one-third of all femes covert could write wills under the stated terms of their settlements.
436 From 1801 to 1830, 26 percent (45/172) of the settlements sampled gave women this privilege, while 29 percent (50/170) gave it to either the feme covert or the survivor of the marriage (see Table IV). As the number of settlements allowing women to write wills declined, those arranging for automatic descent to children increased (see Figure 2).

The reasons for this decline are not clear. One explanation may lie in the increasing standardization of settlements. As the chancellor noted when ordering creation of a trust for Mrs. Smith, there was a "usual" settlement. It consisted of joint control for husband and wife, with descent to their children. Over the period studied, we have seen an increase in settlements allowing for joint control, as well as descent to children. Chancellors ordered this kind of settlement in most cases coming under their jurisdiction, and the increasing use of automatic descent provisions may demonstrate female acceptance of a standard form on this point. Moreover, as marriages became less patriarchal over the period, women may have regarded the right to make wills as less vital to their financial autonomy. The desire to exert control after death dwindled as more women possessed authority during life. Most mothers undoubtedly divided their estates equally among children, even when they did write wills. The change to automatic descent probably represents little difference in the way estates were administered but does demonstrate a weakening of women's desires for explicit protection and control.

[50] Women without the right to make wills through marriage settlements could bequeath personal property if their husbands consented. See *Grimke* v. *Grimke*, 1 S.C. Eq. (1 Des.) 366-382 (1794), and *Smelie* v. *Smelie*, 2 S.C. Eq. (2 Des.) 66-79 (1802). The law on this point is discussed in Blackstone, *Commentaries*, II, 498, and *Laws Respecting Women*, 178-179. Without valid marriage settlements, however, women could never devise real property. Smith, *De Republica Anglorum*, ed. Alston, 127; *Laws Respecting Women*, 149; Holdsworth, *History of English Law*, III, 185; Kent, *Commentaries on American Law*, II, 130-131.

TABLE IV
DESCENT OF SETTLEMENT PROPERTY

Years	Woman Controls		Survivor Controls		Combined*		Automatic to Children		Mixed/Unknown		No. Deeds
	N	%	N	%	N	%	N	%	N	%	
1730-1740	12	52	4	17	16	70	3	13	4	17	23
1741-1750	24	69	1	3	25	71	10	29	0	0	35
1751-1760	26	47	3	5	29	53	24	44	2	4	55
1761-1770	37	35	9	8	46	43	52	49	9	8	107
1771-1780	50	47	6	6	56	52	45	42	6	6	107
1781-1790	39	44	6	7	45	51	43	49	0	0	88
1791-1800	20	39	1	2	21	41	29	57	1	2	51
1801-1810	15	28	2	4	17	31	30	56	7	13	54
1811-1820	14	29	1	2	15	31	27	55	7	14	49
1821-1830	16	23	2	3	18	26	47	68	4	6	69
Total	253	40	35	5	288	45	310	49	40	6	638

* Woman Controls and Survivor Controls

FIGURE 2

DESCENT OF SETTLEMENT PROPERTY

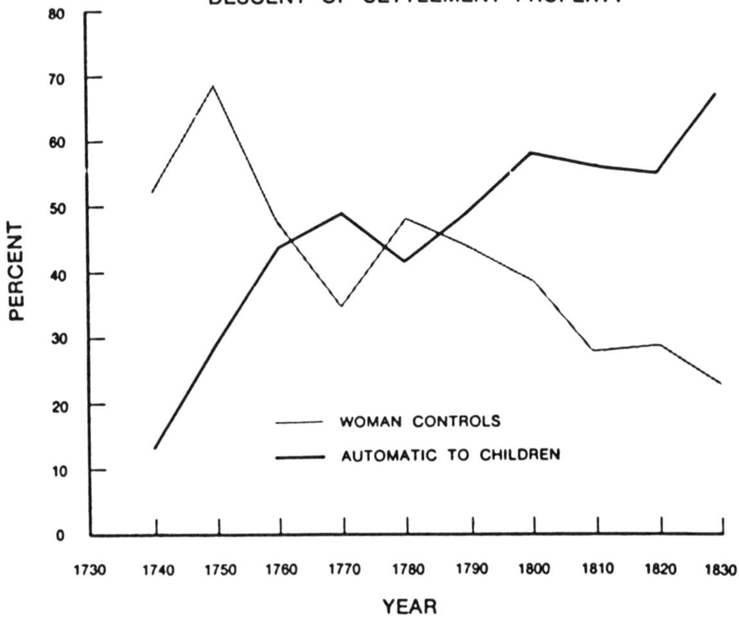

438

Some mothers were fully aware of the potential power of testamentary rights. Mary Ladson, marrying for the first time in 1760, included a clause in her settlement allowing her to write a will. She wanted her estate to be divided among her children "in such shares and proportions and at such times as the said Mary by her last Will and Testament shall give Limit." The widow Jane Wilkie was equally explicit about her desire to decide what property should go to her children. In 1774 she wrote in her settlement, "All such Child or Children shall possess & enjoy all such part & proportion in the manner & form as she the said Jane Wilkie shall point out & direct." Even after the turn of the century, when fewer women possessed the legal ability to write wills, some women still realized the power they held. Elizabeth Legare wrote in 1825 that she intended to use her estate during her lifetime for the provision of her children "at her own discretion," and not otherwise.[51]

Women who had already experienced married life, such as Jane Wilkie and Elizabeth Legare, took special care to protect their property rights in

[51] Marriage Settlements between Mary Ladson and Thomas Poole (1760), Miscellaneous Records, MM, 41-44; Jane Wilkie and Charles Cogdell (1774), Miscellaneous Records, RR, 314-316; Elizabeth Legare and William B. Legare (1825), Marriage Settlements, 9, 185-187.

TABLE V
WIDOWS AND SINGLE WOMEN COMPARED

	Widows		*Single Women*	
Control	*N*	*%*	*N*	*%*
Woman	133	52	59	21
Man	50	19	90	33
Couple	55	21	107	39
Trustee	3	1	10	4
Mixed/Unknown	16	6	9	3
Total	257	100	275	100
Descent				
Woman Controls	150	58	53	19
Survivor Controls	10	4	19	7
(Combined)	160	62	72	26
Automatic to Children	79	31	185	67
Mixed/Unknown	18	7	18	7
Total	257	100	275	100

marriage settlements. Most single women were not so careful. Comparison of settlements made by widows and single women proves valuable for understanding some individuals' needs for separate estates. A woman's marital status frequently acted as a motivating force for the creation of a settlement and for the inclusion of female managerial and testamentary powers.[52]

Of the 638 settlements sampled, 532 recorded a marital status for the woman. During the period 1730 to 1780, widows appeared in over half of the settlements giving status, 56 percent (159/286), while single women constituted 44 percent (127) of the sample. Even if we take into account the high mortality rate in colonial South Carolina and the use of the state as a Revolutionary battlefield, the high percentage of widows is surprising. After 1780, the number of widows declined, but they still made settlements in 40 percent (98/246) of the sample.

When we compare the powers of control exercised by widows with those held by single women, it becomes clear that experienced matrons were more emphatic about managing their own property than were women marrying for the first time (see Table V). Widows held complete

[52] For a discussion of one enterprising widow's experience, see Mary Beth Norton, "A Cherished Spirit of Independence: The Life of an Eighteenth-Century Boston Businesswoman," in Berkin and Norton, eds., *Women of America*, 48-67. Although the woman Norton describes was a Bostonian, the same influences governed her actions in creating a marriage settlement as governed the actions of many South Carolina women.

FIGURE 3

DESCENT OF SETTLEMENT PROPERTY

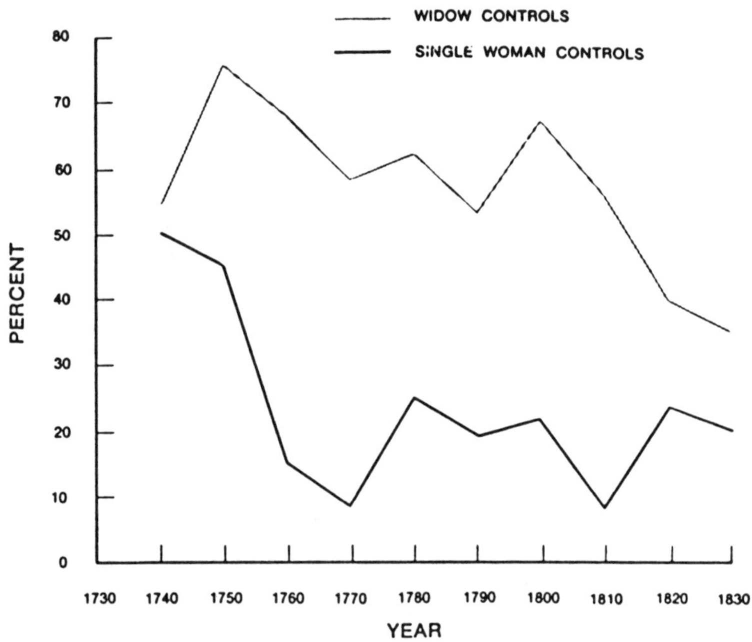

managerial powers and specified the right to make wills at more than double the rate of first brides. Rather than directing settlement property by themselves, most single women divided between giving their husbands authority and arranging for coadministration. They also provided for automatic descent of settlement property in fully two thirds of their deeds, whereas widows did so less than one-third of the time. The settlements of first brides thus demonstrate a less protective attitude than those of experienced matrons. Moreover, after 1740 there was remarkably little change in this pattern either for control or descent (see Figures 3 and 4).

Clearly, the experience of marriage affected the attitudes of women toward property control and management. Before entering a second union, many women demanded the right to administer their own property. Widows' desire for active control may have reflected the fact that their estates were no longer simply gifts from parents and friends but property they had worked for themselves, either alone or with their former husbands. Parents who initiated the settlements of new brides concerned themselves primarily with protecting property from husbands' creditors. They did not seek to provide daughters with the power to control and

FIGURE 4

SETTLEMENTS WITH PROVISIONS FOR CHILDREN

441

devise property as much as they created a fund for family income. Widows, however, frequently demanded the right to manage the property that they had obtained themselves. Elizabeth Meshaw's settlement in 1736 observed, "The said Elizabeth Meshaw since the Death of her said Husband hath by her great pains care Labour and Industry acquired a considerable addition to the Estate and Interest so left her. . . . [P]articularly [she] hath purchased a Tract of Land containing Two Hundred and Fifty Acres." Elizabeth retained the right to devise her estate as she saw fit, without the interference of her new husband. When Christiana Hoff purchased a slave through her own labor, she wrote a settlement in 1772 explicitly denying her husband any rights to it. The case of Elizabeth Baxter may be most revealing. Before Elizabeth, a "merchant," consented to marry Thomas Robinson, a "mariner," in 1771, she executed a settlement of all her personal estate and business property. She reserved absolute control over the property for herself "in order the better to enable her to support & maintain her & her children & which the said Thomas Robinson is at present rendered incapable of doing."[53] Elizabeth

[53] Marriage Settlements between Elizabeth Meshaw and Thomas Snipes (1736), HH, 27-28; Christiana Hoff and John Hoff (1772), PP, 254; Elizabeth Baxter and Thomas Robinson (1771), PP, 6-8, Miscellaneous Records.

was taking no chances. If Thomas could not support her, she would arrange to do so herself. Women such as Elizabeth, who knew the dangers of marriage and widowhood, took special care for their own and their childrens' futures.

Although the number of widows who provided for children in their settlements increased throughout the period, widows remained less likely than young brides to arrange for automatic descent. Widows such as Elizabeth Baxter had the responsibility of caring for the children of their previous marriages and undoubtedly felt pressure to include protective clauses for children in their settlements, yet did so at half the rate of single women. Thus Mrs. Baxter retained the right to devise her estate. Although she clearly was concerned with providing for her children, she did not think it necessary to arrange for their inheritances when she wrote her settlement. Such dispositions could be made later, when she was closer to death. For the moment she worried primarily about living in a male-dominated world with a new husband who could not support her.
442 The failure to arrange for automatic descent implies that many widows did not view settlements primarily as a means of guaranteeing the inheritances of their children. More than anything else, they wanted absolute control over management decisions and the right to bequeath to whomever they pleased. When they chose to remarry, they did so with strings attached.

Although the comparative powers of widows and single women remained largely the same throughout the eighteenth and early nineteenth centuries, one development in the settlements of single women may indicate an increasing desire on their part to exercise authority. There was a gradual but steady increase in the number of settlements allowing couples joint powers of administration. Single women did not feel the need to exercise sole control to the same degree as widows, but they did become less willing to give husbands absolute managerial rights. From 1730 to 1780, only 32 percent (41/127) of their settlements gave couples joint powers of administration, whereas 45 percent (66/148) did so from 1781 to 1830. The number of men with sole powers fell from 39 percent (49/127) to 28 percent (41/148). With regard to the management of property, therefore, the settlements of widows and single women became slightly more uniform over time, with both groups favoring partnerships in managing separate estates.

Widows, heiresses, merchants' wives, the wives of debtors, and women whose parents warned them about the dangers of married life—these were the South Carolina matrons with trust estates. They were frequently women of wealth with a great deal to lose if their husbands proved wasteful or unfortunate in business. Sometimes they were women of small fortunes intent on protecting what little they had. They were intelligent, or experienced, or protected by concerned parents. Above all, given the legal status of women under the common law, they were fortunate.

Courts of chancery in South Carolina offered liberal support for marriage settlements. Judges regarded separate estates as the right of every feme covert, necessary for women's security in many cases and helpful to society in providing some families with economic support. Judges consistently ruled in favor of the creation of separate estates and enforced liberal precedents for administering them. Realizing the delicate position of married women under the common law, chancellors acted to mitigate legal hardships by wholeheartedly supporting women's rights to separate estates. Judicial acceptance of settlements increased in the period studied, demonstrating expansion of women's property rights under equity law. As seen in the cases of *Postell and Smith* v. *Skirving's Executors*, *Johnson* v. *Thompson*, and *Lowndes' Trustee* v. *Champneys' Executors*, equity law promoted the legal rights of South Carolina women. Historians of colonial American law may have been overly optimistic in positing wide use of settlements among femes covert, but they were correct in stressing the legal importance of equity law. Women with separate estates in eighteenth and early nineteenth-century South Carolina enjoyed many of the legal rights of men. It remains to be seen if other jurisdictions duplicated this pattern.

Although chancellors supported the use of separate estates, settlements 443
were rare, used either by wealthy women with valuable family interests to protect or by women with an uncommon perspective on their legal status. Equity proved invaluable to women such as the widow Elizabeth Holson, who wanted to enjoy her own estate without "the Least or Smallest Controul or intermeddling" of her husband, but Elizabeth was one of only a small number of women with marriage settlements.[54] We still do not know why so few women relied on separate estates. Either they were satisfied with their common law status, or they did not regard equity law as a viable alternative. In South Carolina, it may be important that settlements were not necessary to confer feme sole trader status. Independent businesswomen functioned under the common law as long as their husbands demonstrated tacit consent to their activities. But more important, the majority of women apparently regarded equity law protections as superfluous to their needs. For women without much property or for women who perceived their legal status as secure, separate estates served no purpose.

We must learn more about the application of common law principles before we will fully understand the meaning of equity law. Perhaps the harshness of common law rules were mitigated in practice, making separate estates largely unnecessary. If most women did not feel a need to use equity law, then we must reevaluate the effect of common law restrictions on women's lives. We must also consider an alternative possibility: that social custom so oppressed women, they did not consider the possibility of employing separate estates. Community scorn or family opposition may have prevented women from acting on their desire for separate estates. There is some evidence to show that the fear and distrust women exhibited by creating settlements antagonized men. The wording

[54] Marriage Settlement between Elizabeth Holson and John Harth (1779), Marriage Settlements, I, 152.

of settlements, for example, occasionally reveals attempts to appease men's feelings. Some women wrote that their desire for separate estates arose from a fear of the system, not the individual. Such public statements relieved men of responsibility for the anxiety experienced by women and thus saved them face in the community. Otherwise, the mere existence of a settlement attested to the insecurity of a particular woman.

At this point it is impossible to be sure whether male antipathy to settlements prevented most women from making them. Final conclusions await further research on the social customs of families in the South and on the use of common law rules pertaining to the rights of women. Perhaps the words of Sarah Ann Binnikes demonstrate, as well as anything we now have, the attitude of women who wrote settlements. Sarah's settlement stated that its object was to protect her separate interests so that she would not be "defeated or defrauded" out of her property "by the collusive act or device" of her husband. The job of Sarah's trustees was to sue her husband in case he "bargained, sold, or inveigled away" her lands and to demand
444 damages from the court "for any waste which he may commit upon the said lands or injury he may commit upon the said personal or any of the said personal property."[55] There can be no doubt that Sarah Ann did not trust her husband-to-be. It is unlikely that most couples began married life with such distrust. Undoubtedly women as well as men preferred to demonstrate hope, rather than fear, on the day of their marriage. But if experience proved women naive, then we can understand why so many widows insisted on the creation of settlements, and we can also comprehend why they carefully reserved managerial rights for themselves.

[55] Marriage Settlement between Sarah Ann Baxter and Joseph Binnikes (1825), *ibid.*, 9, 159.

The Crime of Precocious Sexuality: Female Juvenile Delinquency in the Progressive Era

STEVEN SCHLOSSMAN
Radcliffe Institute, Harvard University

STEPHANIE WALLACH
Simmons College

The juvenile justice system's discrimination against poor and minority children has been well documented, but the system's discrimination on the basis of gender has been less widely recognized. Drawing on neglected court records and secondary sources, Steven Schlossman and Stephanie Wallach show how girls bore a disproportionate share of the burden of juvenile justice in the Progressive era. The authors note that during the Progressive era female juvenile delinquents often received more severe punishments than males, even though boys usually were charged with more serious crimes. Schlossman and Wallach conclude that the discriminatory treatment of female delinquents in the early twentieth century resulted from racial prejudice, new theories of adolescence, and Progressive-era movements to purify society.

This essay is an historical inquiry into the practice of sexual discrimination against female juvenile delinquents. Although American public policy toward girl offenders first took shape in the middle decades of the nineteenth century—the Victorian era—we have decided to focus on the Progressive era of the early twentieth century. During this latter period scientific and popular literature on female delinquency expanded enormously, and most states adopted the main components

The authors would like to thank Nancy Pottishman Weiss, Merle Borrowman, Geraldine Joncich Clifford, and Sheldon Messinger for their helpful suggestions on earlier drafts of this essay. A portion of the research for this essay was supported by the Spencer Foundation, to which we extend our sincere thanks. Responsibility for errors in fact or interpretation is, of course, our own.

Harvard Educational Review, Vol. 48, No. 1, February 1978.

0017-8055/78/0200-0065$02.35/0

of modern correctional machinery. Our essay spotlights the differences between stated intentions, revealed preferences, and actual outcomes.[1] Although we attempt to develop a broad interpretation, we must emphasize the selectivity of our historical research. We do not pretend to have exhausted available sources, to have explored all possible interpretations of our evidence, or, certainly, to have written the definitive account. Instead, we offer a preliminary synthesis of untapped sources in an effort to call attention to a neglected subject, to encourage additional research on it, and to suggest ways of integrating the topic of female delinquency into the rapidly growing fields of women's history and the history of corrections.

Our essay speaks only indirectly to modern-day issues in juvenile justice. Continuities between past and present will often be apparent, to be sure, but we dare not draw them too explicitly for the simple reason that social scientists know very little about the theory and practice of female juvenile justice between the 1920s and the 1960s.[2] Nonetheless, we do believe it is possible to use history as a force for social change by laying bare the roots and assumptions of anachronistic policies—policies, in this instance, that lag behind our current attitudes toward female sexuality and equal justice for women. Given our reformist goals, it may be useful to explain in advance why we focus on sexual discrimination as opposed to other equally blatant injustices in the correctional system.

Like other critics of American juvenile justice, we decry practices that lead to unwarranted labeling and incarceration of children and that discriminate against poor, minority youth, regardless of sex.[3] We consider it indisputable that, from the early nineteenth century to the present, the juvenile justice system has systematically singled out lower-class children for punishment and ignored middle- and upper-class youth.[4] In this essay, however, our main concern is not with class, ethnic, racial, or age bias, for we believe those themes have been adequately treated elsewhere. Rather, what most interests us now is how, in a correctional system that discriminates consistently against poor, minority children as a whole, females carry a disproportionate share of the burden of injustice.

Discussion of female delinquency is conspicuously absent from most scholarly writing on criminal justice. Despite a persistent hue and cry during the last decade

[1] See Lawrence Cremin, "Foreword," in *American Education and Vocationalism*, eds. Marvin Lazerson and W. Norton Grubb (New York: Teachers College Press, 1974), p. ix.

[2] One reason for the lack of scholarly attention to girl offenders in this period was the emphasis on gang delinquency, in which girls participated very little. There is, however, Paul Tappan's classic *Delinquent Girls in Court* (Montclair, N.J.: Patterson Smith, 1969), originally published in 1947.

[3] See, for example, Lois Forer, *"No One Will Lissen"* (New York: Grosset and Dunlap, 1970); Patrick Murphy, *Our Kindly Parent . . . The State* (New York: Viking, 1974); Lisa Richette, *The Throwaway Children* (New York: Dell, 1969); and Ken Wooden, *Weeping in the Playtime of Others* (New York: McGraw-Hill, 1976).

[4] See, for example, Michael Katz, *The Irony of Early School Reform* (Cambridge, Mass.: Harvard University Press, 1968); Anthony Platt, *The Child Savers* (Chicago: University of Chicago Press, 1969); Alexander Liazos, "Class Oppression: The Functions of Juvenile Justice," *The Insurgent Sociologist*, Fall 1974, 1, 2–24; and Steven Schlossman, *Love and the American Delinquent* (Chicago: University of Chicago Press, 1977).

about spiraling rates of delinquency, despite mounting evidence demonstrating the ineffectiveness of correctional programs, and despite the women's rights movement, girl offenders are largely ignored. Even as the number of females processed through the juvenile courts climbs steadily, an implicit consensus remains that the male teenager defines the delinquency problem in modern America and suffers most egregiously from correctional injustices.[5]

We suggest two main reasons why girl delinquents receive so little attention. First, girls are accused primarily of so-called victimless crimes, that is, offenses that do not involve clear-cut damage to persons or property. If committed by adults, these actions would not be legally punishable; if committed by boys, the same acts would be interpreted less seriously and punished less severely. Thus, rather ironically, the plight of female delinquents receives little scrutiny because they are accused of committing less flagrant violations of legal codes. Second, traditional stereotypes of women as the weaker and more dependent sex rationalize, indeed even legitimate, discriminatory correctional practices in the name of humanitarianism. As the half-century struggle to enact the Equal Rights Amendment makes abundantly clear, one of the most tenacious beliefs in our society is that women require more comprehensive legal protection than do men. Society justifies "preventive" intervention into the lives of antisocial girls under the rationale that they are especially vulnerable to evil forces and temptations. This so-called chivalrous attitude leads to earlier intervention and longer periods of supervision for delinquent girls than delinquent boys.

The sparse historical writing about female delinquency concentrates on reformatories, especially the pioneering nineteenth-century institutions, rather than on the juvenile justice system as a whole.[6] Furthermore, several of the studies are uncritical and Whiggish in their interpretations, seeing a benign humanitarian spirit

[5] For exceptions see Don Gibbons, *Delinquent Behavior* (Englewood Cliffs, N.J.: Prentice-Hall, 1976), 2nd ed., pp. 169–189; William Sanders, *Juvenile Delinquency* (New York: Praeger, 1976), pp. 64–83; Rose Giallombardo, *The Social World of Delinquent Girls* (New York: Wiley, 1974); Meda Chesney-Lind, "Juvenile Delinquency: The Sexualization of Female Crime," *Psychology Today*, July 1974, 8, 43–46; Meda Chesney-Lind, "Judicial Enforcement of the Female Sex Role: The Family Court and the Female Delinquent," *Issues in Criminology*, Fall 1973, 8, 51–69; Kristine Rogers, " 'For Her Own Protection . . .': Conditions of Incarceration for Female Juvenile Offenders in the State of Connecticut," *Law and Society Review*, 1972, 7, 223–246; Sarah Gold, "Equal Protection for Juvenile Girls in Need of Supervision in New York State," *New York Law Forum*, 1971, 17, 570–598; Robert Terry, "Discrimination in the Handling of Juvenile Offenders by Social Control Agencies," in *Becoming Delinquent*, eds. Peter Garabedian and Don Gibbons (Chicago: Aldine, 1970), pp. 78–92; Freda Adler, *Sisters in Crime* (New York: McGraw-Hill, 1975), chap. 4; *Crime and Delinquency*, 1977, 23 (issue theme: "Criminal Justice to Women: Not Fair!"); and Paul Katzeff, "Equal Crime," *Boston Magazine*, December 1977, 107–108, 206, 208–210. For an estimate that girls now form nearly one-quarter of the juvenile court clientele, see Rosemary Sarri and Robert Vintner, "Justice for Whom? Varieties of Correctional Approaches," in *The Juvenile Justice System*, ed. Malcolm Klein, v (New York: Russell Sage, 1975), p. 171.

[6] See the pioneering studies by Barbara Brenzel, "Lancaster Industrial School for Girls: A Social Portrait of a Nineteenth Century Reform School for Girls," *Feminist Studies*, Fall 1975, 3, 40–53; and by Estelle Freedman, "Their Sisters' Keepers: The Origins of Female Corrections in America," Dissertation, Columbia University, 1976.

behind early twentieth-century correctional innovations for girls. Margaret Reeves, for example, conducted an exhaustive survey of girls' reformatory programs in the 1920s and concluded, with few reservations, that they embodied the triumph of social conscience in America and the onward march of correctional science.[7] Recently, Robert Mennel, in his ambitious survey of juvenile correctional history, described Progressive-era policies as "the first sign of a more sympathetic attitude toward female delinquents."[8]

On the basis of our research, we consider the traditional interpretation to be lacking in four principal respects: it offers little empirical evidence of benign or effective treatment of girl offenders; it generally blurs the distinction between the stated intentions of correctional reformers and the actual outcomes of their efforts; it deals inadequately with the fears and prejudices underlying benevolent programs for poor, immigrant children; and it does little to illuminate, even obliquely, the practice of sexual discrimination in the juvenile justice system today. We do not quarrel with historians who emphasize the humanitarian spirit that guided such famous juvenile reformers as Jane Addams, Sophonisba Breckinridge, and Edith Abbott, or such lesser figures as Augusta Bronner, Mabel Elliott, Emma
448 Lundberg, and Edith Burleigh.[9] But we do believe that the humanitarian schemes were often quite repressive in design and even more so in outcome.

Our main arguments can be sketched as follows. Although public response to female delinquency emerged in the Victorian era, not until the Progressive period was female delinquency widely perceived as a social problem requiring extensive governmental intervention. In the Progressive period the abundant literature on delinquency was riddled with stereotypical assumptions about women and, in particular, about immigrant women. These stereotypes laid a basis for more punitive treatment of delinquent girls than delinquent boys. Girls were prosecuted almost exclusively for "immoral" conduct, a very broad category that defined all sexual exploration as fundamentally perverse and predictive of future promiscuity, perhaps even prostitution. But while girls, unlike boys, were almost never accused of violating criminal statutes, they received stiffer legal penalties.

Discriminatory treatment of female delinquents was consistent with racial prejudices in the Progressive period. Ethnic girls—immigrants or daughters of immigrants—were seen as inherently more predisposed to immoral conduct than Yankee girls—daughters of native-born parents. Discriminatory correctional practices also embodied the new wisdom of the behavioral sciences, particularly the theories of adolescence generated by such pioneer psychologists as G. Stanley Hall. Finally, the practice of female juvenile justice reflected the quasi-utopian, but ultimately repressive, pursuit of Progressive-era reformers for a more "pure" society, as revealed in the eugenics, antiprostitution, and sex-education campaigns.

[7] Margaret Reeves, *Training Schools for Delinquent Girls* (New York: Russell Sage, 1929).

[8] Robert Mennel, *Thorns and Thistles* (Hanover, N.H.: University Press of New England, 1973), p. 172.

[9] See especially Robert Bremner, *From the Depths* (New York: New York University Press, 1956); and Walter Trattner, *Crusade for the Children* (Chicago: Quadrangle, 1970).

Female Delinquency: The Emergence of a Social Problem

Public response to female delinquency can be traced at least as far back as the Jacksonian period, although the traditional date of origin is 1856, when Massachusetts opened the nation's first reform school for girls. Well known in the latter half of the century, the Massachusetts example inspired emulation by diverse philanthropic organizations in the East and Midwest. Several state governments responded to the wishes of these organizations and built reformatories for girls. Compared to the huge reformatories for boys erected in the nineteenth century—by the 1850s the New York House of Refuge held over one thousand inmates—the institutions for girls were generally small and makeshift, often consisting of two or three converted farmhouses. Several of the girls' facilities were little more than receiving stations; their primary purpose was to facilitate the smooth operation of boys' reformatories after attempts to house both sexes in the same buildings had proved embarrassing failures.[10]

The female reformatories incorporated the evangelical spirit of Victorian religious revivalism. Until the end of the nineteenth century the image of the female
delinquent remained mainly that of the individual "fallen woman."[11] This image 449
contrasted sharply with that of the male delinquent, who was described less as a sinner than as a carefully nurtured young criminal.[12] To be sure, boys' delinquencies were roundly condemned but were rarely, as was often the case with girls', regarded as indications of innate moral perversity.

Nineteenth-century authors of crime literature wrote endlessly about delinquency—the classic presentation being Charles Loring Brace's *The Dangerous Classes of New York and Twenty Years' Work among Them*[13]—but they paid very little attention to female delinquents. The "dangerous classes" against whom the reformers warned and about whom newspapers printed sensational stories were overwhelmingly male.[14] When the girl offender did appear in the literature, she was treated mainly as a footnote to the problem of boy delinquency. But early in the twentieth century—especially in the decade preceding the First World War—female delinquency began to attract increasing attention as a separate and pressing social problem.

The heightened public awareness of and growing governmental response to female delinquency in the Progressive era are well documented. Articles on girl

10 Brenzel, "Lancaster"; Mennel, *Thorns and Thistles*, chap. 4; Freedman, "Their Sisters' Keepers," chaps. 3 and 4.

11 On the image of the "fallen woman,' see Freedman, "Their Sisters' Keepers," chap. 2; for the emphasis on environmental causes behind male criminality, see David Rothman, *The Discovery of the Asylum* (Boston: Little, Brown, 1971).

12 Schlossman, *Love*, chaps. 2, 3, and 5.

13 Charles Loring Brace, *The Dangerous Classes of New York and Twenty Years' Work among Them* (New York: Wynkoop and Hallenbeck, 1872).

14 Miriam Langsam, *Children West* (Madison, Wis.: State Historical Society of Wisconsin, 1964); Thomas Bender, *Toward an Urban Vision* (Lexington, Ky.: University Press of Kentucky, 1975); and Steven Schlossman, "The 'Culture of Poverty' in Ante-Bellum Social Thought," *Science and Society*, 1974, 38, 150–166.

offenders appeared in a wide range of popular and scholarly journals. The prestigious philanthropic organization, the National Conference of Charities and Correction, began to discuss female delinquency regularly for the first time since the organization's founding in the early 1870s. Several books were devoted in whole or in part to female criminality. While the mass media continued to emphasize the "boy problem," many civic groups began giving equal attention to the "girl problem." Local organizations such as PTAs, juvenile protective associations, women's clubs, and settlement houses sponsored lectures and discussions on the causes and cures of girls' delinquency; they also led campaigns to garner funds for such innovations as girls' clubs, YWCA summer camps, and, to a lesser extent, Girl Scouts.[15]

Governmental investment in the custody and treatment of female delinquents increased dramatically in the Progressive era. The decade between 1910 and 1920 was an especially prolific period for the creation of publicly sponsored reformatories for girls. Whereas between 1850 and 1910 an average of fewer than five new reformatories were created per decade, twenty-three new facilities opened between 1910 and 1920. Furthermore, older ninteenth-century reformatories were expanded in size, staff, and clientele in this decade. Equally important, a number of states took over private girls' reformatories.[16] In short, the involvement of government with female delinquency grew sharply in the Progressive period, reflecting the expanded discussion of the subject in the literature on juvenile crime.

The Practice of Sexual Discrimination

Before trying to explain the rising interest in female delinquency in the Progressive era, it is necessary to demonstrate that girls received discriminatory treatment in juvenile courts and reformatories. The historical sources for such an empirical study are vast but have never been tapped. We have examined the sources selectively and have chosen for close analysis those we believe are representative of three bodies of evidence.

First, we briefly analyze scattered statistical data to demonstrate that juvenile courts treated female delinquents more harshly than male delinquents. Second, we present an overview of cases in a single juvenile court to evoke the actual decision-making process and thereby show that sentimental notions of the "good girl" and conventional ideals of domesticity prefigured punitive treatment for girl delinquents. Third, we look synoptically at the rehabilitative goals and methods of female reformatories to illuminate further the discriminatory nature of treatment. Our goal is to provide empirical evidence for the contention, developed later in

[15] These observations draw upon Schlossman's study of social-reform groups in Milwaukee and of parent-education organizations throughout the country. See Schlossman, *Love,* chap. 7, and "Before Home Start: Notes Toward a History of Parent Education in America, 1897–1929," *Harvard Educational Review,* 1976, 46, 436–467. Also useful is David McLeod, "Good Boys Made Better: The Boy Scouts of America, Boys' Brigades, and YMCA Boys' Work, 1880–1920," Dissertation, University of Wisconsin, 1973.

[16] Reeves, *Training Schools,* pp. 39ff; and Mennel, *Thorns and Thistles,* pp. 171–179.

this essay, that the practice of female juvenile justice coincided with the ideology of treatment. Discrimination on the basis of sex was no accident, we believe, but rather was integral to both the theory and practice of Progressive-era juvenile justice.

The first body of evidence was derived from court records in Chicago, San Francisco, Milwaukee, and New Haven. Several points stand out most prominently from these data: the vast majority of delinquents, boys and girls alike, were poor, ghetto-dwelling children of recent immigrants; however, unlike males, females were brought to court almost exclusively for alleged early sexual exploration; and female offenders were treated more punitively than males.

The ethnic origins of both boy and girl delinquents are revealing. In Milwaukee, for example, more than 90 percent of the children brought into court were the offspring of European immigrants. Of these, three out of four were either German or Polish. In Chicago, San Francisco, and New Haven the ethnic background of delinquents was similar, although southeastern European countries were more frequently represented, reflecting the different patterns of immigrant settlement in these cities.[17]

That the delinquents were predominantly poor is evident in a number of ways. Although it is impossible to compare the incomes of families of delinquent and nondelinquent children or to assess the contributions of different family members to total income, we do have periodic salary data for the fathers of delinquent youth in Milwaukee. These data suggest the truth of the popular impression that delinquents were primarily from the working class. Their fathers' salaries were low, generally reported to be less than ten dollars per week. Moreover, the salaries were highly irregular: many fathers moved frequently from job to job; many were unemployed for long periods because of seasonal hiring, debilitating illnesses (particularly tuberculosis), and drinking bouts. In addition, an analysis of the occupations of delinquents' fathers, using city directories and addresses supplied in court to distinguish individuals with the same names, indicates that the majority were working class or lower on the economic scale, the single largest category being that of "laborer."[18] A further indication that delinquents came mainly from poor, ghetto families is their residence patterns. The majority of Milwaukee delinquents lived in the poorest immigrant neighborhoods surrounding the city's scattered railway network.

Although similar in their social and cultural backgrounds, girl and boy delinquents were treated very differently in court. Consider the types of crimes for which boys and girls made their first courtroom appearances. The majority of boys were charged with offenses that fell under the adult criminal code. In Chicago, for

17 For data on Milwaukee see Schlossman, *Love*, appendix 2, table 6. Our main source for Chicago is Sophonisba Breckinridge and Edith Abbott, *The Delinquent Child and the Home* (New York: Russell Sage, 1912); for San Francisco, Emily Huntington, Leona Jones, Donna Moses, and Ruth Turner, "The Juvenile Court," Bachelor of Arts Thesis, University of California at Berkeley, 1917; and for New Haven, Mabel Wiley, *A Study of the Problem of Girl Delinquency in New Haven* (New Haven, Conn.: Civic Federation of New Haven, 1915).

18 Schlossman, *Love*, pp. 143–144.

example, stealing accounted for more than half of the reported crimes.[19] The charges against girls were of an entirely different nature. The majority were charged under the loose heading of "immorality";[20] however, a charge of "immorality" did not mean that a girl had had intercourse or performed some other mature sexual act. Rather, a girl only had to show "signs" in her appearance, conversation, and bearing that she had probably had intercourse in the past or might do so in the near future. These criteria naturally opened the way to invidious judgments, especially because the delinquents were mainly daughters of immigrants, who were, according to contemporary racial mythology, instinctively emotional and lacking in self-restraint. Thus judges and probation officers would see precocious sexual activity where it did not exist, would prematurely regard unfamiliar cultural patterns of behavior and expression as signs of advanced sexual experience, and would be more pessimistic about the implications of sexual exploration by ethnic than by Yankee girls.

In practice, an extraordinarily wide range of conduct was included under the label of immorality: staying away from home, associating with persons of dubious
452 character, going to dance houses, fornicating, coming home late at night, masturbating, using obscene language, riding at night in automobiles without a chaperone, strutting about in a lascivious manner, and so forth. To the courts, being "on the road to ruin" was but one short step from being "ruined"; hence, so-called predelinquents were treated much like those who actually engaged in mature sexual relations. The ostensible purposes behind such a loose definition of crime were to root out the underlying causes of misconduct as soon as they became evident and to instruct ethnic girls that their Yankee counterparts upheld higher standards of sexual propriety than their own parents practiced or condoned.[21]

The different treatment of boy and girl delinquents was even more apparent in the disposition of cases. Far more frequently than girls, boys received the relatively noncoercive sanction of probation—supervision in the child's own home or in a surrogate home approved by the court. In Chicago, for instance, 59 percent of the boys who appeared in court between 1899 and 1909 were placed on probation, as compared to only 37 percent of the girls. Conversely, significantly higher proportions of girls than boys were incarcerated in reformatories for sentences that could last several years. In Milwaukee twice as many girls as boys were committed, and in Chicago one-half of the girl delinquents, as contrasted with one-fifth of the

[19] Breckinridge and Abbott, *The Delinquent Child*, pp. 28–35. See also Huntington et al., "The Juvenile Court," appendix.

[20] Breckinridge and Abbott, *The Delinquent Child*, pp. 38–40; Huntington et al., "The Juvenile Court," appendix; Alida Bowler, "A Study of Seventy-Five Delinquent Girls," *Journal of Delinquency*, 1917, 2, 157; Mabel Elliott, *Correctional Education and the Delinquent Girl* (Harrisburg, Pa.: Commonwealth of Pennsylvania Department of Welfare, 1928), pp. 34–35; Louise Ordahl and George Ordahl, "A Study of Delinquent and Dependent Girls," *Journal of Delinquency*, 1918, 3, 34–35; and Wiley, *A Study of the Problem*, p. 11.

[21] Bowler, "A Study of Seventy-Five Delinquent Girls," p. 159; Breckinridge and Abbott, *The Delinquent Child*, pp. 35–39; Elliott, *Correctional Education*, pp. 34–35; Ordahl and Ordahl, "A Study of Delinquent and Dependent Girls," pp. 55–59; and Wiley, *A Study of the Problem*, p. 9.

boy delinquents, were sent to reformatories.[22] In sum, girls appeared in juvenile court on noncriminal charges far more frequently than boys; nonetheless, girls received more punitive dispositions.[23]

We turn now to another body of evidence: the day-to-day experiences of girls in juvenile court. From the archival records of the Milwaukee Children's Court we have chosen several cases from between 1901 and 1920 for examination. Transcripts from actual hearings, we believe, provide the most vivid and dramatic demonstration of the assumptions that shaped the definition and treatment of female delinquency in the Progressive era.[24]

Alleged girl delinquents in Milwaukee had their private lives probed in fine detail so that judges and probation officers could assess the underlying causes of misbehavior. Whenever it could be demonstrated that a girl had used vile language, masturbated, or indulged in lascivious thoughts, the court freely employed some type of intervention, usually probation. Consider the case of Annagret Schmitt. Neither the hearing transcript nor the accompanying records provides a precise reason why Annagret was brought into court—a common occurrence, since it was assumed that some form of aberrant sexual expression was behind any

specific accusation. Thus Annagret, like every girl who appeared in court, was subjected to a vaginal examination. The only proof of virginity was an intact hymen. To his own surprise the examing doctor concluded that Annagret was still a virgin, but he informed the court that irritation in her clitoral area indicated she was a regular masturbator. The probation officer, a woman, analyzed the situation as follows: "She masturbates, and she has somewhat injured herself in that way, and probably this is the cause of her conduct at home, and says things [sic] that are not true. . . . [Annagret] most likely is trying to imagine things, and then believes everything is true." Thus, according to the court, Annagret's masturbatory habits explained her penchant for fantasy and justified labeling her a delinquent and placing her under supervision.

In cases of advanced sexual misconduct, the court usually explored the circumstances in excruciating detail. The ostensible goals were to procure evidence

22 Breckinridge and Abbott, *The Delinquent Child*, p. 41; and Schlossman, *Love*, appendix 2, table 3.

23 In arguing that girls received more punitive treatment, we assume that incarceration is, by its very nature, a harsher form of punishment than probation. We are *not* saying, however, that the treatment of girls in reformatories was harsher than that of boys in reformatories.

24 These cases derive from Schlossman's sample of 1,200 cases in Milwaukee (10 percent of the total heard in this period). To the best of our knowledge, the Milwaukee court is the only one to have opened its early records for historical investigation; it is consequently impossible to say whether they are strictly representative of experiences in courts elsewhere. Although selected with an eye toward the exemplary and archetypal, each case was necessarily idiosyncratic because, obviously, no two children or their parents were exactly alike. The cases that follow should be appreciated much like opera highlights, as suggestive of a larger drama and of characteristic patterns of interaction among protagonists. To protect client anonymity we have changed the names of children and parents who appeared in court, although we have tried to retain their particular ethnic origins. For the same reason we have not cited the specific dates or docket numbers of individual cases.

against the male or males involved and to evaluate the girls' attitudes toward men and sex. At times, though, the immediate goal seemed to be nothing other than sheer titillation, much like the famous vice reports in this period. Such reports offered, in the names of science and social reform, pornographic scenes that would have been censored in the commercial media. In court, girls were required to recount, with some attempt to recreate the atmosphere, the steps that led to their sexual encounters, their physical experiences ("How far did he go into you; what did you feel; did you bleed?"), and their later subjective reactions. In pursuing this line of questioning the court's assumptions were transparent; it presumed that a girl's moral condition and potential for rehabilitation depended on just how much of her biological purity had been preserved and on how morally revolted she was by her experiences.

At the same time that the court avidly investigated the girls' sex lives, it preached a conventional code of Victorian morality, highlighting especially the virtues of chastity and the joys of marriage. With all good intentions the court lectured sexually precocious girls on how their behavior was endangering their later salability as wives. Without doubt many of the sexually active girls who appeared in juvenile court were immature and would have benefited from intelligent advice about sex. But the advice the court proffered must have struck these girls as naive and irrelevant to their current needs and past experiences. Consider, for example, one judge's advice to a girl who had contracted venereal disease:

> By and by, three or four years from now, some nice fellow will come along, and you love him, and he will love you, and you will get married, and live right. That ought to be the aim of a girl like you, to look forward to the time you have a good home and a good man.

Quaint moral admonitions like these were the court's main antidote to sexual precocity among girls and, if nothing else, reveal the cultural stereotypes that shaped the legal processing of female delinquents.

As observed earlier, juvenile courts did not distinguish between actual delinquency and predelinquency because they saw their mission as the treatment of underlying causes. The courts aimed to "save" girls once it became apparent they were "on the road to ruin." Consider the case of Sara Wadrewski. Sara's father had brought her into court on a charge of disobedience, alleging that she had refused to work, stayed out late, and gone to parties where the girls dressed like boys. As often happened, a probation officer was on hand to supplement the parents' charges by relating neighborhood gossip. Sara, he intimated, probably had had intercourse with several boys because she was seen lying on the grass with them in a local park. A group of neighbors made similar accusations. To the judge's question, "In what way is she a bad girl?" one neighbor responded, "Why, for the reason that she bums around and doesn't work, and doesn't bring no money home, and runs to parties, and then calls names, calls her brother names, he is a cripple." Sara roundly denied most of the allegations, particularly the charges that she had had group sex, or indeed, that she had ever had "connection." But her protestations of virginity were to no avail; shortly after the initial hearing she was committed to the local Catholic reformatory.

Juvenile court sessions were often like scenes from a Kafka novel. One could never be sure that the disposition of a case would be on the basis of the accusations or on the quality of evidence. Despite these uncertainties it was almost guaranteed that a girl would be sent to a reformatory if either she or her parents, especially her mother, were not blushingly contrite about the girl's sexual adventures. A classic case is that of fifteen-year-old Deborah Horwitz, who freely admitted staying out late at night with many boys and who casually flaunted her sexual desires. In addition to Deborah's self-incriminating testimony, efficient snooping by a probation officer into Deborah's bedroom bureau turned up even more incriminating evidence: five self-photos that the court considered racy (although Deborah got no more racy than opening the top button of her high-necked blouse and removing her hat); and a remarkably candid series of letters to a sailor friend that left no doubt about her initiation into the joys of sex.

In such cases the court's custom was to blame the mother for her daughter's
actions. Mrs. Horwitz, however, would not stand for it: "I got lots of trouble with 455
the other girl, she needs an operation, and I got lots of trouble with the other children." Nor would Deborah accept the court's harsh evaluation of her behavior. Thus the judge intoned:

> Well, Deborah, this is a very serious matter. If you would live a good life you would be a good woman, and be useful to society, but you have started out very bad. There is only one way to reform you and this is to send you to an institution. I cannot let you go home to your parents. . . . How is it, can't you stop?

Deborah responded, "I can stop, of course I can." "Why don't you behave yourself, then?" the judge rejoined. "These boys tell me that you just coax them." "I never coaxed anybody," Deborah maintained. But to no effect. Precocious sexuality in a girl who would not at least feign repentance and whose parents would not at least feign shock was intolerable to the court. Deborah was committed forthwith to the state reformatory for girls.

As these excerpts reveal, the court defined female delinquency wholly in sexual terms and responded to girls on the basis of Victorian views of women's social role and sexuality. We shall have more to say later about the persistence of these Victorian assumptions in the Progressive period. For the present we will extend our study of actual treatment by examining the female reformatories, which, as noted earlier, expanded rapidly in the early twentieth century. Like the juvenile courts, the reformatories operationalized prevailing cultural stereotypes about women and transformed these stereotypes into tools for punishment and rehabilitation.

Female reformatories in the Progressive era had four principal goals. The basic one was the isolation from males of sexually precocious females, preferably in bucolic settings. Elaborate efforts were made to keep all men away from the institutions or, indeed, from anywhere near the girls. In California, for example, sponsors of the female reformatory concluded that the mile separating the male from the female institution was inadequate. A new facility far removed from males was essential to eliminate "the influences that mysteriously emanate from the proximity of the sexes."[25] The mere act of isolating delinquent girls came to be seen as a rehabilitative tool. As such, it served an important, latent economic function by rationalizing a minimal public investment in other, more positive, methods of treatment.

Not only were the institutions situated so as to eliminate sexual temptation, but they were also designed to serve a second long-range function. Safe custody was considered a spur to later marriage. By incarcerating delinquent girls the reformatories removed them from the unregulated sexual marketplace of ghetto streets and forced them to save their sexual favors, moral reputations, and health until they were of marriageable age. Most inmates of female reformatories were fifteen or sixteen years old, too young to marry in most states. A minimal stay of two to three years was therefore considered essential; upon release the girls would be of marriageable age and could seek legitimate gratification for their pent-up sexual energies. The institutions further promoted marriageability by placing the girls, after release, in new social settings where their moral improprieties were not
456 common knowledge and where they could search anew for companionship.[26] Like the isolation of inmates from all contacts with men, the assumption that custodial care could have long-term therapeutic value underlay the marital goals of the reformatories. Thus, it could seriously be argued that custody in female reformatories was itself a form of treatment.[27]

[25] Adina Mitchell, *Special Report on the Whittier State School* (Sacramento, Calif.: State Printing Office, 1896), p. 11. See also Mary Berry, "The State's Duty to the Delinquent Girl," National Conference on the Education of Truant, Backward, Dependent and Delinquent Children, *Proceedings* (1918), pp. 82–83; Mrs. Jennie Griffith, "The Training of Delinquent Girls," Conference of the National Committee on Prisons and Prison Labor, *Proceedings* (1919), pp. 15, 17; Miriam Van Waters, "Where Girls Go Right," *Survey Graphic*, 1922, 1, 365; and Maine Industrial School for Girls, *Annual Report* (Waterville, Me.: Sentinel Publishing Co., 1909), pp. 7–8.

[26] Breckinridge and Abbott, *The Delinquent Child*, p. 8; Huntington et al., "The Juvenile Court," appendix; Olga Bridgman, "An Experimental Study of Abnormal Children, with Special Reference to the Problems of Dependency and Delinquency," University of California, *Publications in Psychology*, 1918, 3, 8; Berry, "The State's Duty," p. 87; Edith Burleigh and Frances Harris, *The Delinquent Girl* (New York: New York School of Social Work, 1923), pp. 32, 38–43; Mary Dewson, "Probation and Institutional Care of Girls," in *The Child in the City*, ed. Sophonisba Breckinridge (Chicago: Chicago School of Civics and Philanthropy, 1912), pp. 360–362; Martha Falconer, "Work of the Girls' Department, House of Refuge, Philadelphia," National Conference of Charities and Correction, *Proceedings* (1908), p. 393; and National Conference of Charities and Correction, *Proceedings* (1903), p. 517. Elliott's *Correctional Education*, a follow-up study of ex-inmates from the Sleighton Farms reformatory in Pennsylvania, left no doubt that marriage was the most important variable in explaining postrelease behavior.

[27] This argument was rarely advanced about the boys' reformatories. In fact, although historians have yet to provide adequate documentation, male reformatories apparently experimented with a variety of new correctional ideas in the Progressive era and participated tangentially in the "progressive education" movement. Elaborate vocational-training programs at a few of the larger reformatories became the envy of "progressive" educators such as David Snedden. In addition, many public reformatories experimented with self-government programs designed loosely along the lines suggested by William George in his famous Junior Republics; many adopted new forms of recreational and military training to improve health and discipline and upgraded their academic

Female reformatories did employ nominally rehabilitative programs, if only to give the girls something to do while their virtue was being protected. These programs embodied traditional stereotypes about women. The institutions attempted to instill in inmates the ideology of domesticity and the minimal skills necessary for its practice. According to correctional administrators, a girl's delinquency alone revealed that she had not learned to revere domestic pursuits. Instruction in domesticity was allied with the reformatories' marital goals: inmates would become so devoted to and skillful at domestic chores that they would easily attract husbands. It was as if, in the moral calculus of the juvenile reformers, a rigorous pursuit of domesticity would compensate for the girls' previous immoralities. Moreover, even if the girls failed to find mates shortly after release, they would at least be trained as domestics and so could support themselves while working in upright, middle-class households.[28]

Inmates were expected to take care of their reformatory cottages with the same pride that middle-class women lavished on their homes. Ideally, the girls would assimilate middle-class domestic values and lower-class domestic skills.[29] In each reformatory cottage, the matron served as the domestic educator, teaching girls both proper attitudes and skills. To increase public regard for the vocational-training programs, reformatory superintendents described them as if they were part of the larger home-economics movement that swept the country in the Progressive era.[30] Actually, the training rarely went beyond the chores necessary for personal hygiene and cottage upkeep, with a cooking class or two added for good measure. As one superintendent blithely argued,

---

offerings for older inmates. Of course we do not believe that these newer correctional programs necessarily rehabilitated inmates. Our point is simply that levels of interest and public investment in rehabilitative programs were greater in boys' than girls' reformatories. For background on the relation between "progressive education" and juvenile corrections, see Walter Drost, *David Snedden* (Madison, Wis.: University of Wisconsin Press, 1967); and Jack Holl, *Juvenile Reform in the Progressive Era* (Ithaca, N.Y.: Cornell University Press, 1971).

28 A widely discussed social "problem" in the Progressive era was the declining availability of trained domestic help; hence it can be argued that the reformatories' emphasis on domestic training was economically functional for the girls. It was also recognized, though, that domestics received wages so low that some were tempted to turn to prostitution for supplementary income.

29 Mary Berry, "Co-Ordination of Industrial and Vocational Work with Parole Administration," National Conference on the Education of Truant, Backward, Dependent and Delinquent Children, *Proceedings* (1920), pp. 52–60; Bowler, "A Study of Seventy-Five Delinquent Girls," pp. 156–157; Burleigh and Harris, *The Delinquent Child*, pp. 8–9; William Fairbanks, "Girls' Reformatories and Their Inherent Characteristics," National Conference of Charities and Correction, *Proceedings* (1901), pp. 254–262; Miss Mary Hinkley, "Problems of Administration: The Responsibilities of a School Toward Its Girls," National Conference on the Education of Truant, Backward, Dependent and Delinquent Children, *Proceedings* (1920), pp. 20–23; Maine Industrial School for Girls, *Annual Report* (1909), p. 15; Griffith, "The Training of Delinquent Girls," p. 17; and Miss Elizabeth Mansell, "An Institution Program for Delinquent Girls," National Conference on the Education of Truant, Backward, Dependent and Delinquent Children, *Proceedings* (1917), p. 35.

30 See Emma Weigley, "It Might Have Been Euthenics: The Lake Placid Conference and the Home Economics Movement," *American Quarterly*, 1974, 26, 79–96; and Barbara Ehrenreich and Deidre English, "The Manufacture of Housework," *Socialist Revolution*, October–December, 1975, 5, 5–40.

> We never have taught typewriting and stenography. I find that in our community you can get about a dozen girls, who want to use a typewriter to one that wants to use a scrubbing brush. It seems to me that if you can get girls to understand that to be a homemaker is about the best thing that can come into the life of a woman, this is almost the best education they can have at the present time.[31]

Another superintendent was candid enough to admit what must often have been true in other reformatories that boasted "scientific" courses in home economics: "We teach the girls in practical cooking, as few are mentally capable of appreciating food values as taught in regular domestic science courses."[32]

The fourth and final goal of the female reformatories, surely their most ambitious, is implicit in the previous remark on inmates' mental limitations. The female reformatories were expected to play a central role in fulfilling the objectives of the eugenics movement, which achieved its greatest popularity at precisely the same time that governmental investment in female corrections significantly expanded.[33]

Eugenicists in the Progressive era sought to improve the "genetic fund" of the American population by discouraging and, if possible, forcibly preventing propa-
458 gation by individuals considered innately inferior in culture and intellect. Almost by definition, the eugenicists identified recent immigrants from southeastern Europe as inferior. Relying on the rediscovery of Mendelian genetic theory in 1900, the eugenicists presented several key arguments: social conditions, such as poverty, and personality traits, such as laziness and courage, were discrete "unit characters" transmitted through heredity; unit characters were immutable; race was the primary determinant of human capacities; in some races socially undesirable unit characters predominated; and social legislation was necessary to encourage breeding of the racially fit and discourage breeding of the unfit. According to the eugenicists, persistent immorality among children was a sign of their genetic inferiority or racial degeneracy. To keep these degenerates from further diluting the nation's "genetic fund" and to prevent the nation from committing "race suicide," eugenicists insisted that permanent institutionalization and, if possible, sterilization were essential. The hereditarily degenerate threatened the eugenicists' vision of a more perfect and efficient world devoid of crime, poverty, and disease—a world quite consistent with the vision of many well-known reformers who outwardly were not eugenicists themselves.

Male and female reformatories were to play a special role in the larger eugenics campaign, as early detectors of innate criminality. In this role, however, the reformatories faced a unique problem: from a clientele composed mainly of chil-

[31] National Conference of Charities and Correction, *Proceedings* (1901), p. 258.

[32] California School for Girls, *Biennial Report* (Sacramento, Calif.: State Printing Office, 1918), p. 9.

[33] For background on the eugenics movement we have relied especially on Mark Haller, *Eugenics* (New Brunswick, N.J.: Rutgers University Press, 1963); Donald Pickens, *Eugenics and the Progressive Era* (Nashville, Tenn.: Vanderbilt University Press, 1968); Rudolph Vecoli, "Sterilization: A Progressive Measure?" *Wisconsin Magazine of History*, 1960, 48, 190–203; Peter Tyor, "Segregation or Surgery: The Mentally Retarded in America, 1850–1920," Dissertation, Northwestern University, 1972; and Allan Chase, *The Legacy of Malthus* (New York: Knopf, 1976).

dren of racially inferior immigrants, how were they to identify those whose inheritance was so inferior as to warrant permanent incarceration or sterilization? By the 1910s the principal method of detection became mental testing, which rapidly evolved through a bewildering variety of forms, culminating in the 1916 Stanford revision of the Binet test—the intelligence quotient (IQ) test. With a seemingly precise instrument like the Stanford-Binet test in hand, psychologists and their helpers administered mental tests with virtual abandon to captive inmate populations. The tests were purported to identify those delinquents whose innate intelligence was so low that, in the judgment of the psychologists, they could never learn to control their instincts and become civilized members of society. These defective delinquents, as they were commonly called, were to be transferred from the reformatories and incarcerated, if facilities permitted, in homes for feeble-minded children— institutions that proliferated in the Progressive era. In sum, the newly devised mental test legitimated eugenic goals by providing a scientific instrument for weeding out from the delinquent population those children whose antisocial behavior was inbred.[34]

Eugenic goals, as we noted, applied equally to male and female reformatories, 459
and IQ and other mental tests were freely administered in both. But the literature on delinquency discussed feeble-mindedness among girls with a special urgency. In part this was because delinquent girls appeared at first to test at somewhat lower levels than delinquent boys.[35] More important, though, were the two widely held beliefs that women bore the primary moral responsibility for determining whether to have children and that women lacked the sexual drives of men. From

[34] *The Journal of Delinquency*, published in California, provided the principal forum for discussing this use of mental tests. Its articles were written mainly by psychologists, physicians, psychiatrists, and correctional workers. The *Journal* came especially under the influence of Lewis Terman and several of his students at Stanford, although other prominent members of its editorial board included William Healy, founder of the Juvenile Psychopathic Clinic in Chicago, and Arnold Gesell, the developmental psychologist from Yale.

[35] See, for example, C. S. Bluemel, "Binet Tests on Two Hundred Juvenile Delinquents," *Training School Bulletin*, 1915, 12, 191. Of all the drawbacks of the early IQ tests administered to delinquents, the most basic one was the leeway given to the examiner. The tests left much room for interpretation; often there was no clear-cut right or wrong answer. In such instances the examiners frequently came to dubious conclusions about inmates' mental ages. Consider the following example from Bluemel (p. 187), in which the examiner asked:

> "What is the difference between pride and pretension?" The first replies: "If you have too much pride, you go to certain places—cafes and dance halls. Some pretend to be proud but are poor." The second replies: "Pride means to be proud, and pretension means to pretend to be something that you are not." The third replies: "Pride is something in you that makes you—if you have enough of it—hold yourself a little above people that are without pride. Pretension is false pride." Obviously, these answers indicate that the three girls are at different mental levels. This fact is also attested by their answers to the other questions; and the answers in their totality permit one to make a fair estimate of their mental ages.

See also Ordahl and Ordahl, "A Study of Delinquent and Dependent Girls," pp. 41–73; and Jean Walker, "Factors Contributing to the Delinquency of Defective Girls," University of California, *Publications in Psychology*, 1925, 3, 147–207.

this perspective, sexually precocious girls were morally and biologically perverse. When this view was joined with the belief that delinquent girls' intelligence was so far below normal that they could never learn to control their instincts, it becomes clear why the specter of female delinquency haunted the eugenics movement and why delinquent girls were more frequently incarcerated than delinquent boys.

Sexual Precocity and the Social Order in the Progressive Era

Having sketched the main elements of female juvenile justice in the Progressive era, we return to our earlier questions: why did public interest and investment in female delinquency burgeon so noticeably in this period, and why were girls treated more punitively than boys?

Perhaps the most obvious explanation of the rising interest in female delinquency in the Progressive period would be that the incidence of female delinquency grew until it simply could not be ignored. Much evidence could be marshaled to sustain this argument. One could turn, for example, to the remarkable
460 data on family breakdown, cultural disintegration, and crime in urban immigrant communities documented in Thomas and Znaniecki's 1927 classic, *The Polish Peasant in America*.[36] Equally familiar are Jane Addams's poignant commentaries on the tensions and communication gulfs between mothers and daughters in *Democracy and Social Ethics* and *The Spirit of Youth and the City Streets*.[37] Similarly, one could assess the moral consequences of growing female participation in the work force. Did the increasingly familiar, "promiscuous" social relations of young men and women at work, mainly in the factory, encourage early sexual experimentation, as many contemporaries feared?[38] Finally, one could point to the pervasive image of the white-slave trade, as embodied in the work of the Chicago Vice Commission or Jane Addams's *A New Conscience and an Ancient Evil*.[39] The image of the white-slave trader fueled the era's antiprostitution campaigns and expressed metaphorically the common view that impoverished women were vulnerable to unscrupulous entrepreneurs. In short, the rising public investment in and sensitivity to female delinquency could be seen as a pragmatic response to a real and growing social problem.

Although this argument is appealing, two serious limitations, one methodological and the other conceptual, persuade us, while not ignoring or denying it, to focus our attention elsewhere. First, the argument encounters the methodological difficulties common to all attempts to calculate the actual incidence of crime, whether in the present or, especially, in the past. We agree with modern-day sociologists and criminologists that official crime data and popular impressions of

[36] William Thomas and Florian Znaniecki, *The Polish Peasant in America*, 2 vols. (New York: Knopf, 1927).

[37] Jane Addams, *Democracy and Social Ethics* (New York: Macmillan, 1902); and *The Spirit of Youth and the City Streets* (New York: Macmillan, 1909).

[38] For example, see "Are Low Wages Responsible for Women's Immorality?," *Current Opinion*, May 1913, 54, 402.

[39] Jane Addams, *A New Conscience and an Ancient Evil* (New York: Macmillan, 1913).

crime waves are unreliable indices of illegal activity in any period.[40] Second, as Edwin Schur and others have argued, the traditional foci in criminological research on the incidence of crime and the personal characteristics of offenders have often obscured the fact that crime is a social and legal artifact.[41] Crime does not exist in the abstract; certain activities become illegal only when so labeled. This holds true particularly for juvenile delinquency because, as we have seen, its legal definition is extremely broad and imprecise.

To reiterate, we do not deny the possibility that rates of female delinquency were actually on the rise in the Progressive era, although it would be nearly impossible, given the broad definition of delinquency, to determine how to measure its incidence. Rather, our point is simply that the public agencies responsible for defining, prosecuting, and punishing antisocial behavior invariably shape a society's awareness of criminal conduct at any moment. Therefore, whatever the actual incidence of delinquency, it is essential to examine the cultural context in which delinquency was defined and the legal and penal context in which codes were enforced.[42]

We believe the heightened sensitivity to female delinquency and the growing governmental investment in correctional institutions can be best understood in relation to three developments that directly and indirectly affected social policies —eugenic solutions to social problems, increasing popularity of theories of adolescence, and the movement for "social purity." We have already dealt with the first development, the pervasive appeal of eugenics,[43] and so will proceed to the second development, the growing popularity of theories of adolescence.

[40] The previously cited texts of Gibbons and Sanders (see footnote 5) are especially sensitive to this difficulty. See also the essays collected under the heading, "The Data of Delinquency: Problems of Definition and Measurement," in *Juvenile Delinquency*, ed. Rose Giallombardo (New York: Wiley, 1966).

[41] Edwin Schur, *Radical Non-Intervention* (Englewood Cliffs, N.J.: Prentice-Hall, 1973).

[42] See especially Platt, *The Child Savers;* and Leon Radzinowicz, *Ideology and Crime* (New York: Columbia University Press, 1966).

[43] The theories and policies proposed in the eugenics movement drew upon several long-term preoccupations of American social reformers. Hereditarian thinking and racial mythologies were staples of American social thought throughout the nineteenth century, existing before the influence of Social Darwinism. Similarly, anti-immigrant hostility was common from the early nineteenth century onward, particularly in the large cities of the Northeast. We believe, nonetheless, that racial mythologies and anti-immigrant prejudice attained, in tandem, a new degree of legitimacy after the rediscovery in 1900 of Mendel's ideas, especially after these were popularized, and distorted, by social scientists whose influence on social policy grew enormously in the Progressive period. For example, Henry Goddard, one of the leading applied social scientists in the country and the first person to translate and adapt the Binet-Simon intelligence tests to American needs, wrote the best-selling bible of the eugenics movement, *The Kallikak Family* (New York: Macmillan, 1912) and led campaigns for literacy tests, restrictive marriage covenants, sterilization laws, and immigration restrictions. Even Jane Addams, a quintessential environmentalist, could endorse "the new science of eugenics" and "its recently appointed university professors" (*A New Conscience*, pp. 130–131). See Charles Rosenberg, "The Bitter Fruit: Heredity, Disease, and Social Thought," *Perspectives in American History*, 1974, 8, 189–235; Ray Billington, *The Protestant Crusade, 1800–1860* (New York: Macmillan, 1938); and Oscar Handlin, *Boston's*

Differential treatment of boy and girl delinquents did not represent a failure in implementation, we believe, but rather was an inevitable outcome of the sexually biased social-science theories of adolescence that matured in the Progressive era.[44] These theories gave the imprimatur of science to traditional Victorian views of women as weak, impressionable, emotional, and yet erotically impassive.[45] Moreover, these theories helped shape juvenile justice in two major ways: they invalidated the most optimistic features of the juvenile court movement as applied to girls, and they legitimated the creation of new reformatories for girls just when institutional care for boys was being widely challenged.

The central role of Clark University president G. Stanley Hall in developing and popularizing new ideas about adolescence has been well documented.[46] Following Hall's lead, reformers of various hues portrayed adolescence as at once the most malleable and the most problematic time of development. Adolescence represented a new stage of life: anything was possible, for better or for worse. Most important, during adolescence a child's permanent character took shape. Jane Addams captured the common viewpoint most poignantly in her paean to the "spirit of youth": in adolescence the human spirit bursts forth anew in unsuspecting children, enthralling them with the enchantment of life, confusing them with the rush of passion and idealism.[47] During this stage of life, the reformers admonished, children required especially solicitous parental care and creative social planning to help them cope safely with the potentials of adolescence.

Not surprisingly, most commentators believed that the female youngsters of poor immigrant families were particularly vulnerable. They grew up in slums, came from inferior racial stock, and were scarred by cultural norms that sanctioned the open display of male sexual interest. However, this concern for the vulnerability of ethnic girls did not lead to extensive social programs for them. The many organizations developed for children in the Progressive era, such as day and evening clubs, scouts, and summer camps, were promoted much less vigorously

---

Immigrants (Cambridge, Mass.: Harvard University Press, 1941). On the growing role of social scientists, see Julius Weinberg, *Edward Alsworth Ross and the Sociology of Progressivism* (Madison, Wis.: State Historical Society of Wisconsin, 1972); Barry Karl, *Charles E. Merriam and the Study of Politics* (Chicago: University of Chicago Press, 1974); Julia and Herman Schwendinger, *Sociologists of the Chair* (New York: Basic Books, 1974); and Chase, *The Legacy of Malthus*, pt. 2.

[44] Although such theories were not nearly as new as their proponents claimed, they did exert considerable influence on Progressive-era social reformers. See Joseph Kett, *Rites of Passage* (New York: Basic Books, 1977), chap. 8; and Steven Schlossman, "G. Stanley Hall and the Boys' Club: Conservative Applications of Recapitulation Theory," *Journal of the History of the Behavioral Sciences*, 1973, 9, 140–147.

[45] Two articles that advance the same argument as it applies to formal criminological theory are Doris Klein, "The Etiology of Female Crime: A Review of the Literature," *Issues in Criminology*, Fall 1973, 8, 3–30; and Dale Hoffman-Bustamante, "The Nature of Female Criminality," *Issues in Criminology*, Fall 1973, 8, 117–136.

[46] See Dorothy Ross, *G. Stanley Hall* (Chicago: University of Chicago Press, 1972); Kett, *Rites of Passage*, chap. 8; and Schlossman, "G. Stanley Hall and the Boys' Club."

[47] Addams, *The Spirit of Youth*.

for girls than for boys.[48] This resulted, in part, because boys were a much more immediate social threat: their delinquencies posed a clear and present danger, whereas girls' delinquencies engendered more long-term fears. But the best explanation, we believe, lies in the fact that adolescent girls were considered much less malleable than adolescent boys. Institutions like girls' clubs and Girl Scouts received less support than their male counterparts because adolescence in girls, as a life stage, was regarded as a much less promising period for reshaping character. Rather than a new beginning, adolescence in girls was the time when character traits instilled earlier were put to the test. Most writers assumed that by the time girls reached puberty the most promising time for shaping their character had long since passed.[49] Thus, while the psychological theories of adolescence provided a new source of "scientific" optimism for preventing delinquency among boys, they gave no such hope for aiding girls.[50]

For similar reasons, we believe, the promise of the juvenile court movement was less widely acclaimed for girls than for boys. As Schlossman argues in his history of

[48] On boys' clubs, see Schlossman, "G. Stanley Hall and the Boys' Club"; on camps, see McLeod, "Good Boys Made Better"; on Boy Scouts, see Jeffrey Hantover, "Sex Role, Sexuality, and Social Status: The Early Years of the Boy Scouts of America," Dissertation, University of Chicago, 1976; and Peter Schmitt, *Back to Nature* (New York: Oxford University Press, 1969), chap. 10. For a more comprehensive synthesis of these and other organizations aimed at youth, see Kett, *Rites of Passage*, chaps. 7 and 8.

[49] In reaching this conclusion we have relied especially upon: Augusta Bronner, "Effect of Adolescent Instability on Conduct," *Psychological Clinic*, 1915, 7, 249–265; Burleigh and Harris, *The Delinquent Girl*; Mary Paddon, "A Study of Fifty Feeble-Minded Prostitutes," *Journal of Delinquency*, 1918, 3, 1–11; Maude Miner, "The Woman Delinquent," New York City Conference of Charities and Correction, *Proceedings* (1911), pp. 152–165; Rheta Dorr, "Reclaiming the Wayward Girl," *Hampton's Magazine*, January 1911, 26, 67–78; Bridgman, "An Experimental Study of Abnormal Children"; Mary Moxcey, *Girlhood and Character* (New York: Abingdon, 1916); Winifred Richmond, *The Adolescent Girl* (New York: Macmillan, 1926); Ruth True, "The Neglected Girl," in *West Side Studies*, ed. Pauline Goldmark (New York: Survey Associates, 1914), pp. 1–134; Emily Lamb, "A Study of Thirty-Five Delinquent Girls," *Journal of Delinquency*, 1919, 4, 75–85; Ordahl and Ordahl, "A Study of Delinquent and Dependent Girls"; Merritt Pinkney, "The Delinquent Girl and the Juvenile Court," in *The Child in the City*, ed. Breckinridge, pp. 349–354; Breckinridge and Abbott, *The Delinquent Child;* Wiley, *A Study of the Problem;* William Thomas, *The Unadjusted Girl* (Boston: Little, Brown, 1923); Miriam Van Waters, "Causes and Cure" and "The True Value of Correctional Education," in the Miriam Van Waters Papers, Box 11, Schlesinger Library, Radcliffe College; Falconer, "Work of the Girls' Department"; Elliott, *Correctional Education*; Huntington et al., "The Juvenile Court"; Walker, "Factors Contributing to the Delinquency of Defective Girls"; Miss Vida Francis, "The Delinquent Girl," National Conference of Charities and Correction, *Proceedings* (1906), pp. 138–145; and Jane Rippin, "Social Readjustment as the Function of the Judge," Conference of the National Committee on Prisons and Prison Labor, *Proceedings* (1919), pp. 25–31.

[50] We quote from Kett, *Rites of Passage*, p. 224: "Hall, moreover, had written very little about girls, a bias fully reflected in both the literature on boys-work after 1900 and in the masculine orientation and sexual segregation of scouting. . . . It was a boy's world, not a girl's and not a man's, a fact which prompted H. W. Gibson, a YMCA tractarian and boys-worker, to reduce all of adolescent psychology to something called 'boyology.' " A very useful compendium which nicely captures the differences in the theories is *Boy Training*, ed. John Alexander (New York: Association Press, 1915).

"progressive" juvenile corrections, the main rehabilitative tool of the court movement was probation.[51] Ideally, probation was to be a means of family education. Probation officers were to function less as agents of law enforcement than as visiting teachers who would instruct parents and children on how to eliminate family stress and how to use community resources to increase economic security and recreational enjoyment. The theory of probation was built firmly on the assumptions that most children became delinquent during their adolescent years, that adolescents were especially malleable, and that the successful rechanneling of youthful energies into lawful pursuits would motivate parents to modify their behavior toward their children and eliminate delinquency-producing conditions in the home. Probation epitomized the belief that adolescents merited several chances to become upright citizens.

Not so—or at least markedly less so—with erring adolescent girls.[52] Writers on female delinquency argued that, while a female's delinquencies were less criminally culpable, they were also less amenable to change through a relatively informal means of supervision like probation. Girls also received probation less frequently than
464 boys because of the greater tendency to blame parents of delinquent girls. Unlike boys, it was argued, girls did not have places other than their homes in which to spend free time safely. Although writers on delinquency recognized that immigrant mothers and youth entered the work force because of poverty, they nonetheless held that rearing a girl imposed special moral responsibilities. Thus all mothers, regardless of economic circumstances, were obliged to keep their girls at home, when not in school or church, and to transform homes into refuges for protecting female virtue. This tendency to hold mothers more directly responsible for the behavior of girl delinquents than of boy delinquents further diminished the likelihood of probation for girls. If the female delinquent was considered less redeemable than her male counterpart, so too was her mother.

As probation was devalued for girl offenders, incarceration was judged more suitable. Earlier we examined the main rationales for female reformatories; here we will present additional justifications that illuminate why girl and boy delinquents were treated differently. One was the belief that girl delinquents, unlike boys, were not at all childlike in their behavior. By usurping the ultimate adult prerogative—sexual intercourse—female delinquents forfeited their right to be regarded merely as innocent, curious children. Moreover, precocious sexual exploration by girls threatened society's attempt to keep children innocent, chaste, and dependent until marriageable age. Female delinquents thereby subverted family government and had to be removed from their natural homes for the protection of neighborhood youth. Finally, imprisonment was seen as a boon to rehabilitation because of the speed with which neighborhood grapevines disseminated the repu-

[51] Schlossman, *Love,* chap. 4.

[52] The citations in note 49 are all relevant here, especially Breckinridge and Abbott, *The Delinquent Child,* pp. 35–38, 72–73, 169; Ordahl and Ordahl, "A Study of Delinquent and Dependent Girls," pp. 60–61; Van Waters, "Causes and Cure," p. 5; Paddon, "A Study of Fifty Feeble-Minded Prostitutes," p. 10; and True, "The Neglected Girl," p. 19.

tations of "bad girls." One writer summed up these diverse rationales for more frequent incarceration of delinquent girls:

> And suppose a boy does bolt? He can try again. Suppose he "goes bad" a second or a third time, either through animal spirits or bad companions? He can begin all over again. Suppose he even stays out nights, and goes into lower forms of degradation? Even then if he can pull himself together physically and morally, he has not lost the chance for a decent manhood and a square deal. But is it so with any delinquent girl? No, a thousand times no! By the publicity of even the appearance in Court her reputation is tarnished, and with her reputation in question, her chance to retrieve herself in the same environment is very small. And in that eighty percent of crimes against the person, does my girl get a fair chance to "try again?" No, the world is against her, evil men are ready to tempt her further, the industrial situation helps to put her at their mercy, and even nature herself gives a last push towards the downward path when she physically handicaps herself. No! My girl who has once become delinquent finds it a 1000 times more difficult to straighten herself than the boy. The delinquent girl must be preserved against the *opportunities* of temptation which are inevitably more fatal to her than to the boy.[53] 465

Clearly, then, the juvenile reformatory was the best possible place to treat delinquent girls—to protect society from them and them from society.

The third and final development behind growing awareness of female delinquency in the Progressive era was the movement for "social purity." More particularly, we want to analyze the relation of the purity ideal to what several historians have described as the "sexual revolution" of the Progressive era or the beginnings of "the modernization of sex." We believe that changes in sexual mores provided the cultural foundation for the burgeoning interest in female delinquency, the expansion of female reformatories, and the differential treatment of boy and girl delinquents. To explicate our position, we will first examine changing sexual mores in the Progressive era and then point up how they shaped new policies toward female delinquents.[54]

53 Francis, "The Delinquent Girl," p. 140.

54 In the 1950s and 1960s the most common historical approach to the subject of morals and sex in the Progressive era was to emphasize its puritanical features. This approach flowed from the interpretation of social-reform movements epitomized by the work of Richard Hofstadter, especially *The Age of Reform* (New York: Knopf, 1955). In the past few years a different historical interpretation has emerged that stresses the loosening grip of Victorian morality on sexual attitudes and holds that "modern" attitudes toward sex first emerged in the Progressive era rather than, as is more commonly thought, in the 1920s. This view rests on several sources of evidence: the work of historical demographers, who argue that rates of premarital pregnancy rose markedly in this period; self-report studies, which indicate that dramatic increases in premarital intercourse occurred; and reexamination of literary sources, which suggests that social discourse in the Progressive era was a good deal less prudish than had been thought. As examples, see Linda Gordon, *Woman's Body, Woman's Right* (New York: Grossman, 1976), pt. 2; Paul Robinson, *The Modernization of Sex* (New York: Harper & Row, 1976); John Burnham, "The Progressive-Era Revolution in American Attitudes Toward Sex," *Journal of American History*, 1973, 59, 885–908; James McGovern, "The American Woman's Pre-World War I Freedom in Manners and Morals," *Journal of American History*, 1968, 55, 315–333; and Carl Degler, "What Ought To Be and

Increasing investment in reformatories for sexually precocious girls reflected a widespread revulsion against the growing frequency and legitimacy of sex as an everyday topic of discussion.[55] The expansion of the government's capacity to punish sexual promiscuity formed one phase of what we term a "sexual counterrevolution." The men and women who led this counterrevolution were, by and large, the same types of middle-class, nonethnic individuals who participated in the better-known political and social reforms of the period. For these men and women, the sexual counterrevolution represented a moral analogue to the cleansing of corruption in the political and economic arenas.[56]

To the counterrevolutionists the public's fascination with sex was inherently dangerous because it threatened the maintenance of conventional family life. They were particularly troubled by many recent changes: the flagrant commercialization of sex in the press; the demystification of sex by doctors, psychologists, and intellectuals; the increasingly open propaganda for dissemination of birth-control devices; and the moral dangers inherent in the discovery of new medical remedies for venereal disease. The counterrevolutionists urged that new strategies were essential to revitalize older sexual ideals, neutralize overstimulated sexual appetites, and purify social discourse on sex. If reticence was no longer possible, purity was.[57]

The counterrevolutionists engaged in three major "reform" campaigns: the wholesale destruction of prostitution; the widespread dissemination of sex educa-

---

What Was: Women s Sexuality in the Nineteenth Century," *American Historical Review*, 1974, **79**, 1467–1490.

While we agree with the historians who argue that the early twentieth century witnessed a marked increase in the public's willingness to discuss sex openly, we are uneasy about the tendency to locate the origins of sexual modernity in the Progressive era. This approach, we feel, exaggerates indications of the new morality and plays down evidence of older Victorian thinking. Most important for the history of female juvenile justice, this interpretation shifts attention away from major efforts in this period to reaffirm Victorian moral and sexual standards as well as to recast older religious commands into new secular, scientific language. Thus we both agree and disagree with the new interpretation.

[55] On the scholarly side, the psychologist Helen Thompson Woolley noted that between 1910 and 1914 "the number of experimental investigations in the field [psychology of sex] has increased to such an extent that whereas it was difficult at that time [1910] to find anything to review, it is now impossible to review all that I could find" ("The Psychology of Sex," *The Psychological Bulletin*, 1914, **11**, 353). If scholars were having a field day with sex, so was the American public: "A wave of sex hysteria seems to have invaded this country," wrote the anonymous author of a piece which has since become an historical classic. "Our former reticence on matters of sex is giving way to a frankness that would even startle Paris." ("Sex O'Clock in America," *Current Opinion*, August 1913, **55**, 113).

[56] This is our impression from reading the literature; we have not conducted empirical research on the social origins of the counterrevolutionists. Certainly Theodore Roosevelt was the most prominent of the individuals who engaged as fervidly in moral as in political reform. Roosevelt popularized the notion of "race suicide" and boasted that one of his greatest achievements was to have exercised enough will power to remain a virgin until marriage (William Harbaugh, *The Life and Times of Theodore Roosevelt* [New York: Oxford University Press, 1975], p. 15).

[57] For general background see David Pivar, *Purity Crusade* (Westport, Conn.: Greenwood, 1973); and David Kennedy, *Birth Control in America* (New Haven, Conn.: Yale University Press, 1970).

tion; and, our main subject, the punishment of sexually precocious girls. Each campaign had a number of concrete, functional goals, but each needs to be seen symbolically as well. Together, the campaigns represented a ritualistic protest against cultural change, a spirited reaffirmation of older moral ideals, and an urgent call for creative new strategies to realize them.

The campaign against prostitution was, ironically, both a contribution to and a sharp reaction against what one author wittily called the arrival of "sex o'clock" in America.[58] Prostitution had been a widespread and fairly well-accepted part of American urban life. To be sure, moralists of many kinds had periodically remonstrated against the easy acceptance of prostitution and were probably responsible for insuring that only one brief effort was made, in St. Louis, to experiment with European methods of regulation.[59] By and large, though, prostitutes sold their services with little interference, and, all evidence indicates, remarkably large percentages of American males used them.[60]

In the Victorian years prostitution was silently tolerated for three principal reasons. For one, prostitutes thrived mainly in the poorer, immigrant neighborhoods, and the feeling was, then as now, that as long as prostitutes remained in the slums, more respectable communities need not worry unduly about them. Second, nineteenth-century popular opinion sanctioned the view that men possessed superabundant sexual energies that required frequent release for mental and physical health. We must be careful not to exaggerate here; for opposite beliefs on male sexuality were also held in the Victorian period. Several reformers argued, for example, that sexual indulgence destroyed men's bodies and minds and that men should be continent in their sexual expression.[61] In retrospect, though, what is remarkable is how easily these contradictory sentiments coexisted—the latter as ideology for public consumption, the former as an "underground" precept guiding actual behavior.[62]

58 "Sex O'Clock in America."

59 John Burnham, "Medical Inspection of Prostitutes in Nineteenth Century America—The St. Louis Experiment and Its Sequel," *Bulletin of the History of Medicine*, 1971, **45**, 203–218.

60 See Roy Lubove, "The Progressives and the Prostitute," *Historian*, 1962, **24**, 308–330; Robert Riegel, "Changing American Attitudes toward Prostitution (1800–1920)," *Journal of the History of Ideas*, 1968, **29**, 437–452; Keith Thomas, "The Double Standard," *Journal of the History of Ideas*, 1959, **20**, 195–216; Egal Feldman, "Prostitution, the Alien Woman and the Progressive Imagination, 1910–1915," *American Quarterly*, 1967, **19**, 192–206; Eric Anderson, "Prostitution and Social Justice: Chicago, 1910–15," *Social Service Review*, 1974, **48**, 203–228; Claudia Johnson, "That Guilty Third Tier: Prostitution in Nineteenth-Century American Theaters," in *Victorian America*, ed. Daniel Howe (Philadelphia: University of Pennsylvania Press, 1976), pp. 111–120; and James Wunsch, "Prostitution and Public Policy: From Regulation to Suppression, 1858–1920," Dissertation, University of Chicago, 1976.

61 A very useful introduction to the ideals and practices of sex in the Victorian period is *Primers for Prudery*, ed. Ronald Walters (Englewood Cliffs, N.J.: Prentice-Hall, 1974). See also Gordon, *Woman's Body*, chaps. 4 and 8; and Patricia Vertinsky, "Education for Sexual Morality: Moral Reform and the Regulation of American Sexual Behavior in the Nineteenth Century," Dissertation, University of British Columbia, 1974, sect. 2.

62 We borrow the term "underground" from Bryan Strong, who writes of the attempt in the early twentieth century "to counteract the underground belief in what was called the 'sexual

The third reason for toleration of prostitution was the Victorian sentimentalization of womanhood.[63] "Respectable" women—the only kind men dared marry—were placed gingerly upon a pedestal and viewed as rarefied creatures without sexual motivation. By nature they were so innocent and gentle that it would have been cruel for husbands to impose their sexual lusts upon them. This viewpoint obviously facilitated public acceptance of prostitution: the practice was rationalized as a protection of the home and domestic life through the absorption of men's excess sexual energies.

In the reform campaigns of the Progressive era, the ambivalences and contradictions of Victorian sexual thinking gave way to the unyielding pursuit of purity and innocence. Under the leadership of the counterrevolutionists, city after city conducted elaborate studies of prostitution, revealing how openly prostitution flourished. Estimates varied, but it was conservatively calculated that well over half of American males from all social classes used or had used prostitutes and that many had contracted some form of venereal disease. Using these facts to support their position, the counterrevolutionists attacked regulation or even the toleration of prostitution as blasphemy. The wholesale destruction of prostitution became their
468 goal, and, to a remarkable extent, they succeeded in wiping out many of the nation's most famous red-light districts in the years before the First World War.[64]

The metaphor of the white-slave trade fueled the antiprostitution campaign, but the extent to which prostitution was centrally organized was always uncertain.[65] Two other well-publicized arguments, though, helped sustain the fight against prostitution. The first resulted from several major scientific advances in detection and treatment of venereal disease. The counterrevolutionists drew grave moral implications from these scientific developments. On the one hand, they insisted, the physical devastation and easy communicability of venereal disease demanded rapid elimination of prostitution to safeguard family health. On the other hand, they asserted, the discovery of effective cures for venereal disease required quick destruction of prostitution, lest men be tempted to greater vice by the knowledge that they need not fear infection.[66]

The second rationale for destroying prostitution also drew upon medical opin-

---

necessity,' which declared that men must exercise their sexual power lest their organs weaken or atrophy for want of use. Belief in a 'sexual necessity,' of course, was inconsistent with the ideal of chastity and continence" ("Ideas of the Early Sex Education Movement in America, 1890–1920," *History of Education Quarterly*, 1972, 12, 145).

[63] See, for example, Anne Scott, *The Southern Lady* (Chicago: University of Chicago Press, 1970); and Barbara Welter, "The Cult of True Womanhood: 1820–1860," *American Quarterly*, 1966, 18, 151–174.

[64] See Gordon, *Woman's Body*, p. 204. While we find her argument intriguing, we do not believe there is sufficient evidence to support Gordon's cause-effect contention that "the basis for the weakening of prostitution between 1910 and 1920 was not the conversion of men to purity; it was the conversion of women to 'indulgence' " (p. 192).

[65] For example, see Clifford Roe, *The Prodigal Daughter: The White Slave Evil and the Remedy* (Chicago: L. W. Walter, 1911); and *War on the White Slave Trade*, ed. Ernest Bell (Chicago: Charles C. Thompson, 1909).

[66] The principal medical spokesperson and organizational leader of the counterrevolutionists

ion, although in this instance it was more a medical assertion than a demonstrable advance in scientific knowledge. The counterrevolutionists contended that a single standard of sexual behavior—that of continence—should prevail for men and women.[67] This ideal, as we observed, also had its supporters in the Victorian era. The twentieth-century proponents of continence did little to challenge the underground Victorian view that men's sexual appetites were ravenous. Instead, they emphatically urged continence as part of the larger Progressive-era moral revival, which included such other popular displays of conscience as the prohibition movement and the campaigns against child labor, dime novels, cheap movies, and the easy availability of narcotic drugs. Furthermore, the counterrevolutionists now gained the concerted support of powerful medical organizations against the underground doctrine of "sexual necessity." Three hundred of the nation's leading physicians, for example, issued a much-publicized manifesto in favor of male continence, which declared in part:

> In view of the individual and social dangers which spring from the widespread belief that continence may be detrimental to health, and of the fact that municipal toleration of prostitution is sometimes defended on the ground that sexual indulgence is necessary, we, the undersigned, members of the medical profession, testify to our belief that continence has not been shown to be detrimental to health or virility; that there is no evidence of its being inconsistent with the highest physical, mental, and moral efficiency; and that it offers the only sure reliance for sexual health outside of marriage.[68]

In sum, the counterrevolutionists, who led the antiprostitution campaign, relied heavily on medical opinion to persuade the American public that Victorian sexual liberties were sinful and unhealthy and that continence was possible through moral exertion and the removal of temptation. Paradoxically, then, at the very time when sex was becoming an accepted part of social discourse, a surprisingly effective campaign was led to eliminate one of the most common figures of nineteenth-century society, the prostitute.

Like the antiprostitution crusade, the sex-education movement drew heavily on medical science. Proponents of sex education saw themselves as progressive, fearlessly attacking the Victorian "conspiracy of silence" about sex. On closer inspection, though, sex education appears to have been anything but a modernizing influence. The sex educators fought mainly against imaginary adversaries, for sex was already an everyday topic of conversation. Moreover, the movement's rhetoric was largely puritanical, revealing deep fears about the moral impact of cultural change.[69]

---

was Dr. Prince Morrow, whose activities are well treated in Burnham, "The Progressive Era Revolution."

[67] See especially Thomas, *The Unadjusted Girl;* and Strong, "Ideas of the Early Sex Education Movement."

[68] Quoted in Maurice Bigelow, *Sex-Education* (New York: Macmillan, 1918), p. 161.

[69] We are especially indebted to the works of Pivar, Strong, and Vertinsky, "Education for Sexual Morality." The best primary sources, in our estimation, are *The Social Emergency*, ed. William

The main goals of sex education were to purify discourse on sex, particularly in the popular press and among children, and to instill moral inhibitions against sexual gratification now that effective birth control and cures for venereal disease were becoming widely available. The sex educators were moral crusaders marching under the banners of medical and pedagogical science. They sought to develop instructional techniques for innocently conveying new medical knowledge about sex to children and, at the same time, imbuing sex with older spiritual meanings. Sex education was a means of pedagogical warfare against the purveyors of sexual titillation. Far from encouraging freer discussion of sex, the sex educators wanted to discipline lust and channel it to conventional moral ends.[70]

While the sex educators claimed to bring discussion of sex into the open, their pedagogical approach was so indirect as to be obscurantist. About the only form of open sexual discussion they could tolerate, in fact, involved the mating of plants. The copulation of pistils and stamens served as a model for teaching children acceptable sexual emotion and was much preferred to analogies between human and animal sexuality.[71] To the extent that sex educators actually discussed human sex, it was always as a form of spiritual communion; intercourse was mainly a melding of chaste minds. The sex-education movement, then, is best conceived as part of a new strategy for realizing Victorian moral ideals in an era growing increasingly comfortable with sex. If adults in the Progressive period had become unduly attracted to sex, their children need not be.[72]

How is the sexual counterrevolution related to our main subject—female juvenile justice in the Progressive era? We believe the sentiments that motivated the antiprostitution and sex-education campaigns also inspired punitive treatment of female delinquents. The expansion of female reformatories was especially significant, for they played important instrumental and symbolic roles in the sexual counterrevolution. First, and most pragmatically, the female reformatories

---

Foster (Boston: Houghton-Mifflin, 1914); Bigelow, *Sex-Education*; and National Society for the Scientific Study of Education, *Education with Reference to Sex* (Chicago: University of Chicago Press, 1909).

[70] Although the sex educators, by and large, wanted nothing to do with Freud, they were advocating a form of creative repression akin to the goals of the early conservative champions of Freud in America. See Nathan Hale, *Freud and the Americans* (New York: Oxford University Press, 1971).

[71] For example, Bigelow writes in *Sex-Education*: "Like eating, [sex] is a necessary function inherited from animals; but there has been an evolution of greater significance. In the animal world, sexual activity has only one function, reproduction; but human life at its highest has superadded psychical and social meaning to sexual relationships, and the result has been affection and the human family. If we reject this higher view of the double significance of sexuality in human life, and insist that only the necessary propagative function is worthy of recognition, it is almost inevitable that most people will continue to accept the hopeless view that human sexuality is on the same vulgar plane as that of the animals; in short, that it is only an animal function. This, I insist, is a depressing interpretation that will never help overcome the prevailing vulgar attitude toward sex" (p. 74).

[72] For assessments of the influence of the sex-education movement, see Strong, "Ideas of the Early Sex Education Movement," pp. 152–153; and Vertinsky, "Education for Sexual Morality," chap. 9.

assisted in the medical effort to eliminate venereal disease. They isolated those girls who were assumed most likely to become disease carriers. If the girls were already carriers, the reformatories prevented them from spreading disease and made treatment possible. Second, and most presumptuously, the incarceration of sexually promiscuous girls was thought to facilitate the moral ideal of male continence. By removing from view a prime source of sexual temptation, the reformatories, it was earnestly hoped, would also eliminate a stimulant of sexual desire in ghetto communities, especially for teenage boys. Third, and most urgently, the reformatories took sexually active girls off the street during the age range when prostitutes were most commonly recruited.[73] Hence reformatories, aided by the juvenile courts' punitive attitude toward sexual precocity among girls, would contribute to the attack on prostitution by cutting off a likely supply of new recruits.

Finally, and most idealistically, the reformatories assumed a special symbolic role in the sexual counterrevolution. In an era becoming increasingly fascinated by all things sexual, reformatories offered a warning that society would still not tolerate girls who showed the same interest in sex as boys and reinforced the traditional belief that "normal" girls were sexually impassive. These sentiments seem to us to have represented, to a large extent, a rearguard defense against emerging modern views on the reality of female sexual desire. But if, in fact, the counterrevolutionists lost the war, they were a powerful enough force in the Progressive era to win important battles. We should not gauge their significance in the early twentieth century by their long-term defeat in the battle for sexual liberation.

In sum, we believe that female juvenile justice in the Progressive era was closely tied to the evolution of sexual mores. In an era of shifting cultural norms, new social policies emerged to defend older moral ideals. As we noted earlier, we do not deny the possibility that there may have been a real increase in female delinquency in the early twentieth century. But we insist that, whether the increase was real or imagined, the public response to female delinquency formed part of a larger cultural reaction, an attempt to revitalize Victorian morality and to punish women —prostitutes and sexually precocious girls alike—who impeded attainment of that goal.

Conclusion

We promised earlier not to draw glib comparisons between past and present because of the incomplete nature of our historical research. But our research unequivocally demonstrates that the roots of sexual discrimination in juvenile

[73] According to Jane Addams, "it has been estimated that at any given moment the majority of girls utilized by the trade are under twenty years of age and that most of them were procured when younger . . . the average age of recruits to prostitution is between sixteen and eighteen years. . . . All the recent investigations have certainly made clear that the bulk of the entire traffic is conducted with the youth of the community, and that the social evil, ancient though it may be, must be renewed in our generation through its younger members. The knowledge of the youth of its victims doubtless in a measure accounts for the new sense of compunction which fills the community." *A New Conscience*, pp. 52, 142.

justice are deep indeed. Despite radically different attitudes today toward the social role and sexual desires of women, our correctional policies share many of the assumptions common in the nineteenth and early twentieth centuries.[74] Perhaps mainstream ideas about the proper role of women and of female sexuality have not changed as much as some may think;[75] perhaps correctional policies always lag behind changes in cultural perception; perhaps we as a society are trying unconsciously to relieve guilt about the passing of older moral standards by continuing to punish the most vulnerable group of females—poor, minority children who today, as in the past, predominate among incarcerated girls. We do not have a ready answer, but we do believe that there is an intimate relation between a society's correctional system and its deepest values and beliefs. And without doubt the values and beliefs that shaped a discriminatory system of juvenile justice in the Victorian and Progressive eras still dominate the administration of female juvenile justice today.

[74] Richard Flaste, "Is Juvenile Justice Tougher on Girls Than on Boys?" *New York Times*, 6 September 1977, p. 48, cols. 1–4.

472 [75] The classic argument, of course, is presented in Betty Friedan, *The Feminine Mystique* (New York: Norton, 1963). In addition to previously cited books and articles, the following historical works shed much light on continuities between past and present: Charles Rosenberg, "Sexuality, Class, and Role," *American Quarterly*, 1973, 25, 131–153; Charles Rosenberg and Carroll Smith-Rosenberg, "The Female Animal: Medical and Biological Views of Women," *Journal of American History*, 1973, 60, 332–356; Rosalind Rosenberg, "The Dissent from Darwin, 1890–1930: The New View of Woman among American Social Scientists," Dissertation, Stanford University, 1974; and Paula Fass, *The Damned and the Beautiful* (New York: Oxford University Press, 1977).

A Guide to Additional Primary-Source Materials on Female Juvenile Delinquency in the Early Twentieth Century

Bowen, Mrs. Joseph. "The Delinquent Child of Immigrant Parents." National Conference of Charities and Correction, *Proceedings* (1909), pp. 255–261.

Bridgman, Olga. "An Experimental Study of Abnormal Children, with Special Reference to the Problems of Dependency and Delinquency." University of California, *Publications in Psychology*, 1918, 3, 2–59.

Bronner, Augusta. *A Comparative Study of the Intelligence of Girls*. New York: Teachers College Press, 1914.

Burleigh, Edith. "The Advantage of Parole Under a Separate Superintendent." National Conference on the Education of Truant, Backward, Dependent and Delinquent Children, *Proceedings* (1916), pp. 80–83.

Burleigh, Edith. "Some Principles for Parole for Girls." National Conference of Charities and Correction, *Proceedings* (1918), pp. 147–154.

DeBolt, Mrs. L. N. "Industrial Employment as a Factor in the Reformation of Girls." National Conference of Charities and Correction, *Proceedings* (1900), pp. 214–220.

Dummer, Mrs. W. F. "Introduction to Roundtable Discussion on the Delinquent Girl." The American Sociological Society, *Publications*, 1921, 16, 185–186.

Dye, Charlotte. "The Defective Delinquent." National Conference on the Education of Truant, Backward, Dependent and Delinquent Children, *Proceedings* (1917), pp. 78–82.

Falconer, Martha. "The Culture of Family Life Versus Reformatory Treatment." National Conference of Charities and Correction, *Proceedings* (1914), pp. 108–110.

Falconer, Martha. "Reformatory Treatment for Women." National Conference of Charities and Correction, *Proceedings* (1914), pp. 253–256.

Goddard, Henry. "The Treatment of the Mental Defective Who Is Also Delinquent." National Conference of Charities and Correction, *Proceedings* (1911), pp. 64–65.

Hamilton, Dr. Alice. "Venereal Disease in Institutions for Women and Girls." National Conference of Charities and Correction, *Proceedings* (1910), pp. 53–56.

Harris, Dr. Mary. "Preparing Delinquent Women for the New Citizenship." Conference of the National Committee on Prisons and Prison Labor, *Proceedings* (1919), pp. 6–14.

Harris, Dr. Mary. *I Knew Them in Prison*. New York: Viking, 1936.

Hoag, Dr. Ernest, and Dr. Edward Williams. *Crime, Abnormal Minds and the Law*. Indianapolis, Ind.: Bobbs-Merrill, 1923.

Hodder, Jessie. "The Next Step in the Treatment of Girls and Women Offenders." National Conference of Charities and Correction, *Proceedings* (1918), pp. 117–121.

Holsopple, Francis. "Social Non-Conformity: An Analysis of 420 Delinquent Girls and Women." Dissertation, University of Pennsylvania, 1919.

Kauffman, Reginald. *The Girl That Goes Wrong*. New York: Macaulay, 1911.

Kenworthy, Dr. Marion. "The Logic of Delinquency." The American Sociological Society, *Publications*, 1921, 16, 197–204.

Lundberg, Emma. "The Child-Mother as a Delinquency Problem." National Conference of Charities and Correction, *Proceedings* (1920), pp. 167–168.

Miner, Maude. *Slavery of Prostitution*. New York: Macmillan, 1916.

Miner, Maude. "The Individual Method of Dealing with Girls and Women Awaiting Court Action." Congress of the American Prison Association, *Proceedings* (1921), pp. 8–12.

Montgomery, Miss Sarah. "Discipline and Training of Girls in Industrial Schools." National Conference of Charities and Correction, *Proceedings* (1908), pp. 198–201.

Morrow, Dr. Louis, and Dr. Olga Bridgman. "Delinquent Girls Tested by the Binet Scale." *Training School Bulletin*, 1912, 9, 33–36.

Morse, Mrs. Frannie. "The Methods Most Helpful to Girls." National Conference of Charities and Correction, *Proceedings* (1904), pp. 306–311.

Murray, Virginia. "The Runaway Girl and the Stranded Girl." National Conference of Charities and Correction, *Proceedings* (1920), pp. 175–180.

National Conference on the Education of Truant, Backward, Dependent and Delinquent Children, *Proceedings* (1915), pp. 49–53, and (1917), pp. 36–41, 82–90.

Renz, Emile. "The Intelligence of Delinquents and the Eugenic Significance of Mental Defect." *Training School Bulletin*, 1914, 11, 37–39.

Rippin, Jane. "Municipal Detention for Women." National Conference of Charities and Correction, *Proceedings* (1918), pp. 132–139.

Sessions, Dr. Kenosha. "Some Deductions from the Wasserman Test." National Conference on the Education of Truant, Backward, Dependent and Delinquent Children, *Proceedings* (1915), pp. 47–49.

Sessions, Dr. Kenosha. "The Delinquent Girls as a Community Problem." National Conference on the Education of Truant, Backward, Dependent and Delinquent Children, *Proceedings* (1918), pp. 76–78.

Smith, Dr. Carrie. "The Unadjusted Girl." National Conference of Charities and Correction, *Proceedings* (1920), pp. 180–183.

Taft, Jessie. "Some Problems in Delinquency—Where Do They Belong?" The American Sociological Society, *Publications*, 1921, 16, 186–196.

Van Waters, Miriam. "Juvenile Court Procedure as a Factor in Diagnosis." The American Sociological Society, *Publications*, 1921, 16, 209–217.

Wald, Mrs. Lillian. "The Immigrant Young Girl." National Conference of Charities and Correction, *Proceedings* (1909), pp. 261–266.

Wilson, Otto. *Fifty Years' Work with Girls, 1883–1933*. Alexandria, Va.: National Florence Crittendon Mission, 1933.

Worthington, George, and Ruth Topping. *Specialized Courts Dealing with Sex Delinquency*. New York: Frederick H. Hitchcock, 1925.

The Woman Suffrage Movement in Texas

BY A. ELIZABETH TAYLOR

In the summer of 1848, when most Americans were discussing the recent war with Mexico and the coming presidential election between the Democrats and the Whigs, a small but determined group of men and women met at Seneca Falls, New York, to hold the world's first woman's rights convention. At this meeting a series of resolutions was adopted, demanding for women a larger sphere of action than the laws and customs of that day allowed. Since one of the resolutions called for enfranchisement, this meeting is usually considered the beginning of the woman suffrage movement.

After the convention adjourned, the delegates returned to their homes to form woman's rights societies. For many years, however, the agitation was confined almost entirely to the North. The Old South was not in sympathy with the philosophy of feminism, and it was not until after the Civil War that the woman's movement reached the South.

The first apparent interest in woman suffrage in Texas came at the constitutional convention of 1868. On July 8 of that year T. H. Mundine of Burleson County offered a declaration stating that all persons meeting age, residence, and citizenship requirements be deemed qualified electors "without distinction of sex." A motion to reject this declaration was tabled, and it was referred to the committee on state affairs.[1]

Several weeks passed without the committee's reporting. Finally on July 30, it recommended the adoption of Mundine's declaration in a report which stated that woman bore "her reasonable portion of the

[1] *Journal of the Reconstruction Convention, Which Met at Austin, Texas* (2 vols., Austin, 1870), I, 245.

I wish to thank Mrs. Jane Y. McCallum who graciously made her woman suffrage collection available to me. From 1927 to 1933 Mrs. McCallum served as secretary of state for Texas. She was the first person to hold that position for longer than four years.

burdens of government" and therefore should not be "denied the right of aiding in the enactment of its laws."[2] A minority report, however, urged the rejection of Mundine's declaration. Its signers stated that although they did not consider women less capable than men, they believed that women's influence would not be increased through enfranchisement. They declared that voting was "unwomanly" and that a "true" woman would shrink "from mingling in the busy noise of election days."[3]

The minority opinion ultimately prevailed, and in January, 1869, the convention rejected woman suffrage by a vote of 52 to 13.[4]

After this rejection, the issue remained dormant until the constitutional convention of 1875, during which two woman suffrage resolu-
476 tions were introduced and were referred to the committee on suffrage.[5] The committee recommended that voting privileges be extended to all male persons except minors, paupers, lunatics, felons, soldiers, and sailors. All other male persons could vote after meeting residence, age, and other requirements. Aliens could vote if they had lived in the state for one year and had declared their intention of becoming citizens. The report failed to mention women and therefore disposed of the question of woman suffrage by ignoring it.[6] On October 7, 1875, the convention adopted this report by a vote of 61 to 20.[7]

A few days before the report's adoption the convention received from Mrs. G. W. Hyatt of Eldorado a petition in behalf of women's enfranchisement. Her petition was referred to the committee on suffrage, but the committee took no action on it.[8] Concerning her petition, one member of the convention wrote Mrs. Hyatt that he knew of only two men in the convention who openly favored votes for women and that only "the fear of ignoring the right of petition, and gallantry

[2] *Journal of the Reconstruction Convention*, I, 578-79.

[3] *Ibid.*, 580.

[4] *Ibid.*, II, 414.

[5] *Journal of the Constitutional Convention of the State of Texas, Begun and Held at the City of Austin, September 6th, 1875* (Galveston, 1875), 92, 192.

[6] *Ibid.*, 238.

[7] *Ibid.*, 308.

[8] Seth Shepard McKay (ed.), *Debates in the Texas Constitutional Convention of 1875* (Austin, 1930), 142-43.

toward her sex on the part of a few, prevented the memorial from being summarily rejected."[9]

In the decade that followed little interest was shown in woman suffrage. In 1887, however, the state Woman's Christian Temperance Union endorsed it.[10] Temperance crusaders were inclined to favor enfranchisement because they thought women would vote for prohibition, and many women became suffragists as a result of their interest in temperance.

Meanwhile, throughout the nation the movement gained momentum. In 1890 the National American Woman Suffrage Association was formed through the amalgamation of the American Woman Suffrage Association and the National Woman Suffrage Association. Also in 1890, Wyoming became the first woman suffrage state, and three years later Colorado adopted woman suffrage.

In the spring of 1893 organized agitation began in Texas when Mrs. Rebecca Henry Hayes of Galveston issued a call for a convention of men and women to meet in Dallas to form a Texas Equal Rights Association. At this meeting forty-eight members organized the association, adopted a constitution, and elected officers. Mrs. Hayes was elected president and Mrs. S. L. Trumbull of Dallas, first vice-president.[11]

The objectives of the organization, which was to be an auxiliary of the National American Woman Suffrage Association, were to "advance the industrial, educational and equal rights of women, and to secure suffrage to them by appropriate State and National legislation." Local equal suffrage societies were to be organized as auxiliaries of the state association, and individuals could join it by paying annual dues of fifty cents. Membership was open to both men and women.[12]

[9] Elizabeth Cady Stanton and others (eds.), *History of Woman Suffrage* (6 vols., New York, 1881-1922), III, 804. Cited hereinafter as *History of Woman Suffrage.*

[10] Helen M. Stoddard, "Texas," *ibid.*, IV, 931.

[11] *Minutes of the First Session of the Texas Equal Rights Association, to which is appended the Constitution and By-Laws and a List of Charter Members* (n.p., n.d.), 2-3. This pamphlet is in the woman suffrage collection owned by Mrs. Jane Y. McCallum of Austin. In addition to her own papers, Mrs. McCallum's collection includes the papers of Minnie Fisher Cunningham, A. C. Ellis, Alice McFadin McAnulty, and Annette Finnigan.

[12] *Ibid.*, 9.

Each charter member was to act as a local organizer and to promote the cause "by means of suffrage literature and lectures."[13]

In October, 1893, a woman's congress was held in Dallas as a feature of the state fair. About three hundred women attended the congress, which was arranged by Dr. Ellen Lawson Dabbs, corresponding secretary of the Texas Equal Rights Association. Among the speakers was Mrs. Hayes, who delivered an address on "Women and the Ballot." In her speech Mrs. Hayes stated: "The ballot means to women the same as it means to men. It is the medium whereby we may clinch our convictions. It is a weapon, a power, a force whereby we may realize the highest form of self-government." She did not expect equal suffrage to purify politics: "I do not believe that the enfranchisement
478 of woman will bring about an instantaneous radical change in the condition of political, social, or religious affairs; but it is a move in the right direction." As long as all men over twenty-one years of age, not "paupers, criminals, or fools," could vote, it seemed but common justice that all women not similarly classed should be granted the franchise.[14]

Realizing that there was strength in organization, the suffrage leaders urged the formation of local societies. In April, 1893, a society of thirteen members had been organized in Denison. The club, the oldest in Texas, became an auxiliary of the state association. In July, 1893, a group at Taylor organized an equal rights society, and in November a similar society was formed at Granger. Dallas, Fort Worth, Belton, and San Antonio organized during the spring of 1894, making a total of seven local societies.[15]

In June, 1894, the state convention was held in Fort Worth with about fifty delegates in attendance. On this occasion several minor changes were made in the association's organization and officers for the coming year were elected. Mrs. Hayes was re-elected president and Mrs. Trumbull, vice-president.[16]

At one of their meetings the suffragists discussed some of the difficulties of their crusade. Mrs. Margaret L. Watson of Beaumont spoke

[13] Dallas *Morning News*, May 11, 1893. The charter membership consisted of thirty-nine women and nine men from twenty Texas towns.

[14] *Ibid.*, November 7, 1893.

[15] *Ibid.*, March 20, August 26, September 2, 9, 30, 1894.

[16] *Ibid.*, June 9, 1894.

of the problem of getting women interested and named ridicule as the most potent weapon against the movement. The cry of "short-haired women" and "long-haired men" kept many people from joining. Mrs. Elizabeth Fry of San Antonio blamed women themselves for their "condition of subjection" and charged that if "they would make a strong demand for their rights, they would get them." Mrs. Trumbull said that only through education could the movement succeed.[17]

Of the public addresses delivered at the convention, one of the most significant was that of Dr. Ellen Keller of Fort Worth. Dr. Keller stated that since women were citizens and were subject to the laws of the land they should be "permitted to help make the laws that govern them." Without equal suffrage, government was not of the people but of "one-half of the people." A just government should allow women to vote or cease to govern them. Voting would make women a "more important factor in the home" and a "more powerful influence in the state." Wherever women had been allowed to vote, they had lost none of their "womanly qualities," and no "social earthquakes" or "political convulsions" had resulted from their enfranchisement.[18]

After the convention adjourned, the suffragists continued their agitation. They organized a society at Beaumont, thereby increasing the number of local clubs to eight.[19] These societies usually met twice each month. Some meetings were for members only, while others were open to the public. The programs dealt with such topics as the legal status of women, parliamentary law, women's occupational opportunities, and current events.

Many individuals devoted time and effort to the movement. Mrs. Hayes traveled more than nine thousand miles in twenty months in the cause. Mrs. Alice McAnulty, Dr. Ellen Lawson Dabbs, Mrs. Elizabeth Fry, and Mrs. Mariana Folsom often spoke in its behalf. Dr. Grace Danforth, who had become a suffragist while studying medicine in Chicago, wrote newspaper articles on the subject. Many newspapers

[17] Clipping from Fort Worth *Gazette,* no date, in McCallum Collection.

[18] Dallas *Morning News,* June 9, 1894.

[19] National American Woman Suffrage Association, *Handbook . . . and Proceedings of the . . . Annual Convention* (Washington, 1884-1921), *1895,* p. 91. Cited hereinafter as N.A.W.S.A. *Proceedings.*

published accounts of suffrage activities, and the Dallas *Morning News* published a weekly suffrage column entitled "Women in Public."

In 1894 the Dallas *Morning News* and the San Antonio *Express* published the opinions of Texas men on woman suffrage. Of the men interviewed, twenty-eight opposed enfranchisement of women and eleven favored it. Those who opposed it maintained that women were already adequately represented by men. Woman suffrage would break up the home and destroy chivalry. It violated the Biblical teachings of the subjection of women. It would mean the enfranchisement of Negro women, and the race problem in the South would thereby be aggravated. Women should not expect to exercise all of the privileges of citizenship because they could not help to defend the country
480 by serving in the armed forces. The men who favored equal suffrage argued that women were taxed without representation, they were mentally and morally qualified to vote, and their enfranchisement would have a salutary effect on politics.[20]

About this same time an *Express* reporter questioned a group of San Antonio women about their attitude toward suffrage. Of those questioned, ten opposed and eleven favored votes for women. The opponents stated that women were willing to let men make the laws, that women had enough rights already, and that they were too preoccupied with home duties to vote. They feared that enfranchisement would destroy chivalry and degrade womanhood. One antisuffragist stated: "God forbid that the day will come when we will see women turned loose upon the nation, a set of raving, tearing politicians, standing elbow to elbow with the rabble and the toughs; unsexing themselves to the detriment of the home and of all social and domestic relations." The advocates of woman suffrage stated that women should be allowed to vote because they obeyed the laws and paid taxes and because they should be the political equals of Negroes and Mexicans. Enfranchisement would bring "new dignity and honor" for women. "If a vote means so much to a man, it certainly ought to be of some benefit to a woman," commented one advocate of enfranchisement.[21]

During the summer of 1894 Texas suffragists endeavored to secure

[20] Dallas *Morning News*, March 20, 1894; San Antonio *Express*, July 29, 1894.
[21] San Antonio *Express*, July 22, 1894.

equal suffrage planks in the state Democratic, Republican, and Populist party platforms. Mrs. L. A. Craig, president of the Dallas society, addressed the Democratic convention, which gave her a courteous hearing but did not endorse votes for women.[22] Mrs. Alice M. McAnulty of Circleville and Mrs. Elizabeth Fry of San Antonio appealed to the Populist convention, but without success.[23] Mrs. B. M. Burchill of Fort Worth had been delegated to attend the Republican state convention but was unable to do so. A written appeal was sent, but it was not adopted by the convention.[24]

In the spring of 1895 A. C. Tompkins of Hempstead introduced the first woman suffrage measure in the Texas House of Representatives. His resolution to enfranchise women by amending the state constitution was referred to the committee on constitutional amendments but was never reported.[25]

Late in 1894 the Texas Equal Rights Association almost split over the question of inviting Susan B. Anthony to lecture in the state. The issue had been introduced in that year's state convention and had provoked much heated discussion. Those who wanted to bring Miss Anthony to Texas argued that her lectures would be a great stimulus to the movement. Others contended that the time was not opportune and that suffrage work should be conducted by Texas women, not by outsiders. The convention adjourned without settling the question, leaving the decision to the state executive committee.[26]

Sometime later the association's president, Mrs. Hayes, announced that she would not support a Texas tour by Miss Anthony and would oppose her coming regardless of what the state executive committee decided. Thereupon the committee declared that Mrs. Hayes by her statement had forfeited her office, and in cognizance of the fact they proceeded to elect Mrs. Elizabeth A. Fry president. Mrs. Hayes refused, however, to recognize the presidency of Mrs. Fry, and she maintained that the committee had no authority to depose her.[27]

[22] Dallas *Morning News*, August 18, 1894.

[23] Stoddard, "Texas," 931.

[24] Dallas *Morning News*, September 2, 1894.

[25] Texas Legislature, *House Journal*, Regular Session, 1895, p. 514. All House and Senate *Journals* hereinafter cited are those of the Texas legislature.

[26] Dallas *Morning News*, June 9, 1894.

[27] *Ibid.*, November 4, December 16, 1894.

For a while the Texas Equal Rights Association found itself in the awkward position of having two presidents. Finally Mrs. Fry acceded, and when the state convention assembled in Dallas in June, 1895, Mrs. Hayes occupied the president's chair. When the convention elected officers for the coming year, a few delegates voted for Mrs. Hayes, but Mrs. Elizabeth Good Houston of Dallas was elected president. Other officers were Mrs. Belle M. Burchill of Fort Worth, vice-president, and Miss Hattie Brewer of Dallas, treasurer.[28]

During the first few months of her presidency Mrs. Houston visited several Texas cities and arranged two suffrage days to be held in connection with the state fair in Dallas. She appointed ten "county presidents" who were "to organize one central and sufficient local clubs . . .
482 to advance the cause of equal suffrage" in their counties.[29]

In spite of these activities, the movement began to decline, and after 1895 suffrage news gradually ceased to appear in the Texas newspapers. The local societies became inactive, and reports from Texas disappeared from the publications of the national suffrage association. By the end of 1896 the Texas Equal Rights Association had ceased to function. Perhaps its decline resulted from the loss of Mrs. Hayes's leadership. Perhaps the movement had been premature from the beginning. In any event, woman suffrage remained a dormant issue during the remainder of the nineteenth century.

Early in the twentieth century the movement was revived when Annette Finnigan and her sisters, Elizabeth and Katherine, organized an equal suffrage league in Houston in February, 1903. About fifty people attended the organizational meeting, at which Annette Finnigan was elected president.[30] A few weeks later this club sponsored a lecture by Carrie Chapman Catt, president of the National American Woman Suffrage Association. Mrs. Catt's lecture was described as "an eloquent and brilliant presentation of the cause of woman suffrage" and was reported to have been well attended.[31]

The Houston suffragists undertook to organize a league in the neigh-

[28] *Ibid.*, June 8, 1895.

[29] *Ibid.*, September 29, October 13, November 17, 1895.

[30] Annette Finnigan, "Outline of History of Woman Suffrage in Texas," MS., in McCallum Collection.

[31] Houston *Chronicle*, March 31, 1903.

boring city of Galveston. They arranged several parlor meetings and formed a club of twenty-five members.[32]

By December, 1903, the membership of the Houston league had increased to seventy-five, and its leaders felt sufficiently encouraged to form a state association. At a two-day convention in Houston the Texas Woman Suffrage Association was organized, with Annette Finnigan as president and Mrs. C. H. Moore of Galveston as vice-president. In their business sessions the women discussed ways of advancing their cause and announced their intention of organizing clubs in every section of the state. The convention's most outstanding speaker was Anna Howard Shaw, who delivered a public lecture on the "Disfranchisement of Women." About five hundred people attended her lecture.[33] 483

During the next year Miss Finnigan attempted unsuccessfully to organize leagues in Beaumont, San Antonio, and Austin. She reported that she found the women "interested" but "too timid to organize." She succeeded, however, in forming a suffrage committee in La Porte.[34]

In December, 1904, a state convention was held in Houston with delegates from Galveston, Houston, and La Porte in attendance. This convention was essentially a conference, and it received little public attention. Many reports were given, and Annette Finnigan was reelected president.[35]

The next year Annette Finnigan and her sisters moved from Texas, and without their leadership suffrage activity declined. The leagues gradually ceased to hold regular meetings, and no further state conventions were held. Once again the suffrage issue had become dormant.

Evidence of renewed interest appeared in 1908 when Anna Howard Shaw gave a series of lectures in Texas under the auspices of the Woman's Clubs. She spoke in Dallas, Austin, San Antonio, and in several other Texas cities. In San Antonio she attacked the legal discriminations against women and urged women's enfranchisement. She considered women "entirely fitted for suffrage" and denied that voting was unladylike. "The depositing of a ballot in the box would not be

[32] N.A.W.S.A. *Proceedings, 1904,* pp. 99-100.

[33] Houston *Post,* December 10, 1903.

[34] Finnigan, "Woman Suffrage in Texas," MS., in McCallum Collection.

[35] *Ibid.*

more unladylike than the depositing of a letter in the postoffice," she said.[36] In Austin she "submitted a very conclusive argument why women should be given the right to vote" and "closed her talk with a plea for government that was really representative and reflected the voice of the people."[37]

A few months later twenty-five persons organized a woman suffrage club in Austin. Within a few weeks it had forty-six members. This club did not attempt to form a state association, nor did it affiliate with the National American Woman Suffrage Association. It maintained its local organization, however, and for several years was the only woman suffrage society in Texas. Its membership in 1911 was fifty-four.[38]

484 The Austin league remained the only woman suffrage club in Texas until February, 1912, when a society of seventy-five women was organized in San Antonio, with Eleanor Brackenridge as president. The society's purpose was "to create a public sentiment in favor of 'votes for women' and to enlist all progressive women in the cause."[39] This organization held frequent meetings and by March 31, 1912, had increased its membership to 144. Interest was further stimulated when Anna Howard Shaw visited San Antonio in May and delivered a public address on woman suffrage.[40] By November, 1912, the society had almost four hundred members and had distributed fifteen thousand pieces of literature.[41]

In April, 1913, Texas suffragists held their first state convention since 1904, when about 150 women and a "sprinkling" of men assembled at the St. Anthony Hotel in San Antonio. Seven Texas cities were represented,[42] and Eleanor Brackenridge was elected state president. The convention's only dissension arose over the endorsement of the proposed federal woman suffrage amendment. Some of the suffragists opposed it as an infringement on the rights of the states. Opinion favoring the federal amendment prevailed, however, and the conven-

[36] San Antonio *Express*, April 28, 1908.
[37] Austin *Statesman*, April 25, 1908.
[38] Mrs. W. L. Duncan's notebook in McCallum Collection.
[39] San Antonio *Express*, February 19, 1912.
[40] *Ibid.*, March 31, May 18, 1912.
[41] N.A.W.S.A. *Proceedings, 1912*, no page number.
[42] Galveston, San Antonio, Dallas, Houston, Austin, Temple, and Del Rio.

tion adopted a resolution urging Congress to pass it. Several prominent persons addressed the convention. Its most distinguished speaker was Mrs. Philip Snowden, a member of the British National Equal Suffrage Association, who reviewed the history of the movement in England.[43]

After 1913 the Texas Woman Suffrage Association held a state convention each year. At its 1914 meeting in Dallas eight local societies were represented. The delegates listened to speeches, planned an educational and organizational campaign, and elected Annette Finnigan, who had returned to Texas, state president. Eleanor Brackenridge was elected honorary president for life.[44] The next year at Galveston the association announced that there were twenty-one local societies in
Texas with a total of 2,500 members. The suffragists pledged $1,600 485
for the promotion of their work and elected Minnie Fisher Cunningham of Galveston state president.[45] A few months later the movement received additional encouragement when the Texas Federation of Women's Clubs endorsed equal suffrage.[46]

At their state convention in Dallas in 1916 the suffragists adopted a new constitution and changed the name of their organization from Texas Woman Suffrage Association to Texas Equal Suffrage Association. They passed a resolution asking the state Democratic convention to include a woman suffrage plank in the party platform and re-elected Mrs. Cunningham state president.[47] Subsequent conventions in Waco (1917) and Austin (1918) re-elected Mrs. Cunningham, who served as state president during the remainder of the movement in Texas.

During 1916 the suffragists focused their attention on organizational activities, and consequently the number of local societies increased rapidly. The state association advised its workers that "home meetings of a few convinced people were better than larger, general meetings for

[43] Dallas *Morning News*, April 2, 3, 1913.

[44] *Ibid.*, April 9, 10, 1914.

[45] *Ibid.*, May 15, 1915.

[46] *Ibid.*, November 11, 1915. In December, 1915, Minnie Fisher Cunningham reported to the national association: "The press of the State is with us, as are the Federation of Labor, the Federation of Women's Clubs, the Farmer's Institute, the Farmer's Congress, the Texas Farm Women, the Texas Press Women, and the W.C.T.U." See N.A.W.S.A. *Proceedings, 1915*, p. 124.

[47] Jane Y. McCallum, "Texas," in *History of Woman Suffrage*, VI, 632; Dallas *Morning News*, May 13, 1916.

the purpose of organizing." It urged the workers to keep their speeches brief and to "touch on the need of mothers for the ballot for the protection of the home and children." The advantages of having an organization were to be explained and an election of officers held. The organizers were told never to engage in "heated arguments" with antisuffragists but to "hear them courteously and attentively, take their names and addresses and have literature sent them bearing on the special point to which they were opposed."[48] So effective was this organizational work that by May, 1916, the number of local societies had increased to eighty,[49] and by June, 1918, there were ninety-eight.[50]

The local societies played an important part in the votes-for-women movement, for on them rested the chief responsibility for promoting
486 favorable sentiment in their communities. These societies endeavored to make more efficient workers of their own members through lectures and discussions on the status of women and on the nature of politics and government. Sometimes they conducted "suffrage schools" in which women were instructed in public speaking, organizational methods, and campaign techniques. They sponsored public speeches, open forums, mass meetings, house-to-house canvasses, parades, and suffrage booths at fairs. They wrote letters and sent petitions to state legislators and to congressmen and gave benefits to raise money for their own treasuries and for donations to the state association.

An important function of both the local and state organizations was the distribution of literature, and many pamphlets and leaflets were

[48] "Points in Organizational Work," MS., in McCallum Collection.

[49] Dallas *Morning News*, May 8, 1916.

[50] There were equal suffrage societies in the following Texas cities: Amarillo, Athens, Austin, Bay City, Beaumont, Blessing, Blooming Grove, Brazoria, Brownsville, Bryan, Burnet, Calvert, Carrollton, Carthage, Cedar Hill, Cleburne, Columbus, Corpus Christi, Corsicana, Creedmoor, Cuero, Dallas, Dawson, Dayton, Denison, De Soto, Dickinson, Duncanville, Elgin, Elkhart, El Campo, El Paso, Farmers Branch, Floresville, Fort Worth, Franklin, Fredericksburg, Frost, Gainesville, Galveston, Garland, Georgetown, Goldthwaite, Gonzales, Grand Prairie, Houston, Hearne, Hico, Hitchcock, Hungerford, Huntsville, Hutchins, Kemah, Kerens, Kleberg, Kountze, Lampasas, Lancaster, Laredo, League City, Malakoff, Manor, Markham, Marshall, Mason, Mexia, Midfields, Mineola, Nacogdoches, Orange, Palacios, Palestine, Paris, Port Arthur, Port Lavaca, Purdon, Refugio, Richardson, Rockdale, Rosenberg, San Antonio, San Augustine, San Benito, San Marcos, Seagoville, Sherman, Swan, Taylor, Temple, Terrell, Texarkana, Texas City, Tyler, Waco, Waxahachie, Wharton, Woodville, and Wortham. In San Antonio and Georgetown there were men's leagues for woman suffrage.

circulated in Texas. One leaflet, for example, told "Why Women Want to Vote." It stated:

> WORKING WOMEN need the ballot to regulate conditions under which they work.
> HOUSEKEEPERS need the ballot to regulate the sanitary conditions under which they and their families must live.
> MOTHERS need the ballot to regulate the moral conditions under which their children must be brought up.
> TEACHERS need the ballot to secure just wages and to influence the management of the public schools.
> BUSINESS WOMEN need the ballot to secure for themselves a fair opportunity in their business.
> TAX PAYING WOMEN need the ballot to protect their property.
> ALL WOMEN need the ballot because they are concerned equally with men in 487
> good and bad government; and equally responsible for civic righteousness.
> ALL MEN need women's help to build a better and juster government and
> WOMEN need MEN to help them secure their right to fulfill their civic duties.[51]

Another leaflet, "Women in the Home," stated: "Women are, by nature and training, housekeepers. Let them have a hand in the city's housekeeping, even if they introduce an occasional house-cleaning."[52] Other leaflets quoted "Eminent People" who favored woman suffrage, told "Why Working Women Need the Vote," and explained "The Political Duties of Mothers."

After the United States entered the first World War, the suffragists participated actively in war work.[53] They sold liberty bonds, planted victory gardens, knitted, sewed, maintained Red Cross auxiliaries, and promoted the war effort in every possible way. Mrs. Cunningham acted as state chairman of the Texas Woman's Anti-Vice Committee, organized to work for the improvement of moral conditions in the vicinities of army camps. Other prominent suffragists were leaders on the home front also. Woman's role in the war effort won many supporters for suffrage. It helped refute the argument that women should not vote because they could not bear arms in defense of their country. Many people began to ask: "Since women are helping to win the war, why shouldn't they vote?"

[51] "Why Women Want to Vote," in McCallum Collection.
[52] "Women in the Home," *ibid.*
[53] McCallum, "Texas," 635-37.

The suffragists realized the psychological value of the war activities of women. One of their leaflets stated: "The country is asking of women service as farmers, mechanics, nurses, doctors, munition workers, etc. . . . Women are asking of the country THE VOTE. Are the Women Going to Get It?"[54] The Texas association distributed a card in the shape of a liberty beil on which was printed: "Women are helping bring Democracy to Europe. Will you help ring the liberty bell for Texas Woman?"[55] Undoubtedly the war hastened the adoption of woman suffrage.

Prior to 1916 the only state suffrage organization in Texas was the Texas Equal Suffrage Association, an affiliate of the National American Woman Suffrage Association. In January of that year, however, the
488 National Woman's Party organized a branch in Texas. The National Woman's Party, originally named the Congressional Union for Woman Suffrage, was led by Alice Paul and differed from the National American Woman Suffrage Association mainly in its attitude toward militancy. Alice Paul, who had campaigned with Mrs. Emmeline Pankhurst in England, favored picketing the White House and other militant tactics. The Texas branch of the National Woman's Party was organized in Houston, and Mrs. Clara Snell Wolfe of Austin was elected state chairman. One hundred charter members were enrolled.[56]

Mrs. Wolfe announced plans for organizing the state along congressional district lines. She was never wholly successful, however, and as late as June, 1918, had secured chairmen for only seven districts.[57] Although the Woman's Party brought to the state several prominent speakers, such as Alice Paul and Doris Stevens, it did not win much favor in Texas. Many people disapproved the militant activities of its national leaders, and the Texas Equal Suffrage Association, the Dallas suffrage society, and others issued statements opposing militancy.[58]

Not until 1915 did the opponents of woman suffrage decide to organize. In March of that year they formed a Texas division of the Na-

[54] "As a War Measure," in McCallum Collection.

[55] "Liberty Bell," *ibid.*

[56] *Suffragist* (Washington, 1913-1921), IV (January 29, 1916), 5.

[57] *Ibid.*, VI (June 29, 1918), 4.

[58] The Texas branch of the National Woman's Party announced its approval of militancy but did not stage any militant demonstrations in the state. Militant suffragism was seldom found outside of the nation's capital and a few large cities in the North.

tional Association Opposed to Woman Suffrage. Mrs. James B. Wells of Brownsville was elected president. The announced purpose of the organization was to tell the people "of the evils which would follow the adoption of a scheme to force upon the Women of Texas the political duties and responsibilities of citizenship."[59]

Although the "antis" announced plans for an extensive organization, they did little actual organizing. They apparently held no state conventions and formed no local auxiliaries. They did, however, distribute antisuffrage literature. One such leaflet, entitled "Votes for Women Means Jury Duty for Women," stated:

> Women in the Suffrage States are serving on juries in murder cases, commercialized vice cases, and whiskey cases.
>
> It must be a grand and glorious feeling for a woman to be drawn as a juror on a murder case, likely to last two months, when the children of the family have contracted the measles.[60]

Other leaflets stated that woman suffrage and socialism went "hand in hand," that women already had adequate legal rights, and that woman suffrage would result in Negro rule in those sections of the South where colored women outnumbered white women.[61]

The Texas legislature took its first vote on woman suffrage during its regular session in 1915.[62] On January 18 Frank H. Burmeister and others introduced a resolution "to authorize females to vote." This resolution was referred to the committee on constitutional amendments, which recommended that it be passed.[63] In the House debate on February 23 W. T. Bagby, leader of the opposition, declared that woman suffrage was contrary to the laws of nature and the Bible. He main-

[59] "Plan of Organization for the Texas Association Opposed to Woman Suffrage," in McCallum Collection.

[60] "Votes for Women Means Jury Duty for Women," *ibid.*

[61] See antisuffrage leaflets in McCallum Collection. Woman suffrage was opposed also by the antiprohibitionists. Although the suffrage association took no official stand regarding prohibition, the general feeling was that woman suffrage was the handmaiden of prohibition. Suffrage leaders in Texas and other states spoke of having to fight the "liquor interests." See Carrie Chapman Catt and Nettie Rogers Shuler, *Woman Suffrage and Politics: The Inner Story of the Suffrage Movement* (New York, 1923), 132-59.

[62] Woman suffrage resolutions had been introduced in 1911 and 1913 but had not been voted upon.

[63] *House Journal*, Regular Session, 1915, pp. 103, 218. During this and subsequent legislative sessions the state suffrage association established headquarters and maintained active lobbies in Austin.

tained that it indicated an "abnormal condition of the mind" and was "allied to Socialism." He concluded by stating that women should not vote because "woman's place was in the home."[64] Other antisuffrage legislators stated that the ballot was not a right but a privilege and that suffrage would "lower" woman and "rob her of those modest charms so dear to us Southern men."[65]

The proponents of the measure countered that women did want to vote, that their disfranchisement was unjust, and that the antisuffrage arguments were ridiculous. When the House vote was taken, 90 legislators voted yea and 32 nay, 19 not voting. The resolution failed by four to receive the two-thirds vote of the whole membership required for a constitutional amendment.[66] During the same legislative session
490 a woman suffrage resolution was introduced in the Senate, but that body took no action on it.

On January 13, 1917, Jess Baker and others introduced in the House a resolution to enfranchise women by a state constitutional amendment. Six days later the committee on constitutional amendments recommended that the resolution be adopted.[67] In the ensuing debate its opponents maintained that women did not want to vote, that woman suffrage was only a fad, that it would undermine the family, and that it would mean the enfranchisement of Negro women. The leading supporter of the resolution, Baker, summarized the arguments in its favor as follows:

> Remember that the women are one-half of the human race, and, therefore, are entitled by inherent right to all the privileges accorded to men. Many women are taxpayers and should have a vote in the election of officials who make and execute laws. Women are eligible to nearly all the offices in Texas, and why shall they not be allowed to vote?
>
> Our present Constitution classes our women, as far as the franchise is concerned with children, idiots, lunatics, paupers and felony convicts. We are only asking you to submit an amendment of the Constitution to the qualified voters of the entire State, which shall take our women out of the above mentioned classes and lift them to a higher plane, where their intelligence and patriotism may have full play.[68]

[64] Dallas *Morning News*, February 24, 1915.
[65] *House Journal*, Regular Session, 1915, p. 617.
[66] *Ibid.*, 617, 846; Dallas *Morning News*, February 24, 1915.
[67] *House Journal*, 1917, pp. 80, 217.
[68] *Ibid.*, 435.

When the House voted on the resolution, 76 legislators voted for it, and 56 voted against it.[69] The measure did not receive the necessary two-thirds favorable majority and failed therefore to be adopted. A similar resolution in the Senate never came to a vote. Bills to allow women to vote in primary elections and to vote for presidential electors were proposed but were not voted upon by either house.

During the next summer Governor James E. Ferguson was impeached and removed from office. Lieutenant Governor W. P. Hobby then became governor of Texas. The suffragists rejoiced over the removal of Ferguson, whom they considered the "implacable foe of woman suffrage and of every great moral issue for which women stood."[70] They believed that his removal had increased their chances of favorable legislation.

In 1918 the suffragists focused their attention on primary suffrage for 491
women. Since primary suffrage could be conferred simply by a legislative act, it was more easily obtainable than full suffrage which could be gained only by a resolution passed by both houses by two-thirds majorities and then ratified by a majority of Texas voters. At a special session in March, 1918, Governor Hobby submitted the "subject of amending the election laws," and a bill providing primary suffrage for women was then introduced by C. B. Metcalfe of San Angelo. On March 12 this measure passed the House by a vote of 84 to 34, and a few days later the Senate adopted it by a majority of 18 to 4.[71] Governor Hobby signed it, and primary suffrage for women became legal in Texas.[72]

The primary suffrage act had exempted women from paying the poll tax in 1918, and therefore they were eligible to vote in the primary in July of that year. They were required to register, however, and only seventeen days remained for that purpose.[73] The state suffrage association urged women to register and endeavored to acquaint them with the nature of voting. A contemporary described the association's activity

[69] *Ibid.*, 436.

[70] McCallum, "Texas," 634.

[71] *House Journal*, Fourth Called Session, 1918, p. 335; *Senate Journal*, Fourth Called Session, 1918, p. 355.

[72] President Woodrow Wilson favored primary suffrage for Texas women. In a letter to Mrs. Elizabeth Herndon Potter, March 8, 1918, he stated: "I feel it a privilege to express my earnest hope that the Legislature of Texas may see its way to adopt a statute which will give women the right to vote in the primaries." In McCallum Collection.

[73] During the seventeen days approximately 386,000 women registered.

as follows: "The suffrage association set to work to assist the new citizens. Omitting only the words 'Official Ballot', nearly half a million reproductions of the long, complicated ballot to be used in the July primaries were circulated; candidates' records were scrutinized; issues were studied; and 'schools of instruction' were conducted all over the State."[74]

The suffragists favored W. P. Hobby for governor and organized "Hobby Clubs" to work for his election. They also supported Annie Webb Blanton for state superintendent of public instruction. Both were elected.

After the 1918 primary election women began to participate actively in Texas politics. Since Texas was a one-party state, primary suffrage
492 was almost tantamount to complete enfranchisement. Women attended party conventions, and in August, 1918, 233 Democratic county conventions endorsed woman suffrage. In September the state Democratic convention meeting in Waco went on record in favor of both the state and federal woman suffrage amendments.[75]

Soon there developed a movement to enfranchise women by an amendment to the state constitution. The plan was for the legislature to adopt a woman suffrage resolution, which would be submitted for ratification in the late spring of 1919. Many Texans favored this plan, but for reasons of strategy Mrs. Cunningham and other suffrage leaders opposed it. They thought that the federal suffrage amendment would probably be approved by Congress during 1919 and preferred therefore to concentrate their efforts in its behalf.

Nevertheless, when the legislature assembled in January, 1919, Governor Hobby recommended that the state election laws be amended to enfranchise women on equal terms with men. He recommended also the disfranchisement of aliens, who under existing law had full voting privileges. A resolution complying with his request passed the Senate

[74] McCallum, "Texas," 638.

[75] Dallas *Morning News*, September 4, 1918. This section of the party platform stated: "We recommend that the Legislature submit an amendment to the State constitution giving women the right of suffrage on the same terms as men. We favor the submission of an amendment to the Federal constitution to the various Legislatures giving the right of suffrage to women on the same terms as men and that the Legislature ratify the same when so submitted."

by a vote of 28 to 0, and the House by a vote of 105 to 0.[76] The resolution was to be submitted to the voters of Texas on May 24, 1919. Unfortunately, the enfranchisement of women and the disfranchisement of aliens were both contained in the same resolution. These two propositions could not be voted upon separately; a voter had to accept or reject both. Ironically, women could not vote on the proposed amendment, since they had only primary suffrage, but aliens, who were then fully enfranchised, could vote on it.

The suffragists planned an intensive crusade to secure ratification. Mrs. Cunningham, who was in Washington lobbying for the federal amendment, returned to Texas to aid in the campaign. Mrs. Jane Y. McCallum, a member of the state executive committee and a former president of the Austin society, acted as director of publicity. Mrs. McCallum was an experienced newspaperwoman and proved to be a competent director.

Publicity was the key to the entire campaign, and the suffragists employed many devices to obtain it.[77] They held mass meetings, circulated petitions, and made house-to-house canvasses. They established suffrage booths in department stores and theater lobbies. They asked ministers to endorse woman suffrage in their Mother's Day sermons. They delivered five-minute talks before clubs and other groups and sponsored public lectures. It was estimated that there were almost fifteen hundred speakers in the field during the campaign.[78] Most of them were Texas men and women, but a few, such as Anna Howard Shaw, came from outside the state.

The distribution of literature was another important phase of this campaign. The suffragists distributed more than 200,000 copies of the *Texas Democrat*, a suffrage newspaper edited by Dr. A. C. Ellis of the University of Texas. They circulated more than three million leaflets, many of which were reprinted in Texas newspapers. One leaflet, en-

[76] *Senate Journal*, Regular Session, 1919, p. 120; *House Journal*, Regular Session, 1919, p. 188.

[77] The campaign was well organized. There were chairmen for the senatorial districts, counties, and precincts. Mrs. McCallum sent them mimeographed outlines of their duties and furnished detailed advice on effective methods of securing publicity in local newspapers.

[78] Report on Organization of the Campaign, May 24, 1919, MS., in McCallum Collection.

titled "Men of Texas," stated: "The women of Texas need your help on May 24. . . . The door of citizenship is and always has been open to the alien by the simple process of naturalization. The door of citizenship to loyal American women who by their service helped you win the war is closed unless your chivalry opens it for us with your vote on May 24th."[79] Another leaflet stated:

We Believe
That "governments derive their just powers from the consent of the governed."
We Believe
That women are people and are governed.
We Believe
That no state can be a true democracy in which one-half of the people are denied the right to vote.
494 *We Believe*
That women need the vote *for the same reason* that men need it.
We Believe
That because laws regulate a woman's life and the lives of her children, and because they tax her property and may even sentence her to death, she should have the right to share in the making of the laws.[80]

A leaflet entitled "Who Represents Her?" asked:

IF a woman is responsible for an accident, if she defaults on her contracts, if she slanders her neighbors, is any man arrested, sued, and bound over to keep the peace?
IF a woman steals from her employer, does her father, husband, brother or son serve out her term in prison?
IF a woman kills somebody, what man represents her in the prisoner's dock during her trial? What man represents her in the electric chair, if she is convicted?
IF a widow or an unmarried woman fails to pay her taxes, is the property of a male relative or of the man next door sold to satisfy the debt to the State?
IF a woman forges a check, does her father, her husband, her employer, go to jail for felony?
WHY is it that the only place in the world where a man wants to represent woman is at the ballot box?[81]

The suffragists valued endorsements by prominent persons. President Woodrow Wilson cabled from Paris that he entertained "the confident hope that the men of Texas would by very great majority render gallant

[79] "Men of Texas," *ibid.*
[80] "True Democracy," *ibid.*
[81] "Who Represents Her?" *ibid.*

justice to the women of the state." Both of Texas' United States senators, C. A. Culberson and Morris Sheppard, urged the approval of the amendment. Many state officials, religious leaders, educators, businessmen, and others endorsed it.

Meanwhile, the antisuffragists were conducting a campaign against the proposed amendment. Mrs. James B. Wells, leader of the "antis," was assisted by Mrs. Ida M. Darden of Fort Worth, who acted as publicity director. They were joined by Mrs. James W. Wadsworth and Miss Charlotte Rowe, both of New York. Mrs. Wadsworth was president of the National Association Opposed to Woman Suffrage, and Miss Rowe was a national field worker.[82] They invited all women who "loved their homes" to join them.

The "antis" distributed more than 100,000 pieces of literature. They 495
advanced the time-worn arguments that women did not want to vote and that their enfranchisement would destroy the home. They insisted also that woman suffrage would lead to socialism and to Negro domination of the South. They said that only two types of women wanted to vote—socialists and Negroes—and predicted that Texas would never adopt woman suffrage.[83]

The suffragists, who had adopted the policy of ignoring the arguments of their opponents, finally decided to answer them, and Mrs. Cunningham and Senator Sheppard published statements in refutation. Both of these statements were widely circulated.

On May 24, 1919, the votes on the proposed amendment were cast. Early returns indicated that woman suffrage was leading. As more precincts reported, however, the woman suffrage majority began to diminish. Final returns showed that it had been defeated by a majority of 25,000 votes.[84]

Many persons immediately concluded that Texas had repudiated woman suffrage. Some said that the primary suffrage act should be repealed. Others maintained that under no circumstances should the legislature ratify the federal suffrage amendment. The suffragists, however, denied that the vote constituted a mandate and maintained that the issue had been confused by the inclusion of the citizenship requirement. They

[82] McCallum, "Texas," 641.

[83] Fort Worth *Star-Telegram*, April 2, 1919.

[84] Dallas *Morning News*, June 15, 1919.

published a leaflet in which returns were analyzed, showing that counties with large alien populations returned large majorities against the proposed amendment.[85] They argued that the alien vote had defeated the amendment and that the state legislature was still bound by the suffrage plank adopted at the state Democratic convention in Waco.

Early in June the federal woman suffrage amendment was submitted to the states for ratification, and Texas suffragists urged the legislature to approve it.[86] Governor Hobby called a special session to convene on June 23. On that day ratification resolutions were introduced in both houses. The House resolution received immediate committee approval, and it was adopted the following day by a vote of 96 to 21.[87]

The Senate resolution received a favorable committee report on June
496 23, but five days passed before it came to a vote. Many senators urged that no action be taken until a referendum could be held and the voters given a chance to express their preference. By the afternoon of June 27, however, it had become evident that most of the Senate favored ratification. The resolution received final approval on the morning of June 28, when the Senate adopted it by a voice vote.[88] Thus Texas became the ninth state in the Union and the first state in the South to ratify the nineteenth amendment.

The ratification of the federal amendment ended the woman suffrage movement in Texas. During the remainder of 1919 thirteen other states approved it. Other ratifications followed in 1920, and with Tennessee's ratification in August of that year the required three fourths of the states was realized. Woman suffrage then became part of the supreme law of the land, and the movement thereby reached its successful conclusion.

[85] "Many Factors Contributed to the Apparent Defeat of Suffrage," in McCallum Collection.

[86] At its regular session the thirty-sixth legislature had adopted a resolution urging Congress to submit this amendment to the states.

[87] *House Journal*, Second Called Session, 1919, p. 102.

[88] *Senate Journal*, Second Called Session, 1919, p. 52.

REYNOLDS v. UNITED STATES: NINETEENTH-CENTURY FORMS OF MARRIAGE AND THE STATUS OF WOMEN

by Carol Weisbrod and Pamela Sheingorn***

INTRODUCTION

This article suggests a social context for the Supreme Court's late nineteenth-century anti-polygamy case, *Reynolds v. United States*,[1] in which the Court held that the first amendment's free exercise clause was not a defense to a prosecution for bigamy.[2] At the time the *Reynolds* case came down questions relating to the role and status of women were integral to the widespread debate over nonmonogamous domestic institutions. The *Reynolds* opinion was decisive legal reaction against certain elements in American society, Mormon polygamy —coexisting with woman suffrage in Utah[3]—and complex marriage at

---

* J.D., Columbia University (1961); Associate Professor of Law, University of Connecticut School of Law.

** Ph.D., University of Wisconsin (1974); Assistant Professor of Art, Baruch College, C.U.N.Y.

The authors are indebted to Jan Deutsch, Jane Isay, Dorothy Lipson, Leon Lipson, Ellen Peters, and Barbara Underwood for their assistance. Errors are our own. Carol Weisbrod's research was supported in part by a grant from the Johnson Fund of the American Philosophical Society.

1. Reynolds v. United States, 98 U.S. 145 (1878) [cited as 1878, although the decision was announced Jan. 6, 1879].

2. For recent discussions of the case, see Davis, *Plural Marriage and Religious Freedom: The Impact of Reynolds v. United States*, 15 ARIZ. L. REV. 287 (1973) [hereinafter cited as Davis, *Impact*]; Davis, *The Polygamous Prelude*, 6 AM. J. LEGAL HIST. (1962) [hereinafter cited as Davis, *Prelude*]; Linford, *The Mormons and the Law: The Polygamy Cases* (pts. 1-2), 9 UTAH L. REV. 308, 543 (1964, 1965). For an argument that the *Reynolds* case is "wrong" *see* Freeman, *A Remonstrance for Conscience*, 106 U. PA. L. REV. 806, 822-26 (1958). *Compare* Cleveland v. United States, 329 U.S. 14, 20 (1946) (Douglas, J.) (upholding conviction under the Mann Act of a Mormon polygamist), *with* Justice Douglas' opinion in Wisconsin v. Yoder, 406 U.S. 205, 247 (1972) (concurring and dissenting in part).

3. Kraditor has reviewed the early history of American woman suffrage:

> In 1838 Kentucky had given its women, under certain conditions, the right to vote in school elections, but it was not until 1861 that the second state, Kansas, adopted school suffrage. Michigan and Minnesota adopted a similar reform in 1875 . . . . [T]he territory of Wyoming decreed full political equality in 1869 . . . .

Oneida,[4] which seemed at the time to threaten the stability of the family.[5] *Reynolds* did not rest solely on the proposition that polygamy and monogamy are alternate forms of marriage and that a multiplicity of forms need not be tolerated. The case was based on the idea that polygamy was a social evil. Plural marriage was viewed in the nineteenth century as an attack on traditional marital institutions and an affront, if not a threat, to the existing social structure. The opposition to the Mormons and the Oneida Perfectionists was rooted in part in the common belief that women were degraded in nonmonogamous systems.[6]

Some nineteenth-century concerns about the status of women

A. KRADITOR, THE IDEAS OF THE WOMAN SUFFRAGE MOVEMENT, 1890-1920, at 3 (Anchor ed. 1971).

Wyoming's enactment of woman suffrage, which included the right to hold office, was
498 followed by the action of the Utah Territory (Feb. 12, 1870) giving women the franchise but not the right to hold office. One commentator has noted, however, that Utah women actually voted on two occasions prior to the vote of Wyoming women. Larson, *Woman Suffrage In Western America*, 38 UTAH HIST. Q. 7, 10 (1970). *See also* Alexander, *An Experiment In Progressive Legislation: The Granting of Woman Suffrage In Utah In 1870*, 38 UTAH HIST. Q. 20 (1970).

George Bernard Shaw saw Mormon polygamy as "[p]olygamy . . . under modern democratic conditions." G. SHAW, *The Revolutionist's Handbook*, in MAN AND SUPERMAN 254 (Penguin ed. 1946).

4. On complex marriage, see text accompanying notes 93 and 94 *infra*. *See generally* M. CARDEN, ONEIDA: UTOPIAN COMMUNITY TO MODERN CORPORATION (1969); R. MUNCY, SEX AND MARRIAGE IN UTOPIAN COMMUNITIES (Penguin ed. 1974); R. PARKER, A YANKEE SAINT (1935); C. ROBERTSON, ONEIDA COMMUNITY, AN AUTOBIOGRAPHY, 1851-1876 (1970) [hereinafter cited as C. ROBERTSON, AUTOBIOGRAPHY]; C. ROBERTSON, ONEIDA COMMUNITY: THE BREAKUP, 1876-1881 (1972); J. WHITWORTH, GOD'S BLUEPRINTS (1975).

5. T.W. Curtis in 1885 observed that it was "curious . . . that the principal objection made to woman suffrage is the same as the one made against the reform in Utah, that it will *destroy the home*!" T. CURTIS, THE MORMON PROBLEM 35 (1885) (emphasis in original) [hereinafter cited as T. CURTIS].

6. The Rev. John W. Mears, writing in *The* (New York) *Independent*, discussed the marital systems of Mormons and Oneida Perfectionists: "These two systems make loud boasts of their superiority over all other social arrangements," he said, "[b]ut the one fact which of itself would be sufficient to dispose of these extravagant claims is the manifest degradation of woman under both of the systems." Mears, *Utah and the Oneida Community*, The Independent, Apr. 10, 1879, at 1, col. 1.

A modern writer has summarized the charges frequently made against polygamy:

> [It] bred vice, incest, forced marriages, sexual slavery, degenerate children, and unbridled male lust. The situation of Mormon women was as bad as the position of female slaves under Southern planters. The morality of the Mormons was a fiction . . . . Polygamy was merely instituted to gratify the lechery and avarice of the Mormon leaders and to perpetuate their power. With the system of the harem came the vices of Turkey and Asia.

A. SINCLAIR, THE EMANCIPATION OF THE AMERICAN WOMAN [THE BETTER HALF] 214 (Harper ed. 1966).

seem odd today. It was thought that women might be injured through, for example, their exercise of the franchise. "If woman were to be admitted to an active participation in politics," said the nineteenth-century intellectual Francis Lieber, "she must do it at the price of her whole peculiar nature, her grace and her attraction." She would then "be distinguished from man by her greater weakness alone, and in consequence become greatly oppressed."[7] Lieber's support of the disenfranchisement of women in their own interest may be an illustration of Dicey's comment that "protection invariably involves disability,"[8] but it is more than that, since the system protected women for reasons beyond—though presumably including—their own welfare. The traditional family was seen as the basis of civilization, and a domestic role for women was considered essential to the stability of marriage. These were the propositions which underlay the nineteenth-century hostility to modification of women's roles. 499

The influence of the *Reynolds* case on the history of the Mormons is obvious. Less well recognized are the role of the case in the history of John Humphrey Noyes' Oneida Community and the relationship to *Reynolds* of the views of the two major centers of the woman suffrage movement, the more radical National Woman Suffrage Association (NWSA) and the more conservative American Woman Suffrage Association (AWSA).[9] Further, the case belongs in the discussion of the history of women's rights in America because women, who had voted in Utah since 1870,[10] were disenfranchised in 1887 as part of the federal antipolygamy campaign. The legitimacy of this campaign was established by the *Reynolds* decision.

A broader point, however, should be made about the *Reynolds* case. The Mormons, the Perfectionists at Oneida, and elements within the suffrage movement all criticized nineteenth-century domestic institutions. While some early feminists may have dreamed of radically restructuring marital institutions, the suffrage movement provided no models. The Mormons and the Perfectionists who lived in social structures completely at variance with those of mainstream

---

7. 2 F. Lieber, Political Ethics 126 (2d ed. rev. Woolsey 1875) (1st ed. Philadelphia 1838).

8. A. Dicey, Lectures on the Relation Between Law and Public Opinion in England 150 n.1 (1905).

9. *See generally* W. O'Neill, The Woman Movement 25 (Quadrangle ed. 1971) [hereinafter cited as W. O'Neill]. *See also* Editorial, *Why There Are Two National Woman Suffrage Associations*, Woman's J., Dec. 3, 1870, at 380, col. 1.

10. *See* note 3 *supra*.

America did offer models, the Mormons arguing that in plural marriage Mormon women "enjoyed a higher social position"[11] than that enjoyed by the women of the outside world, the Oneida Perfectionists urging that Oneida's social principles contemplated a "glorious emancipation for man and woman."[12] These alternative marital structures were not accepted by the great majority of the American people, who stood firmly behind monogamous institutions. As one journalist commented at the time, "[t]he great support of monogamy, even among Gentiles, is, after all, not so much the law as social opinion."[13] The *Reynolds* decision, by giving the majority view the unambiguous force of law, made alternative forms of marriage difficult to sustain.[14]

THE REYNOLDS CASE

500 The *Reynolds* case arose on the following facts. In 1852, the Latter Day Saints in Salt Lake City announced publicly that they were practicing plural marriage.[15] By 1856, the Republican Party platform included a reference to polygamy as a twin relic of barbarism;[16] slavery was, of course, the other. In 1862 a federal statute, the Morrill Act,[17] was passed to deal with bigamy in the territories. The Act provided that "every person having a husband or wife living, who shall marry any other person, whether married or single, in a Territory of the United States, or other place over which the United States [has] jurisdiction, . . . shall . . . be adjudged guilty of bigamy . . . ." Sixteen years after the Morrill Act was passed, a test case[18] involving George Reynolds of Utah, secretary to Brigham Young, finally

---

11. Ivins, *Notes on Mormon Polygamy*, 35 UTAH HIST. Q. 309, 319 (1967) (originally published in 1956 in the *Western Humanities Review*).

12. Circular, June 27, 1852 (Oneida, N.Y.) (predecessor of American Socialist), *excerpted in* C. ROBERTSON, AUTOBIOGRAPHY, *supra* note 4, at 277.

13. 28 NATION 39 (1879).

14. There are occasional indications that the practice of polygamy, though denounced by church and state, nevertheless continues. *See* Comment, *Polygamy in Utah*, 5 UTAH L. REV. 381 (1957). On modern polygamy, see also *Polygamy, Growing in U.S. West, Is Encountering Little Opposition*, N.Y. Times, Oct. 9, 1977, at 1, col. 1.

15. T. O'DEA, THE MORMONS 104 (1957). Linford writes: "The Church of Jesus Christ of Latter-day Saints records the beginning of the practice of patriarchal marriage as July 12, 1843, the date assigned to the revelation which introduced the marriage system of the Church and permitted the Mormon brethren to have more than one wife." Linford, *supra* note 2, at 308-09.

16. Linford, *supra* note 2, at 312.

17. Morrill Act, Ch. 126, 12 Stat. 501 (1862)

18. Reynolds v. United States, 98 U.S. 145 (1878). On *Reynolds* as a test case, *see* Linford, *supra* note 2, at 331-34.

reached the Supreme Court.[19] Reynolds' central argument in the Supreme Court was that his conviction for bigamy could not stand because polygamy was an exercise of rights protected under the religious liberty guarantees of the first amendment, directly operative in the territories.

Reynolds requested the trial court to instruct the jury that if it found from the evidence that he was married "in pursuance of and in conformity with what he believed at the time to be a religious duty, that the verdict must be 'not guilty.' "[20] This request was refused.

Chief Justice Waite, writing for the Supreme Court, considered the jury instruction on the subsequent appeal.[21] The issue was whether religious belief could justify an act made criminal by federal statute.[22] The Court rejected Reynolds' claim that the religious practice of polygamy was constitutionally protected.

Congress, the Court said, could not pass a law for the territories 501
which would prohibit the free exercise of religion, but the antibigamy act was not within the congressional prohibition. The Court found the Morrill Act within the legislative power of Congress, since Congress was "left free to reach actions which were in violation of social duties or subversive of good order."[23] The Court then asked whether those who made the practice of polygamy a part of their religious belief were excepted from the operation of the statute,[24] and concluded that they were not.[25]

---

19. It has been suggested that the delay in enforcement was due to the Civil War and Reconstruction. *See* Davis, *Prelude*, *supra* note 2, at 6.

20. 98 U.S. at 162.

21. The judge instructed the jury that:

> if the defendant, under the influence of a religious belief that it was right—under an inspiration, if you please, that it was right,—deliberately married a second time, having a first wife living, the want of consciousness of evil intent—the want of understanding on his part that he was committing a crime—did not excuse him; but the law inexorably in such case implies the criminal intent.

Id.

22. *Id.*

23. *Id.* at 164.

24. *Id.* at 166.

25. The court stated: "To permit this would be to make the professed doctrines of religious belief superior to the law of the land, and in effect to permit every citizen to become a law unto himself. Government could exist only in name under such circumstances." *Id.* at 167.

Reynolds served 19 months in jail. "Upon his release he was regarded by the Mormons as a 'living martyr' . . . . Ironically, in 1885 he was married a third time . . . ." Davis, *Impact*, *supra* note 2, at 291.

It is the Court's discussion of marriage as a foundation of society which is of interest here.

> Marriage, while from its very nature a sacred obligation, is nevertheless, in most civilized nations, a civil contract, and usually regulated by law. Upon it society may be said to be built, and out of its fruits spring social relations and social obligations and duties, with which government is necessarily required to deal. In fact, according as monogamous or polygamous marriages are allowed, do we find the principles on which the government of the people, to a greater or less extent, rests. Professor Lieber says, polygamy leads to the patriarchal principle, and [*sic*] which, when applied to large communities, fetters the people in stationary despotism, while that principle cannot long exist in connection with
> 502 monogamy. . . .[26]

The decision in the *Reynolds* case has been read in the twentieth century as a statement which "found in polygamy the seed of destruction of a democratic society" and which viewed polygamy as "highly injurious to its female adherents."[27] *Reynolds* sustained a lower court instruction to the jury referring to "pure minded women," "innocent children," and "innocent victims of this delusion."[28] But while the decision refers to the odiousness of polygamy,[29] the *Reynolds* opinion does not detail the injuries to the innocent victims or other evils of the institution.

The evils of Mormon polygamy must, however, have been seen against the background of law and custom relating to the status of women in monogamous America. Contemporary observers were

---

26. 98 U.S. at 165-66. Chief Justice Waite quoted an edited version of Lieber's comments which appeared as a footnote in 2 J. KENT, COMMENTARIES ON AMERICAN LAW 95 *n.h.* (12th ed. O. Holmes 1873). Chancellor Kent cited Lieber to support his statement that "[p]olygamy may be regarded as exclusively the feature of Asiatic manners, and of half-civilized life, and to be incompatible with civilization, refinement, and domestic felicity." *Id.* at 94-95. For Lieber's original, see 2 F. LIEBER, POLITICAL ETHICS, *supra* note 7, at 9.

27. People v. Woody, 61 Cal. 2d 716, 724-25, 394 P.2d 813, 820, 40 Cal. Rptr. 69, 76 (1964).

28. 98 U.S. at 167-68.

29. "Polygamy has always been odious among the northern and western nations of Europe, and, until the establishment of the Mormon Church, was almost exclusively a feature of the life of Asiatic and of African People." *Id.* at 164. Chief Justice Waite referred to the opinion as his "sermon on the religion of polygamy." B. TRIMBLE, CHIEF JUSTICE WAITE 244 n.18 (1938).

aware of the relationship between the polygamy question and the debate over the status of women, and one observer summarized the relation this way: "We are mistaken in supposing the women of Utah are in any greater bondage than are the women of the United States."[30]

NINETEENTH-CENTURY CONVENTIONS OF HOME AND MARRIAGE

Francis Lieber on Monogamy

When Chief Justice Waite noted that the forms of marriage are basic to society and of critical significance to governmental institutions, he cited Professor Francis Lieber's thesis that polygamy leads to the patriarchal principle, and that this principle might fetter those people adhering to it in stationary despotism. Francis Lieber, a German emigré who achieved considerable distinction as a publicist in 503
America,[31] was deeply interested in the forms of marriage. *Reynolds v. United States* constitutes an endorsement of Lieber's views on marriage.[32] It was an invocation of one of the serious intellectual names of the age[33] in connection with a cause he had long defended, and it is possible that Chief Justice Waite did not detail the dangers of polygamy because he assumed that in relying on the opinion of Professor Lieber he had done all that was required.

In *Political Ethics* Lieber had written: "The family cannot exist without marriage, nor can it develop its highest importance, it would seem, without monogamy."[34] In 1865, Lieber, still concerned with the protection of monogamy, had proposed a constitutional amendment declaring polygamy a crime.[35] Lieber set forth in detail his con-

---

30. T. CURTIS, *supra* note 5, at 35 (1885).

31. *See generally* F. FREIDEL, FRANCIS LIEBER: NINETEENTH CENTURY LIBERAL (1947). The citation to Francis Lieber has been described as "an early and unheralded use of social science findings." Galanter, *Religious Freedoms in the United States: A Turning Point?*, 1966 WIS. L. REV. 217, 232.

32. A posthumous endorsement. Lieber died in 1872.

33. A review in *Nation*, noting the "extraordinary favor" with which Lieber's ideas had been received in America, comments: "There must have been something in Dr. Lieber's mind and character remarkably in harmony with the spirit and tendencies of his adopted country to earn for him a reputation like this . . . ." 32 NATION 189 (1881).

34. 1 F. LIEBER, POLITICAL ETHICS, *supra* note 7, at 139.

35. F. LIEBER, *Amendments of the Constitution Submitted to the Consideration of the American People* in 2 MISCELLANEOUS WRITINGS 137, 173 (1881) (reprinting PAPER NO. 83 OF THE LOYAL PUBLICATION SOCIETY (1865)). Polyandry (more than one husband) should also be constitutionally forbidden, he said, for "what does not happen in our days!" *Id.*

ception of monogamy and its significance in an unsigned article published in *Putnam's Monthly* in 1855. Monogamy, he said,

> is one of the primordial elements out of which all law proceeds, or which the law steps in to recognize and protect. . . . Wedlock, or monogamic marriage, . . . is one of the frames of our thoughts, and moulds of our feelings; it is a psychological condition of our jural consciousness, of our liberty, of our literature, of our aspirations, of our religious convictions, and of our domestic being and family relation, the foundation of all that is called polity.[36]

This article specifically addressed the issue of whether Utah should be admitted to the Union and also considered more general questions of alternative forms of marriage. Among the forms cited in
504 Lieber's article were Mormon polygamy and complex marriage as practiced by the Oneida Perfectionists.[37] Lieber's *Putnam's* article placed monogamy "beyond our religion," and "beyond Common Law," in the world of "primordial elements."[38] His arguments, however, would have established monogamy as the only marital system permitted under the law.

American Monogamy

Monogamous marriage in nineteenth-century American law was a relationship between the parties which was described by William Story in 1847 in terms of baron and serf, or hawk and dove.[39] Because the law was repressive to women, Lucy Stone and Henry Blackwell married "under protest" in 1855, writing into their mar-

---

36. [Lieber], *The Mormons. Shall Utah Be Admitted into the Union?*, 5 PUTNAM'S MONTHLY 225, 234 (1855). For attribution, *see* 2 F. LIEBER, MISCELLANEOUS WRITINGS 534 (1881); F. FREIDEL, *supra* note 31, at 262.

37. For another view on the forms of marriage, see Cleveland v. United States, 329 U.S. 14, 25-26 (1946) (Murphy, J., dissenting).

38. [Lieber], *The Mormons, supra* note 36, at 234.

39. In respect to the powers and rights of married women, the law is by no means abreast of the spirit of the age. Here are seen the old fossil foot-prints of Feudalism. The law relating to women tends to make every family a barony, or a monarchy, or a despotism, of which the husband is the baron, king or a despot, and the wife the dependent, serf or slave . . . . [I]f the husband choose, he has his wife as firmly in his grasp and dominion, as the hawk has the dove upon whom he has pounced. The age is ahead of the law. Public opinion is a check to legal rules on this subject . . . .

W. STORY, TREATISE ON THE LAW OF CONTRACTS NOT UNDER SEAL 74 (2d ed. Boston 1847).

riage contract a denunciation of the laws which gave the husband "custody of the wife's person," "the exclusive control and guardianship of their children," and "sole ownership of her personal, and use of her real estate," and finally, "the whole system by which 'the legal existence of the wife is suspended during marriage.' "[40] T. W. Higginson, the noted nineteenth-century reformer who officiated at the Stone-Blackwell marriage, quoted Story's remark many years later, and observed that while women's legal status had been greatly ameliorated since Story wrote, it was not clear "that the final and equitable fulfilment [sic]" had been reached.[41] For Higginson and many others, the issue became focused on suffrage.

While some of the nineteenth-century laws concerning women related exclusively to married women,[42] other laws incapacitated all women, married or single. In either case, the laws were rooted in a particular concept of the roles of men and women in monogamy. In 505
nineteenth-century America the married state was seen as right and natural; the unmarried state was not the norm, and thus it was thought unnecessary to recognize the unmarried state in governmental action. In his concurring opinion in *Bradwell v. Illinois*,[43] Justice Bradley described the unmarried woman as unaffected by "the duties, complications, and incapacities arising out of the married state."[44] Unmarried women, in his opinion, were exceptions. "The paramount destiny and mission of women are to fulfill the noble and benign offices of wife and mother. This is the law of the Creator." The law of the Creator would also be the law of the state since the "rules of civil society must be adapted to the general constitution of things, and cannot be based on exceptional cases."[45]

Political Disabilities of Women

The principal political disability against which women fought in late nineteenth-century America was disenfranchisement. In 1874, in

---

40. The document is quoted in W. O'NEILL, *supra* note 9, at 112-13.

41. T. HIGGINSON, COMMON SENSE ABOUT WOMEN 98 (1882).

42. William Story specifically addressed the legal incapacities of married women. *See* W. STORY, *supra* note 39.

43. 83 U.S. 130 (1872) (fourteenth amendment does not prohibit state's refusal to admit women to the bar).

44. *Id.* at 141. Justice Bradley was joined by Justices Field and Swayne.

45. *Id.* at 141-42. Other explanations have been offered for the legal incapacities of women. John Stuart Mill wrote, "[Women's] disabilities elsewhere are only clung to in order to maintain their subordination in domestic life; because the generality of the male sex cannot yet tolerate the idea of living with an equal . . . ." J. MILL, THE SUBJECTION OF WOMEN 50 (M.I.T. ed. 1970).

the case of *Minor v. Happersett*,[46] the Court found that women's right to vote was not protected by the federal Constitution.

Some conservatives on the suffrage question did not oppose all changes relating to the status of women. A part of the antisuffrage movement was led by women,[47] and this group, of course, did not favor the "degradation" of women. Rather, antisuffrage women, like some antisuffrage men, were interested in achieving such emancipation as was consistent in their view with the laws of nature. Lieber had noted that the progress of civilization was accompanied by the acquisition of greater rights and privileges for women.[48] Some of these changes would be seen as good and humane by Lieber and also by Justice Bradley.[49] Other changes, other "emancipations" or "reforms," however, might lead to catastrophe. In particular, there remained a notable lack of agreement on the issue of the franchise for
506 women. Lieber argued that there was no degradation of women in the refusal of the state to accept votes from women. On the contrary,

---

46. 88 U.S. (21 Wall.) 162 (1874). "If the law is wrong, it ought to be changed," Chief Justice Waite wrote for the Court, "but the power for that is not with us. . . . No argument as to woman's need of suffrage can be considered." *Id.* at 178.

47. *E.g.*, Mrs. Caroline Fairfield Corbin. In one of her later writings she said:

> For the loss of her rights and privileges as wife and mother, woman is to be compensated by equal work and equal wages with man, and the right to vote. With even a glimmering of a perception of the changes implied in the social order by the industrial and political equality of woman, is it any wonder that the overwhelming mass of women, as conceded on all hands, decline the specious bait of woman suffrage?

C. Corbin, The Position of Women in the Socialistic Utopia 10 (1901).

See also Petition to U.S. Senate Against Woman Suffrage (presented by Mrs. General Sherman and Mrs. Admiral Dahlgren), *quoted in* The History of Woman Suffrage 494 (E. Stanton, S. Anthony & M. Gage eds. 1889) [hereinafter cited as HWS]. The petition explained that: "Although we shrink from the notoriety of the public eye, yet we are too deeply and painfully impressed by the grave perils which threaten our peace and happiness in these proposed changes in our civil and political rights, longer to remain silent."

48. Lieber stated:

> [T]hat every step onward has assigned to woman some important element of civilization which, until then, was withheld from her as unfit or unnecessary for her—even education itself; nay, reading and writing not excluded. . . . [W]omen are freely admitted to occupations now which but a short time ago would have been withheld from them.

2 F. Lieber, Miscellaneous Writings, *supra* note 35, at 207. The underlying idea was that "the position which woman occupies in society is one of the gages [sic] by which we try to ascertain the civilization of that society in general." *Id.*

49. Justice Bradley noted: "The humane movements of modern society, which have for their object the multiplication of avenues for woman's advancement, and of occupations adapted to her condition and sex, have my heartiest concurrence." Bradwell v. Illinois, 83 U.S. (16 Wall.) at 142 (1872) (concurring opinion).

a nonpolitical role for women was considered an essential aspect of their nature.

> The nature and consequent duties of woman exclude her from public life; her timidity, bashfulness, delicacy, and inferior grasp of mind, as well as the necessity of acting out those sacred duties more especially assigned to her, require her being more retired than the other sex. A woman loses in the same degree her natural character, as a woman, as she enters into publicity.[50]

For the antisuffrage group, monogamy and the familial organization it ensured, sanctified by natural law and enforced by civil law, required the disenfranchisement of women.

If the issue of suffrage could involve questions greater than the
franchise, reaching the questions of the home and civilization, it could also involve such lesser issues as the right to practice law. In his unsuccessful argument on behalf of Myra Bradwell's right to practice law, Matthew Carpenter pointed out to the Supreme Court that it "seems to be feared that doing justice to women's rights in any particular would probably be followed by the establishment of the right of female suffrage, which, it is assumed, would overthrow Christianity, defeat the ends of modern civilization, and upturn the world."[51] A majority of the Court found that the right of women to practice law was not the sort of claim which could be protected against state invasion by the fourteenth amendment.[52] The Bradley concurrence based its conclusion on the special characteristics, destiny, and mission of women.[53] Similarly, in 1876, Belva Lockwood was refused admission to the practice of law before the Supreme Court.[54]

---

50. 2 F. Lieber, Political Ethics, *supra* note 7, at 124-25. Lieber went on to say: "There are, of course, women whose extraordinary mental organization is such that they form exceptions; but whenever this fundamental principle is abandoned as a general rule, evil ensues, as in every other case of deviation from the laws of nature." *Id.* at 125.

51. Brief of the Plaintiff in Error at 2, Bradwell v. Illinois, 83 U.S. (16 Wall.) 130 (1872).

52. Bradwell v. Illinois, 83 U.S. (16 Wall.) 130, 139 (1872).

53. *See* text accompanying notes 44 & 45 *supra*.

54. Chief Justice Waite indicated:

> By the uniform practice of the Court . . . and by the fair construction of its rules, none but men are permitted to practice before it as attorneys and counsellors. . . . [The Court] dces not feel called upon to make a change until such a change is required by statute or a more extended practice in the higher courts of the States.

Thus the common notion that woman's calling was a higher, nobler sphere than career or politics, that woman's role essentially was domestic, and private, was paralleled by—if it was not reflected in—Supreme Court actions adverse to the cause of women's political rights. These rulings of the late nineteenth-century Supreme Court are a part of that history of American sex discrimination of which Justice Brennan spoke in *Frontiero v. Richardson*,[55] commenting that it was discrimination "rationalized by an attitude of 'romantic paternalism,' which, in practical effect, put women, not on a pedestal, but in a cage."[56]

SOME NINETEENTH-CENTURY DISSENTERS

The Suffrage Movement

508 Early feminists had met in Seneca Falls[57] in 1848, protesting a wide variety of injustices and disassociating themselves from nonfeminist women, who were viewed as unenlightened about the laws under which they lived because they declared themselves satisfied with their present situation.[58] The 1848 meeting ended with a close vote demanding the franchise.[59] As the women's movement concentrated increasingly on suffrage, the public debate on the issue of suffrage and its dangers to the home intensified.[60]

After the Civil War, the tension which had been growing for some time between two factions in the woman suffrage movement

---

Quoted in C. FAIRMAN, RECONSTRUCTION AND REUNION, 1864-1888, 6 OLIVER WENDELL HOLMES DEVISE HISTORY OF THE SUPREME COURT OF THE UNITED STATES 1366-67 (1971). Magrath writes: "[Still] Waite sympathized with the women's rights movement . . . and, with Justices Davis and Miller, unsuccesfully favored admitting women as members of the Supreme Court bar." C. MAGRATH, MORRISON R. WAITE: THE TRIUMPH OF CHARACTER 119 (1963).

A statute directing that women be admitted to practice before the Supreme Court was passed on Feb. 15, 1879. Mrs. Lockwood was admitted on Mar. 3, 1879. C. FAIRMAN, *supra*, at 1367.

55. 411 U.S. 677 (1973). *See* opinion of Justice Brennan, joined by Justices Douglas, White, and Marshall. The opinion goes on to quote the Bradley concurrence in *Bradwell*. *Id.* at 684-85.

56. *Id.* at 684.

57. "[A]n obscure village that happened to be the home of Elizabeth Cady Stanton . . . ." W. O'NEILL, *supra* note 9, at 22.

58. *See id.* at 110-11.

59. "It is," the feminists said, "the duty of the women of this country to secure to themselves their sacred right to the elective franchise." *Id.* at 111.

60. The movement was "constantly confronted by the antisuffragist argument that such a change would contradict the inherent nature of woman and would destroy the home." A. KRADITOR, *supra* note 3, at 82.

finally produced an open split in the movement. The Stanton/Anthony group, based in New York, organized the National Woman Suffrage Association[61] and, for a time, published *The Revolution*. The Stone/Blackwell group, organized as the American Woman Suffrage Association, worked out of Boston and published the *Woman's Journal*. Attempts to unite the two groups were frustrated by "differences in principle and tactics."[62] The Boston group was reluctant to be associated with the more radical ideas of the Stanton/Anthony wing and was particularly threatened by efforts of the NWSA to reform the institution of marriage.[63]

The important differences between the two suffrage groups were reflected in their positions on nonmonogamous marriage practices. The Stone/Blackwell group believed that "[m]onogamy is the rock upon which the church of Woman's Equality is founded,"[64] and that until polygamy was destroyed there could be no equality for wo- 509
men.[65] They denounced the Mormons, free lovers like Victoria Woodhull,[66] and the Oneida Perfectionists.[67] "Let the masculine half of humanity bear the blame," the *Woman's Journal* said, "when John H. Noyes proposes to substitute for the endearing ties of domestic life a system of 'scientific propagation' . . . founded expressly upon the cornerstones of polygamy and incest."[68] Monogamy was as central to the Stone/Blackwell position as it was to Lieber's.

The Stanton/Anthony wing developed a more complex stance.

---

61. This association is hereinafter cited as NWSA.

62. *See* W. O'NEILL, *supra* note 9, at 25.

63. *Id.*

64. *Woman's Rights Versus Polygamy*, Woman's J., June 21, 1879, at 196, col. 1.

65. *Id.* Polygamy "is social barbarism, and so long as it exists, the equality of Woman is impossible." *Id.*

66. On Victoria Woodhull's views, see R. RIEGEL, AMERICAN FEMINISTS 146-47 (1963). Kraditor writes:

> Victoria Woodhull and her sister, Tennessee Claflin, never for a moment represented suffragist thinking. Mrs. Stanton and Mrs. Anthony had defended Mrs. Woodhull in the 1870's only out of a sense of sex solidarity . . . . The very possibility of even such a temporary association with a Woodhull or a Claflin disappeared as soon as the suffrage movement became more than a radical demand by a few individuals.

A. KRADITOR, *supra* note 3, at 93.

67. For a relatively moderate account in the *Woman's Journal*, see Higginson, *The Oneida Community*, Woman's J., Mar. 2, 1872, at 65, col. 1. Although Higginson concluded that it would be a "calamity" for a child to be raised at Oneida, he also noted points to be admired. *See* text accompanying note 100 *infra*. For an account of an Oneida childhood, see P. NOYES, MY FATHER'S HOUSE (1937).

68. *Positivism Versus Woman Suffrage*, Woman's J., Oct. 1, 1870, at 308, col. 4.

The group never advocated polygamy and Mormon women themselves described the women of the National Woman Suffrage Association as "opposed in their feelings to plural marriage and without sympathy for our religious views."[69] But while rejecting the Mormon way of life, some members of the NWSA would occasionally view its evils as merely relative. There were three kinds of polygamy, Mrs. Stanton wrote—Mormon polygamy, bigamy based on fraud, and polygamy involving one wife and many mistresses, "everywhere practiced in the United States."[70] Another NWSA woman put it more succinctly: "The Mormons marry their mistresses, the congressmen don't."[71]

The root of the NWSA position was its dissatisfaction with American monogamy. The suffrage movement had always included a small group prepared to engage in a radical rethinking of the position
510 of women.[72] Though this group could anticipate little success in overturning the traditional domestic system, it was open to the suggestion that the fundamental problem was not disenfranchisement, but rather marriage. "[W]e know that the ballot, when we get it, will achieve for woman no more than it has achieved for man,"[73] said a writer in Susan B. Anthony's *Revolution*. To drop all other demands in order to unite on a demand for the ballot was, she thought, only a very small part of the mission of the radical wing of the movement.[74] Mrs. Stanton argued that social roles and political rights were related, and publicly criticized both the conservatives for claiming that suffrage for women would destroy the family and the timid feminists for answer-

---

69. Woman's Exponent, Dec. 1, 1878, at 102 (resolution thanking the NWSA for its support, adopted Nov. 16, 1878).

70. Stanton, *Address at The Decade Meeting on Marriage and Divorce* in P. DAVIS, HISTORY OF THE NATIONAL WOMAN'S RIGHTS MOVEMENT 70 (1871).

71. Woman's Exponent, Feb. 1, 1879, at 187, *quoting* Sarah Spencer.

72. W. O'NEILL, *supra* note 9, at 29. O'Neill notes that "their minds were open to the possibility that the entire domestic system would have to be restructured as a precondition for sexual equality." *Id.*

73. Bullard, *What Flag Shall We Fly?*, Revolution, Oct. 27, 1870, at 264, *quoted in* W. O'NEILL, EVERYONE WAS BRAVE 19 (1969).

74. The ballot is not even half the loaf; it is only a crust—a crumb. The ballot touches only those interests, either of women or men, which take their root in political questions. But woman's chief discontent is not with her political, but with her social, and particularly her marital bondage. The solemn and profound question of marriage . . . is of more vital consequence to woman's welfare, reaches down to a deeper depth in woman's heart, and more thoroughly constitutes the core of the woman's movement, than any such superficial and fragmentary question as woman's suffrage.

W. O'NEILL, *supra* note 73, at 19-20.

ing that it would not.[75] In private, Mrs. Stanton was decidedly negative toward marriage,[76] and Susan B. Anthony seemed to grow more hostile toward marriage as she grew older.[77]

The statements of some of the Stanton/Anthony group, at least on occasion, indicated that their prime loyalty was to women, *qua* women, and not to domestic institutions at all. Susan B. Anthony, for example, emphasized the independence of women, whatever the domestic structure. Writing to *The Revolution* from Salt Lake City, Miss Anthony said:

> What we have tried to do is to show . . . that the principle of the subjection of woman to man is the point of attack; and that woman's work in monogamy and polygamy is one and the same—that of planting her feet on the ground of self-support. "Independent bread alone can redeem woman from her curse of subjection to man."[78]

---

75. "They are both wrong. It will entirely revolutionize it," said Elizabeth Cady Stanton, *Address at the Decade Meeting on Marriage and Divorce* in P. DAVIS, *supra* note 70, at 70.

76. W. O'NEILL, *supra* note 9, at 27. Mrs. Stanton, he said, "condemned [marriage] as 'opposed to all God's laws.' " *Id.*

77. R. RIEGEL, *supra* note 66, at 70 (1963).

78. 1 I. HARPER, SUSAN B. ANTHONY 389 (1899). S.B. Anthony's letters (1871) from Salt Lake City—one to *Revolution*, the other a letter home—are of interest in considering the response of the radical feminists to polygamy. In her letter to *Revolution* she described the pain involved in the change from polygamy to monogamy undertaken by a secessionist party in Utah.

> The transition of this people into the new life is complicated—is heartrending . . . . One man, a noble, loving, beautiful spirit—nothing of the tyrant, nothing of the sensualist—with four lovely wives, three of whom I have seen, and in the homes of two of whom I have broken bread, with thirteen loved and loving children—wakes up with a new idea. Four women's hearts breaking, three sets of children that must leave their father that the one-wife system may be realized!

Id.

But Susan B. Anthony's conclusion, as expressed in her private letter, was unquestionably antipolygamy. "The system of the subjection of woman here finds its limit, and she touches the lowest depths of her degradation." *Id.* at 390. The letter home concludes:

> The empire totters and Brigham feels the ground sliding from under his feet. These men will be very likely to try the 'variety' plan of Stephen Pearl Andrews, but the women will hate that even worse than polygamy. One man came to me relating a new vision, direct from Christ himself, to that effect, and I said: 'Away with your man visions! Women propose to reject them all, and begin to dream dreams for themselves.'

Id.

On Stephen Pearl Andrews and Victoria Woodhull, see W. O'NEILL, *supra* note 9, at 27-28.

Thus, the men and women in the suffrage movement approached the Mormon question from varying perspectives. For the more conservative wing, monogamy was intrinsically important. For the radicals, discussion of women's political disabilities would start with suffrage but end with a challenge to traditional domestic arrangements.

The Mormons

As a modern historian has said, the Church of Jesus Christ of Latter Day Saints, founded in New York by Joseph Smith, "has outlasted or outdistanced every other sect . . . brought into being in America."[79] The current position of the Mormon movement, another scholar has written, "is a far cry from that of the despised and persecuted minority whose existence was considered a national problem and which was driven across the continent to the wastes of Utah in the middle of the
512 last century."[80] The early history of the Mormons reveals difficulties and persecutions in several states, culminating in the murder of Joseph Smith in 1844. It was Brigham Young who led the Mormons to Utah, where they established a "polygamous theocracy within a monogamous and democratic[81] nation."[82]

The *Reynolds* case, handed down on January 6, 1879, did not instantly destroy polygamy in Utah. The successful federal prosecution of a Mormon polygamist had little immediate impact on Mormon marriages, largely because of problems of proof.[83] Additional federal legislation was found necessary, and in 1882, the Edmunds Act was passed, making it a criminal act to cohabit with more than one woman.[84] This statute also disenfranchised polygamists, bigamists, and cohabitants. Still later, in 1887, the Edmunds-Tucker Act[85] disincorporated the Mormon Church and disenfranchised all the women of Utah—Mormon and gentile, polygamist and nonpolygamist. *Mormon Church v. United States*,[86] decided in 1890, reflects the intensity of the public reaction to polygamy. The practice of polygamy, the Supreme Court said, was "a return to barbarism . . . contrary to the spirit of Christianity and of the civilization which Christianity has

---

79. S. AHLSTROM, A RELIGIOUS HISTORY OF THE AMERICAN PEOPLE 501-02 (1972).

80. T. O'DEA, *supra* note 15, at 2.

81. For a suffragist gloss on "democratic," see the NWSA resolution of Jan. 9, 1879, quoted in text accompanying note 30 *supra*. *See also* note 148 *infra*.

82. S. MORISON, OXFORD HISTORY OF THE AMERICAN PEOPLE 548 (1965).

83. Davis, *Impact*, *supra* note 2, at 291.

84. Ch. 47, 22 Stat. 30 (1882).

85. Ch. 397, 24 Stat. 635 (1887).

86. 136 U.S. 1 (1890) (per Bradley, J.).

produced in the Western world."[87] The Mormons capitulated to the federal government and formally abandoned polygamy with a public statement solemnly placing the responsibility for the change upon the nation which had forced the renunciation.[88] In 1896 Utah gained admission to the Union.[89]

The Perfectionists at Oneida

Founded in Vermont by John Humphrey Noyes, and later reestablished in New York, the Oneida Community was well known, if not notorious, in its own time.[90] Noyes held these central religious ideas: That the second coming had already occurred at the time of the destruction of Jerusalem in 70 A.D. and that there was present salvation from sin.[91] The social system of Oneida derived from Noyes' theological propositions: "Jesus Christ offers to save men from all evil—from sin and death itself; but he always states it as a necessary condition of their accepting his help that they shall forsake all others; and particularly that they shall get rid of their private property."[92] The private property which Oneida disclaimed included both goods and persons. Oneida was committed both to community of goods and to a social system called complex marriage. Although complex marriage as practiced at Oneida was often denounced in the nineteenth

---

87. *Id.* at 49. *See also* Justice Field's comments in Davis v. Beason, 133 U.S. 333, 341 (1890) (upholding Idaho statute requiring voters to swear that they were not practitioners of polygamy and did not advocate or teach it). Justice Field stated that bigamy and polygamy are crimes, tending "to destroy the purity of the marriage relation, to disturb the peace of families, to degrade woman and to debase man."

88. *See* Declaration of Submission, *quoted in* L. PFEFFER, CHURCH, STATE & FREEDOM 533 (1953).

89. Utah's constitution contains a provision forever banning polygamy, as well as a provision for woman suffrage. *See* White, *Woman's Place Is in the Constitution: The Struggle for Equal Rights in Utah in 1895*, 42 UTAH HIST. Q. 344 (1974).

90. The Oneida Community has been described as the "most successful, most widely publicized and most ably defended example of evangelically inspired communitarianism in the United States." S. AHLSTROM, *supra* note 79, at 498.

91. Oneida's theology was sometimes expounded in advertisements in the community newspaper. For example:

> Legal Notice: Notice is hereby given that all claims issued by the old firm of Moses and Law were cancelled 1800 years ago. Any requirement, therefore, to observe as a means of righteousness legal enactments bearing date prior to A.D. 70, is pronounced by us, on the authority of the New Testament, a fraud and imposition.

Quoted in C. NORDHOFF, THE COMMUNISTIC SOCIETIES OF THE UNITED STATES 267 (Dover ed. 1966) (reprinting 1st ed. 1875).

92. *Quoted in id.* at 271.

century as polygamy or free love, the Perfectionists denied that complex marriage was free love, and, in fact, they did not think of the institution as marriage. The Oneida Communists considered themselves to be in this respect more like the celibate (no wife) Shakers than like the polygamous (many wife) Mormons.[93] But every man in Oneida was, in effect, married to every woman, in a system which first involved a form of birth control called male continence and later a form of human genetic experimentation called stirpiculture.[94]

The Perfectionists at Oneida were careful to say they were not advocates of women's rights[95] in the usual sense of that term. Yet within the context of Perfectionist thinking, they sought the fullest development of woman, "compatible with her taking her position as the helpmeet of man in the true order of the transmission of divine power as given by Paul—God the head of Christ, Christ the head of
514 man, man the head of woman."[96] They followed the women's movement with interest,[97] and in their own social environment favored the "*mingling of the sexes* in labor."[98] The Perfectionists were highly critical of the role of women in monogamy, and as part of their 1852 theocratic platform advocated the abandonment of "the entire fashion of the world" particularly "marriage and involuntary propagation."[99]

While the Perfectionists may not have considered themselves advocates of women's rights, others, then and now, have perceived them as sexual egalitarians. In the nineteenth century T.W. Higginson admired the "fidelity" with which the Perfectionists maintained "the equality of the sexes."[100] A twentieth-century historian concluded

---

93. Am. Socialist, Feb. 20, 1879, at 59.

94. For further information on stirpiculture, see C. ROBERTSON, AUTOBIOGRAPHY, *supra* note 4, at 335-55. The word stirpiculture "invented and used by the Oneida Community, is a compound of two words, of which the first is *stirpes*, the Latin word for race, and *culture*, an English word meaning cultivation with a view to improvement." *Id.* at 335. *See also* Shaw's comments on Noyes, G. SHAW, *supra* note 3, at 222-25.

95. Am. Socialist, Jan. 16, 1879, at 21.

96. *Id.*

97. Thus, the Perfectionists said, we "read John Stuart Mill with pleasure; Mrs. Stanton and Miss Anthony and *The Women's Journal* [*sic*] with attention . . . ." Still, they said, "when it comes to doing anything for ourselves, we have to refuse to look at men and women as mutually independent and in a state of competition." Circular, Mar. 18, 1872 (Oneida, N.Y.), *quoted in* C. ROBERTSON, AUTOBIOGRAPHY, *supra* note 4, at 284.

98. Circular, Oct. 8, 1853, *quoted in* C. ROBERTSON, AUTOBIOGRAPHY, *supra* note 4, at 58.

99. Circular, Aug. 29, 1852 (Oneida, N.Y.), *quoted in* C. ROBERTSON, AUTOBIOGRAPHY, *supra* note 4, at 277. *See also* Am. Socialist, Feb. 20, 1879, at 63, "woman in the Oneida Community is made free."

100. Higginson, *The Oneida Community*, Woman's J., Mar. 2, 1872, at 65.

that John Humphrey Noyes had succeeded, "under unique and probably unduplicatable conditions, in abolishing marriage and raising women to a state of absolute equality with men."[101]

In the 1870's some of the clergy of central New York began to urge action against the Perfectionist group. Professor John W. Mears of Hamilton College, who led the anti-Perfectionist movement, called an anti-Oneida conference which was held at Syracuse University on the 14th of February, 1879.[102] The heightened national antipolygamy campaign seems to have affected the timing of the anti-Oneida conference and the *Reynolds* decision played a role by encouraging those opposed to any variation from traditional monogamy.[103]

Oneida's newspaper, *The American Socialist*, tried to defend the Community against these attacks on two levels. Their first argument was addressed to a legal issue: the antibigamy act related only to the territories and had no effect in New York.[104] Their second defense was political: the Perfectionist Community was completely unlike that of the Mormons.[105] But nothing the Perfectionists said or did pro-

---

101. W. O'NEILL, *supra* note 9, at 26.

102. Reports of this meeting appear in the *American Socialist* in early 1879.

103. The *New York Times* noted, "[t]he recent decision of the Supreme Court of the United States establishing the constitutionality of the laws against Utah polygamy gave heart to the movement to eradicate the community." N.Y. Times, Feb. 15, 1879, at 1, col. 7.

104. Am. Socialist, Feb. 20, 1879, at 59.

> Correspondent: Do you not think that the new Polygamy act of Congress [*sic*] has stimulated Dr. Mears and his *confreres* to renewed effort?
>
> Mr. Hinds: It has doubtless given life to this movement, but that act has no reference to Communities like ours, and only affects Territories under the jurisdiction of the United States government.

The Community also insisted more generally that its members were violating no existing laws. Adultery was not then a crime in New York as it had been in Vermont in 1847 when the original Perfectionist Community left Putney. Although prosecution for statutory rape was a possibility, the age of consent in New York in 1879 was ten. *See* D. PIVAR, PURITY CRUSADE: SEXUAL MORALITY AND SOCIAL CONTROL 1868-1900 at 142 (1973). (The age of consent was raised to sixteen in 1887.) Most of the girls at Oneida were older than ten at their sexual initiation. Compare discussion in M. CARDEN *supra* note 4, at 101; R. MUNCY, *supra* note 4, at 192. Clearly proof of any crime, for example, rape or incest, might in some instances have provided the basis for prosecution, but it seems not to have done so in fact. *See* R. PARKER, *supra* note 4, at 282; C. ROBERTSON, BREAKUP, *supra* note 4, at 272; J. WHITWORTH, *supra* note 4, at 161. Nothing ever came of the proposal discussed at the Syracuse conference that the disorderly conduct statute be amended to include persons living in adultery or concupiscence. *See* Am. Socialist, Feb. 20, 1879, at 62. *See also* Am. Socialist, Feb. 27, 1879, at [65] excerpting an article which appeared in *Nation* earlier in February 1879, at 128.

105. Am. Socialist, Feb. 20, 1879, at 59. *See also* J. WHITWORTH, *supra* note 4, at 157-58.

tected Oneida from having outsiders analogize its form of domestic arrangement to Mormon polygamy. A nineteenth-century work on Utah, for example, classified fanatics as sensualists or ascetics, and then remarked, "Of the former class are the Mormons, Noyesites of Oneida, the Antinomians[106] and the followers of St. John of Leyden . . . ."[107]

The link between Oneida and the Mormons had been made and denied from the very earliest days of the Community's history. The Perfectionists had insisted as early as 1852 that Oneida's system was really the opposite of polygamy.[108] Much later, the differences were spelled out in detail:

> The Mormons are supposed to be defiant of civil authority; the Oneida Community claim to be its peaceable sub-
> 516 jects.
>
> The Mormons have their drilled soldiers; the Oneida Community are non-resistants.
>
> The Mormons send out evangelists and compass sea and land for proselytes; the Oneida Community use no such means to increase their numbers.
>
> The Mormons establish themselves in places remote from the centers of civilization; the Oneida Community seek those centers, and shun the wilderness and the desert.
>
> Mormonism is supposed to degrade woman; Oneida Communism elevates and ennobles her.
>
> The Mormons insist that every man has a right to as many wives as he can win and support; the Oneida Community insist that, in the highest form of society, rights in the sense of ownership and social bondage do not exist.
>
> The Mormons are supposed to recruit their numbers largely from the lower classes; the Oneida Community claim to represent the best classes in the churches and society.

---

106. Perry Miller provides a useful formulation of the substance of the antinomian concern. "If the elect are joined to Christ so that they move not of themselves but by the spirit within them, and if they are sure of their vocation, why need anyone study the commandments or fear condemnation for his sins?" P. MILLER, THE NEW ENGLAND MIND: THE SEVENTEENTH CENTURY 369 (Beacon ed. 1961). *See also Antinomianism*, 1 ENCYCLOPEDIA OF RELIGION AND ETHICS 581 (J. Hastings ed. 1908).

107. J. BEADLE, LIFE IN UTAH 333 (1870). On John of Leyden, the sixteenth-century radical Anabaptist, see note 120 *infra* and accompanying text.

108. Circular, Feb. 22, 1852, *quoted in* C. ROBERTSON, AUTOBIOGRAPHY, *supra* note 4, at 273.

> Mormonism is based on a new revelation, and has a new Bible; the Oneida Communists have no new Bible, and base their system on the teachings and examples of Christ and his Apostles.[109]

Nevertheless, the Oneida propagandists failed, and Mormonism and complex marriage continued to be discussed together. Professor Mears had the connection clearly in mind[110] when he commented that the Oneida Community was smaller than the Mormon settlement, but, if on the scale of Utah "would fill the public eye and create more profound and widespread indignation than Utah has ever done."[111] In the *Reynolds* decision itself, Chief Justice Waite may have associated polygamy and complex marriage, for the reference in his opinion to "an exceptional colony of polygamists under an exceptional leadership" is arguably an allusion to Oneida and John Hum- 517
phrey Noyes.[112]

On August 26, 1879, soon after the *Reynolds* decision, the Oneida Community voted to give up complex marriage.[113] The

---

109. Am. Socialist, Mar. 13, 1879, at 84. The caution of the Perfectionists toward the degradation issue should be noted.

110. Rev. Mears wrote, "If polygamy is a great evil and immorality, the organized concubinage of the Oneida Community is still greater." The Independent, Apr. 10, 1879, at 1. Rev. Mears' article opens with a reference to the *Reynolds* case.

111. *Id.*

112. 98 U.S. at 166. The full text of the quotation reads:

> An exceptional colony of polygamists under an exceptional leadership may sometimes exist for a time without appearing to disturb the social condition of the people who surround it; but there cannot be a doubt that, unless restricted by some form of constitution, it is within the legitimate scope of the power of every civil government to determine whether polygamy or monogamy shall be the law of social life under its dominion.

See T. CURTIS, *supra* note 5, at 32, suggesting that the language referred to the Mormons themselves. This construction of Chief Justice Waite's words does not seem consonant with the concern over the political power of the Mormons. It is possible that Chief Justice Waite knew of Oneida through private as well as public channels. John Humphrey Noyes was a cousin of President Rutherford B. Hayes. R. PARKER, *supra* note 4, at 10; Am. Socialist, Feb. 6, 1879, at 42. *See also* C. MAGRATH, *supra* note 54, at 307, referring to the friendship between Chief Justice Waite and Rutherford B. Hayes in the years 1877 to 1881.

113. In September 1879, shortly after the Oneida Community abandoned complex marriage, there was a comment on the matter in the *Woman's Journal*. Lucy Stone wrote, "It is understood that it is not altogether outside pressure which has brought about this result. But when there has been a real wedded love among the members they naturally desired to be protected in their affection." Woman's J., Sept. 6, 1879, at 284. But while some at Oneida may have actively supported monogamist principles, the origin of the internal factionalism may have been elsewhere:

> The point of contention which brought into being two opposing parties was the

Community faced many difficulties, including internal factionalism, and the decision to abandon complex marriage had multiple causes. Still, at least one of these causes clearly was external.[114] A spokesman for the Perfectionists indicated that, in his opinion, the widespread tendency, "wholly without sense or justice," to link complex marriage and polygamy, contributed to their decision. The results of the *Reynolds* case had hastened the Community's action.[115] While the Perfectionists denied similarity between Perfectionism and Mormonism, they could not "be blind to the lessons which the Mormon conflict with the law affords."[116] In the future, Oneida would consist of the celibate and the monogamously married. This decision meant the end of Utopian Oneida. The structure of Oneida Community organization thereafter was fundamentally changed, and soon after, the former community became a joint stock company.[117]

518 The effect of the *Reynolds* decision on the Mormons had been to transform the antipolygamy campaign into a constitutionally legitimate rule of law. For Oneida, *Reynolds* was only one factor among others leading to the breakup of the Community.[118] Most significantly, *Reynolds* reinforced the general proposition that monogamy was the only acceptable form of marriage in America. In 1867 an English writer had observed that "Oneida Creek and Salt Lake City—communities founded by Vermont men—are practical replies to the one great question of our day—What shall be done to reform the abuses

---

> question of the initiation of virgins into the sexual realities of Community life. The initiation of young men posed no problem: sexual relations began routinely for them at puberty. The difficulty arose rather in connection with the young girls. By common consent Noyes had always assumed the responsibility for introducing them to sexual experience. . . . As he grew older, Noyes sometimes delegated the role of "first husband" to one of the several central men. Early in 1879, two of them questioned Noyes's right to decide who was to introduce the young women of the Community to sexual experience.

M. CARDEN, *supra* note 4, at 98-99.

114. The Perfectionists undertook their action "not as renouncing belief in the principles and prospective finality of that institution" but rather "in deference to the public sentiment which is evidently rising against it." Am. Socialist, Aug. 28, 1879, at 276.

115. The stubbornness "of the Mormons in Utah had arrayed the whole power of the law against them." Am. Socialist, Sept. 4, 1879, at 283.

116. *Id.*

117. For an examination of the post-Utopian Oneida, see M. CARDEN, *supra* note 4, at 113-212. "Without faith in Noyes's divine sanction, without a united belief in Perfectionism, and without complex marriage, Oneida lost its justification for existence." *Id.* at 104.

118. This may, however, be the factor imperfectly remembered in those accounts which suggest that Oneida was a victim of hostile state action. *See, e.g.*, W. MCWILLIAMS, THE IDEA OF FRATERNITY IN AMERICA 243 (1973).

of our social and domestic life?"[119] After *Reynolds*, those particular answers were unavailable. The elimination of the Perfectionist and Mormon alternatives strengthened conventional monogamy.

THE *REYNOLDS* CASE: ANOTHER PERSPECTIVE

There may be no certain or logical relation between political equality and any particular form of marriage. While some polygamous arrangements have been based on the subjugation of women,[120] it is possible to imagine forms of polygamy in which women would not be degraded. Thus, in 1903 the English writer, Edward Carpenter, suggested that polygamy arising in a society in which women were free and independent "in their relations to men would be completely different in character from the old-world polygamy, and would cease to act as a degrading influence on women."[121]

However, in any particular society at a given moment the rela- 519
tionship between the forms of marriage and the status of women is real. In America in the late nineteenth century several marriage patterns existed side by side and the variations on monogamy were well known. Were women better off in these institutions than in conventional monogamy? Did these institutions suggest possibilities for future family structures? The contemporary suffrage movement could not afford to ignore issues so central to women's rights in American society.[122]

The members of the suffrage movement could easily have viewed Chief Justice Waite's decision in *Reynolds* as another element in the pattern established by prior decisions.[123] The woman's suffrage

---

119. 2 W. DIXON, NEW AMERICA 54 (1867).

120. Polygamy did not, for example, operate in favor of women's rights in The New Jerusalem of John of Leyden. *See* N. COHN, THE PURSUIT OF THE MILLENNIUM 269-70 (rev. ed. 1970).

121. E. CARPENTER, LOVE'S COMING OF AGE 117 (1903), *quoted in* W. O'NEILL, DIVORCE IN THE PROGRESSIVE ERA 118 (1973).

122. Such questions are still discussed. *See* text note on *Communes, Group Marriage and Other Variant Family Styles* in K. DAVIDSON, R. GINSBURG, & H. KAY, SEX-BASED DISCRIMINATION 209 (1974), exploring an application of Wisconsin v. Yoder, 406 U.S. 205 (1972) to this problem. Kurland has noted that *Yoder* casts "deep shadows" on Reynolds v. United States. Kurland, *The Supreme Court, Compulsory Education, and the First Amendment's Religion Clauses*, 75 W. VA. L. REV. 213, 225 (1973). But *Reynolds* remains the basic statement on variant forms of marriage. *See also* Wilkinson & White, *Constitutional Protection for Personal Lifestyles*, 62 CORNELL L. REV. 563, 572-73 (1977).

123. In the decade preceding the *Reynolds* decision the United States Supreme Court had denied constitutional protection to women's right to practice law, Bradwell v. Illinois, 83 U.S. (16 Wall.) 130 (1872), and to women's right to vote, Minor v. Happer-

movement could not have been surprised that the Justices now condemned Mormon polygamy.[124] The behavior of the Supreme Court had been consistent with the most conservative and paternalistic of contemporary theories of women's rights. In his polygamy decision, Chief Justice Waite had failed to deal with woman suffrage in Utah,[125] a question arguably relevant to the link between polygamy and stationary despotism.

On a critical point Chief Justice Waite cited Professor Francis Lieber, whose anti-Mormon[126] and antisuffrage views rested on the linked propositions that monogamous marriage was the fundamental basis of civilized society and that a primarily domestic role for women was an essential component of monogamous marriage. This philosophy, applied to Utah after 1870 when women were allowed to vote, would result in condemnation of Mormon institutions on separate
520 though related grounds. Polygamy and woman suffrage both were threats to the American home. From this perspective, woman suffrage in Utah would compound rather than cure the defects of Mormon polygamy. *Reynolds* was thus authored by a court whose orientation on the woman question would have made it difficult for even the most conservative and antipolygamy elements of the woman's movement to offer unrestrained endorsement of its decision.

---

sett, 88 U.S. (21 Wall.) 162 (1874). Years later, the NWSA was to recall by resolution (1889) the antifeminism of one judge, Ward Hunt, for his "infamous decision" in the voting trial of Susan B. Anthony. United States v. Anthony, 24 F. Cas. 829 (C.C.N.D.N.Y. 1873); 4 THE HISTORY OF WOMAN SUFFRAGE 155-56 (S. Anthony & I. Harper eds. 1902) [hereinafter cited as 4 HWS].

124. Reynolds v. United States, 98 U.S. 145 (1878).

125. Without suggesting the logical necessity of such a discussion, we may note that a treatment of the suffrage-polygamy issue might have taken a number of forms. The point might have been made, following Lieber, that polygamy in general is bad for women and for society, and so is woman suffrage; or that polygamy in general is bad, suffrage for women in general is good, but the situation of women in Mormon polygamy is so bad that suffrage in Utah is meaningless; or that polygamy in Utah is so bad that although suffrage in Utah is good, and women might have chosen their situation, the evils of polygamy are so great that women cannot be allowed to choose it. It is unlikely that the Court would have been able to agree on any approach to the suffrage question, and it is not impossible that this is one reason why the question was not discussed. On Chief Justice Waite's own position it should be noted that he, along with his predecessor, Chief Justice Chase, headed a list of "Eminent Advocates of Woman Suffrage" in *The History of Woman Suffrage*. 4 HWS, *supra* note 123, at 1076. *See also* C. MAGRATH, *supra* note 54, at 119 (1963). *See generally* note 54 *supra*. *Compare* 3 HWS, *supra* note 47, at 505.

126. Lieber described Mormonism as characterized by "vulgarity," "cheating," "jugglery," "knavery," "foulness," and as bearing "poisonous fruits." [Lieber], *The Mormons*, *supra* note 36, at 233.

The NWSA (Stanton/Anthony group) met in Washington on January 9 and 10, 1879, a few days after the *Reynolds* decision came down. This meeting would have provided the occasion for official applause for the *Reynolds* decision, if the suffragists had believed that approval was in order. But there was no public applause.[127] The Supreme Court's blow to Mormon polygamy, its liberation of the Mormon women of Utah from the yoke of barbarism[128] was not mentioned in the resolutions of the meeting. The NWSA meeting passed a resolution condemning the judges for denying Belva Lockwood admission to the Supreme Court Bar,[129] and then resolved:

> WHEREAS, The general government has refused to exercise federal power to protect women in their right to vote in the various States and territories; therefore,
>
> *Resolved*, That it should forbear to exercise federal 521
> power to disfranchise the women of Utah, who have had a more just and liberal spirit shown them by Mormon men than Gentile women in the States have yet perceived in their rulers.[130]

---

127. The point is not that the resolutions were a direct response to the *Reynolds* decision (the identical resolutions might well have been adopted if the decision had not come down at all), but that there is no resolution approving the decision. This is not likely to be a result of ignorance concerning the Court's decision or a lack of concern with the Court's activities. The suffrage movement was manifestly interested in decisions of the Court affecting women's rights. *See, e.g.*, the resolution on Minor v. Happersett, 88 U.S. (21 Wall.) 162 (1874), and discussions of the *Minor* decision in 2 HWS, *supra* note 47, at 584.

128. The image of Mormon women as bending under the yoke of polygamy was protested by George Tichnor Curtis when he argued on behalf of the Mormons before the Supreme Court. *See* argument in Snow v. United States, 118 U.S. 346 (1886), *reprinted in* G. CURTIS, A PLEA FOR RELIGIOUS LIBERTY 16 (1886).

129. 3 HWS, *supra* note 47, at 128, which introduces the resolutions of the meeting of 1879 by saying that "the resolutions give an idea of the status of the question, and the wide range of discussion covered by the speakers . . . ." *Id.* The *Woman's Exponent* reports the resolutions as adopted. Woman's Exponent, Feb. 15, 1879, at 196. The *Woman's Journal* says: "In the final action on the resolutions . . . [t]he eighth resolution, in opposition to the attempt to take from the women of Utah the elective franchise, was laid on the table for discussion. . . . The tenth, in relation to the Supreme Court of the United States, was adopted. . . ." Woman's J., Jan. 25, 1879, at 29.

130. 3 HWS, *supra* note 47, at 128. The motivation of the Mormons in granting woman suffrage has been variously described. One commentator notes, for example:

> To the Mormons . . . there could be no better way of proving that their system of polygamy was not degrading to women . . . than to declare woman suffrage in Utah, at the very time when Negro suffrage . . . was being offered to the former slaves to protect them from their former masters. . . . [Woman suffrage] would appear to have been a calculated move on the part of the Mormon hierarchy to forestall federal legislation on polygamy.

This resolution, as much as the presence of Mormon women on their platform,[131] reflected the solution of the Stanton/Anthony group to the problem of woman suffrage in a polygamous society.[132] They would support Utah on the question of suffrage, and maintain silence on "religious" questions.[133] In the case of Utah, support of suffrage meant opposition to disenfranchisement, for while it had originally been thought that the franchise for women in Utah might discourage polygamy,[134] it was now said that women would have to be disen-

---

A. GRIMES, THE PURITAN ETHIC AND WOMAN SUFFRAGE 33 (1967). Another historian has said:

> Mormon Utah was at that time threatened by the rapid settlement of the area by "gentiles"—non-Mormons—who came in the wake of the transcontinental railroad. In reaction to the pronounced distaste of the Federal Government and the rest of the nation for the Mormon practice of polygamy, the Utah government
> 522 enacted woman suffrage to prove that Mormon women preferred polygamy and would vote to uphold it. This they did, and as expected, provided a counterbalance in voting strength to the—largely unmarried—non-Mormon population.

G. LERNER, THE WOMAN IN AMERICAN HISTORY 139 (1971). *But see* Alexander, *supra* note 3, at 29-30 (arguing that the Mormons were simply ahead of the rest of the nation in progressive spirit).

131. The Mormon women were Emmeline B. Wells, Editor of the *Woman's Exponent*, and Zina Young Williams. Mrs. Wells was a plural wife; she was born and raised in Massachusetts and had converted to the Mormon faith in 1842. *See* biographical entry in 3 NOTABLE AMERICAN WOMEN 561-62 (1971). As to Mrs. Williams, the *Washington Post* reports:

> A collection was taken, and the appearance of the baskets caused rather an energetic exodus on the part of the audience. But when it was announced that Mrs. Williams, of Utah, would speak, the popular curiosity concerning Mormon women arrested them, and when it was further stated that she was the fourth daughter of Brigham Young, they sat down. . . .

Wash. Post, Jan. 11, 1879, at 1, col. 3. The paper's account of this session was headed *The Females Subside*.

132. It was a serious problem, for involved was the issue of the meaning of the vote for the Mormon women, whether it was free, or controlled, and whether this mattered. In 1871, a history of the suffrage movement had concluded that woman suffrage was of less importance in Utah than in Wyoming because Utah's women were dominated by the church hierarchy. P. DAVIS, note 70, at 70. The *Woman's Journal* viewed the vote in Utah as problematic, pointing out that Brigham Young was "utterly opposed to Woman Suffrage." Woman's J., Feb. 24, 1872, at 61. The Stanton/Anthony group seems not to have addressed the question directly, apparently preferring not to go behind the fact of woman suffrage.

T. W. Curtis suggested at the time that, outside the suffrage movement, the linkage between polygamy and suffrage was largely ignored because suffrage did not fit with widely held views of polygamy. T. CURTIS, *supra* note 5, at 32.

133. One speaker commented that the NWSA had "nothing to do with the religious rights of women in Utah except insofar as they intermingle with and touch woman's political rights." Mrs. Gage, *quoted in* Women's Exponent, June 1, 1879, at 253.

134. This proposal was made in N.Y. Times, Dec. 17, 1867, at 4, col. 5. *See* Larson, *supra* note 3, at 9. Senator Julian introduced legislation under the title "A Bill to Dis-

franchised as part of the battle against polygamy.[135] The women of the Stanton/Anthony group believed that they could support woman suffrage in Utah[136] without taking a public stand on polygamy.[137]

But while the NWSA officially tried to make plain that they did not associate with the Mormons on any issues other than the suffrage question, these disavowals appeared inadequate to some in the suffrage movement. The *Woman's Journal* published a letter on the issue of Mormon women at the NWSA's convention under the title *Polygamy Degrades Womanhood.*[138] The attitude of the Stone/

---

courage Polygamy in Utah," to give the vote to the women of Utah in 1869. Alexander, *supra* note 3, at 24.

135. Disenfranchisement came with the Edmunds-Tucker Act of 1887, *supra* note 85 and accompanying text.

136. The response of the woman suffrage movement to the campaign for disenfranchisement in Utah deserves detailed study. This preliminary observation may be made, however: the evidence does not point in one direction, and observers in the nineteenth century drew somewhat different conclusions from the evidence they used. Thus, contemporary accounts may be used to support the proposition that the nineteenth-century woman suffrage movement worked to save the franchise for Utah's women. "The advocates of the rights of all women stood up boldly for those of Utah, notwithstanding the scoffs and obloquy cast upon them." 4 HWS, *supra* note 123, at 939. *See also* the *Anti-Polygamy Standard* (Salt Lake City) referring to "[o]ur Eastern friends, whose love for female suffrage exceeds their hatred of polygamy." These suffragists "allow their zeal to outrun their reason, when they insist that woman suffrage must be sustained here at all hazards." Anti-Polygamy Standard, Oct. 1882, at 1, col. 1. But T. W. Curtis suggested that the suffrage movement had not done well by the women of Utah. T. CURTIS, *supra* note 5, at 33. One suffrage woman, Lily Devereux-Blake, is quoted as having declared herself "reconciled" to the disenfranchisement, "because of the anomalous condition of local affairs." Daily Tribune, Aug. 11, 1888, *quoted in* R. DWYER, THE GENTILE COMES TO UTAH 202 (1941). A modern historian has concluded that the eastern suffragettes may have even joined other antipolygamy groups to work for disenfranchisement. T. O'DEA, *supra* note 15, at 249.

An inquiry into this question would have to take into account such psychological factors as the desire of Mormon women to believe that they had not been abandoned, and the desire of the radical feminists to believe that they had not betrayed their allies. One would also have to note the increasingly broadened base of the suffrage movement in 1887. When the NWSA protested the disenfranchisement in Utah it also noted as a hopeful sign of the times the endorsement of woman suffrage by the Knights of Labor and by the National Woman's Temperance Union. 4 HWS, *supra* note 123, at 122-23.

137. Privately, however, they might freely express themselves on the question. *See* note 78 *supra*.

138. Woman's J., Mar. 29, 1879, at 97. Amanda Dickinson of St. Louis conceded that "none who knew them would willingly suppose that the leaders of the recent convention of the National Woman Suffrage Association in Washington meant to endorse polygamy . . . ." Still "[s]uffragists everywhere must deeply regret any appearance of affiliation between the advocates of equal rights for Woman and those who advocate or apologize for a system which plunges her into the lowest depths of degradation. . . ." The movement could welcome people of all creeds and conditions of life and could even, "to a certain extent cooperate with free-lovers and polygamists for a good end, as,

Blackwell group prompted Mrs. Stanton to defend the NWSA's position on Utah representatives at the Washington meeting. In a letter quoted in the Mormon *Women's Exponent*, Mrs. Stanton pointed out that if the Mormon Congressman, George Q. Cannon,[139] could sit in the Congress of the United States without compromising the Congress on the question of polygamy, Mormon women could sit on the platform of the NWSA "without making us responsible for their religious faith."[140] From Omaha, on April 5, 1879, Mrs. Stanton wrote to Susan B. Anthony, referring again to Congressman Cannon, and suggesting that if "Congress can stand Cannon with four wives, we might stand the women with only the fourth part of a husband!"[141] Furthermore, she said, "When Congress proposes to disfranchise the women of a Territory, where should they go to plead their case but to the National Woman Suffrage Association?"[142]

524 A report of the January, 1879, NWSA program noted that Mrs. Stanton introduced "Mrs. Wells of Utah, wife of General Wells, the Mormon apostle and polygamist."[143] Mrs. Wells told the meeting that Congress should preserve the franchise held by the women of the territory.[144] Then Susan B. Anthony said that "disfranchisement [sic] is always political degradation to any class affected by it—disfranchisement [sic] and degradation being in politics synonymous terms . . . ."[145] The threatening perception of the NWSA leaders was this: if there was degradation in polygamy with woman suffrage, there was degradation in monogamy without it.

The suffrage movement as a whole may have approved, in private, the result in *Reynolds*, a case in which "polygamy, not Rey-

---

in this free country political parties and public conveyances are open to all." But the movement "must not make itself responsible for the various opinions and practices of its adherents." We can pity and try to understand and sympathize with our fanatical sisters among the Mormons, she concluded, "just as we do with the Hindoo widows who throw themselves on the funeral piles of their husband," but "the spectacle of women in this age and country accepting and defending polygamy is a phenomenon we are utterly unable to comprehend." *Id.*

139. On George Cannon, see 3 DICTIONARY OF AMERICAN BIOGRAPHY 474 (1929). Cannon served in Congress for 10 years. The operation of the Edmunds Act in 1882 caused his retirement by a vote of the House, 123 to 79. *Id.*

140. Elizabeth Cady Stanton, *quoted in* Woman's Exponent, May 15, 1879, at 240.

141. 2 E. STANTON, LETTERS 160 (T. Stanton & H. Blatch eds. 1922).

142. *Id.*

143. Woman's J., Jan. 25, 1879, at 29.

144. *Id.*

145. *Id.* The account of the session in Wash. Post, Jan. 10, 1879, at 1, col. 2, sharpens the Anthony comment: "[d]isfranchisement and degradation [are] synonymous terms."

nolds, . . . [was] on trial."[146] Members of this group may have approved of Oneida's decision to give up complex marriage for similar reasons. Nevertheless, even the most strongly antipolygamy factions of the suffrage movement must have felt ambivalent about a decision in support of monogamy by a court which had ruled against women's political rights.

This ambivalence is illustrated in the *Woman's Journal*. The rhetoric in one issue shows the deep antipolygamy feeling in the Stone/Blackwell group. Responding to an attempt to obtain a presidential pardon for Reynolds, and to Rutherford Hayes' refusal to grant it, the *Woman's Journal* said that if President Hayes would suppress this "relic of barbarism" he would "merit and receive the thanks of universal womanhood" and his name would go down in history with Lincoln's.[147] And again: "All honor to President Hayes! If he succeeds in extirpating this social cancer of polygamy, his name will be remembered in history as "[t]he friend of women."[148] But of the *Reynolds* decision itself, the *Woman's Journal* said very little. Hayes, they seemed to be saying, might be remembered as the friend of women. Suffragists could not be sure about the Court, no matter how strongly Chief Justice Waite denounced polygamy.

Elizabeth Cady Stanton years later addressed her diary in terms that suggest that the ambiguities of the polygamy struggle may never have been forgotten by the generation of feminists who witnessed it. "I still believe in Congress compelling every state to establish within its borders a true republican form of government," she said. "If Congress can forbid polygamy under the national flag, it can forbid disfranchisement."[149]

146. Woman's J., June 21, 1879, at 196.

147. *Id.*

148. *Id.* In private, Hayes expressed his approval of woman suffrage. 4 HWS *supra* note 123, at 1075. *But see* Resolution of January 9-10, 1879, on Hayes' public neglect of the suffrage issue in a presidential message in which "he makes a truly paternal review of the interests of this republic . . . yet forgets to mention twenty million women robbed of their social, civil and political rights." 3 HWS, *supra* note 47, at 128.

149. Aug. 1, 1892, diary entry of Elizabeth Cady Stanton. 2 E. STANTON, *supra* note 141, at 287. It may be noted that *Reynolds* involved a federal antipolygamy act operative in the territories. The question of whether a state might recognize polygamy was therefore technically left open. Lieber's proposed antibigamy amendment to the federal Constitution was not adopted—although federal protection of woman suffrage through a constitutional amendment did ultimately come about—and thus it remains possible to raise the issue of the status of a state law permitting polygamous marriages. *See* H. KRAUSE, FAMILY LAW 4 (1976).

CONCLUSION

The *Reynolds* case is cited in several fields of law. In the field of church and state, the "Supreme Court's concern with the religion clauses of the first amendment begins, for all practical purposes, with the case of *Reynolds v. United States*, where the Court first adopted the Jeffersonian statement that the amendment erected 'a wall of separation between church and State.' "[150] The concepts explored in *Reynolds* "were to cast the molds for subsequent interpretation of religious freedom."[151] In the area of private international law, *Reynolds* is relevant to discussions of *Hyde v. Hyde*, in which an English court refused to take jurisdiction of an action for divorce based on an 1853 Mormon marriage, the court concluding that the Mormon marriage (assumed to be legal in Utah) was not a marriage
526 within the meaning of the English statute.[152] In the history of American federalism, the *Reynolds* case stands for the proposition that while states regulate their own domestic affairs, Congress has the power to regulate marriage in the territories.[153] *Reynolds* can be treated in relation to a general discussion of the nature of marriage and the role of the state in defining marriage as a civil status,[154] and

---

150. P. KURLAND, RELIGION AND THE LAW 21 (1962).

151. Davis, *Impact*, *supra* note 2, at 287.

152. Hyde v. Hyde, L.R.I.P. & D. 130 (1866) discussed marriage as "the voluntary union for life of one man and one woman, to the exclusion of all others." *Id.* at 133. "[T]he basic precept of *Hyde v. Hyde* has not been under direct attack since the unsuccessful attempt at polygamy in the United States in the late Nineteenth Century." Zabel, Hyde v. Hyde, *A Comparative Study of the Law of Marriage in the Sudan and Nigeria* (pt. 1), 1969 UTAH L. REV. 22.

Referring to the proof in *Hyde* that the "law of Utah, equally with the opinions and practices of the Mormon Church, sustained polygamy," J. P. Bishop added, "[b]ut however the law was then, it is not so now," citing the Morrill Act and *Reynolds*. 1 J. BISHOP, NEW COMMENTARIES ON MARRIAGE, DIVORCE, AND SEPARATION 128 (1891). A summary of *Hyde* as a "curious case" involving the validity of a Mormon marriage appears in an editor's footnote in 2 J. KENT, COMMENTARIES, *supra* note 26, at 94 n.1.

As to the recognition of Indian polygamous marriages, see Bartholomew, *Recognition of Polygamous Marriages in America*, 13 INT'L & COMP. L.Q. 1022, 1067-68 (1964). Indian polygamy provided no precedent for Mormon polygamy, perhaps in part for the reason suggested by John Stuart Mill. Polygamy, he said, "though permitted to Mohammedans, and Hindus, and Chinese, seems to excite unquenchable animosity when practised by persons who speak English and profess to be a kind of Christians." J. MILL, ON LIBERTY 112 (C. Shields ed. 1956).

153. 1 J. BISHOP, NEW COMMENTARIES, *supra* note 152, at 70-71.

154. *See, e.g.*, Drinan, *The Loving Decision and the Freedom to Marry*, 29 OHIO ST. L.J. 358, 360-61 (1968).

can, finally, be cited in the field of evidence.[155]

The case is also significant in social and historical terms. Interwoven with the story of the *Reynolds* case are the histories of the Mormons, the Utopian Community at Oneida, and the woman suffrage movement. The "triumph for believers in monogamy"[156] which the *Reynolds* case represented when seen in context was a vindication of a marital institution committed to a primarily domestic and nonpolitical role for women. Viewed in this light, the decision is of a piece with other pronouncements of the late nineteenth-century Supreme Court tending to protect a traditional conception of the monogamous home. The *Reynolds* case effectively ruled out experimentation with radically restructured marital institutions. The case helped define the direction which future reforms would take by establishing that nonmonogamous arrangements, even on a limited scale, were entirely unacceptable. For better or worse, options were available before *Reynolds* which were not available afterwards.[157]

---

155. "If, on the second trial of a cause, it is found that the accused kept away a witness, his evidence given on the first trial may be proved by the prosecution" (citing *Reynolds*). T. COOLEY, PRINCIPLES OF CONSTITUTIONAL LAW 295 n.2 (1880). *See also* MCCORMICK'S HANDBOOK OF THE LAW OF EVIDENCE 609 (E. Cleary 2d ed. 1972). In the *Reynolds* case, Mr. Justice Field concurred on the several points decided except one which related to the "admission of the testimony [of a plural wife] given on a former trial upon a different indictment." 98 U.S. at 168.

156. Wash. Post, Jan. 7, 1879, at 1, col. 1.

157. There has been no attempt here to connect the issues raised to the question of property, despite the view held, for example, by Francis Lieber, that "at all times property and marriage have stood or fallen together." [Lieber], *The Mormons*, *supra* note 36, at 234 n.†. In addition, there has been no effort to assess the value of any of the domestic institutions discussed.